THE KINGFISHER
A-Z
ENCYCLOPEDIA

Editor: Ben Hoare
Art editor: Peter Clayman
Editorial director: Miranda Smith
Art director: Mike Davis
Editorial team: Catherine Brereton, Carron Brown, Sheila Clewley,
Melissa Fairley, Russell McLean, Jennie Morris
Design team: Jo Brown, Jane Tassie
DTP manager: Nicky Studdart
Picture research: Jane Lambert, Cee Weston-Baker
Artwork archivists: Wendy Allison, Steve Robinson
Production: Jo Blackmore, Kelly Johnson
Indexer: Chris Bernstein
Contributors: Jacqui Bailey, Olly Denton, Clive Gifford, Marie Greenwood, Ann Kay,
David Lambert, Keith Lye, Christopher Maynard, Isabelle Paton, Jill Thomas

KINGFISHER
Kingfisher Publications Plc
New Penderel House
283–288 High Holborn
London WC1V 7HZ
www.kingfisherpub.com

First published by Kingfisher Publications Plc in 2002
10 9 8 7 6 5 4 3 2 1

ITR/0702/TPL/GRS/135MA

A CIP catalogue record for this book is available from the British Library

ISBN 0 7534 0776 0

Printed in Malaysia

THE KINGFISHER
A-Z
ENCYCLOPEDIA

KINGFISHER

North America
Myths and Legends
Music
Middle Ages
Mammals
Internet
Insects
Fish
Farming
Europe
Earth
Dinosaurs
Dance
Communication
Birds
Australia
Asia

How to use this encyclopedia

This encyclopedia is fun and easy to use. You can either look up subjects (all of the entries are arranged in alphabetical order) or simply browse through the book. You should find most of the information you want by first looking up the main entry, for example, 'bear' or 'planet'. If the subject you are looking for does not have its own entry, look in the index at the back. Usually, there will be some information about your subject in another article. Throughout the encyclopedia you will find words in bold, like this: **laser**. When you see one, you will know that there is a separate entry on that subject.

The encyclopedia also includes special features on important topics such as aircraft, dinosaurs and the world's continents. These are longer and more detailed than most entries. A list of the special features appears opposite.

Every entry on a country has a quick-reference panel that illustrates the nation's flag and provides details on its government, capital, area, language and currency. On pages 382–383 of the encyclopedia, there is a world map showing the countries of the world.

Having read the entries that interest you, check the guide to useful websites that appears on pages 384–385. These carefully selected websites are excellent research tools that will help you find out more information.

Aardvark

The aardvark is a **mammal** that eats **termites**. When it has smashed open a termite nest with its powerful claws, it pokes its long, sticky tongue in and pulls it out covered with the insects. The aardvark lives in open country in central and southern Africa. It is a shy animal with large ears like a donkey, and is an expert burrower. If caught away from its home it can dig a hole for itself at top speed.

The word 'aardvark' is Dutch for 'earth pig'.

Aardvarks use their keen sense of smell to track down termite nests, then smash them open and lick up the tasty insects.

Abacus

The abacus is a simple counting machine first used in Ancient **Greece** and the **Roman Empire**. It consists of rows of beads strung on wires. Beads on the first wire count as ones, those on the second wire count as tens, those on the third wire count as hundreds, and so on. People still use the abacus in parts of Asia and the Middle East.

The Romans sometimes used small stones as counters. They called these counters calculi and it is from this that we get our word 'calculate'.

Abbreviation

An abbreviation is a shortened form of a word or a group of words. Words and phrases are shortened to save space. Abbreviations are also useful because they are quicker to write, saving us time. Sometimes the first and last letters of a word are used, such as St for 'Saint' or Dr for 'Doctor'. On other occasions, only the beginning of the word is used, as in Sept. for 'September'. A full stop is often placed after the abbreviation to show that it is a shortened form.

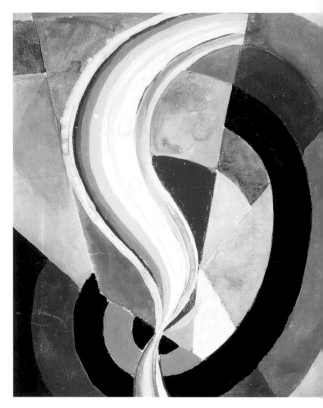

Robert Delaunay painted *Propeller* in Paris in 1923. Delaunay was one of the first European painters to make **abstract art**. He was more interested in patterns and colours than in showing what real things look like.

The **Aboriginal people** of Australia were the first humans to live there. They still make paintings on cave walls and on tree bark. Their subjects are often ancient myths that date back many thousands of years.

Aboriginal people

The term 'aboriginal people' really means the first humans who lived in any country. The aboriginal people of **Australia** arrived there from Southeast Asia more than 40,000 years ago. They had no permanent homes but wandered across the land hunting or gathering their food. Their main weapons were the **boomerang** and the throwing spear.

At first, the Europeans who settled in Australia about 200 years ago treated the aboriginal people very badly. However, the aboriginal people now have rights as Australian citizens, and the **government** has handed over some traditional areas claimed by them.

Abstract art

The main aim of abstract **art** is not to show what people, landscapes or objects actually look like. In abstract art, artists concentrate on the shapes, colours and textures instead. But they can still express all kinds of feelings and ideas in their work. Abstract art can be extremely bold and dramatic, or more delicate and subtle. **Paintings**, drawings and **sculptures** can all be abstract.

Throughout history, many cultures have produced abstract art, including many African and **aboriginal peoples**. In Europe, the first completely abstract art was created in Paris and Moscow in the early 20th century. In the 1950s, the United States, especially New York, became a leading centre of abstract art. Many modern artists have made abstract art, including Pablo **Picasso**, Jackson Pollock and Mark Rothko.

Acceleration

When a car increases speed, it accelerates. If you drop a ball from the top of a tall building, it also starts to accelerate. It reaches a speed of 9.8 m per second after one second. After two seconds it is moving at 19.6 m per second. Every second that it falls, it increases its speed by 9.8 m per second. The ball accelerates because it is being pulled down by the force of **gravity**.

Acid

An acid is a liquid chemical **compound** that is often poisonous. Some acids, such as sulphuric acid, nitric acid and hydrochloric acid, are very powerful and can corrode, or eat away, even the strongest **metals**. Other acids are harmless. These include the citric acid that gives lemons and oranges their sharp taste, and the acetic acid in vinegar. Lactic acid is produced when milk goes sour. All acids turn a special sort of paper called litmus red.

Some substances are the opposite of acids. They are called alkalis or bases, and turn litmus paper blue. Caustic soda is a strong alkali, and alkalis are one of the main ingredients of **soap**.

Acid rain

All rain is very slightly **acid**. The weak acid in rainwater can eat away the limestone in buildings and statues. Limestone is an alkali.

Rain can also react with the waste gases sent out by power stations, cars and factories. When this happens, it falls as weak sulphuric acid and nitric acid, and is called acid rain. After a time, the acid rain slowly poisons lakes and streams, threatening the plants and wildlife that live there. For this reason, people are trying to reduce the amount of waste gases that industrial nations release into the air.

Acoustics

Acoustics is the study of **sound** and how it travels. When an architect designs a concert hall or theatre, he or she must carefully consider the sound quality of the building. Will a full range of sound waves from speech and music reach every seat? Will there be disturbing echoes from the walls and ceiling?

Sound waves travel in straight lines, and they can be reflected or absorbed by the various surfaces that they strike. By choosing different materials to cover each part of a wall or ceiling, architects can turn the sound waves in the best direction.

Acids in laboratories carry warning labels (1). Acids in fruit taste sharp and are harmless (2). The acid in wasp stings (3) causes a painful reaction, while car batteries (4) contain strong sulphuric acid.

Acid rain is the result of pollution from factories mixing with water in the air. It kills wildlife and eats away at buildings.

Great Altar
of Athena

The Parthenon

Statue of the goddess
Athena

The 'Propylaea'
(gateway)

Temple of
Athena

Acropolis

'Acropolis' is a Greek word for the high central part of many ancient Greek cities. The most famous surviving acropolis is in Athens, the capital of modern **Greece**. On top of it are the ruins of ancient temples built in the 400s BCE when Athens was a rich and powerful city. The Parthenon, the largest and most important of these temples, was built to honour Athena, the patron goddess of Athens. It has many giant pillars of white **marble**.

In the early 1800s, many of the Parthenon's marble sculptures were taken away by Lord Elgin, who was the British ambassador to Greece. They are now on display in the British Museum in London. However, many people think the sculptures should be returned to a museum in Athens.

△ The **Acropolis** of Athens, pictured as it looked in about 400 BCE. At the top of the hill stood a temple called the Parthenon.

△ **Acupuncture** is a form of healing using needles. In Chinese medicine, the needles unblock the flow of *ch'i* (vital energy) to restore good health.

Acting *see* Theatre

Acupuncture

Acupuncture is a kind of medical treatment in which thin needles are used to puncture various parts of the body. Usually the needles are inserted only a short way into the patient. Acupuncture was first developed by the Chinese about 5,000 years ago, and it is still used today. In recent years, acupuncture has become accepted in many countries as a branch of alternative **medicine**. It is often used in the treatment of such complaints as headache, asthma and arthritis.

Adhesive

Adhesives are substances that are used to stick things together. There are many different kinds of adhesive. For centuries, people have boiled up animal **bones**, hide and horn to produce an adhesive called glue. Plants that contain a lot of **starch**, such as potatoes and corn, can be made into a paste that is good for sticking paper. Today's artificial adhesives are better than natural ones because they are much stronger. Epoxy resins, for example, are very strong. For any adhesive to work well, the surfaces to be stuck together must be clean. Adhesives have many uses, from envelopes and postage stamps to the construction of **aircraft** and racing cars.

◁ An artificial **adhesive** holds together the plastic material used to make modern canoes.

Adjective

An adjective is any word that describes or modifies a **noun**. 'A grey horse' is more exact than just 'a horse'. We can make it even more precise by writing 'a big, grey horse'. The words big and grey are adjectives describing the noun horse.

Adjectives usually come before the noun, but they can also come after it – 'The pie is delicious.' The word delicious describes the pie. It is an adjective.

Adolescence

Adolescence is the time when a child is growing up to become an adult. The changes of adolescence usually begin to take place in girls of 10 to 13 and in boys of 11 to 14. The changes go on for several years, and the adolescent's body changes in many ways. A girl's hips become wider and her breasts start to develop. She has her first menstrual period. This is a sign that she can one day have babies. A boy's voice becomes deeper and his facial hair starts to grow. Both boys and girls develop hair in their pubic areas and under their arms.

During adolescence, teenagers often feel awkward and have emotional upsets. However, these things soon pass and they become young men and women.

Advertising

Advertising is usually a way of telling somone about things they can buy and persuading people to buy them. Advertisements, or adverts, appear in many different **media**, including **television**, **radio**, **newspapers**, posters and leaflets. **Governments** use adverts too. They tell us things like 'Smoking is bad for your health'.

Today advertising is a huge industry that employs millions of people, including writers, artists, photographers, actors and salespeople. Many who work in advertising are employed by advertising agencies – firms that produce advertisements for clients who have goods or services to sell. Advertising agencies try to make the products and services they are selling appear as desirable and as good value as possible. Many countries have **laws** that stop advertisers making false claims about their products.

Aerosol

An aerosol is something that sprays **paint**, **cosmetics** or insecticides (chemicals that kill insect pests). It consists of a can containing a liquefied **gas** under high pressure. The can also contains the paint or other substance to be sprayed. When a button on the cap is pressed, a tiny nozzle opens and the gas forces out the can's contents in the form of a fine spray. Aerosols used to contain harmful chemicals called CFCs, but in most countries these have been replaced with less damaging substances.

Aesop

Aesop (pronounced 'Ee sop') was an Ancient Greek storyteller. His **fables**, or stories, are today known as *Aesop's Fables*. The characters in the stories are usually animals, but they behave like humans, with the same virtues and weaknesses. Each story teaches its readers a moral and offers useful advice. Aesop's best known fables include *The Tortoise and the Hare*, *The Boy Who Cried Wolf* and *The Wolf in Sheep's Clothing*.

According to legend, Aesop lived in about 620–560 BCE. However, it is likely that Aesop was an imaginary figure, and that his fables were made up by other writers.

Spray

Liquid

When you press down the button on an **aerosol** can, a gas under high pressure forces the liquid up a tube to the top and out as a very fine spray.

One of the most famous stories by **Aesop** tells the tale of a race between a tortoise and a hare. The swift hare is so sure of an easy win that he takes a rest during the race. But he soon falls asleep, allowing the much slower tortoise to win.

AFRICA

Africa is the second largest continent. It stretches from the Mediterranean Sea in the north to the Cape of Good Hope at its tip in the south.

Lappet vultures eat the rotting flesh of dead animals.

The boomslang is one of Africa's most poisonous snakes. It hunts lizards and birds in the treetops.

WILD AFRICA

Large parts of Africa are still wilderness. The scorching Sahara Desert spreads over much of the northern part of the continent. This empty land of sand and gravel is one of the hottest places on the planet. Near the equator, which crosses the centre of Africa, are vast rainforests packed with towering trees. The forests are always damp because they receive lots of torrential rain.

More than one-third of Africa is a high, flat plain, or plateau. Grassland called savanna covers much of the plateau region. Great herds of grazing animals, including elephants, antelope and zebra, roam the savanna. Other animals, such as lions, prey on the grazers.

MOUNTAINS, LAKES AND RIVERS

A giant crack in the surface of the earth, called the Great Rift Valley, runs through East Africa. All along it there are mountains, gorges and deep lakes. The tallest peaks are in Ethiopia, Kenya, Uganda and Tanzania. Africa's largest lake, Lake Victoria, fills a vast hollow in the middle of the Rift Valley. It is like an inland sea, and is surrounded by fertile farmland.

Africa's greatest rivers are the Nile, Niger, Congo, Zambezi and Limpopo. They are used for fishing, as a means of transport and for irrigating (watering) fields.

PEOPLE OF AFRICA

Many different peoples live in Africa. In North Africa are Arabs and Berbers, most of whom follow the Muslim religion. The black peoples who live south of the Sahara Desert make up three-quarters of Africa's population. They belong to over 800 ethnic groups.

There are 53 countries in Africa – more than any other continent. Between them, African people speak over 2,000 different languages.

△ *The Sahara Desert includes large areas of sand dunes, which are whipped into shape by the wind.*

▽ *Waterholes are vital to the animals of Africa's hot, grassy plains – especially in the dry season.*

WAY OF LIFE

Many Africans farm the land, growing crops like cocoa, cotton, sugar, coffee, tea, bananas and rubber. Africa produces three-quarters of the world's palm oil, which is used to make soap and margarine. The continent has extremely valuable mineral resources too, including gold, diamonds, tin and copper. There are rich oil supplies in parts of North and West Africa.

Most African people live in tribal villages, which often have their own culture and way of life. However, Africa's factories and urban areas are growing fast. The biggest cities include Cairo and Alexandria in Egypt, Lagos in Nigeria, Kinshasa in the Democratic Republic of Congo and Cape Town in South Africa.

TUNISIA
MOROCCO
ALGERIA
LIBYA
EGYPT
WESTERN SAHARA
MAURITANIA
MALI
NIGER
CHAD
SUDAN
ERITREA
SENEGAL
GAMBIA
GUINEA-BISSAU
GUINEA
BURKINA FASO
BENIN
NIGERIA
GHANA
COTE D'IVOIRE
SIERRA LEONE
LIBERIA
TOGO
EQUATORIAL GUINEA
CAMEROON
CENTRAL AFRICAN REPUBLIC
DJIBOUTI
ETHIOPIA
SOMALIA
UGANDA
KENYA
RWANDA
BURUNDI
GABON
CONGO
DEMOCRATIC REPUBLIC OF CONGO
Cabinda (Ang.)
TANZANIA
MALAWI
COMOROS
Mayotte (Fr.)
ANGOLA
ZAMBIA
MOZAMBIQUE
MADAGASCAR
MAURITIUS
Réunion (Fr.)
ZIMBABWE
NAMIBIA
BOTSWANA
SWAZILAND
SOUTH AFRICA
LESOTHO

Huge flocks of pink flamingoes gather on the salt lakes of East African countries such as Kenya.

AFRICA FACT FILE

Area: 30,313,000 sq km
Highest mountain: Mt Kilimanjaro, Tanzania, 5,895 m
Lowest point: Lake Assal, Djibouti, 156 m below sea level
Largest lake: Victoria, 68,880 sq km
Longest river: Nile, 6,670 km
Largest desert: Sahara
Number of countries: 53
Largest country: Sudan
Smallest mainland country: Gambia
Smallest island nation: Seychelles
Largest city: Cairo, Egypt, 7 million
Total population: 780 million

EUROPEAN INFLUENCE

For centuries Europeans knew very little about Africa or its people. At the end of the 1400s, the Portuguese found a sea route to India by sailing around the southern tip of Africa. Soon the African coastline was charted, although only a few traders and explorers trekked inland.

In the 1500s, European sailors began to ship slaves from Africa. Up to 14 million slaves were taken to the Americas between 1500 and the 1800s. Usually, traders bought these slaves from tribes on Africa's coasts.

◁ *The Masai women of East Africa wear bright cloth and beaded collars for special ceremonies.*

CONQUERING A CONTINENT

By the 1800s, some European countries started to set up colonies in Africa. The continent was carved up between the English, French, Belgians, Germans, Portuguese and Italians. The European powers brought new ways of life to Africa, but before long many Africans resented foreign rule.

WINNING INDEPENDENCE

During the 1950s and 1960s, most colonies became independent African countries. Many were poor and some suffered bloody civil wars as rival groups fought for power. Today, Africa faces many problems. However, its countries are developing their economies, and richer nations are giving them essential assistance.

Many African people are farmers. This Zambian woman is carrying corn husks.

SEE ALSO
Apartheid, Congo, Egypt, Ethiopia, Kenya, Nigeria, Nile River, Rainforest, Sahara Desert, Savanna, Slavery, South Africa

Afghanistan

AFGHANISTAN
Government: Republic
Capital: Kabul
Area: 647,497 sq km
Population: 26 million
Languages: Pushtu; Dari
Currency: Afghani

Afghanistan is a country in **Asia**. It is a mountainous land lying between the former **Soviet Union**, **Pakistan** and **Iran**. The capital and largest city is Kabul. Nearly all the people, known as Afghans, are Muslims − followers of **Islam**. In 1979, Russian troops invaded Afghanistan to support its **government**, which was friendly to Russia. The Russians withdrew in 1988 and a long **civil war** began. Eventually, a Muslim group, called the Taliban, controlled more than 90 per cent of the land.

Some of the Taliban leaders supported terrorist organizations (see **terrorism**) that attacked both New York and Washington on 11 September 2001. However, later that year, the Taliban were defeated by a rebel force called the Northern Alliance. The rebels received military assistance from other countries, including the US and Britain. Afghanistan now has a new government, but it remains politically unstable.

Africa *see pages 10–11*

Agriculture *see* Farming

AIDS

AIDS (Acquired Immune Deficiency Syndrome) is caused by a **virus** named HIV. The AIDS virus attacks white **blood** cells. These are the cells that fight off viruses and **bacteria** when they enter the body. When white blood cells are destroyed, the patient can become very ill with a **disease** that would not be serious to a healthy person. People with AIDS have no way of fighting disease, and often die.

White blood cell

Genetic material of AIDS virus

AIDS virus

Once the **AIDS** virus has entered the bloodstream, it attaches itself to a white blood cell, multiplies and spreads through the body.

AIDS is passed from person to person in three main ways − by intimate sexual contact, by exposure to blood infected with HIV, and by transmission to a baby in an infected mother's womb. People who have been infected with the AIDS virus may not become seriously ill until years later.

There is no cure for AIDS at present. It is a serious world problem, and kills millions of people every year.

Air

Air is all around us − it surrounds the **earth** in a layer we call the **atmosphere**. We need to breathe air in order to live. Air is colourless and has no smell. Yet it is really a mixture of different gases. We can feel air when the wind blows, and we know air has weight. The average roomful of air weighs more than 45 kg − about the weight of 20 bags of potatoes! Air also carries sound − without it we would not be able to hear, because sounds cannot travel in a **vacuum**.

The chief gas in air is nitrogen, which makes up nearly four-fifths of the air. About one-fifth of the air is **oxygen**, the gas we need to keep us alive. Air also holds some water in very fine particles called vapour. When we talk about **humidity**, it is the amount of water in the air we are measuring.

The air that surrounds the earth gets thinner the higher you go. Mountaineers carry their own air supply because the air at the top of high mountains is too

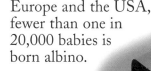

The wandering **albatross** has the longest wings of any bird – up to 3.5 m. It glides low over the ocean, skimming the waves.

thin to breathe properly. High-flying aircraft have to keep the air in their cabins at ground-level pressure so that passengers can breathe normally.

Warm air expands and becomes lighter. When the air around a heater becomes lighter, it rises. Cool air moves into its place. This, too, warms and rises, so the entire room is heated.

Aircraft *see* pages 14–15

Albania

Albania is a small, rugged country that lies between **Serbia** and **Greece** on the eastern shore of the Adriatic Sea. Most Albanians live in remote mountain villages. Albania was ruled by **Turkey** for over 400 years. After World War II it became a communist state (see **communism**), but by 1992, a multi-party system was in place. In 1997, the country was torn apart by an armed rebellion. Order was soon restored, but there have been several other civil disturbances since then.

Albatross

The albatross is a large **bird** that spends most of its life in the air over the oceans. There are 14 different species of albatross. Most albatrosses live in regions south of the **equator**, where they soar gracefully over the waves. They come ashore only

to breed or during fierce storms. Albatrosses often follow ships for days at a time, picking up scraps of food thrown overboard.

Albatrosses settle on the water to sleep and feed. They eat mainly **squid**, **jellyfish** and **fish**. The giant birds drink so much sea water that they need special glands on their head to get rid of all the salt they take in. Every year thousands of albatrosses get tangled up in **fishing** nets and long fishing lines, and die. They are becoming rare as a result.

Albino

Albino animals are born white, with no colouring matter in their skin or hair. They have pink eyes. Albinos inherit their colourless condition from their ancestors (see **genetics**). An albino parent is still able to produce normal young, but these young may later produce albino offspring of their own.

Human albinos are very rare. In Europe and the USA, fewer than one in 20,000 babies is born albino.

ALBANIA
Government: Republic
Capital: Tirana
Area: 28,748 sq km
Population: 3.4 million
Language: Albanian
Currency: Lek

The American *Blackbird* can fly at a height of more than 26,000 m – higher than any other **aircraft**. Up there, the **air** is extremely cold and thin, with very little oxygen.

AIRCRAFT

We live in a world where people take air travel for granted. But it was thousands of years before our dreams of flying like the birds became reality. The first successful powered flight did not take place until the early 20th century.

Montgolfier hot-air balloon

Drawing of a flying machine by Leonardo da Vinci

EARLY DAYS

Myths and legends are filled with extraordinary tales of people who could fly. Brave but foolhardy inventors leaped from high towers wearing wings, but all these attempts ended in failure. In the 1500s, the artist and inventor Leonardo da Vinci drew plans for a helicopter, although such a machine could never have been built in his day.

The age of air travel began with the first balloon flight in 1783. Seventy years later, airships took to the sky. Airships are large, steerable balloons with engines and propellers. At the same time, inventors built the first gliders. Gliding proved that flight was possible by using winged aeroplanes that were heavier than air.

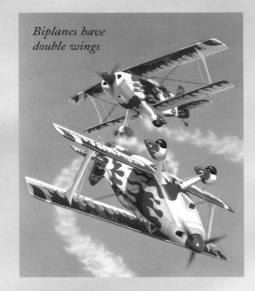
Biplanes have double wings

MILITARY AIRCRAFT

Aircraft were first used as fighting machines during World War I. By 1939, most large countries had an air force. Germany built up a strong air force called the Luftwaffe, which it used in surprise attacks at the start of World War II. The Germans knew that no land battle could be won without control of the skies above the battle area.

As World War II progressed, long-range bombers played a larger part in the tactics of the British, American, German and Japanese air forces. Since then, guided missiles have cut down the part played by bombers, but piloted planes are still needed as a defence against fast strike bombers. Modern fighter aircraft can fly close to the ground at very high speeds, slipping under the enemy's radar screen without being spotted.

CONQUEST OF THE AIR

The development of the petrol engine in the 1880s made powered aircraft a possibility. On 17 December 1903, the Wright brothers climbed into their flimsy aeroplane, the *Flyer*, and made the first-ever controlled flight with people on board. They flew only 36 m. Since that historic flight, progress in aviation has been amazingly rapid. Early aeroplanes had piston engines that drove propellers, pulling the aircraft forwards. Many small aircraft still use propellers, but most large planes have jet engines, which are far more powerful.

GIANT AIRLINERS

Thanks to jet airliners, travelling long distances is now cheap and easy. The Boeing 747 was the first of the big 'jumbo jets'. This highly successful airliner entered service in 1970, and carries up to 560 passengers. It has a wingspan of 60 m, is 70 m long and weighs nearly 320 tonnes. The 747 can fly at a speed of 910 km/h for a distance of 8,000 km.

Boeing 747-400

Passenger seats

Cockpit

Radar equipment

Cargo hold

Wing has curved upper and flat lower surfaces

Large flaps at the back of the wing are extended during landing to increase lift and help reduce speed

HOW AIRCRAFT FLY

An aeroplane's wing creates lift when it slices through the air. It has a curved upper surface and a flat lower surface, which forces the air to travel faster over the top than across the bottom. This creates a sort of upward suction that makes the wing rise, taking the aeroplane up with it. A helicopter rotor blade has the same curved-and-flat shape, which is known as an aerofoil.

HISTORY OF FLIGHT

1783 First balloon flight by Montgolfier brothers
1852 Henri Giffard invents steam-driven airship
1853 George Cayley builds first manned glider
1903 Orville and Wilbur Wright make first powered flight
1919 First trans-Atlantic crossing by air
1927 Lindbergh flies Atlantic alone
1939 First jet plane, the Heinkel *He 178*
1939 First single-rotor helicopter, the Sikorsky *VS-300*
1942 First jet fighter, the Messerschmitt *Me 262*
1947 Bell *XI* rocket plane flies faster than sound
1964 First swing-wing warplane, the US *F-111*
1952 *Comet* is world's first jet airliner
1976 *Concorde* supersonic airliner enters service
1978 First Atlantic crossing by balloon
1981 Solar-powered *Solar Challenger* crosses English Channel
1986 *Voyager* aircraft flies non-stop around world

AIRCRAFT RECORDS

Fastest warplane: Lockheed *SR-71 Blackbird*, 3,529 km/h, USA
Fastest airliner: *Concorde*, 2,333 km/h, Britain/France
Heaviest plane: Antonov *AN-225*, 600 tonnes, Russia
Largest helicopter: Mil *Mi-26*, 55 tonnes, Russia

Chinook twin-rotor helicopter

***F-16* Fighting Falcon**

Rudder for steering

Wingtip fin reduces air resistance

Tail fin

Wing flaps used for take-off and landing

'Black box' records flight details

AIRPORTS

An airport is one of the busiest places in the world. All day and all night airliners take off and land. Airports have three main jobs: they handle passengers, mail and freight; they make sure that all aircraft take off and land safely and on time; and they provide hangars and workshops so that planes can be checked regularly. The centre of operations at an airport is the air-traffic control tower. Inside, ground controllers use computers and radar to guide the pilots who are taking off and landing.

Fuel tanks located inside wings

Jet engines

SEE ALSO
Balloon and Airship, Gliding, Helicopter, Jet engine, Montgolfier brothers, Supersonic flight, Wright brothers

15

The American **alligator** nests on sandy banks. Each female lays about 30 to 40 eggs, and builds a mound of plants and soil to keep them warm. This female is taking her newly hatched babies down to the water.

Alchemy

The **chemistry** of the **Middle Ages** was called alchemy. It was a strange mixture of magic, science and religion. The people who practised alchemy dreamed of producing a magic substance which they called the 'philosopher's stone'. This substance would be able to change cheap metals such as lead into **gold**; it would also cure diseases and keep people young. Needless to say, the alchemists never found the philosopher's stone, but in their search they learned a great deal about chemistry and invented apparatus that chemists still use today.

Alcohol

There are many different kinds of alcohol. The kind we know best is the alcohol in beer, wine and spirits such as whisky. It can make people intoxicated, or drunk. Alcohol is formed by a process called **fermentation**. In fermentation, **yeasts** act on the sugar in grain and fruit to produce alcohol. If strong alcohol is needed, the liquid has to be distilled.

Alcohols are used in the making of perfumes and drugs. They dissolve oils, fats and plastics. The alcohol called glycol is used as an anti-freeze in car radiators because, like all alcohols, it has a very low freezing point.

Alexander the Great was a strong general who ruled over a vast empire. He had a real genius for planning battles and leading troops. Alexander is buried in the city of Alexandria in Egypt.

Alexander the Great

Alexander the Great (356–323 BCE) was a ruler of **Greece** and one of the most powerful generals in history. As a young man he was taught by **Aristotle**, the Greek philosopher.

Alexander became king in 336 BCE. He conquered the Greek city-states and then marched east to conquer Persia, which was at that time the world's greatest empire. By 327 BCE, Alexander's own empire stretched from Greece to India. When his armies reached India they were worn out from marching and fighting. Alexander had to turn back. When he reached **Babylon** he caught a fever and died. He was still only 33.

Algebra

Algebra is a branch of **mathematics** in which letters stand for numbers. It uses various signs to represent connections between the different letters. Algebra equations are statements in which both sides of the equals sign (=) balance each other out; for example x + 3 = 9. Solving an equation means finding the number which makes the statement true.

Algeria

The large North African country of Algeria is bordered by six countries and the **Mediterranean Sea**. The enormous **Sahara Desert** covers most of Algeria, and only a few people, called Berbers, live there. Most Algerians live in a narrow strip along the **Mediterranean**. Algiers is the capital and largest city.

The French seized Algeria in 1830 and stayed there until the country won its independence in 1962, after a long and bitter war. However, many Muslims fiercely opposed the new Algerian **government** because they believed that it was introducing Western values.

Alligator and Crocodile

Alligators and crocodiles are large, powerful animals that belong to the same family of **reptiles**. There are two species of alligator – the American alligator of the southern USA, and the smaller Chinese alligator that lives in the **Yangtze River**. There are 20 species of crocodile, including the Nile crocodile of Africa, and the saltwater crocodile of Australia and southern Asia.

Alligators and crocodiles are aggressive predators that hunt fish, turtles and large mammals. They have become less common because of hunting and damage to their wetland homes.

Alloy

An alloy is a mixture of two or more **metals**. The mixture is often more useful than each metal on its own.

For example, a soft metal such as **copper** can be strengthened by adding **zinc** to form brass, or **tin** to form **bronze**. Pure **iron** is not very strong and rusts easily. It is mixed with chromium, nickel and carbon to make stainless steel, the alloy from which cutlery is made.

Alphabet

An alphabet is a collection of letters, or symbols, used to write down a **language**. The word alphabet comes from the names of the first two letters in the Greek alphabet: alpha and beta. The 26 letters in the English alphabet come from the **Roman** alphabet of 2,500 years ago. Other alphabets in common use today include the Greek, Arabic, Hebrew and Russian, or Cyrillic, alphabets. Most contain symbols for vowels (soft sounds like 'a' and 'e') and consonants (hard sounds like 's' and 't'). But the Arabic and Hebrew alphabets have consonants only.

Alps

The Alps form the largest **mountain** range in **Europe**. They are centred in Switzerland, but stretch from the east of France and southern Germany all the way to the former Yugoslavia. Mont Blanc, 4,807 m high, is the highest peak in the Alps. Thick forests cover the mountains' steep slopes, and there are many lakes in the valleys; the largest is Lake Geneva. The Alps attract many tourists, who go to climb, ski and fish.

Alligators (top) look very like crocodiles (bottom), but have broader, flatter heads. Another difference is that when crocodiles close their jaws, a tooth sticks out on each side.

ALGERIA
Government: Republic
Capital: Algiers
Area: 2,381,741 sq km
Population: 30 million
Language: Arabic
Currency: Algerian dinar

▷ The **Alps** are home to a wide variety of rare mountain wildlife.

Ibex

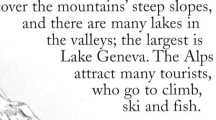

The alpine chough is a species of crow that lives on the highest cliffs and slopes

17

Aluminium

There is more aluminium in the earth's crust than any other **metal**. Most aluminium is produced from bauxite, which is a kind of ore (an ore is a rock or **mineral** containing metals). The bauxite is treated with chemicals and placed in a large electric furnace. An electric current is passed through and aluminium falls to the bottom of the furnace. It is silvery in colour.

Aluminium is light – it weighs only a third as much as steel. It is especially useful where lightness and strength are important, for example in **aircraft** and **tennis** raquets. It is also a good conductor of **heat** and **electricity**, and for this reason it is used for electric power cables and cooking ('tin') foil.

Aluminium is a very useful metal. Among many other things, it is used in tennis raquets, power lines, aircraft and cooking foil.

There are 3,500 kinds of lizard. Lizards make up just over half of the world's reptiles

Amazon River

The Amazon is the mightiest river in **South America** and, at a length of 6,440 km, is the second-longest in the world after the **Nile**. It flows from **Peru** through **Brazil** to the **Atlantic Ocean**. Almost all of the Amazon river basin is dense **rainforest**. In the 1540s, a Spanish explorer saw female Indian warriors on the Amazon's banks, so the river was named after the Amazons (female warriors) of Greek legends.

American Revolution *see* Revolutionary War, American

Amundsen, Roald

Roald Amundsen (1872–1928) was a Norwegian explorer. In 1910, he set out to be the first to reach the **North Pole**, but was beaten by the American, Robert Peary. Amundsen then decided to go for the **South Pole**, which he reached on 14 December 1911, the first person ever to do so. He reached the Pole a month before the ill-fated expedition led by Captain **Scott**.

Andersen, Hans Christian

Hans Christian Andersen (1805–1875) was a Danish storyteller. His fairy tales, such as *The Little Mermaid*, *The Ugly Duckling* and *The Snow Queen*, are still popular all over the world.

Andes

The Andes **mountain** range is the longest in the world. It stretches for more than 7,000 km down the west side of **South America**, running the whole length of the continent. Several peaks are more than 6,000 m high, and Aconcagua, on the border between **Argentina** and **Chile**, is the highest mountain in the Americas at 6,960 m. Many of the peaks are active volcanoes. The Andes are rich in minerals such as copper, silver and gold.

Andorra

Andorra is a tiny, mountainous country on the border between **France** and **Spain**. From 1278 until 1993, it was ruled jointly by the president of France and the bishop of Urgel in Spain.

ANDORRA
Government: Co-principality
Capital: Andorra la Vella
Area: 453 sq km
Population: 66,000
Language: Catalan
Currency: Euro

continued on page 20

LIFE CYCLE OF A FROG

Adult frog

Eggs

Tadpole

Tadpole grows fast

Tadpole develops legs

Baby froglet

Snakes are hunters. The emerald tree boa of South America coils its tail around a branch and waits, perfectly still, until a bird or small mammal comes within reach – then it strikes.

AMPHIBIANS and REPTILES

Amphibians and reptiles are two amazingly varied groups of animals. Amphibians have soft, moist skin, but reptiles are covered with tough scales.

World of amphibians

Amphibians include the frogs, toads, salamanders and newts. They are able to live both in water and on land, but most of them start their lives in water. Common places to find amphibians are pools, streams, ditches, marshes and damp woodland. Amphibians absorb water and oxygen from the air directly through their skins. For this reason they must keep their skins moist.

All amphibians are predators. They hunt a variety of insects and other small animals, usually by hiding and making a sudden lunge to snatch their victims.

World of reptiles

The first reptiles appeared about 360 million years ago. One group of reptiles, the dinosaurs, were the most spectacular creatures this planet has seen. Today, reptiles include the lizards, snakes, alligators, crocodiles, turtles and tortoises. Most reptiles live on land or in rivers and swamps, but some turtles and snakes live in the sea. Many snakes have poisonous bites with which they kill their prey. Turtles and tortoises have armoured shells, or carapaces, for protection.

When baby alligators and crocodiles hatch, they look like miniature versions of their parents.

△ *Most amphibians lay their eggs in water, in a layer of jelly that protects them. The babies are called larvae and the larvae of frogs and toads are known as tadpoles. The larvae can breathe underwater, just like fish. After two or three months, they begin to turn into adults, and are able to leave the water.*

Balancing act

Amphibians and reptiles are cold-blooded animals. This means that their body temperature goes up and down as the surrounding air or water gets warmer and cooler. When it gets too cold, they sunbathe to warm up. But if it gets too hot, they have to take shelter from the sun.

Most amphibians and reptiles live in warm parts of the world. Those that live in cooler regions spend the winter in a deep sleep called hibernation.

◁ *The gliding frog of Malaysia has special webs on its feet that it uses as tiny 'wings'. They allow the frog to glide between trees.*

SEE ALSO
Alligator and Crocodile, Frog and Toad, Hibernation, Lizard, Salamander and Newt, Tortoise, Turtle and Terrapin

▷ *The Australian frilled lizard raises its collar and gapes its mouth to frighten off attackers.*

Predators are **animals** that catch and eat other animals, known as prey. The cheetah's main prey is **antelope**.

continued from page 18

Since 1993, the people of Andorra have elected their own **government** officials. Andorra is surrounded by the **Pyrenees** mountains, and its main industry is tourism.

Angle

An angle is formed when two straight lines meet. The size of all angles is measured in degrees. A 'right' angle forms the corner of a square and has 90 degrees. An acute angle is less than 90 degrees and an obtuse angle is between 90 and 180 degrees.

Anglo-Saxons

Anglo-Saxon is the name given to the group of Germanic tribes who settled in Britain during the 400s and 500s. These tribes were the Angles, Saxons and Jutes. They gradually occupied all of England, and drove the original Celtic people of Britain (see **Celts**) into Wales

◁ Life was hard for ordinary **Anglo-Saxons**. Most of them were farmers, and lived in simple houses made of mud, thatch and timber.

and Cornwall. By the 700s, there were seven main Anglo-Saxon kingdoms: Wessex, Sussex, Kent, Essex, East Anglia, Mercia and Northumbria. About half the words in the English language come from Anglo-Saxon.

Angola

The Republic of Angola is a large country on the coast of the Atlantic Ocean in southwestern **Africa**. It has valuable reserves of **diamonds**.

Portugal claimed Angola in 1482. Native Angolans rebelled against the Portuguese in 1960 and fighting broke out. In 1975, Portugal granted the Angolans full independence. A violent struggle then began between rival Angolan factions, some of them aided by foreign troops. The war ended in 1991 when the **government** and the rebels agreed to a ceasefire. However, despite attempts to keep the peace, fighting continued into the 21st century.

Animals

An animal is any living thing that is not a **plant**. No one knows how many different kinds of animals there are on earth, and hundreds of new kinds are discovered every year. The biggest difference between animals and plants

ANGOLA
Government: Republic
Capital: Luanda
Area: 1,246,700 sq km
Population: 12.4 million
Language: Portuguese
Currency: Kwanza

is in the way they get their food. Animals eat plants or other animals. Plants make their own food out of substances taken in through their roots or leaves. Animals, unlike plants, can also move about at some time in their lives.

Some animals such as the tiny amoeba reproduce simply by splitting in two. In most other animals, the female produces eggs that are then fertilized by the male.

Animals with backbones are called **vertebrates**. Vertebrates include the **birds**, **mammals**, **fish**, **amphibians** and **reptiles**. **Invertebrates** are animals without backbones. **Insects**, **jellyfish**, **molluscs**, **worms**, **spiders** and **snails** are all examples of invertebrates. As invertebrates lack internal bones, some of them have a shell for protection.

Ant

Ants are 'social' **insects** – they live together in colonies. Some colonies are in heaps of twigs, while others are inside chambers deep in the ground. Still others are hills of earth or sand. There are three types of ant – males, queens which lay eggs, and workers or females that neither mate nor lay eggs.

Army ants march cross-country in a great horde that may have as many as several million ants. They devour anything in their path, even cattle.

Antarctic *see* page 23

Anteater

The South American anteater is a curious **mammal** with a long, tapering snout. This snout is specially shaped to winkle ants, **termites** and grubs from their nests. The anteater catches the insects with its long, whip-like tongue.

There are four different kinds of anteater. By far the largest is the giant anteater, which may measure

△ The giant **anteater** uses its long, tube-shaped snout and sticky tongue to catch ants and termites. It may eat up to 30,000 of the insects in a single day.

▽ Leaf-cutter **ants** live in tropical forests in the Americas. Great trails of worker ants climb to the treetops, where the ants cut pieces of leaves. They take the leaves back to the nest and dump them in piles. A fungus grows on the heaps of leaves, and the ants harvest it as food.

over 2 m from the tip of its tail to its snout. Anteaters live in tropical forests, grassy plains and swamps.

Antelope

Antelopes are grazing animals with **horns** and **hoofs**. They look rather like **deer**, but are actually related to goats and cattle. Most antelopes live on the African plains, or **savannas**. They are fast runners and often live in large herds, fleeing suddenly at any hint of danger. Their main enemies are lions, cheetahs and hyenas. Some of the best-known kinds of antelope are the impala, eland, waterbuck, wildebeest, gazelle and the tiny dik-dik, which is hardly bigger than a rabbit.

Antibiotics

Antibiotics are substances, produced by living things, that are poisonous to harmful **bacteria**. Early in the 20th century, scientists began to discover **drugs** that would kill bacteria but not harm the patient. The most important

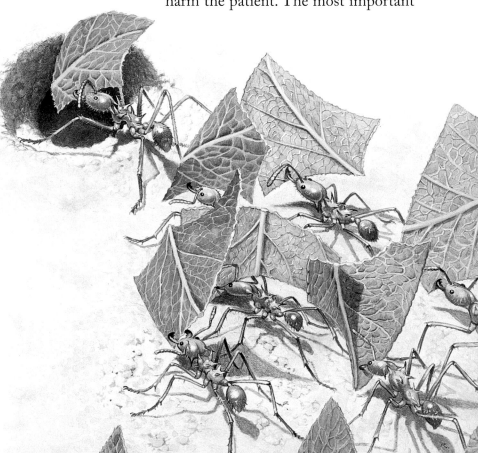

of these drugs was penicillin, a drug produced by a mould. Penicillin was a 'wonder drug' that saved many lives. It was especially useful against pneumonia, a **disease** that inflames the **lungs**. Scientists have found many more useful antibiotics that can fight diseases such as tuberculosis, typhus and whooping cough. But antibiotics do not work against **viruses** – the organisms that cause colds, flu, mumps, measles, **AIDS** and other diseases.

Archaeologists clean finds by brushing away the soil

Each find is recorded and numbered before it is removed

Archaeology is the study of the remains of the past. In 1974, thousands of life-size clay soldiers were found near the tomb of an ancient Chinese emperor.

Apartheid

The word apartheid was used by the white rulers of **South Africa** to describe their policy for keeping apart the white and non-white peoples of South Africa – apartheid means 'apartness' in the Afrikaans language. In the late 1940s, the white South African **government** began to pass a series of laws that made apartheid the official government policy.

Strict apartheid laws kept whites and non-whites apart, and ensured that whites had a much better way of life than the rest of the population. In 1991, the South African government overturned major apartheid laws.

Apes, like these gorillas, are sociable animals that live in family groups. Each group has a large, strong male who rules over all the females, babies and younger males.

In 1994, South Africa's first free elections led to the black African National Congress being the governing party, and **Nelson Mandela** was elected president.

Ape

The apes are our closest animal relatives. We have the same kind of skeleton and blood, and catch many similar diseases.

Apes have large brains, but even the gorilla's brain is only half the size of a human's. Unlike **monkeys**, apes have no tails. There are four kinds of ape: the **gorilla** and **chimpanzee** are African; **orangutans** live in Borneo and Sumatra; and gibbons live throughout Southeast Asia. They are all forest animals.

Apes have extremely nimble hands and fingers for holding food and swinging from branches. They eat a wide variety of leaves, fruits and nuts. Apes are becoming rare in many places because of hunting and because their forest homes are being cut down.

Archaeology

Archaeology is the study of history through the things that people have made and built. They may include tools, coins, pottery, houses, temples and graves. Even a rubbish tip can help to reveal how people lived.

At first archaeological sites were ransacked for their treasures. But, by the early 1800s, archaeologists had begun to uncover sites carefully, noting everything they found and where they found it. Many exciting and important discoveries were made, including the remains of ancient Troy (1871), the early **Greek** civilization at Mycenae (1876), and the tomb of the pharaoh **Tutankhamen** in **Egypt** (1922).

continued on page 24

ARCTIC and ANTARCTIC

The Arctic and Antarctic lie at opposite ends of the earth. They are the coldest places on the planet, and life there is very hard.

Like many Arctic animals, the snowy owl is white to camouflage it against snow.

The polar bear hunts seals, fish and small whales in the frozen seas of northern polar regions. Arctic foxes often follow behind, looking for scraps.

TO THE ENDS OF THE EARTH

The Arctic is the region within the Arctic Circle – an imaginary line drawn around the northern part of the globe. It is made up of the Arctic Ocean, the surrounding seas and islands, and the northern parts of Alaska, Canada, Greenland, Norway, Sweden, Finland and Russia. At the centre of the Arctic is the North Pole. There is no land at the North Pole, only a huge area of frozen sea.

The Antarctic region includes Antarctica, the world's fifth largest continent, which surrounds the South Pole. Nearly all of the Antarctic is covered by a thick ice cap, broken only by a few mountain ranges. This ice cap averages 2,500 m thick. Off the coast of Antarctica there are many islands, icebergs and ice sheets.

Many kinds of whale and dolphin swim to the Arctic and Antarctic to feed. Sperm whales dive deep in search of their favourite food – squid.

POLAR WILDLIFE

Despite the harsh conditions, many kinds of animal live in the Arctic and Antarctic. The Arctic's wildlife includes lemmings, reindeer or caribou, Arctic hares and polar bears. Many Arctic animals spend the winter in burrows underground. Most of the birds migrate (fly south) to warmer areas for the winter, and return in spring to breed. Arctic seas are home to seals, walruses and whales.

Very few animals can survive near the South Pole. However, the Antarctic's seas teem with fish and tiny, shrimp-like animals called krill. They provide food for large numbers of squid, whales, penguins and albatrosses.

ICE AND SNOW

The Arctic and Antarctic get some of the most extreme weather anywhere on earth. In the Arctic, temperatures rise above freezing (0°C) for only four months of the year. However, the Antarctic is even colder – the world's lowest-ever temperature, -90°C, was recorded there. Fierce winds race across the open landscape, creating snowdrifts and raging snowstorms.

It is cold near the North and South poles because the sun never rises high in the sky. In winter, there are days when it does not rise at all. In midsummer, the sun can be seen all day and night – it never gets dark.

POLAR PEOPLES

Several different peoples live in the Arctic, including the Inuit of Canada and Greenland and the Lapps of Norway, Sweden and Finland. They hunt and fish for a living. The only people living in the Antarctic are scientists.

Emperor penguins breed in the Antarctic winter. To survive the bitter cold, they have thick layers of body fat and huddle together in groups.

Arctic   ***Antarctic***

The Arctic and Antarctic circles are imaginary lines around the world. Most of the area inside the Arctic Circle is sea, but the Antarctic Circle is filled by an icy continent called Antarctica.

Even today, one of the fastest ways to travel in the Arctic is on sledges pulled by teams of huskies.

SEE ALSO
Albatross, Amundsen (Roald), Bear, Climate, Iceberg, North Pole, Penguin, Scott (Robert Falcon), Seal, South Pole, Whale

ARGENTINA
Government: Republic
Capital: Buenos Aires
Area: 2,766,889 sq km
Population: 36.5 million
Language: Spanish
Currency: Peso

▽ The **Armada** of 1588 was a huge fleet of Spanish fighting ships. It carried a force of 30,000 people, including priests, surgeons, lawyers and administrators.

continued from page 22

Today, science helps the archaeologist in his or her work. Radiocarbon dating helps tell us when particular objects were made (see **carbon**). **Infrared** and **X-ray** photography can show up designs under the rotted surface of a bronze bowl. Archaeology has even gone under the sea. With modern diving equipment, archaeologists can explore sunken wrecks and other long-lost remains of the past.

Archery

Archery is the use of the bow and arrow, once for hunting and warfare, now mostly for sport. No one knows when bows and arrows were first used, but prehistoric man certainly used them to shoot animals for food and to protect himself. Until the discovery of gunpowder, the **army** with the best archers usually won the battle (see **war**). Modern bows are usually made of laminated wood or fibreglass.

Architecture *see* page 26

Arctic *see* page 23

Argentina

Argentina is the second largest country in **South America**. Most of its people are farmers and ranchers, as much of Argentina's wealth comes from crops and livestock. It is one of the world's top producers of beef and wool.

The chief farming region in Argentina is the pampas, a Spanish word meaning 'flat land'. The pampas lies in the centre of the country around its capital, Buenos Aires. Here, vast farms raise millions of **cattle** and **sheep**. Northern Argentina is an area of tropical forests. In the far south, near the tip of South America, is Patagonia, a cold land of windswept plains and high, snowy mountains. The western part of the country rises steeply to the **Andes** mountains.

Argentina was ruled by **Spain** from 1535 until 1810. Today, most of the population are descended from Europeans, although there are still about 20,000 native Argentinians.

Aristotle

Aristotle (384–322 BCE) was a Greek philosopher and a student of another famous Greek philosopher, **Plato**. At the age of 17, Aristotle went to Athens to become Plato's pupil. He worked there for 20 years and then became tutor to **Alexander the Great**. Aristotle invented the method of thinking called logic. His writings cover many areas, including nature and politics.

Arkwright, Richard

Richard Arkwright (1732–1792) was an English inventor best known for his spinning frame, which made factory production of **cotton** cloth possible.

Arkwright patented his new spinning machine in 1769, after which he built his first spinning mill. He became the pioneer of the modern factory system. His success laid the framework for the **Industrial Revolution**.

Armada

Armada is a Spanish word for a great fleet of armed **ships**. The most famous armada was the fleet that tried to invade England in 1588. The 130 Spanish ships were large, clumsy and heavily armed. The English ships were faster and easier to manoeuvre. The English sent fire ships towards the Spanish fleet, which retreated out to sea. Several Spanish ships were sunk in battle and the Armada was forced to flee around the northern tip of Britain, where many of its ships were wrecked in storms. Only 67 of the original 130 ships finally reached **Spain**.

Armadillo

Armadillos are strange **mammals** that live in Central and South America. Their backs are covered with an armour of bony plates. They have strong claws which they use for digging burrows and tearing open termite nests to find food. There are 20 different kinds of armadillo.

Armour

Armour is covering used to protect the body in battle. It was first worn at least 5,000 years ago and was originally made of tough **leather**. Then metal breastplates, helmets and shields were made. But the rest of the body was still protected by leather or by chain mail, hundreds of small **iron** rings linked together to form a flexible metal coat.

Armadillos get their name from the armour plating on their backs. They roll into a tight ball when under threat of attack.

Suits of plate **armour** were made from silvery steel. They had so many pieces that knights took up to an hour to dress for battle. But although the armour looked difficult to move around in, it was actually quite flexible.

Helmet
Visor
Breastplate
Gauntlet
Leg harness
Leather straps

In the **Middle Ages**, knights rode into battle encased from head to toe in suits of plate armour that weighed up to 30 kg. But as **guns** became more powerful and accurate, heavy armour was no longer of any use, and it gradually died out. Today, lightweight metals and **plastics** are used in bulletproof vests worn by soldiers and the **police**.

Army

The first effective armies appeared in the Middle East more than 3,500 years ago. In the ancient world, Egypt, Greece and Rome all had large armies. Until modern times, infantry (foot soldiers) made up the bulk of most armies, but today's troops do a variety of jobs.

Most armies now consist of combat troops, service troops and staff officers. Combat troops include the infantry, armoured troops (who are equipped with tanks), artillery (who operate the heavy **guns**) and paratroopers (who parachute behind enemy lines).

Service troops provide the food, fuel, ammunition and other supplies needed by the combat troops. They include medical personnel, and engineers who build bridges and prepare landing strips for **aircraft**. The staff is made up of headquarters officers who plan and direct the army operations.

Art *see* page 27

Artery

An artery is a **blood** vessel that carries blood from the **heart** to all parts of the body. **Veins** are different from arteries because they carry used blood back to the heart. Arteries have thick, elastic walls. The largest is the aorta, which is connected directly to the heart itself.

ARCHITECTURE

Architecture is the art of designing buildings and other structures. The main aims of architecture are to make sure that the constructions are strong, look good and are suitable for their purpose.

△ *In 3000–2000 BCE, the Sumerians of ancient Iraq constructed tall pyramid-shaped temples called ziggurats.*

△ *The massive dome of Florence cathedral, built in the Renaissance, was admired across Europe.*

△ *India's Taj Mahal (1650) features domes and minarets (towers) typical of Islamic architecture.*

EARLY ARCHITECTURE

The earliest buildings were simple structures made of dried grass or mud that provided shelter from the sun, wind and rain. More than 5,000 years ago, the ancient civilizations of Mesopotamia (present-day Iraq) started building one-room houses out of sun-baked clay bricks. As workers became more skilled and their construction techniques more advanced, people began to create more elaborate buildings. In the period 2600–1000 BCE, the Ancient Egyptians constructed huge pyramids as tombs for their dead kings. The largest of these pyramids used more than two million stone blocks.

GREEK AND ROMAN ARCHITECTURE

Western architecture as we know it today began to take shape in Greece in around 600 BCE. Over the next 450 years, Greek architects developed a classical style that featured beautiful pillars of stone or marble. Surviving examples of Ancient Greek architecture include temples, such as the Parthenon in Athens, and outdoor theatres.

The Romans copied the Greek architectural style, but also invented their own building techniques, such as curved arches and domed roofs. Arches can support a lot of weight, allowing architects to design larger, stronger buildings. Roman architects built a wide range of structures, mainly in 100 BCE–300 CE, including public baths, palaces, bridges and gigantic sports arenas.

CHANGING STYLES

During the Middle Ages, European architects developed new ways of building with stone. They built everything from fortified castles to churches.

The Gothic style flourished from the mid-1100s to the 1400s. Many of the fine, old cathedrals of Europe were built in the Gothic style. They featured graceful, pointed arches, high ceilings and stained-glass windows.

The Renaissance, which began in Italy in the late 1300s, triggered a new wave of architectural development. The direction of architecture also changed during this period. Instead of concentrating mainly on churches and other religious buildings, architects began to spend more time designing private houses and public buildings such as government offices and town halls.

In the 1500s, architects started to become famous for their work. Since then, the best architects have always been in high demand. They are able to adapt their styles to suit the needs of their clients.

▷ *In the 1980s, a glass pyramid was built in the courtyard of the Louvre Museum, Paris.*

MODERN ARCHITECTURE

In the modern age, the main building materials are still bricks and stone, but architects now have many new materials to choose from for their designs. Concrete and steel, glass and plastic are shaping the new world in which we live. Many other inventions have also helped to revolutionize architecture, such as central heating, electric lighting and air conditioning. When the lift was invented, in 1854, it allowed architects to design much taller buildings. The first steel-framed skyscrapers were erected in Chicago and New York in the late 1800s.

Today, architects work together with engineers and surveyors. They use computers to calculate the different weights and forces within their planned building, and alter the design if necessary. Some modern buildings have very dramatic or futuristic shapes that would have been impossible to build without recent technology.

◁ *New York's Guggenheim Museum was opened in 1960.*

SEE ALSO
Church, Dome, Egypt (Ancient), Greece (Ancient), House, Mosque, Parthenon, Pyramid, Skyscraper

ART

Art is any creative work used to portray images and to express feelings. People produce art in many ways and in many different forms, including painting, drawing, printing, sculpture, photography and film.

△ *Cave paintings made up to 30,000 years ago exist in places as far apart as Africa, China and Europe. This cattle-herding scene was painted on rock in the central Sahara Desert.*

THE STORY OF ART

In the past, art usually had a practical purpose. The earliest cave paintings, for example, probably had a religious or ritual meaning. In Ancient Egypt, Greece and Rome, rulers and wealthy people used art to show off their importance and power. They owned decorated pottery, mosaics and statues, which often depicted gods, goddesses and mythical scenes.

In Europe, during the Middle Ages, art was used to teach people about their religion and to help them pray. To us, medieval paintings sometimes look rather 'flat' and unnatural. This is partly because artists did not know how to make their images appear three-dimensional. They first began to find out how to do this from the late 1300s onwards in Italy. The new, more realistic style spread across Europe during the 1400s and 1500s. This period – the Renaissance – was a time when artists tried out many new techniques.

In the 1600s, artists started to illustrate non-religious subjects, such as portraits of ordinary people, still lifes (collections of objects) and everyday scenes. They also signed their work so that people knew who they were. Medieval artists never signed their work.

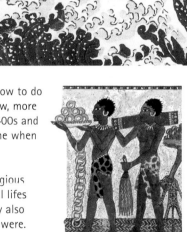

◁ *Ancient Egyptian tombs were covered with wall paintings of gods, religious ceremonies and hunting expeditions.*

△ *Japansese art includes dramatic natural scenes. This print,* The Great Wave, *was made by Hokusai in 1831–1833.*

The invention of photography in the mid-19th century had a big impact on art. Because photographs were so lifelike, many artists decided to create art that was less realistic instead. In France, painters introduced a new, 'loose' style called Impressionism, in which they used bold strokes of colour to give the impression of changing lighting effects. Since then, art styles have continued to change. Some artists have made abstract art, which has no obvious subject, and is more about their ideas and feelings. Artists now produce a wide variety of work in many different styles.

◁ *Sandro Botticelli, a leading artist of the Italian Renaissance, painted* Spring *in about 1478.*

△ *Modern sculptors use many different materials to make sculptures with interesting shapes and textures.*

SEE ALSO
Abstract art, Impressionism, Michelangelo, Painting, Picasso, Renaissance, Sculpture, Van Gogh

ASIA

Asia is the largest continent. It covers one-third of the earth's land area. More people live in Asia than in all the other continents put together.

LAND OF EXTREMES
Asia stretches from the Mediterranean Sea in the west to the Pacific Ocean in the east, and from the Arctic Circle in the north to sun-drenched, tropical islands in the south. Asia is so wide that the sun rises almost 11 hours earlier in Turkey than in Japan.

The far north of Asia is mainly an area of tundra – a treeless wilderness that is frozen for most of the year. Vast forests and grasslands lie to the south of the tundra. Much of western Asia is barren desert. Asia has many mountain chains, including the mighty Himalayas, which form a barrier across the heart of the continent. Further south are fertile plains and lush rainforests.

The buildings of ancient Petra in Jordan were carved out of solid rock. This beautiful city was built in 400 BCE by the Nabateans, an Arab people.

△ *Many of the fastest growing cities are in Southeast Asia. They are leading centres of industry and commerce.*

ANCIENT CIVILIZATIONS
Some of the world's earliest civilizations grew up in Mesopotamia (modern Iraq), the Indus Valley (modern Pakistan) and China. These peoples built the first large cities and invented written languages, legal systems and farming techniques. They also made many advances in architecture, mathematics and science.

By the 1500s, Asia included four of the most powerful states in the world – the Ottoman Empire of the Middle East, the Safavid Empire of Iran, the Mogul Empire of India and China's Ming Dynasty. Their wealth came from trade.

▽ *Major Japanese cities are connected by a high-speed train called the* Shinkansen, *which travels at up to 300 km/h.*

△ *Chinese people celebrate their New Year with street processions led by huge dragons.*

BIRTHPLACE OF RELIGION
Asia is the birthplace of all the world's major religions. India gave rise to both Hinduism, in about 2000 BCE, and Buddhism, 1,500 years later. Buddhism is now the main religion in large parts of East Asia, including Tibet, China, Japan and Thailand. Israel was the home of Judaism and Christianity, which later spread to Europe and the rest of the world. Islam was founded in the Arabian Peninsula in the 600s, and is now practised by Muslims right across the globe. However, Sikhism has relatively recent origins. It was established in the Punjab region of northern India in the early 1500s.

THROUGH THE AGES
Europeans began to visit Asia in the 1400s, and trade quickly developed between the two continents. All kinds of goods were traded, such as spices, silk, ceramics and jewels. Later, for several centuries, China and Japan closed their doors to Europe, halting trade and other contacts. During the 1800s, much of Asia was colonized by European powers, whose armed forces were stronger and better equipped. The colonists created large plantations for growing tea, coffee, rubber and cotton.

After World War II (1939–1945), during which Japan occupied parts of East Asia, many of the colonies won their freedom. Several countries adopted the communist political system, among them the Soviet Union, China and North Korea. With the breakup of the Soviet Union in 1991, eight new Asian states were created, including Kazakhstan and Tajikistan. Today, there are 50 independent nations in Asia, from tiny states like Brunei and Bahrain to powerful giants such as Russia and China.

A R C T I C   O C E A N

Siberia

RUSSIAN
FEDERATION

al Mountains

ZAKHSTAN

ZBEKISTAN

KYRGYZSTAN

MONGOLIA

TAJIKISTAN

NORTH
KOREA

SOUTH
KOREA

JAPAN

CHINA

NEPAL

BHUTAN

INDIA

MYANMAR

BANGLADESH

LAOS

THAILAND

VIETNAM

CAMBODIA

SRI LANKA

INDIAN
OCEAN

BRUNEI

MALAYSIA

SINGAPORE

TAIWAN

PACIFIC
OCEAN

South
China
Sea

PHILIPPINES

*Irian
Jaya*

INDONESIA

EAST TIMOR

*Giant pandas live in China's
mountain forests, and eat
nothing but bamboo.
Fewer than 1,000
now survive.*

NATURAL WORLD

Thousands of animals and plants live in Asia's
varied landscapes. The highest mountains are
home to yaks and snow leopards, while grey
wolves and reindeer inhabit the far north. The
rainforests of the south and southeast shelter
the widest variety of wildlife, including tigers,
Asian elephants, colourful birds and venomous
snakes. But hunting and deforestation (cutting
down forests) are making many species rare.

ASIA FACT FILE

Area: 45,066,400 sq km
Highest mountain: Mt Everest,
Nepal/Tibet border, 8,848 m
Lowest point: Dead Sea, Israel/Jordan,
399 m below sea level
Largest lake: Caspian Sea, 56,015 sq km
Longest river: Chang (Yangtze), 6,380 km
Largest desert: Arabian
Number of countries: 50
Largest country: Russia (77 percent of
which is in Asia)
Smallest mainland country: Brunei
Smallest island nation: Maldives
Largest city: Tokyo, Japan, 26 million
Largest population: China, 1.2 billion
Total population: 3.6 billion

BOOMING POPULATIONS

Parts of Asia are very heavily
populated. Places with the highest
populations include the river valleys
of China, the Indonesian island of Java
and the valley of the Ganges River in India.
By contrast, Siberia's forests and the remote
grasslands of Mongolia have few residents.

In recent years, China and several Southeast
Asian states have joined Japan to become big
economic powers. They have huge factories,
making a range of high-technology products.

*Rice is the staple food across
East Asia. It is grown in
flooded fields, or paddies.
In hilly areas, narrow
terraces are cut into
the slopes.*

SEE ALSO

China, Communism, India, Indonesia,
Japan, Korea, Middle East, Pakistan,
Religion, Russia, Southeast Asia, Turkey

The **asteroid** belt between Mars and Jupiter contains rocks of all sizes. The rocks frequently crash into each other and break up. Ceres, the largest asteroid, is about 1,000 km across.

Arthur, King

King Arthur was a legendary British ruler of the 500s. His kingdom was supposed to have been in western **England**. Many stories grew up around King Arthur's court, and his Knights of the Round Table. The stories were first written down by Sir Thomas Malory in the 1400s.

Asia *see* **pages 28–29**

The **Atlantic Ocean** is the world's second largest ocean. It covers 17 percent of the earth's surface area.

Asteroid

Asteroids are countless thousands of rocks left over from the time when the **sun** and **planets** were being formed. Most of them can be found in the wide gap between the orbits of **Mars** and **Jupiter**. Asteroid collisions formed the craters that can be seen on the **moon** and **Mercury**. Occasionally, asteroids still hit the **earth**. Telescopes now look out for rocks that pose a threat.

Astrology

Astrology is the art of foretelling the future by observing the movements of the **sun**, **moon**, **planets** and **stars**. It is based on the zodiac, an imaginary circle in the sky in which the sun,

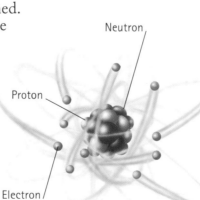

Neutron

Proton

Electron

The nucleus of an **atom** consists of protons and neutrons. Electrons move in fixed orbits all around the nucleus.

moon and planets move. Also in this circle are the 12 **constellations** or groups of stars that look like different shapes. Each shape is a sign of the zodiac and occupies a month in the astrologer's calendar. The 12 signs of the zodiac are Capricorn, Aquarius, Pisces, Aries, Taurus, Gemini, Cancer, Leo, Virgo, Libra, Scorpio and Sagittarius. Some people believe that persons born under each sign have special character traits.

Astronomy

Astronomy is the scientific study of objects in space, and is the oldest science of all. Early observations of the night sky enabled people to divide the year into months, weeks and days, based on the movements of the **sun**, **earth** and **moon**. The development of the **calendar** helped early astronomers to forecast the appearance of **comets** and the dates of **eclipses**. For many centuries, people believed that the earth was the centre of the universe. In the 1540s, Nicolaus **Copernicus** revived the idea that the sun was at the centre of our **solar system**. In 1608, Hans Lippershey invented the **telescope**, an important new tool for astronomers. Modern radio telescopes use giant dishes to collect radio waves sent out by objects in space, such as **pulsars** and **quasars**.

Atlantic Ocean

The Atlantic is the second largest **ocean** in the world, after the **Pacific**. It lies between Europe and Africa in the east and the Americas in the west. Its average depth is more than 1,800 m. There are several strong currents in the Atlantic, including the **Gulf Stream**, which carries warm water towards the coasts of western Europe.

Atmosphere

The atmosphere is the blanket of **air** and moisture that surrounds our planet. It gives us **oxygen** to breathe, keeps the earth's temperature at just the right level, and shields us from most of the sun's harmful **ultraviolet** rays.

Most air is concentrated in the lowest layer of the atmosphere, which extends from sea level to about 18 km high. The final layer of the atmosphere, at 500 km high, is the start of outer space.

Atom

Everything is made of atoms. We cannot see atoms – they are far too small. Look at the full stop at the end of this sentence. It contains about 250,000 million atoms! But even atoms are made up of smaller pieces.

The simplest atom is that of the light gas **hydrogen**. The centre is a tiny body called a proton. Around it spins an even smaller electron. Other atoms are much more complicated than the hydrogen atom. The **carbon** atom, for example, has at its centre six protons and six other things called neutrons. Around these spin six electrons. The largest normal atom is a **uranium** atom.

Atomic bomb
see **Nuclear energy**

AUSTRIA
Government: Republic
Capital: Vienna
Area: 83,849 sq km
Population: 8 million
Language: German
Currency: Euro

▽ The **Aztecs** worshipped many gods – of war, rain, sun and wind – and carried out human sacrifices to win the gods' favour. Captives taken in battle were killed by priests, who cut out their still-beating hearts using ceremonial daggers made of stone.

Australia *see* **page 32**

Austria

Today, Austria is hardly much bigger than Ireland. But once it was one of the largest and most powerful nations in **Europe**. For almost 700 years, from 1278 to 1918, Austria was ruled by a dynasty of kings and queens called the **Hapsburgs**. Their lands covered most of Central Europe. The Austrian Empire collapsed after **World War I**. But there are many relics of the mighty Hapsburg emperors. Vienna, Austria's capital city, is filled with beautiful churches, castles, statues and parks.

Ayers Rock *see* **Uluru**

Aztecs

The Aztecs were a civilization that created a powerful empire in **Mexico** during the 1300s and 1400s. Aztec emperors used well-trained warriors to conquer nearby peoples. The Aztecs built large cities, and erected stone **pyramids** with broad stairways leading to a temple at the top. The last Aztec ruler was Montezuma. He was killed by Spanish troops led by Hernando **Cortes** in 1519–1521.

AUSTRALIA

Australia is the world's smallest and driest continent. It is a huge island about three-quarters the size of Europe.

Sydney is Australia's oldest and largest city. It is built around a large bay on the country's east coast. The dramatic shape of the Sydney Opera House has made it world-famous.

The didgeridoo is an aboriginal instrument that produces a deep, droning sound.

Map labels: Cape York Peninsula, Coral Sea, Timor Sea, Darwin, Cairns, Great Barrier Reef, Tanami Desert, Great Dividing Range, Great Sandy Desert, Alice Springs, Brisbane, AUSTRALIA, Gibson Desert, Lake Eyre, Carnarvon, Great Victoria Desert, Lake Torrens, Darling, Geraldton, Nullarbor Plain, Sydney, CANBERRA, Murray, Mt Kosciuszko, Perth, Adelaide, Melbourne, Esperance, Albany, Tasmania, Hobart

DESERTS AND PLAINS

Much of Australia is dry, flat desert. The rest of inland Australia is covered with areas of grass and scattered trees and bushes. These hot plains are some of the world's most remote and thinly populated areas. The Australians have a special name for them – the outback.

MOUNTAINS AND FORESTS

Australia has few mountain ranges. The main one is the Great Dividing Range, which runs down the east coast. It separates the vast inland deserts from a strip of fertile land by the sea. Forests of eucalyptus trees grow on the mountain slopes.

Lush rainforests flourish in the far northeast of the country, where the climate is much wetter. Tasmania is a large, mountainous island off the southeastern tip of Australia.

CORAL REEFS

One of Australia's most spectacular natural wonders is the Great Barrier Reef, which lies off the coast of Queensland. It stretches for over 2,000 km, and is made up of more than 2,500 smaller reefs and coral islands.

▽ *The Great Barrier Reef is home to a tremendous variety of sea life.*

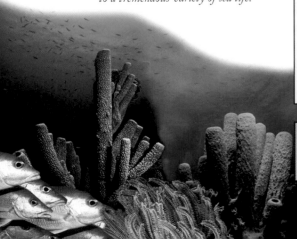

PACIFIC POWER

Australia is one of the main economic powers in the Pacific. Ranchers raise huge herds of cattle and sheep on the inland plains, where it is too dry for crops. Australia's sheep stations produce one-third of the world's wool. Mining and wine-making are also very important.

HISTORY

The first inhabitants of Australia were aboriginal peoples. They wandered across the country hunting and gathering food. In the late 1700s, settlers began to arrive from Britain, searching for a new way of life. Today, Australia retains strong links with Britain, and its head of state is still the British monarch. However, its government is completely independent. Most Australians live in large coastal cities, such as Sydney, Melbourne and Perth.

A WORLD APART

Australia became an island 65 million years ago. Since then, its plants and animals have gradually evolved (changed) into new and different forms. Many species are unique to Australia – they do not live anywhere else.

Australia's eucalyptus trees have fire-resistant bark and can grow in desert conditions. Typical Australian animals include koalas, kangaroos and wombats, which are all marsupials. Unlike any other mammals, female marsupials have a special pouch on their belly in which they carry their young offspring.

▽ *Kangaroos have become so common that in many areas they are pests.*

AUSTRALIA FACT FILE

Area: 7,686,849 sq km
Highest mountain: Mt Kosciuszko, 2,228 m
Largest lake: Eyre, 9,583 sq km
Longest river: Murray, 2,589 km
Number of states: 6 (Western Australia, South Australia, Queensland, New South Wales, Victoria and Tasmania)
Number of territories: 2 (Northern Territory and Australian Capital Territory)
Government: Federal state system
Capital: Canberra
Largest city: Sydney, 3.7 million
Population: 19 million
Language: English
Currency: Australian dollar

SEE ALSO
Aboriginal people, Canberra, Desert, Emu, Great Barrier Reef, Marsupial, Sydney, Uluru

△ Charles **Babbage** with his mechanical calculating machine, which he built in the 1830s but never completed. It is now in the Science Museum, London.

Babbage, Charles

Charles Babbage (1792–1871) was a British inventor and mathematician who is often called 'the father of the computer'. In 1833, he began working on an 'analytical engine' which was intended to perform any arithmetical calculation. Although Babbage's engine worked by using wheels and levers, it contained the key parts of a modern **computer** – including a memory. Numbers and instructions were to be fed in on punched cards. But Babbage's invention was never finished.

Babylon

Babylon was one of the greatest cities of the ancient world. It lay on a fertile plain between the Tigris and Euphrates rivers in a region that is today called **Iraq**. Babylon rivalled even **Egypt** in its wealth and splendour.

The city of Babylon was founded in about 2300 BCE and it continued to flourish for 2,000 years. It became a major centre of trade and religion. The Babylonian people were also skilled in **mathematics** and **astronomy**. A strong Babylonian king, Nebuchadnezzar (ruled 605–562 BCE), built magnificent palaces and pyramid-shaped temples. He also built the Hanging Gardens of Babylon, one of the **Seven Wonders** of the ancient world. The Gardens were filled with plants and flowers, which cascaded down high stone terraces.

▽ **Babylon** was the capital of the Babylonian empire. Its main entrance, the impressive Ishtar Gate, was guarded by two large fortresses. Inside the city walls were temples, palaces and the famous Hanging Gardens of Babylon.

Bach, Johann Sebastian

Johann Sebastian Bach (1685–1750) was one of the greatest composers of all time. He was born at Eisenach in **Germany**, and all his family were musical. From an early age Bach played the **violin** and the viola. At the age of 38, Bach moved to Leipzig, where he lived for the rest of his life. There he wrote some of his greatest pieces of **music** – mostly for choirs and for the **organ**.

When Bach died, his music was forgotten almost at once. Nearly one hundred years passed before people rediscovered his music and realized what a genius he had been.

Bach composed hundreds of pieces of music, but his most famous works are the Brandenburg Concertos, the St Matthew Passion and the Mass in B Minor.

Bacteria

Bacteria are tiny living things that cannot be seen with the naked eye. They are some of the simplest kinds of life. Bacteria are more like **plants** than **animals**. They come in various shapes – some are rod-like, some spiralled and others are round.

There are thousands of different kinds of bacteria. They are found in huge numbers almost everywhere you look. Many bacteria live in the **soil**. They help to break down animal and vegetable matter and make the soil rich. Some bacteria even live inside our bodies. They help with the digestion of our food.

Bacteria multiply extremely fast. Some of them can divide into two every 20 minutes. From a single bacterium there can be millions of bacteria in only a few hours.

Although most bacteria are quite harmless, some cause **diseases**. These kinds are known as germs. Pimples and boils are caused by bacteria. A few are deadly once they get inside the human body. We now have **antibiotics** (drugs) such as penicillin that destroy bacteria. But because bacteria multiply so quickly, they change into new kinds

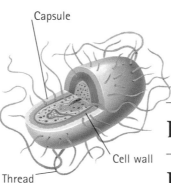

Bacteria are simple cells. They are surrounded by a cell wall and a protective outer capsule. Some are covered with threads that help them move or attach themselves to other cells.

Capsule

Cell wall

Thread

of bacteria that are not affected by the drugs. New drugs have to be made to kill the new bacteria.

Badger

Badgers are **mammals** that are related to ferrets, weasels and **otters**. They have thickset bodies, long blunt claws for digging and powerful jaws. There are several kinds of badger, including the European badger, the American badger and the honey badger of Africa.

People rarely see badgers during the day because they are nocturnal (active at night). After sunset, they emerge from their underground dens to begin feeding. Badgers eat almost anything, from roots and fruits to worms, mice and other small animals.

Bahamas *see* Caribbean

Balboa, Vasco Núñez

Vasco Núñez de Balboa (1475–1519) was a Spanish soldier and explorer who was the first European to set eyes on the **Pacific Ocean** in the New World. Balboa joined a Spanish expedition to **South America** in 1501, exploring the north coast of the continent. He later led an expedition across the narrow strip of land that is now known as the Isthmus of **Panama**. There, from a mountaintop, he looked down upon the Pacific Ocean.

Balkans

The Balkans are a group of countries in southeastern Europe. They include **Greece**, **Albania**, **Romania**, **Bulgaria**, **Bosnia-Herzegovina**, **Croatia**, **Serbia** and the European part of **Turkey**. The Turks ruled much of this region from the 1300s to the 1800s. It was in the Balkans that Archduke Ferdinand of Austria was assassinated in 1914. This event triggered **World War I**.

The **badger** of Europe and Asia has a striking pattern of stripes on its head.

Ballet

Ballet is a precise form of dancing that is usually performed in a theatre. A kind of ballet first appeared in **Italy** in the 1400s, but ballet as it is danced today began in **France**. Traditional, or classical, ballet follows strict rules. There are standard positions for the arms, legs and hands, and set movements that make the **dance** flow smoothly.

Classical ballet makes use of splendid costumes, elaborate scenery and full **orchestras**. Many ballets tell a story, but the dancers do not speak any words. They **mime** (act out) the story, using their bodies. *Giselle*, a tragic story of a young village girl who dies in love-stricken grief, was written by Adolphe Adam and first staged in 1841. The Russian composer **Tchaikovsky** wrote three long-time favourites: *Swan Lake* (1890), *Sleeping Beauty* (1890) and *Nutcracker* (1892).

Modern ballets often look different from classical ones. They borrow dance steps from many different styles of dance. Sometimes, instead of telling a story, they dwell on certain moods.

Balloon and Airship

Balloons and airships use gases that are lighter than air to fly. Balloons can only drift in the wind, but airships can be flown and steered.

The first piloted balloon was launched in 1783. It was built by the French **Montgolfier brothers**. A fire was burned under the balloon to fill it with hot air, and hot air rises, lifting the balloon. In the same year, the first

Hot air rises inside balloon

German *Zeppelin* **airship**

Air vent on side for changing course

Burner

Gas cylinder

△ A modern **balloon** uses a gas burner to heat the air inside a lightweight bag. This takes the balloon up, because hot air rises.

▽ Professional **ballet** dancers spend a long time practising to improve their timing and balance.

gas-filled balloon took to the air. The gas used was **hydrogen**. To descend, the pilot opened a valve and let out some gas. Today, balloons are used to study the **weather**, and hot-air ballooning is a popular sport.

Most airships are larger than balloons. The simplest sort looks like a cigar-shaped bag under which is slung a cabin and **engines**. The first successful airship flew in 1852. By the early 1900s, there was a number of airship passenger services. But a series of disasters brought the age of airships to an end. They were not safe enough for passenger use because they were filled with dangerous hydrogen gas. Modern airships are lifted with helium, a safer gas that does not catch fire. They are used for tasks such as making films and advertising products.

Baltic States

The Baltic States are Estonia, Latvia and Lithuania. They are situated north of **Poland**, on the southern shore of the Baltic Sea. Formerly part of the Russian Empire, the Baltic States became independent countries in 1918. In 1940, during **World War II**, they were seized by the **Soviet Union** and became Soviet republics. German troops invaded and controlled the Baltic States until they were driven out by the Soviet army at the end of the war.

In 1991, while the Soviet Union was in a state of political turmoil, Estonia, Latvia and Lithuania declared their independence and became completely free from foreign control. They have kept their own literature, traditions and languages, although most people can speak Russian.

Bandicoot

Bandicoots live in **Australia** and **New Guinea**. Like **kangaroos**, they belong to a large group of mammals called **marsupials**. In common with all marsupials, female bandicoots have pouches of loose skin in which they carry their young. Bandicoots have greyish-brown fur and are similar in size and shape to rats, though some can be larger. They make their nests in underground burrows and feed on insects, worms and roots.

Bangladesh

Bangladesh is an Asian country that came into being in 1971. Before then, it was part of **Pakistan**. It is one of the world's most densely populated countries and most of the people are very poor. In the rainy season, branches of the **Ganges** and Brahmaputra rivers flood the flat land. A cyclone in 1991 killed 125,000 people.

After years of rule by the military, Bangladesh adopted a parliamentary system in 1991, but there is still political turmoil. The largest cities in Bangladesh are Dhaka, the capital, and Chittagong, the main port. Rice, jute, tea and sugarcane are the main crops.

Bank

Banks are companies that take people's **money** for safekeeping. When your money is first put in the bank, this is called 'opening an account'. Every time you put more money in, you make

Bar codes are patterns of stripes that can be read by a laser scanner. Each bar code stands for a number.

BANGLADESH
Government: Republic
Capital: Dhaka
Area: 143,998 sq km
Population: 128 million
Language: Bengali
Currency: Taka

Basketball is played at a fast and furious pace on indoor courts. There are two teams of five players.

a deposit. If you wish to take some out, you make a withdrawal. Banks do not only hold money in safety. They also make loans to people and businesses, and they provide other ways of making saving and spending easier.

Barbados *see* Caribbean

Bar code

You will have noticed a pattern of black and white stripes on many cartons and packages. This is called a bar code. The stripes make a number in **binary** code, and each product that you buy has a different number. At the store's checkout, a machine called a scanner reads the bar code using **laser** light. The scanner turns the bar code into a signal that goes to the store's cash register. A **computer** inside the cash register searches its memory to find the price of each item and calculates the final bill. It also works out how many products have been sold and orders new supplies when necessary.

Barometer

High **air** pressure is a sign of good **weather**. Low air pressure is a sign of changing and bad weather. A barometer is an instrument used to measure such changes.

There are two kinds of barometer, the aneroid and the **mercury**. The aneroid is more widely used. Inside it is a flat metal box. The air inside the box is at very low pressure. The metal walls of the box are so thin they will bend easily, but they do not collapse because a spring keeps them apart. As air pressure drops, the spring pushes the sides of the box apart. As it rises, they are squeezed together. These movements are picked up by levers and gears that move a pointer around to show different measurements.

Baseball

Baseball is the national **sport** of the **United States**. No one knows quite how it began, but it may have come from a similar English game called rounders. Baseball was probably first played in **New York**, where Alexander Cartwright founded the *Knickerbocker Baseball Club* in 1845.

Today, baseball is played between two teams of nine people each. It is played on a field that has a square, known as the diamond, marked on it. The diamond has four bases 27.5 m apart. In the game, each batter tries to advance around the bases safely and score a run. A team bats until three players are out.

The pitcher throws a ball to the batter, who stands in an area called the home plate. When the batter swings at a pitch (pitched ball) and misses, or if they hit a foul ball, it is called a strike. Three strikes and the batter is out. A batter can also be caught out, or is out if a fielder picks up and throws the ball to a base before the batter reaches it.

Baseball is big business in the United States. It is also popular in Central and South America, Cuba, Japan and the Philippines.

Basketball

Basketball is an American **sport** that has won popularity all over the world. It has been played at the **Olympics** since 1936. Professional basketball is played by two teams of five players. Each team tries to score points by shooting a ball into a net, or basket. The basket is 3 m from the floor and 46 cm in diameter at the top. The ball can be advanced by bouncing it along the floor (dribbling) or by passing it to a team-mate. A player cannot take more than one step while holding the ball. The opposing players try to block him or her without making contact. Successful shots are worth two or three points depending on how close to the basket the player is standing.

Bat

Bats are the only **mammals** that can truly be said to fly. Their wings do not have feathers, but are made of a sheet of skin stretched between the long 'finger' bones. In most bats, the wings are also joined to the legs and tail.

There are nearly 1,000 different kinds of bat. Most of them live in the tropics and warm parts of the world. Where winters are cold, bats **hibernate**. Many bats eat ripe fruit, especially in tropical areas. Other bats feed on insects, which they catch in midair.

Most bats are nocturnal – they sleep in the day and fly at night. Scientists have shown in experiments that bats do not need good eyesight for flying. They find their way in the dark by using a **sonar** system. They make a series of high-pitched shrieks, and use the echoes bouncing off objects to tell where they are.

Clawed thumb for clinging to trees

Rodrigues fruit bat

Wings made of thin sheet of leathery skin

Tail used to brake or change direction in flight

Battery

Positive terminal

Negative terminal

Lead plates

Plastic casing containing sulphuric acid

△ Most vehicles have a **battery** that powers their electrical systems. While a vehicle is running, its engine drives a generator that recharges the battery.

Batteries make **electricity** from chemicals stored inside them. Dry batteries such as those used in many radios, torches and calculators make electricity for only a limited time. In dry batteries, a pastelike chemical mixture is packed around a **carbon** rod. When the chemicals are used up the battery cannot be recharged.

Car batteries can be recharged with electricity and used again and again. They contain pairs of **lead** and lead oxide plates bathed in dilute sulphuric **acid**. As the battery is used, the chemicals in the plates change until no more electricity is produced. But feeding an electric current into the battery changes the chemicals in the plates back to their original state. A current will then flow again.

The images on the **Bayeux Tapestry** were worked in eight colours of wool on small strips of linen, which were then sewn together to make one long strip.

Bayeux Tapestry

After **William the Conqueror** invaded England in 1066, one of his relations had a **tapestry** embroidered to record the conquest. This masterpiece is called the Bayeux Tapestry. It is a piece of linen 70 m long on which there are 72 colourful scenes telling the story of William's victory. Latin words explain what is happening in the pictures. The tapestry is kept under glass in a museum at Bayeux, France.

Bear

Bears are found in most parts of the world except for Australia and Africa. They have short, powerful limbs and heavy, broad heads with strong jaws. They also have long claws for digging and tearing. Bears do not have sharp eyesight, but their sense of **smell** is excellent. Although bears usually move slowly and often look clumsy, they can run quite fast if they have to, and most kinds of bear can climb trees.

Alaskan brown bear

European brown bear

Polar bear

Sun bear

◁ Despite their size, **bears** are usually shy. They attack only if disturbed or cornered.

There are seven species of bear, which include several of the world's largest **carnivores**. The largest bear of all is the Alaskan brown bear, which can weigh over 750 kg. It is actually the same species as the grizzly of western North America and the brown bear of Europe and Siberia. The polar bear lives in snowy **Arctic** regions, where its all-white coat provides it with perfect camouflage. All of the five remaining bears have black coats. They are the American black bear, the Asian black bear, the spectacled bear, the sloth bear and the sun bear. Bears that inhabit cold areas **hibernate** for the winter.

Brown and black bears eat almost anything, including leaves, roots, fruits, honey, worms, fish and small animals. Polar bears hunt small whales and seals. Sloth bears are more fussy – they feed only on ants and **termites**.

Beaver

Beavers are large **rodents** more than 1 m long, including the tail, that weigh over 25 kg. They live in woods by the side of lakes and rivers in many parts of North America and Europe. Beavers are good swimmers and can stay under water for up to 15 minutes. They have a broad, flat tail covered in scaly skin.

The tail is used for steering when they swim. Beavers eat leaves, twigs and bark, mainly from alder and willow **trees**.

Beavers need pools in which to build their homes, and often block up, or dam, streams with mud and sticks to make one. They cut down trees with their sharp teeth and drag them to the pool to strengthen the dam.

Becket, Thomas à

Thomas à Becket (1118–1170) was an Archbishop of Canterbury who angered King Henry II of England by demanding special rights for the Church. He was exiled but returned later and once more angered the king.

After years of quarrels, Henry is said to have shouted, "Who will rid me of this turbulent priest?" Four knights mistakenly thought the king wanted Becket killed, and murdered him in Canterbury Cathedral in 1170.

Bee

There are many different kinds of bee, but the best known kind is the honey bee. Honey bees live in hives or colonies of about 50,000 worker bees.

△ **Thomas à Becket** was Archbishop of Canterbury during the 1100s. He was brutally murdered in his own cathedral for standing up against King Henry II. In 1173, three years after his death, Becket was made a saint.

▽ **Beavers** dam streams with mud, sticks and trees that they have cut down. When a pool has formed behind the dam, they build a safe island home, known as a lodge. The lodge has an underwater entrance.

Inside a honey **bee** hive there are hundreds of cells made of wax. The queen bee lays eggs in the cells. Larvae (grubs) hatch out of the eggs and are fed by the workers. Worker bees collect nectar and pollen from flowers, and take it back to the hive to be made into honey as food.

Queen honey bee

Each hive of honey bees is established by a large queen bee. She mates with stingless male bees called drones. There are several hundred drones in each hive, and their only purpose in life is to find a queen bee to mate with. After mating, they die.

Worker bees are all female and do not breed. A worker bee's life is very short, usually about four weeks, so the queen has to lay many **eggs** to provide enough bees. From time to time a new queen hatches. One of the queens leaves the hive with a swarm of about half the workers to seek another home.

Beekeepers are people who look after hives of honey bees and collect the sweet honey that the bees produce. They feed the bees **sugar** syrup to replace the honey they remove.

There are other types of bee which do not live in large colonies. These are called solitary bees.

Beethoven, Ludwig van

Ludwig van Beethoven (1770–1827) was a German musician who composed many great pieces of **music** that have become famous all over the world. His compositions included concertos, symphonies, choral and chamber music (see also **orchestra**). When he was young, Beethoven became well known as a brilliant pianist. He met **Mozart**, and he later studied under another famous composer, **Haydn**. Beethoven began to go deaf at the age of 32, but continued to compose music even when he was totally deaf.

Beetle

Beetles are **insects**. More than 300,000 different kinds of beetle are known. Some beetles are as small as a pinhead. Others are very large. The African goliath beetle grows up to 10 cm long and can weigh 100 g.

Beetles start their lives as eggs which hatch into grubs, or larvae. The larvae then turn into chrysalises, or pupae, before the adult beetles emerge.

Many beetles and their larvae are destructive pests. Weevils, wireworms and Colorado beetles do great damage to crops, and woodworms eat through timber. However, some beetles can be extremely useful. Ladybirds are small, colourful beetles that eat harmful insects such as aphids and greenflies.

Burying beetles and dung beetles are also useful – they clear away dead animals and dung, which the beetles later use as food.

Burying beetles bury the corpses of small birds and mammals by digging soil from under them. Then the beetles lay their eggs on the buried animals for their grubs to feed on when they hatch.

Beethoven was one of the greatest pianists of his time. He played to Mozart in 1787, at the age of just 17.

Giraffe beetle

Beijing (Peking)

Beijing, formerly called Peking, is the capital of **China**. In 1267, the Mongol conqueror Kublai Khan made it the capital of his empire. Modern Beijing is a major centre of industry and learning. Its population is more than 11 million. In the centre of the city are the palaces of the ancient Chinese emperors. Ordinary citizens were not allowed to step inside the palaces' high walls, which is why the imperial zone of Beijing became known as the 'Forbidden City'.

Belgium

Belgium is a small country situated between **France**, **Germany** and the **Netherlands**. Its capital is Brussels. Belgium's population consists of two main groups – the Germanic Flemings of the north, and the French-speaking Walloons of the south. Because of its central and strategic position, Belgium has been invaded and fought over throughout the course of European history. Today, the headquarters of the **European Union** (EU) and **NATO** are both in Brussels.

Bell, Alexander Graham

Alexander Graham Bell (1847–1922) was an American who invented the **telephone**. Through his work with devices to help the deaf, Bell became interested in sending voices over long distances. On 10 March 1876, his voice was transmitted by telephone for the first time.

Berlin

Berlin is the largest city in **Germany**, and has been the German capital since 1990. It is one of Europe's main cultural and economic centres.

Beetles come in many shapes, but they all have six pairs of legs and a hard case covering their back.

BELGIUM
Government: Constitutional monarchy
Capital: Brussels
Area: 30,513 sq km
Population: 10 million
Languages: Flemish, French and German
Currency: Euro

Berlin was largely destroyed by heavy bombing during **World War II** (1939–1945), but at the end of the war, rebuilding was rapid. In 1945, when Germany was split into two countries, East and West, Berlin was divided into four zones between the Americans, British, French and Russians.

In 1948, the Russians quarrelled with the other allies and blockaded Berlin by cutting its road and rail links with West Germany. But Britain and the USA flew in supplies to keep the city going. After a year, the Russians gave up and re-opened the roads and railways.

In 1961, the communist government of East Germany built the Berlin Wall to separate the eastern and western parts of the city (see **communism**). It was difficult for people to cross between the two halves of the divided city. In 1989, after massive public protests, the Berlin Wall was demolished.

Bernhardt, Sarah

Born in France, Sarah Bernhardt (1844–1923) became one of the most famous actresses of her time. Her excellent speaking voice won her the admiration of audiences everywhere she went. Her best known performance was in *Camille*, a play by French writer Alexandre Dumas (see **theatre**).

Bible

The Bible is the sacred book of two religions: **Judaism** and **Christianity**. Jews and Christians consider the Bible to be the Word of God. Many of their religious beliefs, ceremonies and holidays are based on the text of the Bible.

At the heart of **Beijing** are many palaces dating from the age of the emperors, who ruled China for 2,000 years until 1911.

One story in the **Bible's** Old Testament tells how God spoke to Moses from a burning bush. God told Moses to lead the Jewish people out of Egypt and into Israel.

The Bible is in two parts. The first is called the Old Testament, which begins by describing God's creation of the heavens and the earth. Then it records the history of the Jewish people and the teachings of their prophets before the birth of **Jesus**. The second part of the Bible, called the New Testament, records the life and sayings of Jesus and his disciples (personal followers).

For centuries, all Bibles were hand-written. The first printed one was produced in the mid-1400s. The Bible has always been the best-selling book – more than 2.5 billion copies have been sold since 1816. It has been translated into over 1,500 languages.

Bicycle

Penny farthing **bicycles** were heavy and clumsy. They had solid tyres and a step at the back to help the rider climb on.

The bicycle is a two-wheeled vehicle powered by its rider, who turns two pedals by foot. The earliest bicycles were invented in the 1700s. They were simply two **wheels** joined by a rod, with a seat on top. Riders pushed them along the ground with their feet.

The first bicycles with pedals did not appear until 1865. These machines were known as 'bone-shakers' because the seats had no springs. The next major development was the 'penny farthing', which had an enormous front wheel and a tiny rear wheel. The modern style of bicycle appeared in the 1880s. It had a chain-driven rear wheel and air-filled tyres, and this basic style has changed very little since then except for the addition of **gears**.

Binary system

The modern racing **bicycle** is made from lightweight materials. It is streamlined in shape and has as many as 15 or 20 gears.

The binary system is a number system that uses only two numerals – 0 and 1. Our everyday decimal system uses ten numerals – 0 to 9. In the decimal system you multiply a number by 10 by moving it one place to the left – 20, 200 and so on. In the binary system, when you move a numeral one place to the left you multiply its value by two. A 1 by itself is 1. Move it a place to the left and it becomes 1 times 2, or 2. It is written 10. Move it another place to the left and it becomes 1 times 2 times 2, or 4. It is written 100.

Electronic devices such as **computers** use the binary system to perform calculations and other operations.

Biochemistry

Biochemistry is the study of chemical reactions that take place inside the tiny **cells** that make up all living things. It is a vast subject. Biochemists find out about the **food** people must eat to be healthy. They help farmers by finding out what foods are needed by plants and animals. They help fight **disease** by developing chemicals that kill harmful **bacteria**. Biochemists are also discovering more and more about the chemistry that makes us what we are (see **cloning** and **genetics**).

Biology

Biology is the study of living things and how they relate to each other. The part of biology that deals with **plants** is called **botany**. The study of **animals** is known as zoology. Biologists study everything from the tiniest amoeba, which consists of just one **cell**, to a mighty oak tree or a human being.

One of the earliest biologists was the ancient Greek thinker **Aristotle**, who was the first to dissect, or cut open, and classify animals. There was little interest in biology for more than a thousand years, until the **Renaissance**, when scholars such as Leonardo **da Vinci** tried to discover how living things grew and worked. In the 1600s, William **Harvey** showed how the **blood** travels around the body.

The invention of the **microscope** opened up whole new areas of study for biologists. They were able to learn more about the animal and plant cells that are the building blocks of life. The study of other microscopic organisms, such as **bacteria**, helped people like Louis **Pasteur** understand more about disease and how to prevent it.

In the 1800s, the English naturalist Charles **Darwin** revolutionized biology with his theory of **evolution**. Today, biology is divided into many separate sciences.

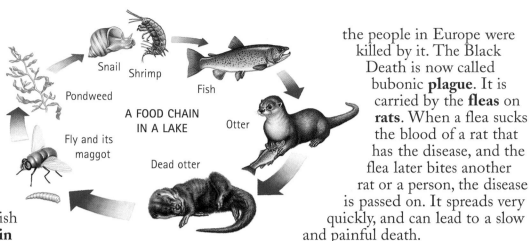

A FOOD CHAIN IN A LAKE

Pondweed · Snail · Shrimp · Fish · Otter · Dead otter · Fly and its maggot

the people in Europe were killed by it. The Black Death is now called bubonic **plague**. It is carried by the **fleas** on **rats**. When a flea sucks the blood of a rat that has the disease, and the flea later bites another rat or a person, the disease is passed on. It spreads very quickly, and can lead to a slow and painful death.

Birds *see* page 45

Birth control

Birth control is the means by which people can control the number of children they have. It is sometimes known as family planning. Birth control has been used since ancient times but modern methods were not widespread until the 1800s and 1900s.

There are many methods of birth control. Some of them work by stopping the sperm of the male from fertilizing the egg, or ovum, of the female. This is known as contraception.

Some people are forbidden by their religion to practise certain kinds of birth control. However, birth control is now encouraged in many countries with large **populations**.

△ **Biology** is the study of living things. The complex links that connect plants and animals are known as food chains. For example, in the food chain above, pondweed produces energy from the sun, soil and water. It is eaten by snails and shrimps, which are in turn eaten by fish. An otter eats the fish. Fly maggots feed on the dead otter, and return nutrients from its body to the soil and water.

▽ **Black holes** are shaped like funnels. Objects are pulled into the funnel, like water going down a drain. Once inside, the space debris cannot escape.

Black hole

Stars are made up mostly of **hydrogen** gas. It is the turning of this hydrogen into helium that makes stars like our **sun** shine and give out heat. When a massive star uses up all its hydrogen fuel, it collapses. This collapse is called a supernova explosion. All that is left after such an explosion is a tiny star. The material in this star is so squashed together – so dense – that even **light** waves find it impossible to escape from them. As the light waves cannot get out, we call them black holes.

Bison *see* Cattle

Black Death

The Black Death was a terrible **disease** that was at its worst during the **Middle Ages**. In one outbreak in the 1300s, 25 million people died of the disease. About one-third of all

Nearby star

Black hole

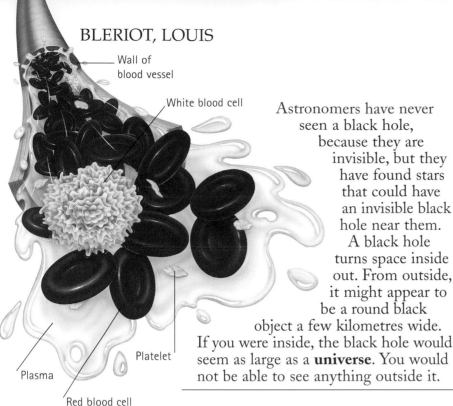

Wall of blood vessel

White blood cell

Platelet

Plasma

Red blood cell

Blood travels around the body through a network of thousands of blood vessels. Each drop of blood contains 250 million red blood cells, 375,000 white blood cells and about 16 million platelets.

Louis **Blériot** made his epic flight across the English Channel in an aeroplane that he had designed and built. In doing so, he won a prize of £1,000 offered by the *Daily Mail* newspaper.

Astronomers have never seen a black hole, because they are invisible, but they have found stars that could have an invisible black hole near them. A black hole turns space inside out. From outside, it might appear to be a round black object a few kilometres wide. If you were inside, the black hole would seem as large as a **universe**. You would not be able to see anything outside it.

Blériot, Louis

Louis Blériot (1872–1936) was a famous French airman. He was a pioneer of aviation and designed and built a number of early aeroplanes. On 25 July 1909, Blériot took off from Calais in one of his own **aircraft**. Twenty-seven minutes later he touched down at Dover on the south coast of England, becoming the first man to fly the English Channel. Blériot went on to design other aircraft and became the owner of a large aircraft company.

Blood

Blood is the fluid that nourishes our bodies and removes waste products. The **heart** pumps blood round the body, through a complex system of blood vessels – **arteries**, **veins** and capillaries. Blood takes in food from the digestive system, and **oxygen** from the **lungs**, and carries them to all the **cells** in the body. Each cell takes exactly what it needs from the blood, and the blood carries away cell waste, including

water and carbon dioxide. Blood also carries special body chemicals to where they are needed, kills germs and keeps the body at the right temperature.

Blood is made in the marrow of the **bones**. The adult human body contains about six litres of blood. This blood is made up of a pale liquid called plasma, and many millions of red blood cells, or corpuscles. Corpuscles are tiny red discs that give the blood its colour.

The blood also contains smaller numbers of white blood cells, or white corpuscles. White corpuscles attack germs that enter the body by absorbing them. Often many white corpuscles are killed in the fight against disease or infection. Large numbers of dead white corpuscles collect as pus. Other blood particles, called platelets, help our blood to clot when we bleed. This helps scratches and other wounds to heal more quickly.

We can all be classified into blood groups A, B, AB or O, according to the type of blood we have. Blood groups are important when patients are given blood transfusions. Transfusions are given to replace either diseased blood, or blood that has been lost in an injury. The blood a person is given is generally the same blood type as their own.

Blues

The blues is a kind of **music** that developed among black musicians in the **United States**. Blues music was first played in the late 1800s, in the southern states near the mouth of the **Mississippi River**. It is an extremely varied type of music, and many blues musicians have created their own individual styles of playing.

The main instruments used in traditional, or 'country', blues are the classical guitar, **piano** and harmonica. Other instruments used include **guitars** and **drums**. The words to the songs are frequently sad, and are often about loneliness or problems in love.

continued on page 46

BIRDS

Birds come in all shapes and sizes, and live all over the world. They are the only animals to have feathers.

The anhinga uses its spearlike bill to stab fish.

The peregrine falcon is the fastest flying bird. It accelerates to as much as 320 km/h when swooping out of the sky to attack other birds.

WORLD OF BIRDS

Birds are vertebrates (animals with backbones). There are nearly 9,000 different types of bird. They range in size from tiny hummingbirds that weigh less than 2 g to the colossal ostrich, which reaches over 150 kg and stands as high as an adult human.

Birds can live almost everywhere, including hot deserts, polar ice caps and the middle of cities. Some rainforests are home to more than 400 species (varieties) of bird.

Toucans have massive bills for splitting open tough fruit. Each kind of toucan has a differently coloured bill.

RAISING A FAMILY

All birds lay eggs. After laying her eggs, the female sits on them to keep them warm. This is called incubation. Sometimes, both parents take it in turns to incubate the eggs. Eggs need at least ten days to hatch, and those of some birds take as long as two months.

Most birds build a nest to protect their eggs and young. Common nest-sites are trees, bushes and cliffs. Some birds, such as pheasants and ducks, lay their eggs straight on the ground.

▽ *Barn swallows build a cup-shaped nest of dried mud. Feeding hungry chicks is very hard work.*

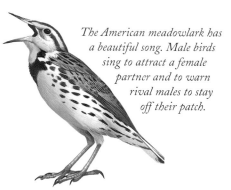

The American meadowlark has a beautiful song. Male birds sing to attract a female partner and to warn rival males to stay off their patch.

THE POWER OF FLIGHT

Birds developed from scaly reptiles that lived during the age of the dinosaurs. Their scales changed over millions of years into feathers, and their front legs became wings. Birds have hollow bones for lightness in the air and strong breast muscles for working their wings. Large birds such as eagles and storks can flap their wings slowly and float, or soar, on air currents. Small birds need to flap their wings fast to stay in the air.

Some birds can fly for thousands of kilometres. Their long journeys are called migrations. Other birds, like penguins, cannot fly at all.

LIVING TOGETHER

When it is time to breed, most birds get into pairs. To attract a suitable mate, the males sing or show off their plumage. They may also perform special dances or make dramatic display flights. Some birds breed together in large groups, or colonies. Each colony is made up of lots of breeding pairs.

▷ *Gannets nest on the ledges of sea cliffs.*

PERFECTLY FORMED

The appearance of a bird tells us a lot about what it eats and where it lives. For example, eagles have hooked beaks for tearing meat, and woodpeckers have sharp, pointed bills for hammering tree trunks. Waterbirds like swans need waterproof plumage and webbed feet for swimming on lakes and ponds. Birds that spend a lot of time in the air, such as swallows, often have long wings and streamlined bodies to help them fly fast and smoothly.

The cassowary is a giant flightless bird found in the rainforests of New Guinea and Australia.

> **SEE ALSO**
> Albatross, Cuckoo, Dodo, Duck, Egg, Falcon, Feather, Hummingbird, Migration, Nest, Ostrich, Owl, Penguin, Woodpecker

Blues music was a major influence on jazz musicians such as Duke Ellington (1899–1974). They liked its strong rhythms and its very varied style.

continued from page 44

The blues influenced a style of piano music called 'boogie-woogie', which was popular in the 1930s. Blues music also contributed to the development of **jazz**, and has been a big influence on many rock musicians.

Boat
see **Ships and Boats**

Boer War

The Boer War (1899–1902) was fought in **South Africa** between the Boers – settlers who originally came from the **Netherlands** – and the British. The slow and badly led British troops were no match for the fast and determined Boers in the early days of the war. But, in the end, Britain's overwhelming strength won. There were about 450,000 soldiers in the British armies during the Boer War, and only about 60,000 Boers.

Bolivia

BOLIVIA
Government: Republic
Capital: La Paz
Area: 1,098,581 sq km
Population: 8.1 million
Language: Spanish
Currency: Boliviano

Bolivia is a land-locked country in central **South America**, west of **Brazil**. Most of Bolivia is an enormous plain stretching from the Brazilian border to the eastern foothills of the **Andes** Mountains. High in the Andes lies the great Bolivian plateau, over 4,000 m high. Two-thirds of Bolivia's people live here. The capital is La Paz, the highest capital in the world, and Lake Titicaca, at 3,812 m above sea level, is one of the highest lakes in the world.

Bolivia was ruled by **Spain** from 1532 until 1825. It gained independence with the help of Simón Bolívar, a Venezuelan general, after whom Bolivia is named. More than half the people are native Bolivians, a third are *mestizos* (people who are part-European, part-Bolivian) and the rest are direct descendants of Europeans. Bolivia is the world's second largest producer of **tin**, and **mining** is the country's main industry.

Bone

Bones make up the hard framework that supports the flesh and organs of all **vertebrates** (animals with backbones). All bones are made up of the same thing, mostly calcium – an element found in limestone and chalk, and in certain foods, especially **milk** and **cheese**. Bones are hard on the outside but soft on the inside. Bone marrow, in the hollow centre of the bone, is where new red **blood** cells are made.

The human **skeleton** has four kinds of bones – long bones, such as arm and leg bones; flat bones, such as the skull; short bones, including ankle and wrist bones; and irregular bones, such as those that make up the backbone. If bones are broken they will knit together again if they are rejoined or set properly. The **cells** in the broken ends of the bone produce a substance that helps the ends to grow together again. A mended bone is as strong as it ever was. But as people get older their bones become brittle and break more easily.

Book

Books are used for storing and passing on all kinds of knowledge, ideas and stories. Some of the earliest books were made by the Ancient Egyptians. These were written by hand on rolls of **paper** made from the papyrus plant.

By the time of the **Roman Empire**, many books were handwritten on parchment or vellum. This material was made from animal **skin**. It was cut into sheets that were fastened together to look much the same as a modern book. During the **Middle Ages**, monks made many beautiful books. These were carefully decorated, or illuminated, by hand with bright colours and sometimes gold and silver.

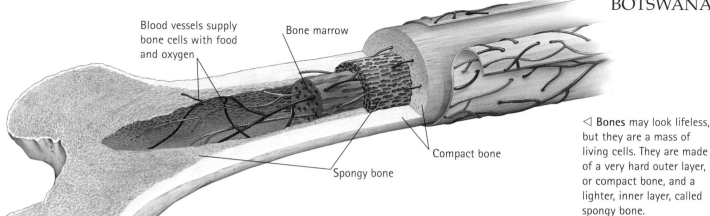

Blood vessels supply bone cells with food and oxygen

Bone marrow

Compact bone

Spongy bone

◁ **Bones** may look lifeless, but they are a mass of living cells. They are made of a very hard outer layer, or compact bone, and a lighter, inner layer, called spongy bone.

In the 1400s, printing on paper was introduced to Europe. At first this was very slow because much of the work still had to be done by hand. Then Johannes **Gutenberg** invented a machine with movable type that could print books quickly. Today, millions of books are produced every year, in all the languages of the world.

Boomerang

The boomerang is a wooden throwing stick used mainly by the **aboriginal people** of Australia. There are two kinds. One is very heavy and is thrown straight at the target. The other is lighter. It is shaped in a special way so that, when it is thrown skilfully, it is possible to make it return to the thrower.

Bosnia-Herzegovina

Bosnia-Herzegovina was formerly a republic of **Yugoslavia**, but became independent in 1992. Its people are Croats, Muslims and Serbs. Fighting broke out between the Bosnians and the Serbian-dominated Yugoslav army as the Serbs attempted to make Bosnia-Herzegovina part of Yugoslavia again. Muslims and Croats were forced out of parts of Bosnia conquered by the Serbs. This was called 'ethnic cleansing'.

The fighting in Bosnia-Herzegovina was some of the worst in Europe since **World War II**. A peace agreement was signed in 1995, with **NATO** troops remaining to enforce it.

Botany

Botany is the study of **plants** and how they grow. There are more than 400,000 different kinds of plant. They vary from tiny algae that can be seen only with a microscope, to massive redwood **trees** nearly 100 m high. Other types of plant include **grass**, **flowers**, **ferns**, **moss** and fungi (see **fungus**).

Without plants there would be no animals, because animals depend on plants for all their food. There would be no **cattle** for us to eat if there was no grass for the cattle to eat. Animals also breathe the gas **oyxygen** that all plants release.

By studying the way in which the features of one generation of plants are passed on to the next generation, scientists are able to grow bigger and better crops. They can breed varieties that are better at fighting plant disease.

In 1753, the Swedish botanist Carl von Linné, who is usually known as Linnaeus, invented the first real system for naming plants. He gave every plant a name made up of two Latin words.

Botswana

Botswana is an African country that lies far from the sea. It is bordered by **Zimbabwe**, **South Africa** and **Namibia**. In 1885, the country, then called Bechuanaland, came under British control. It gained independence in 1966. Botswana is a hot, dry country that includes the Kalahari Desert. Mining of **diamonds** and other minerals is the most valuable industry, but cattle raising and tourism are also important.

BOSNIA-HERZEGOVINA
Government: Republic
Capital: Sarajevo
Area: 51,125 sq km
Population: 3.8 million
Language: Serbo-Croat
Currency: Marka

BOTSWANA
Government: Republic
Capital: Gaborone
Area: 581,730 sq km
Population: 1.6 million
Languages: Setswana and English
Currency: Pula

Boudicca

Boudicca, who is often called Boadicea, was the ruler of a British tribe in about the year 60 CE. Her tribe, the Iceni, belonged to an ancient people known as the **Celts**.

The Roman rulers in Britain said that the Iceni lands should become part of the **Roman Empire**. Led by Queen Boudicca, the Iceni tribe at once rebelled. A strong Roman army quickly crushed the rebellion and Boudicca poisoned herself.

◁ **Boudicca** was a fierce Celtic queen who led her people into battle against the heavily armed Roman forces. Half of England joined Boudicca in the rebellion.

Boxing

People have fought with their fists since ancient times. But modern boxing was born in 1867 when the Marquess of Queensberry drew up a set of rules. Boxers today are divided into weight categories, from flyweights (below 51 kg) to heavyweights (any weight over 86 kg). Judges award points after each three-minute round for skill in attack and defence. Amateur contests usually consist of three rounds of three minutes each, with one-minute rests between rounds. Professional contests can be of any number of rounds up to 12 or 15.

Brain

The brain controls all the other parts of the body. In some tiny **insects** it is no larger than a speck of dust. But **mammals** have large brains in relation to their size. Human beings have the largest brains of all. The brain controls involuntary (automatic) activities such as breathing and blood pressure. It also controls **muscles** and the organs of balance, feeling and movement.

The human brain uses a fifth of all the energy produced in the body. It is largely made up of grey and white matter. Grey matter contains **nerve** cells, and white matter contains nerve fibres that carry messages from the nerve cells to the body. These nerve fibres leave the brain in large bundles and reach out to all parts of the body. Messages from the body are travelling back along the fibres to the brain all the time. Different parts of the brain control different parts of the body. For example, most thinking is done in the front part. Sight, on the other hand, is controlled from the back of the brain.

BRAZIL
Government: Republic
Capital: Brasília
Area: 8,511,965 sq km
Population: 168 million
Language: Portuguese
Currency: Real

▽ **Bronze** can be cast into shape by heating it until it melts and pouring it into a mould. This bronze shield is 2,000 years old.

Brazil

Brazil is by far the largest country in **South America** and the fifth largest country in the world. Much of Brazil is low-lying, and contains the huge basin of the **Amazon River** and the world's largest **rainforest**. Until recently, only tribes of native people lived here. Over half of Brazil's people live in cities that include Rio de Janeiro, Sao Paulo and Belo Horizonte. Brasília, a specially built modern city, has been the capital of Brazil since 1960.

Brazil was ruled by **Portugal** from the early 1500s until 1822, and most people still speak Portuguese. Many Brazilians work on farms. The country leads the world in producing **coffee**, and oil is becoming a more important product. Brazil also produces a lot of beef, cocoa, cotton, maize, sugar cane and tobacco.

Bread

Bread is one of our oldest **foods**, dating back to at least 2000 BCE. It may be made from wheat, maize, oats, barley, or rye flour (see **cereal**). At first bread was flat, but the Egyptians added **yeast** to make the dough rise. Today, most bread is baked with yeast.

Fluid

Bony skull

Membranes

BRAIN

BRAIN

Brain stem

Spinal cord

▷ The **brain** is the body's control centre, responsible for action, thought, memory, behaviour and emotion. It is protected by a bony skull, three layers of membrane and a pool of fluid.

Breathing

Breathing is something we rarely have to think about. As soon as a baby is born, it starts to breathe, and we go on breathing all our lives. It is the **oxygen** in the air that we need. Like all other animals, we must have oxygen to stay alive. This oxygen is used with the food we eat to give us energy to move about and keep our bodies going.

We draw air into our **lungs**. From there it goes through tiny tubes which allow the oxygen to pass into the **blood** vessels. Oxygen goes around our bodies in the blood. We breathe out another kind of gas – carbon dioxide.

When you breathe in, your rib cage is pulled upwards and air is sucked into your lungs. These actions happen in reverse when you breathe out.

Bridge

Bridges are used to take roads, paths and railways over rivers, valleys or other obstacles. The first bridges were probably fallen tree trunks placed across a river or small valley.

The **Romans** were among the first great bridge builders. Some of their stone bridges are still standing today. In the **Middle Ages**, bridges in towns often had shops and houses built on top of them. Modern bridge building began with **iron** bridges in the 1700s. By the end of the 1800s, steel was being used. Today, there is a great variety of bridges. There are three main kinds of bridge. These are the beam, the arch and the suspension bridge.

A modern beam bridge works in the same way as a simple tree trunk bridge. It is made of strong girders, or beams, that stretch from one bank to the other. Sometimes the middle of the bridge rests on pillars.

An arch bridge may have one arch or more. In the past, arch bridges were usually built from stone, but today some are made of steel or **concrete**.

Suspension bridges are hung by strong steel cables from tall towers. The towers also have cables fixed to the ground.

British Isles
see **United Kingdom**

Bronze

Bronze is the **alloy** (mixture) of **copper** and **tin**. It is extremely useful because it is much stronger than pure copper. Bronze does not occur naturally, and was first made in the countries at the eastern end of the Mediterranean in about 3000 BCE. It took another 1,000 years to reach Europe.

Bronze Age

Bronze changed the lives of the **Stone Age** people in Europe. With bronze, they could make better weapons and tools much more quickly. Bronze weapons were much stronger and sharper than their old stone or **flint** axes and knives. The Bronze Age people used bronze to make a whole range of objects, including pots, shields, helmets and ornaments.

▷ The Golden Gate **Bridge** in San Francisco, California, USA, is one of the world's best known suspension bridges. It is 1,280 m long.

BULGARIA
Government: Republic
Capital: Sofia
Area: 110,912 sq km
Population: 8.2 million
Language: Bulgarian
Currency: Lev

As the Stone Age gave way to the Bronze Age, huts were replaced by towns and people began to build palaces and temples. The Bronze Age lasted until about 800 BCE. At this time **iron** started to be used in Europe.

Buddha

The word Buddha means 'Enlightened One'. This name is given to great teachers of the Buddhist religion. The first Buddha was Siddhartha Gautama, who was born in about 563 BCE in northern **India**. For most of his life he travelled around India teaching people. Buddha taught his followers that the only way to true happiness was to be peaceful and kind to other people and animals, and to avoid evil.

Buddhism

Buddhism is a **religion** that was first practised in Asia about 2,500 years ago. Like the Hindus (see **Hinduism**), Buddhists believe that after they die they are born again as an animal or human being. This belief is known as reincarnation. Buddhists think that if they are very good, they will eventually end up in a kind of heaven – Nirvana. Buddhists spend a long time meditating.

There are now 350 million Buddhists all across the globe, but mainly in India, Tibet, China, Japan and Southeast Asia.

Bulgaria

Bulgaria is a country in Eastern **Europe**. Like several of its neighbours, Bulgaria was governed by the communist party during the second half of the 20th century. It became a fully democratic republic in 1990.

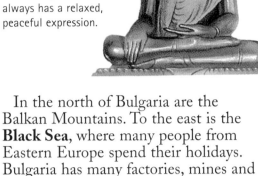

▷ Many statues and images of **Buddha** show him sitting with crossed legs, a pose known as the 'lotus position'. He always has a relaxed, peaceful expression.

In the north of Bulgaria are the Balkan Mountains. To the east is the **Black Sea**, where many people from Eastern Europe spend their holidays. Bulgaria has many factories, mines and farms, but it is a relatively poor country compared with Western Europe.

Burma *see* Myanmar (Burma)

Butterfly

Butterflies are flying **insects**. They are related to **moths**, and live in most parts of the world, even as far north as the Arctic Circle. All butterflies begin their lives as **caterpillars**, which hatch from eggs. When a caterpillar is fully grown it changes into a chrysalis with a hard skin. Inside this the chrysalis changes into an adult butterfly. When it is ready, the butterfly breaks out and flies away to find a mate and lay eggs of its own.

Byzantine Empire

The Byzantine Empire was founded by the Roman emperor Constantine I in 330 CE. It was an eastern division of the **Roman Empire**. Constantine decided to move the empire's headquarters to the east. He built a new city as his capital, which he called **Constantinople** after himself. It is now Istanbul, and is the capital of modern **Turkey**. In the 500s, the Byzantine Empire ruled most of the lands around the Mediterranean Sea and Black Sea. The Byzantine Empire lasted until 1453, when Constantinople was captured by the Turks.

Butterflies come in many colours, shapes and sizes. The largest kind is Queen Alexandra's birdwing of New Guinea (below), which has a wingspan of 28 cm. At the other end of the scale, the dwarf blue of South Africa measures just 14 mm from wingtip to wingtip.

Cactus

There are hundreds of different cacti, but they all have one thing in common. They are able to grow in very hot and dry **climates**. Cacti can do this because they store water in their fleshy stems. They are covered with prickly spines instead of leaves. The spines protect the plants' stores of water from raids by thirsty **desert** animals.

Cacti come in all shapes and sizes, from small pincushion-sized specimens to the giant saguaro cactus that may reach 15 m in height.

△ A group of **Caesar**'s enemies plotted to kill him. On 15 March 44 BCE, they stabbed him to death in the Roman Forum, the great meeting-place in the centre of Rome.

▽ **Cacti** grow in dry places, especially deserts. They make ideal nest-sites for birds, including owls and woodpeckers. Cacti also provide food for a variety of small animals.

Caesar, Julius

Julius Caesar (about 102–44 BCE) was a great leader of the **Roman Empire**. He is most famous for his part in turning the Roman Republic into an empire ruled by one person.

Caesar first became powerful when he commanded an army that conquered what is today France and Belgium. In 55 BCE, he crossed the English Channel and invaded Britain. He later rebelled against the Roman Senate (the main **government** of the entire Roman Empire), when he led his victorious armies into Italy. Caesar captured Rome without a struggle, and in 48 BCE he defeated Pompey, his main rival for power. Caesar then became the sole ruler of the Roman Republic.

Caesar made many enemies who hated what he was doing to the Republic. A group of them murdered him in Rome.

Calculator

About 5,000 years ago, the **abacus** was invented. This was the first calculator. Then, in 1642, the French scientist Blaise Pascal built the first machine for adding numbers. It worked by turning dials. After this, mechanical adding machines were used for years in offices

Saguaro cactus

Prickly pear

The Aztecs of Central America made a **calendar** from a huge stone shaped like the sun. It had the face of the Aztec sun god in the centre, and signs for the days around the edge.

CAMBODIA
Government:
Constitutional monarchy
Capital: Phnom Penh
Area: 181,035 sq km
Population: 11.7 million
Language: Khmer
Currency: Riel

and shops. They were useful but slow, and could not do difficult calculations.

Everything changed in the 1970s, when the **silicon chip** was invented. Now it was possible to make small **electronic** calculators that can add, subtract and divide as fast as we can press the keys. More advanced calculators can also do more difficult calculations needed in science.

Calendar

Every civilization has used some kind of calendar to keep track of days, weeks, months and years. Calendars are used to plan the planting and harvesting of crops, and also to mark special holidays and **festivals**. Western countries use the Gregorian calendar, which was first introduced by **Pope** Gregory XIII in 1582. It is based on the time it takes the **earth** to orbit (travel around) the **sun** – 1 year, or 365 days. The Chinese calendar is based on the orbit of the **moon** around the earth.

Cambodia

Cambodia is a flat, low-lying country in Southeast **Asia**. It changed its name to Kampuchea in 1976 and back to Cambodia in 1988. Most of Cambodia's

people live in small villages and grow rice, vegetables and fruit. The country was formerly part of the French colony of Indochina. It became independent in 1955. Since then, Cambodia has seen bitter **civil war** and **famine**, which killed more than 2.5 million people between 1976 and 1978. In 1993, after free elections, Cambodia became a constitutional **monarchy** again.

Camel

With its wide splayed feet, gangly legs, humped body and long thick neck, the camel has a unique appearance. It is one of the few **mammals** that can stand up to extreme heat and still do work carrying heavy loads.

Camels are ideally suited to making long journeys across **deserts**. Their padded feet grip well on loose sandy ground. They are powerful and swift, and can go for days without eating or drinking, living off the **fat** stored in their humps. Camels will eat almost anything, including the thorny shrubs and thistles found in deserts.

There are two kinds of camel – the single-humped camel of North Africa and the Middle East, and the Bactrian or two-humped camel of the Gobi Desert in **Mongolia**.

Camera

Modern cameras work in much the same way as those of 100 years ago. A shutter opens to let **light** from the scene being photographed pass through a glass **lens** to fall on the film. The amount of light that gets through can be varied by adjusting the size of the hole through which the light passes – the 'aperture'. The light forms an upside-down image of the scene on the film. The film is then developed with chemicals. The image on the developed film is printed onto a special type of paper. The result is a photograph (see also **photography**).

▽ **Camels** are vital beasts of burden in the desert regions of North Africa, the Middle East and Asia.

Today, most cameras have many different parts to help us take photographs in all kinds of situations. Flashguns produce a strong burst of light to illuminate subjects in dim conditions or at night. Long telephoto lenses allow us to zoom in on things that are a long way away. There are even cameras that work underwater.

Taking pictures with early cameras was a slow process. The first real camera, invented by the Frenchman Louis Daguerre (1787–1851) in the 1830s, needed a very long exposure time. The subject had to sit motionless for as much as ten minutes, usually with his or her head in a clamp to keep it still. Modern cameras have fast shutter speeds of less than one-thousandth of a second for taking photographs of very fast-moving objects.

Digital cameras do not use film – the image is converted into digital form and stored on disk. The number of separate photographs they can take depends on the size of their memory chip.

Film advance lever — Viewfinder — Film — Light — Lens — Diaphragm — Shutter

◁ When you take a photo, the **camera**'s shutter flicks open and shut again to let the right amount of light hit the film. The aperture controls the strength of light that reaches the film.

CAMEROON
Government: Republic
Capital: Yaoundé
Area: 475,442 sq km
Population: 14.7 million
Languages: French, English and various African languages
Currency: CFA Franc

Cameroon

Cameroon is a republic on the west coast of **Africa**. Most of the country's people live in scattered tribal villages and are farmers. Cocoa, coffee, cotton, **peanuts** and bananas are the chief crops. Oil is also produced.

Canada

Canada is the second largest country in the world, after **Russia**. In the Arctic, Canada reaches almost as far north as **Greenland**. To the south, it extends to the same **latitude** as southern France. The distance from Canada's Pacific coast in the west to its Atlantic coast in the east is further than from North America to Europe. But in spite of its size, two-thirds of the population of Canada lives in a narrow belt of land no more than 200 km from the border with the **United States**.

In the east of Canada are the **Great Lakes** that lie on the border with the United States. These huge inland seas empty into the St Lawrence River, which flows to the Atlantic Ocean. The two largest cities are Montreal, in the east, and Toronto, in the centre. However, the capital is **Ottawa**.

In the past, Britain and France each governed all or parts of Canada. Today, about 24 percent of Canadians regard French as their mother tongue.

Canada's vast forests have made it the world's largest producer of 'pulpwood' for making **paper**. The country also has enormous mineral reserves, especially of **oil** and **iron**, which have helped make Canada one of the ten leading industrial nations in the world.

Canal

A canal is an artificial waterway built to carry water traffic. Until the 1500s, canals could be built only across flat country. With the invention of canal locks, however, they could be built across high ground too. Canal locks use a system of locking gates and channels to change the water level. Before a boat or **ship** can enter a lock, the level of water inside the lock must be the same as that in the lower pool. Early canals could only be used by narrow, shallow-bottomed boats.

CANADA
Government: Confederation
Capital: Ottawa
Area: 9,976,130 sq km
Population: 30.5 million
Languages: English and French
Currency: Canadian dollar

△ Graphite is a pure form of **carbon**. Its atoms (top) arc arranged in layers that easily slide over each other. For this reason, graphite is one of the softest solids. The 'lead' used in pencils (above) is a mixture of graphite and clay.

△ The world's earliest **car** was a three-wheeled steam carriage invented by Nicholas Cugnot of France in 1769.

These canal boats were pulled along by horses that walked on paths running alongside the canal. Some canals, such as the **Suez Canal** and the **Panama** Canal, are big enough to let ocean liners pass through them. The Panama Canal is 80 km long and links the Atlantic and Pacific.

Canberra

Canberra is the capital of **Australia**. It is a small city in which the main activity is **government**. All the major departments of government have their headquarters here. Canberra has little industry. The city was founded in 1908 by an Act of the Australian parliament, and it expanded soon after the end of **World War I** in 1918.

Cancer

Cancer is a **disease** that causes **cells** in the body to grow uncontrollably. These cancerous cells can mass together to form a swelling known as a tumour. A severe tumour is described as malignant,

and often leads to death. No one yet understands why this happens, but treatments can sometimes be successful. Finding a cure for cancer is one of the greatest challenges facing modern **medicine**, and researchers all over the world are working hard at it.

Cancer is especially likely to affect older people. There are about 100 different kinds of cancer. Some of the most common include breast cancer, **lung** cancer and bowel cancer.

Car

Motorised vehicles were invented as long ago as the mid-1700s, but the first successful motor cars were not built until the 1880s. Since then cars have made enormous changes to the world we live in. The cars themselves have changed too. Clumsy 'horseless carriages' have become the fast, comfortable and reliable cars of today.

Most cars have petrol **engines**. Petrol is burned inside the engine, generating enough power to turn the wheels of the car. Other cars run on diesel instead of petrol (see **diesel engine**).

▽ Modern **cars** are designed on computers. The design teams try to make their cars as safe, efficient, comfortable and attractive as possible.

Petrol tank

Engine

Battery

Water from radiator cools the engine

Brake pads apply pressure to brake discs to slow car down

Gear stick for selecting gears

Driveshaft

Gears connect the driveshaft to the wheels

The driver makes the car accelerate (go faster) by pressing the accelerator pedal. This makes more petrol or diesel go into the engine.

Cars are pushed along by either their front or back wheels. As the engine's pistons go up and down, they turn the driveshaft, which is linked to the wheels by **gears**. The clutch pedal allows drivers to change into another gear. If they want maximum power they use a low gear – for example, first gear. The car needs plenty of power for starting or going up a steep hill. When drivers travel along a clear road at speed they use top gear. Most cars have four or five forward gears, plus reverse.

Carbon

Carbon is an important **element** that is found in every living thing – both plant and animal. Many of the things we use every day contain carbon, such as sugar and paper. Forms of carbon also exist as **coal**, **oil**, **diamonds** and graphite.

Radiocarbon dating is a method of finding out the age of many objects that are less than 50,000 years old. It works by measuring the amount of radiocarbon in an object. All living things contain radiocarbon. When they die, the radiocarbon begins to decay.

Caribbean

The Caribbean is a region that lies to the east of **Central America**, between North America and South America. It includes dozens of islands, forming a chain about 3,200 km long. The largest Caribbean islands are **Cuba**, **Jamaica**, **Puerto Rico** and Hispaniola (which is divided into two countries – **Haiti** and the **Dominican Republic**). Among the smallest islands are Barbados, **Grenada** and the Virgin Islands.

Another name for the Caribbean islands is the West Indies. This is because when the explorer Christopher **Columbus** first saw them in 1492,

he mistakenly thought that he was near India. Many Europeans later arrived to settle in the region. Today, the people of the Caribbean reflect its mix of cultures. They speak Spanish, French or English, often with local accents and variations.

Tourism is by far the largest industry in the Caribbean. Tourists flock to enjoy the beautiful sandy beaches and warm waters. The main crops include sugarcane, bananas and coffee.

Carnivore

Carnivores are a group of **mammals**. Most carnivores feed on the flesh of other animals, although they sometimes eat insects and plants as well. A few of them, such as the giant panda, are totally vegetarian. But what all carnivores have in common is a set of powerful jaws for chopping up food, curved claws for tearing and long sharp teeth.

Carnivores include **cats**, **dogs**, **hyenas**, **bears**, **raccoons** and **badgers**.

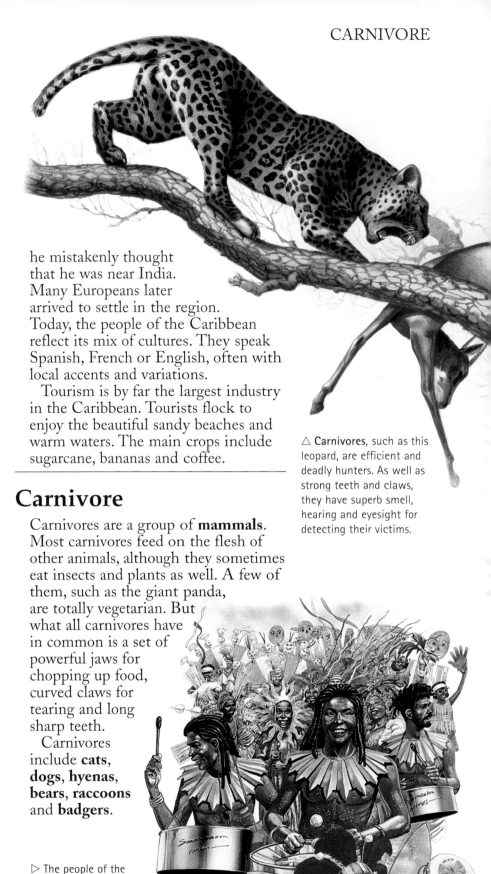

△ **Carnivores**, such as this leopard, are efficient and deadly hunters. As well as strong teeth and claws, they have superb smell, hearing and eyesight for detecting their victims.

▷ The people of the **Caribbean** stage a carnival in spring each year. Many of them wear spectacular costumes. Empty oil drums are made into dish-shaped musical drums called steel pans.

Castles often had double walls for extra protection. They also had plenty of towers for shooting at attackers from different directions at once.

△ The **cats** kept as pets all over the world were first domesticated (tamed) in Africa more than 4,000 years ago, probably by the Ancient Egyptians.

▽ The **caterpillar** of the monarch butterfly is highly poisonous. Its pattern of stripes warns hungry animals to leave it well alone.

All carnivores have very good smell, hearing and eyesight. They are also fast and skilled at hunting down their prey. Some carnivores, such as wolves and hyenas, hunt together in packs. **Lions** hunt in groups called prides. In this way they can kill animals much larger than themselves. Other carnivores, like the **leopard** and **tiger**, hunt alone.

Carroll, Lewis

Lewis Carroll (1832–1898) is the pen-name of an English writer called Charles Dodgson. Dodgson was a mathematics professor at Oxford University, but he is best known for his children's stories. The most famous is *Alice in Wonderland*. The story was written for the daughter of a fellow professor at the university.

Cartoon

Most people think of short, funny **films** with amusing characters and talking creatures when they speak of cartoons. But the word cartoon was originally used by artists to describe the rough sketches they produced when planning a **painting** or a **tapestry**.

In the 1840s, **newspapers** started to print drawings that made fun of politicians and other important people. These were also called cartoons.

The traditional way of making cartoon films is to join together lots of individual drawings. Each of the drawings is a little different from the one before. When they are shown one after another at a very fast speed it looks as if the scene is moving. To create a cartoon, the original sketch is drawn onto sheets of transparent film, called 'cels', then photographed onto film.

Since the 1980s, many cartoons have been made by a new technique called **computer** animation. The artists use computers to produce all the images, and can create exciting special effects.

Castle

Castles are fortified homes built by rulers and lords in the **Middle Ages**. Safe behind the thick stone walls of their castles, the owners and their supporters could fight off attacks by bandits and angry mobs of people, and sit out long sieges by invading armies. Some castles are still lived in, but many are now in ruins.

The first castles were constructed in about 950. They included a hill or mound surrounded by a ditch. From the late 1000s, some larger castles had a stone tower called a keep. As castles developed they became larger and more comfortable. Instead of having all the living quarters crowded into the keep, small 'villages' of huts sprang up inside the castle walls.

All kinds of tactics and siege machinery were needed in an attack on a heavily fortified medieval castle. Troops rushed the ramparts from giant siege towers wheeled up to the walls. Powerful catapults hurled stones against the walls or into the castle to spread confusion. Archers kept up a steady hail of arrows to force the defenders back from the walls, while troops with scaling ladders swarmed up them.

Cat

Cats belong to the group of **mammals** called the feline family. Although cats range in size from domestic breeds to **lions** and **tigers**, they all have many things in common. Cats have short, rounded heads, long face whiskers, sharp teeth that serve as weapons for grabbing and biting their prey to death, and powerful claws. All cats except the **cheetah** can retract (pull back) their claws into a sheath of skin when they are not in use. Cats' long tails help them balance, jump and climb.

There are about 38 kinds of cat. One of these – the domestic cat – has been bred into numerous different varieties. Wild cats are usually loners, but lions and cheetahs live in family groups.

Caterpillar

All **insects** have a life cycle with three main stages – first the egg, then the larva and finally the adult. 'Caterpillar' is simply another name for the larva of a **butterfly** or a **moth**.

Butterflies and moths usually lay their eggs on plants. After the eggs hatch, small, soft, worm-like creatures – the caterpillars – emerge. Caterpillars spend their whole time feeding. Their only purpose in life is to eat, grow and prepare for the change into adults. For this reason they have powerful jaws for chewing up plants. Many feed on crops and can cause great damage.

As caterpillars grow, they become too large for their skins. After a while, the skin stretches and splits and they emerge with a new one. This happens several times. The last 'skin' is quite different from the others. It forms a hard layer, which makes it impossible for the caterpillar to move. In this state it is called a chrysalis. Inside the chrysalis, the caterpillar changes into a butterfly. A moth caterpillar spins a cocoon around itself before turning into a chrysalis.

Cathedral
see Church

Cattle

Cattle are large, grass-eating animals. **Grass** is difficult to digest, and all cattle have four **stomachs** to make this easier. During **digestion**, the food is returned to the mouth to be chewed and swallowed again. When cattle do this, we say they are 'chewing the cud'.

The best known kinds of cattle are cows, oxen and buffalo. They provide us with **milk**, meat and hides for making **leather**. Bison are the largest cattle, with massive bodies covered in shaggy hair. Once huge herds of millions of bison roamed the plains of North America, where they were hunted by the **Native Americans**. But when European hunters arrived, they killed far too many bison, and now they survive in only a few national parks.

Cave

A cave is an underground hollow or passage. The largest caves are formed when slightly **acid** water flows or seeps through limestone rock. The **water** gradually dissolves the rock, sometimes leaving behind a whole network of caves. After a cave has been formed, water may go on dripping through the walls and ceiling. This often creates odd-shaped deposits of **minerals** called stalactites and stalagmites.

△ **Cattle** are still used to plough fields and pull carts in many parts of the world.

▽ A **cave** in limestone rock takes thousands of years to form. It may feature several vertical shafts, side passages, caverns and underground lakes and streams.

Rainwater seeps into rock

Rainwater becomes an underground stream

Stalactite grows down from roof

Stalagmite rises up from floor

The Neanderthals were **cave-dwellers** who lived in Europe and the Middle East until 35,000 years ago. At that time it was much colder than it is now, and caves provided vital shelter.

Cave-dweller

Caves are ideal places to shelter from the weather and from wild animals. They were among the first dwelling-places used by **human beings**. The mouth of a cave is often dry and it is possible to build a **fire** inside when the weather is cold. In hot weather, caves give shelter from the sun. Also, with walls all around them, the cave people could fight off dangerous animals from the cave mouth.

The remains of ancient cave-dwellers have been found in sites all around the world – in China, southern Asia, Africa and Europe (see **prehistoric people**). Here, bits and pieces of their tools and weapons have been dug up, along with bones of the animals they hunted. On the walls of some caves, paintings of animals have been found.

Cell

Cells are the smallest living parts of plants and animals. Single cells can only be seen under a **microscope**. Even a tiny bit of human **skin** contains millions of them. Cells are usually round in shape. A few are spiralled and some, like **nerve** cells, have many treelike branches.

In 1665, the English scientist Robert Hooke examined a piece of cork under a microscope and saw that it was made up of tiny compartments. He named them cells and this term has been used ever since.

Every living thing is made up of cells. They differ in shape, size and function, but all have a control centre called the nucleus. **Animal** cells have a thin cell wall, or membrane. **Plant** cells have a thicker cell wall containing cellulose, a stiffening substance. Plant cells also have chloroplasts, tiny structures that contain a green substance called chlorophyll. Plants use chlorophyll to make their own food, in a process known as **photosynthesis**.

Celts

The Celts were an ancient people of northwestern Europe. At one time, over 2,000 years ago, they lived all over Britain, France and parts of Spain and Germany. In about 400 BCE, they even crossed into Italy and attacked Rome.

Celtic people were tall and warlike. They lived in tribes made up of a chief, nobles, free men and women, and slaves. The tribes often fought each other. The Celts were highly skilled metal-workers and often decorated their weapons and armour with bright designs and curious creatures. They were also gifted poets and musicians. The Celtic **religion** was known as Druidism, and their priests were called druids.

When the armies of the **Roman Empire** spread out, many Celts fled to remote regions. In the lands that the Romans conquered, the Celtic way of life was soon lost. It was only in far-off corners of Europe that the Celtic language and customs survived.

Up until a few hundred years ago, Celtic speech was very common in **Ireland, Wales**, Cornwall (a county in southwestern England), **Scotland** and Brittany (a region of northwestern France). Today, although less common, Celtic speech can still be heard. Celtic languages include the Welsh language and Irish and Scottish Gaelic.

The **Celts** had no written language, but passed on stories of their gods and history in songs and poems.

An animal cell

Thin cell wall

Nucleus

Census

Nearly all countries of the world regularly count the number of people living in them. This **population** count is called a census. Most countries take a census every ten years. A census can also provide useful facts about what jobs people do, how much money they earn, what kind of homes they live in, whether they are married or single and how many children they have.

In ancient Rome, census takers made lists of people and their property. They used these lists to make sure that each person paid the right amount of **tax**. When **William the Conqueror** invaded England in 1066, his officials made a count of all the country's land and property. This census was listed in the **Domesday Book**.

△ **Cells** are tiny building blocks that make up plants and animals. Within each cell are many even smaller structures, each of which does a different job. For example, some produce energy, while others fight off invading bacteria.

inject poison into victims. All centipedes are active hunters. They feed mainly on worms, insects and snails.

Centipedes are found in most parts of the world. The largest centipede is a 46-legged giant that lives in the **rainforests** of South America. It is about 25 cm long and 2.5 cm thick.

Centipedes look similar to another group of creatures, known as millipedes. The main difference between them is that centipedes have two legs on each body segment, whereas millipedes have four.

Central America

Central America is a strip of land between the **United States** and **Mexico** to the north, and South America to the south. It consists of the republics of Belize, **Guatemala**, **El Salvador**, **Honduras**, **Nicaragua**, **Costa Rica** and **Panama**.

Lowland plains, thick forests and swamps lie along the coasts of Central America. In the centre are high mountains.

Centipede

Centipedes are long **invertebrates** (animals without backbones). Their bodies are made up of many parts, often up to 100 or more. Each body part has a pair of legs. The head has long antennae (feelers), powerful jaws and two stinging claws that are able to

▽ **Centipedes** are fierce hunters. Many can move very fast to catch prey or scurry away from danger.

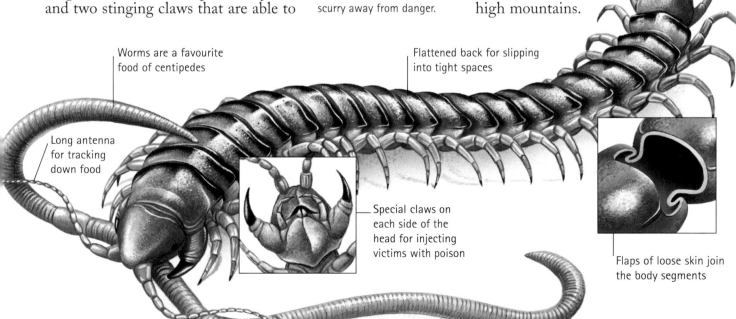

Worms are a favourite food of centipedes

Flattened back for slipping into tight spaces

Long antenna for tracking down food

Special claws on each side of the head for injecting victims with poison

Flaps of loose skin join the body segments

Central America is a hot area. Most of the large cities are in the cooler highlands.

Central America does not include Mexico. However, people often use a different term – Latin America – to describe all of the area from Mexico south to Brazil and Argentina. This is because the people who live there mainly speak Spanish or Portuguese, which come from ancient Latin.

The people of Central America farm tropical crops such as sugarcane, coffee, cotton and bananas. There is relatively little industry in the region.

In the 1500s, Spanish soldiers and settlers arrived in Central America. Much of the land became Spanish colonies. Before then, the region was home to various tribes, including the **Maya**. In 1838, Guatemala, Honduras, Costa Rica, Nicaragua and El Salvador all gained independence from Spain. Panama separated from **Colombia** in 1903, but Belize remained a British colony until 1981.

△ **Central America** includes seven countries. Most people who live there speak Spanish, and many are Roman Catholics.

△ A carving of a *menorah*, the special candlestick lit by Jewish families during the holiday of **Chanukah**.

Cereal

Cereals are the **seeds** of a group of plants that belong to the **grass** family. Throughout human history they have been the most important of all types of **food**. In prehistoric times, cereals were collected from wild plants. Later, when they began to be grown on farms, cereals became the most important food of early civilizations.

Some cereals, such as **rice** and maize, are eaten in their natural form. Rice is the main food crop for half the world's population. Other cereals, such as **wheat** and rye, are ground into flour before being baked or cooked. Pasta is made from a mixture of plain wheat, flour and water. Cereals are also used to make alcoholic drinks like beer and whisky (see **alcohol**), and some are grown as animal feed.

Wheat   Barley   Rye

Rice

Millet

Maize

△ **Cereals** are grasses that are grown for food. They include several of the world's major crops.

Chalk

Chalk is a pure white, soft and crumbly form of limestone. Land that is rich in chalk is found in southern England, in France and in parts of North America.

Most chalk was formed between 135 and 65 million years ago. It is made up of the crushed **shells** of countless tiny sea creatures. When these creatures died, their empty shells built up in thick layers at the bottom of warm, shallow seas. As the shape of the surface of the **earth** changed, these chalk layers were lifted up out of the seas to become dry land.

We usually think of chalk as something that we use to write, but it is also used in many other ways. Mixed with other substances, chalk is used to make ink, **paints**, medicines, **rubber**, **paper** and even toothpaste.

The famous white cliffs of Dover on England's south coast, are made of thick layers of chalk formed in the Cretaceous Period, 100 million years ago.

Chameleon

Chameleons are a group of **lizards** found in Africa, Asia and parts of southern Europe. They have narrow bodies with a crest along the back, and helmeted or horned heads. The most unusual thing about chameleons is that they can change the colour of their skin.

Most chameleons live in trees. They move very slowly and sit on branches for hours, as still as statues, waiting until **insects** come close to them. The chameleons catch the helpless insects with their long, sticky tongues, which shoot out with such speed that the insects seem to vanish without a trace.

Chanukah

Chanukah (also written Hanukkah) is a Jewish holiday that lasts for eight days each December (see **Judaism**).

Jewish families light candles and exchange presents on each night of Chanukah to celebrate an ancient miracle. Long ago, the Jewish people had just one day's supply of oil for their temple, but miraculously it lasted for eight days until they managed to get a new supply.

Chaplin, Charles

Charlie Chaplin (1889–1977) was one of the most famous comic **film** actors of all time. He is best known for his role as a gentle, well-meaning tramp who was always making mistakes and getting into trouble.

Chaplin was born in London, but he spent most of his working life in the United States. He started as an actor on stage, but he became famous for the parts he played in silent films in Hollywood. Chaplin also wrote, directed and produced the films that he made in later years.

Charity

A charity is an organization that exists to help people in need or to do work that is for the public good. Unlike a commercial business, its main aim is not to make money. Many charities rely on donations to keep going.

When times are hard, people have always given a helping hand to one another. This could be anything from a few coins to a free meal or a bed for the night. Many **religions** say that their followers should offer assistance to the poor or the sick.

The first charitable organizations probably appeared in the **Middle Ages**. They were able to help only small numbers of people. Modern charities do all kinds of work. For example, some help homeless people and

△ Charlie **Chaplin** starred in dozens of silent films. He was often called the 'world's funniest man'.

△ **Charlemagne** ruled over much of western Europe in the early Middle Ages.

others distribute food and supplies to people who are suffering from **famine** or natural disasters like **earthquakes**. Charities also raise money for **schools**, museums and **hospitals**, they help protect the environment and they fund important medical research.

Charlemagne

Charlemagne (742–814) was a great military leader. In the 700s, he founded an enormous empire that covered most of western **Europe**.

In the year 768, Charlemagne became the king of the Franks, a people who lived in the country we now call **France**. Through his skill in war, he took over northern Spain, Italy and Germany. He fought for the Christian Church in Rome, and in return, the **pope** crowned him Holy Roman Emperor on Christmas Day in the year 800.

Charlemagne's court was a great centre of culture and learning. Artists and scholars travelled there from far and wide. When Charlemagne died, his sons fought among themselves. Eventually his empire was divided between his grandsons, Charles, Louis and Lothar.

Charles I

Charles I (1600–1649) is known in history as the only English king to have caused his people to rebel and execute him. He came to the throne in 1625, but it was not long before he made enemies almost everywhere. Finally, in 1642, the country was split by **civil war**. The war lasted for several

◁ A **chameleon** can swivel each eye separately to help it look all around itself. It is also able to change colour to match its surroundings. This helps the chameleon to hide from its enemies.

they are joined together. If a piece of wood is burned in a **fire**, this is a chemical reaction. The wood turns to ash and, at the same time, heat and light are given off. It took chemists a long time to find out that burning is the joining together of the wood with the gas **oxygen** from the air. There are many kinds of chemical reactions.

The true science of chemistry as we know it began only in the 1600s. Chemists at this time began to find out how chemicals really work. Then they discovered the **elements**, from which all the millions of substances on earth are made. There are only about 100 elements, each of them made up of tiny **atoms**. The atoms of elements often join together to make different substances. The **salt** you put on your food consists of atoms of the elements sodium and chlorine.

years and thousands of people died in the fighting. But Charles refused to give in.

One of the reasons that Charles was unpopular is that he married a Catholic. He also imposed high taxes to pay for wars that people did not want, as well as trying to limit the powers of the English **parliament**. In 1649, Charles was put on trial. He was found guilty of treason, and the court sentenced him to death.

Charles I of England was put on trial in 1649. The charges against him were very serious. In the end, the court found him guilty and he was beheaded.

Cheese

Most cheese is made from cows' **milk** but it can be made from the milk of goats, sheep, buffalo and even reindeer. To make cheese, the milk is turned sour so that it will curdle. The solid bits, called the curds, are taken away from the liquid, or whey. They are then pressed into a firmer shape. Finally, the cheese is dried and left to ripen.

Chemistry

Chemistry is the study of materials – solids, liquids and gases. A chemist finds out what things are made of and how

CHILE
Government: Republic
Capital: Santiago
Area: 765,945 sq km
Population: 15 million
Language: Spanish
Currency: Peso

Chess

Chess is a game that has been enjoyed for hundreds of years. It is played by two people on a board with 64 black and white squares. Each of the two players has 16 pieces which they line up on either side of the board. Every piece can only be moved around the board in a special way. They are used to attack and retreat, to defend each other, and can be captured and taken out of play. The most important piece for each player is the 'king'. The game is won when one player manages to capture the other player's king.

Chile

Chile is a narrow country that stretches for 4,265 km down the western coast of **South America**. The area that people can inhabit is made even narrower by the **Andes** mountains, which lie along the country's eastern border. Chile has over a quarter of the world's **copper** resources. Its people speak Spanish and are mainly Roman Catholics. In 1973, a military government seized power, but in 1988 the Chilean people voted for an end to military rule.

Chimpanzee

Chimpanzees are the most human-looking of all the **apes**. Fully grown, they are about 1–3 m tall and are able to walk upright, although they usually walk on all fours, using their hands to help push themselves along. Chimps are found in the tropical forests of West and Central **Africa**. They live in family groups. Chimps take good care of their young, and are playful and intelligent animals. Tame chimpanzees can learn to talk in sign language and perform simple tasks.

Chimpanzees are among the noisiest of all **mammals**. They scream and shriek, drum on trees, slap the ground and keep up an almost constant hooting and muttering.

China

China is the third largest country in the world, and the nation with the greatest **population**. There are more than one billion Chinese people – a fifth of the earth's total population. China has the oldest continuous civilization of any country.

Natural barriers, including deserts and the **Himalayas** mountain chain, cut China off from its neighbours on mainland **Asia**. In the east are great plains and rivers, including China's longest river, the Chang (**Yangtze River**) and the slightly shorter Huang Ho (Yellow River). It is here that most of the people live. Many Chinese people are city-dwellers, and work in factories. But there are also millions of farmers living in the countryside.

For more than 3,000 years China was an empire. It was ruled by emperors who were members of royal families known as dynasties. The magnificent imperial palaces can still be seen in

中
国
人

China's main language, Mandarin, is written in picture-signs or characters. The symbols above read 'Chinese People'.

CHINA
Government: People's Republic
Capital: Beijing
Area: 9,596,961 sq km
Population: 1.2 billion
Languages: Mandarin Chinese
Currency: Yuan

China's capital city, **Beijing**. In about 200 BCE, one emperor ordered the construction of the **Great Wall of China** to keep out invading peoples from the north. It stretches for more than 2,400 km and is the longest fortification ever built.

Chinese inventions include **paper**, **printing**, ink, **silk**, porcelain, fireworks and gunpowder – all discovered long before such things were known in Europe or elsewhere. Today, more people speak Chinese than any other language. It is written in picture-signs. There are as many as 40,000 of these symbols, although only about 5,000 of them are in everyday use.

Since 1912, China has been a republic. A bitter **civil war** between Nationalists and Communists ended in 1949 with the victory of the Communists (see **communism**). **Mao Zedong** was one of the most important communist leaders. He tried to make China into a superpower by speeding up the growth of its factories and farms. While Mao Zedong was in power, China became isolated from the rest of the world. Later leaders increased contacts with the West, but many people who opposed the regime were imprisoned. In 1997, Britain handed over its colony of **Hong Kong** to Chinese rule.

Some **chimpanzees** have learned how to use a stick as a tool to dig termites from their nest. Young chimps learn the trick by watching their older relatives.

Chocolate

The chocolate we eat is made from the beans of the cacao **tree**. The beans grow inside pods, which hang from the trunk and branches of the tree. To make chocolate, the beans are first roasted, then ground up to give an oily liquid called 'chocolate liquor'. Other ingredients may then be added to the liquor. **Milk** chocolate, for example, has milk and **sugar** added to it.

△ **Chocolate** is made from cacao trees. First, the trees' huge pods are cut off with a large knife. The beans inside are then dried and roasted.

▽ **Christianity** began in the area that is now Israel, but has spread throughout the world. Saints (below) are holy people who have led a good life and have taken part in a miracle.

Christianity

Christianity is one of the world's largest **religions**. About two billion people call themselves Christians. They follow the teachings of **Jesus** and believe that he is the son of God who came to earth in human form.

Christianity is 2,000 years old. In fact, the main **calendar** used in many countries today is dated from the year in which it was thought that Jesus was born. Christians accept the **Bible** as their holy book and Sunday is their holy day, when they go to church, pray and observe other religious traditions.

In some ways, Christianity grew out of the religion of **Judaism**. But the teachings of Jesus upset the Jewish and Roman leaders of the time, and in the year 29 he was crucified (executed by being nailed to a cross).

After the death of Jesus, his followers, or disciples, spread his teachings far and wide.

There are many different forms of Christianity. The Roman Catholic Church is the oldest and largest Christian church. The **pope** is its head. For hundreds of years, popes have lived in **Vatican City** in Italy. The main church service of Catholics is called the Mass.

In Greece and Russia, the Eastern Orthodox Church is the main form of Christianity.

Protestants are Christians who do not belong to either the Roman Catholic or Eastern Orthodox churches. They believe that the things written in the Bible are more important than what church leaders say. Some passages in the Bible can be explained in different ways. Protestants believe that people should make up their own minds about what these mean.

Protestantism began in the 1500s, when a German called Martin **Luther** led a movement to change the Roman Catholic Church. This period is now called the **Reformation**. Luther's followers became known as Protestants because they protested against the teachings and policies of the Roman Catholic Church.

Christmas

This **festival**, celebrated by Christians on 25 December, marks the birth of **Jesus**. It is not known if Jesus was actually born on this date. In fact, the first mention of a festival of Christmas comes from a **Roman** calendar over 300 years after his death. Christmas customs vary from country to country, but people often exchange gifts, send greeting cards and decorate their homes.

Church

Christian churches are as varied as the countries in which they are found. They come in all shapes and sizes – from tents and tiny wooden huts to towering stone cathedrals. But all churches are used for the same purposes. They serve as places of prayer, as venues for religious services and as places that house all kinds of religious objects.

In most churches, the main entrance is at the west end and the altar is located at the east end.

Throughout the ages, churches have been built in many different styles of **architecture**. In the 1000s and 1100s, most churches were built in the Romanesque style. They had wide, rounded arches and low, round **domes**. In the **Middle Ages** in western Europe, a style known as Gothic appeared. Gothic churches had pointed spires, soaring arches, stone carvings and stained-glass windows. Building a cathedral such as Chartres in France or Canterbury in England was a huge task that took many years. Modern churches often have plainer interiors and use a variety of materials.

△ **Churches** are at the heart of many Christian communities. In the past, they served as important meeting-places, and gave shelter and charity to people in need.

Wooden roof timbers

Stained-glass window

Many stone carvings include spires, pinnacles and statues

▽ Many **churches** have the same basic floor plan, whether they are small parish churches or huge city cathedrals.

Chartres Cathedral, France (built from 1194 to 1260)

Huge stone foundations provide a firm base for the building above

Strong side supports called buttresses help to hold up the heavy roof and arches

Most churches, especially Catholic ones, are built in the shape of a cross. Worshippers sit in the centre, in a section called the nave. They all face towards the altar and the place where the choir sings. On either side are the two wings, called transepts, which give the building its cross shape.

Transept

Altar

Choir

Nave

△ Churchill was Britain's most important leader during World War II.

△ This government poster from the Spanish Civil War shows crimes supposedly carried out by the enemy.

Churchill, Winston

Sir Winston Churchill (1874–1965) was a British prime minister, war leader and writer. Although he was a senior minister in **parliament** before and during **World War I**, he was not very powerful. But in 1940, when **World War II** threatened Britain, the country chose him as its prime minister. As a wartime leader, Churchill showed great courage and determination. His rousing speeches helped the people of Britain to fight against Germany and her allies. He told the people: 'I have nothing to offer but blood, toil, tears and sweat.'

Cinema *see* Film

Circus

The **Romans** first used the word 'circus' to describe a large open-air space where exciting displays of horse-riding, chariot racing, acrobatics and wrestling were held. The modern type of circus began in the 1700s, and circus acts today include jugglers, clowns and acrobats. Some circuses include acts performed with trained animals such as elephants, bears, tigers and lions.

Civil rights

People have always fought for the right to govern themselves. But this does not always mean that people have freedom in their own lives, and sometimes they must fight for this freedom – for their civil rights. The most important of these rights are freedom to follow your own **religion**, freedom to say what you like in speech and in **newspapers**, equality in **law**, and the right to elect and dismiss a **government**.

In the United States, civil rights were an important issue for black people in the 1950s. Dr Martin Luther King led the movement for racial equality and civil rights in the USA (see **racism** and **King, Martin Luther**).

Civil war

Civil war happens when an entire country is divided into two or more groups that fight each other over their different political or religious beliefs. Sometimes friends and even families are forced to take opposite sides in the fighting. Major civil wars took place in **Britain** (1642–1649), the **United States** (1861–1865), **China** (1926–1935) and **Spain** (1936–1939).

Civil War, American

The American Civil War took place in the **United States** from 1861 to 1865. It was fought between the government (Union), backed by the northern states, and the southern states (Confederacy). In 1861, a number of southern states tried to break away from the United States and form their own country.

▽ More than 600,000 soldiers died in the **American Civil War**. The Battle of Gettysburg, 1–3 July 1863, was the bloodiest battle ever fought on American soil.

The main argument was over **slavery**. People in the northern states wanted to free the black slaves who still worked on the big farms, or plantations, in the southern states. These quarrels finally led to civil war.

When war broke out, 11 states left the Union to join the Confederacy. At first the Confederates, under General Lee, won many battles, but they were defeated at the Battle of Gettysburg in July 1863. The Union army, under General Grant, began to win the war. In April 1865, the Confederate army surrendered to General Grant.

The North had much more industry than the South, and in the end that decided the war. After the war, many people in the South were very bitter. The war had destroyed their prosperity. However, most people in the North felt it was more important that slavery be ended and the Union be preserved.

Civil War, English

In the British Isles, the most recent civil war lasted from 1642 to 1649. It was fought between King **Charles I** and the English **parliament**. By this time it was established that, although the king ruled the country, he could **tax** the people only if Parliament agreed. Charles believed that God had given him the right to do this alone. In 1629, he got rid of Parliament and tried to rule without it.

Another important disagreement was about **religion**. Charles was married to a Catholic, but most English people at that time were Protestants. They were suspicious of Charles because several of England's enemies, including France and Spain, were Catholic countries.

In 1642, the king called his friends and supporters to arm themselves. They were called Royalists. Parliament had its own army. Its soldiers were known as Roundheads because many of them had short, closely shaved hair. The Roundheads had a great general

called Oliver **Cromwell**. He was strict and trained his army carefully.

After numerous battles, sieges and skirmishes, the Royalist forces lost the war. Charles was captured and put on trial. In 1649, he was executed. For some years, Parliament ruled without a king, with Cromwell as its leader.

Clay

Clay is **rock** that has been broken down by millions of years of weathering. It is made of tiny particles that make a thick sticky paste. Clay particles are so small and closely packed together that a layer of them is waterproof. When a layer of clay lies underground, rain that seeps down into the soil cannot go through it. The water forms an underground pool, or reservoir. People can get the water out by digging wells.

Clay is easy to mould and can be baked hard in an oven, or kiln. It is used for making pots, tiles and bricks.

Cleopatra

Cleopatra (69–30 BCE) was a queen of **Egypt**. She married the Roman leader Julius **Caesar** and lived with him in Rome. After Caesar's death in 44 BCE, Cleopatra met Mark Antony, who jointly ruled the **Roman Empire** with Octavian. She soon fell in love

△ Martin Luther King was a leader of the **civil rights** movement in the USA. He demanded justice for black people and led numerous protest marches and rallies.

△ Wet **clay** can be made into differently shaped pots using a potter's wheel.

▽ The **English Civil War** was decided at the Battle of Naseby on 14 June 1645. Parliament's soldiers, the Roundheads, won a great victory over royalist forces.

Royalist soldier

Roundhead soldiers

Queen **Cleopatra** of Egypt is famous for causing a war by falling in love with the Roman leader Antony. Her fascinating life has inspired many writers, including Shakespeare.

One of the earliest kinds of **clock** was the sundial. As the sun moves across the sky, the position of its shadow changes on a grid, indicating the time.

Cloning is a technique for making exact copies, or clones, of living things. In 1996, scientists cloned a sheep called *Dolly*. Her offspring was identical.

with Antony, and Antony left his wife, Octavian's sister, to live with her. Octavian did not trust Cleopatra or Antony and started a war with them. He defeated them in a naval battle near Greece in 31 BCE.

Cleopatra and Antony fled to Egypt, and decided to kill themselves. Antony stabbed himself and died in Cleopatra's arms. Cleopatra then died by allowing an asp (a poisonous snake) to bite her.

Climate

Climate is the usual **weather** of a place over a long period of time. The weather can change from day to day, but the climate stays the same.

The **sun** has the greatest influence on the climate. It heats the land, the seas and the air. Countries near the **equator** get more of the sun's rays and usually have a hotter climate than places further north or south. The sun's rays do not get to the **Arctic and Antarctic** easily. They have very cold climates.

When the sun heats the air it causes **winds** that can make the climate hotter or colder. The winds may also carry rain or dry air, which can make the climate wet or dry.

The earth can be roughly divided into several climate zones. Within each zone there are local variations. For example, high mountains may get different weather from lowland plains. Climates can also change over time. Many scientists think that the whole world is becoming warmer, a process called **global warming**.

Clock

Long ago people measured **time** by putting a stick in the ground and watching its shadow move with the sun. Sundials work in the same way. However, sun clocks work only when the sun is shining. The first mechanical clocks were made in Europe in the 1200s, although the Chinese probably

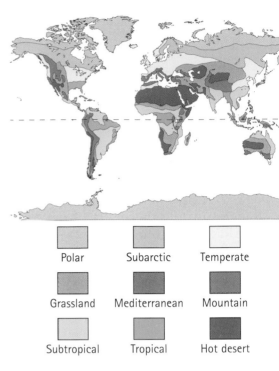

Polar	Subarctic	Temperate
Grassland	Mediterranean	Mountain
Subtropical	Tropical	Hot desert

THE WORLD'S CLIMATE ZONES

had simple clocks as early as the 600s. European clocks were first used in **churches** and **monasteries** to mark the time of services.

Early clocks were poor time-keepers and could lose or gain an hour a day. In 1581, the Italian astronomer **Galileo** discovered that the **pendulum** could be used to measure time. This helped people make much more accurate clocks. Further improvements were made, and ordinary clocks are now accurate to within a few minutes a year.

Today's scientists need very accurate clocks. They invented first the electric and then the quartz crystal clock. A quartz clock – the type used in most watches – tells the time by measuring the vibrations of a quartz crystal inside.

Cloning

Clones are organisms, or living things, that have exactly the same genetic material (see **genetics**). Many examples of clones exist in nature. The offspring of very basic organisms with a single cell, such as **bacteria** and **yeast**, are always clones. Some plants and simple animals like flatworms produce clones through a process called asexual reproduction – that is, without joining a male and female cell together (see **reproduction**). Clones also occur in advanced animals and humans from time to time. Identical twins are clones of each other, but are rare.

Recently, scientists discovered how to clone living things in the laboratory. They first used the technique to clone **frogs** in the 1960s. In **Scotland** in 1996 a team of scientists cloned a **sheep** – the first **mammal** to be cloned. One day researchers may be able to clone a human, but many people think that would be dangerous and wrong.

The ability to clone animals and plants could be very useful in **farming** and **medicine**. However, cloning is extremely difficult and expensive at the moment.

Clothing *see* Fashion

△ **Coffee** comes from beans that are found inside the fruit of the coffee tree. These berries are bright red when ripe.

△ **Coins** were first made in ancient China. Virtually every country now makes them, and collecting coins can be a satisfying hobby.

Coal

Coal is a **fuel** that is found in layers, or seams, under the ground. It is known as a **fossil** fuel because it was made millions of years ago from deposits of dead **plants**. Coal is used for heating and in making **electricity** and chemicals.

Coffee

Coffee is a drink made from the beans of the coffee **tree**. The tree bears red berries which contain **seeds** or beans in yellow pulp, surrounded by a tough skin. The skin and pulp are removed and the beans dried and roasted until they are brown. Then they are ground to brew the coffee we drink.

Coin

The first **metal** coins were minted (made) in about 800 BCE. Before then, all **trade** had been done by barter – by exchanging goods. For a long time, coins were made of precious metals such as **gold** and **silver**. Then people realized that any metal would do as long as everybody agreed that each coin was a symbol for a certain value.

College
see University and College

Ventilation fan

Shaft mine

Slope mine

Drift mine

Main shaft

Ventilation shaft

Coal seams

Opencast mine

◁ **Coal** is mined in various ways according to how deep it is. When it reaches the surface, opencast and drift mines are used. Slope mines are used for slightly deeper layers of coal, and shaft mines extract coal from deep underground.

△ *The printing press enabled books to be made faster and more cheaply. It used small pieces of metal type that could be moved again and again to print different texts.*

THE PRINTED WORD

Early written communication was produced on clay tablets, stone, wood, pressed reeds or animal skins. The Chinese invented paper over 2,000 years ago, but until the Middle Ages, few people could read or write. Every book was written out by hand, usually by professional scribes or monks. As a result, books were expensive and rare.

In the mid-1400s, German metalsmith Johannes Gutenberg invented the first printing press. For the first time, books became widely available. Newspapers appeared from the 1600s onwards. The printed word allowed new ideas about the world to be communicated faster and to a greater number of people than ever before.

△ *The world's network of telephone lines hums with millions of calls and emails every day.*

COMMUNICATION

Communication is the process of sharing ideas and information with others. It can take many forms from making a gesture or facial expression to speaking and listening, reading a newspaper or sending an email over the internet. Communication can be between two people or between millions, such as when a TV programme is broadcast around the world.

▽ *Invented in 1878, the manual switchboard allowed many telephones to be connected through a single telephone exchange. The operators had to connect each caller and receiver separately.*

SPOKEN AND WRITTEN LANGUAGE

Tens of thousands of years ago, prehistoric peoples gradually developed spoken languages. But before the invention of written languages, the only way of recording communication was to remember it or make paintings. The Sumerians of Mesopotamia (present-day Iraq) created the first written language in about 3500 BCE. It used small pictures to show objects and ideas. The Ancient Egyptians invented hieroglyphics – another form of picture writing.

In about 1000 BCE, a new way of writing grew up in the Middle East, which used an alphabet of 22 symbols. Each symbol represented a different sound and the symbols could be written together to form words. This became the basis of writing used in much of the world today. Other types of alphabet include Arabic, Chinese and Braille, the patterns of raised dots that enable blind people to read.

◁ The Sumerian language, cuneiform, was written down on clay tablets with a carved reed implement called a stylus.

△ A communications satellite stays over the same spot on earth. It receives and passes on television and telephone signals from one point on the planet to another.

TELECOMMUNICATION

Telecommunication is the ability to communicate over long distances. It was attempted in historic times using flags, drums, messengers and smoke signals. During the 1800s, communication systems using electrical signals carried down wires were invented. The first was the telegraph, which was developed in the 1830s and 1840s in Russia, Britain and the USA. Before long, thousands of kilometres of telegraph wires had been strung up.

In 1876, Scottish inventor Alexander Graham Bell found out how to send the human voice down telegraph cables, creating the telephone. The telephone developed rapidly. Within 21 years, there were a million telephone lines in the world. Today, the total is over one billion.

THE COMMUNICATIONS REVOLUTION

The different methods that allow us to communicate are called media. In the 1900s, new communications technology provided people with many more types of media. Recorded sound, photography and the cinema all became available to millions of people. Italian Guglielmo Marconi created the first wireless telegraph, which transmitted messages using radio waves instead of wires. Broadcasting, where a message is sent from one source to many receivers, began with the first radio programmes in the 1920s. Television followed in 1936.

Since 1962, satellites have relayed telephone calls and TV pictures across the globe. The arrival of personal computers in the 1970s vastly improved and speeded up existing forms of communication. Computers also led to the birth of the World Wide Web and email.

SEE ALSO
Book, Computer, Film, Hieroglyphics, Internet, Language, Newspaper, Photography, Printing, Radio, Recording, Satellite, Telephone

Colombia

Colombia is a country in northern **South America**. The **Andes** mountains cover about a third of its area. Most of the people live in the northwest, where the highlands are fertile. The Colombians won independence from **Spain** in 1819 under the leadership of Simón Bolívar. The country is a democratic republic but has many social problems, including a huge trade in illegal drugs. **Coffee** is Colombia's main commercial crop.

Colosseum

The Colosseum of Rome was a giant sports stadium built by the Ancient Romans. It held more than 50,000 people and was the largest building of its kind in the **Roman Empire**. It still stands in the centre of Rome but is mostly in ruins.

The floor, or arena, was used for **gladiator** combats, battles between men and animals and fights between different kinds of animals. The floor could also be flooded so that mock sea battles could be fought on it.

The **Colosseum** of Ancient Rome was completed in 80 CE. It had four storeys and a canvas roof that protected spectators from the sun and rain.

COLOMBIA
Government: Republic
Capital: Bogota
Area: 1,141,748 sq km
Population: 40 million
Language: Spanish
Currency: Peso

Colour

The first person to find out about coloured **light** was Isaac **Newton**. He shone sunlight through a piece of **glass** called a prism.

◁ **Colour** is what we see when light from an object reaches our eyes. A tomato looks red to us because it reflects red light back into our eyes, but takes in all the other colours of light.

The light that came out of the prism was broken up into all the colours of the **rainbow** – red, orange, yellow, green, blue, indigo and violet. Newton had found out that white light is a mixture of several colours added together.

When sunlight falls on rain, we may see a rainbow. Rainbows are caused by the drops of **water** behaving like tiny prisms. They break up the sun's light into a spectrum of colours, which are always in the same order, from red to violet.

A red flower looks red to us because it absorbs (soaks up) all the other colours and reflects only red to our eyes. A green leaf absorbs all the colours of light except for green.

Coloured light behaves differently from coloured pigments (the substances that give inks and **paints** their colour). All the colours in light combine to make white light, but mixing coloured pigments results in black.

Columbus, Christopher

Christopher Columbus (1451–1506) was a sailor and explorer. In 1492, he claimed several islands off America for **Spain**. Although Columbus returned to America three more times, he died believing that he had reached Asia.

Columbus – like many people of his time – knew that the earth was not flat but round. Sailors from Europe used to sail east to the 'Indies' (Asia). They brought back rich cargoes of **gold** and **spices**. Columbus thought that if he sailed west instead he could reach the Indies quicker. Ferdinand and Isabella, king and queen of Spain, gave him ships and money to make this voyage.

In 1492, Columbus sailed west with three ships. After three weeks, on 12 October, they reached an island in the Americas. Columbus named it San Salvador – an island in the Bahamas.

Comet

Comets travel around the **solar system** in loops, or **orbits**. Sometimes they pass close to the sun. At other times they move far beyond the path of **Pluto**, the outermost **planet**. Their orbits may last from several years to many centuries.

Comets are clouds of frozen gas, ice, dust and rock. The largest are only a few kilometres across, but their bright tails may be millions of kilometres long. One of the most famous comets is named after the English astronomer Edmond **Halley**.

△ As a **comet** travels towards the sun, the sun's rays knock particles out of the comet and push them away to make a long tail. The tail is made of glowing gas and dust.

Commonwealth

A commonwealth is a group of countries or people who hold regular meetings and try to help each other. The Commonwealth of Nations is a commonwealth made up of many of the countries that were once ruled by Britain. Most of these countries now have their own **governments** and laws

▽ Christopher **Columbus** made four voyages across the Atlantic to America. On his first expedition, in 1492, he sailed with three ships, the *Santa María*, the *Pinta* and the *Niña*.

but some of them still have the queen or king of Britain as their **monarch**. The Commonwealth came into being at a meeting held in 1926. Its members include **Canada, Australia, New Zealand, India, Pakistan** and many African, Pacific and Caribbean countries.

Communication

see **pages 70–71**

Communism

Communism is a set of ideas about the way a country should be run. The main idea of communism is that people should share their wealth and property. Doing this makes people more equal because nobody is very rich or very poor.

In most communist countries, the people own the factories and farms but it is usually the **government** that runs them. The government controls almost everything, and personal freedoms are often restricted. There may be strict

An early European **compass**. The needle in a compass always points north and south because the earth itself is a giant magnet. The needle lines up parallel with the earth's magnetic field.

Communism is a way of organizing a country so that everybody can share its wealth and property. The image below shows a meeting of the Chinese Communist Party in 1949. Large posters of the party leaders form a backdrop to the speeches being made.

government control of the **media**, including newspapers, television, films and books. The purpose of all these strict government controls is to organize the country for the benefit of everyone.

Many countries became communist during the course of the 20th century. They included the **Soviet Union**, **China**, **Cuba** and North **Korea**, and several countries in Eastern Europe. **Lenin** and **Stalin** of the Soviet Union and **Mao Zedong** of China were among the most important communist leaders of the last century.

Communism has not always been a successful form of government. Many of the people in communist countries have remained poor.

Compact disc
see **Recording**

Company

A company is an organization that exists to make money – a profit – for the people who own it. It does this by selling goods or providing a useful service of some kind. Companies range in size from a single employee, or worker, to thousands of employees.

A company must keep records of the money and goods that come into and go out of the business. This is known as keeping accounts, or accounting. An accountant's job is to study whether the company is doing well or badly.

Some of the earliest companies grew up in Europe in the **Middle Ages**. They bought and sold products such as wool, timber and food (see **trade**). Today, many companies are owned by shareholders. These are people who have bought a share of the company. Shares in companies are bought and sold at places called **stock exchanges**.

Compass

A compass is an instrument for finding the way. A magnetic compass always points to the earth's magnetic poles, which are close to the **North Pole** and the **South Pole**. It works by **magnetism**. It has a magnetic needle fixed to a pivot so that it is free to swing around. The needle always points north and south when it is at rest. With a compass showing where north and south are, it is easy to travel in a straight line in any direction you wish to go.

Compound

Compounds are chemicals that are made up of two or more **elements**. For example, **salt** is a compound made up of the elements sodium and chlorine. Compounds are formed when elements come together and make a new substance that is completely different from the elements. **Water** is a compound of the gas elements **hydrogen** and **oxygen**, and it is very different from either of them.

There are millions of compounds in the world. They can be

very simple, like water (with three **atoms** in each molecule), or complex like some plastics (with hundreds of atoms in their molecules).

Computer

Computers are playing an ever-larger part in our lives. They have led to enormous advances in science and technology. For example, computers can guide aeroplanes and spacecraft, control life-saving medical equipment and operate automatic cash machines that give us money in the street. This book was designed, edited and produced using computers!

Computers can do all these things because they are able to do millions of calculations each second. First the computer receives data, or information, put in by the user. Then it processes the data according to its programme, and produces a result.

All computers use a language called the **binary system**. There are only two numbers in the binary system – 1 and 0. Computers use this system because they have been designed to work with electrical currents. They can recognize the difference between a large current and a small current flow. If there is a large current, they register 1 and if there is a small current, they register 0. When we type on a computer keyboard, we are making lots of electrical currents flow through tiny circuits in **silicon chips**. It is these tiny currents that give us the answers we need.

A computer has four basic parts. An input device, such as a keyboard, mouse or joystick, is used to enter data into the computer. Then the computer's 'brain' – the central processing unit or CPU – processes the data and performs the tasks it has been told to do. The resulting information is sent to the computer's output device, such as a screen

△ The Chinese thinker, **Confucius**, taught people to respect one another.

DEMOCRATIC REPUBLIC OF CONGO
Government: Republic
Capital: Kinshasa
Area: 2,345,409 sq km
Population: 50 million
Languages: French and various Bantu languages
Currency: Congolese Franc

▽ **Computers** can be used to direct robots, such as this one that sprays paint on to new cars.

or printer. And finally the computer's memory unit stores programmes and data. These can also be stored on removable disks (see **recording**).

Computers can be linked to each other using a network of telephone lines and cables. The **internet** is a globe-spanning computer network, allowing messages and information to be sent across the world in seconds.

Concrete

Concrete is a mixture of cement, gravel and **sand**, together with water. The paste-like concrete sets hard and is used to make buildings, **roads**, **bridges** and **dams**. The cement that is the starting-point for concrete is usually made from limestone and **clay**. These materials are crushed and mixed, then heated in an oven called a kiln. When cool, the mixture is ground into cement powder. Concrete is often strengthened by placing steel rods in it when it is soft.

Confucius

Confucius (551–479 BCE) lived nearly 2,500 years ago in **China**. He was a famous philosopher (thinker) who taught people how to live and behave in a good way. The Chinese people followed his teaching for centuries.

Congo (Zaire)

The Democratic Republic of Congo, which was known as Zaire between 1971 and 1997, is a huge country in **Africa**. It includes most of the Congo River basin. The Congo River is the second longest river in Africa – only the **Nile** is longer. It is an important means of transportation for the peoples of central Africa. Thick forests and **savanna** (grassland with trees) cover much of Congo's land. The country is very rich in minerals, including **copper**, cobalt

SOUTHERN HEMISPHERE

NORTHERN HEMISPHERE

Constellations are groups of stars that form patterns in the night sky. People who live north of the equator (in the northern hemisphere) see different stars from those who live south of the equator.

△ **Conifers** include firs, pines, spruces, larches and cedars. Most of them have needle-like leaves which they do not lose in winter.

▽ **Continents** lie on huge plates of rock, which move because they are floating on a layer of semi-liquid rock called magma.

and **diamonds**, but most of its people live by farming.

The country was once ruled by **Belgium**, but it became independent in 1960. Since then, it has suffered from a long **civil war**. Across the Congo River lies the Democratic Republic of Congo's smaller neighbour, the Republic of Congo.

Conifer

Conifers are **trees** and shrubs that have cones instead of **flowers** for making seeds and pollen (the powdery grains that plants use to fertilize each other). Many conifers are found in cooler parts of the world. Vast forests of conifers cover much of **Canada** and **Russia**.

Conservation

Humans use **plants, animals, soil, water** and **minerals** for nearly everything that they make. Conservation means using these valuable resources wisely and protecting them for use in the future. It also means preserving areas of outstanding natural beauty.

Today, the need to conserve wildlife and natural resources is a major world problem. It involves the study of **ecology**, the branch of **biology** that deals with the relationship between all living things and their surroundings. Conservationists are people who try to find a balance between the needs of

human beings and care of the natural environment. Without care, the world's fast-growing **population** will cause increasing damage to wild **habitats** such as forests, marshes and seas.

There are many different aspects to conservation. It includes recycling (re-using) useful materials such as paper, plastic, glass and metal. It also includes saving energy and reducing the amount of harmful **pollution** produced by factories and vehicles. Another concern of conservationists is to try to stop plants and animals from becoming extinct (vanishing forever). The best way of doing this is to create nature reserves that protect an entire habitat.

Constantinople

Constantinople is the old name for the city of Istanbul in **Turkey**. It lies between Asia and Europe, and was the most important city in the western world for more than a thousand years.

Constantinople was named after the Roman emperor Constantine. In 330 CE, he founded the city on the site of the ancient Greek town of Byzantium. He divided the **Roman Empire** into two to make it easier to rule. Constantinople was the capital of the eastern half – the **Byzantine Empire**.

After the last Roman emperor was overthrown in 476 CE, Constantinople and the Byzantine Empire continued to be powerful. The city was a great centre of **Christianity**, learning and **trade** until it was invaded by the Ottoman Turks in 1453. It became a Muslim city, and was renamed Istanbul.

Volcano

Ocean floor

Hot magma rising from deep below the surface

Constellation

Stars form patterns known as constellations in the night sky. In early times, these were named after ancient gods, heroes, animals and objects whose shapes people saw in the patterns. Examples include Orion the Hunter, Leo the Lion, Lyra the Lyre.

Astronomers have named a total of 88 constellations over the whole sky. Twelve of them form a wide track where the **sun** appears to travel in the course of the year, and where the **planets** are usually found. These are the constellations of the Zodiac.

△ **Conservation** includes the battle to protect rare wildlife. In Africa, wardens burn piles of confiscated elephant tusks to deter the illegal trade in ivory.

Continental shelf

Continents do not end where their coasts meet the sea. Their true edge lies far out under the sea. Each continent is ringed by a gently sloping shelf of land under the sea – the continental shelf. This shelf sometimes stretches for hundreds of kilometres from the shore. Beyond the continental shelf is the deep **ocean** floor.

Most sea life is found on the continental shelf. Sunlight shines through the water, helping plants, fish and other animals to grow.

△ **Constantinople** was attacked by the Ottoman Turks in 1453. They crushed the defenders, and turned the Christian city into a new Muslim capital.

Continent

A continent is a large area of land. There are seven continents – **Africa, Antarctica, Asia, Australia, Europe, North America** and **South America**.

The continents are not fixed. They are made of **rock**, but the great heat in the centre of the **earth** has made the surface rocks break into huge pieces called plates. These plates are floating on top of a layer of hot, molten (partly melted) rock called magma. As the magma moves, the plates slide along on top of the magma, taking the continents with them. This movement is very slow. A continent moves only a few centimetres each century.

The shapes of North and South America, Europe and Africa look like jigsaw pieces that would fit closely if they were pushed together. The continents have this appearance because they used to be one giant piece of land that later broke up. The name for this process is 'continental drift'.

People who study **geology** have found evidence showing that South America was once in contact with Africa. Geologists think that the movements of the continents pushed up some pieces of land to make mountains such as the **Alps**, the **Andes** and the **Himalayas**. The mountains are continually getting higher as the earth's plates push against each other.

Contraception
see **Birth control**

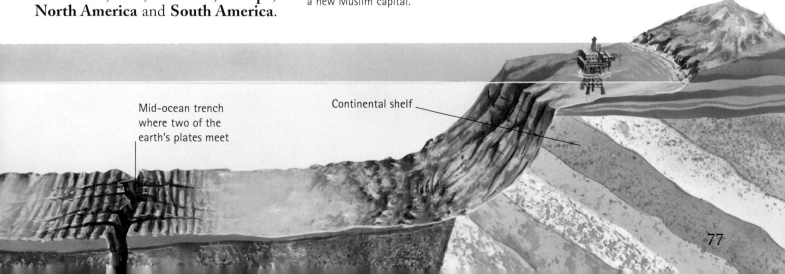

Mid-ocean trench where two of the earth's plates meet

Continental shelf

Cook, James

James Cook (1728–1779) was a British sea captain and explorer. His expeditions took him round the world and all over the **Pacific Ocean**. In 1770, Cook landed in Botany Bay, **Australia**, to claim the continent for Britain. **New Zealand** and many Pacific islands also became British colonies as a result of his trips.

Captain **Cook** was the first European explorer to visit the Antarctic and Hawaii. He also led voyages to the South Pacific and Australia.

Copernicus, Nicolaus

Nicolaus Copernicus (1473–1543) was a Polish scientist. He is sometimes called the father of modern **astronomy**. Copernicus showed that the **earth** is not the centre of the **universe**, as people used to believe. Instead, the earth and the **planets** revolve around the **sun**. Copernicus also showed that the earth itself moves round, or rotates, each day.

Copper

Copper is a reddish-brown **metal**. It was one of the first metals that people used. Copper is very soft when it is pure. But if it is mixed with other metals it makes **alloys** such as brass and **bronze**, which are harder and better for making tools. Copper lets heat and **electricity** pass through it very easily, so it is often used for pots, pans and electric wires.

Cotton has green fruits called bolls. When they are ripe, they split open to reveal a fluffy mass of white fibres and seeds.

Coral

Corals are tiny animals that live in warm, shallow seas. They have soft bodies, but build hard, chalky, 'skeletons' around themselves for protection.

△ **Cowboys** are known as *gauchos* in South America. Many of them still lead a traditional way of life on the plains of Argentina.

Most corals live in groups, or colonies. These can have many shapes, from lacy fans to stubby branches, usually in beautiful colours. Some colonies form thick underwater walls called reefs. Coral reefs support the richest variety of animals anywhere in the sea. The world's largest coral reef is the **Great Barrier Reef**, which lies just off the east coast of **Australia**.

Cortès, Hernando

Hernando Cortès (1485–1547) was a Spanish soldier and explorer who in 1519 landed on the coast of **Mexico**. With a force of only 600 soldiers and a handful of horses he conquered the great **Aztec** empire. His horses and guns helped convince the Aztecs he was a god. Cortès marched on their capital Tenochtitlàn, captured the Aztec emperor Montezuma, and by 1521, had taken control of Mexico.

Cosmetics

Cosmetics have been used since prehistoric times when **cave-dwellers** decorated their dead with dyes and paints. Lipstick, eye-shadow, nail varnish and hair dye were widely used by the Ancient Egyptians. The Greeks and Romans bathed with scented oil and wore perfumes to make their bodies and clothes smell sweet. Most modern cosmetics are made from a base of **fats** and oils, to which a variety of natural and artificial substances is added.

Costa Rica

Costa Rica is a small Spanish-speaking country lying between **Nicaragua** and **Panama** in Central America. It was

◁ **Coral** reefs provide homes for many sea animals, which find shelter in crevices or burrow into the coral itself.

a Spanish colony from 1530 to 1821 and became independent in 1848. Costa Rica is a largely agricultural country, the chief crops being coffee, bananas, sugarcane and cocoa. **Rainforest** covers much of the rest of the land.

Cotton

Cotton grows in warm and tropical places all around the world. It is one of the most important plants grown by people. Its fibres are spun into yarn and then woven into cloth (see **weaving**). The seeds are used for oil and cattle food. Cotton oil is used to make soaps, paints and cosmetics.

Cowboy

There are still many people in the western USA who ride **horses** and herd cows, but the great days of the cowboys lasted only 40 years, from the 1860s to 1900. At that time, there were **prairie** grasslands stretching from Texas north to Canada. **Cattle** were grazed there and then driven in great herds by cowboys to the railroad stations.

The cowboys' life was simple and hard. They travelled light, and usually owned nothing more than their horse, saddle, bed-roll and clothes.

Crab

Crabs belong to a group of animals called **crustaceans**, and are closely related to **lobsters**. Crabs have hard, thick **shells** that cover their flat bodies. They also have long, spidery legs for walking underwater, swimming and burrowing. The first pair of legs have pincers, which are used for attacking and holding prey. Crabs have their eyes on the end of short stalks. These can be pulled into the shell for safety.

Most crabs live only in the sea, but there are some kinds that live in rivers or lakes and some tropical kinds that live on forested islands.

Cricket

Cricket is a **sport** that was probably invented in England in the 1300s. It is played with a bat and a ball by two teams of 11 players on an oval grass pitch. The teams take it in turns to 'bat' and to 'field'.

A member of the fielding side, the bowler, throws the ball to the batsman, who stands in front of three wooden stumps. The stumps have two small sticks resting on top of them, called bails, and the bowler tries to knock them off with the ball. If the bowler is successful, the batsman is 'out'. The batsman is also out if a member of the fielding side catches a ball that he or she has just hit before it hits the ground.

The batsman scores 'runs', or points, by hitting the ball and by running the short distance to where the bowler was standing. There are two batsmen, who run back and forth between the two wickets, or bases, swapping positions as they do so.

Cricket is played mainly in Britain and former British colonies, such as **India**, **Australia**, **Pakistan**, **Zimbabwe** and several **Caribbean** nations.

Croatia

Croatia is a small country in the **Mediterranean**. It was formerly a republic of **Yugoslavia**, but it declared its independence in 1991. This was followed by fighting between Croatia and the Yugoslav army. The army was dominated by another Yugoslav republic, **Serbia**. Croatia has a long coastline with many islands. Steep mountains sweep down to the coast, separating the sea from inland plains.

Crocodile
see **Alligator and Crocodile**

Crabs that live in the sea feed on small animals like worms and scraps of meat lying on the seabed.

COSTA RICA
Government: Republic
Capital: San José
Area: 50,700 sq km
Population: 3.6 million
Language: Spanish
Currency: Colón

CROATIA
Government: Republic
Capital: Zagreb
Area: 56,533 sq km
Population: 4.5 million
Language: Croatian
Currency: Kuna

The **Crusades** were a series of eight wars between Christian knights (left) and the Muslim Turks (right), called Saracens.

Cuba is one of the world's leading producers of cigars. They are rolled by hand from dried tobacco leaves.

CUBA
Government: Communist
Capital: Havana
Area: 114,524 sq km
Population: 11.2 million
Language: Spanish
Currency: Peso

Cromwell, Oliver

Oliver Cromwell (1599–1658) was the only ruler of Britain never to have been a **monarch**. He came to power after the English **civil war** of the 1640s. Cromwell fought against **Charles I** with the army of the English **parliament** and became its leader. After Charles I was executed, Cromwell became the head of the country but he never declared himself king. In 1660, two years after Cromwell's death, Charles's son was restored to power as King Charles II.

Crusades

The Crusades were wars between followers of **Christianity** and **Islam** in the **Middle Ages**. They took place in Palestine, the Holy Land. In 1071, Turkish Muslims captured the city of **Jerusalem** and stopped Christians from visiting the holy places in Palestine. A few years later, the Byzantine emperor in **Constantinople** joined forces with the **Pope** to drive the Turks from the Holy Land. They started the first Crusade. Their armies took Jerusalem from the Muslims in 1099.

There were seven more Crusades after the first one. Many of them failed because the Crusaders quarrelled with each other. The third Crusade, in 1187, was defeated by a great Muslim general called Saladin. The Muslims took back much of the Holy Land.

During the Crusades, Europeans learned more about the eastern parts of the world. When they returned to Europe, they took back with them new things such as spices, silk and paper.

Crustacean

Crustaceans are a large group of about 10,000 **invertebrates** (animals without backbones). They include sandhoppers, woodlice, barnacles, prawns, shrimps, **lobsters**, **crabs** and water fleas. Most of them live in the sea.

All crustaceans have numerous joints in their bodies and legs. They often have claws, or pincers, on their front legs. They use these for defence and to grab prey. Many crustaceans live inside **shells**, which keep their soft bodies safe.

Cuba

Cuba is an island in the **Caribbean**. It was ruled by **Spain** from the 1500s until 1898, when the **United States** took Cuba from Spain. In 1902, the island gained independence. Cuba became a communist country in 1959 under its leader Fidel Castro (see **communism**). Cuba has large farms growing sugarcane and **tobacco**, but forest covers the centre of the island.

Curie, Marie and Pierre

Marie Curie (1867–1934) and Pierre Curie (1859–1906) were scientists who worked together, and finally married each other. She was Polish, he was French. They studied **radioactivity** and discovered the element **radium**, for which they were given the **Nobel Prize** for physics in 1903.

Cyclone *see* Hurricane

Czech Republic

The Czech Republic is in Eastern Europe. It used to be part of the country known as Czechoslovakia, which split into two nations, the Czech Republic and **Slovakia**, in 1993. Much of the Czech Republic is covered by mountains. Prague, its capital, is one of the most historic cities in Europe.

In 1938, **Germany** took control of western Czechoslovakia. This ended with the defeat of Germany in **World War II**. Czechoslovakia was then ruled by a communist government, but in 1989 the government fell and was replaced by a more democratic government.

Dali, Salvador

Born in Spain in 1904, Salvador Dali was one of the most inventive artists of the 1900s. His **art** was often bizarre, and many of the people who saw his work were at first shocked. Dali's **paintings** are unsettling because they are full of weird objects and strange landscapes. They frequently feature illusions, or 'tricks of the eye'. Dali made many other things beside paintings, including **sculptures**, **films**, furniture and even pieces of **jewellery**.

Dali belonged to a group of artists and writers called the Surrealists, who claimed to produce their work without having to think about what they were doing. Dali used to say that he was just painting his **dreams**. He died in 1989.

△ Salvador **Dali** often made sculptures from unusual combinations of objects. He created his famous 'lobster telephone' in 1936.

Dalai Lama

The Dalai Lama is the religious leader of **Tibet**, a disputed area that currently forms part of southwest **China**. Tibet has its own form of **Buddhism**. The teachers of Tibetan Buddhism, called lamas, live in monasteries and instruct people in the ways of the Buddhist **religion**. The most important lama of all is known as the Dalai Lama.

Followers of the Dalai Lama believe that he is the reincarnation of a godlike buddhist teacher who lived long ago. When a Dalai Lama dies, the other lamas search for a young boy they believe to be the next reincarnation to take his place.

▽ Many **dams** are curved so that the great weight of water behind them pushes against the sides of the valley instead of against the dam wall.

Dam

A dam is a barrier built across a **river** to control its flow. Modern dams are usually made of **concrete**, and include some of the largest structures built by people. There are several reasons for building dams. The main one is to make a reservoir – an artificial **lake**.

continued on page 84

DANCE

Dance is one of the oldest human arts. It is the rhythmic movement of the body, usually in time to music.

△ Before a game, the All Black rugby team of New Zealand performs a ritual dance that helps build the players' team spirit.

▽ Traditional Indian dances have close links with the Hindu religion. The dancers enact tender love stories and tales of epic battles between gods and demons.

WHY PEOPLE DANCE

Humans seem to have a powerful urge to dance. This may be because moving the body in rhythm is a natural way of expressing our feelings. For example, children often jump up and down when they are excited and sway gently when they are happy and resting. Dance can tell a story and create an atmosphere. It is also great fun. Many people dance simply to enjoy themselves.

AN ANCIENT ART

Dance is almost as old as human civilization itself. Prehistoric cave paintings in Africa and southern Europe show people dancing. Dance later became part of religion. It was used to bring rain, make crops grow and guarantee good hunting. Warriors performed war dances to make themselves feel brave before a battle. People also danced at ceremonies and feasts.

WORLD OF DANCE

Every country has its own dance traditions, which often evolved from the simple dances of ordinary people. Gradually, set moves and steps were introduced. Some dances became very formal, with strict rules for the dancers. The first formal social dances were held in Japan 1,500 years ago.

◁ Many dance styles have their origins in traditional folk dances. These ballet dancers are wearing costumes based on those of Ancient Greece.

Costumes, makeup and lighting effects help dancers to create the characters they are playing. In modern ballets, the dancers often wear one-piece leotards.

THE BEAUTY OF BALLET

Ballet emerged during the Renaissance (1400s) at the royal courts of Italy and France. It is like a language, but it uses music and dance instead of words. Ballet dancers mime (act out) the story using their whole bodies. They show feelings by exaggerating their movements.

A new ballet is the result of a partnership among many people. The choreographer has the idea for the ballet and arranges the dance movements. He or she works closely with the composer, who writes the music. Then there are the set, costume and lighting designers.

△ Ballet dancers start classes when still young. They learn the basic steps and how to move to music.

◁ Some ballet steps take a lot of practice to perfect. The grand jeté is a large leap in which the dancer stretches both legs out, like doing the splits in midair.

CHANGING STYLES

When the way people live changes, the way they dance often changes too. Many new dances have emerged over the last 200 years. In the 1800s, the waltz swept across Europe and North America. It was a type of ballroom dance with swift, gliding turns. At first, the waltz caused an uproar because the man and woman held each other so closely. Tap dancing, a combination of African, Irish and English traditions, developed among black Americans. Rock'n'roll burst onto the scene in the 1940s and 1950s. It gave birth to disco, which is now danced all over the world.

CARNIVAL TIME

Dancing plays a major part in many festivals. In spring, the people of Central and South America organize a five-day-long carnival in which people flood the streets in breathtaking costumes, and dance to samba music. In China, the Chinese New Year is celebrated with giant dragons that are 'brought to life' by teams of dancers.

△ In parts of West Africa, voodoo queens stage ritual dances. They enter a trance while slowly swaying from side to side. Local people believe that the voodoo queens can perform spells.

◁ On the island of Java, people perform a traditional horse dance. The dancers imagine they are possessed by the spirits of horses.

SEE ALSO
Ballet, Exercise, Festival, Mime, Music, Opera, Pop music, Skating, Theatre

continued from page 81

A reservoir stores **water** to be sent over long distances in pipes so that people can use it for drinking, washing and cooking. Dams are also built to store water for **irrigation** (watering fields) in the dry season. In hot countries, people have been doing this for hundreds of years.

Whenever water is at a height from which it can fall, it can be made to do work. Dams are often built to harness this power. In the past, small dams were built to force streams of water into narrow channels. The rushing streams turned water wheels that drove machinery. Today, huge dams build up an enormous pressure of water, which can be released by opening gates. When the dam gates are open, water gushes down wide pipes, and hits the blades of **turbines**, making them spin and turn **generators**. The generators produce **electricity** (see **hydroelectric power**).

Danger sports

A **sport** is a game or activity involving physical skills, often in competition with other players or teams. 'Danger sports' is a term for a range of sports in which there is an added element of risk, or 'danger', to the participants. However, despite their name, danger sports are less perilous if people use the correct equipment and take the appropriate safety precautions.

Danger sports include hang **gliding**, snowboarding (see **skiing**), whitewater rafting (travelling down fast-flowing rivers in inflatable rafts) and potholing (exploring underground **caves**). Rock climbing involves scaling cliffs using ropes and harnesses. Rock climbers often descend by abseiling – attached to a rope, they gradually 'walk' down the rock face. Skydiving is a danger sport that began in the 1940s. Skydivers jump from a high-flying **aircraft**, and fall through the air for several minutes before opening their parachute.

Dark Ages

Early scholars gave the name Dark Ages to the period in **Europe** after the fall of the **Roman Empire** in the 400s. During the Dark Ages, which lasted for about 500 years, the Goths, Vandals and **Huns** swept down into Europe from the north and east. The invaders destroyed many of the fine buildings and works of **art** that had existed in Roman times. This is why the period was called the Dark Ages.

Towards the end of the Dark Ages, the **Vikings** began to venture out of their homelands in **Norway**, **Denmark** and **Sweden** in search of treasure and better farmland. They were settlers and traders as well as fierce warriors.

Despite the destruction and warfare that took place during the Dark Ages, civilization did not come to an end as historians once thought. Learning, art, crafts and **trade** continued to flourish throughout Europe. For **Ireland**, the period was a golden age. Some of Europe's first Christian churches were built there, and beautifully illustrated **Bibles** such as the *Book of Kells* were produced.

△ Rock climbing is a very popular **danger sport**. It requires a combination of strength, agility, fitness and good concentration.

▽ During the **Dark Ages**, raiders from Scandinavia threatened large parts of Europe. They attacked many towns, villages and churches, forcing people to flee for their lives.

Darwin, Charles

Charles Darwin (1809–1882) was an English biologist and thinker. In 1859, he published his greatest book, *On the Origin of Species*. Darwin put forward the theory that all living things have evolved, or are descended, from earlier living things. They are alive because they have won the struggle to survive.

Darwin noticed that within every species of **animal**, **plant** or **bacteria**, there are variations between different individuals. For example, they may be a different size, shape or colour, or they might behave in a different way. Darwin realized that some of these variations can increase the living thing's chance of survival. His ideas have become known as the theory of **evolution**.

When Darwin's book was published, it outraged many people. Christians objected because they thought it was against the teachings of the **Bible**. Today, most people accept Darwin's theory, although some think that it conflicts with their religious beliefs.

Da Vinci, Leonardo

Leonardo da Vinci (1452–1519) was an Italian artist and inventor. He lived during the **Renaissance**. One of his most famous **paintings** is the *Mona Lisa* (painted about 1503), which hangs in the Louvre Museum, **Paris**. It is a portrait of a woman who is smiling mysteriously. Many people have wondered at what she was smiling.

As well as paintings, da Vinci made thousands of detailed **drawings** of human bodies, plants, animals, rocks and water. He was also interested in **architecture**, **music** and **engineering**,

△ Leonardo **da Vinci** was a creative genius. This is an illustration of what his planned flying machine might have looked like.

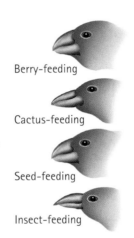

Berry-feeding

Cactus-feeding

Seed-feeding

Insect-feeding

△ When **Darwin** visited the Galapagos Islands, in the Pacific, he noticed that the finches there had differently shaped beaks. He also noticed that each finch ate a different sort of food. This gave him the idea that livings things can change, or evolve, to suit their surroundings.

▷ **Day and night** happen because the earth spins on its axis as it circles the sun. Only part of the globe faces the sun at any one time. We say that this region is in daylight. The other side of the world is in darkness, or 'night'. As the earth spins, different parts of the earth fall into the zone of darkness.

and worked as an engineer for members of the Italian nobility and for the French king. Among the many things da Vinci designed are cranes, forts, **bridges** and **canals**. The canals had locks so that boats could travel up and down sloping ground.

Da Vinci also drew ideas for things long before they had been invented and actually built. His drawings include a **helicopter** and a machine-gun.

Day and night

The **earth** spins as it moves around the **sun**. The part facing the sun is light, while the part facing away from the sun is dark. The light part is 'day' and the dark part is 'night'. Because the earth is spinning, day and night follow each other continuously.

Scientists describe a 'day' as the time the earth takes to spin around once, or complete one turn. If you measure how long it takes between one sunrise or sunset and the next, you will find that it is almost exactly 24 hours.

Days vary in length between different points on the earth. This is because the earth's axis is tilted at an angle to its path around the sun. As a result, some parts of the **planet** receive longer periods of daylight than others. In addition,

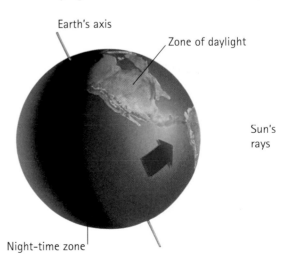

Earth's axis

Zone of daylight

Sun's rays

Night-time zone

most parts of the earth receive different amounts of daylight at different times of year. These differences are a major feature of the **seasons**.

D-Day

D-Day – 6 June 1944 – was one of the turning-points of **World War II**. On this day, a huge force of soldiers from the Allied countries landed on the coast of Normandy in northern **France**. At that time, France was occupied by the armies of Hitler's **Germany**.

The D-Day invasion force was the largest the world had ever seen. It involved 132,500 troops – British, Americans, Canadians and their allies – as well as 1,200 **ships**, 4,100 landing-craft and 10,000 **aircraft**. The supreme commander of the force was the US general, Dwight Eisenhower (1890–1969). The force set off before dawn from England's south coast. On the same day, a Russian **army** attacked Germany from the east. After heavy fighting, in which many thousands of troops died, the Germans were forced to retreat. They finally surrendered to the Allies on 7 May 1945.

△ The **D-Day** landings in France were the result of months of planning. All the preparations took place in secret, so that the German forces occupying France were taken by surprise.

Deep-sea fish

Most of the **animals** and **plants** that live in the world's seas and **oceans** stay in the top 200 m. Below this, conditions become less and less suitable for living things. At a depth of 1,000 m, it is very cold and very dark. No sunlight penetrates that far. Plants cannot live at such depths because they need **light** to make their food through photosynthesis. But some animals can live at great depths. Their bodies are designed to withstand the enormous pressure deep down.

Anglerfish   Hatchet fish

Lantern fish

Viper fish

△ **Deep-sea fish** look very different from fish that live in higher levels of the ocean. Many of them have huge eyes, jaws and teeth.

Most deep-sea animals are quite small, and they often have enormous jaws, **teeth** and **eyes**. Many of the **fish** also possess light-producing organs. These 'lights' help the fish communicate with other members of their species in the darkness. Some deep-sea fish use their lights as lures, to attract prey within range of their jaws. Other animals found at great depths include **jellyfish**, **crustaceans** and **corals**.

Deer

Deer are **mammals** related to **cattle** and **antelopes**. They are different from their relatives because they have antlers rather than permanent **horns**. Male deer, or stags, shed their antlers and grow a new set every year. Female deer, or does, lack antlers. The exception is the reindeer, known as the caribou in **North America**, in which both sexes have antlers and keep them all year.

In early spring, **blood** starts to flow into two hard lumps on the male deer's forehead. The blood carries a bony substance that makes the antlers grow rapidly. At first, they are covered with a soft, hairy **skin** called velvet. In early summer, the antlers are fully grown. The blood supply is then cut off and the velvet dies. The male deer rubs off the velvet until his antlers are hard and shiny. Some antlers can be very large. Those of moose measure up to 2 m across.

Most species of deer live in the woods and **forests** of the Northern Hemisphere. But there are also species in **South America** and southern **Asia**. Although deer are wild animals, some of them can be tamed successfully. Reindeer can be trained to pull sledges, and their meat and hides are used by the Lapp people of Scandinavia. Deer are also farmed for their meat, which is called venison.

De Gaulle, Charles

Charles de Gaulle (1890–1970) was a French general and statesman. He fought in **World War I**, and in 1916 was badly wounded. After the war, he continued his **army** career. When **World War II** broke out in 1939, he was put in command of a tank division. After the Germans occupied **France** in 1940, de Gaulle escaped to **London** and formed the Free French Movement, which organized the resistance struggle against the German forces.

In 1944, de Gaulle returned from exile and became head of the French **government**. But two years later, he resigned when the political parties could not agree. By 1958, France was in serious political trouble. The French settlers in **Algeria** and the French army were rebelling. De Gaulle was elected president of France in 1959, and finally resolved the Algerian problem. He was one of the most powerful European leaders, and stayed in office until 1969.

△ In 508 BCE, **democracy** came to Athens. The people of the city met on Pnyx Hill to debate important issues.

Delta

When a **river** flows across a flat plain into the sea, it flows very slowly. On its way, it deposits **soil** and **sand** on the plain. In time, this sediment begins to build up into mudbanks. The river creates many small channels through the mud, which often change direction. This maze of mudbanks and channels is called a delta. This is because its shape often resembles the Greek letter delta (△).

The **Mississippi** delta stretches 320 km into the Gulf of **Mexico**. Another large delta is formed by the **Nile River** in **Egypt**.

△ **De Gaulle** led the 'Free French' fighters who were struggling against the German forces during World War II. He was French president in 1945 and 1959–1969.

Male red deer

▷ In summer, male **deer** rub their antlers against branches to remove the outer layer of dead skin.

Democracy

Democracy is a type of **government** in which the people take part in ruling the state. In most democracies, people can elect their own government. The representatives of different political parties stand for **election**, and people vote for the candidate they prefer. Usually, the candidates and parties with the most votes then form a government.

Elections are held regularly, which gives the people the chance to elect a new government. In a true democracy, people can say, read and believe what they like. They cannot be imprisoned without a proper trial.

There are many kinds of democracy. The most common form has an elected **parliament** made up of officials from the various political parties. Its leader is often known as the prime minister. In some countries, such as the **United Kingdom**, **Spain** and the **Netherlands**, there is a hereditary monarchy as well as a parliament. But usually the **monarch** plays little or no part in politics. In many countries, called **republics**, the head of state is an elected **president**. An example of this kind of democracy is the **United States of America**. Its parliament is called Congress, and it is made up of two separate chambers – the Senate and the House of Representatives.

Denmark

DENMARK
Government:
Constitutional monarchy
Capital: Copenhagen
Area: 45,069 sq km
Population: 5.3 million
Language: Danish
Currency: Danish krone

Denmark is a small country in northern **Europe**. It forms part of Scandinavia, which also includes **Norway, Sweden, Finland** and **Iceland**. Denmark consists of a peninsula called Jutland, which is surrounded by about 600 islands. To the west is the North Sea, to the east is the Baltic Sea, and to the south is **Germany**. Denmark is a flat country whose soil and **climate** are ideal for agriculture. Dairy and pig **farming** are especially important.

Descartes, René

René Descartes (1596–1650) was a French thinker who was interested in many different subjects, including **mathematics**, **physics**, **astronomy** and **law**. He thought that all the **sciences** were connected, rather like the links in a chain. Descartes devoted a lot of time to searching for a system that would link together all knowledge.

Descartes' revolutionary ideas influenced many other thinkers. He has often been called the 'father of modern **philosophy**'.

Desert

Not all deserts are hot and sandy. Some are cold, and others are rocky. But all deserts are extremely dry. Any area in which less than 25 cm of rain falls in a year is classified as a desert. Most of the world's large deserts are in the tropics.

◁ **Deserts** are tough places for people as well as animals. Most people live in oases – pockets of fertile land where an underground spring rises to the surface.

This is a scene from *David Copperfield* by Charles **Dickens**. Dickens' writing both entertained and informed his readers about social problems.

This is because the air is too hot and dry for rainbearing clouds to form. Other deserts exist because they are located far from the sea's moist **winds**, or because they lie behind high **mountains** that block rain-bearing winds (see also **weather**).

There are three main types of desert. The first is rocky, where any soil is blown away by the wind. The second has large areas of gravel. The third is made up of **sand** dunes, and is burning hot by day and bitterly cold at night.

It is difficult for **plants** and **animals** to live in such conditions. Some plants, like the **cactus**, store moisture in their fleshy stems. Others have **seeds** that lie apparently lifeless in the ground for long periods. When a shower of rain falls they burst into life and can **flower** and produce new seeds within weeks. Many desert animals shelter from the sun by day and come out only at night. Some never drink, but get all the moisture they need from their food.

The world's largest desert is the **Sahara** in **Africa**. The driest desert is the Atacama in **South America**, which lies to the west of the **Andes** mountains. Cold deserts include the icy continent Antarctica, a large part of the Arctic (see **Antarctic** and **Arctic**), and the Gobi Desert of central **Mongolia**. In total, deserts cover about one-seventh of the land on **earth**.

Detergent

Strictly speaking, the word 'detergent' means any substance that will clean things. **Soap** is a detergent. But today, the word detergent usually means synthetic, or artificial, detergents such as most washing powders. Detergents are similar to soaps, but they can reach dirty areas better than soaps and they do not leave a deposit, or scum, behind.

Developing world

The 'developing world' is a term that describes the world's poorer countries, many of which are in **Asia**, **Africa** and **South America**. These nations are still in the process of developing some of the features typical of wealthier states, such as modern industries, **hospitals**, **schools**, **roads**, **railways** and other important public services.

Life is usually hard for the majority of people in developing countries. They often suffer from bad living conditions, especially in the towns and cities. Parts of the **population** do not have easy access to clean drinking **water**, doctors and medicines, which leads to more frequent outbreaks of **disease**.

Many countries in the developing world supply the rest of the world with **food**, **minerals**, **timber** and **textiles**, as well as providing cheap labour. This pattern of wealth in one part of the world and poverty in another is very difficult to change. The wealthy countries do not want to give up the wealth and power they have been used to for so long. This means that many developing countries continue to get poorer, while the rich countries continue to get richer.

Diamond

Diamonds are made of pure **carbon**, the same **mineral** that is found in **coal**. They are usually colourless, although a few are blue, pink or yellow.

Diamonds have many smooth, flat sides that meet in sharp edges. This type of substance is known as a crystal. Other crystals include snowflakes, **salt** crystals and **sugar** crystals.

Diamonds are harder than anything else in the world. They are formed by great **heat** and pressure deep beneath the surface of the **earth**. They have to be cut in a special way to catch the **light** and 'sparkle'. After cutting, they are polished. Diamonds are not only worn as **jewellery** – they are used in industry for drilling and cutting materials such as **glass** and **metal**.

Dickens, Charles

Charles Dickens (1812–1870) was a famous English writer. His books give us a vivid picture of life in Victorian England in the mid-1800s (see also **Victoria, Queen**). Several of Dickens' novels are about children, especially poor children and orphans. He tried to improve the lives of the poor by making their suffering more widely known through his books. He also created some of the best-known characters in English literature. Some of his most important books are *Oliver Twist*, *David Copperfield*, *Great Expectations* and *A Christmas Carol*.

△ **Diamonds** occur naturally in rock. By the time a diamond has been removed from its lump of rock, cut into shape and polished, it has lost about 50 percent of its weight.

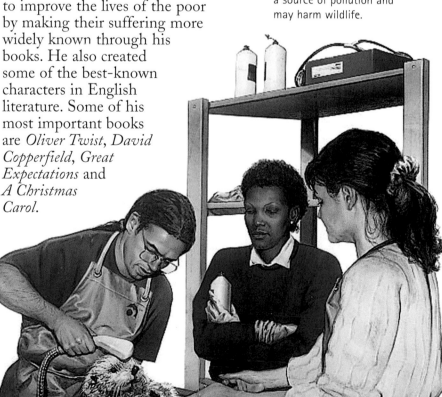

▽ **Detergents** can be used to clean the fur of animals that have been affected by oil spills. But if they are washed into rivers and seas, detergents become a source of pollution and may harm wildlife.

Dickinson, Emily

Emily Dickinson (1830–1886) was one of America's greatest poets, and is considered to be among the most important poets of the 1800s. Her **poetry** is recognized for its originality, variety and beauty. She wrote about the difficulty in making sense of the world, and of how quickly and strangely life passes. Dickinson was a very private person, who refused to publish any of her poems during her lifetime. She lived all her life at her parents' home in Massachusetts, **USA**.

Dictator

A dictator is the leader of a country who rules with absolute power and authority. In the **Roman Empire**, a dictator was a magistrate who was given absolute power to deal with emergencies when decisions had to be made quickly. Today, the term is used to describe a tyrant who uses force to take away people's rights and freedoms. Often, those who try to oppose a dictator are imprisoned, killed or forced to leave the country until the dictator is finally overthrown. A dictatorship is the opposite of a **democracy**,

△ General Franco became a **dictator** in 1939, when he took control of Spain. During the Spanish Civil War (1936–1939), his rebel forces had defeated Spanish government troops.

▽ **Diesel engines** are used on railways throughout the world, such as on this mountain railway in the south of Mexico. In diesel trains, a diesel motor produces the electricity that drives the train.

in which the people choose their own government in elections. Some dictators of the 1900s include Adolf **Hitler** of **Germany**, Benito **Mussolini** of **Italy**, Francisco Franco of **Spain** (1892–1975), and Antonio Salazar of **Portugal** (1889–1970), all of whom believed in a political theory known as **fascism**. Many people now think that Josef **Stalin**, who led a cruel regime in the former **Soviet Union**, should also be called a dictator.

Dictionary

A dictionary is a **book** that tells us what words mean. The words are arranged in alphabetical order from A to Z. Often the meanings, or definitions, include a brief history of the words and an explanation of how they are used and pronounced. One of the first large dictionaries of the English language was produced by Dr Samuel Johnson (1709–1784).

Diesel engine

Diesel engines are a type of **engine** in which **fuel** is burned inside the engine. They are named after the German inventor, Rudolf Diesel (1858–1913), who built his first successful engine in 1897 to replace the **steam engine**. The fuel used in diesel engines is known as diesel. It is produced from **oil**, as is petrol. Diesel engines are cheaper to run than petrol engines, but they are also heavier and more difficult to start. As a result, they were not widely used in **cars** until the 1970s. But their main use is still to drive large machines such as trains (see **railway**), tractors, **ships**, buses and trucks. A properly working diesel engine causes less **pollution** than a petrol engine.

A diesel engine is similar to a petrol engine, but instead of using a spark from a spark plug to ignite the fuel, the diesel engine uses **heat** that is made by a piston squeezing **air** inside a cylinder. If air is tightly compressed – pushed into a much smaller space than it filled before – it becomes very hot. This heat sets fire to the diesel fuel, which burns instantly, like a small explosion. The burning fuel produces hot gases, which push the piston down and thus drive the engine.

Digestion

Digestion is the way in which the **food** that **animals** eat is broken down into substances that can be used by the body. In humans, this takes place in the digestive tract, or alimentary canal, a long tube that runs from the mouth to the anus. Digestion starts in the mouth, where the **teeth** and special chemicals in the saliva help to break the food down. The food then passes down a tube called the oesophagus. **Muscles** in the oesophagus push and squeeze the food through to the **stomach**. There, **acids** and more chemicals help to turn the food into a creamy **liquid**. A muscle at the lower end of the stomach opens from time to time to release food into the small intestine.

Inside the small intestine, bile from the **liver** and juice from the pancreas help to break down the food still further.

Oesophagus

Swallowed food

Liver

Small intestine

Large intestine

Stomach

Pancreas

Rectum

Anus

△ In humans, **digestion** involves many different organs. Food passes from the mouth to the stomach and intestines. After all the useful substances have been removed, faeces are excreted from the anus.

▽ Sleeping sickness is a common **disease** in parts of Africa. It is caused by a tiny parasite which is carried by the tsetse fly. When an infected fly bites someone, the parasites enter their bloodstream. There, the parasites breed rapidly, causing fever, headaches and sleepiness.

Parasite

Human red blood cell

Tsetse fly

Much of it passes through the thin walls of the intestine into the bloodstream. The remainder enters the large intestine, where liquids and salts are absorbed until only solid waste material is left. **Bacteria** living inside the large intestine digest any remaining food products. The final waste product is passed out of the body as faeces.

Dinosaurs
see **pages 92–93**

Disease

Diseases make us ill. Some are caused by **bacteria**, or germs, that invade our bodies. Others are caused by **viruses** or **parasites**. Some diseases are passed down from parents to children in the genes with which they are born (see **genetics**).

The body resists diseases through its immune system. Special **cells**, such as white **blood** cells, fight the invading organisms. The body also produces antibodies to fight disease. Antibodies produced to 'defeat' diseases such as measles or chickenpox stay in our systems and usually prevent us from having the same disease again – we become immune. Many **drugs** and **inoculations** have been developed to help us fight diseases, although some diseases have no known cure.

△ Apatosaurus, *also known as* Brontosaurus, *was a huge plant-eater that could reach leaves growing in the treetops. It weighed up to 30 tonnes.*

DINOSAURS

Dinosaurs were a type of reptile that first appeared on earth about 230 million years ago. Some dinosaurs were only the size of a chicken, but others were the largest land animals that ever existed. The dinosaurs became extinct about 65 million years ago.

▽ *In the late Triassic period, about 220 million years ago, a herd of* Coelophysis *is washed away in a flash flood. In 1947, scientists discovered their fossilized remains at Ghost Ranch, New Mexico, USA.*

WORLD OF DINOSAURS

The word dinosaur means 'terrible lizard', but this is misleading because the dinosaurs were not actually lizards. They belonged to a group of reptiles called the archosaurs, which also included primitive crocodiles and giant flying creatures called pterosaurs. The dinosaurs roamed the planet for over 160 million years. They lived during three different geological periods – the Triassic, Jurassic and Cretaceous – which are often known collectively as the 'age of reptiles'.

MANY DIFFEFRENT KINDS

Scientists have so far identified more than 500 types of dinosaur, but there are probably many more that remain undiscovered. The dinosaurs ranged in size from chicken-sized species such as *Compsognathus* to giants such as *Argentinosaurus*, which weighed up to 100 tonnes and was largest land animal ever to walk the earth. There were two main groups of dinosaur – the Saurischia, which had hipbones arranged like a lizard's, and the Ornithischia, which had hipbones arranged like a bird's. Each species of dinosaur had a different diet and lifestyle. Some were vegetarian, while others were hunters or scavengers.

THE PLANT-EATERS

Most dinosaurs were herbivores (plant-eaters). The world's climate was much warmer during the Triassic, Jurassic and Cretaceous periods than it is today, and the tropical conditions provided an abundant supply of vegetation to eat. The largest plant-eaters, such as *Brachiosaurus* and *Diplodocus*, walked on all fours. Their long necks allowed them to reach the leaves and cones of tall trees. Smaller species walked on their back legs and grazed lower down.

THE MEAT-EATERS

The meat-eating dinosaurs, or theropods, had razor-sharp claws on their feet for bringing down prey, and strong jaws full of teeth for tearing flesh. They walked upright, using their long, heavy tails for balance. The theropods hunted a wide range of dinosaurs and other animals, and fed on carrion (dead remains) as well as fresh meat.

Elasmosaurus

Ichthyosaurus

Kronosaurus

Teleosaurus

◁ *The swimming reptiles that lived in the sea, and the flying reptiles, such as pterosaurs, were not dinosaurs. The dinosaurs lived only on land.*

◁ Deinonychus, *whose name means 'terrible claw', was a fast-moving hunter with a 12cm-long retractable claw on the inside of each back foot.*

WAY OF LIFE

Like all reptiles, dinosaurs laid eggs. Fossilized nests suggest that a female dinosaur would lay 10–40 eggs in a shallow hole on the ground. The baby dinosaurs hatched 3–4 weeks later, and probably left the nest quickly to fend for themselves. It is likely that many plant-eating dinosaurs lived in herds to make it harder for the meat-eaters to attack them. Some of the predators hunted in packs, like wolves, while others waited in ambush.

▷ *Plant-eating dinosaurs had several methods of defence, including swinging their tails at their attackers.*

Brachiosaurus
(plant-eater)

Ankylosaurus *had a bony, clublike tail*

Stegosaurus' *tail was armed with spikes*

Diplodocus' *tail was long and whiplike*

▽ *The dinosaurs evolved into many different species. Most of the largest dinosaurs were plant-eaters.*

Compsognathus
(meat-eater)

Diplodocus
(plant-eater)

Velociraptor
(meat-eater)

Allosaurus
(meat-eater)

Stegosaurus
(plant-eater)

OTHER REPTILES

Dinosaurs could neither swim nor fly, but many of the other reptiles alive at the same time could. Pterosaurs used their leathery wings to glide on rising air currents. The largest pterosaurs had a wingspan of up to 12–15 m – wider than a hang glider. Many reptiles lived in the sea, including the long-necked elasmosaurs. Almost all of these reptiles died out at the same time as the dinosaurs.

END OF THE DINOSAURS

No one knows for certain why the dinosaurs died out. The most popular theory suggests that the earth was hit by a huge meteorite. This would have thrown up a cloud of dust that blotted out the sun for months or even years, killing many plants and animals. Some scientists believe that gradual climate change was to blame, perhaps caused by frequent volcanic eruptions over a period of 500,000 years. But although the dinosaurs became extinct, many other types of animal survived.

▽ Tyrannosaurus rex *lived in North America 95–65 million years ago. It had a massive head packed with 15cm-long teeth. Instead of chasing its prey, it may have launched surprise attacks.*

DINOSAURS FACT FILE
Earliest: *Eoraptor*, which first appeared about 230 million years ago
Heaviest: *Argentinosaurus*, up to 80–100 tonnes
Tallest: *Sauroposeidon*, up to 18 m
Smallest: *Microraptor*, 40 cm long
Largest meat-eater: *Gigantosaurus*, up to 13 m long and 8 tonnes in weight
Largest skull: *Triceratops*, up to 3 m long
Longest tail: *Diplodocus*, up to 13 m
Most teeth: *Edmontosaurus*, up to 1,200
Largest egg: *Hypselosaurus*, 30 cm long and 25 cm wide

SEE ALSO
Amphibians and Reptiles, Fossil, Meteorite, Prehistoric animals

Disney, Walt

Walt Disney (1901–1967) was an American film-maker best known for his **cartoons** and **films** for children. Disney characters, especially Mickey Mouse and Donald Duck, are famous all over the world. Walt Disney began his work in the 1920s. His cartoon artists, or animators, produced characters and settings that moved realistically. Full-length Disney cartoon features include *Snow White and the Seven Dwarfs*, *Pinocchio* and *Bambi*.

Distillation

When saltwater from the sea is boiled in a saucepan, it turns into steam. If the steam then hits a surface such as a window, it cools and becomes a **liquid** again. But the boiled **water** has changed – it is now pure fresh water. The **salt** is left behind in the pan. This boiling and cooling of liquids to make them pure is called distillation.

△ During the festival of **Diwali**, Hindus decorate their homes and streets with lights. They also hold feasts, and stage parades and firework displays.

△ The **dodo** died out because introduced rats and pigs plundered all of its eggs and chicks.

▽ **Dolphins**, such as these spotted dolphins, live in groups, or schools. They hunt as a team, working together to track down their main prey – fish.

Distillation is often used to separate different liquids mixed together. The mixture is heated and the liquid that boils at the lowest temperature evaporates (turns to a **gas**) first and is separated from the other liquids. Then the liquid with the next lowest boiling point evaporates, and so on. This process is called fractional distillation. It is used to separate the materials in the crude **oil** from oil wells. Distillation is also used to make spirits such as whisky and gin (see **alcohol**).

Diwali

Diwali (also written Divali) is one of the most important **festivals** in **Hinduism**. It is held in October each year, and celebrates Rama, the Hindu **goddess** of wealth and beauty.

Dodo

About 400 years ago, a Dutch ship landed on Mauritius, a remote island in the **Indian Ocean**. The crew found flocks of turkey-sized **birds** that had no proper wings and could not fly. In time, people called the birds dodos, from the Portuguese word *doudo*, meaning 'stupid person'. But people introduced **rats** and **pigs** to the island, which began eating dodo eggs and chicks. By the 1690s, the dodo had become extinct.

Dog

Humans have been keeping dogs for as long as 10,000 years. Dogs are often pets, but many do useful work such as herding sheep or guarding buildings. They can be trained to serve as guide dogs for blind people and to sniff out illegal **drugs** hidden inside bags or vehicles.

The first domesticated dog probably descended from a **wolf**. There are now more than 100 breeds of domestic dog, and many different colours, shapes and sizes. Other kinds of wild dog include **foxes**, North America's coyotes, the **jackals** of Asia and Africa, and the Australian dingo.

Dogs are **carnivores** and all belong to the same family. They have superb senses of **smell**, **hearing** and **sight**.

△ Domestic **dogs** are bred for specific purposes. For example, this greyhound has been bred for speed. It can reach 57 km/h.

Doll

Children all over the world play with dolls. Dolls may be made of **wood**, china, **plastic** or many other substances. The very first doll may have been just a forked twig that resembled a human. Homemade dolls can cost nothing. Some old dolls may be very valuable.

Dolphin and Porpoise

Dolphins and porpoises belong to the same group of **mammals** as **whales**. Like all mammals, they breathe air, suckle their young on milk and are warm-blooded. They have sharp **teeth** and their heads end in beaklike snouts. Dolphins and porpoises are highly

△ The **Dome** of the Rock, Jerusalem, was completed in 691 CE. It is a Muslim shrine known as al Aqsa.

DOMINICAN REPUBLIC
Government: Republic
Capital: Santo Domingo
Area: 48,734 sq km
Population: 8.4 million
Language: Spanish
Currency: Peso

intelligent and communicate with each other using a sophisticated 'language' of whistles and clicks. They use **sonar** – an underwater **radar** system – to navigate and to locate **fish** to eat. There are about 45 species of dolphin and porpoise in the world, of which the largest is the orca, or killer whale.

Dome

Domes are roofs shaped like upturned pudding bowls. Some domes are made from bricks or stones. Other domes are made of **concrete**, steel or **plastic**. Domed roofs cover many **mosques** and **churches**. Famous examples include the Dome of the Rock, **Jerusalem**; St Sophia, Istanbul; St Peter's, **Rome**; and St Paul's Cathedral, **London**. The world's largest dome – the Louisiana Superdome in the American city of New Orleans – has a span of 223 m.

Domesday Book

Twenty years after the Norman invasion of 1066, **William the Conqueror** ordered that a great survey of property owners in England should be made. It became known as the Domesday Book. William wanted to find out how much land people owned so that he could be sure that he was getting all the **taxes** that were due to him. This survey, or **census**, was completed in 1086.

Dominican Republic

The Dominican Republic occupies the larger part of the island of Hispaniola in the **Caribbean** Sea. The rest of the island is occupied by **Haiti**. It has large **forests**, and its main crop is **sugar**.

Donkeys can carry heavy loads for their size. They have large heads, long ears and a short mane.

Many **drugs** are made from plants, animals or minerals. For example, an extract from this foxglove flower is used to produce a drug that fights heart disease.

Eider **ducks** live at sea. We use their soft feathers, or eiderdown, to fill duvets, pillows and cushions.

Donkey

Donkeys are small, sturdy relatives of **horses**, and are descended from the wild asses of **Africa**. They are sure-footed and can carry large loads over rough ground. Donkeys are still used for work in southern **Europe**, **Asia**, North Africa and **South America**.

Dragon *see* Myth and Legend

Drawing

Drawings are pictures or designs that are usually made with pencil, pen, **chalk** or some similar material other than **paint**. Drawings are produced for all kinds of reasons, and play an important role in **architecture**, **art**, **engineering** and **fashion**. Some drawings are precise. In others, a powerful effect is produced by using few lines and little detail.

Dream

Dreams occur when our **brains** are active during **sleep**. Some dreams are of everyday occurrences. Others may be just a series of jumbled images. People often dream of falling, being chased or of water. Frightening dreams are called nightmares. On waking, we may not remember what we have dreamed.

We do not know exactly why people dream. Dreams may be sparked off by indigestion or a similar physical cause, such as a cramped sleeping position. External noises may also cause dreams.

Drug

Drugs are chemicals that affect the way the body works. Doctors give drugs to patients to help them fight **disease**. **Antibiotics** are a common type of drug, which attack certain kinds of germs. These drugs help cure people suffering from pneumonia and other illnesses. Drugs such as aspirin and paracetamol help to relieve **pain**. The strongest painkillers are anaesthetics. General anaesthetics are used to send patients to sleep during operations (see **surgery**).

Some people need to take drugs containing **vitamins** or other essential substances. But people sometimes take drugs simply because they can give a pleasant feeling. These drugs include cocaine, cannabis, **alcohol** and nicotine, which is found in **tobacco**. However, many of these drugs are addictive (habit-forming), and some can cause illness or even death.

Drum

Drums are important percussion instruments (**musical instruments** that are played by being struck). The **sound** is made by hitting a tightly stretched sheet of skin or plastic called a drumhead. A kettledrum has one drumhead stretched over the top of a metal basin. A bass drum or a side drum has two drumheads, one across each end of a large open 'can'.

Duck

Ducks are web-footed water **birds** related to **swans** and **geese**. The two main groups of ducks are dabbling ducks, which feed at the surface of the water, and diving ducks, which dive underwater in their hunt for food. The mallard, one of the best-known dabbling ducks, lives on ponds, **lakes** and **rivers** across the northern half of the world.

DVD *see* Recording

Dye

Dyes are substances used to colour **textiles** and other materials. Some dyes are extracted from **plants**, but most modern dyes are made from chemicals. To dye an object, you dip it in water containing dissolved dye.

Eagle

Eagles are large **birds** of prey. They spend hours soaring high in the sky or perched on a rock or in a tree, and use their sharp **sight** to scan their surroundings. When an eagle spots its prey it swoops down from the air and pounces. It seizes its victim with sharp talons and tears off pieces of flesh with a strong, hooked beak.

There are more than 50 species of eagle in the world. They feed on a variety of prey, from small mammals to birds, fish, snakes and lizards. Eagles are related to **hawks** and **falcons**.

Ear

Our ears equip us with the sense of **hearing**, and allow us to keep our balance. Each ear has three

△ The golden **eagle** preys on medium-sized animals such as rabbits.

main parts – the outer ear, middle ear and inner ear. The outer ear is the part we can see, and the tube that leads from it into the head. **Sounds** reach the outer ear as vibrations, or sound waves, in the air. The cuplike shape of the ear collects these sound waves and sends them into the tube, known as the ear canal.

Next, the sound waves reach the middle ear. Here, the waves make the eardrum move to and fro. This is a thin 'skin' across the entrance of the middle ear. The moving eardrum makes tiny **bones** vibrate inside the middle ear. These are called the hammer, anvil and stirrup.

The vibrations travel on into the inner ear, where they make liquid move in the cochlea. This structure looks like a snail's shell. **Nerves** inside the cochlea turn vibrations into electrical messages that travel to the brain. The inner ear also has three hollow loops containing liquid. These loops send signals to the brain to help us keep our balance.

Eardrum · Hammer · Anvil · Stirrup · Hollow loops · Nerve to brain · Inner ear · Middle ear · Outer ear · Ear canal · Cochlea

△ **Ears** are complicated, delicate organs. Sound waves travel from the outer ear to the cochlea, where they become electrical messages.

EARTH

△ *The upper layer of land on earth is made up of topsoil (1), subsoil (2), fragmented rock (3), and hard bedrock (4).*

Our planet, earth, is one of the nine planets that move around the sun. It is a giant ball of rock with a central core of intensely hot, dense metal. Unlike the other planets in the solar system, the earth is surrounded by a blanket of gases called the atmosphere, and much of its surface is covered in water. These are the conditions that allow the earth to support life.

▷ *The earth formed from a vast cloud of dust that surrounded the sun. The dust clumped together and over millions of years became a rocky planet.*

TURNING EARTH

The earth is constantly moving around the sun along an elliptical (oval-shaped) path called its orbit. It travels at an average speed of 30 km per second, and takes 365.25 days – one year – to make a complete orbit. During this time, the earth covers a total distance of 958 million km. As well as orbiting the sun, the earth rotates in a circle on its axis – an imaginary line joining the North and South poles. It does this once every 24 hours. As the earth spins, one side faces the sun and is in daylight, or day, while the other side faces away and is in darkness, or night.

△ *This diagram uses different colours to represent the tectonic plates of the earth's crust. The arrows show the direction in which each plate is moving.*

CHANGING SEASONS

The earth is tilted towards the sun at an angle of 23.5°. As the earth moves along its orbit, the parts that are tilted towards the sun receive more light and warmth – they experience summer. As the earth travels further along its orbit, these places tilt away from the sun – they experience winter.

INSIDE THE EARTH

The earth's solid inner core is almost pure iron, while its outer core consists mainly of semi-liquid iron and nickel. The outer core is slowly circulating all the time, and powerful electrical currents within it generate the earth's magnetic field. Surrounding the core is the mantle – a mixture of minerals and metals, such as quartz, silicon and aluminium. It is topped with a rocky crust.

VIOLENT EARTH

The surface of the earth is made up of about 20 tectonic plates, like jigsaw pieces. On top of them lie the continents. The plates are not fixed but move slowly, causing the continents to collide and tear apart. This movement is known as continental drift. When two plates collide, the land crumples and mountains are formed. When two plates move apart, molten magma rises up from beneath the surface to create new land or ocean floor. At certain points on the earth, neighbouring plates rub together. This creates a massive build-up of pressure, which eventually escapes in the form of volcanic eruptions and earthquakes.

Magma

◁ *The earth's rocks, sand and soil are made up of minerals. Many minerals are formed deep underground from 'lakes' of hot magma.*

Lighter minerals form at top

Denser minerals form at bottom

EARTH FACT FILE

Age: about 4,550 million years

Diameter: 12,714 km (from North Pole to South Pole through the earth's centre)

Circumference: 40,076 km (around the middle of the earth at the equator)

Area of water: about 362 million sq km – 71 percent of the earth's surface

Area of land: about 148 million sq km – 29 percent of the earth's surface

Highest mountain: Mount Everest, Asia, 8,848 m above sea level

Greatest ocean depth: Marianas Trench, Pacific Ocean, 11,034 m

Hottest place: Al'Aziziyah, Libya, where 57.7°C was recorded in 1922

Coldest place: Vostok, Antarctica, where -89.2°C was recorded in 1983

Crust

Mantle

Outer core

Inner core

FROM CRUST TO CORE
The earth has four main layers. The crust is the planet's solid outer layer. Its thickness varies from 6 to 30 km. The crust floats on the mantle, a 2,900 km-thick layer of semi-molten (partly melted) rock. Beneath the mantle is the outer core, which extends for 2,240 km. It is made mainly of metals, which are molten and under huge pressure. The earth's centre is the inner core – a solid ball about 2,240 km across where the temperature is over 6,000°C.

WATERY WORLD
Over 70 percent of the earth's surface is covered with water. About 97 percent of this water is the salt water in seas and oceans. The rest is the freshwater in lakes, rivers, glaciers, ice sheets and snow. Although we usually see only their surface, the oceans are vast and deep – the average depth of the oceans is 5,000 m and the deepest ocean trenches reach down 11,000 m. The immense volume of water on the earth helps to regulate the planet's climate. It is continually recycled – it evaporates from the rivers, lakes, seas and oceans to form water vapour, which in turn forms clouds and falls as rain. Every living thing needs water to survive.

LIFE ON EARTH
The earth's distance from the sun is ideal – not too hot like Venus, nor too cold like Mars. This allows it to support a tremendous variety of plant and animal life, from tiny bacteria to human beings. Life on earth began millions of years ago. Simple plants evolved, which began to release oxygen. Gradually, enough oxygen built up to create the atmosphere. Animals rely on the atmosphere for the oxygen they breathe.

CLIMATE ZONES
The earth has a range of different climates. Polar regions are snowy and icy. Tropical areas, near the equator, are hot and wet. In between are the temperate regions, which have warm summers, cool winters and moderate rainfall.

SEE ALSO
Atmosphere, Climate, Continent, Desert, Earthquake, Gravity, Mountain, Ocean, Orbit, Planet, Seasons, Solar system, Weather

An **earthquake**'s shock waves begin underground in a region called the hypocentre. They reach the earth's surface directly above, at the epicentre. From here, they spread out in all directions.

Earthquake

An earthquake is when the surface of the **earth** shakes. It is caused by the sudden release of pressure through weak parts of the earth's crust called fault lines. About half a million earthquakes happen every year. Most are so weak that only special instruments called seismographs prove they have taken place. A seismograph shows earth tremors as changes in a line traced on a turning drum. Tremors vibrate the weight that holds the tracer.

Tremors can happen when **volcanoes** erupt, when the roof of an underground **cave** falls in, or when there is a landslide. But the largest earthquakes occur when one huge piece of the earth's crust slips suddenly against another piece. This may take place deep underground, but the shock waves travel up through the earth's crust and make the surface shake. A seabed earthquake may trigger a tsunami – a massive ocean **wave** that travels great distances at speed.

Only one earthquake in 500 does any damage, but some earthquakes cause terrible destruction. In 1906, a powerful earthquake and the massive **fires** it caused destroyed most of **San Francisco**, USA. When an earthquake

shook the Kwanto Plain, Japan, in 1923, 570,000 buildings collapsed. One of the most devastating earthquakes of recent times hit the Chinese city of Tangshan in 1976. As many as 750,000 people are thought to have died.

Earthworm *see* Worm

Easter

Easter is the most important religious **festival** in **Christianity**. On Easter Day, Christians remember the resurrection of **Jesus**. Easter falls on a different date each year, but it is always a Sunday in April or late March.

At **Easter**, Christians give each other decorated eggs to symbolize the new life that returns to nature at about this time.

Echo

An echo is a **sound** bounced back from a wall or some other hard object. Sound always travels at the same speed, so we can use echoes to find how far off objects are. A ship's **sonar** uses echoes to find the depth of the sea. Echoes also help **bats** to fly in the dark. **Radar** is a device for tracking moving objects that uses the echoes from **radio** signals.

Echoes are reflected sound waves. Sometimes, if you face a cliff and shout, sound waves from your voice hit the rock and bounce back.

Eclipse

An eclipse happens when the shadow of one **planet** or **moon** falls on another. If the shadow hides all of the planet or moon there is a total eclipse. If it hides only a part, there is a partial eclipse.

The only eclipses you can easily see without a **telescope** take place when the **sun**, moon and **earth** are in line. When the earth lies between the sun and the moon, the earth's shadow falls on the moon. This is an eclipse of the moon. When the moon lies between the earth and the sun, the moon's shadow falls on a part of the earth. An eclipse of the sun, or solar eclipse, can be seen from that region. About two or three of each kind of eclipse happen every year.

Ecology

Ecology is a branch of **biology**. It is the study of the relationship between living things and their surroundings, or environment. Ecologists are scientists who study how living things and their surroundings affect each other.

Ecology shows us that most species of **plants** and **animals** can live only in a particular kind of environment such as a **lake, forest, desert** or **mountain**. These places are called **habitats**.

Within each habitat lives a variety of plants, all of which are suited to the habitat's **soil, temperature**, sunshine, rainfall and so on. The animals living in the habitat eat the plants or one another. So the plants and animals are linked in what ecologists call a **food chain**. If some species die out and vanish from the food chain, those that eat them lose their food and may die too.

Habitats are always changing. Often these changes are good for some plants and animals, but bad for others. For example, if a pond dries up, its fish will die, but the dead fish will provide food for a heron. Human activities can also change habitats. For example, we may cut down a wood to make way for a new field. We change the natural landscape by **farming** the land, and by building cities and roads. **Pollution** from our factories poisons the **water**, soil and **air**. Ecologists study the ways in which we change the natural environment, and can help us to limit the damage we do. Taking steps to protect the natural world is called **conservation**.

Economics

Economics is the study of people's needs, such as food, clothing, goods and housing, and the ways in which people meet these needs. Economists study the ways in which a community's needs can be met. No country has enough resources to supply all the things that its people want. It has to decide the best way of using the resources that it has. Many economists believe that this is the most important decision nations must make.

There are several different economic systems, including **communism** and capitalism. In the capitalist economic system, most of the land, resources and industries are owned by private individuals and **companies** rather than by **governments**.

Ecuador

Ecuador is a country in northwestern **South America** and it lies on the **equator**. Its name is Spanish for equator.

△ **Ecology** is the study of living things and of where they live. Inside this huge greenhouse in the Sonoran Desert of Arizona, USA, ecologists have created replicas of seven major world habitats, including a rainforest, a grassland and a 4.5-million-litre saltwater ocean.

▽ During an **eclipse** of the sun, or solar eclipse, day becomes night. When the moon moves in between the earth and the sun, it temporarily casts a shadow on to part of the earth.

ECUADOR
Government: Republic
Capital: Quito
Area: 283,561 sq km
Population: 12.4 million
Language: Spanish
Currency: Sucre

▽ The greatest pyramids of **Ancient Egypt** were built on the banks of the Nile River at Giza, near the modern city of Cairo. This illustration shows a royal boat approaching the pyramid complex.

Most of eastern Ecuador is dominated by the **Andes** mountains. More than half of Ecuador's population live in the high mountain valleys, where they keep herds of **sheep** and **llamas**. However, the country's chief products are **coffee**, bananas, **sugar** and **oil**.

The Galapagos Islands lie 960 km off the Pacific coast of South America. They belong to Ecuador and have a unique range of wildlife. One of the first scientists to visit them was the English biologist, Charles **Darwin**.

Edison, Thomas

Thomas Alva Edison (1847–1931) was an American inventor. As a boy, he spent only three months at school, but he went on to produce more than 100 **inventions**. The most famous are the electric light (see **electricity**) and the phonograph for **recording** and playing back **sounds**. Edison finished building his phonograph in 1877. It was a hand-operated device that played recordings made on tin-foil cylinders.

Eel

Eels are long, slim **fish** with tiny scales and fins like narrow ribbons. The two best-known species are the European and American freshwater eels, which have a remarkable life cycle.

When it is time to breed, the adult eels leave their **rivers**, streams and marshes, and swim thousands of kilometres far out into the **Atlantic Ocean**. There, they spawn (release their eggs and sperm). After spawning, the adult eels die.

When they hatch, the tiny young eels are transparent and look nothing like their parents. These babies find their way all the way back to their parents' original homes in **North America** and **Europe**. The young eels grow up in fresh water and stay there until they are ready for their long journey back across the Atlantic. The eels' long journeys are an example of **migration**.

Egg

An egg is a female **cell** that will grow into a new **plant** or **animal**. Most eggs only grow if they are joined with, or fertilized by, male cells. The male cells of animals are usually known as sperm (see **reproduction**). In most **mammals**, the fertilized eggs grow inside the mother's body. However, all **birds** and most **fish**, **amphibians** and **reptiles** lay eggs that contain enough food for the young to grow inside the egg.

Egypt

Modern Egypt dates from 642 CE, when Egypt was conquered by Muslim soldiers from Arabia. Egypt has over 60 million people, more than any other nation in **Africa** apart from **Nigeria**. Its capital, Cairo, is the largest African city. Most Egyptians are Arabs, and **Islam** is the main religion.

The **Nile River** flows through Egypt to the **Mediterranean Sea** on the country's north coast. Water from the river creates large areas of fertile farmland, where **cotton** and other crops are grown.

In the east is the **Suez Canal**, which allows **ships** to sail from the Mediterranean to the **Red Sea**.

Egypt, Ancient

About 5,000 years ago, the Ancient Egyptians began to build one of the world's first great civilizations. For the next 2,500 years, Ancient Egypt was one of the strongest and wealthiest states on earth.

The population of Ancient Egypt was probably no more than six million. Scarcely any of the people lived in the hot sand and rock **deserts** that cover most of inland Egypt. Almost all of them settled near the banks of the mighty **Nile River**.

Each year, the river overflowed and left rich mud on nearby land, creating ideal conditions for **farming** to flourish. Farmers learned to dig and **plough** their fields, and could grow two crops a year in the warm, fertile **soil**. The farmers grew more than enough grain, fruit and vegetables to feed themselves. The surplus food was used to feed the rest of Egypt's population – merchants, craftspeople, miners, priests and noble families, as well as the **pharaohs** who ruled over the entire land.

Most Ancient Egyptians were poor and lived in simple mud-brick huts with palm-leaf roofs. Wealthy Egyptians lived in large, well-furnished **houses** and could afford luxury foods such as meat and cakes. They wore fine clothes, **jewellery** and even **cosmetics**.

The Ancient Egyptians were highly skilled at **architecture** and **engineering**, and built splendid cities, temples and tombs. They constructed impressive **pyramids** as tombs for their dead pharaohs. Building a pyramid was an enormous task, which took thousands of workers many years to complete. The workers cut huge stone blocks for the pyramid, ferried them down the Nile on rafts and then hauled them into place. Each block weighed up to 2.5 tonnes.

Inside a bird's **egg**, the chick is fed from the yolk. When the chick hatches, its feathers and claws are fully formed.

EGYPT
Government: Republic
Capital: Cairo
Area: 1,001,449 sq km
Population: 62.6 million
Language: Arabic
Currency: Egyptian pound

Inside each pyramid, the Ancient Egyptians would place the mummy (preserved body) of a pharaoh. They believed the dead went on living, so they placed food and furniture beside each mummy. Thieves later emptied almost all of the tombs. But the boy pharaoh **Tutankhamen**'s tomb was discovered almost intact in 1922.

The dry Egyptian air has preserved many examples of **hieroglyphics**, a system of picture writing that was written on fragile **paper** made from the papyrus plant. Hieroglyphics and wall **paintings** tell us a great deal about how the Ancient Egyptians lived. The **art** they made often depicted gods such as Ra, the sun god, or Osiris, the god of the dead (see **god and goddess**).

The Ancient Egyptians also believed in the sphinx – a creature with the body of a lion and the head of the pharaoh. The most famous sphinx guards the huge pyramid of Khafre at Giza.

In time, foreign armies equipped with **iron** weapons conquered the Ancient Egyptians. Their land fell under foreign rule after 525 BCE. When the Egyptian queen **Cleopatra** died in 31 BCE, Egypt became part of the **Roman Empire**.

Eid

An Eid is a religious **festival** of **Islam**. Muslims celebrate two Eids each year – Eid ul-Adha (Festival of Sacrifice) and Eid ul-Fitr (Festival of the Breaking of the Fast). Eid ul-Adha occurs at the end of the 12th month of the Islamic **calendar**. Animals such as sheep or goats are sacrificed

◁ The people of **Ancient Egypt** believed in life after death. Their bodies were mummified (preserved) before burial to prevent decay. First, the internal organs were removed. Then the body was placed in salt for 40 days to dry. Finally, it was rubbed with spices and oils, and tightly wrapped in bandages.

in memory of the prophet Abraham, who was so faithful to God that he was prepared to sacrifice his own son.

Eid ul-Fitr is a joyful feast held at the end of **Ramadan** – the Islamic month of fasting. During Ramadan, Muslims fast (do not eat or drink) from dawn until sunset every day.

Einstein, Albert

Albert **Einstein** helped to develop the first atomic bomb, but he became very concerned about the need to control nuclear weapons after World War II.

Albert Einstein (1879–1955) was an important scientist whose main area of research was **physics**. He was born in **Germany** but in the 1930s went to live in the **USA**. His theory of relativity was a new way of looking at **time**, **space**, **matter** and **energy**. Einstein proved that a small amount of matter could be transformed into a vast amount of energy. This made it possible for people to use **nuclear energy**.

Elasticity

When you pull a **rubber** band, it stretches. When you let go, it springs back to its original size. The rubber band is elastic – it has elasticity. If you drop a rubber ball, the part of the ball that hits the ground is flattened. Then the ball springs back into its original round shape. As this happens, the ball pushes on the ground and jumps up – it bounces. The ball has elasticity.

Elasticity exists because the molecules that make up an elastic material try to stay at a certain distance from each other. If they are squeezed more tightly together, they immediately push apart. If they are pulled apart, they try to come together again. All solids and **liquids** have some elasticity.

Election

Most countries, local regions and public organizations hold elections from time to time. Elections give people the chance to elect, or choose, a new **government**,

In many **elections**, people vote by making a mark next to the candidate's name on a piece of paper. The papers, or votes, are posted in a sealed box, to be counted later.

Polevaulting relies on **elasticity**. When the pole hits the ground, it bends. Because the pole is highly elastic, it starts to straighten out, hurling the vaulter over the bar.

council or leader. We do this by voting. Voting is essential to the political system called **democracy**.

In democratic countries, voters go to a certain building on election, or polling, day. They are given a piece of paper printed with the names of all the candidates. Each voter puts a cross in secret against the name of the person they want to elect. Sometimes, the rules of the election say that the voter has to choose several candidates.

Many elections are decided by a system in which the candidate with the most votes wins. But others are decided by another system, called proportional representation. In this system, the number of candidates elected from each party is calculated according to the percentage of the total vote that the party receives.

Only adults may vote in political elections. In many countries, people earn this right when they reach 18.

Electricity

Electricity is an invisible form of **energy**. It is used to power electric trains, light bulbs, **computers**, **radios**, **televisions** and many other devices.

The electricity that we use flows through **wires** as electric current. An electric current flows when tiny particles called electrons jump between the **atoms** that make up the **metal** in the wire. Current can flow only if a wire makes a complete loop called a circuit. If a gap is made in the circuit, the current stops flowing. Switches are devices that open and close gaps in circuits.

The unit of electric current is the amp – short for ampère. An average domestic light bulb carries no more than one amp. A **lightning** flash can peak at about 20,000 amps. A nuclear **power station** can deliver 10 million amps. Voltage is a unit of measurement that describes how powerfully a source of electricity, such as a **battery** or a **generator**, sends an electric current.

Batteries are a highly convenient source of electricity. The electric current they produce can be used to start **cars**, illuminate torch bulbs and work radios. But most of the electricity we use is produced in power stations. Inside a power station's generators, coils of wire are made to rotate between powerful magnets (see **magnetism**). This makes an electric current flow through the coils of wire.

Electricity travels from the power station through a network of overhead power lines and underground cables to wherever it is needed. This network is called the electricity grid. The current flowing through the power lines has a very high force, or voltage. Before it reaches homes and factories, devices called transformers reduce the voltage of the current to a lower level that can be used safely.

In a house, electric current flows out of the plugs in the walls and through any electrical equipment that is in use. Then it returns to the generator in the power station through another set of wires. This completes the circuit.

The electricity used in houses is in the form of alternating current – it flows in one direction and then in the opposite direction. Each movement back and forth happens about 50 times a second. This is so fast that we do not notice, for example, that lights flicker.

△ **Electricity** produced by the power station travels along a network of high-voltage power lines. It passes through a series of transformers and substations, where the current is changed to the lower voltage used in homes and factories.

▽ **Electricity** can be generated by turbines that harness the power of the wind. They are built in groups, called wind farms, which are located in exposed places where it is always windy. There are plans to build many offshore wind farms like this one in the future.

paint on circuit boards. Electronic engineers work out which components need to be put together to make circuits that can perform specific tasks. These circuits are found in all kinds of devices, including **computers**, **television** sets, **radios**, pocket **calculators**, **telephones**, digital watches and **radar**. Without electronics, **aircraft** could not fly and **space exploration** would be impossible.

Element

Everything that you see around you is made up of chemical ingredients called elements. In each element all the **atoms** are of the same kind.

Electronics

Electronics is an important branch of **engineering** that involves the study of **electricity**. It deals with the way in which tiny particles called electrons flow through certain solid materials, **gases** or a **vacuum**.

Modern electrical devices contain tiny electronic parts such as **silicon chips** and **transistors**. These parts, or components, are joined together by lines of metallic

Labels on diagram:
Nuclear power station
Substation
Substation
Large factory
Underground transformer
Homes
Transformer

△ Every **element** behaves in a different way. For example, metals burn with different coloured flames. The picture above shows (from left to right) the flames of calcium, copper, sodium, lithium, potassium, barium and lead.

△ **Emus** live on Australia's grasslands. They gather in small flocks, and move from place to place in search of seeds, berries and fresh leaves to eat.

Different elements can be joined to make more complicated substances called **compounds**, but an element cannot be broken up into a simpler kind of substance.

Chemists have found more than 100 different elements, of which 92 occur naturally. Scientists have produced some of the other elements in laboratories. At ordinary room **temperatures**, some elements are **gases**, some are **liquids** and some are solids.

Elephant

Elephants are the largest living land **animals**. A large bull (male) elephant may stand twice as high as a human and weigh as much as seven family cars. Elephants have huge ears, a long trunk, **ivory** tusks and very thick **skin**. There are two species of elephants. The African elephant has larger ears and tusks than the Indian, or Asian, elephant. Most African elephants roam the grassy plains, or **savannas**, of East Africa, although they also live in forests. Indian elephants mainly live in thick **rainforests**.

Elephants are plant-eating **mammals**, or **herbivores**. They use their trunks to pull up grass and plants, and scoop food and water into their mouths.

Elizabeth I

Elizabeth I (1533–1603) was a famous English queen. She never married, and ruled alone for 45 years. During the 1500s, there was much religious conflict in **England**, **Scotland** and the rest of **Europe**. A Protestant, Elizabeth tried to unite her country and end the wars of religion, but she had her Catholic rival, **Mary Queen of Scots**, put to death.

In 1588, Elizabeth's navy crushed the Spanish **Armada** and made England powerful at sea. England became a wealthier and more important country. Many writers, poets and scholars lived in Elizabeth's reign, including the playwright **Shakespeare**. People often call her reign 'the Elizabethan Age'.

Elizabeth II

Elizabeth II (b. 1926) is queen of the **United Kingdom** of Great Britain and **Northern Ireland** and head of the British **Commonwealth**. Her husband is the Duke of Edinburgh. Her eldest son, and heir to the throne, is Charles, Prince of **Wales**. Elizabeth II's official residences are Buckingham Palace, London, and Windsor Castle, Berkshire.

El Salvador

El Salvador is the smallest country in **Central America**, but it has more people per square kilometre than any other Central American country. Many of its people are farmers, and the most

◁ Hunters have killed thousands of African **elephants** for their ivory tusks. The species is now endangered.

important crops are **coffee**, maize and **sugar**. El Salvador has had several conflicts with its neighbour, **Honduras**, and suffered a 12-year **civil war** which ended in 1992.

Emu

Only the **ostrich** is larger than this big Australian **bird**. An emu can run at up to 50 km/h on its long, strong legs. It cannot fly because it is far too heavy and its wings are small and weak.

Energy

Energy is the ability to do work. It exists in several forms, but there are two main kinds – potential energy and kinetic energy. Potential energy is the 'energy of position', or stored energy. For example, the water stored behind a high **dam** has potential energy. Kinetic energy is the 'energy of movement'. When water from the dam falls through pipes and works **turbines** to generate **electricity**, it has kinetic energy.

Other forms of energy are electrical, **heat**, chemical, **sound** and **nuclear**. Energy can be changed from one form into another. For example, the chemical energy of petrol is turned into kinetic energy as it works the moving parts of a car's **engine**, to electrical energy in the car's headlights, to sound energy in the car's horn, and so on. At every stage, some energy is turned into heat energy – this is why the car's engine becomes very hot. However, energy is never 'lost' or destroyed.

The **sun** gives us most of the energy we use on **earth**. Energy from the sun is called radiant energy.

Engine

Engines are **machines** that change potential (stored) energy into useful energy that does work. People have used simple engines such as **windmills** and waterwheels for hundreds of years.

▷ Elizabeth I of England wore elaborate costumes, makeup, wigs and jewels. Her dramatic appearance impressed people, which increased her power and prestige.

The first **steam engines** were developed in the early 1700s. They provided power for factory machinery, and were later used to drive **ships**, trains and **cars**. Today, steam still drives some machines, such as the steam turbines in nuclear **power stations**. However, steam engines have been largely replaced by **internal combustion engines**. These include petrol engines and **diesel engines**. In internal combustion engines, **fuel** burns inside the engine.

In a petrol engine, petrol mixes with **air** inside a cylinder. A spark sets the mixture alight, and it explodes. This happens over and over again. Hot gases from the explosions push a piston to and fro inside the cylinder. The moving piston drives the crankshaft around, which turns the vehicle's **wheels**. Most petrol engines have up to eight cylinders.

The first **jet engine** was designed in 1930, and **rockets** followed not long afterwards. Jet engines are used in many **aircraft**. Rocket engines are used in **missiles** and **space exploration**.

EL SALVADOR
Government: Republic
Capital: San Salvador
Area: 21,041 sq km
Population: 6.1 million
Language: Spanish
Currency: Colón

▽ In a petrol **engine**, air and petrol are mixed to produce explosions. The explosive force drives pistons, which turn the crankshaft. As the crankshaft rotates, it turns the vehicle's wheels.

Waste gases out

Cylinder

Air in

Spark plug

Piston

Crank

Fuel in

Crankshaft

EUROPE

Europe is the second smallest continent.
Its moderate climate, fertile land and rich
resources make it ideal for human habitation.

A FERTILE CONTINENT

Europe is a peninsula that lies to the west
of the continent of Asia. It lies on the same
tectonic plate (section of the earth's surface)
as western Asia. Europe has a long history of
human settlement. This is mainly because
a greater proportion of its land is suitable
for farming than that on any other continent.

◁ The Alps lie
at the heart of
Europe, and are
a major tourist
destination.

CHANGING LANDSCAPES

The north of Europe is covered
with mountains and vast forests
of conifer trees, and lies partly
in the Arctic Circle. It includes
Scandinavia – Norway, Sweden,
Denmark and Finland – and
part of western Russia.

A zone of flat, lowland
plains covers much of central
Europe. It stretches from the
United Kingdom east to the
Ural Mountains of Russia. In this
region lie many of Europe's great
rivers, such as the Rhine, Danube and
Volga. The warm summers, cool winters and
plentiful rainfall are ideal for growing wheat,
barley, oats, potatoes and vegetables.

ICELAND

Norwegian Sea

Faroe Is.

Shetland Is.

Orkney Is.

ATLANTIC OCEAN

REP. OF IRELAND

North Sea

DENMARK

NORWAY

SWEDEN

FINLAND

ESTONIA

LATVIA

Baltic Sea

LITHUANIA

Russian Federation

UNITED KINGDOM

NETHERLANDS

BELAR

English Channel

Channel Is.

BELGIUM

GERMANY

POLAND

LUXEMBOURG

Bay of Biscay

CZECH REPUBLIC

LIECHTENSTEIN

SLOVAKIA

Carpathians

FRANCE

SWITZERLAND

AUSTRIA

HUNGARY

MOLD

ALPS

SLOVENIA

ROMANIA

CROATIA

PORTUGAL

Pyrenees

MONACO

SAN MARINO

Appennines

BOSNIA HERZEGOVINA

Adriatic Sea

UNION OF SERBIA AND MONTENEGRO

BULGARIA

SPAIN

ANDORRA

Corsica

VATICAN CITY

MACEDONIA

Majorca

Ibiza

Minorca

Sardinia

ITALY

ALBANIA

Strait of Gibraltar

GREECE

Aegean Sea

Sicily

Ionian Sea

MALTA

Mediterranean Sea

◁ Rotterdam, on
the Netherlands
coast, is the busiest
port in the world.
It is used to export
and import a huge
range of products,
from chemicals to
steel, machinery,
textiles and grain.

THE MEDITERRANEAN

The southern part of Europe is separated from the north
by several mountain ranges. From west to east, these
are the Pyrenees, Alps, Carpathians and Caucasus. The
Mediterranean region includes Portugal, Spain, southern
France, Italy and Greece. It has a much warmer climate
than the rest of Europe, with mild winters and hot, dry
summers. The mixed landscape of rolling hills and plains
is used to grow crops such as citrus fruits and olives.

RUSSIAN

FEDERATION

KRAINE

Caspian
Sea

Caucasus

lack Sea

△ The warm climate of the Mediterranean region is ideal for growing vines, which produce the grapes used in wine-making.

△ Europe has a large motor industry, with many highly automated vehicle-assembly plants.

POWERFUL EMPIRES

Throughout history, Europe has had a huge influence on world politics. The system of democracy – where the government is chosen by the people – was developed in Ancient Greece about 2,500 years ago. Democracy is now the main political system across much of the world. Laws introduced by the Roman Empire, which controlled much of Europe until it was finally defeated in 476 CE, still influence many legal systems today.

CONQUERING THE GLOBE

During the Middle Ages, European explorers began to explore unknown lands. England, Spain, France and Holland used their military strength to establish colonies abroad. The trade that flowed in and out of Europe from the colonies made these states extremely wealthy. In the 1800s, Belgium and Germany also founded colonies. Most European colonies became independent states after World War II.

CULTURE AND RELIGION

Europe has been a leading centre of learning since the days of Ancient Greece. Impressive Ancient Greek and Roman ruins are scattered across the south of the continent. During the Renaissance (1350–1500s), Europeans became interested in many new ideas about science, art and literature. Europe is also an important centre of Christianity. The headquarters of the Roman Catholic Church are in the Vatican City in Rome, Italy, while the Orthodox Church flourishes in the east and southwest.

COMING TOGETHER

The map of Europe has often changed, mainly due to wars between rival countries. Both World Wars were begun and fought largely in Europe. After World War II, Europe was divided between the non-communist states of the West and the Russian-backed communist states of the East. This period was called the 'Cold War'. In the late 1980s, the communist governments of Eastern Europe finally crumbled. Today, 15 European states have formed the European Union. This organization attempts to improve the cooperation between its members.

Fertile plains cover much of eastern Europe. In some areas, farmers still use teams of oxen to plough fields and pull carts.

EUROPE FACT FILE

Area: 10,534,600 sq km

Highest mountain: Mount Elbrus, southwest Russia, 5,633 m

Largest lake: Ladoga, northwest Russia, 68,880 sq km

Longest river: Volga, 3,531 km

Number of countries: 45

Largest country: Russia (23 percent of which is in Europe)

Smallest country: Vatican City

Largest city: London, UK, 7.2 million

Largest population: Germany, 83 million

Total population: 727 million

SEE ALSO

Alps, Ancient Greece, European Union, Explorer, Farming, Renaissance, Roman Empire, Vikings, World War I, World War II

△ Many climbers tried to reach the summit of Mount **Everest** before two finally succeeded in 1953. They were New Zealander Edmund Hillary and a Sherpa tribesman from Nepal, Tenzing Norgay.

ETHIOPIA
Government: Republic
Capital: Addis Ababa
Area: 1,221,900 sq km
Population: 63 million
Language: Amharic
Currency: Ethiopian birr

Engineering

Engineers do many different types of jobs. Metallurgical engineers separate **metals** from other substances to make them usable. Chemical engineers use chemicals to make such things as **soap**, **paint** and **plastics**. Civil engineers plan and design structures such as **bridges**, **roads**, **railways**, **tunnels** and airports. Electrical engineers work with devices that use or produce **electricity**. The newest branch of electrical engineering is **electronics**, which includes the study and design of **computers**.

England

England is the largest country in the **United Kingdom** of Great Britain and **Northern Ireland**. It covers an area of 130,439 sq km – roughly three-fifths of Great Britain's total area. England's neighbours are **Scotland** and **Wales**. Northern Ireland lies to the west, across the Irish Sea.

England is named after the Angles, a group of **Anglo-Saxons** who settled there about 1,500 years ago. Today, England is densely populated, with a population of nearly 50 million.

Equator

The equator is an imaginary line around the world, halfway between the **North Pole** and the **South Pole**. It divides the earth into the Northern Hemisphere and the Southern Hemisphere.

Estonia *see* Baltic States

Ethiopia

Ethiopia is a huge country in the northeast of **Africa**. It was formerly called Abyssinia. Much of Ethiopia consists of rocky **mountains** and open areas of high ground called plateaux. Here, farmers grow grain and **coffee**.

For many years, Ethiopia suffered from drought (a long period with no rain) and **civil war**. **Famine** was widespread. In the 1980s, a worldwide campaign raised money to send food and medical supplies to the country.

European Union

The European Union (EU) is a group of nations that work together to make it easier for goods, **money** and people to travel between the countries in the Union. Its members are **Austria**, **Belgium**, **Denmark**, **Finland**, **France**, **Ireland**, **Italy**, **United Kingdom**, **Greece**, **Luxembourg**, the **Netherlands**, **Portugal**, **Spain**, **Sweden** and **Germany**. Several other European countries have applied to join these 15 nations.

The headquarters of the European Union are in Brussels, Belgium. In 2002, 12 members of the EU adopted a single unit of currency – the euro.

Everest, Mount

Mount Everest is the world's highest peak. It rises 8,848 m above sea level. The **mountain** stands in the **Himalayas** on the borders of **Nepal** and **Tibet**.

Evolution

The theory of evolution states that the **plants** and **animals** alive today are descended from other forms that lived long ago. This slow process of change has been going on for many millions of years – ever since life first appeared on **earth** – and it is still happening. Much of the evidence for evolution comes from **fossils** – the remains of extinct plants and animals. Fossils give us an idea of what the ancestors of today's species looked like.

The theory of evolution says that plants and animals must adapt to their surroundings, or environment, if they are to survive. Those which adapt best are most likely to survive.

For example, in the past, some **giraffes** may have had longer necks than others. The long-necked giraffes would have been able to feed on leaves that were too high for short-necked giraffes to reach. During food shortages, the taller giraffes would have been more likely to survive than the shorter ones. In time, all the short-necked giraffes died out – leaving only giraffes with long necks.

Charles **Darwin** was one of the first to put forward the theory of evolution. He published his idea in 1859.

Exercise

Exercise usually means activities that strengthen the **muscles** and improve **health**. Many **sports** are good ways to exercise, but it is better to take regular gentle exercise than to take strenuous exercise only once in a while. Brisk walking is one of the best exercises.

Explorer

Explorers are people who travel to find out about little-known places. There have been explorers ever since **Stone Age** people started to wander across continents. In the 1200s, Marco **Polo** reached China from Europe, but the great age of exploration did not begin until the 1400s.

Famous western explorers include Vasco da **Gama**, Hernando **Cortés**, Christopher **Columbus**, Ferdinand **Magellan**, James **Cook**, David **Livingstone** and Roald **Amundsen**.

Explosion

Explosions occur when people **heat** or strike certain solid or **liquid** substances. These suddenly turn into hot **gases**. The gases fill more space than the solids or liquids, so they rush violently outwards. High explosives such as dynamite explode faster and do more damage than low explosives such as gunpowder.

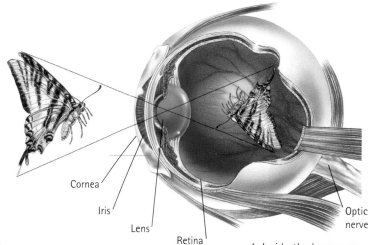

Cornea

Iris

Lens

Retina

Optic nerve

Eye

Eyes are organs that provide **animals** with information about the appearance of objects. A human eye behaves much like a **camera**, by bending **light** rays to form images of objects.

Light rays enter the eye through a layer of transparent skin called the conjunctiva. The rays pass through a hard, transparent layer called the cornea. This bends the rays. The **lens** brings them into focus on the retina at the back of the eye. The focused image is 'received' by light-sensitive **nerve** endings on the retina, which send the **brain** a message along the optic nerve. The iris – the eye's coloured part – is a **muscle** that opens and closes to let more or less light through. This allows us to see in dim or bright light.

△ Inside the human **eye**, the image on the retina is upside down. The brain turns it over so that we see things the right way up.

▽ **Explorers** have added greatly to our knowledge of the world. In 1947, Norwegian Thor Heyerdahl used a log raft to sail from Peru, across the Pacific to the Polynesian islands. This showed that it would have been possible for people to make a similar voyage thousands of years ago.

F

The Goose That Laid Golden Eggs is a **fable** about greed. A farmer had a goose that laid eggs made of gold, which made him very rich. He greedily cut the goose open, hoping to find even more treasure, but there was none. As the goose was dead, there were no more eggs.

Fable

Fables are stories that are usually told to teach a lesson. Their main characters are often animals that can speak and act like human beings. Some of the most famous fables include those of **Aesop**, an Ancient Greek storyteller. Aesop's fables, such as *The Wolf in Sheep's Clothing* and *The Ant and the Grasshopper*, are told to this day. Many modern writers have produced fables to comment on how they see the world. One of the best-known modern fables is *Animal Farm* (1945) by George Orwell (1903–1950).

The largest **falcon** in the world is the gyrfalcon, which lives in the Arctic regions of Europe, Russia and North America. The gyrfalcon preys on other birds, and nests on cliff ledges.

Falcon

Falcons are fast-flying **birds** of prey. They are found all over the world, and include species such as the peregrine falcon, the merlin and several types of kestrel. Falcons have sharp talons for killing prey, and strong, hooked beaks for tearing flesh. They swoop down on their victims from above, hitting them with their outstretched talons.

Falkland Islands

The Falklands are a group of cold, windswept **islands** that lie in the South **Atlantic Ocean** about 770 km east of the southern tip of **South America**. The islands are a British colony, and **sheep** farming is the main occupation. In 1982, **Argentina** invaded the Falklands, but the Argentine troops were defeated by British forces.

Famine

Sometimes a country does not have enough **food** to feed its **population**, and eventually some of the people may starve to death. This situation is known as famine. Many of the countries in the **developing world** suffer famine, often because there has not been enough rain to grow sufficient food. Nations that are unaffected by the famine send food supplies to help the starving people.

Faraday, Michael

Michael Faraday (1791–1867) was an English scientist who is best known for his experiments with **electricity**. He showed that it could be made to flow along a **wire** when the wire was passed between the poles of a **magnet**. Today, this is how most electricity is produced in large **generators**.

Farming *see* page 114

Fascism was perhaps at its strongest across Europe in the years before World War II, as can be seen by the size of this Nazi rally held in Germany in 1936.

Fascism

Fascism is a political belief. It takes its name from the Latin 'fasces' – a bundle of rods with an axe that was the symbol of authority in Ancient Rome. Fascism first appeared in **Italy** in 1919 when Benito **Mussolini** founded the Italian Fascist Party. In 1922, Mussolini seized power to become **dictator** of Italy.

Fascist political ideas include the belief that the **government** of a country must be all-powerful. Its citizens must work hard and obey the government for the good of the nation. Fascists believe in strict discipline and training for all people, including children. Anybody who opposes a fascist government is made an outlaw. In fascist Italy, many people were jailed, exiled or executed because they did not agree with the Fascists. All the other political parties were made illegal.

Fascism became popular in many other countries between the two **World Wars**, and fascist governments came to power in **Germany**, **Spain** and **Portugal**. The supporters of Germany's fascist party, the National Socialist Workers' Party, were known as Nazis. In 1933, Adolf **Hitler**, the Nazi leader, became German chancellor. Hitler's fascist policies led to the outbreak of World War II.

Fashion

Most people in the world wear some sort of clothing. What they wear depends on the **climate** and how they live. Styles of clothing also change according to the latest fashion.

The earliest clothes were **animal** skins. In the ancient world people began to wear loose, draped tunics. By the **Middle Ages**, the dress of poorer people was still simple, but the wealthy dressed in fine **silk** and damask (a luxurious, shiny fabric) from East **Asia**. During the **Renaissance** (1350–1500s), the new wealth and interest in **art** made rich, colourful fabrics popular. In the 1700s in **Europe**, clothes became very elaborate to match the grand buildings of the period. People wore huge wigs and wide, stiffened skirts, which were often beautifully embroidered.

By the 1900s, fashions had become more practical, especially for women. Today, many people throughout the world dress in a similar way in clothes such as jeans, T-shirts and jackets. Clothes are often made from modern **textiles** that contain artificial fibres such as nylon and polyester.

How styles change from year to year is decided by fashion designers. Fashion is big business. Every season there are spectacular shows where models display the latest designs.

Fat

Fat is an important **food** for both **animals** and **plants**. The tissue of these living things contains fat. Fat in a pure state may take the form of a **liquid**,

continued on page 115

△ Some clothing **fashions** are extremely elaborate. This is the costume worn by the actors of Japanese 'kabuki' drama, which combines a story with dances and songs.

△ In Ancient Greece, the **fashion** was to wear light, loose-fitting clothes made of wool or linen.

▽ Stiff ruffs made of starched linen and worn around the neck were the height of **fashion** in England during the 1500s.

FARMING

Farming is the business of growing crops and raising livestock on the land to produce food, drink, textiles and other products.

△ Combine harvesters are machines that can cut and beat corn at high speed.

△ Irrigation was invented in the Middle East in about 4000 BCE. It is a system for watering fields to help crops grow.

ORIGINS OF FARMING

Farming began about 13,000 years ago when Stone Age people started to herd wild animals. By 7000 BCE, people had learned that scattered seed would grow, providing food for themselves and their animals. The first crops were probably wheat, barley and millet, cultivated with sticks and hoes. In 3000 BCE, farmers in Mesopotamia (modern Iraq) invented the ox-drawn plough. The plough revolutionized agriculture because farmers could now turn over long lines of soil to make their crops grow better.

▽ Milk is produced on dairy farms from cattle, although goats and sheep may also be kept for milk. On modern dairy farms, cattle are milked by automatic milking machines.

△ Rice is the staple food of over half the world's population. At first, the rice plants are grown in dry fields but then the crop is transplanted by hand to rice paddies (pools of shallow water).

AGRICULTURAL REVOLUTIONS

Dramatic developments have taken place in farming over the last 500 years. Crop rotation began in the 1600s when it was realized that fodder crops such as turnips, peas and clover put goodness back into the soil. Each year, farmers alternated fodder crops with cereals such as wheat. Farmers also began feeding their livestock during the winter, and developed larger, fatter breeds of cattle, sheep and pigs. In the 1800s, as fields grew ever larger, tractors started to replace horses and oxen. Combine harvesters were first introduced in the USA in the 1830s.

FARMING TODAY

Today, most farms in developed countries are mechanized, with few people working on them. Poultry are often reared indoors in cages – this is known as battery farming. But while many countries produce an excess of food, poorer nations still suffer famine. Many new farming methods and crops have been brought to the developing world to try to solve the problem.

▷ The traditional farming year begins in late winter when the fields are ploughed. The crops are sown in spring, and harvested at the end of summer.

ORGANIC FARMING

By the 1900s, farmers were commonly using chemicals such as fertilizers and pest-killers. These massively improved crop yields. But some farmers are returning to more 'natural' organic farming methods because many people are concerned about the chemicals in their food.

SEE ALSO
Cattle, Cereal, Fertilizer, Food, Irrigation, Pig, Plough, Sheep, Vegetable, Windmill

continued from page 113

such as vegetable oil, or a solid, such as butter. Fat is a store of **energy**. A unit of fat contains twice as much energy as the same amount of **protein** or **starch**.

Fats play an important part in our diet. We get most vegetable fat from the **seeds** and **fruits** of plants, where it is stored. In animals and **human beings**, fat is stored in tiny 'droplets' in a layer under the **skin** and in the **cells** of the body. Meat, and dairy products such as butter, **milk** and **cheese**, are our main sources of animal fats. Animal fats are also important in the manufacture of **soaps**, **perfumes** and polishes.

Fawkes, Guy

Guy Fawkes (1570–1606) was the most famous member of a group of plotters who attempted to kill King James I of England (1566–1625) by blowing up the English **Parliament** with gunpowder. They were protesting against laws which tried to control the rights of Roman Catholics. The plot failed, and Fawkes was arrested on 5 November 1605 in the cellars of the House of Lords in London. Together with the other conspirators, he was executed. Every November, the defeat of the 'Gunpowder Plot' is celebrated across Britain with **firework** displays.

Feather

The only **animals** to possess feathers are **birds**. Feathers protect birds, keep them warm and give their bodies a smooth, streamlined shape. Feathers also form the broad surface area of the wings that allows birds to fly. Each feather is made of a central hollow tube, from which spring many branches and side-branches. The side-branches are 'zipped' together by tiny hooks, or barbs, to form a flat surface.

Feathers are replaced once or twice a year. This process is called moulting. Old feathers that are worn and broken fall out. New ones grow in their place.

△ A close-up of part of a **feather** shows the interlaced network of tiny hooked branches.

△ In **fencing**, the fighters are protected from injury by wire-mesh masks, thick jackets and a glove worn on the hand holding the foil – the weapon.

▽ This illustration shows Guy **Fawkes** and his fellow conspirators, who in 1605 plotted to blow up the English Parliament. Fawkes is the third from the right.

Fencing

Fencing can be described as the **sport** of 'friendly duelling'. Fencers wear a special glove, padded jacket and face mask. They fight with blunted swords. The winner is the one who scores the most points by touching their opponent with their sword. In the past, fencing was a form of sword practice for real duels, but today it is a popular sport and an **Olympic Games** event.

Fermentation

With time, **milk** goes sour, **bread** dough rises, and grape juice turns into **wine**. All these are examples of fermentation.

Fermentation is caused by the action of microscopic **fungi** such as **bacteria**, **yeast** and mould. These tiny living things break substances down into simpler forms. People have been using fermentation since the earliest times to make bread, beer, wine and **cheese**. But it was not until the 1800s that the French scientist Louis **Pasteur** found out how fermentation really works.

Fermi, Enrico

Enrico Fermi (1901–1954) was an Italian scientist. In 1938, his studies of the **atom** were rewarded with a **Nobel Prize**. In 1942, during **World War II**, Fermi built the first atomic reactor. He constructed it in an empty squash court under a football stadium in Chicago, **USA**. There, he set off the first artificial nuclear chain reaction.

△ **Ferns** do not have seeds or flowers. Instead they produce spores – minute structures each consisting of a single cell – from which new ferns develop.

△ **Festivals** often play a big part in the life of local communities. This masked stilt dancer is performing at a village festival in Mali, North Africa.

FIJI
Government: Republic
Capital: Suva
Area: 18,274 sq km
Population: 801,000
Languages: Fijian and English
Currency: Fiji dollar

Fern

The ferns were some of the earliest land **plants** on **earth**. Today, their delicate, feathery leaves look much the same as they did millions of years ago. There are about 10,000 different species of fern. They are found all over the world, usually in damp, shady places such as under **trees**.

Fertilizer

Fertilizers are chemicals that are dug into the **soil** to nourish it. They help **plants** to grow larger and healthier by giving them the chemical nutrients they need to grow. The most important fertilizers are calcium, phosphorus, potassium and **sulphur**.

Festival

A festival is a period of celebration which may last for anything from a day to several weeks. The word festival comes from the Latin *festa*, meaning feast. Festivals are often held for religious reasons. Important religious festivals include **Ramadan** and **Eid (Islam)**, **Chanukah** and **Passover (Judaism)**, **Christmas** and **Easter (Christianity)** and **Diwali (Hinduism)**. In **Buddhism**, festivals are held to celebrate events in the life of **Buddha**, and to honour the Buddhist monks.

Fibre optics

An optical fibre is a flexible **glass** strand thinner than a human **hair**. Along this superfine fibre a beam of **light** can travel very easily. The light can then be used to carry **telephone** conversations and **television** pictures, or to allow surgeons to see inside our bodies. The fibres are made of specially pure glass designed to reflect the light in towards the centre of the strand. Using **laser** light, signals can be sent for more than 50 km before they have to be amplified, or increased in power. This means that optical fibres are far more efficient than the **copper** cables that were once used, as well as being much thinner and lighter.

Fiction

Fiction is literature that describes imaginary events and people. The main form of fiction is the novel – a written story. The opposite of fiction is non-fiction – any form of **writing** that has been produced to supply us with information or facts. Non-fiction includes text **books** and encyclopedias.

Novels developed from short stories written in **Italy** in the 1300s. One of the first famous novels was *Don Quixote* (1615), by the Spanish writer Miguel de Cervantes (1547–1616). Some of the first English novels with believable, or true-to-life, stories were written by Daniel Defoe (1660–1731). Defoe's best-known novel is *Robinson Crusoe* (1719), which tells the tale of a shipwrecked sailor.

There are many kinds of novels. For instance, some are adventure tales, such as *Treasure Island* (1883) by Robert Louis **Stevenson**. There are horror stories such as **Frankenstein** (1818) by the English writer Mary Shelley (1797–1851), humorous novels like *The Adventures of Tom Sawyer* (1876) by Mark **Twain**, and satirical novels such as Jonathan **Swift**'s *Gulliver's Travels* (1726), in which Swift pokes fun at human society. All novels are meant to entertain us, but many of the best novels also offer new ways of looking at life. For example, Charles **Dickens** made his readers aware of how harsh life was for poor people in England in the mid-1800s.

Fiji

Fiji is a country made up of hundreds of **islands** in the **Pacific Ocean**. The largest island is Viti Levu. Fiji became a British territory in 1874, but gained its independence in 1970. In 1987, Fiji's army leaders seized power. Civilian rule was restored in 1990, but in 2000, the **government** was again overthrown. New **elections** were held in 2001.

Film

The art of making moving pictures came from a **machine** called the kinetoscope, which was invented by an American, Thomas **Edison**, in 1891. Soon after, two French brothers, Auguste Lumière (1862–1954) and Louis Lumière (1864–1948), built a similar device of their own – the 'cinématographe'. This machine projected pictures from a piece of film on to a screen. The pictures were shown one after the other so quickly that the images on the screen appeared to move. In 1896, in **Paris**, the Lumière brothers gave the world's first public film show. Soon many people in **Europe** and **North America** were making films.

These early films did not look much like the ones we are used to seeing today. They were only in black and white, the movements were jerky and there was no sound. At first, films were made to show news and real events, but by 1902 film-makers began to invent their own stories, using actors to play the different parts. The first 'talkie', as films with sound became known, was *The Jazz Singer*, which opened in 1927.

As the film industry grew, enormous sums were spent on lavish productions. However, after **World War II**, a more realistic type of film became popular. In the 1950s, the growing popularity of **television** led to a decline in film-making, because people stayed at home to watch TV rather than go to the cinema. But the film industry began to recover in the 1970s, when modern blockbusters were born. These films were full of dramatic special effects.

Hollywood – a suburb of **Los Angeles** in California, **USA** – has long been the film-making capital of the world. However, most countries have their own film industries. One of the largest is in Mumbai (formerly Bombay), **India**.

Fingerprint

Fingerprints are marks we leave behind whenever we touch something. You can see them by pressing your fingertips into an ink pad and then onto a sheet of white **paper**. Everybody has patterns of lines and swirls on their fingers, but each person's fingerprints are different. Because of this, **police** officers can use fingerprints to help identify criminals.

Finland

Finland is a country in northern **Europe** between **Sweden** and **Russia**. Northern Finland stretches north of the **Arctic** Circle. Thousands of **lakes** and **rivers** dot the Finnish landscape, forming a great inland waterway. About 75 percent of the land is covered by **forests** of **conifer** trees such as spruce, pine and larch. Finland's main industries are logging and making wood products, such as **paper**.

△ Fingerprints never change and are unique to each person. Detectives often check the scene of a crime for fingerprints, which they use to try to identify the criminals.

FINLAND
Government: Republic
Capital: Helsinki
Area: 337,032 sq km
Population: 5.2 million
Language: Finnish
Currency: Euro

▽ Making a **film** often involves a large team of people, including actors, camera operators, lighting designers, sound recordists and technicians. The film's director controls what is seen on screen.

△ *Angelfish live on coral reefs, which are home to a greater variety of fish than any other part of the ocean.*

△ *The bright colours of the lionfish are a warning to other animals that its spines are highly poisonous.*

△ *When a pufferfish is threatened, it rapidly gulps water to 'inflate' its body to twice its normal size.*

◁ *Sea horses have a most unusual life cycle. The female lays her eggs in a pouch on the male's belly. When the eggs hatch, the male pushes the tiny babies out through the opening of his pouch.*

△ *The hammerhead shark has a long flap on either side of its head. Scientists think that these flaps may help the shark pinpoint its prey.*

FISH

Fish were the first vertebrates (animals with backbones) to develop on earth, about 500 million years ago. They live in water, and breathe oxygen through their gills.

WORLD OF FISH

There are 22,000 different species of fish, which are found in all kinds of water habitats throughout the world. About 60 percent of all fish species live in the saltwater of seas and oceans. The rest are freshwater fish, found in rivers, streams, lakes and ponds.

Sea fish constantly lose water and must drink a lot, whereas freshwater fish take in water through their skin.

Inside a typical bony fish

Spinal cord

Scale

Barbel (helps the fish locate food by touch)

Gills

Heart

Pectoral fin (for steering)

Swim bladder (helps the fish float)

TYPES OF FISH

Fish are divided into two main groups. Bony fish have bony skeletons and are covered with overlapping scales. There are about 20,000 species of bony fish, including salmon, sardines and eels. Cartilaginous fish have skeletons of flexible cartilage, or gristle, and are covered with tiny, tooth-like bumps that feel like rough sandpaper. There are more than 600 species of cartilaginous fish, including sharks and rays.

FOOD AND FEEDING

Most freshwater fish have a varied diet that may include water plants, snails, insects, larvae, worms and other fish. Most of the fish that live in seas and oceans are meat-eaters. They feed on a wide range of prey, such as shrimps, squid and other fish. However, some sea fish graze on algae or feed on plankton – tiny plants and animals floating in the water.

SHAPES AND SWIMMING

To help them move easily through the water, many fish have a streamlined shape and a tail shaped like a crescent or a fork. The fins of a fish have different uses. The tail fin pushes the fish forwards, the pectoral and pelvic fins are for steering, and the anal and dorsal fins help the fish to stay upright in the water.

Inside the body of a bony fish is a gas-filled bag called a swim bladder. This holds the fish up in the water and allows it to float, in a similar way to a lifejacket. Sharks and other cartilaginous fish lack swim bladders, and must keep moving to avoid sinking to the seabed.

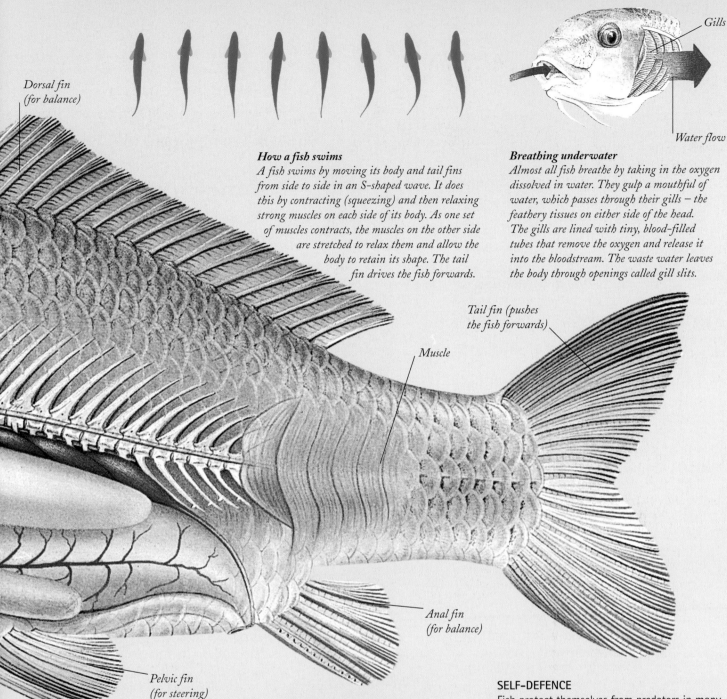

Dorsal fin
(for balance)

Gills

Water flow

How a fish swims
A fish swims by moving its body and tail fins from side to side in an S-shaped wave. It does this by contracting (squeezing) and then relaxing strong muscles on each side of its body. As one set of muscles contracts, the muscles on the other side are stretched to relax them and allow the body to retain its shape. The tail fin drives the fish forwards.

Breathing underwater
Almost all fish breathe by taking in the oxygen dissolved in water. They gulp a mouthful of water, which passes through their gills – the feathery tissues on either side of the head. The gills are lined with tiny, blood-filled tubes that remove the oxygen and release it into the bloodstream. The waste water leaves the body through openings called gill slits.

Tail fin *(pushes the fish forwards)*

Muscle

Anal fin *(for balance)*

Pelvic fin *(for steering)*

SENSES
Most fish have good senses of sight and smell, and some species possess whiskerlike feelers, known as barbels, around their mouths. Fish also have a special structure called the lateral line – a row of tiny holes running along the side of the body. Tiny hairs in these holes pick up vibrations in the water, allowing the fish to detect a predator or food before it comes into view. In addition, sharks and some types of bony fish are able to sense the minute electric currents given off by animals. This helps them to find prey in dark or muddy water.

REPRODUCTION
Some species of sharks and rays give birth to live young, but most fish hatch from eggs. The female fish usually lays enormous numbers of eggs – hundreds or many thousands – which are then fertilized by the male. Eggs laid in rivers, lakes and near to the seashore sink to the bottom, where they may be hidden among plants. In the open ocean, the eggs float in the water and are often eaten by fish and other marine animals. However, enough eggs are produced to guarantee that some will survive. Almost all newly hatched fish are independent straight away, but some African cichlids shelter their young in their mouths.

SELF-DEFENCE
Fish protect themselves from predators in many ways. Some fish live in large shoals (groups) because predators are often confused by the sheer number of bodies, and find it harder to attack. Other fish use camouflage to hide. A few fish, such as stingrays and lionfish, have poisonous spines, while flying fish can escape their enemies by shooting out of the water and gliding through the air on their winglike fins.

SEE ALSO
Deep-sea fish, Eel, Fishing, Goldfish, Lake, Migration, Ocean, Plankton, River, Salmon, Sea horse, Shark, Tropical fish, Tuna, Water

Fiord

The coasts of **Norway, Greenland** and the South Island of **New Zealand** are broken up by a series of steep-sided valleys called fiords. These are where the sea has invaded the land. Narrow strips of water wind inland along the dramatic **mountain** gorges.

Fiords were formed when the great **glaciers** of the **Ice Ages** gouged out valleys as they flowed down to the sea. When the ice melted, the sea flooded the valleys. Fiords are very deep and so make perfect shelters for large **ships**.

Fire

The ability to make and use fire is one of the great advantages people have over **animals**. Early **human beings** were frightened by fire. But in ancient times, people discovered that two **flints** struck sharply together produced a spark. Later, a flint was struck against a piece of **iron** to make a spark that could be used to light an easily burned material called tinder.

Once humans had learned to make and control fire, it became a necessary part of life. Fire provided illumination and warmth at night, cooked food and scared away animals. However, even today fires that get out of control may cause terrible damage and suffering.

Fireworks

Fireworks are devices that produce spectacular displays of **lights, colours,** smoke and noise. They were invented in **China** centuries ago, but only became known in **Europe** in the 1300s.

Fireworks are often launched into the air by **rockets**. They are made to explode by gunpowder – a black powder produced from charcoal (charred **wood**), **sulphur** and saltpetre (potassium nitrate). Fireworks' brilliant colours are given off by different combinations of burning chemicals.

Fireworks were invented by the Chinese hundreds of years ago.

Gill net

Trawl net

Purse seine net

The fishing industry uses three main types of net. Gill nets trap fish by their gills. Trawl nets have a funnel shape and are dragged along the seabed. Purse seine nets encircle fish, then are pulled shut.

Fir tree *see* Conifer

Fish *see* pages 118–119

Fishing

Fishing is one of the most important industries. Each year, about 60 million tonnes of **fish** are caught in the **oceans, rivers** and **lakes** of the world. Fish are a good source of **food** because they are rich in **protein**. They are also used as **animal** feed and as **fertilizer**, and oil from fish is used to make **soap**.

Most fishing takes place at sea, and often the catch is made far from the home port. The fish must be preserved or they will quickly spoil. In the past, fish were often dried, smoked or salted because there were no **refrigerators**. Today, fish are packed in ice or frozen. Some fishing fleets include very large factory **ships**. These take fresh fish straight from the other ships, and can package the fish while still at sea.

The best places to fish are where the sloping seabed is no more than 180 m deep. These coastal waters lie above the **continental shelf**, and are the feeding-grounds of huge numbers of fish. However, improved fishing techniques and the growing number of fishing boats mean that too many fish are now being caught. The stocks of many fish species have suffered large declines, depriving both humans and animals of a valuable food supply.

Fitzgerald, Ella

Ella Fitzgerald (1918–1997) was an American **jazz** singer whose many **recordings** are still played all over the world. She sang with lots of different jazz musicians during her long career. She became famous for the beautiful tone of her voice, and for her ability to improvize – to change her songs and add new parts while on stage.

Flag

Flags are pieces of coloured cloth, usually decorated with bold markings. They have special fastenings so that they can be flown from masts and poles. Flags are used by countries, **monarchs**, **armies** and **ships**, and by organizations such as political parties, **sports** teams and the **scouting** movement.

Flags have been used as emblems since the time of the Ancient Egyptians. Their flags were flown on long poles as battle standards, held by 'standard-bearers'. Flags showed which soldiers belonged to which ruler or general.

Today, national flags are flown as a symbol of a country's **history**, its power and its importance. Flags are also used for signalling. Since 1857, ships at sea have used an international code for flag signals. For example, a yellow flag means that a ship is in quarantine because of illness on board. Other well-known signals are a white flag – a sign of truce during war – and a flag raised only to half-mast – a sign that people are mourning someone's death.

Flame

When something is heated enough to make it burn, it will also often burst into flames. These flames are **gases** that are given off during burning. Bright flames that give off plenty of **light**, such as those of candles, **wood** or **coal**, have tiny **carbon** particles in them that glow brightly. Flames are not all equally hot. Wood fires burn at about 1,000°C. The flames of acetylene **welding** torches are about 3,000°C.

Flamingo

Flamingoes are large water **birds** that live on shallow **lakes** in the warmer parts of the world. The bright colour of their **feathers** ranges from pale to deep pink. Flamingoes wade through the shallows on their stiltlike legs in

A **flamingo**'s body is not much larger than that of a goose, but its long legs and neck can make it up to 1.8 m tall. The bright pink colour of its plumage comes from its food and from minerals dissolved in the water.

This greatly magnified image of a **flea**'s body shows the large abdomen where blood is stored.

Pointed **flint** tools such as these were used by early cave-dwelling humans about 50,000 years ago.

search of tiny **plants** and **animals** to eat. When feeding, they tuck their heads right under the water's surface and use their broad, hooked beaks like sieves to filter **food** from the water and mud.

Flamingoes nest together in huge gatherings called colonies. The largest colonies have many thousands of birds.

Flea

Fleas are tiny, wingless **insects** less than 3 mm long. They live on the bodies of **birds** and **mammals**, including **human beings**. Fleas are **parasites**, and feed on their hosts by biting through the skin and sucking the **blood**. Fleas carry germs and other **bacteria** from one host to another. **Rat** fleas, for example, used to pass bubonic **plague** to people.

Fleming, Alexander

Alexander Fleming (1881–1955) was a British doctor who discovered the **antibiotic** called penicillin. It is one of the most important **drugs** known. Penicillin fights infections caused by many kinds of **bacteria**. Although the drug fights the infection, it does not usually harm the body. Penicillin has saved millions of lives.

Fleming discovered penicillin by accident in 1928, when he noticed an unknown kind of mould (see **fungus**) growing in his laboratory. For his work, Fleming was awarded the 1945 **Nobel Prize** for **medicine**.

Flint

Flint is a **mineral** that is a form of **quartz**. It is found in layers of **chalk** and limestone. A lump of flint is dull white on the outside and shiny grey to black on the inside. Flint is very hard, but it can be chipped into sharp-edged flakes. **Stone Age** people made tools and weapons out of flint. Because flint gives off a spark when struck against **iron**, it can be used for starting a **fire**.

Flood

There are two main kinds of flood – those caused by **rivers** overflowing their banks, and **ocean** floods caused by high **tides** and strong **winds** blowing from the ocean towards the land. Rivers usually flood in the spring when spring rains add to the water produced by melting snow and ice. The water level in the rivers rises so much that they burst their banks.

Throughout **history**, three great rivers have flooded regularly – the **Nile** in Egypt, the **Mississippi** in the USA, and the Huang Ho or Yellow River in China. Two huge **dams** were built across the Nile at Aswan to produce **hydroelectric power** for generating **electricity**. Before the Aswan dams controlled the waters of the Nile, the annual floods created a zone of fertile land in the middle of a sandy **desert**.

The best-known flood story is that in the Book of Genesis in the **Bible**. The event on which this Old Testament story is based may have taken place in about 3000 BCE, when the Euphrates River flooded a vast area of southern Mesopotamia (present-day Iraq).

Flower

There are more than 250,000 different species of flowering **plant**, ranging from small, ground-hugging plants to spectacular **orchids**, spine-covered **cacti** and giant, long-lived **trees**. The flowers that these plants produce come

△ **Flowers** are the part of a flowering plant that is involved in reproduction. They make seeds that will form a new generation of the same type of plant.

▽ Much of Bangladesh lies in a **flood** zone. The floods create fertile land where farmers can reap two or three harvests a year. But unexpected floods may destroy crops.

in a dazzling array of colours, sizes and shapes. Some flowers grow singly, while others grow in tight clusters. Many flowers have bright colours, a strong scent and produce a sweet nectar, but some are drab and unscented by comparison.

Whatever they look like, flowers all have the same part to play in the life of the plant. Flowers help plants to reproduce themselves (see **reproduction**). Inside each flower there are male parts called stamens, which are made up of anthers and filaments, and female parts called pistils, which are made up of stigmas, styles and ovaries. The stamens contain hundreds of powdery grains of pollen, which fertilize the pistils. Fertilization occurs when pollen grains are transferred from the stamens of one plant to the pistils of another plant of the same variety. Once this has happened, **fruits** begin to form and grow. The fruits contain the **seeds** that will eventually grow into a new generation of plants.

The flowers that we grow in our gardens and use to decorate our homes are all descended from wild flowers. But cultivated flowers such as roses, lilies and orchids often look different to their wild relatives – over many years, they have been specially bred to improve their appearance and scent and to make them easier to grow.

Fly

Flies are one of the largest groups of **insects** in the world. They have two pairs of wings – one pair for flying and a smaller set behind the main pair to help them maintain balance in the **air**. Most flies do not live long. In warm weather, the life cycle of a housefly – from **egg** to maggot to adult – may be complete in just one week.

Some flies feed on decaying matter, while others bite **animals** to feed on their **blood**. Horseflies often attack

Flower
Flower stalk
Flower bud
Leaf
Stem

horses and cattle in big swarms. Blowflies lay their eggs in open wounds on the skin of animals. The maggots that hatch from the eggs eat into the animals' flesh and cause great harm. Houseflies lay their eggs in piles of rotting matter.

Some types of fly are dangerous to humans because they spread **diseases** such as cholera and dysentery. Tsetse flies, which live in the tropics, spread sleeping sickness, a serious disease that causes sleepiness and high fever. Even ordinary houseflies can pose a health risk to humans because they pick up harmful **bacteria** from manure and rotting food, and carry them into our homes, where they leave the germs on our fresh food.

A **fly** has a pair of huge compound eyes, each of which is made up of many thousands of microscopic six-sided lenses.

Food

Food is any substance that is a source of nutrition to a living thing. Without food, nothing can live. Humans need food for a variety of reasons. It gives us the **energy** to move about and stay warm, and keeps our bodies healthy. The three main kinds of human food are **proteins**, **fats** and carbohydrates. We also need certain **minerals** and **vitamins**. A 'balanced diet' – one that includes all of these things – is necessary for good **health**.

Today, we eat a huge variety of different foods, which may be skilfully prepared, decorated and cooked before being eaten. An increasing proportion of our food is prepared in factories. It may be bottled, canned, frozen or dried before it is sold to us.

Food chain

When you eat **fish** from the sea, such as **tuna**, you are taking part in a food chain that began somewhere in the **ocean**. There, tiny floating **plants** and **animals** called **plankton** were eaten by tiny fish. The tiny fish were eaten by

In this **food chain**, grass makes its own food using energy from the sun. The grass is eaten by rabbits, which in turn provide food for a red fox.

larger fish, and these fish were in turn eaten by even larger fish such as the tuna.

Every living thing has its place in a food chain, and most belong to several different food chains. A food chain begins with green plants, which manufacture their own food from **water**, chemicals in the **soil** and **air**, and sunlight. This process is called photosynthesis. Unlike plants, animals cannot make their own food. Instead, some of them eat plants, and the rest eat other animals. When animals or plants die, **bacteria** that live in the soil break down the animal or plant tissues. The chemicals that make up the animals or plants are released into the soil. These chemicals act as **fertilizers** to enrich the soil and help the green plants to grow. And so the food chain begins all over again.

Football *see* Sport

Ford, Henry

Henry Ford (1863–1947) was a pioneer **car** manufacturer in the **USA**. In 1903, he founded the Ford Motor Company, which is today one of the world's largest **companies**. Henry Ford was the first to use assembly lines on which the cars were put together from standard parts. Conveyor belts brought the parts to the workers, who each performed a particular task. By building his cars in this way, Ford was able to produce hundreds a day, and they were cheap enough for ordinary people to buy. Henry Ford's biggest success was the Model T, launched in 1908.

Henry **Ford**'s Model T was the first mass-produced car in the world. More than 15 million Model Ts were sold between 1908 and 1927.

Forest

A forest is a large area of land covered mainly with **trees** and other **plants**. It is one of the world's most important **habitats**, and forests occupy almost 30 percent of the **earth**'s land area.

1 Ammonite dies and falls to seabed

2 Soft parts of body rot away

3 Empty shell is covered with sand and mud

4 Over millions of years, shell is compressed and turned to stone

5 Forces of erosion break up the ground, and bring fossil up to surface

6 Fossil hunter cracks open stone to reveal fossil

△ This diagram shows how the **fossil** of an ammonite – a type of mollusc that lived in the sea 150 million years ago – was formed.

▽ **Forests** once covered twice as much of the earth's land as they do today. Huge areas of forest have been felled to provide timber, or to make way for fields, roads and towns. However, it is important to control the rate at which forests are cut down because they provide us with firewood, building materials, natural foods and many other useful products.

There are three basic types of forest. Tropical **rainforests** are found near the **equator**, where the **climate** is hot and wet. In these conditions, many kinds of trees and plants grow very quickly. Coniferous forests are found mainly in the cold, northern areas of **Canada**, **Europe** and **Asia**. These forests are made up largely of **conifers**, such as spruce, fir, larch or pine, which do not shed their leaves in winter.

The third type of forest is known as broad-leaved, or deciduous, forest. Broad-leaved trees drop their leaves in winter, and include species such as oak, beech, birch and willow. Broad-leaved forests are found in the temperate regions of the world, which have mild winters, warm summers and rain all year round. The **United States**, Europe and the cooler parts of **Africa** all have large broad-leaved forests.

Forests grow in layers. At ground level **fungi**, **mosses**, **ferns** and wild **flowers** grow in the forest **soil**. Then comes a layer of larger bushes and shrubs. Above this is a layer of smaller trees. Finally, the tops of the tallest trees form a layer called the forest canopy.

Fossil

Fossils are the hardened remains or impressions of **animals** and **plants** that lived millions of years ago. A fossil may be a shell, **bone**, tooth, **leaf** or **skeleton**, or even sometimes an entire animal.

Most fossils have been found in areas that were once in or near the sea. When a plant or creature dies its body sinks to the seabed. The soft parts rot away, but the hard skeleton becomes buried in the mud. Over millions of years, more and more mud settles on top of the skeleton. Eventually, these layers of mud harden into **rock**, and the skeleton becomes part of that rock. **Water** seeps through the rock, slowly dissolving the original skeleton. It is replaced by stony **minerals** which form exactly the same shape – creating a fossil.

Fossils lie buried until movements in the **earth**'s crust push up the seabed and it becomes dry land. In time, water, ice and **wind** wear away the rock and the fossil is exposed. The oldest known fossil is over three billion years old.

Fox

Foxes are **mammals** and belong to the same family as domestic **dogs**. They are active, fast-moving hunters that have superb senses of **smell**, **sight** and **hearing** for catching their prey. The commonest species is the red fox, which is found in **Europe**, North **Africa**, **North America** and parts of **Asia**. It hunts small **birds**, **insects**, and **rodents** up to the size of **rabbits**. The red fox live in holes in the ground called 'earths',

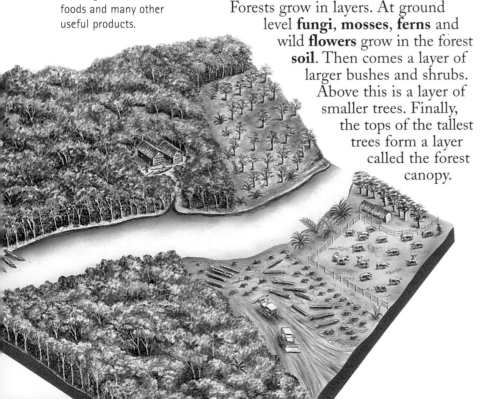

which it either digs itself or takes over from rabbits or **badgers**. Recently, more and more red foxes have been found in cities. They live under the floors of buildings or in any hidden place they can find, and eat scraps from dustbins. Other species of fox include the grey fox of North America, and the bat-eared fox, which lives in the open **desert** country of Africa.

Fraction

If you cut a cake into equal parts, each part is a fraction of the whole cake. Each half can be written as a number – $\frac{1}{2}$. If the cake is cut into four, each quarter is written $\frac{1}{4}$. The number above the dividing line in a fraction is called the numerator. The number below is called the denominator.

France

France is the largest country in western **Europe**. In ancient times, France was inhabited by **Celts**, but Julius **Caesar** conquered it and for 500 years it was part of the **Roman Empire**. The Franks, from whom the country got its present name, invaded in the 400s CE.

Throughout much of the **Middle Ages**, France was divided into many small parts, which often had their own rulers. However, the French kings gradually became more powerful, and united the different territories into a single country. The city of **Paris**, on the Seine River in the northern half of France, became the country's capital.

France has a temperate **climate** and a very varied landscape. Farmland covers about half of the country, and much of the population is employed in **farming**, **fishing** and forestry. France produces a large amount of grain, **vegetables** and **fruit**, and it is famous for its **wines**.

For centuries, the French and English were enemies and fought many wars. The rival nations were at war, almost without a break, from 1337 to 1453.

The kit **fox** lives in North American deserts and spends the daytime in a deep burrow where the air is quite cool. It comes out at night to hunt for insects, rodents and other small animals.

This period is known as the **Hundred Years' War**. In 1789, France was shaken by a violent uprising called the **French Revolution**. During the Revolution, which lasted for several years, the French people overthrew their monarchy and turned France into a **republic**.

After the Revolution, a general called **Napoleon** came to power in France, and made himself emperor. He went to war and conquered most of Europe before he was finally defeated at the Battle of Waterloo in Belgium in 1815. Later, France became a republic again. During the two **World Wars**, France was a battleground for Allied armies and the invading German forces. It was one of the first members of the **European Union**, and today is among Europe's wealthiest states.

FRANCE
Government: Republic
Capital: Paris
Area: 547,026 sq km
Population: 58.6 million
Language: French
Currency: Euro

Francis of Assisi

Francis of Assisi (1182–1226) was named after the town in central **Italy** where he was born. After recovering from a severe illness at the age of 22, Francis decided to become a priest. He gathered around him a band of monks,

Francis of Assisi lived in poverty and devoted his life to the service of God. He was fond of birds and animals whom he called his brothers and sisters.

△ Anne **Frank**'s diary describes the hardships Jewish people faced in the 1930s under the German Nazis. The Nazis inflicted appalling suffering on Jewish people, and forced them to wear a yellow star to show they were Jews.

▽ During the **French Revolution**, the working-class people of Paris built barricades across the city's streets, from which to defy troops and police.

who became known as the Franciscans. The monks spent their lives preaching, and caring for the poor and the sick. Francis himself spent his final years in private prayer, and in 1228, two years after his death, he was made a saint.

Frank, Anne

Anne Frank (1925–1945) was a young Jewish girl who kept a secret diary while hiding from the German Nazis during **World War II**. In 1933, Anne's family fled from **Germany**, where the Nazis were persecuting **Jews** and other groups in society. The Frank family sought refuge in Amsterdam in the **Netherlands**. But in 1940, Germany invaded the Netherlands, and in 1942 the Franks decided to go into hiding. For 25 months, the whole family lived inside a cramped attic above a shop.

Anne's diary is a powerful and moving account of the difficulties her family faced while in hiding. It records what it was like to be a Jew during World War II. In 1944, the Franks' attic was discovered. Anne, her sister and her mother were taken away by the Nazis, and died in a concentration camp.

Franklin, Benjamin

Benjamin Franklin (1706–1790) was an American politician and scientist. He was born in Boston, **USA**, the youngest of 17 children.

Franklin became a printer and then went on to publish a yearly almanac which made him his fortune. Later, he became involved in America's **Revolutionary War**, which brought the USA freedom from British rule. Franklin was one of the politicians who signed America's Declaration of Independence, and he helped draw up the peace treaty at the end of the war.

Franklin's scientific inventions include bifocal spectacles, and the **lightning** conductor − a rod that protects buildings from lightning. By flying a kite during a thunderstorm, Franklin proved that lightning was a form of **electricity**.

French Revolution

The French Revolution, which erupted on 14 July 1789, was one of the most important **revolutions** in **history**. It led to enormous changes in the political, religious and cultural life of **France**, and its effects were felt in many other countries around the world as well.

In the France of 1789, the king and nobles were seen as people who spent vast sums of money on luxuries. They built themselves lavish palaces and mansions, while many people starved in misery. Involvement in wars, such as the American **Revolutionary War**, had drained the treasury, so the people had to pay even higher **taxes**. At the same time, food prices had doubled after the harvest had failed. More and more of the French people, including farmers, shopkeepers, townspeople, merchants and even some nobles, wanted major changes to be made.

There was no **parliament** to stop the king from treating his subjects badly, and eventually, in 1789, the French people's anger exploded into revolution. Food riots broke out, and mob violence spread. The king, **Louis XVI**, tried to flee the country, but was arrested and later beheaded. In the 'Reign of Terror' that followed, nearly 20,000 people were executed as enemies of the Revolution.

A new **government** was established in 1790 which tried to introduce the ideas of the Revolution. But the new leaders quarrelled among themselves. In 1799, the government was overthrown by a French general called **Napoleon**.

Freud, Sigmund

Sigmund Freud (1856–1939) was an Austrian doctor who made a great contribution to our understanding of the human mind. Freud was awarded a degree in **medicine** in 1881, and began to study mental illness. He taught that the 'subconscious' – the thoughts and memories we are not aware of – held the key to a person's mental state. To 'open up' the subconscious, Freud developed a special system called psychoanalysis – a kind of medical examination of the mind.

Friction

When two things rub together, it causes friction. Friction makes it hard to move something across a surface. Smooth objects cause much less friction than rough objects, so when things need to go fast it helps to reduce friction. This is why the **wheels** of a train and the rails of the track are very smooth. When we want things to slow down, we add friction – for example, by applying the brakes in our **cars**.

If two things rub together at great speed, the friction produces **heat**. If you rub your hand fast against your leg you can feel the heat generated by the friction. Without friction, the world would be a strange place. We could not walk because our shoes would not grip the ground, and cars would stand still no matter how fast their wheels turned.

Frog and Toad

Frogs and toads are a large group of **amphibians**. This means that they can live both on land and in **water**. They breathe through their **skin** as well as their **lungs**. Like all amphibians, frogs and toads have a complex life history. In spring, the adults lay mounds of jelly-like **eggs**, or spawn, in a pond or some other damp place. The eggs hatch into larvae, known as tadpoles, which gradually develop legs and turn into miniature versions of their parents.

Fruit

Fruits are the ripe **seed** cases of any flowering **plant**. The fruits protect the seeds as they develop and help spread them when they are ripe. Some fruits scatter their seeds on the **wind**. Others are eaten by **birds** and **animals**, which then spread the seeds.

Arrow-poison frog

Midwife toad

△ Frogs and toads are found all over the world. There are about 2,500 different species.

▽ Fruits spread their seeds in many different ways. This squirting cucumber shoots out its seeds in a jet of liquid, which is produced by water pressure building up inside the fruit.

Seed

Squirting cucumber

127

△ A **fuse** (left) is fitted inside ordinary household plugs. Too large a current will cause the wire inside the fuse to melt, thus breaking the circuit (right).

▽ A **fungus** is neither a plant nor an animal, but belongs to a separate kingdom of living things – the fungi. There are more than 100,000 different species of fungi, including mushrooms, toadstools, moulds and yeasts. The toadstool shown below is called fly agaric.

To most of us 'fruit' means juicy **foods** such as apples, pears, oranges and bananas. These fruits are important in our diet. They give us **mineral** salts, **sugar** and **vitamins**. The water, skins and seeds of fruit help our **digestion**.

Fuel

Fuels are substances that give off **heat** when they burn. They provide us with the **energy** we use for cooking food, heating buildings, powering **aircraft**, **cars** and **machines**, and producing **electricity**. The most important fuels are **oil**, **coal** and **natural gas**, which are called the **fossil** fuels because they were formed underground from the remains of prehistoric **plants** and **animals**.

Some fuels give out more heat than others. A kilogram of coal gives nearly three times as much heat as a kilogram of wood. Oil gives nearly four times as much, and **hydrogen** gas about ten times as much. The radioactive element **uranium** can give over 500,000 times as much heat as hydrogen.

As the earth's supplies of fossil fuels are used up we will have to make more use of **nuclear energy**, **solar energy**, and **wind** and **hydroelectric power**.

Fuel cell

A fuel cell is a special kind of electric **battery** that keeps on making **electricity** as long as **fuel** is fed into it. The main use for fuel cells is in **space exploration**. Fuel cells supplied the electricity in the various Apollo spacecraft that flew to the **moon** in 1969–1972. These cells used **oxygen** and **hydrogen** as fuel, which combined together to produce electricity and **water**. The water was not wasted – the Apollo astronauts drank it.

Fungus

A fungus is a simple, plantlike organism with no roots, stems or leaves. Fungi also lack the chemical chlorophyll that allows green **plants** to make their food through the process of photosynthesis. So fungi have to find a ready-made supply of food. Some feed as **parasites** on living plants or **animals**. Others feed on animal and plant remains.

There are more than 50,000 species of fungus. Some have only a single **cell**, while other fungi are made up of chains of cells. These produce tiny, threadlike growths that spread through the substance on which the fungus feeds.

Many types of fungus grow a large fruiting body that sheds tiny particles called spores. New fungus plants grow from the spores. **Mushrooms** are the fruiting bodies of fungi that are hidden underground. The fungus family also includes moulds. Uncovered food is a perfect place for moulds to grow.

Fuse

A fuse is a safety device in an electric circuit. It contains fuse **wire**, which is made so that it will melt at a low **temperature**. If too much **electricity** flows through the circuit, the wire 'fuses', or melts, breaking the circuit.

In this way, an electric fuse stops the wire in the circuit from becoming too hot and possibly setting fire to nearby objects. Electric current must pass through fuse wire to get from the outside power line to the electric wiring in a house. Inside the house, each electric plug also has a fuse.

G

Vostok I

Galaxy

Someone once called galaxies 'star islands' in space. A galaxy is made up of a huge group of **stars**. Our **sun** is just one star of about 100,000 million stars that belong to the **Milky Way** galaxy. A beam of **light** would take about 100,000 years to shine from one side of the Milky Way to the other. Yet the Milky Way is only a medium-sized galaxy.

There may be as many as 10,000 million more galaxies beyond the Milky Way. The nearest large galaxy is called Andromeda. The light from this galaxy takes more than two million years to reach us.

Some galaxies have no particular shape. Others have spiral arms made up of many millions of stars. The Milky Way and Andromeda galaxies both look like this. There are also galaxies that look like saucers or balls. Edge on, a spiral galaxy looks like a flat disc with a swollen middle – the nucleus. From above, it looks like a whirlpool of stars.

Astronomy has shown that **radio** waves are sent out from many galaxies. Strong radio waves also come from strange starlike objects known as **quasars**, which are very powerful **energy** sources. Some people think that a quasar may be the beginning of a new galaxy. Scientists think that galaxies may form where **gravity** pulls huge clouds of **gas** together.

Gagarin, Yuri

Yuri Gagarin (1934–1968) was the first human being to travel into space. The Soviet cosmonaut rocketed upwards in *Vostok I* on 12 April 1961. He circled the **earth** once in 108 minutes and landed by parachute within 10 km of the planned spot. After his famous flight, Gagarin continued to train as a cosmonaut, but he was killed in a plane crash in March 1968.

▽ The Milky Way **galaxy** belongs to the Local Group – a collection of about 30 galaxies.

Galileo

Galileo Galilei (1564–1642) was an Italian **mathematics** teacher and one of the first true scientists. One of his experiments showed that a **pendulum** took the same time to make a long swing as it did to make a short one. He also learned that light objects fall as fast as heavy ones. He built a **telescope**, and became the first person to use this tool for studying the **moon** and **planets**. What Galileo saw made him believe **Copernicus**' idea that the **earth** was not the centre of the **universe**. Later, scientists such as Isaac **Newton** built on Galileo's theories.

△ With his telescope, Galileo saw that the moon was not smooth, but was covered with craters.

Galleon

This kind of heavy, wooden sailing **ship** was used for carrying fighting men and cargoes over **oceans** in the 1500s. A galleon was four times as long as it was wide. It had a special deck to carry cannons. There were square sails on its two front masts and three-cornered lateen sails on its one or two rear masts. Lateen sails helped galleons to sail against the **wind**.

△ Galleons were faster and easier to manage than some other ships.

Gama, Vasco da

Vasco da Gama (c. 1469–1524), a Portuguese navigator, discovered how to sail from **Europe** to the **spice**-rich lands of **India** by way of southern **Africa**. He left Lisbon with four **ships** in July 1497 and reached Calicut, southern India, in May 1498. On the journey home, 30 of the 90 crewmen died of scurvy (a **disease** caused by a lack of **vitamin** C), and only two of the four ships reached Lisbon.

Gambia

Gambia is mainland **Africa**'s smallest country. It is on the west coast, and is about half the size of **Wales**. Most Gambians earn their living by **farming**,

GAMBIA
Government: Republic
Capital: Banjul
Area: 11,295 sq km
Population: 1.3 million
Languages: English, Mandinka and Wolof
Currency: Dalasi

with peanuts as the main crop. Once a British colony, Gambia became an independent **republic** in 1965.

Gandhi, Indira

Indira Gandhi (1917–1984) was prime minister of **India** from 1966 until 1977 and from 1980 until her death. Her father, Jawaharlal Nehru (1889–1964), became India's first prime minister after independence. For years she helped her father, then went into politics herself. When in power, Mrs Gandhi fought for economic progress, social reforms and national unity. In 1984, she was killed by two Sikhs, members of a religious group (see **Sikhism**). Her son Rajiv succeeded her as prime minister, but was assassinated in 1991.

Gandhi, Mahatma

Mohandas Karamchand Gandhi (1869–1948) is sometimes called the 'father of modern India'. This frail-looking Hindu lawyer helped to free **India** from British rule by disobeying British laws peacefully. In 1920, he told Indians to spin cloth for their own clothes instead of buying it from Britain.

People admired Gandhi's beliefs, his kindness and his simple way of life. He was called the Mahatma, meaning 'Great Soul'. In 1947, Britain gave India independence. Soon after, one of his fellow Hindus shot Gandhi for preaching peace between Hindus (see **Hinduism**) and Muslims (see **Islam**).

Ganges River

The Ganges is the greatest **river** in **India**. It flows for about 2,500 km and drains an area three times the size of Spain. The river rises in the **Himalayas** and flows southeast through India and **Bangladesh** to the Bay of Bengal. Rich farmlands and great cities line its banks. Hindus believe the river is sacred.

Garden

Gardens are pieces of land kept especially for growing lawns, **flowers**, **fruits**, **vegetables**, or attractive shrubs and **trees**. There were gardens in Egypt 4,500 years ago. Later, **Babylon** was famous for its hanging gardens. **Renaissance** Italy had gardens with fountains, pools, terraces and steps.

In the 1700s, European landscape gardeners placed natural-looking lawns and trees around large houses. In the 1800s, gardens were laid out in cities where anyone might walk. Today, many houses have some sort of garden.

△ Wealthy Romans had grand villas in the country, with **gardens** laid out in patterns. They also grew olives, and kept sheep and goats for food and milk.

Garibaldi, Giuseppe

Giuseppe Garibaldi (1807–1882) was an Italian patriot who helped turn **Italy** from a collection of small states into a united and independent country. After two periods of exile in the **United States**,

△ Giuseppe **Garibaldi**, one of Italy's greatest heroes, fought against foreign rule in Italy during the 1800s.

Garibaldi led his followers, the Redshirts, against the Austrians, who then controlled Italy. In 1860, he gained control of Sicily and southern Italy, then he invaded the mainland and captured the important city of Naples. This victory helped make possible the uniting of Italy under King Victor Emmanuel (1820–1878).

Gas

Gases are substances with no shape or size. A gas takes up the size and shape of any container that holds it. This can happen because gases are made of **atoms** moving freely in space. When a gas becomes cold enough, it turns into a **liquid**. Liquids have a fixed size but no fixed shape. If that liquid becomes much colder still, it turns into a solid. Solids have a fixed shape and size.

The gas we use to cook with and heat our homes is called **natural gas**. This gas is found underground in many parts of the world.

▽ Mahatma **Gandhi** led India to independence from Britain in 1947.

Polished emerald gem

Rough emerald gem

Emerald gem in rock

△ An emerald is a type of **gem**. Gems found in rocks look quite dull in their natural state. Experts cut them out of the rock, and shape and polish them.

▽ Most cars have four or five forward **gears** and one reverse gear. A car's gearbox is the link between the engine and the car's wheels.

Oil and natural gas collect in porous **rocks** (rocks that allow liquids to soak through). They are trapped between impervious rocks (rocks that will not allow liquids to pass through).

Gear

A gear is a **wheel**, or cog, with teeth along its rim. These teeth can fit into the teeth of other gears. **Metal** rods, or axles, are fitted into the centre of each gear. If one axle is turned, the gear attached to it turns. This makes the second gear and its axle turn too.

Gears are used to increase or decrease the speed at which wheels turn. They are also used to increase or decrease the turning power of wheels.

Gear wheels turn at different speeds in proportion to the number of teeth they possess. If a small gear wheel fits into a large gear wheel with twice as many teeth, the big wheel will turn at only half the small wheel's speed, but will have twice the turning power of the small wheel. When a **car** is in low gear, this is what happens. The car goes slowly, but it has plenty of power.

Gem

Some **rocks** contain hard crystals that can be cut to show clear, brilliant colours. These gems are often used

in making **jewellery**. **Diamonds** are among the rarest, finest gems but blue sapphires, green emeralds and red rubies are also much sought after. Pearls are gems produced by **oysters**. Artificial gems are made from **glass** and **plastic**.

Generator

Generators produce electric current. Huge generators in **power stations** provide **electricity** for homes and factories. The largest generators can light 20 million 100-watt electric lamps. But there are tiny generators too. A **bicycle** dynamo is a generator that you can hold in one hand.

If a loop of **wire** is turned between the ends of a horseshoe-shaped magnet (see **magnetism**), an electric current flows in the wire. Generators work by changing the **energy** of motion into electrical energy. The energy to work a generator's moving parts can come from **wind**, flowing **water**, or steam produced by **heat** from **fuels** such as **oil** or **coal**. Large generators have thousands of coils of wire which are made to turn very quickly between powerful magnets.

Genetics

Each **animal** or **plant** passes on certain characteristics to its offspring. For example, we say that someone has 'his father's eyes' or 'her mother's hair'. The **science** of genetics explains why living things look and behave as they do.

Heredity works in an amazing way. Each individual produces sex **cells**. If a male and a female cell join, the female cell grows into an individual. Inside every cell there are tiny chromosomes, largely made of a chemical called DNA (deoxyribonucleic acid).

Gear cog

Gear stick

Flywheel (inside the car wheel)

Axle

Different parts of each chromosome, called genes, are arranged on the DNA. Genes carry coded messages that contain the information needed to make a new plant or animal look and behave as it does. They determine its sex and the characteristics it inherits from its parents.

Scientists are now able to isolate different genes within DNA. This means that they have the potential to modify or change DNA, for example by taking out genes that cause hereditary **diseases**. However, many people worry that in the future scientists may misuse genetic modification by creating individuals to a specific design.

Genghis Khan

Genghis Khan (1167–1227) was a **Mongol** chief who cruelly attacked many Asian peoples and established a mighty empire. His real name was Temujin, meaning 'iron-smith'.

At only 13 years old, he took his dead father's place as chief of a small Mongol tribe of **nomads**. He soon won power over nearby tribes as well. In 1206, he became known as Genghis Khan, meaning 'Very Mighty King'. Genghis Khan formed a huge army of tough, hard-riding nomads on the great grasslands of Central **Asia**. Then he set off to conquer the lands around him. His troops pushed southeast to **Beijing** in **China**, and south into **Tibet** and what are now **Pakistan** and **Afghanistan**. In the southwest, they invaded Persia (modern **Iran**) and southern **Russia**.

After Genghis Khan died, other Mongol rulers won more land and made the empire even larger.

Geography

Geography is the study of the **earth**'s surface. Geographers examine everything on the earth – the land, sea, **air**, **plants**, **animals** and people. They explain where things are found, how they got there and how they affect one another.

There are many different areas, or branches, of geography. For instance, physical geography studies things such as **mountains**, valleys, **lakes** and **rivers**. Meteorology studies the **weather**. Economic geography deals with **farming**, **mining**, manufacturing and **trade**. Human geography divides the peoples of the world into cultures.

Geology

Geology is the study of the **earth** itself. Geologists are scientists who discover what things the earth is made of,

△ **Genghis Khan** put together a huge, organized army. Each warrior had five ponies, ridden in turn so that they would not get tired. When the Mongols besieged a city, most of the inhabitants were killed and the surrounding land was laid waste.

▽ Inside each cell are strands of DNA, which contain a sequence of genes (see **genetics**) that make up an individual's characteristics.

Cell

Genes are contained within the centre, or nucleus, of a cell.

Chromosomes contain strands of DNA. There are 23 pairs of chromosomes in each human cell.

Genes are arranged on a corkscrew-shaped chemical called DNA, found within each chromosome.

GERMANY

Government: Federal
republic
Capital: Berlin
Area: 356,755 sq km
Population: 82.1 million
Language: German
Currency: Euro

▽ **Geology** helps us to
understand the structure
of the earth. To do this,
geologists study rocks,
which also give clues to
the history of the earth.

where they are found, and how they
got there. They also study the different
chemicals in **rocks** and **minerals**.
They try to find out how rocks are
formed, and how they are changed by
movements beneath the surface of the
earth. **Volcanoes** and **earthquakes**
give useful clues about movements
deep down underground.

Geologists study the history of
the earth. They have found rocks
3,800 million years old, and **fossils**
showing that **evolution** began over
3,400 million years ago. We now
know that the earth was formed
about 4,550 million years ago.

Geologists also help engineers choose
where to build a **road** or **tunnel** (see
engineering). They help miners to find
coal, **oil** or **natural gas** underground
(see **mining**), and they told us what
the **moon** is made of by studying rocks
brought back by astronauts.

Geometry

Geometry is a branch of **mathematics**.
It can help establish the shape, size
and position of an object, or how much
a container holds. People draw lines
and measure **angles** to help them solve
geometric problems.

Germ *see* Bacteria, Virus

Germany

Until the late 1800s, Germany was a
country of separate states and cities,
each with its own ruler. They were
united by Otto von Bismarck
(1815–1898), the prime
minister of Prussia, one
of the most powerful
of these states. The
united Germany
became a great
nation, but after
World War II, the
area was divided into two

countries – West Germany and
East Germany. East Germany was
a communist country, closely allied to
the **Soviet Union**. The two Germanys
remained separate until 1990, when
they were finally reunited under a
federal **government**.

Germany lies in the middle of
Europe and has the largest **population**
of any western European nation.
Farms and cities stand on a low, flat
plain to the north, while the south is
a region of wooded **mountains**. In the
far south, the tall peaks of the **Alps**
rise thousands of metres above sea
level. Germany's major **rivers** are
the Rhine, the Elbe and the Oder.
They flow north towards the North
Sea and the Baltic Sea.

Before reunification, West Germany
was the richest nation in Europe. Its
mines and factories produced more
coal, **steel**, **cars** and **television** sets than
any other western European nation.
East Germany, less than half the size
of West Germany, had mines and
factories too, but much of its industry
was old-fashioned and unproductive.

Once the rich West and the poorer
East were united, there were problems
to be faced. In East Germany, prices
rose and many people lost their jobs
as inefficient businesses closed. **Taxes**
were raised to pay for the costs of
unification. However, Germany is
still a very prosperous nation and the
German people are working together
to overcome any remaining difficulties.

Geyser

Geysers are hot springs that now
and then squirt out steam and scalding
water. Water fills a deep crack in the
ground, often near a **volcano**; hot rock
heats the water deep underground,
but the weight of the water above it
stops the hot water from boiling until
it is much hotter still. Then it turns to
steam that forces the water upwards,
emptying the crack. The next eruption

happens when the crack is full again. There are many geysers in parts of **Iceland**, the **USA** and **New Zealand**.

Ghana

Ghana is a nation in West **Africa**. The country is hot, with plenty of rain in the south where Ghana meets the **Atlantic Ocean**. The land here is low, with tropical **forests** and farms. The north is drier, with grasslands. Most of Ghana's people are farmers, and grow crops such as cocoa. Another major occupation is mining **diamonds** and **gold**. **Lake** Volta provides **hydroelectric** **power** to make **electricity** for the whole of Ghana. This enormous man-made lake covers a greater area than any other artificial lake in the world.

Gibraltar

This small British colony, won from **Spain** in 1704, is a rocky peninsula that juts out from the tip of southern Spain. Most of Gibraltar is a **mountain** called the Rock. Gibraltar guards the western end of the **Mediterranean Sea**. It has an important port and British naval base.

△ The tallest **geyser** ever known was the Waimangu geyser in New Zealand. In 1904, this squirted steam and water nearly 460 m into the sky.

△ An adult male **giraffe** may stand as tall as 5 m. Giraffes have several different coat patterns, which vary from place to place.

Giraffe

Giraffes are the tallest **animals**. They have long legs and a long neck. Yet this neck has only seven **bones**, the same as any other **mammal**. Giraffes live in the hot grasslands of **Africa**.

A giraffe's long neck and legs enable it to eat the leaves from branches that are far above the reach of other browsing animals (see **evolution**).

Glacier

Glaciers are rivers of ice. Most form high up in **mountains** where snow falls and never melts. As snow piles up, the lower layers are crushed and turn to ice. This begins to flow very slowly downhill through valleys. Most glaciers take a year to flow as far as

GHANA
Government: Republic
Capital: Accra
Area: 238,537 sq km
Population: 18.7 million
Languages: English (official) and various African languages
Currency: Cedi

you can walk in five minutes. The **rocks** they carry grind against the sides and floor of each valley until they make it deep and wide. Glaciers gradually melt when the **climate** warms up. During the **Ice Ages**, glaciers spread worldwide. Many valleys in the **Alps** and **Rocky Mountains** once held glaciers.

Gladiator

Gladiators were men trained to fight to the death in shows to entertain crowds in Ancient Rome (see **Roman Empire**). Many gladiators were criminals, prisoners of war or slaves. Some fought with a sword and shield. Others had a three-pronged spear and a net. Most fights ended when one gladiator killed the other.

Gland

Glands are organs that produce substances needed by the body. There are two kinds – endocrine and exocrine glands. Endocrine glands send their substances, called **hormones**, directly

△ Successful **gladiators** became famous in Rome. They were well-fed and received medical care, and could eventually earn their freedom.

Hair

Oil gland

Sweat gland

△ Sweat **glands**, deep in the skin, produce watery sweat. Skin also contains oil glands that make oils to keep skin soft.

The glacier picks up moraine (rubble), which piles into ridges.

The top of the valley is eroded into an armchair shape called a cirque.

△ As a **glacier** travels slowly down a mountainside, deep cracks called crevasses appear on the surface. Melting ice forms a lake at the bottom of the glacier.

into the bloodstream (see **blood**). One main endocrine gland is the thyroid. The hormone it produces controls the rate at which the body uses **energy**.

Exocrine glands release their substances through tubes, either into the intestines or onto the **skin**. Sweat, tears and saliva all come from the exocrine glands.

Glass

Glass is one of our most useful materials. It is easy to shape and cheap to make. It is also transparent, so you can see through it. Glass can be made as flat sheets, thick castings or delicate wafers. It can be made into curved **lenses** for **cameras**, **microscopes** and other optical instruments. It can be blown into bottles, or drawn out into tubes, **wires** and very thin fibres.

Glass is made by mixing and heating **sand**, limestone and soda ash. When these ingredients melt, they become glass. Ingredients can be added to make glass that is heat-proof, extra-tough or coloured. Glass is a good electrical insulator as it does not conduct current easily. It also resists common chemicals and nuclear radiation.

Gliding

Gliding is flying without using **engine** power. Gliding **aircraft** called sailplanes have long narrow wings. This gives them extra lift. The glider is launched by a winch or a towing aircraft. Once aloft, it loses height very gradually, kept up by rising **air** currents. If the air is rising as fast as the craft is falling, the glider may stay at the same level above the ground. If the air is rising at a faster rate, the aircraft can climb.

In 1853, the first glider to carry a man flew across a valley in Yorkshire, UK. Modern sailplanes can do much more than that. In 1986, one sailplane reached a height of 11,500 m over California, **USA**.

Hang-gliding is a sport in which the pilot is suspended from the glider by a harness and a trapeze-like bar. The wing is light – usually 22 to 44 kg in weight – so that it can be carried and launched by one person. Take-off is from a hill, cliff or mountain steep enough to achieve flight. While in the air, pilots use their body weight to control the glider.

Global warming

Global warming is the slow rise of the **earth**'s **temperature**, which in turn causes changes in **climate**.

The earth's **atmosphere** is made up of **gases**, such as carbon dioxide, that trap the heat **energy** from the **sun**. Without these gases, the sun's **heat** would simply escape into space, and the earth would be a lot colder. The gases are known as greenhouse gases because they keep heat in the atmosphere in a way similar to how heat builds up in a greenhouse.

However, the balance of these gases has been upset by human activity, for example burning **fossil** fuels such as **coal** and petrol, and there now is far more carbon dioxide in the atmosphere. This traps in more of the sun's heat than the earth needs. The resulting rise in temperatures may lead to higher sea levels and changes in rainfall patterns, which will have an impact on all living things.

Glue *see* Adhesive

Goat

Goats are taller, thinner and more agile **animals** than their close relatives, the **sheep**. Goats have hooves and hollow **horns** and the male has a beard.

Wild goats, found in the **mountains** of Central **Asia**, the **Middle East** and **North America**, live in herds and eat **grass** and leaves. Domestic goats are kept in many lands. They provide **milk**, meat and skins. Two kinds, Angora and Cashmere goats, are famous for their silky wool which is woven into fine cloth (see **weaving**).

God and Goddess

The word god or goddess is used to mean the person who created and controls the **universe**. People have always worshipped some sort of powerful god. The civilizations of Ancient **Greece**, Ancient Rome (see **Roman Empire**) and Ancient **Egypt**, believed in several gods, each of which created one part of the world. The stories about these gods and goddesses are called **myths and legends**.

Most major world religions – **Islam**, **Judaism**, **Christianity** and **Hinduism** – teach that there is one God who controls the universe. Worshippers of Islam, the Muslims, use the Arabic word 'Allah' for God.

△ Hang-**gliding** is a popular sport. The glider's design was the result of NASA research into spacecraft re-entry as part of the US space programme.

▽ **Global warming** is a result of too much carbon dioxide in the atmosphere. The gas traps in the sun's heat and is increasing the earth's temperature.

Normally, when the sun's rays pass through the atmosphere, most of them are absorbed by the earth's surface, and some are reflected back into space.

Global warming occurs when some of the sun's rays reaching the earth's surface are kept within the atmosphere, which raises the earth's temperature.

Jews, Sikhs and Muslims forbid the creation of any idols (images of God). Whereas Hindus have many different images and names for God, such as Vishnu and Kali.

Gold

Gold is a soft yellow **metal** that never **rusts**. Thin veins of gold formed in **rocks** long ago by hot **gases** and **liquids** rising from deep in the **earth**. Half of the world's gold is mined in **South Africa**. If washed out of the rocks, lumps of gold, called nuggets, may collect in the beds of streams and **rivers**.

Gold is beautiful and scarce, so it is valuable. Most of the world's gold is kept in brick-shaped bars called ingots in **banks**. **Jewellery** is made from gold mixed with other substances to make it harder.

△ The elephant-headed Hindu **god** Ganesh is the legendary scribe of a sacred Hindu text known as the *Mahabharata*.

△ The Romans worshipped many **gods**. Jupiter was king of the gods while Diana was **goddess** of the moon and hunting.

Goldfish

Goldfish are a type of carp that are usually gold, gold and black, or gold and white in colour. They are easy to keep as pets in tanks or ponds. Goldfish came originally from **China**, but have since been taken across the world. They can reach 30 cm long, and may live for over 20 years.

Golf

Golf is an ancient Scottish game that dates from well before the 1400s. Today, golf is one of the most popular **sports** worldwide. The golfer's aim is to hit a small ball from the starting-point, or tee, into a small hole in the fewest number of strokes. A complete game has 18 holes.

Goose

A goose is a large, powerful **bird** with a long neck, webbed feet and a loud, honking call. Geese live on both land and **water**. The male goose is called a gander and young geese are called goslings.

Gorbachev, Mikhail

Mikhail Gorbachev (b. 1931) became general secretary of the Soviet Communist Party and leader of the **Soviet Union** in March 1985. As leader, he tried to reform the Soviet economy, and promoted a more open society. He became the first **president** of the USSR in 1989. Later, he faced growing opposition to his policies, and resigned at the end of 1991.

Gorilla

Gorillas are the largest of the **apes** – a large male may be as tall as a man. They live in family groups in the warm forests of central **Africa**, eating **fruit**, roots, tree bark and leaves, and making beds of twigs in the **trees**.

◁ In the late 1800s, there were **gold** rushes in Canada, South Africa, New Zealand, the USA and Australia, as people massed to seek their fortune.

The Canada **goose** flies as part of a distinctive V-shaped formation when with other geese.

Government

Every country needs a government to make **laws**, control **trade** and finance, and look after relations with other countries. Most governments fall under one of two headings – totalitarian or democratic. **Democracy** is a system in which the people vote for their leaders and can remove them from power if they fail. Totalitarianism is a system in which one person or a group has complete control over the people and cannot be voted out of office. A dictatorship is when one person controls a country.

There are different kinds of democracies. The **United Kingdom** is a monarchy, with a **monarch** as head of state. The country is, however, governed by **parliament**. The **United States** is a **republic** with a **president** as head of state. The US government is divided into three branches – Congress makes the laws, the executive proposes and enforces the laws, and the judicial branch decides which laws agree with the Constitution of the United States.

Grammar

Grammar is the study of the ways in which words are formed and arranged to make sentences. Words are classified as parts of **speech** according to what they do in a sentence. There are four kinds of word – **verbs** (action words), **nouns** and pronouns (naming words), **adjectives** (describing words for nouns or pronouns) and adverbs (describing words for verbs and adjectives).

To be a sentence, there must be a

△ The **Grand Canyon** is the deepest gorge anywhere on land. The layers of rock show the earth's history over millions of years.

△ **Grass** is home to many insects. It provides a good hiding-place from predators such as birds.

subject (noun) and a verb. The order of words in a sentence is very important. 'The dog bites the girl' means something different from 'The girl bites the dog', but exactly the same words are used. It is usual in English for the subject of a sentence to come before the verb. Exceptions to this rule are called idioms – 'There goes the boy.'

Grand Canyon

The Colorado River carved this deep gash in the **earth**'s surface. The canyon crosses a desert in Arizona, a state in the west of the **United States**. The canyon is about 350 km long, up to 20 km across, and about 2 km deep.

Granite

Granite is a hard **rock** made largely of crystals of **quartz** and feldspar. Quartz is transparent, like **glass**. Feldspar is pink, white or grey. Granite also has specks of dark **minerals** in it, and is used in buildings and monuments.

Granite was once a mass of hot, melted rock underground. As the rock cooled, it hardened. Then movements of the **earth**'s crust forced it up to the surface.

Grass

Grasses are flowering **plants** with long, thin leaves growing from hollow stems. Bamboo is as tall as a tree but most grasses are short. **Herbivores** such as **sheep** and **cattle** eat grass. We eat the seeds of cultivated **cereal** grasses such as **wheat** and **rice**.

Grasshopper

These **insects** have feelers, wings and long back legs. Grasshoppers eat leaves, and those called **locusts** damage crops. Many males 'sing' by rubbing their back legs on their wings. A grasshopper can jump 20 times its own length.

Gravity

Gravity is the pull that tries to tug everything towards the middle of the **earth**. It is gravity that makes objects fall, stops us flying off into space, and keeps the **moon** circling the earth. When we weigh something, we are measuring the force with which gravity pulls that object down. The more closely packed the substances in an object are, the heavier it seems.

All **planets** and **stars** exert a pulling force called gravitation. The larger and denser a star or a planet is, and the nearer it is to other objects, the more strongly it pulls them towards it. The **sun** is at a great distance from the planets, but it is so huge that its gravitation keeps the planets circling it.

GREECE
Government: Presidential parliamentary republic
Capital: Athens
Area: 131,944 sq km
Population: 10.5 million
Language: Greek
Currency: Euro

▽ The **Great Wall of China** is made from earth and stone. Watch-towers were built every 200 m along it. Chinese sentries sent warning signals from the towers if anyone attacked the wall. The signal was smoke by day and a fire at night.

Great Barrier Reef

This is the longest **coral** reef in the world at about 2,000 km long. It stands in the sea off the northeast coast of **Australia**. Much of the reef's surface lies just underwater and is a danger to ships.

Most of the Great Barrier Reef is built by millions of tiny, soft-bodied creatures called coral polyps, related to the **sea anemone**, which live in colonies and build stony cases to protect themselves. A coral reef is made of many colonies.

In the 1960s, part of the reef was destroyed by crown-of-thorns starfish, which feed on the polyps. Today, boats, **pollution** from oil spills and rubbish, and people breaking up coral to sell to tourists are the main threats to the reef.

Great Lakes

This is the world's largest group of freshwater **lakes**. Lake Michigan lies in the **United States**. Lakes Superior, Erie, Huron and Ontario are shared by the United States and **Canada**. The lakes were formed when a huge sheet of ice melted 18,000 years ago. **Rivers** and **canals** connect the lakes to each other and to the **Atlantic Ocean**.

Great Wall of China

Over 2,000 years ago the first emperor of **China**, Shih Huang Ti, built this wall to keep out China's enemies from the north. The Great Wall is the longest wall in the world. It stretches for 2,400 km from western China to the Yellow Sea.

Greece

Greece is a country that lies in southeast **Europe**. Rocky **mountains** cover most of the land, and peninsulas poke out into the sea like giant fingers. Greece includes the island of Crete and

Doric   Ionic   Corinthian

△ There were two main types of architecture in **Ancient Greece** – the Doric and Ionic. From the 400s BCE, the Corinthian style became popular.

△ The semicircular theatre in Athens, **Ancient Greece**, could hold over 10,000 people.

many smaller islands in the Aegean and Ionian seas. Greek summers are hot and dry, while winters are mild and wet. Many of the people work in the capital city, Athens. Greek farmers grow lemons, grapes, wheat and olives.

Greece, Ancient

The first great peoples in Greece were the Minoans and the Mycenaeans. The Minoans lived in Crete. They had rich cities and farms, and led a peaceful life. The Mycenaeans lived on mainland Greece and were warriors and sailors. Both civilizations ended about 1200 BCE.

Around this time, new groups of people began to move to Greece from the north. Instead of making Greece one kingdom, they built separate cities. They often fought with each other, but sometimes they joined together to fight enemies. Two of the strongest cities were Athens and Sparta. In the 400s BCE, Athens was ruled by a **democracy**.

The Greeks loved the **theatre**, **art** and **poetry**. They had many great thinkers, or **philosophers**, including **Aristotle**, **Plato** and Socrates. Greek cities had many graceful buildings. They were decorated with beautiful **sculpture**. In 339 BCE, Greece was conquered by Philip of Macedonia, the father of **Alexander the Great**.

Greenland

Greenland is the world's largest **island**, but it holds no more people than a large town. This is because Greenland has

such a cold **climate**. Most of it lies in the **Arctic**. Thick ice covers seven-eighths of the island. Bare **mountains** make up much of the rest. **Vikings** discovered it nearly 1,000 years ago. It lies northeast of **Canada**, but today, it belongs to **Denmark**. Greenland has enjoyed home rule since 1979.

Most Greenlanders live in villages of wooden houses near the coast. Some are Danes, many are **Inuit**. A lot of Greenlanders work in the country's thriving **fishing** industry.

Guatemala

More people live in Guatemala than in any other **Central American** country. Nearly half of them are Indians, descendants of the **Maya**. Guatemala is a land of dense jungles, **volcanoes**, dry **deserts** and sparkling **lakes**. Most of the people earn their living by **farming** – **coffee**, **cotton** and bananas are the main products. The country was conquered by the Spanish in 1524, declared its independence in 1821, and became a **republic** in 1839.

Guerrilla warfare

Guerrillas are 'hit and run' fighters. Often they do not wear uniforms and live in places where they can easily hide, such as **forests** or **mountains**. The word *guerrilla* is Spanish for 'little war'. Guerrilla tactics are most often used by small groups of people who are fighting against a larger, more organized force.

GREENLAND
Government: Part of Denmark, but with home rule
Capital: Godthåb
Area: 2,175,600 sq km
Population: 59,000
Languages: Inuit, Danish and Greenlandic
Currency: Danish krone

GUATEMALA
Government: Republic
Capital: Guatemala City
Area: 108,889 sq km
Population: 11.1 million
Language: Spanish
Currency: Quetzal

Guevara, Che

Che Guevara (1928–1967), born Ernesto Guevara de la Serna in **Argentina**, was a leading communist figure (see **communism**) in the Cuban Revolution (1956–1959). In the 1960s, he held **government** positions in **Cuba** under president Fidel Castro (b. 1926).

In 1966, Guevara led a guerrilla group in **Bolivia** but, in 1967, he was captured and shot by the Bolivian army.

Guinea

Guinea is a country on the west coast of **Africa**. It has over seven million people. Some of the world's largest deposits of bauxite, from which **aluminium** is made, are in Guinea.

Guitar

The guitar is a stringed **musical instrument**. It consists of a body with a flat back and a long 'neck'. The strings (made of nylon, **steel** or cat-gut) and a series of **metal** pieces, called frets, run along the neck to the body. The player strums or plucks the strings with one hand, and uses the other to press the strings against the frets. Different notes are made according to where the strings are pressed.

Most guitars have six strings. Acoustic guitars are wooden, with a round hole in the front of the body to amplify the sound. Electric guitars are made of metal or **plastic**, and lack the hole in the body so they use a separate electric amplifier.

Guinea pig

The guinea pig, also called a cavy, is a **rodent** from **Peru**. Guinea pigs are up to 29 cm long and may be brown, grey, white, black or a mixture. Some have long silky **hair**, or hair that forms swirls called rosettes. They eat **grass** and hay. Many people keep guinea pigs as pets.

GUINEA
Government: Republic
Capital: Conakry
Area: 245,857 sq km
Population: 7.3 million
Language: French
Currency: Guinea franc

△ Large **guns** called cannons had wheeled bases to move them around. They fired large metal cannonballs.

△ Gutenberg's printing press was an important achievement, but he never made much money from it.

Gulf Stream

This **ocean** current is like a giant river flowing through the sea. It carries warm water from the Gulf of **Mexico** northwards along the eastern coast of the **United States**. The Gulf Stream is up to 60 km wide and 600 m deep. One branch of the Gulf Stream crosses the **Atlantic Ocean** and brings warm water to northwestern **Europe**. If it were not for the Gulf Stream, winters in northern Europe would be much more severe.

Gulf War

On 2 August 1990, Iraqi forces under President Saddam Hussein (b. 1937) invaded the small country of Kuwait. The **United Nations** imposed economic sanctions on **Iraq** then voted to use force to restore Kuwait's independence. The Gulf War was fought from 16 January to the defeat of Iraq on 28 February 1991. The allied forces against Iraq included **France**, the **United States** and the **United Kingdom**.

Gull

Few **birds** are more graceful than gulls gliding and soaring over the sea. They have webbed feet and swim well, but most stay near land. They catch **fish**, but also scavenge for food on the shore.

Gulls breed in noisy crowds called colonies. Many colonies live on islands, which helps keep their **eggs** safe from predators such as **rats** and **foxes**.

Gun

Guns are weapons that fire bullets or other **missiles** from a tube open at one end. Guns were probably invented in the 1200s. By the 1300s, guns fired missiles that could pierce **armour** and break down **castle** walls. Big guns called cannons were first used in about 1350.

In the 1800s, guns fired pointed shells that exploded when they hit. Soon, shells could be fired further and hit targets more often than before.

Troops first used hand-held guns in the 1300s. Inventors developed pistols and revolvers for firing at nearby targets. Then muskets, rifles and machine-guns were developed to shoot distant targets.

Gutenberg, Johannes

Johannes Gutenberg (c. 1395–1468) was a German goldsmith sometimes called the father of **printing**. In his day, people slowly copied **books** by hand or printed them from wooden blocks where each letter was carved separately. About 1440, Gutenberg learned to make **metal** letters called type. He placed them in rows to build pages. Each page was held together by a frame, which he fixed to a press. He then pressed the inky surface of his type onto sheets of **paper**. His movable type helped him to make copies of a book faster and more cheaply than before.

Guyana

Guyana is a hot, rainy country on the northeast coast of **South America**. Most people live along the coast in a narrow strip of flat land about 20 km wide. **Sugar** cane and **rice** are grown here. Valuable **minerals**, including **gold** and **diamonds**, are found in the hilly region inland. Guyana produces bauxite to make **aluminium**.

Once a British colony, Guyana became independent in 1966 and a **republic** in 1970.

Gymnastics

Gymnastics are exercises that help to make and keep the body fit. The **Olympic Games** have separate gymnastic exercises for men and women. Women perform graceful steps, runs, jumps and somersaults on a narrow wooden beam. They swing to and fro between a high bar and a lower one. They leap over a vaulting horse and perform floor exercises to **music**.

Men hang from a high bar and from rings, swinging up and down, and to and fro. Using two parallel bars, they swing, vault and do handstands. They grip hoops that jut up from a pommel 'horse', and swing their legs and body. They also leap over a vaulting horse.

Gypsy

Gypsies are a group of people found all over the world. Some speak a **language** called Romany. Some live in houses, others travel all the time and live in caravans. Gypsies prefer to earn an independent living, for example by trading goods or selling arts and crafts.

The name 'gypsy' comes from the word 'Egyptian'. It was once thought gypsies came from **Egypt**, but they probably originated from **India** 600 years ago.

Gyroscope

A gyroscope is a **wheel** that spins in a special frame. No matter how the frame tilts, the wheel's axle points in the same direction. Even **gravity** and the **earth**'s **magnetism** do not affect the axle.

On a **ship** or **aircraft**, a **compass** made from a gyroscope always points north. Gyroscopes can also keep an aircraft on course without the pilot steering.

GUYANA
Government: Republic
Capital: Georgetown
Area: 214,969 sq km
Population: 856,000
Language: English
Currency: Guyanese dollar

▽ Modern competitive **gymnastics** developed from German and Swedish systems of exercise. Children and adults perform simpler exercises in gymnastics classes.

△ The astronomer Edmond **Halley**'s greatest achievement was to predict the appearance of a comet. This 2 km-long ball of rock, dust and ice was later named Halley's Comet.

H

Habitat

A habitat is the home of a particular species of **animal** or **plant**. It provides all the things that the species needs to survive, such as **food**, **water** and shelter. There are many thousands of different habitats across the world, including grasslands, swamps, **forests**, **deserts**, **rivers**, **lakes** and **oceans**.

Biologists group similar types of habitat together in general categories known as biomes. For instance, the North American prairie and the East African **savanna** are just two of the habitats that belong to the grassland biome. Within each habitat, there are also many small, specialized living places known as microhabitats. For example, the microhabitats in a typical forest might include the topmost leaves of a tall **tree**, behind the bark on a tree trunk, a clump of flowers on the forest floor and underneath a rotting log.

Hair

Hair grows like living threads from the **skin** of **mammals**. It is made from the same substances as **nails and claws**, **hooves**, **feathers** and **reptiles**' scales. Hair helps to keep the body warm, and protects the skin. Each hair root is enclosed in its own case, or follicle, which has a **blood** supply, a tiny erector **muscle** and a **gland**.

There are many kinds of hair. For example, **cats** have plenty of soft, thick fur, and **porcupines** are protected by sharp, stiff hairs called quills.

Haiti

Haiti is a small country in the western part of the island of Hispaniola in the **Caribbean** Sea. Much of the country is covered by rugged **mountains**, but there are fertile valleys and coastal plains where **coffee** and other crops are grown. Nine-tenths of the people are descended from African slaves. In 1677, Haiti became a French colony. It gained its independence in 1804, following a rebellion.

Halley, Edmond

Edmond Halley (1657–1742) was an English astronomer who is best known for his study of **comets**. He noticed that the path followed by a comet which

◁ In 1791, the Caribbean island of **Haiti** (then known as Santo Domingo) was shaken by a violent slaves' revolt. As many as 100,000 slaves rebelled against their owners, setting fire to the plantations of sugar and coffee. France sent troops to the island, but after a bitter war Haiti eventually won its independence.

HAITI
Government: Republic
Capital: Port-au-Prince
Area: 27,750 sq km
Population: 7.8 million
Language: French
Currency: Gourde

he had seen in 1682 was very much like those reported in 1607 and 1531. Halley decided that these sightings must all be of the same comet and predicted that it would return in 1758. On 25 December 1758, it did. Halley's Comet reappears regularly once every 76 years or so – it will next pass near to the **earth** in 2061.

Handel, George Frideric

George Frideric Handel (1685–1759) was a German-born British composer who is today known mainly for his oratorios – pieces of **music** written for large choirs. Handel's most popular work is the oratorio *Messiah* (1742). He also composed orchestral music, such as the *Water Music* (1717) and *Royal Fireworks Music* (1749), for royal events, and wrote a number of **operas**.

Hannibal

Hannibal (247–183 BCE) was an emperor of the Carthaginian Empire, which in ancient times was one of the most powerful states in the **Mediterranean**. He fought several wars with the **Roman Empire** to keep control of the valuable trade routes that passed through Carthage, his empire's capital on the coast of North **Africa**.

Hannibal was a brilliant general, and his excellent military strategies allowed him to defeat armies much larger than his own. But although Hannibal won many important battles, in the end he was never able to conquer the Romans.

△ Despite its name, the black-tailed jack rabbit is in fact a type of **hare** that lives in North America's hot deserts. Its huge ears give off heat, which helps the animal stay cool.

▽ In 218 BCE, **Hannibal** led an army from Spain across the Alps to Italy. As well as 40,000 troops, he took 37 elephants, which he planned to use to frighten the enemy troops of the Roman Empire.

Hapsburgs

Many of **Europe**'s kings and emperors belonged to the Hapsburg royal family. Its name comes from a Swiss **castle** called *Habichtsburg* ('Hawk's Castle'), which was built in 1020 by a German bishop. The owners of the castle became the counts of Hapsburg.

In 1273, Count Rudolf of Hapsburg (1218–1291) was elected **Holy Roman Emperor**, and in 1276, Rudolf seized **Austria**. Later Holy Roman Emperors were mostly Hapsburgs. Members of the Hapsburg family also married foreign princesses, and so increased their power by gaining the countries their wives inherited. By the 1500s, the Hapsburgs ruled much of Europe, from **Spain** in the west to **Hungary** in the east. However, they began to lose power in the 1700s due to wars and revolts. **Napoleon** ended the Holy Roman Empire in 1806, and **World War I** finally smashed the Hapsburgs' huge Austro-Hungarian empire.

Hare

A hare is a type of **mammal** related to the **rabbit**. It has long ears, powerful, muscular legs and a short tail. Unlike rabbits, which are naked and blind at birth, young hares are born with fur and eyes that can open. They are known as leverets.

Hares live in open country in fields and on plains, moors and high **mountains**. They do not dig their own burrows, and when resting they simply crouch in a dip in the ground. Hares can run extremely fast to escape their predators, and may reach a speed of up to 70 km/h.

Harp

The harp is the oldest of all stringed instruments. Early harps were little more than bows with strings of different lengths stretched across them. Modern harps have a wooden frame, with the strings attached between the hollow sounding-board and the top of the instrument. There are seven foot pedals that can change the pitch of the strings. The harpist sits with the sounding board between the legs, and plucks the strings with fingers and thumbs.

Strings

Sounding-board

Pedals

△ Concert **harps** produce a rich, powerful sound. The pedals are used to change the pitch of the strings.

Harvey, William

The English doctor William Harvey (1578–1657) was the first to show that **blood** flows around the body in an endless stream. Harvey proved that a beating **heart** squeezes blood through **arteries** and flaps in the heart, and that the blood returns to the heart through **veins**. He calculated that the amount of blood pumped by a heart in one hour weighs three times more than an adult.

Hawk

Hawks are **birds** of prey related to **falcons** and **eagles**. They have superb **sight** for spotting prey, hooked beaks and razor-sharp talons for catching and killing victims, and long tails for steering while in midair. Many species of hawk look rather like falcons, but they usually have broader wings with more rounded tips. Female hawks are always larger than the males.

Hawks are found all over the world except on Pacific islands. The goshawk lives across the northern regions of **North America**, **Europe** and **Asia**, and is strong enough to kill prey as large as **ducks** and **rabbits**. Other types of hawk include sparrowhawks and buzzards.

Arteries (shown in red) carry blood without oxygen

Veins (shown in blue) carry blood with oxygen

△ William **Harvey's** experiments in the 1620s led him to discover how blood circulates in humans. He realized that the heart pumps blood through the arteries and around the body, and that the blood returns to the heart through the veins.

Haydn, Franz Joseph

Franz Joseph Haydn (1732–1809) was an important Austrian composer who wrote 104 symphonies. Many of them used the **orchestra** in a powerful new way. He also wrote fine pieces for the **piano** and numerous quartets (works for four stringed instruments). Later, both **Mozart** and **Beethoven** were influenced by Haydn's **music**.

Health

Good health is perhaps one of the most important things in life. There are certain rules which help us to stay healthy. We should eat a balanced diet that includes the right kinds of **food**, and drink plenty of clean, fresh **water**. We should take regular **exercise**, which strengthens our **muscles** and keeps us fit. Exercise helps the **blood** to circulate around our bodies, cleaning out waste and supplying plenty of **oxygen**. It is also important to ensure that we get enough **sleep**. The number of hours' sleep we need depends on our age. Young babies sleep for 20–22 hours each day, whereas older people often need only 6–7 hours.

Hearing

Hearing is the sense that allows people to pick up **sound**. The sense organ making this possible is the **ear**. Deaf people cannot hear – they either were born without hearing or, at some time, their ears were damaged by an illness or in an accident. All **vertebrates** (**animals** with backbones) have hearing organs, and some species can hear much better than people. **Cats** and **dogs**, for example, pick up more sounds than we can. **Bats** use their exceptional hearing to find their prey. They utter a series of high-pitched squeaks and listen for the **echoes** that bounce back off flying **insects**.

Heart

The heart is a powerful, muscular **pump** that maintains a continual flow of **blood** around the body through **veins** and **arteries**. In a typical adult person, the heart goes on working at between 70 and 80 beats per minute until death. It was the English doctor William **Harvey** (1578–1657) who discovered how the heart works.

A human heart is about the same size as a clenched fist. It is divided into two halves, each of which has a small upper chamber, called the atrium, and a larger lower chamber, called the ventricle. The atria (plural of atrium) collect the blood flowing into the heart. The ventricles are strong **muscles** that pump blood into the arteries.

The right atrium receives **oxygen**-poor blood from all over the body through large veins called the superior (upper) vena cava and the inferior (lower) vena cava. This blood is pumped by the right ventricle through the pulmonary arteries to the **lungs**, where it absorbs oxygen. The left atrium receives the oxygen-rich blood from the lungs through the pulmonary veins. The left ventricle pumps this blood out to the body's **cells** along the large artery called the aorta.

Heat

Heat is a form of **energy** that we can feel but not see. When something burns, heat is produced. The **sun** gives out enormous amounts of heat, which is produced by **atoms** joining together or 'fusing' inside the sun. This same kind of energy can be released by a **hydrogen** bomb on **earth**.

Most of the heat we use comes from burning **fuels** such as **coal** or **natural gas**. Heat is also be made by **friction**, or rubbing things together, and it is produced when **electricity** travels along a coil of **wire**. This is what makes the coils inside a toaster glow red.

We can measure how hot a thing is by finding its **temperature**. This is done with a **thermometer**. When a substance gets hot, the molecules, or tiny particles, of which it is made move around more quickly. Often the substance expands as this happens. **Metals** are the **elements** that expand the most when they are heated.

Heat energy moves around in three ways – by conduction, convection and radiation. It travels from a region of higher temperature to a region of lower temperature. Conduction carries heat through solid objects, known as conductors. For example, if you dip a spoon into a hot drink, it soon starts to feel warm. Convection carries heat through **liquids** and **gases**. Radiation is a process that carries heat energy in straight lines through empty space. This is how heat from the sun reaches the earth.

△ A radiator gives off, or radiates, heat. The heat travels through the air by the process of convection. As air above the radiator becomes warm, it rises. Cooler air moves in to take its place, creating a convection current.

▽ This front view of the human **heart** illustrates the main blood vessels carrying blood to and from the heart, and the coronary artery that supplies the heart's thick muscle wall.

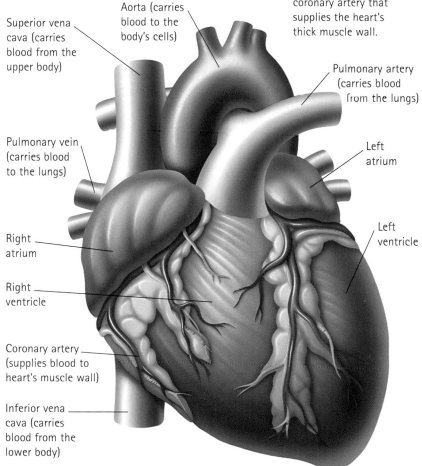

Superior vena cava (carries blood from the upper body)

Aorta (carries blood to the body's cells)

Pulmonary artery (carries blood from the lungs)

Pulmonary vein (carries blood to the lungs)

Left atrium

Right atrium

Left ventricle

Right ventricle

Coronary artery (supplies blood to heart's muscle wall)

Inferior vena cava (carries blood from the lower body)

Hedgehog

The hedgehog is a **mammal** that has a covering of spines on its back for protection. The spines are modified **hairs**. When threatened, the hedgehog rolls up into a prickly ball.

There are several species of hedgehog, found in **Europe**, North **Africa** and parts of **Asia**. The best-known species lives in woods, hedgerows and gardens across much of Europe. It emerges at night to hunt for **snails**, **slugs**, **worms** and **insects**, which it tracks down with its excellent sense of **smell**. During the winter, hedgehogs enter a form of deep sleep known as **hibernation**.

△ Hedgehogs are useful animals in gardens because they eat slugs and insect pests. Despite having short legs, they can roam up to 1.5 km each night in their search for food.

Helen of Troy

In the legends of Ancient **Greece**, Helen of Troy was the most beautiful woman in the world. She was the daughter of Zeus, the king of the **gods**, and Leda, a human. Helen married Menelaus, king of Sparta, but later ran away with Paris, prince of Troy. Menelaus followed with a large army, and so began the **Trojan War**. The story was told by the poet **Homer**.

Helicopter

The helicopter is an extremely useful **aircraft** that was invented in the 1930s. It can take off and land vertically, and therefore is able to work in areas too small for ordinary aircraft. In addition, it can fly in almost any direction and hover in midair.

Helicopters do not have fixed wings. Instead they have a moving wing called a rotor which acts as a wing and a propeller. The pilot controls the craft by changing the angle, or 'pitch', at which the blades of the rotor pass through the air. A smaller rotor on the tail keeps the helicopter from spinning around. Helicopters are used for a variety of purposes, but are especially useful for rescue missions, aerial observation and transporting troops to remote locations.

▽ Helicopters play a major part in many search and rescue missions. They were used to rescue people stranded during the devastating floods that hit the African country of Mozambique in early 2000.

Henry V

Although Henry V (1387–1422) ruled as king of **England** for only nine years, he changed the course of English history during his short reign. By the time he died, England had become the strongest kingdom in **Europe**.

In the period 1403–1408, the young prince Henry led an army against the Welsh rebels. In 1413, he succeeded his father, Henry IV (1367–1413), and immediately set about increasing the power of the English throne. Henry revived an earlier claim to the French throne, and in 1415 invaded **France**. He was a brilliant soldier, and led his troops to a celebrated victory at the Battle of Agincourt. Henry's force included 900 men-at-arms and 3,000 archers. The French had at least three times as many heavily armed troops, but they were badly led and organized.

In 1417, Henry returned to France to try to conquer Normandy. But after a long military campaign, Henry died near **Paris** in 1422 without achieving victory.

Henry VIII

Henry VIII (1491–1547) belonged to the Tudor dynasty, and became king of **England** in 1509. His father was Henry VII (1457–1509), the first Tudor king. Henry was a popular but ruthless ruler, and is remembered for his lavish court and efficient government.

Henry was married six times, and broke away from the Roman Catholic Church when **Pope** Clement VII (1478–1534) refused to grant him permission to divorce his first wife, Catherine of Aragon (1485–1536). In the period 1536–1540, Henry closed 800 **monasteries**, turning out 10,000 monks and nuns and selling or making gifts of their lands. He did this to break the power of the papacy in England, and to raise money. He founded the Protestant Church of England, and established himself as its head. Henry also fought several wars with **Scotland** and **France**.

△ **Henry VIII** abolished the authority of the pope in England, and declared himself the head of the English Church.

Heraldry

In the **Middle Ages**, a knight in full **armour** was hard to recognize as his face was hidden by his helmet. So knights began to use special designs worn on their surcoats and shields.

In 1415, **Henry V** led his troops to a great victory over a much larger French army at Agincourt in northern France.

△ **Herbs** such as marjoram (above) can be used fresh from the garden, or they can be cut and dried for storage. Some herbs are also used to make herbal medicines, which can help treat a variety of illnesses.

These designs became coats-of-arms, family emblems that no one else could wear. Heralds were officials who kept records of coats-of-arms and awarded new ones. There are names for the different colours and patterns used in heraldry, and the shapes form the basis of the designs of many modern **flags**.

Herb

Herbs are **plants** with soft, rather than woody, stems. Some herbs are added to **food** during cooking, while others are important for their healing qualities and are made into herbal **medicines**. Herbs used in cooking include mint, parsley, thyme, garlic, rosemary, basil, fennel, sage and chives. Most can be grown quite easily, although they came originally from the warm, sunny lands of the **Mediterranean** region.

Herbivore

Herbivores are a group of **mammals** that feed mainly on **plants**. There are many kinds of herbivores, including **cattle, deer, elephants, goats, horses** and **sheep**. Some herbivores eat only **grass**, while others feed on the leaves, **seeds** and **fruits** of a variety of plants. Many herbivores have complex **digestion** systems that can extract the goodness from the toughest plant matter.

Heredity *see* Genetics

Hibernation

When a **mammal**, an **amphibian** or a **reptile** hibernates, it goes to **sleep** for the winter. It does this because in winter **food** is scarce. Going to sleep during the cold **weather** saves the animal from starving to death.

Before hibernation, **animals** eat as much food as they can find. The dormouse, for example, stuffs itself until it is plump and round. As autumn approaches, it makes a snug nest, curls into a ball, and falls into a sound sleep. In fact, its **heart** beats so slowly, the dormouse looks dead. Its body uses hardly any **energy** while in hibernation, in order to make its store of **fat** last as long as possible. In spring, the thin and hungry dormouse wakes and emerges from its nest to look for food.

In cold **climates**, many of the animals hibernate, but not all sleep right through the winter. For example, **squirrels** wake up on mild days and eat food they had hidden away in the summer.

△ During **hibernation**, the body temperature of a dormouse falls and its heartbeat slows down. The dormouse will not wake even if it is touched.

△ These picture-signs are an example of Egyptian **hieroglyphics** – one of the world's oldest forms of writing. The symbols, or hieroglyphs, were carved on the walls of temples, tombs and monuments, and inscribed on a kind of paper called papyrus.

◁ The **Himalayas** are the world's highest mountain range. The name literally means 'home of the snows'.

Hieroglyphics

Hieroglyphics are ancient **writing** systems. The modern Western **alphabet** has 26 letters. However, about 5,000 years ago, the people of Ancient **Egypt** began to use picture-signs instead of letters. Later, these signs developed into hieroglyphs – special marks that stood for things, people and ideas.

Hieroglyphic writing was difficult to produce, and only a few people knew how to create it. When the Ancient Egyptian civilization died out, the secret of reading it was lost – no one could understand the hieroglyphs carved on stones and written on papyrus scrolls. Then, in 1799, a French explorer found the Rosetta Stone, which is now in the British Museum in **London**. On the stone was something written in two known **languages**, and also in hieroglyphs. By comparing the known languages with the hieroglyphs, experts were at last able to translate the signs.

Several other ancient cultures also used hieroglyphic systems, including the Hittites, who lived in the region that is now **Turkey**, and the **Aztec** and **Maya** civilizations of **Central America**.

Himalayas

The Himalayas are a chain of high **mountains** that forms a huge barrier across **Asia**, dividing **India** in the south from **Tibet** and **China** in the north. Many of Asia's largest **rivers** begin in the Himalayas, and are fed by the melting snow and ice.

Until **aircraft** were invented, hardly any outsiders had ventured into the Himalayas. Even today, there are few **roads** or **railways** in the mountains. Often the only way to travel is on foot, over steep mountain tracks. **Horses, yaks, goats** and even **sheep** are used to carry heavy loads.

The highest mountain in the world lies in the Himalayas. This is Mount **Everest**, which is 8,848 m high.

Hinduism

Hinduism is one of the world's great **religions**. Most Hindus live in **Asia**, and particularly in **India**. Their religion is thought to be 4,000 years old.

Hindus believe that God is present in all things. Only priests, known as Brahmins, can worship the supreme God. Ordinary people worship other **gods**, such as Vishnu, God of Life. Hindu gods all have different characters. Shiva has four arms, and is often shown dancing. Kali is the wife of Shiva. Ganesh, Shiva's son, has the head of an **elephant** and Hindus believe that praying to him will bring success.

The most important holy **books** of the Hindus are called the *Vedas* – the Books of Knowledge. Of these, the main manuscript is the *Rig Veda*, a collection of more than 1,000 hymns composed in the ancient **language** Sanskrit. Hindus also believe that certain animals, such as the cobra and the cow, are sacred and must never be killed or eaten. Unlike many other faiths, Hinduism was not started by one teacher – its beliefs accumulated gradually over many centuries.

△ One of the chief gods in **Hinduism** is Shiva, who Hindus believe is both a creator and a destroyer. In this sculpture, Shiva is depicted dancing in a halo of flames.

▽ The **hippopotamus** rests in the water during the heat of the day, and becomes active again in the evening.

Hippopotamus

The name hippopotamus means 'river horse', but in fact the hippo is related to the **pig**, not the **horse**. It is a huge, heavy **mammal** and lives in **Africa**. Of all land animals, only the **elephant** is larger.

Hippos live near **rivers** and **lakes**. They spend most of their time in the water and are good swimmers. Their eyes are on the tops of their heads so they can stand underwater and peep out without being seen. Hippos can stay submerged for nearly ten minutes without coming up for breath.

In spite of their fearsome-looking jaws, hippos eat only **plant** food. They browse on water weeds and **grasses**, and at night often come ashore to feed.

History

History is the story of the past. People who study history are called historians. They often write about important events such as **wars** and **revolutions**, and about rulers and **governments**, because these affect nations. However, historians are also interested in the lives of ordinary people, and in what they did and thought about.

Nowadays, we think of history as being written down in history **books**. But in earlier times, before books and **printing**, history was passed on by word of mouth. People told stories about their rulers, wars and adventures, and also about their own families. It was in this way that the stories of Ancient **Greece** were collected by the poet **Homer** to form the *Iliad* and the *Odyssey*. Some early stories such as these were made up in verse, and sung to **music**. This made it easier for people to remember the stories correctly.

In Ancient **Egypt**, scholars recorded the reigns of the **pharaohs**, and listed the victories they won in battle. These accounts were often written on stone

△ The **history** of ancient civilizations often has to be pieced together from clues that have survived over the years. This huge stone head, one of eight carved by the Olmecs of Mexico over 3,000 years ago, may represent an important Olmec ruler.

tablets in the form of **hieroglyphics**. The scholars of the **Roman Empire** and ancient **China** were also very interested in history. It was they who first took the writing of history seriously, and they described how their civilizations rose to power.

In **Europe** during the **Middle Ages**, many people could not read or write, and printing had not been invented. It was the priests and monks who preserved ancient books and kept the official records and documents. These records include the **Domesday Book** (1086), which tells us much of what we know about **England** at the time of **William the Conqueror**. It was not until the 1700s and 1800s that history became an important branch of study in the **universities** of Europe.

Historians get their information from hidden remains, such as things found buried in old graves, as well as from old books. The study of hidden remains is called **archaeology**. But history is not just concerned with the distant past. After all, history is our story – what is news today will be history tomorrow. So modern historians are also interested in **recording** the present. They talk to old people about their lives, and they keep records on **film** and tape of the events of today. **Television** has become a very important source for historians.

Hitler, Adolf

Adolf Hitler (1889–1945) was the *Fuhrer*, or leader, of **Germany** during **World War II**. An ex-soldier, born in **Austria**, Hitler became head of the Nazi party which took over Germany in 1933. At that time, Germany was still weak after its defeat in **World War I**.

◁ Events that change the course of **history** are called turning-points. This photograph was taken at the Yalta Conference (1945), where Allied leaders met to discuss how to rebuild Europe after World War II. It shows (left to right) Winston Churchill of Britain, President Roosevelt of the USA and Josef Stalin of Russia.

Under Hitler's leadership, the Nazis promised to avenge this defeat and create a new German empire. In 1939, Hitler led Germany into World War II. His armies conquered much of **Europe**, including **Poland**, Czechoslovakia (see **Czech Republic** and **Slovakia**), Austria the **Netherlands** and half of **France**.

Hitler's policies were an extreme form of the political theory known as **fascism**. He held strongly racist views, and millions of Jews, gypsies and other groups in society were killed in Nazi death camps. But, by 1945, Germany had lost the war. Hitler killed himself in the ruins of **Berlin** to avoid capture.

△ Adolf **Hitler** had a humble background, but rose to become leader of the German Nazi party. During political unrest in 1933, he was appointed chancellor of Germany.

plate is developed and a black-and-white pattern, the hologram, appears. When the hologram is lit up by a laser beam and viewed from the other side, it produces a three-dimensional image of the original object. The image seems real, with width, depth and height, but it is not in the object's original **colour**. Instead, the hologram takes its colour from the laser beam.

Holography was not developed until the 1960s, and scientists are still looking at practical uses for the technology. For example, holograms could prove to be useful in **medicine**, as a way of probing the human body.

HIV *see* AIDS

Hobby

Any activity that is enjoyed during your spare time is a hobby. It can be collecting things such as **stamps**, **coins** or **rocks**. It can be a creative hobby such as **drawing**, **painting**, **photography** or **weaving**. Or it can be an activity such as **chess**, **tennis**, **swimming** or **sailing**. Part of the fun of any hobby is enjoying it with other people who share your interest.

△ Skateboarding is a **hobby** that has grown in popularity in recent years. Keen skateboarders learn how to perform special moves and tricks.

Holland *see* Netherlands

Holography

Holography is a way of making realistic, three-dimensional pictures called holograms. It is done by using **laser** light instead of a **camera**.

To make a hologram, a laser beam is split into two. One beam hits the object and is reflected onto a photographic plate, and the other beam, angled by **mirrors**, strikes the plate directly. The photographic

Holy Roman Empire

For over 700 years, a large part of **Europe** was loosely united as the Holy Roman Empire. At different times the empire included **Italy**, **Germany** and **Austria**, and parts of the **Netherlands**, **France** and **Switzerland**. The first 'emperor of the Romans' was the

▽ The emperors of the **Holy Roman Empire** had the right to be crowned by the pope in Rome.

Honduras

Honduras is a mountainous country in **Central America**. It has a long coastline with the **Caribbean** Sea and a shorter one with the **Pacific Ocean**. About one-third of the land is covered with tropical **rainforest**. Most of the population are farmers. They live mainly in small villages in the west of the country and near the large banana plantations on the northern coast.

In 1502, the explorer Christopher **Columbus** discovered Honduras, and the country became a colony of **Spain**. Honduras declared its independence in 1821, and became a **republic** in 1838.

French king **Charlemagne**, who was crowned by **Pope** Leo III (d. 816) on 25 December 800. The word 'holy' was not added to the emperor's title until later. After a while, the popes began to have more trouble than help from the emperors, and there were many disputes between the empire and the Roman Catholic Church. By the end of the 1400s, most of the emperors were from the **Hapsburg** royal family of Austria. As some German states grew larger and stronger in the 1500s, so the emperors began to lose power. By the 1800s, the emperor was really only emperor of Austria and **Hungary**.

Homer

Homer was a poet and storyteller in Ancient **Greece**. He probably lived in around 700 BCE but we know little else about him. All there is are two great poems said to be by Homer, the *Iliad* and the *Odyssey*. These poems tell us much of what we know about Ancient Greek **history** and **myths**. The *Iliad* tells the story of the **Trojan War**, and the *Odyssey* recounts the adventures of Odysseus, a Greek hero.

△ **Homer's** *Odyssey* tells how Odysseus and his men encountered the Sirens, three female monsters whose beautiful voices lured sailors to their doom on the rocky coastline. Odysseus had himself tied to the mast and his men plugged their ears so they would not be tempted.

HONDURAS
Government: Republic
Capital: Tegucigalpa
Area: 112,088 sq km
Population: 6.3 million
Language: Spanish
Currency: Lempira

Hong Kong

Hong Kong is a 1,046 sq km area in southeastern **China**. Part of it is a small **island** and the rest is a strip of land called the New Territories on the mainland. The **United Kingdom** governed Hong Kong from 1842 until 1997, when it was returned to China. Since then, it has been a Special Administrative Region of China.

Hong Kong has a very large natural harbour surrounded by **mountains** – its name in fact means 'fragrant harbour'. The capital is Victoria, and another busy city is Kowloon. Many of the people work in **trade**, **fishing** and manufacturing. Tall apartment blocks have been built for housing, but there is still little room for the millions of people who crowd this small area.

Hoof

A hoof is the hard covering of **horn** that protects the feet of some **mammals**. **Animals** with hooves are divided into two main groups, those with an even number of toes, and those with an odd number of toes. The animals with an even number of toes include **deer**, **antelopes**, **cattle**, **goats**, **camels**, **pigs** and **sheep**. All these species have either two or four toes. Animals with only one toe include **horses** and **zebras**. Domestic horses have their hooves cut and trimmed, and wear iron horseshoes.

Hormone

Hormones are chemical messengers found in all **animals** and **plants**. In many animals, hormones are produced in organs called **glands**, which are found in several parts of the body. From these glands, the different hormones are carried in the **blood** to other parts of the body.

The pituitary gland located in the centre of our head produces several hormones. These 'master' hormones

△ **Hong Kong** is one of Asia's leading centres of shipping, commerce and manufacturing.

▽ Although a horse's **hoof** (below) is made of tough horn, it can still be worn down by walking on hard surfaces such as roads. This is why many horses are fitted with horseshoes.

control the hormone secretion of several other glands. The thyroid gland in the neck, for example, is stimulated by the pituitary gland to produce a hormone that controls how fast **food** is used up by the body. Too little of this hormone makes people overweight. The hormone adrenalin is produced in the adrenal glands, just above the **kidneys**. It is controlled by **nerve** messages, and is released when we are frightened or excited. When adrenalin flows, the **heart** beats faster, the blood pressure rises and the body prepares itself for strenuous physical exertion.

Many hormones can now be made in the laboratory. They are then used to help people suffering from **diseases** caused by the lack of certain hormones. **Insulin** is a hormone used to treat diabetes, a disease in which too much **sugar** stays in the blood.

◁ The two massive **horns** on the brow of *Triceratops* grew to over 1 m long. This plant-eating dinosaur probably used its fearsome horns to fend off attacks by meat-eating predators such as *Tyrannosaurus*, and it may also have used them in combats with rivals of the same species.

Horn

Horn is a form of hard **skin**. Human finger and toe **nails** are made of horn, as are the **feathers** and beaks of **birds**, and the scales of **reptiles**. In addition, many animals grow horns – bony growths covered with a layer of horn, and fixed to the animal's skull. **Cattle**, **sheep**, **goats** and most **antelopes** have curved horns. **Deer** horns are branched antlers made of bone covered with skin. Every year the antlers fall off and a new set grows back in their place.

Horse

The horse was one of the first wild animals to be tamed. Today, there are only a few wild horses left, such as

Przewalski's horse, which lives in the remote grasslands of **Mongolia** and northern **China**. Many so-called 'wild' horses, such as the mustangs of **North America**, are actually descended from domestic horses that have run wild.

The horse is valued for its speed and strength. But the earliest kind of horse was a small, rather doglike creature, with a way of life quite unlike that of modern horses. Called *Eohippus*, it lived millions of years ago. It had four toes on its front feet and three toes on its back feet, and it was small enough to hide from its enemies in the undergrowth.

Later, horses emerged to live on the open plains. There was no undergrowth in which to hide, so they escaped from enemies by running away. Gradually, their legs grew longer and they lost all their toes except one. Finally, after millions of years of **evolution**, the modern horse appeared. It too has only one toe on each foot, and actually runs on tiptoe. Its toe has become a **hoof**.

Horse-riding

People have been riding horses since about 3000 BCE. Horses remained the fastest form of transport until the 1820s, when the first regular **railways** were developed. Today, farmers and ranchers still use horses to carry out their work in some parts of the world, but many people ride horses simply for pleasure. It takes a great deal of skill to ride a horse well.

One of the most important things a rider must learn is how to tell a horse what to do. There are two kinds of signal used for this. The first, called natural aids, are given by hand, leg and voice commands. The second are artificial aids. These include using reins and whips. Command signals must be given smoothly and correctly, otherwise the horse will become confused about what its rider wants it to do. People can test their horse-riding skills by taking part in races and cross-country events.

▽ **Horses** are built for speed, and even young foals are able to gallop. No one knows when horses were first tamed, but they were being used for riding and pulling carts in Egypt and Central Asia about 5,000 years ago.

Many modern **hospitals** are huge organizations that employ hundreds of people doing all kinds of jobs. Running a large hospital is an extremely costly and complicated exercise.

Hospital

Hospitals are places where sick people, or patients, are cared for. Doctors and nurses look after the patients and try to make them better.

There are two main types of hospital. One, the general hospital, deals with everything from accidental injuries to infectious **diseases**. The other type of hospital specializes in certain conditions. For example, there are psychiatric hospitals for people who are mentally ill; maternity hospitals where women give birth; and geriatric hospitals for the elderly. In hospitals attached to medical schools, student doctors gain experience through treating real patients.

In ancient times, temples dedicated to the gods of healing used to have a hospital area. Sick people came there to pray and be treated. Later, in the **Middle Ages**, hospitals attached to **monasteries** were run by monks and nuns. But over the last 200 years, non-religious hospitals have become the most common. In many countries, hospitals organized by the state provide inexpensive or free medical treatment for all people. Healthcare is one of the main things on which **governments** spend the **money** that they have raised through **taxes**.

Hotel

Hotels are places where travellers or tourists can stay. Before 1800, there were no hotels as we now know them. Travellers spent the night at taverns or inns. Wherever people travelled, there were inns that gave food and shelter to travellers and their horses. Today, large hotels are like small towns, and provide a wide range of facilities such as swimming-pools, restaurants and shops.

△ Some of the world's first **hotels** sprang up in the USA, such as this one in San Francisco, California, which was built in about 1850.

House

The first houses were simple shelters made of mud, branches, leaves or animal hides. Later, people learned how to make bricks by drying wet **clay** in the sun. For thousands of years, brick, **wood** and stone were the materials from which almost all houses were built.

Modern houses are built to keep out cold, draughts and rain, and to keep in warmth. Double-glazing of windows and insulation in the roof and walls help to do this. Many homes have central-heating and, in hot **climates**, air-conditioning. In crowded cities, homes are built on top of one another to form blocks of flats.

▽ **House** design has gone through major changes, but there are still certain basic similarities between modern houses and the shelters of our earliest ancestors. For example, all houses must provide a way of cooking food, some form of heating, a water supply and a method of dealing with waste.

Modern home · Rubbish tip · Open fire · Prehistoric home · Solar panel · Well · Central-heating radiator · Sewage pipe · Electrical power · Water pipe

Hovercraft

Propeller

Fan

Flexible
rubber skirt

△ A **hovercraft** has fans on each side that suck in air and push it underneath the craft to lift it up. Extra fans at the rear propel the vehicle forwards.

A hovercraft is a special type of vehicle that rides on a cushion of **air**. The air is blown downwards by fans, and held in by a skirt or side wall around the craft. Hovercrafts work best over **water** but can also cross beaches and flat land. They are much faster than ordinary **ships**. Since they do not have to push against the water but simply skim smoothly through the air, they can easily manage speeds of 120 km/h. Their advantage over **aircraft** is the size of the load they can carry. A large hovercraft can hold dozens of **cars** and up to 400 passengers.

Human beings

Human beings are **mammals**, and we are very like our closest relatives, the **apes**. We have the same kind of **blood**, **bones**, **muscles** and other parts inside our bodies. But the main difference between humans and any other **animal** is the size of our **brain**. The human brain is enormous compared to body size.

Humans use their brain to think things out, and when they have found a solution to a problem, they can talk about it with other humans. This is why humans are the most successful animal alive today. All people belong to the same species, which is classified as *Homo sapiens* ('thinking man').

△ The tiny ruby-throated **hummingbird** nests across the eastern USA, and flies to Central America for the winter. This is a remarkable feat for such a small bird.

▽ **Human beings** are descended from apelike animals that lived in Africa about four million years ago. These creatures gradually evolved (changed) into modern humans.

Human body

The human body is rather like a **machine** with many parts. Each part has a special job, and all the parts work together to keep you alive and healthy. Like all machines, your body needs fuel, which it gets in the form of **food**. The **oxygen** you breathe in from the **air** helps turn the food you eat into **energy**, which allows you to work, think and grow.

Your body is made up of millions of tiny **cells**. A group of cells that work together is called tissue. For example, cells that allow you to lift things are called **muscle** tissue. Tissues that work together make up an organ. The **heart** is an organ that pumps **blood**. Other organs are the **brain, ears, eyes, liver, lungs, stomach** and **skin**.

Organs that work together are called systems. You have a **digestion** system (the mouth, **stomach** and intestines), a circulation system (the heart, **arteries** and **veins**), and a nervous system (the brain and **nerves**). The study of the human body is called anatomy.

Hummingbird

Hummingbirds are among the smallest **birds** in the world. They are found only in the New World, from southern **Canada** to the tip of **South America**.

15 million years ago   4 million years ago   2 million years ago   1.5 million years ago   130,000 years ago   100,000 years ago

The tiniest of the 320 different species is the bee hummingbird of **Cuba**, which measures less than 5 cm in length.

Hummingbirds can beat their wings up to 70 times a second. This is what causes their distinctive humming sound. It also allows hummingbirds to hover in midair, and to fly backwards and sideways like **helicopters**. In this way, the birds dart from **flower** to flower and feed while flying. They drink the sweet nectar and take tiny **insects** from deep within the cups of flowers.

Hundred Years' War

England and **France** were at war, almost without a break, from 1337 until 1453. This period is called the Hundred Years' War. The war was started by the English king Edward III (1312–1377), who thought that he was the rightful heir to the French crown. Edward assembled an army, which landed in France in 1346. His foot soldiers and archers routed the French at Crécy in 1346 and at Poitiers in 1356.

A treaty was signed in 1360, but the war started again in 1369. In the early 1400s, **Henry V** of England decided to try again for the French crown. He invaded northern France in 1415, and at the Battle of Agincourt, his bowmen mowed down the French cavalry. A new peace treaty was signed in 1422.

Henry married the daughter of the French king and was named heir to the French throne. But the two kings died and war broke out again. This time, the French were led by a young peasant girl, **Joan of Arc**. By 1453, the English had been driven from all of their lands in France, except for the town of Calais.

Hungary

Hungary is a landlocked country in central **Europe**. The Danube **River** flows across the country on its way to the Black Sea, almost dividing it in two. **Ships** can sail upriver as far as

Budapest, the capital and largest city. Hungary is low-lying and fairly flat. To the east it becomes a vast grassy plain, where herds of sheep, cattle and horses are grazed. **Farming** is important, but more of the people work in industry and in **mining** than on farms.

When the Austro-Hungarian Empire collapsed after **World War I**, Hungary became an independent **republic**. In 1956, the **Soviet Union** forced Hungary to adopt **communism**, but in 1989 a more democratic system was introduced.

Huns

The Huns were a group of wandering warriors who swept into **Europe** in about 400 BCE from the plains of Central **Asia**. They conquered large parts of **Germany** and **France**. Their most famous general was Attila, who attacked **Rome** and nearly destroyed the **Roman Empire**. However, the Huns' power declined suddenly after Attila's death in 453 BCE.

Hunting

Hunting was the main way by which prehistoric humans lived, and in ancient times in places such as **China** and **Egypt** it became a popular sport for wealthy people. Nowadays, hunting is an activity that is mainly carried out to provide a source of **food** or to control pests. Growing numbers of people around the world want to preserve wild animals, not kill them (see also **conservation**).

HUNGARY
Government: Republic
Capital: Budapest
Area: 93,030 sq km
Population: 10 million
Language: Hungarian
Currency: Forint

▽ **Hunting** was a very popular sport for wealthy people in ancient China. All sorts of game was caught, either shot with bow and arrow or chased by hounds, cheetahs and falcons.

Hurricane

A hurricane is a severe storm. To be called a hurricane, a storm must have **wind** speeds of at least 120 km/h. Hurricanes form over **oceans** near the **equator**, where the **air** is very moist. Hurricanes in the **Pacific Ocean** are known as typhoons, and those in the **Indian Ocean** are called cyclones.

During a hurricane, winds whirl around in a great circle and may reach speeds of over 320 km/h. The largest hurricanes have measured 1,600 km across. At the centre of the hurricane is a narrow column of air that spins very slowly. This is called the 'eye' of the hurricane.

If a hurricane reaches the coast, it may cause immense damage to buildings and property. However, **satellite** pictures help scientists to predict the route a hurricane will take, which usually gives people enough time to evacuate the area.

△ **Hurricane** winds spiral upwards at great speed within a wall of storm clouds. They rotate around a narrow central column of slow-moving air.

Hydroelectric power

More than one-fifth of the world's **electricity** is produced using the **energy** of fast-flowing **water**. This is called hydroelectric power. Most hydroelectric plants are found below artificial **dams**, but some are powered by natural **waterfalls**.

Water is heavy, and when it falls through large pipes from a high dam it can be made to turn the paddle-shaped blades of **turbines**. Shafts connected to the blades turn electric **generators**, as in **coal**- or **oil**-fired **power stations**.

Hydrofoil

Much of the **engine** power of a **ship** goes into overcoming the drag of the **water** around the vessel's hull, or underside. A hydrofoil solves this with underwater 'wings' called foils,

△ **Hydrofoils** can travel faster than other boats due to their 'wings' that lift them out of the water. They are mainly used for short-distance express passenger services.

which lift the craft right out of the water. The wings are attached to the hull of the hydrofoil at the bow (front) and the stern (back), and lift the hull as the craft gathers speed. As the water's drag grows less, the hydrofoil shoots ahead, travelling much faster than an ordinary boat can.

Hydrogen

Hydrogen is a **gas**. It is thought to be the most abundant **element** in the whole **universe**, and is the single most important material from which **stars**, including our **sun**, are made.

Hydrogen is the lightest of all the elements – it is more than 14 times lighter than **air**. It is colourless, and has neither **smell** nor **taste**. Hydrogen burns very easily. Huge volumes of hydrogen are always being burned in the sun. It is this fierce burning that gives us **light** and **heat** on **earth**.

Hydrogen is a very important part of the bodies of all **plants** and **animals**. It is also contained in the fossil fuels – **coal**, **oil** and **natural gas**. At one time, hydrogen was used to fill airships (see **balloon and airship**), but because hydrogen catches fire easily, it proved to be too dangerous for this purpose.

Hyena

Hyenas are four species of meat-eating **mammals**. Although they have a similar shape to **dogs**, they are more closely related to the **cat** family. Hyenas often scavenge their meals from the kills of other animals such as **lions**, **leopards** and **cheetahs**, although they sometimes make kills of their own. They have very powerful **teeth** and jaws for crushing the **bones** and making the most of their source of left-over food.

Hyenas are found in parts of **Africa** and southern **Asia**, and live in groups called packs. They feed at night, and spend the day resting in holes or caves.

△ The spotted **hyena** lives in southern Africa. It has a loud cry that resembles human laughter.

Ice Ages

The Ice Ages were times when vast sheets of ice covered parts of the **earth**. Each period lasted for thousands of years. In between were warmer periods. The last Ice Age ended about 20,000 years ago, but the ice might return again.

During the Ice Ages, the **weather** was very cold. Endless snow fell and **glaciers** grew and spread. At times, the glaciers covered much of **North America** and **Asia**, and **Europe** as far south as southern **England**. In some places, the ice piled up more than a thousand metres high.

The sea level was lower during the Ice Ages than it is today. A land bridge was formed between North America and Asia, and the first people to live in America crossed this 'bridge' from Asia.

Iceberg

An iceberg is a chunk of a **glacier** or an ice shelf that has broken away and is floating in the **ocean**. The iceberg floats because when **water** freezes it expands, so ice is less dense than water. Only part of the iceberg is visible – most of it is hidden under the surface. Icebergs are found in the freezing waters of the **Antarctic** and **Arctic**.

△ **Icebergs** pose a serious threat to shipping because they extend far below the waterline. Some icebergs reach as much as 950 m beneath the surface.

▽ During the **Ice Ages**, animals and early humans had to cope with bitterly cold conditions. Many of the mammals developed thick coats of shaggy fur to keep them warm.

Icebergs can be very large – some weigh millions of tonnes and may be up to 150 km long. They provide an ideal resting place for **penguins** and **seals**, but are dangerous to **ships**. Sometimes they float south from the Arctic into the **Atlantic Ocean**, and on the night of 14–15 April 1912, a liner called the *Titanic* hit an iceberg in the north Atlantic on her maiden voyage. The ship sank, and about 1,500 of the passengers and crew drowned.

Ice hockey

Ice hockey is a team **sport** played on an ice rink that is 60 m long and 26 m wide, with a goal at either end. The players, six in a team, wear ice skates and hold a long-handled stick with a curved blade at the bottom. They use this to drive the puck, a rubber disc, around the rink. Both teams try to shoot the puck past the opposing team's defence and into their goal nets. Each game is divided into three 20-minute periods. Ice hockey is a fast-moving sport, and the players must wear padded clothing for protection.

Woolly mammoth

Woolly rhinoceros

Iceland

Iceland is a mountainous island that lies just south of the **Arctic** in the north **Atlantic Ocean**, between **Norway** and **Greenland**. Warm waters from the **Gulf Stream** keep most of the country's harbours free of ice all year round.

Iceland is a volcanic island, with numerous **volcanoes** and hot springs. Water from some of the springs is used to heat homes. The northern part of the island is covered by **glaciers** and a wilderness of stone and lava (cooled volcanic matter).

Iceland was discovered by the **Vikings** in 874. Today, most of the population live in the south and east where the land is lower. They live by **farming** and **fishing**. Iceland became an independent country in 1944 after breaking its ties with **Denmark**.

△ Impressionism was a style of art in which loose brushstrokes were used to give the impression of a scene. This painting of a field of poppies was made in 1873 by Claude Monet, one of the best-known impressionist painters.

ICELAND
Government: Republic
Capital: Reykjavik
Area: 103,000 sq km
Population: 278,000
Language: Icelandic
Currency: Króna

Immigration

Immigration is when people settle in a country in which they were not born. Throughout **history**, millions of people have travelled to live in new lands. The act of leaving one's country in this way is called emigration.

People leave their native country, or emigrate, for many different reasons. Sometimes they are fleeing persecution, **war** or natural disasters such as **famine** or outbreaks of **disease**. People who emigrate for these reasons are known as refugees. Sometimes people emigrate because they hope to improve their standard of living. The period from the early 1800s until the 1930s saw some of the heaviest immigration in history. About 60 million people moved to a new country. Most moved from **Europe**, and more than half emigrated to the **United States of America**. The main reception centre in the USA at that time was Ellis Island, near the city of **New York**. The other countries that people emigrated to in this period included **Australia** and **South Africa**.

Immunity

Immunity is the long-term protection against **disease** that is acquired by **animals**, including **human beings**. People develop immunity through their immune system. This constantly cleans the **blood** and body tissues, and attacks invading germs (see **bacteria**). When the body detects the presence of germs, it immediately starts to fight them. It produces antibodies – substances that attack certain disease-causing germs. These antibodies stay in the body to stop more of the same kind of germs from invading the body again. For example, if you have had measles, you are unlikely to catch measles again.

Vaccination is a process that allows us to acquire immunity to diseases that we have never caught previously.

The doctor or nurse puts a substance in our body that contains a tiny amount of a particular type of germ. This is often done by means of an injection. The quantity of germs we are given is far too small for us to become unwell, but our bodies still produce antibodies to fight the germs. From then on, our body is protected against these germs.

Impressionism

In the 1860s in **France**, some artists began to paint in a new way. Instead of working indoors, they started to paint outside in the open air. They painted scenes from nature and everyday life rather than grand historical scenes, and tried to catch the ever-changing **light**.

In 1874, the group held an exhibition in **Paris**. Their **art** was laughed at, and one **newspaper** poked fun at a **painting** called *Impression: Sunrise* (1872) by Claude Monet (1840–1926). It called the group 'Impressionists', and the name stuck. However, before long, people began to appreciate the lively style of the Impressionists. In addition to Monet, the leading Impressionists were Edouard Manet (1832–1883), Camille Pissarro (1830–1903), Edgar Degas (1834–1917), Alfred Sisley (1839–1899) and Pierre Auguste Renoir (1841–1919).

Inca

The Inca were a people who ruled a great empire in **South America** from the 1200s until the 1500s. In the 1400s, the empire grew until it stretched for almost 3,200 km along the west coast of South America, from present-day **Ecuador** to **Chile**. The centre of the empire was in **Peru**.

The Inca king and his nobles ruled over the people in the empire. They laid down strict rules and told the farmers and craftsmen what to grow and make. The Inca built many **roads** through their lands.

In the 1500s, Spanish soldiers led by Francisco Pizarro (c.1478–1541) reached America. They captured the Inca king Atahualpa (c.1500–1533) and said they would free him in return for **gold**. The Inca brought treasure to free the king, but the Spanish still killed him. By 1569, the Spaniards had conquered the whole Inca empire.

India

India is a large country in southern **Asia**. It has a **population** of about one billion – only **China** has more people. To the north of India are the snowy peaks of the **Himalayas**. Many people live in the fertile northern plains, which are crossed by the great **Ganges** and Brahmaputra **rivers**. The south is high, flat land, with **mountains** called the Ghats along the coast.

India is very hot and dry in summer. Parts of the country are almost **desert**. But **winds** called **monsoons** bring heavy rain to the northeast every year. The Shillong Plateau in eastern India is one of the wettest places in the world, with an average of 1,087 cm of rain a year.

Most Indians are farmers who live in villages, growing **rice**, **wheat**, **tea**, **cotton** and jute, a natural fibre used to make sacks and rope. India also has fast-growing industries. Its many bustling cities such as Kolkata (formerly Calcutta) and

INDIA
Government:
Federal republic
Capital: New Delhi
Area: 3,287,590 sq km
Population: 997 million
Languages: 16 official languages, including Hindi and English
Currency: Rupee

▽ The **Inca** were skilled engineers, and constructed a network of roads that covered all of their empire. They even built highways in the Andes mountains.

Mumbai (formerly Bombay) are among the world's largest. Hindi and English are the two main **languages**, but there are hundreds of others. Most Indians practise **Hinduism**, but many follow the **religion** of Islam. There are also many other religions in India, including **Buddhism** and **Christianity**.

British trading companies began to visit India in the 1600s, and it became a British colony during the 1800s. In 1920, Mohandas **Gandhi** began a long campaign against British rule, and in 1947, India won independence. The British **government** partitioned (divided) its former colony into two separate countries – India and **Pakistan**.

Indian Ocean

The Indian Ocean is the world's third largest **ocean**, with an area of 73,500,000 sq km. It stretches from **Africa** in the west to **Indonesia** and **Australia** in the east. Two very large islands lie in the ocean – **Madagascar**, off southeastern Africa and **Sri Lanka**, off the southern tip of **India**. Strong **winds** from the ocean, called **monsoons**, bring heavy rainfall to **Southeast Asia** each summer. The ocean's warm waters support large **coral** reefs.

INDONESIA
Government: Republic
Capital: Jakarta
Area: 1,904,000 sq km
Population: 207 million
Language: Bahasa Indonesian (Malay)
Currency: Rupiah

▽ The new factories of the **Industrial Revolution** were built near canals and railways so that raw materials could brought in, and finished goods taken to markets easily. Factory owners built houses and schools for the workers, but many industrial areas turned into slums.

Indonesia

Indonesia is a country in **Southeast Asia**. It is a chain of over 3,000 **islands** around the **equator**. The islands stretch over a distance of 4,800 km.

More than half of Indonesia's people live on Java, where the capital Jakarta is located. Most of the people are farmers and major crops include **rice**, **tea**, **rubber** and **tobacco**. Indonesia also produces **oil** and other **minerals**, as well as timber from its **forests**.

Parts of Indonesia became a colony of the **Netherlands** in the late 1700s, but the country gained independence in 1949. Indonesia formerly included East Timor, but in 1999, the people of East Timor voted to break away and form a new independent state.

Industrial Revolution

The Industrial Revolution is the name given to the great changes that took place in **Europe** in the 1700s and 1800s, when people began to use **machines** to make goods in factories, instead of by hand at home.

The new machines were run by **steam engines**, and could make things much faster than people could by hand. **Mining** and **metal**-working became more important and the first regular **railways** were constructed. Many people moved from the countryside and began to work in factories in the fast-growing towns. Another reason why people moved to urban areas was the major changes taking place in **farming**. Improved methods of growing and harvesting crops meant that fewer workers were needed on the farms.

Inflation

Inflation is a word used to mean rapidly rising prices. Every time prices go up, **money** is worth less because people need more money to buy the same things. In turn, people ask for higher wages. If wages rise, then the cost of making things in factories goes up. This often makes prices rise again. Because prices and wages affect

△ After World War I, **inflation** in Germany was so high that it was called hyperinflation. The value of the German currency – the mark – was reduced to almost nothing. In late 1923, a loaf of bread cost 200 billion marks. Workers took their wages home in wheelbarrows, and children played with stacks of worthless notes.

each other like this, inflation is hard to stop. There are many reasons why inflation starts. If inflation becomes high, money can become worthless. Some countries have experienced 'hyperinflation', when prices increase by over 50 percent every month. This means an inflation rate of over 13,000 percent a year.

Infrared rays

When you feel the **heat** from a **fire** or the **sun**, you are feeling infrared rays. They are called infrared because they lie just beyond the red end of the **light spectrum**. This means that we cannot see infrared rays, although they behave in the same way as visible light rays. For example, they can be reflected.

Photographers use a special type of film that is sensitive to infrared rays to take pictures in total darkness (see also **photography**). Infrared-sensitive film can be used to take pictures in which hot and cold areas show up as different colours. White areas are the hottest and blue are coolest.

Male stag beetles have large jaws that are used in fights over females.

Crickets have long back legs for hopping, and rub their wings together to chirp loudly to attract a mate.

Earwigs are flat with pincers at the end of their tail, and have wings that fold away.

Aphids have soft green or brown bodies and are less than 3 mm in length.

▽ The praying mantis (below, right) is a fierce predator. It uses its huge front legs to grab prey, such as beetles.

INSECTS

There are insects all over the world, except in the sea. Their bodies are divided into three parts, and they have six jointed legs.

Abdomen

Common wasp

An insect's legs are made up of small segments and flexible joints.

Thorax

Most winged insects have two pairs of wings.

Antennae provide insects with a sense of smell.

▷ Bumblebees are social insects that collect the pollen from flowers and store it in pollen sacs on their back legs. The pollen is used as food for the colony.

Many insects have large compound eyes with hundreds of tiny lenses.

▽ Ants live in communal nests, such as this one made by leaf-cutter ants in South America.

Head

WORLD OF INSECTS

There are more than three million different kinds of insect, ranging from tiny fleas that can only be seen through a microscope, to 13 cm-long Goliath beetles. Insects are split into about 29 groups, including bees, flies, ants, grasshoppers, beetles and butterflies.

All insects have three body parts – the head, the thorax and the abdomen – and three pairs of legs, which are joined to the thorax. Most insects also have two pairs of wings. The body of every insect is covered with a tough body case called an exoskeleton.

▷ An insect, such as this housefly, has four stages in its life cycle. It begins with an egg, which turns into a larva. The larva grows by shedding its skin, and forms a chrysalis, or pupa. This finally splits open to reveal an adult.

SOCIAL LIFE

Some insects, including ants, bees and termites, live in large, highly organized colonies. Each insect within the community has a job to do, such as hunting for food, caring for the larvae or guarding the nest. There is a queen in every group and only she can lay eggs.

HELPERS AND PESTS

Without bees and other flying insects, flowering plants would not be pollinated and fruit trees would not bear fruit. Bees also give us honey. Scavenging insects such as dung beetles are useful because they feed on animal dung and help keep soil fertile. However, some insects are pests that cause damage to crops, while others carry diseases.

> SEE ALSO
> Ant, Bee, Beetle, Butterfly, Caterpillar, Flea, Fly, Grasshopper, Invertebrate, Locust, Mosquito, Moth, Parasite, Termite, Wasp

Instinct

People have to learn to read and write, but a newborn baby will grasp tightly enough with its hands to support its own weight. This kind of behaviour is called instinct. Parents pass on instincts to their offspring through heredity (see **genetics**).

Animals do many things by instinct. For example, **birds** build their **nests** this way. Some animals, such as **insects**, do almost everything by instinct. They have set ways of finding food, defending themselves against predators or escaping. **Bees** and **wasps**, for instance, sting as an instinctive reaction to danger. Species that act only by instinct are said to lack **intelligence**, and they cannot easily change their behaviour.

Insulin

Insulin is a **hormone** that controls the body's use of **sugar**. It is produced in the pancreas **gland**. When not enough insulin is produced, the body cannot use or store sugar properly, a condition known as diabetes. Many people with diabetes have to give themselves daily injections of insulin.

Insurance

Insurance is a way of safeguarding against loss, damage or injury. A person with an insurance policy pays a certain sum of **money** to an insurance **company** every year. If they lose or damage something they have insured, the company gives them money to replace it or to pay for its repair. It is possible to insure all kinds of property, including **houses** and other buildings. People often take out health insurance policies to pay for medical treatment should they become unwell.

Internet *see pages 168–169*

Intelligence

When a person uses experience and knowledge to solve a new kind of problem, they are showing intelligence. Intelligence depends on being able to learn. Creatures that act only by **instinct** lack intelligence. **Human beings**, **apes**, **dolphins** and **whales** are the most intelligent **animals**.

Inuit

The Inuit people live in the cold **Arctic** lands of **Greenland**, **North America** and northeast **Asia**. At one time, the Inuit lived in tents in summer and built snow homes called igloos for the winter. They hunted in boats made of animal skin and canoes called kayaks, and caught **fish** with harpoons. **Dogs** pulled their sledges. However, many Inuit no longer lead this kind of life.

Invention

An invention is the creation of something completely new. Many important inventions have come from

continued on page 170

△ A herring gull chick's natural **instinct** is to peck the red spot on its parent's beak. This encourages the parent to cough up food from its throat pouch for the chick to eat.

▽ The **Inuit** hunters of Canada were probably the inventors of the igloo. It was built from blocks of frozen snow cut with an ivory-bladed snow knife. The gaps between the blocks were filled with loose snow.

INTERNET

The internet is a globe-spanning computer network that gives people rapid access to information, knowledge, entertainment and opinions from around the world.

△ *The internet is a bit like a library with a huge number of books – finding the web page you want can sometimes seem quite daunting. Search engines greatly speed up the process of locating web pages.*

LINKING COMPUTERS TOGETHER

A computer network is two or more computers linked in some way so that they can send and receive data (information) from each other. The world's largest computer network is the internet, or 'net'. Millions of computers can join the internet using standard software. Internet users are able to share and exchange a variety of information, including images, sounds and text messages.

EARLY DAYS

The internet began in the USA in the late 1960s as a military communications system called ARPANet. This was a network of defence computers designed so that it could survive and continue working even if parts of the system were destroyed during a war. ARPANet gradually developed into the internet, first as a way for scientists and academics to share information, and then, by the early 1990s, for the general public as well.

GETTING CONNECTED

Some computers have a permanent connection keeping the machines linked to the internet all the time. However, most personal computers, or PCs, are not permanently linked. They need a device called a modem for this, and use a company called an Internet Service Provider (ISP) to gain access to the internet via a telephone line. The modem converts computer data into a signal that can be sent down a phone line. When receiving information from the internet, the modem performs the opposite operation – it converts the phone signal into data that the computer can understand.

THE INTERNET EXPLOSION

Connecting to the internet is known as 'going online', and any computer connected to the internet is called a host. The numbers using the internet have risen sharply. In early 1981, there were just 213 hosts. By 1991, there were 376,000 and in 2001, the figure had risen to over 130 million. People without access to the internet at home, school or work may hire a computer at a cyber café for a small charge.

△ *Many goods and services can be chosen, ordered and paid for over the internet.*

▽ *Today, there are websites in many different languages, created by people and organizations all over the world.*

▽ *People can use the internet to view live video clips, such as these images from a recent NASA space mission.*

△ *Using email, people can send messages to each other in minutes. Over nine billion emails are sent every day.*

△ *The internet provides information on plays, films, concerts, exhibitions and many other forms of entertainment.*

THE WORLD WIDE WEB

The World Wide Web allows people to 'surf the net' quickly and efficiently. It is a massive, linked collection of websites, which in turn consist of separate web pages. Each web page is a document that has its own address known as a URL. By clicking on hot spots on the screen, users can jump to different web pages.

SEE ALSO
Communication, Computer, Media, Telecommunication, Telephone

USES OF THE NET
A huge range of activities is carried out on the internet, from education to online games that can link dozens of players. E-commerce is where companies do business over the internet. Thousands of companies have websites that allow customers to view and order products online using a credit card. The ability of the World Wide Web to handle images and sound files has not just made websites more appealing to view. Museums can now show their exhibits on the internet, while many radio stations release their programmes in the form of sound files that people can download from the internet.

△ *The internet is often referred to as the 'Information Superhighway' because it carries vast amounts of computer data. It is also called 'cyberspace', a word first used in 1984 in William Gibson's science-fiction novel* Neuromancer.

HISTORY OF THE INTERNET
1965 Three computers are linked over a phone line in the USA to form an early computer network
1969 ARPANet created by US military
1971 First email sent
1974 Telenet, the first commercial version of ARPANet, starts running
1977 First modem for personal computers invented
1984 Domain name system, which gives computers a unique location ending in .com, .org etc, is introduced
1991 World Wide Web invented
1994 First internet shops and banks
1998 First e-auctions on the internet
2000 World Wide Web is estimated to contain over one billion web pages

IRAN
Government: Islamic republic
Capital: Tehran
Area: 1,648,000 sq km
Population: 63 million
Language: Farsi (Persian)
Currency: Rial

IRAQ
Government: One-party republic
Capital: Baghdad
Area: 434,924 sq km
Population: 22.8 million
Language: Arabic
Currency: Dinar

▷ Iran has many examples of traditional Islamic architecture. The Madrasa-i Chahar Bagh was built in the city of Isfahan in the 1700s as a college for religious studies. It features the tall minarets, or towers, found on every mosque.

continued from page 167

the work of one person, while others have been created by many people working as a team. It is not known who developed many of the earliest inventions such as the **wheel, plough, pottery, weaving** and **metal** tools.

Throughout **history**, civilization has been driven forward by inventions. Each invention has been based on those that came before it, and has made further progress possible. Some important inventions of the last 600 years include the **printing press** (c.1440), **telescope** (1608), **steam engine** (1765), **camera** (1816), **telephone** (1876), **radio** (1895), **aircraft** (1903), **television** (1925), **laser** (1960) and **silicon chip** (1961).

Invertebrate

Invertebrates are **animals** that have no spine, or backbone. There are more than one million different species of invertebrate, with many more waiting to be discovered. They include all the **insects, spiders, scorpions, worms, molluscs, crustaceans, starfish, jellyfish** and many others.

Iran

Iran is a country in the **Middle East**. It lies between the Caspian Sea in the north and the Persian Gulf in the south. **Deserts**, snowy **mountains** and green valleys cover most of the land. Much of the country experiences hot, dry summers and cold winters.

The old name for Iran is Persia, and the Iranian **language** is Persian. The main **religion** is **Islam**. Many Iranians are **nomads** who travel around with flocks of **sheep** or **goats**. Iranian women weave beautiful rugs from **wool** or **silk**, which are famous for their intricate patterns and rich colours. Iran's most important product is **oil**.

Iran has a long **history**. In about 550 BCE, the Persian leader Cyrus and his army established an empire that stretched from **Greece** and **Egypt** to **India**. The Persian empire was then the largest in the world. **Alexander the Great** conquered Persia in about 330 BCE. Later, the country was ruled by Arabs and **Mongols**. During the 1900s, Iran was ruled by emperors, or shahs. In 1979, the **government** of Iran changed and the shah left the country. Religious leaders now rule this Islamic **republic**. From 1980 to 1988, Iran fought a long and bitter war with **Iraq**.

Iraq

Iraq is a country in the **Middle East**. Much of it is a dry, sandy and stony plain that is cool in winter and very hot in summer. The Tigris and Euphrates **rivers** flow through the plain to the Persian Gulf. Their water allows the farmers to grow **rice, cotton, wheat** and dates. Iraq is also one of the largest **oil** producers in the world. Pipelines carry the oil from the north of the country across the **desert** to ports in **Syria** and the **Lebanon**.

Many Iraqis are **nomads** who live in the desert and tend flocks of **sheep** and **goats**. But four million people work in Baghdad, the capital city. Some of the world's first cities, such as Ur, were built near Iraq's big rivers. Later, the powerful Babylonian empire built the famous city of **Babylon** there.

Modern Iraq is a **republic**, with Saddam Hussein (b. 1937) as its **dictator**. It fought a war with **Iran** from 1980 to 1988. In 1990, an Iraqi army invaded Kuwait, but it was forced to leave after the **Gulf War** in 1991.

Ireland

Ireland is the second largest **island** of the **British Isles**. It is a land of green fields, rolling hills, **lakes** (known as loughs) and winding **rivers**. The Shannon, which flows through Ireland's flat central plain, is the longest river in the British Isles. Low **mountain** ranges line the coasts.

The Irish **climate** is mild and moist, and a lush carpet of green **grass** covers much of the land, giving the country the nickname the Emerald Isle. Much of the country's economy is based on **farming** and **fishing**.

England gained control of Ireland in the 1500s, after which Protestants from England and **Scotland** settled there. When Ireland became self-governing in 1921, the six Protestant-dominated northern counties stayed part of the **United Kingdom** and became known as **Northern Ireland**. In the Republic of Ireland, most of the people are Roman Catholics. The division of the island causes continuing tensions.

Iron and Steel

Iron is the cheapest and most useful of all **metals**. It is often mixed with **carbon** and other ingredients to create steel, which is a strong building material.

Iron is one of the most plentiful metals in the **earth**'s crust, where it occurs in the form of a rocky material called iron ore. Before it can be used, the iron ore has to be melted down, or smelted, in a

IRELAND
Government: Republic
Capital: Dublin
Area: 70,284 sq km
Population: 3.7 million
Languages: Irish Gaelic and English
Currency: Euro

∇ **Iron** is extracted from its ore in a blast furnace. Most of the iron is then processed again to make steel or steel alloys.

blast furnace. The iron is then made into cast iron, wrought iron or steel. Cast iron is hard but not as strong as steel. Red-hot molten cast iron is poured into moulds to make such things as **engine** blocks. Wrought iron is softer than cast iron, and is used for chains and gates. Steel is extremely hard and strong. Sometimes other metals such as tungsten and chromium are added to the steel to produce steel **alloys**. These are used to make many different things, from nails to **bridges**, buildings and other objects that carry heavy loads.

Irrigation

Farmers and gardeners who water **plants** are irrigating them. Irrigation makes it possible to grow crops and **flowers** in dry **soils**, even in a **desert**. Farmers in **China**, **Egypt** and **Iraq** have been irrigating large areas of land for thousands of years.

Many countries store **water** in **lakes** made by building **dams** across **rivers**. **Canals** take water from the lakes to farms – one irrigation canal in **Russia** is 850 km long. Ditches or pipes carry water from each canal to the fields. In each field, the water flows between the rows of plants, sometimes spurting up from holes in the pipes and sprinkling the plants like a shower of rain.

1 Iron ore, limestone and coke (a form of carbon) are put into the furnace. These raw materials react with each other to produce poor-quality pig iron.

2 The pig iron is poured into the converter. Oxygen is blown onto the pig iron to turn it into steel.

3 The molten steel can be cast into different shapes while still fluid.

△ The symbols of **Islam** are the crescent and star.

ITALY
Government: Republic
Capital: Rome
Area: 301,225 sq km
Population: 58 million
Language: Italian
Currency: Euro

ISRAEL
Government: Republic
Capital: Jerusalem
Area: 20,770 sq km
Population: 6.1 million
Languages: Hebrew and Arabic
Currency: Shekel

Islam

Islam is the second largest **religion** after **Christianity**, with more than one billion followers known as Muslims. Many Muslims live in the **Middle East**, southern **Asia** and **Africa**. Islam was begun by the Prophet **Muhammad**, an Arab born in about 570 in the city of **Mecca** (in modern **Saudi Arabia**).

Muslims believe in one all-powerful **god** called Allah. The word 'Islam' means 'submission' in Arabic, and Muslims try to submit to Allah's will and live their lives according to his word. They pray five times a day, give gifts to the poor each year and fast from dawn to sunset during the holy month of **Ramadan**. Muslims also try to obey the rules for good living set out in the **Koran**, the Islamic holy **book**. If possible, Muslims must also make a pilgrimage to Mecca at least once during their lifetime. There are two main Islamic **festivals** – **Eid ul-Adha** (Festival of Sacrifice) and Eid ul-Fitr (Festival of the Breaking of the Fast). Islam has no organized church and no priests. Instead, there are holy men and teachers. The Muslim place of worship is called a **mosque**, and the Muslim holy day is Friday.

Island

An island is a piece of land surrounded by **water**. Some islands are chunks of land that became separated from **continents**. Other islands are **volcanoes** that have risen up above sea level.

Israel

Israel is a small country on the eastern shore of the **Mediterranean Sea**. The state of Israel was created in 1948 as a homeland for Jewish people from around the world (see also **Judaism**). More than half of the land is **desert** or dry, rocky **mountains**, but there are also fertile plains, where farmers grow oranges, **cotton**, grain and **vegetables**.

The capital of Israel is **Jerusalem**, which is regarded as a holy place by Jews, Christians and Muslims.

The Israelis have fought several wars against their Arab neighbours. In 1994, a treaty was signed between Israel and the **Palestine** Liberation Organization (PLO) which granted limited self-rule to two mainly Arab regions within Israel – the West Bank and Gaza Strip. However, the bitter conflict between Jews and Palestinians continues.

Italy

Italy is a country in southern **Europe**. It sticks out into the **Mediterranean Sea**, and includes the **islands** of Sicily and Sardinia. Much of Italy is covered with hills and **mountains**. The snowy peaks of the **Alps** cross northern Italy, while the Apennines run like a backbone down the middle of the country. The farmers grow large quantities of grapes, lemons, pears, olives, oranges and **wheat**. Northern Italy is mainly industrial and produces **cars** and **machines**.

Italy was where the **Roman Empire** was founded, and the Roman Catholic Church established its headquarters at the **Vatican** in **Rome**. From the 1300s to the early 1500s, Italy was the centre of the **Renaissance**.

Ivan the Terrible

Ivan IV (1530–1584), was the first tsar, or emperor, of **Russia**. He is known as 'Ivan the Terrible' because he was a cruel ruler who killed his own son, but he also conquered Russia's neighbours to make it into a stronger nation. During his reign, **Moscow** became Russia's capital.

Ivory

Ivory is a hard, creamy white substance that forms long **teeth**, or tusks, in the **elephant**, **hippopotamus** and **walrus**. Elephants have long been hunted for their ivory, but are now protected.

Jackal

The jackal is a member of the **dog** family. There are three species, found in eastern **Europe**, the **Middle East**, southern **Asia** and North **Africa**. Like most wild dogs, they are both hunters and scavengers, and use their superb senses of **hearing** and **smell** to track down food after dark. They hunt a wide range of small animals. By day, jackals hide in thick undergrowth.

Jaguar

One of the big **cats**, the jaguar lives in the **rainforests**, grasslands and swamps of the northern half of **South America**

◁ The golden **jaguar** often lives near water and is expert at fishing. It waits on the bank, and flips fish out of the water with a paw.

JAMAICA
Government:
Constitutional monarchy
Capital: Kingston
Area: 10,991 sq km
Population: 2.6 million
Language: English
Currency: Jamaican dollar

◁ The golden **jackal** is known as 'the howler' by Arabs because of its loud yapping and cries, which are usually heard at night.

and in parts of **Central America**. It is the largest species of American cat, and can weigh up to 150 kg. The jaguar's coat is rich yellow with black spots, and resembles that of the **leopard** of **Africa** and **Asia**. However, unlike the leopard, many of the jaguar's spots are in the centre of rings of dark fur.

Jaguars are good tree-climbers and, unusually for a cat, are also excellent swimmers. They hunt mainly at night for **rodents**, peccaries (a type of wild **pig**), **deer** and other **mammals**. They also eat **turtles**, **frogs** and **fish**.

Jamaica

Jamaica is a tropical **island** in the **Caribbean** Sea. Its name means 'island of springs' – there are many streams flowing from springs on the sides of the country's forested **mountains**.

More than two and a half million people live in Jamaica, most of whom have African ancestry. Many people work on farms that grow bananas, oranges, coconuts, **coffee** and **sugar** cane. Jamaica also has large mines to extract bauxite – the ore from which **aluminium** is produced. Its capital, Kingston, is an important port.

JAPAN
Government:
Parliamentary democracy
Capital: Tokyo
Area: 377,708 sq km
Population: 126 million
Language: Japanese
Currency: Yen

Jazz musicians often start by playing a tune or rhythm, and develop it as the mood takes them.

Jellyfish tentacles are covered with powerful stinging cells that paralyse passing animals, and pull the victims up to the jellyfish's waiting mouth.

Japan

Japan is a long string of islands in the **Pacific Ocean** off the mainland coast of eastern **Asia**. Its largest island is Honshu, followed by Hokkaido to the north, and Kyushu and Shikoku to the south. **Mountains** cover much of Japan. The highest is a snow-capped **volcano** called Fujiyama, or Mount Fuji, which last erupted in 1707. There are also large **forests**, and many **waterfalls** and **rivers**. Northern Japan has cool summers and cold winters, while the southern islands have a much warmer **climate**.

Japan is a crowded country, with more than 126 million people. To feed this population, Japanese farmers grow huge amounts of **rice**, and the country has one of the world's largest **fishing** fleets. However, Japan still has to import large quantities of **food**.

Japan does not have many **minerals**, so has to buy most of the minerals it needs from other countries. But because of its advanced technology and efficient factories, it is a great industrial power. Japan is one of the world's top producers of **cars**, **ships** and **electronic** equipment such as **radios** and **television** sets.

During the 1800s, Japan became one of the world's most powerful nations. It fought against the Allied powers in **World War II**, but in 1945 the **USA** dropped atomic bombs on the cities of Hiroshima and Nagasaki, which forced Japan to surrender. After the war, Japan became a fully democratic country (see **democracy**), and the once all-powerful emperor became the head of state, with only ceremonial duties.

Jazz

Jazz is a kind of **music** that began in the **USA** in the late 1800s. The players use unexpected rhythms, and often improvize – that is, they make up the notes and melodies on the spur of the moment. However, they must fit the music made by the rest of the band.

The main instruments used in jazz are the saxophone, trumpet, **piano**, **guitar** and **drums** (see also **musical instruments**). The development of jazz has been influenced by various other styles of music, especially the **blues**.

Jefferson, Thomas

Thomas Jefferson (1743–1826) was the third **president** of the **United States**, and one of the most important founders of the country. He was a champion of **democracy** and liberty, and the main author of the Declaration of Independence (1776), which forms the foundation of American **government** to this day. This document has had an immense influence all over the world. Its most important parts state that 'all men are created equal', and have the right to 'Life, Liberty and the Pursuit of Happiness'.

Jellyfish

A jellyfish is a kind of **invertebrate** (**animal** without a backbone) that lives in the **ocean**. It has a soft body and is armed with stinging tentacles, which it uses to catch and kill prey. It eats mainly small **fish**, shrimps, floating **plankton** and other jellyfish.

Jerusalem

Jerusalem is the capital of **Israel**, and is located high up in hilly country. It is a holy city for **Judaism**, **Christianity** and **Islam**. Huge walls surround the

▽ Jerusalem's centre is a centuries-old maze of streets and closely packed buildings. There are numerous holy sites, including synagogues, mosques and churches.

city's oldest part. In 1948, Jerusalem was divided between Israel and **Jordan**, but Israel captured the whole city during a war in 1967. Since then, the tensions between Jerusalem's Jewish and Muslim residents have frequently erupted into violence. There have been several attempts at drawing up a peace settlement, but so far without success.

Jesus Christ

Jesus Christ was a religious leader on whose life and teachings **Christianity** was founded. Most Christians believe that he is the Son of God, and that he was sent to earth to save humanity. The life of Jesus is described in the New Testament of the **Bible**.

Jesus was born in Bethlehem (in present-day **Israel**) around 4–1 BCE. His date of birth is not certain, but has long been celebrated on 25 December – **Christmas** Day. His mother was Mary. When Jesus grew up, he travelled throughout the Holy Land, teaching and healing sick people. The Bible tells how Jesus performed miracles to show people the love of God.

Jesus had twelve followers known as apostles, who were chosen to spread his teachings throughout the world. However, he also had enemies. In the end, one of the apostles, Judas Iscariot, betrayed Jesus to his opponents in the **Roman Empire**. The Romans crucified Jesus on a cross, but the New Testament says that he was resurrected (came to life again) and rose to heaven. Jesus' followers were convinced he was the Messiah, and they began to convert people to Christianity.

△ A **jet engine** has rotating blades at the front, which suck in air. The air is compressed, or squashed, and ignited with aviation fuel. This creates hot gases, which are forced out of the rear of the engine, pushing the aircraft forwards.

▽ **Joan of Arc** was burned at the stake by her English enemies, who claimed she was a witch.

Jet engine

A swimmer travels forwards by pushing **water** backwards, and a jet **engine** works in a similar way. It drives an **aircraft** forwards by pushing **gases** backwards. **Air** is sucked into the front of the jet engine, and is blown into the combustion chamber. There, the air is ignited using aviation **fuel** – kerosene or paraffin. The burning fuel produces extremely hot gases, which shoot out of the back of the engine as exhaust. **Rockets** work in a similar way, but do not need a supply of air.

Jews *see* Judaism

Jewellery

Ornaments worn to decorate the body are called jewellery. The most common kinds are earrings, necklaces, brooches, bracelets and rings. Jewellery has been found that dates from earliest human history. In addition to its use as personal decoration, jewellery has been worn as a symbol of wealth and status, and for religious reasons. Expensive jewellery is often made of **gold** or **silver**, and set with **diamonds** or other **gems**.

Joan of Arc

Joan of Arc (1412–1431) was born into an ordinary peasant family in **France**, but was to lead an **army** against the English during the **Hundred Years' War**. When still only 17 years old, Joan claimed that God told her to rid France of its English invaders. She left the farm where she worked, and persuaded France's king,

Charles VII (1697–1745), to let her lead his army. Joan won five battles, but was captured by the English and burned as a witch. However, she had managed to save France. In 1920, the **pope** made her a saint.

Johnson, Samuel

Samuel Johnson (1709–1784) was an English writer. He was famous for his witty remarks, and for the sharpness of his opinions on people, politics and literature. As well as writing novels, Johnson compiled one of the first English **dictionaries**.

Jordan

Jordan is a small country in the **Middle East**, in the northwest corner of the Arabian Peninsula. Most of the country lies on a plateau 1,000 m above sea level. The Jordan **River** and the salty Dead Sea lie to the west of the plateau.

In 1967, **Israel** captured Jordanian land west of the Jordan River. This area is known as the West Bank. In 1988, Jordan renounced its claims to the West Bank, and passed responsibility for the area to the **Palestine** Liberation Organization (PLO).

Judaism

Judaism is the **religion** of the Jewish people. It teaches that there is one true God, who revealed himself to the Jews and has given the human race rules by which to live. The Jewish holy **book** is the Hebrew **Bible**. This consists of the first five books of Moses (the Torah), historical accounts of the tribes of **Israel**, and books written by kings and prophets (messengers). Christians include all of this material in their Bible, calling it the Old Testament.

One of **Judaism**'s most sacred sites is the Western Wall in Jerusalem, which is all that remains of King David's Temple (above).

JORDAN
Government:
Constitutional monarchy
Capital: Amman
Area: 97,740 sq km
Population: 4.7 million
Language: Arabic
Currency:
Jordanian dinar

Jews try to live their lives according to the Bible's Ten Commandments. They believe that God gave the Law to Moses on top of Mount Sinai after Moses led their ancestors out of **Egypt**, where they had been slaves. This flight from Egypt is known as the Exodus, and is commemorated in one of Judaism's most important **festivals – Passover**. Other Jewish festivals include **Yom Kippur**, when sins are confessed and forgiveness asked, and **Chanukah**.

Today, Jews live throughout the world, but regard Israel as their spiritual and historical home. Jews pray in buildings called **synagogues**, and their teachers are known as rabbis. The Jewish holy day is the Sabbath, which lasts from sunset on Friday to sunset on Saturday.

Jupiter

Jupiter is the largest of the **planets** in our **solar system**. It is twice the size of all the other planets put together. Jupiter's force of **gravity** is extremely powerful – anyone on Jupiter would weigh twice as much as on **earth**. Astronomers think that most of Jupiter is made up of hot, **liquid hydrogen**. The planet appears to have light and dark belts around it, and it is circled by 28 moons. Jupiter spins so fast that a **day and night** last less than ten 'earth hours'. But a **year** on Jupiter is 12 times longer than an 'earth year' because it is further from the **sun**.

JUPITER FACTS
Average distance from sun: 778 million km
Nearest distance from earth: 630 million km
Average temperature: –150°C
Diameter across the equator: 142,800 km
Atmosphere: Hydrogen, helium
Number of moons: 28
Length of day: 9 hours 50 minutes
Length of year: 11.9 earth years

KAZAKHSTAN
Government: Republic
Capital: Astana
Area: 2,717,000 sq km
Population: 14.9 million
Languages: Kazakh, Russian and German
Currency: Tenge

△ **Kangaroos** are the largest type of marsupial. This picture shows a family group of eastern grey kangaroos, which live in eastern Australia and grow up to 2.4 m long, including the tail.

Kangaroo

Kangaroos are **marsupials** that live in **Australia**. Most of them live on grassy plains and in dry, open country known as the 'bush'. Kangaroos feed on **grass** and other **plants**. They move about in groups, springing along on their large, powerful back legs. Their long tails help them to keep their balance.

There are many species of kangaroo. Red and grey kangaroos are the largest. When it stands on tiptoe, a fully grown red kangaroo may be taller than an adult human. Grey kangaroos can run at up to 55 km/h. Smaller members of the kangaroo family are called **wallabies**.

Kazakhstan

Kazakhstan is a large country that was a **republic** of the former **Soviet Union** until 1991. It stretches from the Caspian Sea in the west to **China** in the east. Much of country is steppe (a type of grassland) or **desert**. There are rich deposits of **metals** and **minerals**, such as **lead**, **iron**, **coal** and **oil**. For centuries, the people of Kazakhstan lived as **nomads**, herding livestock from place to place. This lifestyle changed after **Russia** conquered the country in 1800, advancing **farming** and industry.

KENYA
Government: Republic
Capital: Nairobi
Area: 582,646 sq km
Population: 29.4 million
Languages: Swahili and English
Currency: Shilling

Kennedy, John Fitzgerald

John F. Kennedy (1917–1963) was the 35th **president** of the **USA**. After serving with the US navy in **World War II**, Kennedy entered politics and was elected to the House of Representatives – the lower chamber of the US **parliament**. He became president in 1960 at the age of 43, the youngest person ever to win this office.

The 'Kennedy era' was a time of great optimism and prosperity in the United States. To many people, Kennedy was a symbol of this strength. The **Soviet Union** was a major rival of the USA in this period known as the Cold War. Kennedy forced the Soviet Union to halt its efforts to base **nuclear** missiles in **Cuba**, and relations between the two nations improved. In 1963, Kennedy was assassinated in Dallas, Texas, by Lee Harvey Oswald (1939–1963).

Kenya

Kenya is a country in East **Africa**. Its southwest border touches the shores of **Lake** Victoria, and the **Indian Ocean** lies to the southeast. The **equator** runs across the middle of the country. Much of the land is covered by **mountains** and flat-topped hills. The rest is mainly **savanna** – a type of open grassland with scattered acacia **trees**. The savanna is home to herds of grazing **mammals**,

177

Vein from kidneys

Artery to kidneys

Kidney

Cutaway kidney

Ureter

Bladder

Urethra

△ The **kidneys** are part of a system for cleaning the blood of impurities and excess liquid. These drain off down the ureters into the bladder, and leave the body through the urethra as urine.

▽ **Kiwis** are nocturnal, flightless birds unique to New Zealand's forests.

including **antelope zebra** and **elephant**, as well as **carnivores** such as **lions, leopards** and **hyenas**. There are several huge national parks where animals are protected, and these attract tourists from all over the world. Tourism is a major part of Kenya's economy.

Kenya was a British colony from 1895 until 1963, when it became an independent state. However, it remains a member of the British **Commonwealth**. Some Kenyans, such as the Masai, herd **cattle**. Others grow crops such as maize, **tea** and **coffee**, much of which are sold abroad.

Kidney

All **vertebrates** (**animals** with a backbone) have two kidneys. These are bean-shaped, reddish-brown organs. Human kidneys are about the size of a person's fist, and lie on each side of the backbone at about waist level.

Kidneys clean the **blood**. They do this by filtering out waste matter and straining off any **water** that the body does not need. Blood pumped from the **heart** flows into each kidney through an **artery**. Inside the kidneys, the waste matter and surplus water are removed from the blood and mixed to make urine. The urine drips slowly into the bladder. The filtered blood flows out of the kidney through a **vein**.

King, Martin Luther

Martin Luther King (1929–1968) was an American **civil rights** leader who worked for racial justice through peaceful means. He was born in Atlanta, Georgia, and became a Baptist minister like his father. It was in Montgomery, Alabama, where he was pastor, that he began his civil rights crusade.

In 1956, King organized a boycott of buses in Montgomery as a protest against the unfair treatment of black passengers. During the next ten years, he led many peaceful demonstrations and meetings all over the **USA**. Success came when the US Congress passed civil rights laws in 1964 and 1965.

King was awarded the **Nobel Prize** for Peace in 1964 for his campaigns of non-violence. However, in 1968, at the age of just 39, he was assassinated in Memphis, Tennessee.

Martin Luther King's speeches were an inspiration to many people, and still have great influence to this day. One of his most famous speeches was in 1963, when he spoke to a crowd of 200,000 people who had come to **Washington D.C.** to march for civil rights for all people. In his speech he said: 'I have a dream that one day this nation will rise up and live out the true meaning of its creed: "We hold these truths to be self-evident, that all men are created equal".'

Kiwi

This strange **bird** from **New Zealand** gets its name from the shrill cries made by the male. The kiwi is a stocky brown bird as large as a chicken. It has tiny wings but cannot fly, and instead runs on its short, strong legs. Its **feathers** are shaggy and look very much like the **hair** of **mammals**.

Kiwis are shy birds that live in **forests**. By day, they sleep in burrows. At night, they emerge to hunt for **worms** and grubs.

Kiwis have very poor **sight**, and use their superb sense of **smell** to locate food. Unusually for birds, their nostrils are located at the tip of their long, thin beaks. The females lay very large **eggs**, which are incubated by the males.

Young **koalas** hold tightly to their mothers' backs as they climb through the eucalyptus trees that form their habitat.

Knight

In the **Middle Ages**, a knight was a soldier on horseback who fought for his ruler. In peacetime, he served his master in his household. Although, in theory, anyone could become a knight, **horses** and **armour** were so expensive that few people could afford them, and knighthood became an honour usually given to the wealthy. Boys trained for it from the age of about seven.

Knights lost their usefulness in **war** when the introduction of **guns** changed fighting methods. The British **monarch** still makes people knights as a reward for special service to the country, but these are purely honorary.

Reef knot

Clove hitch

There are many different types of **knot** for various purposes. Choosing the right knot is half the skill of knot-tying.

Knot

A knot is a way of fastening rope, cord or thread. Knots are especially important for sailors and **mountain**

Armies of heavily armoured **knights** first emerged in Europe during the 800s, and dominated warfare on the continent until the 1300s.

climbers, although most people need to tie a knot at some time.

Knots are used to make a noose, tie up a bundle, or join the ends of small cords. There are also bends and hitches. A bend is used to tie the ends of rope together, and a hitch is used to attach a rope to a ring or post. Common knots include the reef knot, bowline, clove hitch, half hitch and sheet bend. Rope ends can also be joined by weaving them together. This is called a splice.

Koala

The koala is a **marsupial** that resembles a small, chubby **bear**. It lives in the **forests** of eastern **Australia**, and also visits parks and large **gardens**. The koala climbs slowly among the branches of **trees** and rarely descends to the ground. Its only food is the leaves of eucalyptus trees. Forest **fires** and **hunting** nearly made the koala extinct, but many koalas now live on protected reserves.

◁ Muslims believe that the **Koran**'s sacred text was revealed to the Prophet Muhammad by the Angel Gabriel.

Koran

The Koran is the holy **book** of **Islam**. Its name means 'a recitation'. It contains 114 chapters of Arabic verse, and says that there is one God whose prophets (messengers) included Abraham, **Jesus Christ** and **Muhammad**. The book teaches Muslims to be humble, generous and just. It is said that the Koran was revealed to Muhammad by the Angel Gabriel, or Jizreel. The way it is written has influenced Arabic literature.

Korea, North

North Korea forms the northern half of the Korean Peninsula in **Asia**, which juts out from **China** into the Sea of **Japan**. It was created in 1948, when the Korean Peninsula was divided into two separate states – North Korea and **South Korea**. North Korea has many **mountains**, and **forests** cover large areas. **Farming** is the main occupation, and the main crops are **rice** and **silk**. Heavy industry, such as steel-making (see **iron** and **steel**), is also important.

NORTH KOREA
Government: Communist
Capital: Pyongyang
Area: 120,538 sq km
Population: 23.4 million
Language: Korean
Currency: Won

North Korea adopted **communism**, and from 1950 to 1953 it fought a war with South Korea. During the war, it was helped by two other communist powers in Asia – **China** and the **Soviet Union**. South Korea was supported by forces from the **United Nations** (mainly the **USA**). After the war, North and South Korea remained hostile, but in the late 1990s, relations between them gradually began to improve. There is now an uneasy peace in the region.

Korea, South

South Korea was born in 1948 as a result of the division of the Korean peninsula into two independent nations. It is smaller than its northern neighbour, **North Korea**, but its **population** is twice as large and its industry more developed. It manufactures **cars**, **ships**, **textiles**, steel (see **iron** and **steel**) and a wide range of **electronic** products. South Korea's capital, Seoul, is one of the world's largest cities, with more than 10.5 million people.

SOUTH KOREA
Government: Republic
Capital: Seoul
Area: 98,484 sq km
Population: 46.8 million
Language: Korean
Currency: Won

Kremlin

This is the oldest part of **Moscow** in **Russia**. Some of its buildings date from the 1100s. For most of its history, the Kremlin has been the seat of the Russian **government**, and it used to be the residence of Russia's tsars, or emperors.

Kublai Khan

The grandson of the warlord **Genghis Khan**, Kublai Khan (1216–1294) was leader of the **Mongol** empire when it reached the peak of its power in **Asia**. Kublai became Great Khan in 1259. He conquered **China** and set up his capital at Cambulac (modern **Beijing**). It was the first time China had been completely overcome by outside forces. Kublai Khan also forced neighbouring countries in **Southeast Asia** to accept him as their ruler.

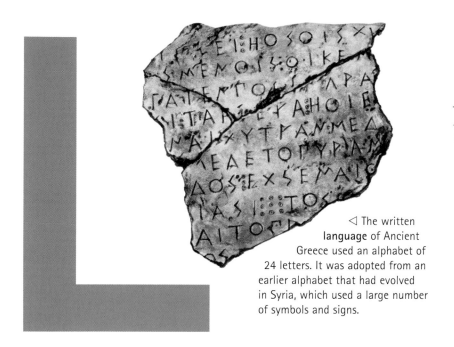

◁ The written **language** of Ancient Greece used an alphabet of 24 letters. It was adopted from an earlier alphabet that had evolved in Syria, which used a large number of symbols and signs.

Lake

A lake is an area of **water** that fills a hollow in the surface of the **earth**. The world's largest lake is the salty Caspian Sea, which lies between **Europe** and **Asia**, east of the Caucasus **mountains**. The largest freshwater lake is Lake Superior, one of the **Great Lakes**.

Many lakes were formed during the **Ice Ages**. They began in valleys carved by **glaciers**. When the glaciers melted, they left behind mud and stones that formed natural **dams**. The meltwater from the glaciers piled up behind the dams to form lakes.

Lakes provide an important **habitat** for many kinds of **plant** and **animal**,

LAOS
Government: People's Republic
Capital: Vientiane
Area: 236,800 sq km
Population: 5.1 million
Language: Lao
Currency: Kip

and are used by people as a source of water, for **fishing** and for transportation.

Language

Language is the way in which **human beings** communicate with each other. It includes **speech**, **writing** and sign language. Many other **animals** have ways of communicating, including special body movements and **sounds**. But speaking is something that only humans can do. Spoken language came first, and later people invented a way of writing it down. Today, there are 4,000–5,000 languages in the world. Some of the most widely spoken are Mandarin Chinese, English, Hindi, Arabic, Spanish and French.

Laos

Laos is a country in **Southeast Asia**. Its capital and largest city is Vientiane on the Mekong **River**. It has a tropical **climate**, and most of the land is covered

▽ Many **lakes** are fed by rivers and streams, which often form a marshy delta where they enter the lake. Other rivers drain water out of the lake, and over time may cut a valley or gorge.

Gorge

Hollow carved by glaciers to form lake

Marshy delta

River flowing into lake

181

with **forests** and **mountains**. Nearly all of the **population** earn their living by **farming**. **Rice** is the main crop. Laos came under the control of **France** in 1893, but won independence in 1949.

Lapland

Lapland is a region in the **Arctic** in the far north of **Sweden**, **Norway**, **Finland** and **Russia**. The land is windswept **tundra** or **forests** of **conifers** and birch **trees**. Lapland is named after the people who live there, the Lapps, who are mainly **nomads**. They travel the land with herds of reindeer, sleep in tents and eat reindeer meat. Other Lapps are fishers or farmers, and live in villages. The Lapps' traditional clothing is made from reindeer hides and **wool**. They speak a **language** with the same roots as Finnish.

Laser

A laser is a device that concentrates **light** to produce a narrow, powerful beam. Many lasers have a ruby crystal or **gas** inside them. Bright light, **radio** waves or **electricity** are fed into the laser. This makes the **atoms** of the crystal or gas jump around very fast. The atoms give off strong light.

The light of lasers can be used for many things. Doctors use small laser beams to burn away tumours and tiny areas of **disease** in the body. Laser beams are also used to make precision cuts in **surgery**, repair damaged **eyes** and correct short- or long-sightedness (see **lens**). Dentists can use lasers to drill holes in **teeth**. Lasers are used in factories to cut **metal** and join tiny metal parts together. Some lasers are strong enough to cut through materials as hard as **diamonds**.

Another use for lasers is to measure distance. The laser beam is aimed at

Artificial ruby rod

Coiled fluorescent light

Mirror

Mirror

Laser beam

Inside this **laser**, a bright light is aimed at a ruby crystal. This energises the ruby's atoms, so it flashes light. Mirrors concentrate the laser beam.

Lines of **latitude** and **longitude** are drawn in a grid over the earth's surface, and allow us to locate places quickly.

△ People accused of breaking the **law** may have to go to court, where lawyers argue the case. They present evidence and question witnesses. A jury decides whether the accused is guilty or not.

objects far away, and the distance is measured by counting the **time** it takes for the light to travel there and back. Laser beams can also carry radio and **television** signals. A single laser beam can send many **telephone** calls and television programmes without mixing them up (see **fibre optics**).

Latitude and Longitude

Lines of latitude and longitude are imaginary lines drawn on **maps**, atlases and globes. They form an interlocking network that allows us to pinpoint places with great accuracy. Everywhere on **earth** has a different position of latitude and longitude.

Lines, or parallels, of latitude show how far north or south of the **equator** a place is. They are measured in degrees (written as °). The equator lies at 0° latitude. The **North Pole** has a latitude of 90° N ('north'), and that of the **South Pole** is 90° S ('south'). Lines, or meridians, of longitude show far east or west a place is. Greenwich in **London** lies at 0° longitude. A place halfway around the world from London is at 180° longitude.

Latvia *see* Baltic States

Law

Laws are the official rules that people live by. They control many of the things that people do, and help them live together in peace. In a **democracy**, laws are proposed by the **government**, passed by an elected body such as a **parliament**, and enforced by the **police** and courts.

The first written laws were enacted in **Babylon** 4,000 years ago. The ancient Jews based their laws on the Ten Commandments given to Moses by God, as related in the **Bible** (see **Judaism**).

The Romans (see **Roman Empire**) developed many new kinds of law, such as family law, property law and criminal law, some of which are still in use around the world.

Someone who is accused of breaking the law may be summonsed to court, and is known as the 'defendant'. In the court, two teams of lawyers put each side of the case. The prosecution tries to prove that the defendant is guilty, and the defence attempts to show that he or she is innocent. Then it is up to the jury – a randomly selected group of members of the public – to decide. The judge determines the punishment.

△ **Lead** was formerly used in cosmetics, before it was known that the metal is toxic to humans.

Lead

Lead is a heavy, blue-grey **metal** that does not **rust**. It is used for many things, but its greatest single use is in **batteries** for **cars**. Lead shields protect workers from dangerous radiation in the **X-ray** departments of **hospitals** and in **nuclear** power stations (see also **radioactivity**). Lead is mixed with **tin** to make solder, which is used for joining pieces of metal. Many items are now made without lead because lead can be poisonous to humans. It interferes with the production of red **blood** cells, and may damage organs such as the **brain**, **kidneys** and **liver**.

Leaf

A leaf is the **food** factory of a green **plant**. To make food, the leaf needs **light** from the **sun**, carbon dioxide from the **air** and **water**. Air enters the leaf through tiny holes called stomata. Water is drawn up from the ground by the plant's roots. It flows up the stem and into the leaf through tiny tubes called veins. Inside the leaf is a green substance called chlorophyll. The chlorophyll uses light, carbon dioxide and water to make **sugar**. This process is called photosynthesis.

The sugar then passes through tubes to the other parts of the plant. The byproduct of photosynthesis is **oxygen**, most of which passes into the air.

In the autumn, broad-leaved or deciduous **trees** shed their leaves. The water supply to the leaves is shut off, which destroys their green **colour** and gives the leaves yellow, orange and red tints. **Conifers** are trees with needle-shaped leaves that are not lost in winter.

▽ A **leaf** is designed to catch as much sunlight and lose as little water as possible. It is held out to the light by stiff veins, and its upper surface has transparent cells that allow light to reach the internal structures where food is made. The leaf's waterproof outer layer stops the leaf drying out.

Leakey family

The Leakey family discovered **fossils** in East **Africa** that traced the **evolution** of modern **human beings** from early apelike ancestors. Born in **Kenya**, Louis Leakey (1903–1972) unearthed the fossil remains of a primitive human species in a gorge in **Tanzania**, which he suggested was our true ancestor. In 1978, Louis' wife, Mary Leakey (1913–1996), found human footprints that were made 3.5 million years ago. The Leakeys' son, Richard (b. 1944), discovered many more early human remains in Africa during the 1970s.

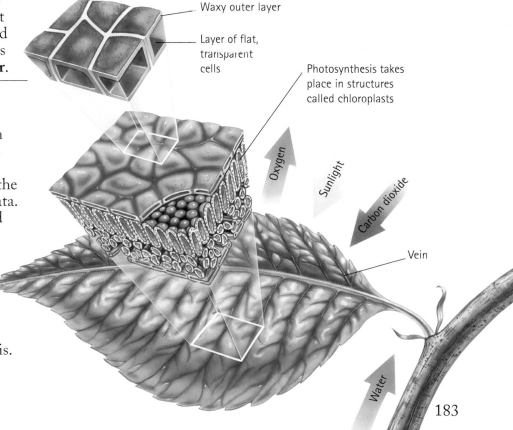

Waxy outer layer

Layer of flat, transparent cells

Photosynthesis takes place in structures called chloroplasts

Oxygen

Sunlight

Carbon dioxide

Vein

Water

183

LEBANON
Government: Republic
Capital: Beirut
Area: 10,400 sq km
Population: 4.2 million
Language: Arabic
Currency: Lebanese
pound

△ Lenin's revolutionary ideas led to the defeat of Russia's old regime ruled by emperors, or tsars, and to the birth of communist rule in Russia.

Leather

Leather is made from the **skin**, or hide, of **animals**. Most leather comes from **mammals** such as **cattle**. First, the skins are cured by being soaked in salt **water**. Then the remaining **hair** and meat is taken off. Next the skins are treated with a chemical called tannin, which comes from **tree** bark. This process is called tanning, and it makes the skins strong and waterproof. Finally, the leather is oiled to soften it and is dyed different **colours**. It is now ready to be cut, shaped and stitched or glued into the final product.

Lebanon

Lebanon is a country in the **Middle East** that borders the **Mediterranean Sea**. It lies between **Syria** and **Israel**. Lebanon's coast is flat, but inland there are dry, rocky **mountains**.

Lebanon has been a trading centre for centuries. Ancient Lebanon was part of the Phoenician Empire. The Phoenicians were great traders all over the Mediterranean. Later, Lebanon became part of the **Byzantine Empire**, ruled from **Constantinople**. It was famous for the fine cedar **wood** that came from its **forests**.

Since 1975, Lebanon has experienced instability caused by rivalries between **religions** and political groups. The

country was torn apart by a **civil war** in 1975–1976, and there were further outbreaks of fighting in the late 1970s and throughout the 1980s. Lebanon has also suffered as a result of the ongoing conflict between **Israel** and Palestinians based in southern Lebanon (see also **Palestine**).

Legend
see Myths and Legends

Lenin, Vladimir Ilyich

Vladimir Ilyich Lenin (1870–1924) helped to make **Russia** the world's first communist country. Like the German Karl **Marx**, Lenin believed in a political system known as **communism**. He wanted every country to be run by the workers and no longer split into the wealthy and the poor.

For many years, Lenin lived outside Russia, and wrote **books** and articles for communist **newspapers**. In 1917, he returned to Russia and became the leader of the Bolsheviks, a communist group, who overthrew the **government**. This event is called the **Russian Revolution**. Lenin played a major part in Russia's new communist government until his death in 1924.

Lens

Lenses make objects look larger or smaller. Artificial lenses are usually made of **glass** or **plastic**, but the lens inside your **eye** is made of **protein**.

Convex lens

Object

Virtual image

Concave lens

Virtual image

Object

◁ **Lenses** come in two main forms: convex and concave. Light rays passing through a convex lens bend outwards, making the virtual image appear larger than it really is. The virtual image is what we see. A concave lens bends the rays inwards and the image looks smaller.

binoculars, **telescopes**, periscopes and **cameras**. The human eyeball acts like a large convex lens, and focuses **light** rays onto the back of our eye. However, some people's eyes cannot focus properly, and they may be unable to see clearly. Their vision can usually be corrected with spectacles, and in some cases, through **surgery**. Short-sighted people have difficulty in seeing distant objects, and use spectacles that have concave lenses. People with long sight cannot focus on nearby objects, and use spectacles with convex lenses.

Leopard

Leopards are big **cats** that live in much of **Africa** and in parts of southern **Asia**. They are also found in **Southeast Asia** and the **Middle East**, but have become rare there. Leopards inhabit a range of **habitats**, including open grasslands, **forests**, **mountains** and even the edges of **deserts**. Most leopards have spotted coats similar to those of the **jaguar**, but some called panthers are almost entirely black. Leopards are powerful and agile hunters. They catch and eat a wide range of **animals**, including **mammals**, **reptiles** and **fish**.

Library

A library is a place where **books** and documents are stored so that people can refer to them. Some libraries also store other things, such as old manuscripts, **maps**, **drawings** and **recordings**. One of the world's largest libraries is the Library of Congress in **Washington D.C.** in the **United States**, which has over 80 million different items in its vast collection.

△ The **leopard** often drags its kills, such as this antelope, up into trees. There, the big cat can devour its prey at leisure, and other predators are unable to feed on the carcass.

A lens has smooth sides, which are often curved. There are two kinds of simple lens. A lens where the middle is thicker than the edges is called a convex lens, and magnifies objects. A lens in which the edges are thicker than the middle is called a concave lens, and reduces the size of objects. Many kinds of device use convex lenses, including **microscopes**,

LIBYA

Government: Islamic
Arab Socialist
Capital: Tripoli
Area: 1,759,540 sq km
Population: 5.4 million
Language: Arabic
Currency: Libyan dinar

Libya

Libya is a large country in North **Africa**. It has a small **population** for its size because most of the country lies in the barren **Sahara Desert**. Most Libyans are Arabs, and **farming** is the chief occupation. Libya also has rich supplies of **oil**. The country became part of the Turkish Ottoman Empire in the 1500s (see **Turkey**), and was a colony of **Italy** from 1912 until the end of **World War II**. In 1952, Libya became an independent monarchy as the United Kingdom of Libya.

In 1969, **army** officers overthrew the king and took control, and Colonel Muammar Muhammad al-Qadhafi (b. 1942) became head of the country's **government**. Since then, al-Qadhafi has led a revolution in Libyan life. He has often argued that Arab countries should unite and promote the **religion** of **Islam**. However, under al-Qadhafi Libya has funded **terrorism** and revolutionary groups in other parts of the world. In 1992, the **United Nations** imposed economic sanctions on Libya, which remain in force today.

Lichens

Lichens are simple living things that are made up of fungi (see **fungus**) and algae living together. They lack roots, **leaves** and **flowers**. Some lichens grow as crusty patches on **rocks**, **trees** and walls. They grow very slowly – a patch no larger than your hand may be hundreds of years old. Other lichens grow as small, shrubby tufts close to the ground. Lichens can live in places that are too dry, cold or hot for green **plants**.

Liechtenstein

Liechtenstein is one of the smallest countries in the world. It lies between **Switzerland** and **Austria** in the **Alps**. Many international **companies** have their headquarters in Liechtenstein because businesses pay less **tax** there than elsewhere. Tourism also brings **money** into the country.

Light

Light is a form of **energy** that we can see. Some things, such as **stars**, electric lightbulbs (see **electricity**) and certain types of chemical, produce light. However, most do not produce light, and are visible only because they reflect it. For example, we can see the **moon** and **planets** in the sky only because they reflect light from the **sun**.

Sunlight is normally the brightest light visible to humans. Bright sunlight seems white, but is made up of the **colours** of the **rainbow** (see **spectrum**). The English scientist Isaac **Newton** first showed this by making a sunbeam shine through a prism – a 3-D triangle made of **glass**. Seven colours of light emerged from the prism – red, orange, yellow, green, blue, indigo and violet.

A prism splits light into separate beams, each with its own wavelength. This is easy to understand if you think of light travelling in waves. The distance between the tops of the waves is the wavelength, and we see each wavelength as a different colour. Long waves are red, short waves are violet, and the wavelengths inbetween show up as the other colours in the rainbow.

Light travels at more than 300,000 km a second. Even so, it takes eight minutes for the light from the sun to reach **earth**, a distance of about 150 million km. A light **year** is the total distance a beam of light travels in one year. Astronomers (see **astronomy**) use light years to measure how far away stars are. Some stars are millions of light years' distance from the earth.

LIECHTENSTEIN

Government:
Constitutional monarchy
Capital: Vaduz
Area: 157 sq km
Population: 32,000
Language: German
Currency: Swiss franc

nation at the end of the American **Civil War**. But on 14 April 1865, on a visit to Ford's Theatre in **Washington D.C.**, he was shot dead by John Wilkes Booth (1838–1865), an actor who supported the defeated Southern states.

Lindbergh, Charles

Charles Augustus Lindbergh (1902–1974) was an American pilot who became the first man to fly the **Atlantic Ocean** solo. He took off from **New York** on 20 May 1927, and landed the next day in **Paris, France**. His 5,600-km flight had taken 33½ hours. Lindbergh's voyage made him an international hero. Later, he helped to plan air tours to **South America** and over the Atlantic.

Lion

Lions are big **cats** with plain, sandy coats. They live in the southern and eastern regions of **Africa**, and in a tiny part of western **India**. An adult male lion weighs about 180 kg and has a large, shaggy mane. The female is smaller, and has no mane. Lions usually live in groups called prides. A typical pride has one adult male, several adult females and all their cubs. Each pride defends its own hunting territory.

Lightning

Lightning is a naturally occurring form of **electricity**. It is a sudden, massive flow of electric current between two clouds or between a cloud and the ground (see **weather**). Lightning is caused by the movement through the **atmosphere** of **atoms** with positive and negative charges. A huge surge of charged atoms causes a flash and a bang – thunder (see **thunderstorm**).

There are three types of lightning. Streak lightning flashes in a single line from cloud to earth. Forked lightning happens when the lightning divides to find the quickest way to earth. Sheet lightning happens inside a cloud.

Female **lions**, or lionesses, are less heavy and faster than the males, and hunt for all the lions in their pride. They usually hunt together, which means they can tackle larger prey than if they hunted alone. Lions feed mainly on zebra, gazelle and antelope.

Lincoln, Abraham

Abraham Lincoln (1809–1865) was **president** of the **United States** from 1861 to 1865. He had little schooling, but studied **law** on his own. In 1854, a law was passed allowing people in the USA's new western territories to own slaves (see also **slavery**). Lincoln joined the anti-slavery Republican Party in 1856, and was elected president in 1860. He started a second term of office in 1865, just as he was trying to unite the

▷ **Lindbergh's** historic flight across the Atlantic in 1927 inspired many other pioneering pilots. He made the trip in a single-engine aircraft, named the *Spirit of St Louis* in recognition of the financial support given by nine St Louis businessmen.

Liquid

A liquid is a substance that is able to flow and change its shape. If a liquid is poured into a container, it takes the shape of the container but its **volume** remains the same. As a liquid becomes hotter, the **atoms** inside it move faster. They begin to leave the liquid, and a **gas** is formed. When the liquid reaches a certain **temperature**, called the boiling point, all of it turns into gas.

When a liquid cools, its atoms slow down. At freezing point, they settle down into fixed positions and the liquid becomes a solid.

Different liquids have different freezing and boiling points. **Water**, **milk**, **mercury** and **oil** are all liquid at ordinary room temperatures.

This cutaway of the **liver** shows the mass of blood vessels inside the organ. The liver performs over 500 different functions that control the chemical makeup of our blood.

△ **Llamas** are hardy animals, well-adapted to the harsh conditions of the Andes mountains.

▽ Some **lizards**, such as this thorny devil, have evolved spikes and spines to protect them from predators. The thorny devil lives in Australian deserts, and feeds mainly on ants.

Lister, Joseph

Joseph Lister (1827–1912) was an English surgeon who pioneered a way of stopping patients from dying of infections after operations. He used antiseptics to kill **germs** on surgeons' hands and instruments (see **surgery**).

Literature
see **Fiction, Poetry**

Lithuania
see **Baltic States**

Liver

The liver is a flat, triangular organ tucked under the ribs on the right side of the body. It makes the digestive juices that burn up the **fat** that you eat, and manufactures the **proteins** contained in **blood**. It also gets rid of any poisonous substances in the blood, such as **alcohol**, or modifies them so that they are harmless. Another function of the liver is to store essential **minerals** and **vitamins**.

Livingstone, David

David Livingstone (1813–1873) was a Scottish doctor and missionary who explored southern and central **Africa**. He travelled there to help stop traders selling Africans into **slavery**, and to spread **Christianity**. Livingstone made three long journeys between 1841 and 1873. He discovered the Victoria Falls and searched for the source of the **Nile River**. In 1869, after no one had heard from him for several years, the *New York Times* sent a journalist, Henry Stanley (1841–1904), to find him. After a long search, Stanley met Livingstone in 1871 near Lake Tanganyika in **Congo**.

Lizard

Lizards are **reptiles** with dry, scaly skin. Most species have four legs, but some have none and resemble **snakes**. A few lizards are born live like **mammals**, but most of them hatch from **eggs**.

There are about 3,500 species of lizard, most of which are found in hot countries. Lizards that live in cooler regions often spend the winter in a form of **hibernation**. The main prey of lizards is **insects**, but the world's largest lizard, the 2.5 m-long Komodo dragon, may attack and kill **mammals** as large as wild **pigs** and **deer**.

Llama

The llama belongs to the **camel** family, but has no hump. It stands about 1.5 m high at the shoulder and has long, thick **hair** to keep it warm on the cold slopes of the **Andes** mountains in **South America**, where it lives. All llamas are descended from wild ancestors that were tamed by the **Inca** at least 4,500 years ago. Today, South American people still use llamas to carry heavy loads, and make clothes and ropes from llama **wool**. Llamas are also farmed for their wool in many other parts of the world.

Lobster

The lobster is a **crustacean** related to prawns, shrimps and **crabs**. Its body has a hard shell (see **shellfish**). It has four pairs of legs and a pair of huge claws for grabbing **food**. When a lobster feels threatened, it tucks its tail under its body. This drives **water** forwards, which pushes the lobster backwards to escape.

A **lock** contains a bolt that slides into a metal panel in the door frame when the correct key is inserted. In the lock shown above, notches in the key slot into metal plates called tumblers to move the bolt.

Key
Tumbler
Bolt

△ By day, **lobsters** hide among rocks or in holes dug into the seabed. They emerge at night to hunt prey such as prawns and small fish and to scavenge for dead animals.

Lock and Key

There are two main kinds of lock. In the simplest, when the key is turned a piece of **metal**, called a bolt, moves out and fits into a slot. The key has a few notches that are made to fit exactly with similar notches in the lock. The second is the Yale lock, invented in 1860. In a Yale lock, the key turns a cylinder when several small metal pins

in the lock are pushed to the right height by the notches on the key. As there are many possible combinations for the heights of the pins, a Yale lock offers more security than simpler locks.

Locust

The locust is a type of **grasshopper** that lives in **Africa**, southern **Asia** and **Australia**, and which sometimes breeds in enormous numbers. A large swarm may contain hundreds of thousands of locusts. It may travel far across both land and sea to find new feeding-places, and when it lands, the locusts often eat all the **plants** there. Swarms of locusts can destroy crops over huge areas.

London

London is the capital of the **United Kingdom**. It is the largest city in Europe, with a **population** of 7.2 million people. It lies on the Thames River, which flows eastward to the North Sea.

London began as a Roman settlement called Londinium. In the **Middle Ages**, it became the main home of the English kings, and the location of the country's **parliament**. London also grew into an important port and trading centre. During the 1600s, the city's crowded buildings allowed **plague** to spread quickly, and the Great Fire of 1666 destroyed much of the city centre. Parts of London were heavily bombed in **World War II**.

▷ **London** stands on the Thames and its most famous river crossing is Tower Bridge, which was completed in 1894. The central section of this bridge opens to let large ships through.

Louis XIV of France was called the 'Sun King' because of the splendour of his court and of the royal palace at Versailles.

The French king **Louis XVI** proved to be a weak and unpopular ruler, and was executed during the French Revolution.

LUXEMBOURG
Government:
Constitutional monarchy
Capital: Luxembourg
Area: 2,586 sq km
Population: 432,000
Languages: French and Letzeburgesch
Currency: Euro

Today, London is one of the world's major financial centres, with many **banks**, **insurance** companies and a busy stock exchange. Thousands of tourists visit London to see buildings such as Buckingham Palace, the Tower of London and the Houses of Parliament.

Longitude
see **Latitude and Longitude**

Los Angeles

Los Angeles is the second largest city in the **United States**, after **New York**. It is surrounded by huge suburbs, and more than 13 million people live in the wider Los Angeles area. The city is in California, with the **Pacific Ocean** to the west and the San Gabriel **mountain** range to the east. Los Angeles has a large port and business district. Many tourists flock to Hollywood, a hilly suburb where many **films** are produced.

Loudspeaker

A loudspeaker turns electric signals into **sound** waves. The most common kind of loudspeaker has a **plastic** cone fixed to a **wire** coil. Inside the coil is a magnet (see also **magnetism**). Electric signals flow through the coil, making it move to and fro, which in turn makes the cone vibrate. **Air** around the cone also starts to vibrate and these air vibrations reach our **ears** as sounds.

Louis XIV

Louis XIV (1638–1715) ruled **France** for 72 years. He came to the throne when only four years old, although a chief minister, Cardinal Mazarin (1602–1661), governed in his name until 1661. Louis was determined to strengthen the power of the French monarchy, and claimed to rule by absolute power. He once boasted to his courtiers that 'I am the State.'

Louis built a vast palace at **Versailles**, which was like a small town. He forced the nobles to live there and serve him personally to prevent rebellions.

Louis XVI

Louis XVI (1754–1793) of **France** was criticised by his people for being more interested in hunting and entertaining than in important affairs of state. His unpopularity ensured that his attempts to reform the **government** finances were doomed. In July 1789, the **French Revolution** erupted, and in 1791, Louis tried to flee the country with his queen, **Marie Antoinette**. They were captured, and guillotined in 1793.

Lungs

Lungs are organs used in **breathing**. They are two large, sponge-like masses in the chest which absorb **oxygen** from the **air** and remove waste carbon dioxide from the **blood**. Air flows to the lungs down the windpipe, or trachea. Inside the lungs are thousands of tiny tubes called bronchioles, which end in cups known as air sacs, or alveoli. This is where the lungs give oxygen to the blood and take away carbon dioxide.

Luther, Martin

Martin Luther (1483–1546) was a German priest whose quarrel with the Roman Catholic Church started the Protestant **Reformation**. He objected to the way priests forgave people's sins in return for **money**. He also believed that God's teachings lay in the **Bible**, and this was more important to him than what the **popes** and bishops said.

Luxembourg

Luxembourg is one of the smallest countries in **Europe**. The **European Union** has offices in the capital city, which is also called Luxembourg.

△ **Madagascar** is home to a wealth of plants and animals found nowhere else on earth, such as these ring-tailed lemurs (above). These mammals live in troops of up to 20 animals, and eat fruit and leaves.

Machine

A machine is any device that makes work easier by allowing us to use force to complete a task. The machine is stronger than a person trying to carry out the task on their own because it exerts a greater force. When a force is used to move something, we say that work is done.

All of the machines we see working around us are related to one or other of six simple machines: the lever, **screw**, **pulley**, inclined or sloping plane, wedge, and **wheel** and axle.

There are many kinds of levers. The simplest is a long pole, pivoted or balanced on a log and used to lift a heavy **rock**. The screw can pull things together or push them apart – with a screw jack, someone can lift a **car** that weighs far more than they do.

A simple pulley is used in the winding mechanism that raises **water** from a well. The inclined plane makes it easier to raise heavy loads to higher levels – it takes less work to pull a load up a slope than to lift it vertically. The wedge helps us to split things – chisels, knives, nails and axes are all types of wedge.

Probably the most important of all simple machines is the wheel and axle – used not only for moving loads, but also

△ The pulley is a simple **machine** that helps us lift heavy objects. It changes the direction of a force, so by pulling down on the rope, a person can raise a large load. If several pulley wheels are joined together, this increases the size of load that can be lifted with the same effort.

MADAGASCAR
Government: Republic
Capital: Antananarivo
Area: 587,041 sq km
Population: 15 million
Languages: Malagasy and French
Currency: Malagasy franc

as a component of all sorts of other machines, such as **clocks**.

Madagascar

Madagascar is the fourth largest **island** in the world. It is in the **Indian Ocean**, about 400 km off the east coast of **Africa**. Madagascar has fertile coastal plains, thick **forests**, a rugged central plateau and a warm, tropical **climate**. Large areas of land have been stripped bare of natural vegetation to supply timber for export and to create new farmland. The main crops are **coffee**, **rice**, **sugar** cane and vanilla. A unique range of wildlife lives on Madagascar, including **parrots** and **lemurs**.

Between the 800s and 1300s, Arabs set up colonies in Madagascar. In the 1800s, the island came under French control, but it won independence in 1960.

Madrid

Madrid is the capital city of **Spain**. It was chosen by King Philip II (1527–1598) as his capital because it was in the middle of the country. Madrid is the seat of the country's **parliament**. It has many elegant buildings, including the Prado, which has one of the finest collections of **paintings** in the world.

Magellan, Ferdinand

Ferdinand Magellan (1480–1521) was a Portuguese sailor and **explorer**. He set out to find a new sea route to **Asia**, heading west and rounding the southern tip of **South America**.

In September 1519, Magellan sailed west from Seville in **Spain**, around Cape Horn (in the south of present-day **Argentina**) and into the **Pacific Ocean**. His expedition consisted of five **ships** and 270 sailors of several nationalities. Magellan was killed in 1521 during a confrontation between his crew and the residents of Cebu, an **island** in the **Philippines**. But one of his ships returned safely to Spain in September 1522, having completed the first ever round-the-world voyage. This epic journey provided the first positive proof that the **earth** is round. Although Magellan did not live to complete the voyage, the expedition could not have succeeded without his brave leadership.

Magic

Many early peoples used magic. It was their way of attempting to control what happened around them. They chanted magic words, enacted special **dances** and produced magical **paintings**.

△ Many **magic** tricks appear to be impossible, but work because the audience is taken in by the magician's cleverly planned actions and words. Some rely on secret devices that are prepared in advance.

▽ **Magellan** was killed when local villagers in the Philippines attacked his expedition after a dispute.

All through **history**, people have believed that certain things (such as talismans or charms) or people (such as **witches** and sorcerers), have magical powers. Magic is often closely tied up with **religion**. But most people today think of magic as the conjuring tricks performed by magicians.

Magna Carta

The Magna Carta is a signed agreement, or charter, that was drawn up in **England** in the time of King John (1167–1216). Not even the great barons, or nobles, of the time could argue with the king.

King John improved methods of record-keeping and strengthened the **law** courts, but was an unpopular ruler. He was forced to rule harshly and to demand extra **taxes** from the people in order to pay for the war with **France**, which he had inherited from the reign of his elder brother, King Richard (1157–1199). In 1215, the English barons met and demanded that John sign the Magna Carta, or 'great charter'. This document marked the beginning of a new system of **government** in which the king had to rule according to the law.

Magnetism

Magnetism is a kind of force belonging to magnets, which attract **metals**, particularly **iron** and **steel**. The **earth** is a huge natural magnet. Invisible lines of magnetic force spread out around the **planet**, joining the north and south magnetic poles. We call this the earth's magnetic field.

The needle in a **compass** is a magnet. It always turns to face magnetic north. In ancient times, people noticed that a kind of iron ore called a lodestone suspended from a string would always swing to point in the same direction. A lodestone is a natural magnet. Another name for it is magnetite.

An electromagnet is made by coiling **wire** around a metal core and passing **electricity** through the coil. As soon as the current is broken, the magnetic field ceases to exist. Electromagnets can be altered in strength, and made more powerful than ordinary magnets. They are able to produce magnetic fields strong enough to drive **generators** and electric **motors**.

Malaria

Malaria is a common and deadly tropical **disease**. It is caused by a tiny **parasite**, which is carried by the female Anopheles **mosquito**. When an infected mosquito bites someone, parasites pass into that person's bloodstream. Inside the **blood**, the parasites multiply, causing a serious illness that is often fatal.

Drugs are used to treat malaria, but they are not always effective because over time new strains of malarial parasite evolve that are not affected by the drugs. Scientists try to destroy the mosquitoes and the swamps in which they breed. However, so far it has proved impossible to exterminate the **insects** completely.

Malaysia

Malaysia is a country in **Southeast Asia**. It consists of two parts, Peninsular Malaysia, and East Malaysia or Sabah,

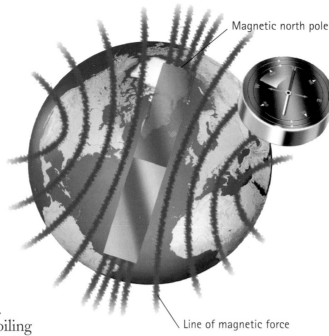

Magnetic north pole

Line of magnetic force

which is part of the **island** of Borneo. These two regions lie 650 km apart, and are separated by the South China Sea. Malaysia's **climate** is hot, humid and rainy, and the country has large areas of **rainforest**.

Malaysia is a fast-growing nation. Its capital, Kuala Lumpur, is a large, modern city with many **skyscrapers**. The country exports **rubber**, **tin** and timber, but some people are worried that its logging industry is cutting down too many **forests**. Malaysia developed modern industries in the late 1900s, and manufactured goods are now the most valuable exports.

Malaysia is a member of the **Commonwealth**. It is ruled by a sultan, who is head of state, and a prime minister, who is head of **government**.

Maldives

The Republic of Maldives is a long chain of **islands** southwest of **India** in the **Indian Ocean**. Although there are about 2,000 islands, the country's total area is small. Most of the people make their living by **fishing**. Scientists think that some islands in the Maldives will vanish in the future because of rising sea levels caused by **global warming**.

MALAYSIA
Government:
Constitutional monarchy
Capital: Kuala Lumpur
Area: 329,749 sq km
Population: 22.7 million
Languages: Malay,
English and Chinese
Currency: Ringgit

MALDIVES
Government: Republic
Capital: Malé
Area: 298 sq km
Population: 269,000
Language: Divehi
Currency: Rufiyaa

Malta

Malta is an island in the **Mediterranean Sea**. Since ancient times it has been a vital naval base, as it guards **trade** routes to the East. For centuries, Malta was ruled by the Knights of St John, but in 1813 it became British. During **World War II**, Malta survived heavy bombing raids. Since 1962, it has been self-governing, and it is now a **republic**. The capital, Valletta, has an old harbour surrounded by fine buildings.

Mammals *see* pages 196–197

Mammoth

During the **Ice Ages**, woolly mammoths roamed the plains of **North America** and **Europe**. They looked like shaggy-haired **elephants** with long, curling tusks. But they lived in a much colder **climate** than the elephants of today.

Mammoths lived together in herds, and ate **grass** and other **plants**. Their enemies included **wolves** and fierce sabre-toothed cats (see **prehistoric animals**), and **cave-dwellers** hunted mammoths for food. Sometimes a group of hunters drove a mammoth into a pit, where it was killed with spears.

The frozen bodies of mammoths have been dug up by scientists in the icy **tundra** of **Siberia**. Mammoth remains have also been found in tar pits in California. The last mammoths died out about 30,000 years ago.

Mandela, Nelson

Nelson Mandela (b.1918) was one of the most important political leaders in **Africa** during the 20th century. The son of a tribal chief, he was born in the Transkei territory of **South Africa** and became a lawyer. After **World War II**, the white South African **government** introduced the policy of **apartheid** – separate development for white and

MALTA
Government: Republic
Capital: Valletta
Area: 316 sq km
Population: 379,000
Languages: Maltese and English
Currency: Maltese lira

After 28 years as a political prisoner, Nelson **Mandela** became an emblem of black peoples' struggle for equality in South Africa.

Mao **Zedong** was chairman of the Chinese communist party for 27 years, and his strong leadership inspired the Chinese people.

non-white people. Mandela helped form the African National Congress (ANC) in 1944, which began a campaign of non-violent opposition to the government. In 1962, Mandela was arrested and put in prison. People all over the world demanded his release, and he was eventually freed in 1990.

In 1991, President de Klerk (b.1936) took measures to end apartheid. Fully democratic **elections** were held in 1994, and Mandela was elected **president**. He was South Africa's first black head of state. Mandela retired in 1999, and was succeeded by Thabo Mbeki (b.1942).

Maori

The Maori are the native people of **New Zealand**. It is thought that they came in canoes from islands in the **Pacific Ocean** to New Zealand in the 1300s. The Maori were fierce warriors who fought with clubs made of **bone** or greenstone (a kind of jade). They waged a long, hard struggle against the Europeans who began to settle in New Zealand in the mid-1800s. This conflict did not end until 1865, and there were further outbreaks of fighting for years afterwards. Today, the Maori continue to play an important part in the life of New Zealand, and their **population** is increasing at a faster rate than that of non-Maoris.

Maori people are skilful at **weaving**, **dancing** and carving in **wood**. Maori carving is full of decoration. Every part of the surface of their work is covered with curves, scrolls and spirals. Tattooing is also an important Maori **art**.

Mao Zedong

Mao Zedong (1893–1976) was a great Chinese leader. He was the son of a farmer, and trained to be a teacher. In 1921, Mao helped to form the Chinese Communist Party (see **communism**) and fought against the Chinese nationalists under Chiang Kai-shek

(1887–1975). In 1934, Mao led 90,000 communists on a 368-day march through **China** to escape nationalist forces. This feat was called the 'Long March'. In 1949, when Mao and the communist armies had defeated the nationalists, Mao became head of the Chinese **government**.

Mao wanted China to become as strong and wealthy as the **USA**, and brought about radical changes in culture and **economics**. His strict policies meant that all aspects of life came under state control. However, many of Mao's plans for his country did not work. He resigned from his job as head of government in 1959, but carried on as chairman of the Chinese Communist Party. Mao had many arguments with the communists of the **Soviet Union**. He also wrote several **books** about **guerrilla warfare**.

After Mao's death in 1976, China's new leaders criticized his rule and increased contacts with the West.

The **Marathon** of the Sands is a gruelling race in the Sahara Desert that covers about 230 km in six days – further than five normal marathons.

Map

We need maps to help us find our way and to discover details of the world's **geography**. There are many kinds of map. Political maps show country boundaries and the positions of important towns, **roads** and **railways**. Physical maps show natural features such as **mountains**, **rivers** and **lakes**. **Weather** maps show **temperatures** and **air** conditions.

Maps are drawn to different scales. The scale of some maps is so large that you might be able to find your **house** on one. The scale of other maps is

Using a **map** and compass, it is possible to locate your exact position. Maps often have contour lines to show features such as hills and valleys. Each contour line joins up different points at the same height.

Guglielmo **Marconi** with his wireless telegraph, which could send radio signals across the world.

so small that it is possible to squeeze the whole world onto a page of an atlas.

At first, a lot of guesswork went into mapmaking. Today, aerial **photography** is used to make extremely accurate maps. The pictures are taken from an **aircraft** flying at a constant height. Each photograph overlaps the next one slightly, so no detail is lost. **Satellites** are used to produce weather maps.

Charts are maps of the sea. They tell sailors about lighthouses, **rocks**, channels and the depth of **water** in various places. Detailed maps of the seabed can be produced using **sonar**.

Marathon

The marathon is a long-distance race of 42.19 km that has been run in the **Olympic Games** since 1896. Its name commemorates a famous run by the Greek soldier Pheidippides, who ran from the town of Marathon to **Athens** in 490 BCE to bring news of a Greek victory over the Persians.

Marble

Marble is a **rock** that is formed when limestone is squeezed and made very hot inside the **earth**. Pure marble is white, but most of the rock has other substances in it which give it many colours. Marble has long been used in **architecture** and **sculpture**. It is easy to shape and can be polished until beautifully smooth.

Marconi, Guglielmo

Guglielmo Marconi (1874–1937) was a famous physicist who discovered how to transmit **radio** waves. His father was Italian and his mother Irish. Marconi built a **machine**, the telegraph, for sending radio signals, and in 1901 he sent the first message across the **Atlantic** (see also **communication**).

MAMMALS

There are a greater variety of mammals than any other animal group. They are found all over the world, and they live on land, in water and underground.

△ The slender loris is active only at night. Its huge, saucerlike eyes help it find insects and other prey in the darkness.

WORLD OF MAMMALS

Mammals are warm-blooded animals, which means they can stay active and keep their bodies warm in cold weather. Most of them are covered with fur. Even sea mammals such as dolphins and whales have a thin layer of hair on their bodies. Unlike other animal babies, young mammals feed on milk from their mother's body. Mammals are named after the mammary glands (breasts) that produce this milk.

TYPES OF MAMMAL

The first mammals evolved from reptiles about 230 million years ago. They were small and ate insects. When the dinosaurs died out, many other types of mammal began to evolve. Today, there are 4,200 species of mammal, divided into three groups. These are placental mammals (which give birth to fully developed young), marsupials (mammals whose young develop in a pouch) and egg-laying mammals.

▷ Mammals such as this two-humped, or Bactrian, camel suckle their babies with milk. The milk contains everything that the young need to develop and grow.

△ Lynxes are large cats with tufted ears. The fur of the North American lynx is covered with spots, but the larger Siberian lynx has a plain coat.

△ Echidnas are unusual mammals that lay eggs. They feed on insects and have spines for protection.

EGG-LAYING MAMMALS

The duck-billed platypus and the echidna are Australian mammals that lay eggs. They are the most primitive mammals alive today, and have beaklike mouths with no teeth. The milk that the females produce does not come from teats, but oozes from a slit in the skin on the belly.

PLACENTAL MAMMALS

Placental mammals are the largest group of mammals. They include a tremendous variety of species, such as rodents, elephants, seals and human beings. Placental mammals develop inside the mother's body, and obtain food and oxygen through the placenta (the part of the womb that connects mother and baby). Some species can run just minutes after birth, but others rely on their parent or parents for months.

MARSUPIALS

Marsupials are mammals that nurse their babies in pouches on the female's body until the young are big enough to fend for themselves. Most marsupials, such as kangaroos, bandicoots and koalas, live in Australia and New Guinea. Other species, including opossums, live in America.

THE RIGHT TEETH

Mammals eat a wide range of foods, and have teeth to suit their diets. Carnivores such as cats and dogs have sharp teeth for seizing prey and tearing flesh. Herbivores such as horses and cattle have broad, grinding teeth for eating plants.

RODENTS

Almost half of all mammals are rodents, including mice, rats, voles, squirrels, beavers and porcupines. Rodents have sharp incisors (front teeth) for gnawing through food and burrowing. Many species dig underground tunnels in which to live. Most rodents live for only 1–2 years, but they breed rapidly.

◁ The Mongolian gerbil lives in the deserts of Central Asia and feeds on plant shoots and seeds.

> **SEE ALSO**
> Blood, Bone, Carnivore, Evolution, Food, Hair, Herbivore, Hibernation, Marsupial, Rodent, Prehistoric animals, Reproduction

△ Some South American monkeys, such as this female spider monkey and her baby, can hang from trees by their tails.

WAY OF LIFE

Mammals have adapted to life in all kinds of different habitats. Camels, for example, can survive in hot deserts where food and water are scarce. They store fat in their humps, which they convert into energy when needed. Polar bears have thick fur to keep them warm in the Arctic. In common with other bears and many rodents, they hibernate (enter a deep sleep) during the winter. Antelopes and other grazing mammals form huge herds on Africa's grasslands. They have highly efficient digestion systems for extracting nutrients from plants. One group of mammals – the bats – can fly, and have taken to the air. Their 'wings' are actually modified forelimbs.

MARINE MAMMALS

Whales, dolphins and porpoises spend their entire lives in the sea. Unlike fish, they breathe air and must surface to fill their lungs. They have streamlined bodies, flippers and powerful tails. Many whales filter plankton (microscopic floating animals) from the water. Dolphins are high-speed predators that hunt fish and squid.

▽ Killer whales, or orcas (below left), prey on sea mammals such as harp seals. Seal pups are easier to catch than adult seals.

Margarine

This is a **food** like butter, made from vegetable **fats** and **oils**. **Vitamins** are usually added to make it nearly as nutritious as butter. Margarine was first produced in 1867 by the French chemist Hippolyte Mège-Mouriés (1817–1880). He won a prize offered by the French **government** for finding a cheap substitute for butter. Many people now eat margarine and similar spreads because they are low in unhealthy saturated fats.

△ The French queen **Marie Antoinette** showed great courage at her trial, but was condemned to death in October 1793. She was executed on the guillotine.

Marie Antoinette

Marie Antoinette (1755–1793) was the Austrian-born wife of **Louis XVI** of **France**. A beautiful and vivacious young woman, she spent **money** lavishly. She spent most of her time inside the royal palace at **Versailles**, near **Paris**, and became a symbol to the poor people of France of all they hated about the royal court. When the **French Revolution** broke out in 1789, the king and queen were taken to Paris by force.

They escaped, but were swiftly recaptured and executed on the guillotine in 1793.

Mars

The **planet** Mars is about half the size of the **earth**, and takes about two years to travel around the **sun**. It has huge **volcanoes** and deep gorges, far larger than those on earth. Most of Mars is covered with loose **rocks**, scattered over a dusty, red surface, which is why Mars is called the 'Red Planet'. It has a North Pole and a South Pole, both covered with thick snow or frost. The planet's thin atmosphere is made almost entirely of carbon dioxide, and strong winds whip up dust storms.

Seen through a **telescope**, the red surface of Mars is criss-crossed by thin grey lines. Some early astronomers (see **astronomy**) thought that these lines were **canals** that had been dug by intelligent beings to irrigate the **soil**. But space probes sent to Mars in 1965, 1969 and 1976 (see **space exploration**) found no trace of the canals. The American *Viking* spacecraft landed on the planet itself, and took samples of its soil, but were unable to find any evidence of life.

Mars has two tiny moons – Phobos and Deimos. Phobos, the larger of the two, is only about 24 km across. Both of the moons are probably **asteroids** that were dragged towards Mars and began to **orbit** the planet.

▽ Several space probes to Mars, including *Viking I*, *Viking II* and *Pathfinder*, found no evidence of alien life forms on the planet. But in early 2002, NASA scientists detected frozen water under the surface of Mars, raising new hopes that it may once have supported life.

MARS FACTS
Average distance from sun: 228 million km
Nearest distance from earth: 78 million km
Average temperature: –30°C
Diameter across the equator: 6,794 km
Atmosphere: Carbon dioxide
Number of moons: 2
Length of day: 24 hours 37 minutes
Length of year: 687 earth days

Marsupial

Marsupials are a group of **mammals** that raise their young inside a pouch. They include **kangaroos**, **wallabies**, **bandicoots**, **opossums** and **koalas**. Most marsupials live in **Australia** or **New Guinea**, but there are also a few species in **North America** and **South America**.

A newly born marsupial is extremely small, and is blind, deaf and naked. It crawls into its mother's pouch and stays there, feeding on her **milk** until it can look after itself. There are about 250 species of marsupial, most of which live in **forests** or on grasslands. Many marsupials are nocturnal.

△ The common wombat is a heavily built **marsupial** with powerful front feet for digging its extensive burrows. A young wombat stays with its mother for at least a year.

▽ Tae kwon do is a **martial art** based on Korean kick fighting. This black-belt student is demonstrating the power of a flying kick by breaking a piece of wood.

Martial arts

The martial arts are various forms of combat that come from east **Asia**. They include judo, karate and aikido, all from **Japan**, and kung-fu from **China**. Judo, meaning 'the gentle way', is the most popular martial art. It developed from jujitsu, at that time a violent way of fighting that could maim or kill. Today, judo is a safe **sport** practised by men, women and children. It has been an **Olympic** sport since 1964, and is used in many parts of the world for self-defence. A trained student of judo can quickly unbalance an opponent and throw them to the floor.

Marx, Karl

Karl Marx (1818–1883) was a political thinker and writer whose ideas brought about enormous social and political changes. Marx was born in **Germany** and his ideas were the starting-point of **communism**. He believed that people who own property, the capitalist class, exploit those who work for them in order to become wealthier. Marx also thought that the workers would one day rise up against the capitalists and take control. Marx wrote several **books**, the most famous of which is *Das Kapital*, which took 30 years to write and was still incomplete when he died in 1883.

Marx often collaborated with another German thinker, Friedrich Engels (1820–1895). The two men's writings later inspired several communist **revolutions**, notably the **Russian Revolution** of 1917.

Mary, Queen of Scots

Mary, Queen of Scots (1542–1587) was **Scotland**'s last Roman Catholic **monarch**. The daughter of James V of Scotland (1512–1542), Mary was educated in **France**, and did not return to Scotland until she was 19. By that time,

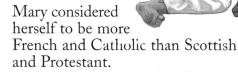

Mary considered herself to be more French and Catholic than Scottish and Protestant.

Mary was the second in line to the English throne after her Protestant cousin **Elizabeth I**. In 1567, Mary was forced to give up the Scottish throne, and later she was imprisoned for 20 years in **England** for plotting against Elizabeth. She was executed on the queen's orders in 1587.

Mathematics

We all use simple mathematics every day. For example, we add up the **coins** in our pockets to find out how much **money** we have, or look at a **clock** and work out how much **time** we have left before going somewhere. In business, people are constantly using some kind of mathematics, often, nowadays, with the help of **calculators** and **computers**. The branch of mathematics that deals with numbers is called arithmetic. **Algebra** uses symbols such as x and y instead of numbers. **Geometry** deals with lines, **angles** and shapes such as triangles and squares.

Matter

Everything you can see and touch is matter – and so are some things you cannot. Matter is anything that has **volume**, or takes up space. Scientists say that matter has mass – the amount of matter in something. The mass of something always remains the same. The pull of **gravity** gives you weight, but your weight can change. If you go to the **moon** you will weigh only one-sixth as much as you do on **earth**, but your mass will still be the same.

Matter can be grouped into three main forms – solid, **liquid** and **gas**. This **book** is solid, the **water** that comes from a tap is liquid, and the **air** that we breathe is made of gases. The solid, liquid and gas forms are called the three states of matter.

Nearly all matter can exist in all three forms. If air is made cold enough it becomes a liquid. A gas can be turned into a solid by cooling it.

MAURITIUS
Government: Constitutional monarchy
Capital: Port Louis
Area: 2085 sq km
Population: 1.1 million
Languages: English and French
Currency: Rupee

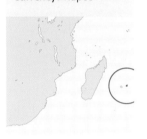

▽ The **Maya** built huge pyramids and palaces using only stone hand tools. The Castillo pyramid in Chichén Itzá was 30 m high and its base measured 55 sq m. Four staircases led up to a temple at the top of the pyramid.

Solids such as **iron** can be turned into liquids by heating them. In the **sun**, iron exists as a gas because it is so hot.

Mauritius

Mauritius is a small **island** nation in the **Indian Ocean**. Most of the island is surrounded by **coral** reefs. The island is thought to be the peak of an ancient **volcano**, and has many volcanic hills.

Mauritius is one of the most densely populated places in the world. There are about 500 people for every square kilometre of the island. The chief crops are **sugar** cane and **tea**, and **fishing** is important in coastal regions. Tourism is a fast-growing industry.

Maya

The Maya first lived in **Central America** in the 400s. They grew maize, sweet potatoes and **vegetables**, and became wealthy through **trade** with neighbouring peoples. Later, the Maya built stone cities, with richly decorated palaces, temples and **pyramids**. Today, many of these great buildings are still standing, hidden in the **rainforest**. The Maya were also skilled in **astronomy** and **mathematics**, and they developed an advanced **writing** system that was a form of **hieroglyphics**.

The Maya did not use **metals** until very late in their **history**. They built with stone tools, and had no knowledge of the **wheel**. Their lives were controlled by **religion**. They worshipped many **gods**, including a **sun** god, rain gods, **soil** gods and a **moon** goddess who looked after women.

Measure

see **Weights and Measures**

Mecca

The city of Mecca in western **Saudi Arabia** is the birthplace of the Prophet **Muhammad**, who founded the **religion** of **Islam**. It is the holiest place in the world for Muslims. In the centre of Mecca is the Great **Mosque**, and in the mosque's courtyard is the Ka'ba, which houses the sacred 'Black Stone'. Muslims believe that the stone was given to Abraham by the Angel Gabriel. It is kissed by **pilgrims** to Mecca.

Today, the world's **media** can keep us informed of events as they happen. Satellite trucks allow TV crews in a war zone or at the scene of a disaster to broadcast their reports almost instantly. Reporters use mobile phones and laptop computers to email stories to their newspapers.

Media

The media is the channel through which news and views are publicised. It includes **newspapers**, magazines, **television**, **radio** and the **internet**. The media offers a window on the world, bringing events from other countries close to home. It can be aimed at providing information or entertainment, or it may be **advertising** something.

News put out through the media can affect public opinion. This means that today's media **companies** are extremely influential and powerful. Sometimes **governments** try to censor, or control, the output of the media. However, the freedom of the media to print or broadcast what it likes – as long as it is true – is an important civil right. In many countries, there are **laws** that protect the media's independence.

Two million Muslims make the pilgrimage to **Mecca** each year. They perform rituals such as walking around the holy shrine, or Ka'ba, a black structure containing a stone that dates from ancient times.

Medicine

Medicine is the **science** of healing. It includes the prevention, diagnosis and treatment of all types of **disease** and sickness. Early doctors relied on **magic** cures, prayers and charms. **Acupuncture** is an ancient form of medical treatment that was developed in **China** 5,000 years ago. In Ancient **Greece**, doctors

The **Mediterranean Sea's** attractive coastline and pleasant climate make it a major tourist destination.

examined patients and prescribed herbal remedies. But medicine could not progress in a scientific way until the 1700s when doctors began to learn how the **human body** works.

Medicine has advanced faster during the last 200 years than in the whole of human **history**. The development of anaesthetics (pain-killing **drugs**) in the 1800s allowed enormous progress to be made in **surgery**. Scientists have discovered all kinds of other important drugs, such as **antibiotics**, and diseases such as tuberculosis and smallpox have been almost wiped out. Doctors can now transplant organs such as the **heart** and the **kidney**. Modern **hospitals** are full of sophisticated equipment such as **X-ray** machines, **ultrasound** scanners and life-support **machines**.

Mediterranean Sea

The Mediterranean Sea is surrounded by three **continents** – **Europe**, **Africa** and **Asia**. It is joined to the Black Sea by a narrow strait, or passage, and flows out into the **Atlantic Ocean** through the Strait of **Gibraltar**. The **Suez Canal**, opened in 1869, cuts across **Egypt** and allows large **ships** to sail from the Mediterranean into the **Red Sea**.

Melbourne

Melbourne is the second largest city in **Australia** and the capital of the state of Victoria. It has a **population** of nearly three million people. The city lies at the mouth of the Yarra **River** on Port Phillip Bay. Melbourne was the capital of Australia from 1901 to 1927, until it was changed to **Canberra**.

Mendel, Gregor

Born in **Austria**, Gregor Mendel (1822–1884) was a monk who became famous for establishing the basic laws of heredity. Heredity is the passing on of characteristics such as **eye** colour and **skin** colour from parents to their children (see **genetics**).

Mendel grew up on a farm, where he became interested in **botany** – the branch of **biology** that deals with **plants**. When Mendel entered a **monastery**, he began to grow peas. He noticed that when he planted the **seeds** of tall pea plants, only tall pea plants grew. Then he tried crossing tall pea plants with short pea plants by taking pollen from one and putting it in the other. He found that again he had only tall plants. But when he crossed these new mixed tall plants with each other, three-quarters of the new plants were tall and one-quarter were short. Mendel had found out that characteristics such as tallness and shortness are controlled by genes

A **mercury** barometer helps forecast the weather by measuring air pressure. It contains a glass tube full of mercury, which rises or falls when the air pressure changes. This makes a pointer move over a scale.

Mercury has a dry, airless surface pockmarked with craters, and there is also evidence of ancient lava flows. During the day, the planet is baked by heat and radiation from the nearby sun. Its dense core is made of iron and nickel.

passed on from each parent. Mendel also showed that some genes – for example, the gene that produces tallness in pea plants – are stronger than others.

Mercury (metal)

Mercury is the only **metal** that is a **liquid** at ordinary **temperatures**. When mercury is poured onto a table it forms small bead-like drops. This is because of the attraction between mercury's molecules. Mercury is used in **thermometers** and **barometers**.

Mercury (planet)

The **planet** Mercury is one of the smallest in our **solar system**, and the closest to the **sun**. A day on Mercury lasts 59 of our days. During the long daylight hours, it is so hot that even **lead** would melt. During the equally long night, the **temperature** drops to as low as −170°C. Little was known about Mercury's surface until the space probe *Mariner 10* flew past the planet in 1973, 1974 and 1975. It showed Mercury to have a thin atmosphere and big craters like those on our **moon**.

MERCURY FACTS
Average distance from sun: 58 million km
Nearest distance from earth: 45 million km
Average temperature: 140°C
Diameter across the equator: 4,878 km
Atmosphere: Almost none
Number of moons: 0
Length of day: 59 earth days
Length of year: 88 earth days

Metal

About two-thirds of the **elements** on **earth** are metals. The most important metals are **iron** (used for making steel), **copper** and **aluminium**.

People have used metals since early times. Iron, copper and **tin** were the first metals to be used. They were made into tools and weapons. **Gold** and **silver** were also discovered at a very early stage and used for **jewellery**.

Most metals are solid unless they are heated, and many are shiny. They all let **heat** and **electricity** pass through them. Copper and silver are the best for this. Some metals are soft, and are easy to beat into shapes or pull into thin **wires**. Other metals are brittle – they break easily – and a few are so hard that they are difficult to work with.

Metals can be mixed to form **alloys**, which have different properties to the metals from which they are made. For example, **bronze** is an alloy made from tin and copper, and is stronger than either of them.

The earth has a huge supply of some metals, such as iron and aluminium, while others, such as gold and platinum, are rare. Metals may be found pure, or mixed with other elements in **minerals**. Many metals are found as ores, which are **compounds** of metal and **oxygen**.

Meteor

A meteor is a lump of **metal** or stone that travels through space at great speed. Millions of small meteors fall to the **earth** every day, but most burn up in the **atmosphere**. The burning

△ As a **meteor** enters the earth's atmosphere, friction heats it and makes it glow. Meteors may be chips off comets, the moon or Mars, but most are asteroid debris.

MEXICO
Government:
Federal republic
Capital: Mexico City
Area: 1,972,547 sq km
Population: 96.6 million
Language: Spanish
Currency: New peso

▷ Much of the fruit and vegetables that **Mexico** produces is sold at its colourful street markets, but the country also exports large quantities of food. Important crops for export include coffee, cotton, corn and bananas.

meteors are called shooting stars, and are visible on clear nights. Large meteors that reach the earth's surface are known as meteorites. The violent impact may create a large hole, or crater.

Mexico

Mexico is a country in **North America**. It lies between the **USA** in the north and **Central America** in the south. Much of the country is hilly, with fertile uplands. The highest **mountains** reach over 5,700 m. In the southeast, the low Yucatán Peninsula sticks out far into the Gulf of Mexico, the western part of the **Caribbean** Sea. Seven-tenths of Mexico has little rainfall, but lush **rainforests** grow in the south.

The first people in Mexico were Indians, including the **Aztecs**. Spanish settlers arrived in Mexico in 1519, and the country was under **Spain**'s control until 1821, when it won independence. Today, many Mexicans are *mestizos*, of mixed European and North American origin. Most white people

Michelangelo worked on this statue of Moses from about 1513 to 1516. His statues were often larger than life and are famous for their accurate carving.

In an optical **microscope**, the image can be seen by looking down through the eyepiece, which contains a series of magnifying lenses.

▽ The **Middle East** produces much of the world's oil, which is drilled from underground rocks that lie beneath the desert.

are descendants of the Spanish settlers. Many Mexicans are farmers, or work in the country's large **oil**, **natural gas**, **iron and steel** and chemical industries. However, widespread poverty has led to a steady stream of people trying to enter the USA illegally in search of jobs (see **immigration**).

Michelangelo

Michelangelo Buonarroti (1475–1564) was a painter and sculptor who lived in **Italy** at the time of the **Renaissance**. He is famous for the large-scale **paintings** he made of religious and historical subjects, and for his wonderfully lifelike **marble** statues. He also made a large number of beautiful **drawings**.

Michelangelo's patrons included the **pope**, nobles and wealthy townspeople. He spent four and a half years painting huge pictures in the Sistine Chapel in the **Vatican City** for Pope Julius II (1443–1513). This massive undertaking was finally completed in 1511. One of Michelangelo's best-known statues is David (1504), which stands 4 m high. Michelangelo was also the chief architect of St Peter's, a spectacular **church** that towers over the Vatican.

Microphone

A microphone picks up **sound** waves and turns them into electric signals. These can be made into a **recording** or sent out as **radio** waves. They can also be fed through an amplifier and

loudspeakers, which make the sound louder. A **telephone**'s mouthpiece has a microphone in it that turns **voices** into electric signals (see **communication**).

Microscope

A microscope is an instrument used for looking at tiny objects. It magnifies things, or makes them look larger. Objects that are invisible to the naked **eye** are called 'microscopic'. Many microscopic **plants** and **animals**, including **bacteria**, can be seen if you look at them through a microscope.

Microscopes work by using **lenses**. The simplest microscope is a magnifying glass, which has only one **lens**. The lenses in many microscopes work by bending **light** rays. Small microscopes can magnify about 100 times, but big microscopes used by scientists may magnify up to 2,000 times. The electron microscope is much more powerful – it can magnify up to 2 million times. Instead of bending light rays, it bends beams of electrons (see **atoms**).

Middle Ages
see **pages 206–207**

Middle East

The Middle East is a group of countries in southwest **Asia** lying between **Africa** and **Europe**. Much of the region is **desert**, with rugged **mountain** ranges in eastern **Turkey**, **Afghanistan** and **Iran**. Most people live along the coasts, in inland valleys, or around an **oasis**. The main **rivers**, the Euphrates and Tigris, rise in Turkey and flow through **Syria** and **Iraq** to the Persian Gulf. They are used to irrigate the farmland that lies on their banks (see **irrigation**).

In parts of the Middle East, nomadic tribes herd **goats** and **sheep** (see **nomad**). The region's chief resource is **oil**. **Saudi Arabia** has about a quarter of the world's known oil resources, and other leading oil producers include Iraq, Iran, Kuwait, Qatar, **Oman** and the **United Arab Emirates**.

Many of the people in the Middle East are Arabs, and follow the **religion** of **Islam**. During the second half of the 20th century, there were several wars between Arab countries and the mainly Jewish state of **Israel**.

Migration

Migration is the regular movement of **animals** between one place and another. Some animals migrate every year, but others migrate only twice in their life. These journeys are made to reach new feeding or breeding areas, and are usually linked to the **seasons**.

Animals migrate by **instinct**. They do not have to plan their journey, and are believed to use a range of methods to find their way. Some follow natural features such as **mountains, rivers** and coastlines, while others use their sense of **smell**. **Birds** may be guided by the **sun** or the **stars**, or by sensing the **earth**'s powerful magnetic field (see **magnetism**).

Birds are the greatest migrants. Every autumn, swallows and martins leave **Europe** and fly south to spend the winter in **Africa**. **North America**'s swallows and martins fly south to **South America**. These trips may be 10,000 km long. In spring, the birds fly north again to breed.

But birds are not the only animals that make long migrations. **Butterflies, turtles, fish, whales** and many grazing **mammals** migrate too. Whales and fish make long journeys through the **ocean** to find food and breed. The **eels** of Europe's rivers and marshes swim thousands of kilometres across the **Atlantic Ocean** to breed. After mating, the adults die. The young eels that hatch take years to swim back to Europe. Vast herds of caribou, or reindeer, migrate from the **tundra** in the **Arctic** to spend the winter in **forests** further south.

Milk

Milk is a **food** on which all baby **mammals** live. It comes from the mammary **glands**, or breasts, of the baby's mother. The baby sucks the milk from its mother's nipples or teats.

Milk contains all the things that a baby needs. At first, the milk is pale and watery, but later it is much richer and creamier. It is full of **fat, sugar, starch, protein, vitamins** and essential **minerals**. It also protects the baby from **diseases** and infections.

People also use milk from animals such as **cattle, sheep, goats** and even **camels** and caribou, or reindeer. The milk is consumed as a drink, and is used to make foods such as cream, butter, yoghurt, **cheese** and ice cream.

The monarch butterfly's **migration** from North America to Mexico covers more than 3,000 km. The butterfly gathers in huge swarms at its winter home, and makes the return trip in the following spring.

Milky Way

When you look at the sky on a clear, moonless night you can see a pale cloud of **light**. If you look at it through binoculars or a **telescope**, you will see that the cloud is really millions of **stars**. All these stars, and most of the other stars we see, are part of our **galaxy**, which is called the Milky Way. Astronomers (see **astronomy**) think that the Milky Way has about 100,000 million stars

continued on page 208

▽ This view what the **Milky Way** might look like from several hundred light-years above our galaxy. It has a structure of spiral arms and a densely packed central bulge of older stars.

MIDDLE AGES

In European history, the Middle Ages stretched from the fall of the Roman Empire in around 470 CE to the dawn of the Renaissance at the beginning of the 1400s. It was a 1000-year period of turbulence and strife.

△ *Stained-glass windows were a type of 'painting' that reached its greatest height in churches in France in the 1100s. The windows told stories about everyone and everything, from Biblical events to the kings and queens of the day.*

Following the Roman Empire's collapse, much of western Europe was overtaken by barbarians. Their influence began to spread south until it reached nearly to the Mediterranean.

CHRISTIANITY UNDER THREAT

In the southeast of Europe, Islam had begun to reach many countries from its base in the Middle East. By c.750 CE, Arabs controlled much of northern Africa and eastern Asia, and had become powerful rivals to the Byzantine Empire. They tried to sack the Byzantine capital Constantinople in 674–678 but failed. If the Byzantine Empire and Christianity wished to survive the onslaught from barbarians in the north and Arabs in the south, then a new rule would have to be established.

▽ *Most large European towns held a market once or twice a week, and the main square would be filled with traders shouting their wares.*

△ *In Europe, most people worked the land for a living, paying their dues to their feudal lord or to the Church. They would sow seed by hand and use a horse to pull the plough.*

THE EMPEROR CHARLEMAGNE

In an attempt to consolidate power and bring peace to Europe, the pope crowned the king of the Franks, Charlemagne (747–814), Christian emperor in 800. Charlemagne's strong 14-year reign was a brief, settled period of enlightenment, but it ended with his death. The power structure of this relationship, between emperors and popes, became a dominant feature of the Middle Ages.

△ *In the Middle Ages, women were considered inferior to men. A wealthy woman would be educated because she needed to run the household.*

EUROPE AT WAR

After the death of Charlemagne, the Vikings began a series of raids and conquests that lasted almost 200 years. Their influence was felt from present-day Russia in the east to Ireland in the west. Viking raids on northern Europe ended with their leader's defeat by King Harald of England in the 1000s.

By this time, the march of Islam seemed unstoppable and it had become a major threat to European Christianity. Large parts of Spain and southern Italy had been conquered by the North African Arabs or Moors. In 1095, the pope urged all Christians to drive back the Arabs and recover the holy Christian sites in Palestine. This call resulted in the Crusades, which cost the lives of thousands of Arabs and Europeans, and lasted for nearly 200 years.

After the threats from the Vikings and Islam had passed, the European nations started to fight each other in an attempt to gain power and wealth. The Hundred Years War (1337–1453) was fought by the kings of France and England over the sovereignty of France.

A decisive battle was won by the English king Henry V at Agincourt in France in 1415, but a century later England had lost all her French possessions. The Hapsburg royal family in Austria and the Hohenzollerns of Germany fought long wars to conquer new lands for their respective peoples.

A FEUDAL SOCIETY

Life in Europe in the Middle Ages was very harsh for the poorest peasants. For much of the time, Europe was divided into kingdoms, dukedoms and other states. Agriculture was the source of wealth for the majority, and the richest landowners were mainly monarchs and the Church. In this feudal society, the peasants were allowed to live on the land and to farm it as long as they surrendered most of their crops to their lord, who in turn paid the king. Peasants also paid large taxes to the Church in the form of tithes. Many also worked in the houses of the wealthy as servants.

In contrast to the hand-to-mouth existence of the poor, the rich lived a comfortable and even luxurious life. The rich lords and their families often held lavish feasts and banquets to celebrate special occasions. These were formal meals that lasted for hours and included many dishes of spiced meats as well as drinks of mead (a kind of beer) and wine.

NATURAL DISASTERS

Plagues and pestilence were common throughout Europe and spared neither rich nor poor. The Black Death (a form of bubonic plague) swept through Europe from Asia in 1347 and wiped out 25 million people, almost a third of the population of Europe.

▷ *Sieges on castles were a common feature of the wars that took place during this period. Foot soldiers stood little chance against the sword of a fully armed knight.*

TRADE AND PROSPERITY

During the latter half of the Middle Ages, the growth in technology and industry allowed merchants and craftspeople to form into trade guilds. These were powerful organizations that imposed regulations and rules, and tried to control prices across Europe as a whole. They also encouraged a spread of skills throughout the region, and this in turn promoted trade between countries. The guilds also helped raise the living and working conditions of the lowest classes.

When the Middle Ages finally came to an end in the 1400s with the beginning of the Renaissance, the Christian society of Europe began a period of stability and expansion through art, learning, trade and exploration.

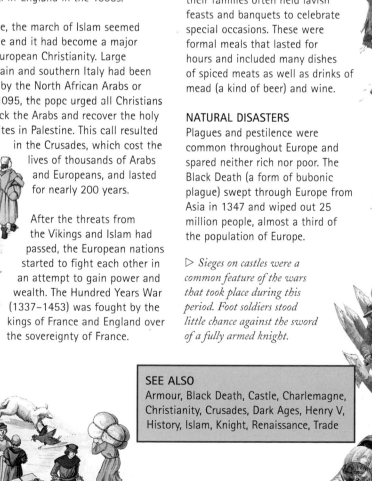

SEE ALSO
Armour, Black Death, Castle, Charlemagne, Christianity, Crusades, Dark Ages, Henry V, History, Islam, Knight, Renaissance, Trade

continued from page 205

including the **sun**. The Milky Way stretches for 100,000 light-years. A light-year is the distance light travels in one **year** at a speed of 300,000 km a second. Our own **solar system** is 30,000 light-years from the centre of the Milky Way.

Mime

Mime is the art of acting in silence. A mime artist does not speak. Instead, their movements tell the story. The face, hands and body are used to show how the artist feels. Mime artists are like dancers. They must control every movement with great care so that the audience can follow the story.

In Ancient **Greece** and the **Roman Empire**, mime included some speaking, but much of the story was told with gestures. The actors wore masks. Gradually, mime came to be face, hand and body interpretations only, and the speaking parts were lost. Mime is used a lot in **dance**, especially **ballet**.

Mineral

The **rocks**, **sand** and **soil** of the **earth** are made up of materials called minerals. There are over 3,000 kinds of mineral, but only 30 of them make up the majority of the **planet**'s rocks.

Some minerals, such as **gold** and platinum, are made up of only one **element**. Others, such as **quartz** and **salt**, consist of two or more elements. Some minerals are **metals**, such as **copper** and **silver**. Other minerals, like **sulphur**, are non-metallic.

Pure minerals are made up of **atoms** arranged in regular patterns, known as crystals. Minerals form crystals when they cool from hot **gases** and **liquids** deep inside the earth. Crystals can grow very large if they cool slowly.

Azurite

Malachite

Realgar

Galena

△ Many of the **minerals** found on earth form three-dimensional shapes called crystals. Each mineral has differently shaped crystals.

Whether they are large or small, crystals of the same mineral nearly always have the same shape. Minerals that can be cut to a beautiful shape and polished are called gemstones. **Gems** include rubies, **diamonds**, sapphires and emeralds.

Mining

Mining is the process of taking **minerals** out of the **earth**. It is one of the most important industries. When minerals lie in one place in large quantities, they are known as ores. People mine minerals such as **gold**, **silver**, **tin**, **coal** and **salt**. They also mine stone for building.

Mines can be quarries (open pits) or underground **tunnels**. **Quarrying** is used to extract ores that lie close to the surface of the **soil**. First the soil is removed, then giant excavators scoop up the **rock** that contains the minerals. Today's underground mines can reach as deep as 3 km below the surface. Problems with drainage and ventilation have been solved using **machines**, which pump out **water** and circulate fresh **air**. Another form of mining is dredging, in which minerals are scooped up from the beds of **rivers** and **lakes**.

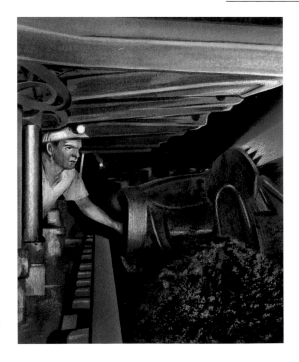

Mirror

A mirror is made from a sheet of **glass** that has a very thin layer of **silver** or **aluminium** sprayed on the back. This is then painted to protect the **metal** surface from scratches. Mirrors were first made in this way in the 1500s in **Venice**. Before that date mirrors were usually made of solid pieces of highly polished metal such as silver or **bronze**.

◁ **Mining** is hard and dangerous work. Deep mines have always suffered from cave-ins, flooding and poisonous gases. In the future, some mining may be carried out by robots.

Light is reflected from a smooth surface, and the reflection, called an image, is what we see when we look into a mirror. However, the image is reversed. If you raise your left hand, the image raises its right hand.

A plane mirror has a flat surface. A convex mirror curves outwards like the back of a spoon. A concave mirror curves inwards like a hollow bowl.

Missile

A missile is a weapon powered by a **rocket** engine and armed with an explosive warhead. A guided missile is guided to its target by **radio** or **radar** commands or by a device inside the missile. One type of guided missile is the ballistic missile. A ballistic missile follows a path that is partly outside the earth's **atmosphere**. It is guided as it flies up into the air, but when its rocket **engine** burns out, it returns to **earth** on an unguided path.

The only defence against a ballistic missile is to fire another missile at it before it hits its target. Such defensive missiles are called 'anti-ballistic missiles'. However, some missiles are armed with warheads that split up into several separate warheads as they descend. This makes defence much more difficult.

Mississippi River

The Mississippi River is the longest **river** in the **United States**. It rises in Minnesota in the north and flows 3,779 km southwards to the Gulf of **Mexico**. It has over 250 tributaries – smaller rivers that flow into it. This vast network of rivers is extremely important for North American shipping and industry.

The waters of the Mississippi carry a huge quantity of mud. As a result, its **delta**, the coastal zone where most of the mud is dumped, is growing out to sea at a rate of 1 km every 10 years.

Warhead

Fuel tank

Rocket engine

Missiles are very effective weapons and have totally changed the way wars are fought. Most of a missile is taken up with fuel tanks for its rocket engine.

△ **Moles** have supersoft fur that lies flat in any direction. This helps them to squeeze down tunnels.

▽ A tremendous variety of **molluscs** live in the sea, including 1) whelks, 2) limpets, 3) cuttlefish, 4) cockles and 5) mussels.

Modem *see* Internet

Mole

Moles are small burrowing **mammals**, found all over the world. They spend most of their lives underground. Moles have narrow snouts and huge, clawed feet for tunnelling quickly through the **soil**. Their **eyes** are almost sightless but they have excellent **hearing** and very sensitive noses for finding **food** by **smell**. Moles feed on **worms** and **insect** grubs. They store some of their food to eat in the future, and have separate chambers for sleeping and raising their young.

Mollusc

Molluscs are one of the largest groups of **invertebrates** (**animals** without backbones). There are about 70,000 different species, including **snails** and **slugs**, **octopuses**, cuttlefish, **squid**, mussels, whelks, cockles, scallops and limpets. After **insects**, molluscs are the most numerous of all animals. Molluscs live in many **habitats**, but most are found in the sea.

All molluscs have soft bodies and no **bones**. For this reason, many molluscs grow shells to protect themselves. As a mollusc grows, its shell grows with it. The shell is made of the **mineral** calcium carbonate, which is produced from the **food** the mollusc eats.

MONACO
Government:
Constitutional monarchy
Capital: Monaco-Ville
Area: 1.9 sq km
Population: 32,000
Language: French
Currency: Euro

▽ A **monastery** in Europe during the Middle Ages was like a small town. The most important building was the church, but there were also dormitories for the monks, a hospital for caring for the sick, and gardens. Cloisters were half-covered courtyards where monks could go for quiet prayer.

Monaco

The tiny country of Monaco lies on the French coast of the **Mediterranean Sea**. It is called a 'principality' because it is ruled by a prince. Since the 1200s, all of Monaco's rulers have come from the Grimaldi family.

Monaco's main industry is tourism. With a population of 32,000 in an area of 1.9 sq km, Monaco has a greater **population** density than any other country in the world – 16,800 people per square kilometre. More than half of the people of Monaco are French.

Monarch

A monarch is a person who inherits a country's throne and is head of state for life. In the past in some countries, the monarch was elected, but he or she is usually the eldest child of the existing monarch. A family of monarchs is called a dynasty. There have been several royal families in the British Isles, such as the House of Tudor, which ruled **England** from 1485 until 1603. One of Europe's most powerful royal families was the **Hapsburgs**, to which many of the continent's emperors and kings belonged.

Monarchs around the world have had many different titles, such as king, queen, emperor, sultan and shah. Many monarchs have ruled with absolute power, and sometimes it was believed that the monarch was responsible only to God. This system of **government** is the opposite of **democracy**, in which the people choose their government and officials in regular **elections**. But throughout **history**, there have also been other forms of monarchy. Constitutional monarchy, for example, is where the monarch's duties are largely ceremonial, and the real power lies with politicians.

Monastery

A monastery is a place where monks live in a separate community. The monks lead a religious life and obey strict rules. Monks are always male, but there are also nuns, who live in all-female religious communities in convents. Monasteries are especially important in **Buddhism** and **Christianity**.

Christian monasteries began in **Egypt** in about 300. The monks worked as farmers, labourers and teachers, and helped the poor. One of the most famous early Christian monks was St Benedict (c. 480–547), who founded the Benedictine order in **Italy**. He divided the day into periods of prayer, religious study and work. Another important Italian monk was Francis of Assisi (1182–1226), who founded the Franciscan order. Life in a Buddhist monastery revolves around meditation, the study of religious texts and taking part in ceremonies. In parts of **Asia**, such as **Thailand** and **Myanmar**, boys as young as eight are sent to monasteries to train to become Buddhist monks. One of the most well-known Buddhist monasteries is the Potala, which stands on a rocky outcrop near Lhasa, the capital of **Tibet**. It was the home of the **Dalai Lama**.

Money

We use money every day to pay for things we buy. We pay with either **coins** or **paper** notes. This kind of money is known as cash. There is also another kind of money that includes cheques and credit cards.

Almost anything can be used as money. In the past, people used shells, beads, cocoa beans, **salt**, grain and even **cattle**. **Metal** coins were first used in **China** as long ago as 800 BCE. They were also used in Ancient **Greece** and the **Middle East**. At that time, coins were valuable because they were made of either **gold** or **silver**. Later, people began to use coins made of cheaper metals. The metal itself had no value, but the coins were still worth the amount stamped on them. Paper money was invented in China in about 600 CE. Today, a country's money is backed by its **government** and **banks**.

Mongolia

Mongolia is a **republic** in the heart of **Asia**, between **Russia** and **China**. It is a high, flat country. Much of the land is **desert** or grassy plateaux, with high **mountain** ranges in the west. The Gobi Desert covers a large area in the south.

Mongolia is a thinly populated country, and its people are descended from the **Mongols**. Until recently a communist state (see **communism**), Mongolia now has a multi-party system.

Mongols

The Mongols were **nomads** who lived on the great plains of Central **Asia**. They herded huge flocks of **sheep**, **goats**, **cattle** and **horses**, which they grazed on the vast grasslands of the region. They lived in tents called yurts, which were made of light **wood** and **animal** hides.

MONGOLIA
Government: Republic
Capital: Ulan Bator
Area: 1,565,000 sq km
Population: 2.4 million
Language: Mongolian
Currency: Tugrik

▽ The banded **mongoose** is famed for its ability to attack and kill venomous snakes, such as this cobra. It relies on speed to grab the snake before it bites.

▷ Red howler **monkeys** roar from the treetops at dawn to lay claim to their territory. They live in large family groups in the forests of Central and South America.

The Mongols were superb horsemen and highly trained warriors. In the 1200s, they formed a mighty **army** led by **Genghis Khan**. Swift-riding hordes of Mongols swept through **China**, **India**, Persia (present-day **Iran**) and as far west as **Hungary**. Under Genghis Khan, and later his grandson **Kublai Khan**, the Mongols conquered half the known world, but they were unable to hold their empire together. Within 100 years, the Mongol empire had been taken over by the Chinese.

Mongoose

The mongoose is a small **mammal** that lives in **Africa** and southern **Asia**. It is a relative of weasels and stoats. It has a long body, a bushy tail and short legs. The mongoose lives in a burrow and feeds on small **birds**, **rodents** such as **rats** and **snakes**.

Monkey

Monkeys are **mammals** that belong to the primates – the same group of **animals** as **apes** and **human beings**. Most monkeys have long tails and thick fur all over their body. They are usually smaller than apes. Monkeys' hands and feet are used for grasping food, branches and other objects, and are very similar in design to those of humans. Many monkeys use their long tails as an extra 'arm' or 'leg' when swinging through the **trees**.

Monkeys live in family groups called troops, and spend much of their time playing, fighting and grooming each other. Each troop of monkeys has its own territory where it lives and feeds.

There are about 200 different species of monkey. Most live in the tropics, especially in **forests**, in **Central America**, **South America**, **Africa** and **Asia**. More and more monkey species are becoming rare, mainly due to **habitat** destruction and **hunting**.

Monsoon

Monsoons are **winds** that blow from land to sea during winter, and from sea to land during summer. They occur mainly in southern **Asia**. The summer monsoon carries moisture from the sea, and rain falls over the land. Summer monsoons bring the rainy season. In **India**, 1,700 mm of rain falls from June to September, and only 100 mm in all the rest of the year.

△ The **moon's** surface is pitted with craters, almost all of which were made by meteorites crashing into it.

MOROCCO
Government: Constitutional monarchy
Capital: Rabat
Area: 458,730 sq km
Population: 28.2 million
Language: Arabic
Currency: Dirham

◁ **Monsoon** winds bring torrential rain that causes serious floods in southern Asia, especially India and Bangladesh.

Moon

A moon is a natural **satellite** that travels around, or **orbits**, a **planet**. The **earth** has only one moon, but other planets in our **solar system** may have many moons. **Jupiter**, for example, has 28.

The earth's moon is our nearest neighbour in space. It loops around this planet, never coming closer than 356,400 km. It travels at about 3,660 km/h and takes $27\frac{1}{3}$ days to complete the circuit. The moon was probably formed at the same time as the earth, but the **rocks** on its surface are older than those on the earth's surface because the moon has not changed in 4,000 million years.

The moon is a dry, lifeless world, with no **air** or **water**. **Gravity** on the moon is just one-sixth of the gravity on earth, yet the moon's gravitational pull affects us every day. It is the moon's pull that causes the **ocean tides** to rise and fall.

Mormonism

Mormonism is a **religion** founded by the American Joseph Smith (1805–1844) in 1830. Its name comes from the *Book of Mormon*, which Mormons believe is a sacred **history** of ancient American peoples. Mormonism began in **New York**, but the Mormons were persecuted for their beliefs and driven out. They finally settled in Salt Lake Valley, Utah.

Morocco

Morocco is a country in northwest **Africa**. It has two coastlines. To the west is the **Atlantic Ocean** and to the north is the **Mediterranean Sea**.

Most of Morocco's 28 million people are farmers. They grow **wheat**, maize, **fruit** and olives, and some keep **sheep**, **goats** and **cattle**. Most of the people are Muslims, followers of **Islam**. The largest city is Casablanca.

Morse code

Morse code is a simple way of sending messages. It is an **alphabet** of dots and dashes, and each letter has its own dot and dash pattern. The code was created by Samuel Morse (1791–1872), an American artist and inventor, to send messages along a telegraph **wire**. The telegraph operator presses a key at one end to send a signal along the wire to a sounder at the other end. A short signal is a dot and a long signal is a dash. The first official telegraph message was sent in 1844.

Today, Morse code is used regularly only by **ships** and by amateur **radio** operators. However, it is also used by people in emergencies, when radio signals are too weak for other systems to work.

△ The first messages in **Morse code** were sent in the mid-1800s using a telegraph machine.

Mosaic

A mosaic is a picture made from small pieces of coloured stone or **glass** set into plaster or cement. The pieces are arranged to make a design or a portrait, or to show a scene. Mosaic-making is an ancient **art**. The Sumerians of Mesopotamia (present-day **Iraq**) made mosaics almost 5,000 years ago.

Mosaics are a very practical way of decorating floors and walls, as they can be washed without being spoiled. In the **Roman Empire**, villas and palaces had dazzling mosaics showing scenes of everyday life. Mosaics were also used to make pictures of saints, angels and **Jesus Christ** in **churches** all over **Greece**, **Italy** and **Turkey**.

△ This **mosaic** is of the Emperor Justinian, who ruled the Byzantine Empire during the 500s.

▷ **Moscow**'s Red Square is dominated by the onion-shaped domes of St Basil's Cathedral and the fortress walls of the Kremlin.

Moscow

Moscow is the capital of **Russia**. It is also the largest city in the country, with a **population** of more than eight million people. Moscow lies on a plain across the Moskva **River**. It is Russia's main industrial and business centre – everything is made in Moscow, from **cars** to **clothing**. It is also the political and cultural centre of the country.

Moscow was first made the capital of Muscovy in 1547, during the reign of **Ivan the Terrible**, the first tsar (emperor) of Russia. The city grew up around the **Kremlin**, an ancient fort from which the Muscovy princes used to defend their country. Moscow remained the capital of the tsars until 1712, when Peter the Great (1672–1725) moved the capital to St Petersburg. However, Moscow remained important, even after it was largely burned down during **Napoleon's** occupation of 1812.

After the **Russian Revolution** of 1917, Moscow became the seat of the **Soviet Union's** government. In 1992, it became the capital of Russia once again.

Mosque

A mosque is a building used for worship by Muslims. It may also serve as a tomb or as a place where Muslims receive religious instruction (see **Islam**). Most mosques have up to six towers called minarets, from which official criers known as *muezzins* call people to prayer. There is also usually

The world's largest **mosque** stands beside the sea in Casablanca, Morocco. It can hold 100,000 worshippers and a laser beam on top of its 176 m-high minaret can be seen 50 km away.

When a female **mosquito** bites, she injects a special substance into her victim that makes the blood flow more easily. This is why mosquito bites itch.

a courtyard containing a fountain or well. This is where Muslims wash before they begin to pray, as laid down by the holy **book** of Islam – the **Koran**. Inside the mosque, there is an arch called the *mihrab*, which is set in the wall nearest to the holy city of **Mecca**. Muslims face this arch when they pray.

Mosquito

A mosquito is a small **insect** that looks like a **fly**. It has a slender, tube-shaped body, three pairs of long legs and two narrow wings. Female mosquitoes bite and suck **blood**. They have sharp tubes called stylets with which they pierce tiny blood vessels in their victims. The male mosquitoes live on the juices of **plants**. Some kinds of mosquito spread **diseases** such as **malaria** and yellow fever.

Moss

Moss is a kind of **plant** that grows in low, closely packed clusters. It has slender stems covered with tiny leaves. Instead of proper roots that reach into the **soil**, mosses have a mass of fine hairs that soak up moisture and **food**.

Moth

Moths are flying **insects** that resemble **butterflies**. However, there are several differences. Moths have plumper bodies than butterflies.

Some **moths**, such as this garden tiger, are just as colourful as butterflies. Strong coloration is often a warning sign to potential predators that the moth tastes foul or is poisonous.

Their antennae are like tiny combs, or have feathery hairs on them, while butterfly antennae end in tiny knobs. Many moths fly in the evening and at night, whereas butterflies are active only in the daytime.

Motor, electric

An electric motor is a **machine** that changes electrical **energy** into mechanical energy. There are electric motors all around us. They drive things such as **refrigerators**, **vacuum** cleaners, electric **clocks**, hair dryers, washing machines and some trains (see **railway**).

A simple motor is made up of a coil of **wire** held between the poles of a magnet (see **magnetism**). When an electric current flows through the coil, the coil becomes a magnet with a north pole and a south pole. Since like poles repel and unlike poles attract, the coil swings round between the poles of the magnet until its north pole is facing the south pole of the magnet and its south pole is facing the magnet's north pole. The direction of the current in the coil is then reversed so that the coil's poles are also reversed. The coil then has to swing round again to line up its poles with those of the magnet. The electric motor keeps on turning because it keeps getting a series of magnetic pushes.

The **motorcycles** used in Grand Prix racing are built especially for the racetrack, and are far more powerful than ordinary motorbikes.

Motorcycle

The first motorcycle was built in 1885 by the German engineer Gottlieb Daimler (1834–1900). He fitted one of his petrol **engines** to a wooden **bicycle** frame. Today's motorcycles are more complicated **machines**.

A motorcycle's engine is similar to that of a **car**, but smaller. It is either a two-stroke or a four-stroke engine, and it may have from one to four cylinders. The engine can be cooled by either **air** or **water**. It is started with an ignition button on the handlebars. This turns the engine and starts it firing.

Mountain

A large part of the **earth**'s surface is covered by mountains. The greatest mountain ranges include the **Alps** of **Europe**, the **Rocky Mountains** of **North America**, the **Andes** of **South America** and the **Himalayas** of **Asia**. There are also mountains under the **oceans**. The peaks of these submerged mountains may rise up above the sea's surface as **islands**.

Mountains are formed by movements in the earth's crust. Some mountains are formed when two great land masses move towards each other and squeeze up the land inbetween. The Alps were formed in this way. Other mountains are heaps of ash and lava that poured out when a **volcano** erupted.

Mountains are constantly being worn away by a process known as erosion. The hardest **rock** is worn away by rain, **wind**, **sun** and frost. **Rivers** and **glaciers** cut deep valleys into mountainsides.

Mouse

A mouse is a **rodent**, like its relative the **rat**. There are many species of mice, which live in a wide range of **habitats**. Mice breed very quickly. A female can have 40 babies a year, and the young can themselves breed at 12 weeks.

▷ In **mountain** areas, different plants grow at different altitudes. This is because the weather conditions change the higher you go.

Permanent snow

High-altitude alpine plants

Pastures

Coniferous trees

Broad-leaved (deciduous) trees

Mozambique

Mozambique is a **republic** in southeast **Africa**. It was ruled by **Portugal**, but became independent in 1975. **Farming** is the most important industry in this hot, tropical country. Mozambique's ports of Maputo and Beira are used for importing and exporting goods to the inland regions of Africa. In the 1980s, **famine** and **civil war** caused widespread hardship in Mozambique, and in 2000, **floods** devastated huge areas.

Mozart, Wolfgang Amadeus

Frequently described as one of the greatest ever composers, Wolfgang Amadeus Mozart (1756–1791) began writing **music** at the age of five. He was born in **Austria**, and by the time he was seven years old, was playing at concerts all over **Europe**. Mozart wrote over 600 pieces of music, including many beautiful **operas** and symphonies. But he earned little **money** from his hard work. He died at just 35.

Muhammad

The Prophet Muhammad (570–632) was the founder and leader of the **religion** of **Islam**. He was born in **Mecca** in what is now **Saudi Arabia**. Muhammad believed that God had asked him to preach to his people at the age of 40. He taught that there

continued on page 217

MOZAMBIQUE
Government: Republic
Capital: Maputo
Area: 801,590 sq km
Population: 17.3 million
Language: Portuguese
Currency: Metical

△ The harvest **mouse** lives in fields and hedgerows, and weaves a domed nest the size of a tennis ball.

MUSIC

Music is an art form that consists of organized sounds played in time. It is perfomed on special occasions, or simply for enjoyment.

One of the earliest known musical instruments is the 'bull-roarer'. It was made from a bone and a piece of cord and made a strange screaming noise when whirled about the head.

MUSIC FOR ALL

The word 'music' comes from the 'muses', or goddesses, of Ancient Greece, who were said to inspire songs and dance. Music is often called a 'universal language' because it is an art form that everyone in the world can understand. Even without musical training, anyone can share the feelings and emotions that are conveyed by musical notes or song.

A gamelan is a kind of orchestra from Indonesia. It includes up to 40 drums, gongs, xylophones and chimes, which are played together to make a magical tinkling sound.

MUSIC WITH A PURPOSE

Although the precise origins of music are unknown, it seems likely that the earliest music was connected with religion, magical practices and dance. Simple musical instruments that are thousands of years old have been found in some Stone Age sites. African tribal music is one of the oldest surviving musical forms. It is always accompanied by the rhythm of drums.

MUSIC AS ART

With the growth of civilizations, people turned music into art. For example, the ancient *ragas* of India were tunes with beautiful rhythms. In the tomb paintings of the Ancient Egyptian pharaohs, musicians play versions of the lyre, the harp and different forms of pipe.

THE CLASSICAL ERA

Musical notation – the way in which music is written down – was probably invented by Italian monks in the 800s. It meant that the same piece of music could be taken to different places and played by many musicians. In the Middle Ages, most Western music was centred around the church, but during the Renaissance there was a big increase in non-religious music. The first orchestras appeared in the 1600s, and featured new instruments such as violins, violas and cellos. Gradually, more instruments were invented, and orchestras grew in size.

MODERN MUSIC

Since the late 1800s, many different types of music have been developed, including blues, jazz, pop music, reggae and R&B ('Rhythm and Blues'). The invention of the radio and record-player allowed new musical styles to spread, and meant that people could listen to music in the comfort of their homes. People could buy and play their favourite pieces of music again and again. There are now many methods of recording music, including onto vinyl records, tapes or cassettes, CDs, DVDs and digital sound files.

△ The Etruscans, who lived in Italy before the Romans, made rich and varied music with instruments such as lyres and double flutes.

During the 1700s and 1800s, music enjoyed a golden age in Europe. This picture shows the child prodigy Wolfgang Amadeus Mozart playing the piano while on a concert tour of Europe.

MUSICAL THEORY

As painters and sculptors use lines, colours and shapes, so musicians use the properties of sound. They use notes of different pitch (highness or lowness) and combine them with the beat of a rhythm to make a melody, or tune. They sometimes add harmony, which is when two or more notes of different pitch are played together. Tone or timbre – the quality of sound produced by different instruments or voices – is another aspect of music.

In recent years, computers have revolutionized the production of music. They allow musicians to make music that is without human flaws of rhythm and timing. Many genres have come out of computer music, including dance music, where repetitive beats are combined with influences from every other conceivable form of music.

The 'classic' rock or pop band has keyboards, electric guitar (left), bass guitar and drums (below).

continued from page 215

was only one God, called Allah. In 622, Muhammad was forced out of Mecca, and this is the year from which the Muslim **calendar** dates. After his death, his teachings spread rapidly.

Muscle

Muscles are the things that make the parts of our bodies move. There are two different kinds of muscle. Some work when your **brain** tells them to. When you pick up a chair, your brain sends signals to muscles in your arms, in your trunk and in your legs. All these muscles work together, and you are able to pick up the chair. The second kind of muscle works even when you **sleep**. Your **stomach** muscles go on churning **food**, and your **heart** muscles go on pumping **blood**.

Muscles can only pull, not push, so they often work in opposing pairs. One contracts (tightens) as the other relaxes (stretches).

Mushroom and Toadstool

Mushrooms and toadstools are both forms of fungi (see **fungus**). They grow in damp places in woods and fields. Some taste excellent, but others are poisonous and may cause death if eaten. Mushrooms and toadstools lack the chlorophyll that allows **plants** to make their own **food** using the **sun**'s **energy**. Instead, they feed on decayed matter in the **soil**, or are **parasites** that feed off plants.

Most of a mushroom or toadstool consists of a mass of threadlike fibres hidden underground. The part we can see is a soft, fruiting body that scatters millions of tiny particles called spores from which new fungi grow.

Music *see* page 216

▷ There are 640 **muscles** in the human body, each of which moves a particular part of the body.

Musical instrument

There are four main kinds of musical instrument. Woodwind instruments produce a musical note by vibrating **air** inside a tube. They include the clarinet, oboe, bassoon, flute, piccolo and recorder. In brass instruments such as the trumpet, tuba and trombone, the vibration of the player's lips makes the air in the instrument vibrate. String instruments work in one of two ways. The strings of the instrument are either made to vibrate by a bow, as in the **violin**, cello and double bass, or the strings are plucked, as in the **guitar** and **harp**. In percussion instruments, a tight piece of **skin** or a piece of **wood** or **metal** is struck to make a note. Percussion instruments include **drums**, cymbals, tambourines and the **xylophone**.

Muslims *see* Islam

Mussolini, Benito

Mussolini (1883–1945) was the leader of **Italy's** fascists (see **fascism**). In 1922, he persuaded the king of Italy to make him prime minister. Soon afterwards, he made himself **dictator**. He wanted military glory, and led Italy into **World War II**. His armies were defeated, and he was shot by his own people.

Myanmar

Myanmar is a country in **Southeast Asia**. It was known as Burma until 1989. Most of its people are farmers and follow the **religion** of **Buddhism**. During the 1900s, Myanmar suffered civil unrest, and it has had a military **government** since 1958.

MYANMAR
Government: Military
Capital: Yangon
Area: 676,552 sq km
Population: 45 million
Language: Burmese
Currency: Kyat

MYTHS and LEGENDS

Myths and legends are stories about heroes and religious beliefs. Most of these tales date from ancient times, and many are still told today.

According to Greek mythology, the hero Perseus killed the monster Medusa by cutting off her head. The sight of her head, which had snakes for hair, turned people to stone. Here, in a fit of rage, Perseus holds it up to King Polydectes and his courtiers.

ANCIENT ORIGINS

Every society has its own myths and legends, some of which are hundreds or even thousands of years old. Myths and legends first appeared before writing was developed, and were passed on through the generations by word of mouth. Later, people began to write the stories down, and artists illustrated them.

In Greek mythology, the magical winged horse Pegasus was tamed by the hero Bellerophon, who rode the stallion on many adventures.

MYTH OR LEGEND?

In ancient times, people knew little about nature or science, and they told myths to explain the world and their place in it. Myths grew up around things such as the rising and setting of the sun, the seasonal flooding of a river or a sudden storm. The collected myths of a civilization are known as its mythology. By studying mythology, we can learn a lot about early people's way of life.

Unlike myths, which early people regarded as true or sacred, legends are folktales that may be based on fact. Legends often concern the exploits of heroes, gods and creatures such as giants, dragons, mermaids and witches. Although stories about legendary characters such as Robin Hood and King Arthur are probably made up, there may have been historical figures who inspired them.

△ *The Ancient Egyptians believed in many gods and goddesses. Some were represented with the heads of animals that they considered to be sacred.*

GODS, GODDESSES AND SPIRITS

In ancient times, nature was vital to people's survival. If the crops failed or hunting was unsuccessful, there would be nothing to eat. These things were so important that humans came to believe that they were the work of powerful beings. People started to worship gods and spirits to make sure that they were helped. For example, if the sun god was happy, the sun would shine at the right times. But if he was angry, the sun could scorch the earth or disappear forever, leaving the world in cold and darkness.

The Ancient Greeks thought that the sun was the god Apollo driving a flaming chariot across the sky. For Ancient Egyptians, the sun was the god Ra sailing through the heavens. The Japanese, Aztecs and Native Americans also had sun gods.

The Zuni, a Native American tribe, believe that the first people came from inside the earth, and were trained by the medicine man Yanauluha to farm the land.

GREEK AND ROMAN MYTHOLOGY

The people of Ancient Greece developed a complex belief system of gods and spirits, which was later adopted by the Romans. The Greeks and Romans told long stories and epic poems about these supernatural beings as a form of entertainment. For example, in the 700s, the Greek poet Homer wrote poems such as the *Iliad* and *Odyssey*.

Zeus (called Jupiter by the Romans) was the most important Greek god. King of the gods, he ruled over them and hurled thunderbolts when he was angry. Other deities (gods and goddesses) included Hades (Pluto), god of the underworld, and Athene (Aphrodite), goddess of wisdom.

Garuda is a half-man, half-eagle creature that appears in Hindu mythology. He is said to be the sun in the form of a bird. In this picture, Garuda is carrying the god Vishnu and his wife Lakshmi.

ABORIGINAL MYTHS

'Dreamings' are stories told by the aboriginal people of Australia to explain how the world was made. They tell how, in a period called the 'Dreamtime', spirits walked the earth and created living things, including people. The spirits taught human beings how to survive and then returned to sleep in the earth. The routes that the spirits made are called 'songlines', and defined the land's features.

SEE ALSO
Aboriginal people, Arthur (King), Aztecs, Egypt (Ancient), God and Goddess, Greece (Ancient), Homer, Native Americans, Religion, Roman Empire, Vikings, Witch

Legends were at the heart of Norse culture. Sigurd is a legendary Norse warrior who killed the dragon Fafnir and captured his treasure. But the gold carried a curse, and in the end Sigurd himself was killed.

SCANDINAVIAN LEGENDS

The Norse (who were known as Vikings from the 800s to the 1100s) and other northern European peoples believed in many gods and warrior heroes. The most powerful Norse god was Odin – god of the sky, war, law and poetry. Odin ruled the other gods, and was married to the goddess Frigga. He rode an eight-legged horse called Sleipnir. Other Norse gods include Odin's son Thor, god of thunder, and Loki, a trickster god. Giants, dwarves and dragons also featured in many Norse legends.

▽ *The Norse believed that giants posed a constant threat to gods and humans alike. Here, Surt leads the fire giants of Muspell against the gods in what would be the last battle – and the end of the world.*

219

Nail and Claw

Nails and claws are made of hard **skin**, like animals' **horns**, and grow at the end of toes and fingers. When they are broad and flat they are called nails, but if they are sharp and pointed they are claws. Human nails are of little use. But most **birds**, **mammals** and **reptiles** use their claws to attack and to defend themselves from predators.

A close look at an animal's claws will tell you much about its way of life. **Cats** and birds of prey have very sharp claws. They are hooked for holding onto and tearing prey. **Anteaters** have long, strong, curved claws for tearing apart **termites**' nests.

The claws of birds, reptiles and mammals are vital to their survival. The claws of all members of the cat family can be retracted (pulled back) into the paws at will.

△ Claws are made of the same material as nails. Prehistoric animals, such as the dinosaur *Deinonychus*, had large, sharp claws to slash and kill prey.

Namibia

Namibia is in southwest **Africa**. Most of the country is located on the plateau of Table Mountain, more than 1,000 m above sea level. The east of the country forms part of the Kalahari **Desert**. As a result, there is not much good farmland. The main industry is

NAMIBIA
Government: Republic
Capital: Windhoek
Area: 824,292 sq km
Population: 1.7 million
Languages: Afrikaans, English and others
Currency: Namibian dollar

mining. Much of the land of the native San people – who have been living in the deserts of Namibia and **Botswana** for over 30,000 years – has been encroached on by international mining corporations. In 1915, the country became a South African territory under the League of Nations. In 1946, the **United Nations** said that **South Africa** had no rights over Namibia, but South Africa disputed this. In 1989, it was finally agreed that South Africa would hand over power to the black majority. After a long armed struggle against South African control, independence was achieved in 1990.

Nanak, Guru

Guru Nanak (1469–1539) founded the Sikh religion (see **Sikhism**) in the 1400s in the area of present-day **Pakistan** and northwest **India** known as Punjab.

Guru (meaning spiritual guide or teacher) Nanak was concerned by the tensions between Hindus (see **Hinduism**) and Muslims (see **Islam**). He gathered together a small group of like-minded followers to search for an understanding of God (see **god and goddess**), uncluttered by ritual. He based his religion on a simple desire to get close to God and do God's will.

Sikhs believe in one god called Satguru, which means true teacher, who created the world. Satguru's will is made known through wise teachers – ten human gurus (Nanak and his nine successors) – and from a book, the *Adi Granth* ('first book'). Guru Nanak chose his successor, and in his own lifetime established him as Guru Angad.

The first Sikh *gurdwara* (temple) was built in Kartarpur (present-day Pakistan), where Guru Nanak ended his days after being a wandering preacher.

As a mark of equality, Sikhs often eat communally in a shared *langar* (dining room) attached to the *gurdwara*. The gurdwara is also a community centre.

Napoleon Bonaparte

Napoleon Bonaparte (1769–1821) attended the best military school in **Paris**, and by 1792 he was a captain of artillery. Three years later, he saved **France** by crushing a royalist rebellion in Paris. Soon, he was head of the French **army** and had won great victories in **Italy**, **Belgium** and **Austria**. In 1804, he crowned himself emperor of France in the presence of the **Pope**.

Napoleon was a small man. His soldiers adored him and called him 'the little corporal'. With political skills equal to his skills as a general, Napoleon reorganized the **government** of France and drew up a new French code of **law**. Many of his laws are still in force today.

Napoleon set out to conquer the whole of **Europe**, but he could not defeat Britain at sea. Frustrated by this failure, he tried to stop all countries from trading with Britain, but **Russia** would not cooperate. In retaliation, Napoleon led a great army into Russia in the winter of 1812. This campaign ended in disaster because his troops were defeated by the bitter **weather**. He met his final defeat at the Battle of Waterloo in 1815, where he was beaten by the British under the Duke of Wellington (1769–1852) and the Prussians under Gebbard von Blücher (1742–1819). He was imprisoned by the British on the lonely **Atlantic** island of St Helena, where he died in 1821.

Native Americans

The original inhabitants of **North America** are called Native Americans. They formed hundreds of groups, such as the Cherokee in the Appalachian **Mountains** and the Sioux on the Great Plains. From the early 1600s, Europeans began to settle in their lands. As the Europeans spread out over the

△ The Iroquois were a group of **Native American** tribes who existed mainly through hunting. They lived in village communities in the woodland areas of what is now New York State.

▽ Napoleon Bonaparte made his reputation at the Battle of Marengo in Italy in 1800. He led a brilliant counter-attack which crushed the Austrian army. He was finally defeated at Waterloo in 1815.

continent during the next 250 years, many Native Americans died through warfare and exposure to new **diseases**. The remainder were forced to live in reservations (pockets of land) put aside for them by the Europeans.

NATO (North Atlantic Treaty Organization)

NATO is a defensive alliance set up after **World War II**. In 1949, 12 countries signed a treaty in which they agreed that an attack on one member would be considered an attack on them all. The 12 were **Belgium**, **Canada**, **Denmark**, **France**, **Iceland**, **Italy**, **Luxembourg**, the **Netherlands**, **Norway**, **Portugal**, the **United Kingdom** and the **United States**. **Greece** and **Turkey** joined in 1951, West **Germany** in 1954, **Spain** in 1982, and the **Czech Republic**, **Hungary** and **Poland** in 1999. In 1990, the united Germany replaced West Germany in NATO.

The purpose of the alliance is to unify and strengthen the military defences of the nations of western **Europe**. Each member nation contributes soldiers and supplies to NATO forces. The members of NATO also cooperate on political and **economic** issues.

In the 1960s some NATO members felt that the United States had too much power within the alliance. France withdrew her NATO forces in 1966, but remained a member. With the collapse of many of the communist **governments** (see **communism**) of eastern Europe in 1990, NATO had to examine its role for the future. In 1991, NATO forces were restructured as the Cold War came to an end. A possible new role for NATO could be peacekeeping in troubled parts of the world using smaller forces.

Natural gas

Natural gas is a type of **gas** which occurs naturally underground and does not have to be manufactured. It is usually found in **oil** fields, but is sometimes found on its own. When there is only a little natural gas in an oil field, it is burned off. If there is plenty, it is piped away and used for heating and to produce **electricity**.

Natural gas is found in large quantities in **Russia**, in Texas and Louisiana in the **United States**, and in the North Sea oil fields. Half the world's supply of natural gas is used by the United States.

▽ Pipelines take the oil and **natural gas** from oil rigs to land. An oil rig is a platform fixed to the sea bed, which drills into the rocks below and pumps up the oil and natural gas from these rocks.

▽ Modern **navigation** uses satellite technology to beam radio signals from place to place. The instruments are very accurate and allow ships, aircraft and spacecraft to know their precise position.

Navigation

Navigation means finding the way, usually in a **ship** or an **aircraft**. For hundreds of years, navigators at sea used the changing positions of the **sun** and **stars** to work out their **latitude**.

Knowing the difference between the **time** on the ship and the time set at 0° **longitude** at Greenwich helped them to work out their position more precisely.

Today, many navigational instruments are **electronic** and are very accurate. **Radio** beacons and **satellites** send out signals from which a ship can find its position. Then the navigator uses a **compass** to keep the ship on the right course. **Computers** help ships, aircraft and **spacecraft** navigate so exactly that their position is known precisely.

A sextant can be used to work out a ship's position by measuring the angle between a star or the sun and the horizon. Once the angle has been measured, the star's position at that particular time can be looked up in a very accurate table. This allows the position of the ship to be calculated. By taking a series of sextant readings, the ship can be kept on the right course.

Satellite

Radio signals

Radio beacon

Neanderthal
see Cave-dweller

Nepal

Nepal lies between **India** and **Tibet**. The north of the country is in the Himalaya **Mountains** (4,200 m above sea level). Most of the people live in the fertile central valley and keep **sheep**, **goats** and **yaks**. The capital, Kathmandu, lies at 1,340 m above sea level and is the only city in the country.

Tourism is a main source of income for Nepal. Visitors travel there from all over the world to climb the world's highest mountain, **Mount Everest** (8,848 m).

In 2001, the crown prince assassinated his father, mother and other members of his family. The royal family's authority has been damaged as a result.

Neptune

The **planet** Neptune is named after the **Roman** god of **water** and the sea. It is a large planet far out in the **solar system**, about 4.5 billion km from the **sun**. Only **Pluto** is further away. It takes Neptune 164.8 years to circle the sun. The **earth** takes 365 days.

Being so far from the sun, Neptune is a very cold place. Scientists think its **atmosphere** is rather like **Jupiter's**, which is mostly made up of the gas **hydrogen**. Neptune has eight **moons**, and scientists have recently discovered a system of thin rings around the planet.

Early astronomers (see **astronomy**) were unable to see Neptune, but they knew it had to be there. They could tell there was something affecting the **orbit** of the nearby planet, **Uranus**.

In 1845, two astronomers, Englishman John Adams (1819–1892) and Frenchman Urbain Leverrier (1811–1877), used **mathematics** to work out where Neptune should be. The following year astronomers used this information and spotted the planet.

NEPAL
Government: Monarchy
Capital: Kathmandu
Area: 147,181 sq km
Population: 23.4 million
Languages: Nepali, Maithir and Bhojpuri
Currency: Nepalese rupee

△ **Nerves** are bundles of fibres that contain cells called neurons. They carry impulses from parts of the body to the brain.

▽ If we could observe **Neptune** from its largest moon, Triton, it would look like this. The light from the sun would be no brighter than that of a star.

Nerves

Nerves are tiny fibres made up of **cells** called neurons. They form a complex network all through the body – the nervous system. When a part of the body touches something, nerves send a message, or impulse, through the spinal column to the **brain**. If we feel **pain**, a message is sent back to tell the **muscles** to move away from whatever is causing the pain. Nerves also carry the **senses** of **sight**, **hearing** and **taste**. The sense organs have special nerve endings that respond to **heat**, **light**, cold and other stimuli. The **eye**, for example, contains the large optic nerve, which responds to light stimuli and transmits messages from the eye to the brain. The brain makes sense of the messages transmitted.

Nerve cells are covered with a layer of **fat** called a myelin sheath. Without this layer, nerve cells cannot transmit their messages properly. Sufferers of the **disease** multiple sclerosis (MS) lose the use of their muscles as the disease destroys these fatty layers.

NEPTUNE FACTS
Average distance from sun: 4.5 billion km
Nearest distance from earth: 4,497 million km
Average temperature: -210°C
Diameter across the equator: 48,400 km
Atmosphere: 85% hydrogen, 13% helium and 2% methane
Number of moons: 8
Length of day: 18 hours
Length of year: 164.8 earth years

Nest

A nest is a home built by an **animal** or **bird**, where it has its young and looks after them. Birds build nests when they are ready to lay **eggs**. With some birds, the female builds the nest, but with others the male will help. Some nests are very complicated, and may be lined with **wool**, **hair** or **feathers**. Others have a more simple design or are quite untidy.

Coots live on open stretches of **water**, but build their nests on piles of stones or sticks raised above the water.

The South American oven bird builds a nest shaped like an old-fashioned oven, from mud and pieces of **grass**.

A few mammals such as mice (see **mouse**) and **squirrels** make nests for their young, but these are not as intricate as birds' nests.

Some **insects** make the most elaborate nests of all. These are not at all like birds' nests. They are often built for a whole group, or colony, of insects. There will be one queen, who lays eggs, and hundreds or even thousands of workers to look after them. Most **bees** and wasps make this sort of nest. Some wasps build their nests out of paper. **Termites** make huge mud nests. The complex pattern of cells in the hornet's papery nest makes a safe home for the young.

△ The male weaverbird hangs from a branch and weaves long strips of grass to make his **nest**. This is also how he attracts a mate – if the nest is good enough, a female will line it with feathers.

NETHERLANDS
Government: Democracy (government at The Hague)
Capital: Amsterdam
Area: 33,939 sq km
Population: 15.8 million
Language: Dutch
Currency: Euro

Netherlands

The Netherlands is one of three nations – the others are **Belgium** and **Luxembourg** – known as the Low Countries because they do not rise high above sea level. More than a third of the Netherlands is below sea level as much of the farmland has been reclaimed from the sea and marshes.

The sea often floods the flat land near the coast, so sea walls have been built for protection against storms (see **weather**).

Living so near to the sea, the people of the Netherlands, who are known as the Dutch, have a long and successful history of seafaring, **trade** and exploration. Rotterdam is the busiest port in **Europe**.

The country has one of the highest **population** densities in Europe with about 400 people per square kilometre. Most live in the Randstad – the group of major cities that includes Rotterdam, Amsterdam and The Hague. The Randstad lies in the provinces of North and South Holland. The Netherlands itself is often known as Holland.

The Netherlands is a prosperous country and was one of the first members of the European Community. It has a queen, but is governed by a democratic parliament (see **democracy**).

New Guinea

New Guinea is one of the world's largest **islands**. It lies to the north of **Australia**, in the **Pacific Ocean**. It is inhabited by people whose ancestors travelled to the islands from **Southeast Asia** about 40,000 years ago. They developed a way of life that depended on raising pigs and growing yams. This is still the basis of **farming** today.

The island is divided into two parts. The west is called West Papua (formerly Irian Jaya), and belongs to Indonesia. The east is called **Papua New Guinea**. About four million people live there. It used to belong to Australia but became independent in 1975. The capital is Port Moresby. Most of the people live in the central highlands. Over the centuries, isolated villages in the **mountains** have developed their own **languages** – resulting in Papua New Guinea having more than

800 languages. As a result, many people in the Pacific Islands speak pidgin, a shared language used for trading. New Guinea's main exports are **tea**, cocoa, copra (coconut), **copper** and **gold**.

Tourism brings foreign income to the Pacific Islands and gives the islanders a reason to preserve traditions of **dance**, **music**, and cooking.

Newspaper

Newspapers are just what their name says they are – papers that print news. They first appeared in the 1400s, just after **printing** was invented. Printers produced pamphlets telling people what was happening in the country and what people thought about it.

The format of today's newspapers first appeared in the 1700s. Nowadays, there are newspapers in almost every country in the world, in many different **languages**. Some are printed every day, some every week.

One of the oldest newspapers is *The Times*, which is printed in **London**, in **England**. It began in 1785 as the *Universal Daily Register*. It changed its name to *The Times* in 1788. Other famous newspapers are the *New York Times* and the *Washington Post* in the United States, *Pravda* in Russia and *Le Monde* in France.

Newt
see Salamander and Newt

Newton, Isaac

Sir Isaac Newton (1642–1727) was an English mathematician (see **mathematics**) and scientist who made some of the world's greatest scientific discoveries (see **science**). He left Cambridge **University** in 1665 when the **plague** shut down the entire university. In the 18 months before the university reopened, Newton did much of his most important work.

Newton's experiments showed that white **light** is a mixture of all the **colours** of the **rainbow** (the **spectrum**). By studying the spectrum of light from a **star** or other glowing object, scientists can now find out what that object is made of. Newton's studies of light led him to build the first reflecting **telescope**.

Newton also discovered **gravity**. He realized that the same kind of force that makes apples fall from **trees** also gives objects **weight** and keeps the **planets** in **orbit** round the **sun**.

Newton determined the laws of motion that are still used in **physics** today. His discoveries made many later **inventions** possible.

New York

New York City is the largest city in the **United States**. More than 14 million people live in New York and its suburbs.

The city stands mainly on three **islands** that lie at the mouth of the Hudson **River**. The **island** of Manhattan is the heart of New York, and many of its most famous sights such as Fifth Avenue, the main shopping street, are found there.

Ships from every continent dock at New York's port, which is the world's largest. New York is also one of the world's great business centres and is famous for having the greatest collections of skyscrapers in the world.

New York probably has the most mixed population of any city in the world. Its black community is the largest in the United States. The world's largest Jewish population lives in the New York area. The city has a Little Italy and a Chinatown.

△ **New York** City is often called the 'city that never sleeps'. In Manhattan, the streets are organized on a grid pattern, and run either from north to south or from west to east.

△ **New York** is home to some of the tallest buildings in the world, including the Empire State Building, at 381 m tall.

NEW ZEALAND
Government: Democracy
Capital: Wellington
Area: 270,534 sq km
Population: 3.8 million
Languages: Maori and English
Currency: New Zealand dollar

NICARAGUA
Government: Republic
Capital: Managua
Area: 130,000 sq km
Population: 4.9 million
Languages: Spanish and English
Currency: Cordoba

▷ The **Niagara Falls** is one of the most spectacular sights in North America. It is made up of two huge waterfalls, the Horseshoe Falls in Canada and the American Falls in the United States.

New Zealand

New Zealand is a remote **island** nation in the **Pacific Ocean**, 1,600 km southeast of **Australia**. It is actually two **islands**. North Island is famous for its hot springs and **volcanoes**. South Island has a range of **mountains** called the Southern Alps and many **lakes**.

Both islands have plains and valleys. The mild climate helps farmers to grow grains, **vegetables** and apples. They also raise **sheep** and **cattle**. New Zealand is the world's third largest producer of sheep and **wool**. The estimated number of sheep is about 45 million.

There are nearly four million New Zealanders or kiwis, nicknamed after the flightless **kiwi** bird. About 85 percent of the people live in a city or town. Auckland is the largest city, but the capital is Wellington. Both cities are located on North Island.

New Zealand is a member of the **Commonwealth**. Many of its people are descended from British settlers. Others are **Maori**, descended from Pacific Islanders, who lived in New Zealand before the British settlers

arrived after 1769. By the end of the 19th century, most Maori had been decimated by **warfare** and **disease**. However, their numbers are growing again and now pure-blood Maori and the decendants of mixed marriages make up 14 percent of the **population**. The New Zealand **government** has also returned lands to the Maori and Maori is now an official **language** taught in schools.

Niagara Falls

The Niagara Falls are **waterfalls** on the Niagara **River** in **North America**. **Water** from most of the **Great Lakes** flows through this river. Each minute, about 450,000 tonnes of water plunge about 50 m over the falls.

The falls stand on the border between **Canada** and the **United States**. Most of the water plunges down the Horseshoe Falls in Canada. The rest plunges down the American Falls in the United States.

People can gaze down on the falls from observation towers, or take a boat that sails close to the wild waters.

The sheer size of Niagara Falls has challenged people's courage and ingenuity for many years. Charles Blondin (1824–1897) walked across the top of the falls on a tightrope on 30 June 1859.

As the water plunges over the edge of Niagara Falls, it slowly erodes (wears away) the **rock**. In this way, the position of the falls is gradually changed. The falls are about 11 km further north than they were when the water first flowed over them thousands of years ago. In another several thousand years, Niagara Falls as we know them will have disappeared.

Nicaragua

Nicaragua is a country that stretches across **Central America** from the **Pacific Ocean** to the **Caribbean** Sea. Most of the people live on the western coast, where the land is flat and good for **farming**. A line of high **mountains** runs down the centre of Nicaragua. Farming is the main industry – **cotton**, **coffee**, **fruit** and **sugar** are the main products. But the country suffers from **economic** problems, partly caused by natural disasters. In 1998, **Hurricane** Mitch destroyed much of Nicaragua, **Honduras** and **Guatemala**. Some 10,000 people were killed. The mountains are also frequently shaken by **earthquakes**.

Politics also plays a part in the economic instability. Corrupt regimes protecting the advantages of the wealthy few have faced armed rebellion from **communist** groups in Central America.

Nigeria

This nation in western **Africa** is named after the Niger **River** that flows through it to the **Atlantic Ocean**. The **Sahara Desert** stretches across the country.

Nomadic people (see **nomad**) such as the Tuareg live by herding – travelling with their **camels** and **goats** in search of pasture. Other peoples settle by oases (see **oasis**) and grow dates and grains. Life is hard as the Sahel – an area of semi-**desert** – is steadily becoming drier.

Niger also has one of the fastest growing **populations** in the world. Almost half of its people are under 15.

In 1995, international sanctions were declared against Nigeria and the country was suspended from the **Commonwealth**, but membership was restored in 1999 when democratic **elections** (see **democracy**) were held.

NIGERIA
Government: Democracy
Capital: Abuja
Area: 923,768 sq km
Population: 12.6 million
Languages: Hausa, Yorba, Ibo and English
Currency: Naira

△ Florence **Nightingale** worked to improve the awful conditions of wounded soldiers in hospital during the Crimean War.

Nightingale, Florence

Florence Nightingale (1820–1910) was one of the pioneers of modern **nursing**. She was from a wealthy background and could have had an easy life, but instead she chose to work caring for the sick. Florence Nightingale trained as a nurse, and then founded a training **hospital** in **London, England**.

In 1854, she took 38 nurses to **Turkey** to tend British soldiers wounded in the Crimean War (see **warfare**). Her hospital was a dirty barracks that lacked **food, medicines** and bedding. She cleaned it up, found supplies, and gave the wounded every care she could. Her work saved many hundreds of lives.

Florence Nightingale was called 'the lady of the lamp' by the soldiers.

Nile River

The Nile **River** in **Africa** is generally thought to be the longest river on **earth** – an astonishing 6,670 km – though some people believe that the **Amazon** is longer. The Nile rises in Burundi in central Africa and flows north through **Egypt** into the **Mediterranean Sea**.

The Nile is very important to farmers, who rely on it to irrigate their crops (see **irrigation**). Huge underground pipes carry **water** from the river underneath the **desert** to cities.

▷ The banks of the **Nile** in Egypt have fertile land which is good for farming. The Ancient Egyptians used the Nile for irrigating crops and transport.

Nobel prize

These **money** prizes are given each year to people who have helped humankind in different ways. Three prizes are for **inventions** or discoveries in **physics**, **chemistry**, and physiology and **medicine**. The fourth is for literature. The fifth prize is for work to make or keep peace between peoples and the sixth is for **economics**. Money for the prizes was left by the Swedish chemist Alfred Nobel (1833–1896), who invented the **explosive** dynamite.

When Alfred Nobel died in 1896, he left $9 million US dollars to set up the prizes that now bear his name. The interest that this money earns each year is used for the prizes.

△ The Tuareg people of the Sahara Desert, Africa, are **nomads**. They live by trading camels and goats, and sleep in tents made of animal skin.

Nomad

People without a settled home are nomads. Many nomads live in lands too dry to farm. These people keep herds of **animals** and travel to find fresh pasture for them. They live in portable homes, such as tents. Many nomads still live in or near the great **deserts** of **Africa** and **Asia**.

Northern Ireland

Northern Ireland consists of six counties in the northeast corner of the **island** of **Ireland**. It is part of the **United Kingdom** of Great Britain and Northern Ireland. Northern Ireland

△ On the north coast of **Northern Ireland** lies the Giant's Causeway. This natural staircase into the sea was made when volcanic rock cooled and shrank to form thousands of six-sided columns.

was separated from the rest of Ireland in 1921, when the Republic of Ireland (Eire) won independence from the UK. Political problems in Northern Ireland date back to the 1600s, when many English and Scottish Protestants settled there. From the 1960s, protests by the minority Catholics (outnumbered by Protestants in Northern Ireland) against unfair treatment led to civil disorder. Bombings and other terrorist acts (see **terrorism**) have led to great loss of life, though the British and Irish **governments** are trying to settle Northern Ireland's future peacefully.

North Pole

The North Pole is the furthest northern place on **earth**. Its **latitude** is 90° north. It is the northern end of the earth's axis – this is an imaginary line around which the earth spins, like a wheel spinning around its axle.

The North Pole lies in the centre of the **Arctic Ocean**. Here, the surface of the sea is always frozen. The **sun** does not rise in winter or set in summer for many weeks. The first person to claim to have reached the North Pole was the American **explorer** Robert E. Peary (1856–1920). He and his team arrived in 1909 using sledges pulled by **dogs**.

The first **ship** to reach the North Pole was the US nuclear **submarine** *Nautilus*. It travelled under the ice-covered pole on 3 August 1958.

Northwest Passage

This was a longed-for sea route from **Europe** to **Asia** through the frozen waters of the **Arctic Ocean** north of **Canada**. **Explorers** took nearly 400 years to find it. Ice continually hindered **ships** trying to sail through the passage.

It was Norwegian Roald **Amundsen** (1872–1928) whose ship first sailed through the Northwest Passage in 1906. In 1969, an **oil** tanker broke a path through the ice, but the ice is so thick that ships cannot regularly use this route.

Norway

Norway is **Europe**'s sixth largest country. This long, northern kingdom is wide in the south, but narrow in the centre and the north. **Mountains** with **forests**, bare **rocks** and snow cover much of Norway. Steep inlets called **fiords** pierce its rocky coast.

Summers in Norway are cool and the winters long. It is very cold in the **Arctic** north, but the rainy west coast is kept fairly mild by the **Gulf Stream**.

Noun

A noun is a word used as the name of something – a person (Mary), an animal (lion), a thing (book), a place (America) or a quality (kindness).

The subject of a sentence – what a sentence is about – is always a noun or a pronoun. A pronoun is a word that is used in place of a noun. The most common pronouns are I, we, you, he, she, it and they.

Nuclear energy

The tiny nucleus at the centre of an **atom** contains the most powerful force ever discovered. This force

NORWAY
Government: Constitutional monarchy
Capital: Oslo
Area: 324,219 sq km
Population: 4.5 million
Language: Norwegian
Currency: Krona

▽ British navigator John Franklin (1786–1847) set off to find the **Northwest Passage** in 1845. His ships froze into the ice, and Franklin and his men eventually all died.

gives us **nuclear energy** – sometimes called atomic energy. The heaviest **element** with the largest atom is **uranium**. The nuclear **fuel** used in nuclear **power stations** is a rare form of the metal called uranium-235.

Nuclear energy can be controlled to provide us with power. In a nuclear power station, control rods are lowered into a reactor to keep the reaction stable. But the uranium still gets very hot and so a coolant – a **liquid** or a **gas** – moves through the reactor. When the hot coolant leaves the reactor, it goes to a boiler to make steam. It is this steam that powers **generators** to make **electricity** for our homes and factories.

NORTH AMERICA

North America is the third largest continent after Asia and Africa. It stretches from the Arctic Ocean in the north to the tropics of Panama in the south. North America includes the countries of the Caribbean and Central America, the United States of America and Canada.

△ *Cowboys herd cattle on the ranches of Texas, USA.*

LANDSCAPE

North America is a continent of great variety. Its climate ranges from bitter cold tundra in the north, to hot, dry deserts and tropical rainforest in the south. The Rockies in the west and the Appalachians in the east form two of the continent's mountain ranges. In the centre of the continent lie great plains where two of North America's largest rivers, the Missouri and the Mississippi, flow. In Alaska and northern Canada, few, if any, trees grow in the harsh climate. There are huge evergreen forests elsewhere in Canada and in the northern United States, which provide North America with much of its timber. Natural wonders include the Niagara Falls and the Grand Canyon.

PEOPLES OF NORTH AMERICA

North America is a melting-pot of people and cultures. It was home to native populations, such as the Inuit in northern Canada and the Native American peoples all over the continent, for thousands of years before the first explorers arrived in the 1400s. Immigrants from Europe seeking a new life for their families followed in the footsteps of the explorers. Much of the native Americans' land was taken by European settlers and the native population suffered greatly through warfare and exposure to new diseases. Today, the continent is largely populated by descendants of the immigrants.

△ *The New York Stock Exchange in Wall Street is a leading international stock market and the financial centre of North America.*

From the 1600s, huge plantations were developed by the European settlers. They needed plenty of labour to grow tobacco and cotton, so they shipped slaves across the Atlantic Ocean from Africa. Over 300 years, more than a million slaves were transported. The issue of slavery was fiercely debated by the northern and southern states, and caused a civil war that tore North America apart during 1861–1865. Slavery was abolished after the war, but many African-Americans still lived in poverty and did not have equal rights. In the 1960s, civil rights campaigners protested against discrimination and did much to increase racial equality. African-Americans make up 12 percent of today's North American population.

Most of the continent's population live in eastern North America, and Mexico City is the continent's largest city. English and Spanish are the main languages spoken, and French is spoken in parts of Canada.

INDUSTRY

Half the world's manufactured goods are produced in North America, which is mainly due to the vast natural resources of the continent, such as timber. Americans have also been involved in most of the technological advances of the past few decades, developing industries, such as computing, that have confirmed the continent's position at the forefront of world industrial production. The industries are found mainly in Canada and the United States, which are extremely wealthy and powerful countries as a result. In comparison, most of the countries of Central America and the Caribbean are extremely poor. Many of these smaller countries in North America do not share the same natural resources as the United States and Canada, and their basic economies are weaker as a result.

▽ *Lynx live in the Canadian tundra where they hunt birds and small mammals.*

SEE ALSO
Canada, Caribbean, Central America, Civil War (American), Grand Canyon, Immigration, Inuit, Mexico, Native Americans, Niagara Falls, Revolutionary War (American), Slavery, Tobacco, Tundra, United States of America

ARCTIC
OCEAN

*Chukchi
Sea*

*Greenland
Sea*

Bering Strait

*Beaufort
Sea*

ALASKA

*Baffin
Bay*

Davis Strait

Cape Farewell

*Gulf of
Alaska*

*Great Bear
Lake*

*Great Slave
Lake*

C A N A D A

*Labrador
Sea*

*Hudson
Bay*

Labrador

**PACIFIC
OCEAN**

*Lake
Athabasca*

*Reindeer
Lake*

*Laurentian
Highlands*

*Lake
Winnipegosis*

*Lake
Winnipeg*

*Lake
Manitoba*

WASHINGTON

Lake Superior

Ottawa ■

MAINE

VERMONT
NEW
HAMP.

MONTANA

NORTH
DAKOTA

MINNESOTA

*Lake
Huron*

*Lake
Ontario*

OREGON

IDAHO

WISCONSIN

*Lake
Michigan*

NEW YORK

MASS.

RHODE I.
CONNECTICUT

Coast Range

WYOMING

SOUTH
DAKOTA

Great Plains

MICHIGAN

Lake Erie

PENNSYLVANIA

NEW JERSEY

**ATLANTIC
OCEAN**

*Great
Salt Lake*

UNITED STATES

IOWA

DELAWARE

*Great
Basin*

NEBRASKA

OHIO

WEST
VIRGINIA

Washington DC ■

MARYLAND

CALIFORNIA

NEVADA

UTAH

INDIANA

VIRGINIA

*Colorado
Plateau*

COLORADO

Z OF AMERICA

KANSAS

MISSOURI

KENTUCKY

NORTH
CAROLINA

ARIZONA

NEW
MEXICO

OKLAHOMA

TENNESSEE

Appalachians

Sierra Madre

ARKANSAS

SOUTH CAROLINA

Baja California

Gulf of California

TEXAS

MISSISSIPPI

ALABAMA

GEORGIA

LOUISIANA

FLORIDA

MEXICO

*Gulf of
Mexico*

Nassau ■

BAHAMAS

Havana ■

Mexico City ■

*Yucatán
Peninsula*

CUBA

**DOMINICAN
REPUBLIC**

HAITI

Port-au-Prince ■

Santo
Domingo ■

ST KITTS
& NEVIS

ANTIGUA &
BARBUDA

DOMINICA

Kingston ■

JAMAICA

ST LUCIA
BARBADOS

ST VINCENT
& THE GRENADINES

Belmopan ■
BELIZE

Caribbean Sea

GRENADA

TRINIDAD AND
TOBAGO

GUATEMALA

HONDURAS

ARUBA

NETHERLAND
ANTILLES

Guatemala City ■

Tegucigalpa ■

San Salvador ■

NICARAGUA

Managua ■

*Lake
Nicaragua*

San Jose ■

COSTA RICA

Panama City ■

PANAMA

be enormously large. The famous Greek scientist Archimedes (287–212 BCE) estimated the number of grains of **sand** it would take to fill the **universe**. He did not know the number, but he said it was finite – an exact number. He also knew that some numbers are infinite. If we go on counting 1, 2, 3, 4, 5… and so on, we will never come to the end. This set of numbers is infinite.

Number

In the **Stone Age**, people wrote a number such as 20 or 30 by making 20 or 30 separate marks. In many ancient **caves**, the marks that these early peoples made can still be seen.

As time progressed, people invented special signs or groups of signs to show different numbers. These signs are called numerals. For centuries, many people used Roman numerals, but these are rather clumsy. For instance, the Roman numerals for 38 are XXXVIII.

The modern system is more simple and uses Arabic numerals that were first used in **India**. The most important numeral in today's system is the 0. If we write 207, we mean two hundreds, no tens and seven ones. Without the 0 we would not be able to write 207.

The earliest known written numbers were those used by the Babylonians about 5,000 years ago. All the great civilizations have had their own way of **writing** and using numbers.

There are many very large numbers. The **population** of the world is very large. The number of blades of **grass**, and of leaves on the **trees** must

△ Many **nurses** work in hospitals in shifts – some look after patients during the day and others watch over them at night. Nurses also visit people in their own homes, and work in community centres and doctor's surgeries.

▽ A well-balanced diet contains all the **nutrients** a person needs to keep healthy. A wide variety of food and liquids need to be eaten and drunk regularly to ensure enough nutrients are taken in.

Nursing

People who are very ill or old require nursing in their homes or in a **hospital**. Nursing can mean feeding, washing and giving treatment ordered by a doctor. It is hard work and requires special skills. Men and women train for several years before becoming nurses. Modern nursing owes much to the example set by Florence **Nightingale**.

The word 'nursing' comes from the Latin word *nutricia*, meaning nourishing. Records from Ancient **Egypt** and **Greece** mention various nursing practices, including the giving of herbal remedies. The Roman armies employed male nurses to care for the wounded (see **Roman Empire**).

Nutrition

Nutrition is the process by which we take in and use **food**. **Human beings** need food to keep their bodies running smoothly and to provide **energy**.

Malnutrition is a weakening of the body which can be caused by eating food that lacks enough of the nutrients to keep the body strong and healthy. Nutrients can be divided into six groups: **proteins**, carbohydrates, **fats**, **vitamins**, **minerals** and **water**. No one nutrient is more important than another. Each has its own work to do. A well-balanced diet contains all of them.

Octopus

There are about 50 species of octopus. They are soft-bodied **molluscs** that live in the sea. Octopus means 'eight feet', but the eight tentacles of an octopus are usually called arms. The largest octopus has arms about nine metres across, but most octopuses are no larger than a person's fist. Unlike most molluscs, octopuses do not have a shell. They have instead a tough **skin** that protects the organs in their bodies.

The octopus hides in underwater **caves** or crevices, or creeps about the seabed searching for **food**. Its two large **eyes** keep a watch for enemies. If danger threatens, the octopus may confuse an enemy by squirting an inky **liquid**. The ink hangs in the **water** like a cloud. The octopus can also propel itself forwards fast by squirting water backwards from a tube in its body.

The octopus is the most intelligent of the **invertebrates** (animals without backbones). It can be trained to find its way through a maze and is able to solve simple problems, for example it can remove the stopper from a sealed jar containing food.

In many countries, particularly those bordering the **Mediterranean**, octopuses are a favourite food.

Oasis

An oasis is a fertile place in a **desert** where **plants** are able to grow. It may be simply a small clump of **palm** trees, or a much larger irrigated area (see **irrigation**). Oases are found where there is **water**. This can come from **rivers**, wells or underground springs that reach the surface at that point. These sources of water may be fed by rain that falls on nearby **mountains** and seeps through **rocks** beneath the surface of the desert. People can make oases by drilling wells and digging irrigation ditches.

△ Suckers on the tentacles of an **octopus** are used to grip crabs, shellfish or other prey. The tentacles pull the victim towards the octopus' mouth, which is hard and pointed, like the beak of a bird.

▽ An **oasis** may be only a spring and a small group of palms. However, some oases are much larger. A variety of plants and animals makes their home in these oases, and some support large towns.

OCEANS

Oceans cover nearly three-quarters of the surface of the earth. If you put all the world's water in 100 giant tanks, 97 of them would be full of water from the oceans.

OCEANS OF THE WORLD

There are four oceans. The largest and deepest is the Pacific Ocean. The second largest is the Atlantic, which is only half the size of the Pacific. The Indian Ocean is smaller but deeper than the Atlantic Ocean. The Arctic Ocean is the smallest and shallowest ocean of all.

The oceans are never still. Winds crinkle their surface into waves. The Gulf Stream and other currents (some warm, others cold) flow like rivers through the oceans, and every day, the ocean surface falls and rises with the tides. In winter, polar sea water freezes over, and icebergs from polar seas may drift hundreds of kilometres through the oceans.

△ *The salt water oceans and seas of the world cover nearly 71 percent of the earth's surface.*

▽ *An atoll begins as a coral reef around a volcanic island (1). As the islands sinks, the reef grows upwards (2). Eventually, the island disappears and all that remains is the atoll, surrounding a lagoon (3).*

PLATE MOVEMENTS

The earth's crust is made up of a small number of large plates of solid rock. These float on the moving molten rock underneath and also move in relation to one another. New crust is formed at the edge of the plates. The plate movements mean that the ocean floor is always changing shape. It is constantly being created and destroyed by the movements.

WATER CYCLES

The oceans are always losing water as water vapour, which is drawn up into the air by the sun's heat, but most is returned as rain. Rain water running off the land carries salts and other minerals to the oceans. If a square tank one kilometre long and one kilometre high were filled with sea water, it would hold four million tonnes of magnesium. In fact, the oceans supply most of the magnesium used in the manufacture of things such as aircraft components, fireworks, flares and batteries.

Continental shelf covered with salts and minerals washed off the land

Continental slope

Seamounts – underwater volcanoes

Spreading ridge with central valley, flanked by steep mountains

Abyssal plain

Abyssal hills forming ridges

OCEAN FACT FILE

ARCTIC OCEAN
Surface area: 14,350,000 sq km
Average depth: 990 m
Greatest depth: 4,600 m

INDIAN OCEAN
Surface area: 73,500,000 sq km
Average depth: 3,890 m
Greatest depth: 7,450 m

ATLANTIC OCEAN
Surface area: 106,000,000 sq km
Average depth: 1,800 m
Greatest depth: 9,144 m

PACIFIC OCEAN
Surface area: 166,242,000 sq km
Average depth: 4,280 m
Greatest depth: 11,022 m

THE OCEAN FLOOR

The shape of the ocean floor is very similar to the shape on land. There are mountains and valleys, ridges and volcanoes, plains and hills. A typical ocean floor has a continental shelf and slope leading down onto an abyssal plain, with abyssal hills rising to an abyssal ridge containing a rift valley. Beyond these may be a deep ocean trench.

MARINE LIFE

Oceans are home to countless living things. Most of the life is found within a layer of water about 100 m deep, where the sunlight penetrates. The minerals in sea water help to nourish tiny plants drifting at the surface. The plants are food for tiny animals, some of them one-celled. These tiny animals (zooplankton) and plants (phytoplankton) are collectively known as plankton and are the basis for the entire ocean food chain. All sea creatures depend for their food either on plankton itself or on animals that feed on plankton. For example, zooplankton feeds on phytoplankton, but both are eaten by small fish. These in turn are eaten by larger predators, who probably feed one of the top predators, maybe a shark.

EXPLORING THE DEPTHS

The exploration of the deepest levels, more than 10,000 m down, was first carried out using special underwater vehicles called bathyscaphes. Today, mini-submarines are still used to explore the seas, studying the life there, shipwrecks such as the *Titanic* and the geology of the ocean floor.

The deepest marine trench in the world is the Marianas Trench off the island of Guam in the Pacific Ocean. This trench marks the point

△ *There is an enormous variety of species living in our oceans – some very strange – each occupying its own space at particular levels.*

where the fast-moving Pacific plate meets the slower-moving Philippine plate. Its deepest point, Challenger Point, was measured accurately in 1984 by a Japanese survey vessel using a multi-beam echo-sounder to make an 'echo map' of the ocean floor. They found that the trench plunges deeper into the earth (10,924 m) than Mount Everest, the world's tallest mountain, rises above sea level (8,854 m).

1 Herring 2 Sperm whale 3 Prawn 4 Kat-tail
5 Angler fish 6 Grenadier 7 Cod 8 Gulper eel
9 Sea spider, tube worms, clam, white ghost crab
10 Tripod fish 11 Viper fish 12 Swallower
13 Lantern fish 14 Swordfish 15 Yellowfin tuna
16 Giant squid 17 Hammerhead 18 Barracuda
19 Portuguese man-of-war 20 Plankton
21 Green turtle 22 Sea lion 23 Common dolphin

SEE ALSO
Antarctic and Arctic, Atlantic Ocean, Earth, Echo, Indian Ocean, Minerals, Mountain, Pacific Ocean, Salt, Water

Ocean trench

Volcanic islands forming

235

△ **Oil** travels south from Alaska to ports through the Trans-Alaska pipeline. This pipeline was built on supports above the ground, to prevent it thawing the permafrost.

△ Sunflower seeds are rich in an **oil** which is used to make margarine, and is a good substitute for olive oil in salads and cooking, or for herb oils for skin treatments.

Oil

Oils are **fats** and other greasy substances that do not dissolve in **water**. Oil is also mineral oil which was formed millions of years ago from dead **plants** and **animals**. The oil is trapped under **rocks** deep underground, and engineers drill holes down through the surface of the rocks to reach it.

Oil deposits are found on land, and also off-shore in the **ocean** bed. The world's largest known oil deposits lie in the **Middle East**, in the countries of **Saudi Arabia**, **Iran**, **Iraq** and Kuwait. The biggest part of an oil-drilling platform is the derrick – the tall **metal** tower that houses the drilling

equipment. The drill bit, at the end of the drill pipe, cuts through rock with sharp metal teeth. By examining the fragments of rock cut by the drill, scientists can tell when they are getting near an oil deposit. The oil gushes up or can be pumped up (see **pump**) to the surface.

Oil refineries separate the oil into many different chemicals. As well as producing petrol and paraffin, oil by-products can be used to make artificial **fertilizer**, many kinds of **medicine**, **plastics**, **perfumes**, **soaps**, **detergent**, paint and even animal feed.

We may need to find new ways to make these things because the world's supplies of oil are running out. Today, scientists are working on new ways of extracting oil from shale, a kind of rock, and from tar sands.

Olympic Games

This competition is the world's oldest sports event. The first Olympics took place at Olympia, **Greece**, in 776 BCE. The Greek Games ended in 394 CE. Modern Olympic Games began in 1896.

The modern international Olympics are held every four years, each time in a different country. Athletes from different nations compete in races, jumping, **gymnastics**, football, yachting

▷ The **Olympic Games** have witnessed the triumph of many international athletes over the years. These are some of the winners between 1896 and 1996.

Thomas Burke, USA, 100 metres

Canadian ice hockey team

Attilio Pavesi, Italy, cycling

Dawn Fraser, Australia, swimming

Joe Frazier, USA, boxing

Nadia Comaneci, Romania, gymnastics

Steffi Graf, Germany, tennis

Jan Zelezny, Czech Republic, javelin

and many more contests (see **sport**). More than 6,000 people from more than 100 countries take part. The winners are awarded medals, but no prize **money**.

The opening ceremony of each Olympic Games features the lighting of the Olympic flame with a torch. Brought all the way from Greece, the torch is carried by athletes and sportspeople of all nationalities.

Since 1924, a separate Winter Olympics has taken place, held two years after the summer Olympics.

Oman

Oman is a country in southeast Arabia on the Persian Gulf. On the fertile coastal plain, **fruit** (particularly dates) and **vegetables** are grown. **Oil** is the main source of income. Many of Oman's people are **nomads**.

Opera

An opera is a play with **music**. The 'actors' are singers who sing all or many of their words. An **orchestra** in an orchestra pit below the level of the stage accompanies the singers.

The first opera was performed in **Italy** nearly 400 years ago. Famous composers of serious opera include **Mozart**, Verdi, Puccini and **Wagner**. Some shorter, less serious operas are called operettas. Operettas of the 1800s gave rise to the tuneful musical comedies of the 1900s.

Opinion poll

Politicians and manufacturers want to know what people think of their party's policy or the goods they make. In these circumstances, they can employ a research firm to conduct an opinion poll – to ask questions and analyse the answers. It would be impossible to ask

OMAN
Government:
Absolute monarchy
Capital: Muscat
Area: 212,417 sq km
Population: 2.3 million
Languages: Arabic,
English, Urdu
Currency: Rial Omani

△ **Opera** is a popular form of entertainment. Wagner even designed an opera house at Bayreuth in 1876, so that he could put on a complete performance of his *Ring* cycle.

△ When an American **opossum** baby reaches about three months in age, it can ride around on its mother's back.

questions of everyone, everywhere, so a carefully selected group of people, called a sample, is chosen to represent a larger group. The sample may be only one percent of the larger group, but it must contain the same kind of people. For example, if 20 percent of the larger group is under 18 years of age, then 20 percent of the sample group must also be under 18.

The questions may be asked by a trained interviewer or they may be printed on a questionnaire. The answers are then analysed and the results show the opinions of the larger group.

Some people say that opinion polls can be unfair. In **election** polls, for example, many people want to be on the winning side and therefore may switch their votes during the campaign to the candidate whom the polls show to be ahead. Careful studies have, however, failed to show that this 'bandwagon effect' exists.

Opossum

Opossums are **marsupials** that live in North and **South America**. Some look like **rats**, others look like **mice**. The Virginia **opossum** is as large as a **cat** and is **North America**'s only marsupial. It feeds after dark and climbs **trees**, clinging on with its tail. Opossums have keen eyesight and hearing, and eat anything they can find, alive or dead. If danger threatens, the Virginia opossum lies still and pretends to be dead. If someone pretends to be hurt, we say he or she is 'playing possum'. A female Virginia opossum has up to 30 babies at a time, each no larger than a honeybee, but only a small number survives. Like all marsupials, opossums give birth to their babies when they are still in a very immature state, so the young rely on their parent to stay alive.

Orang-utan

This large, red-haired **ape** lives on the **islands** of Borneo and Sumatra in **Southeast Asia**. Its name comes from Malay words meaning 'man of the woods'. The male is as heavy as a man, but not as tall. Orang-utans use their long arms to swing through the branches of **trees** as they hunt for **fruit** and leaves to eat. Each night, they make a **nest** high up in the trees. A leafy roof helps to keep out rain.

Orang-utans live alone or in small family groups. People are their main enemies. Hunters catch the young illegally to sell to **zoos**, so orang-utans are in danger of becoming extinct.

△ The **orang-utan** is the second largest ape after the gorilla, and a fully grown male can weigh up to 90 kg. Its arms are longer than its legs and it has a high forehead. The male orang-utan grows a moustache and beard but the rest of his face is hairless.

Orbit

An orbit is the curved path of something that spins around another object in space. Artificial **satellites** and the **moon** travel around the **earth** in orbits. Each **planet**, including the earth, has its own orbit around the **sun**.

Every orbit is a loop rather than a circle. An orbiting object tries to move in a straight line but is pulled by **gravity** towards the object that it orbits. People used to think that planets moved in circular orbits, but actually the shape is more like a flattened circle, or ellipse.

Orchestra

An orchestra is a large group of musicians who play together. The word orchestra originally meant 'dancing place'. In ancient Greek **theatres**, dancers (see **dance**) and musicians performed on a space between the audience and the stage. When **opera** was invented in **Italy**, the theatres arranged their musicians in the same way. Gradually, people began to use the word orchestra to describe the group of musicians, and not the place where they performed.

The modern orchestra owes much to the composer **Haydn**. He arranged its musical instruments into four main groups: strings, woodwind, brass and percussion. Most orchestras have a conductor. Soloists rehearse with an orchestra, and the conductor has the job of coordinating all the musicians, who may number over a hundred.

Orchid

There are more than 15,000 species of these rare and lovely flowering **plants** that live in **rainforests**. Many grow on **trees**. Their roots draw nourishment from the damp **air**. Usually each kind of orchid is fertilized by one kind of **insect**.

◁ Many bees and hummingbirds in the rainforest feed on the nectar and pollen from **orchid** flowers. They help pollinate the orchids by carrying the pollen from plant to plant.

But some can be pollinated by **snails** or **hummingbirds**.

The common spotted orchid grows in damp or dry grassy places and in open woods. Its **habitats** are being threatened by modern **farming** methods.

Organ

Pipe organs are **musical instruments** with many pipes of different heights and widths. The largest organ has more than 30,000 pipes. Each pipe makes a special **sound** as **air** flows through it. An organist plays an organ by pressing keys arranged in rows called manuals. Each manual controls a different set of pipes. Levers or knobs called stops allow the organist to combine different groups of pipes. **Electronic** organs sound similar, but have no pipes.

△ Some more powerful church **organs** have one or more keyboards and several banks of pipes. They were often highly decorated.

Ore *see* Mineral

Ostrich

This is the largest living **bird**. An ostrich may weigh twice as much as a man and stand more than 2 m high. Ostriches cannot fly. If an enemy attacks, they run away, but they can kick hard enough to rip open a **lion**.

Ostriches live in **Africa**. They roam in large herds, led by a male. The females lay large, white **eggs** in a **nest** dug in the **sand**. Ostriches can live for 50 years or more.

△ The **ostrich** is the only bird with two-toed feet. Although it cannot fly, it can run at up to 70 km/h on its strong legs.

Apart from laying the largest egg, the ostrich has broken records for the number of eggs it lays - up to 15 at one time.

Ottawa

Ottawa is the capital of **Canada**, and its third largest city, with a **population** of about one million. It is in the province of Ontario in southeast Canada, and the Ottawa and Rideau **rivers** flow through the city.

Ottawa's best-known site is the Parliament buildings, which stand on a hill above the Ottawa River. It includes the tall Peace Tower with its 53 bells. Ottawa also has several universities and museums.

Early British settlers began building Ottawa in 1826, and named it after the nearby Outawouais **Native Americans**. More than one citizen in three is French-speaking.

Otter

Otters are large relatives of the weasel. They have long, slender bodies and short legs. An otter hunts in **water** for **fish** and **frogs**. Thick fur keeps its body dry, and it swims swiftly by waggling its tail and body like an **eel**, using its webbed hind feet as paddles.

By night, otters hunt up and down a **river**, or roam overland to find new fishing-grounds. They love to play by sliding down a bank of snow or mud. The number of otters in the wild is going down steadily, and they are now quite rare. This could be due to **pollution**, but no-one is sure.

▷ **Otters** move quite slowly on their webbed feet on land, but fast enough to catch animals such as rabbits. They are superb hunters in water, catching mainly fish and frogs.

Owl

These **birds** of prey hunt mainly at night. They have soft **feathers** that make no **sound** as they fly, and their large, staring **eyes** help them to see in the dimmest **light**. Owls also have keen **hearing** – some can catch mice in the pitch-dark simply by listening to the **sounds** they make. An owl can also turn its head around 180 degrees to look backwards.

When an owl eats a **mouse** or small bird, it swallows it complete with **bones** and fur or **feathers**. Later, the owl spits out the remains in a pellet.

There are more than 130 species of owls. Some of the largest and smallest owls live in **North America**. The great grey owl of the north is as long as a man's arm. The elf owl of the south is the smallest in the world – smaller than a sparrow. It has a short tail and tiny feet, and is small enough to nest in holes made by woodpeckers. In the **desert**, it is often found nesting in the saguaro **cactus**.

Barn owls are one of the world's most widespread species, but they are far less common today than they once were. This may be because there are fewer deserted buildings

△ Wax candles have a wick that is burned to provide light. **Oxygen** is needed to keep the flame burning.

△ People harvest tonnes of **oysters** each year for food. Pearl oysters are also farmed for their pearls which are used in jewellery.

▽ Most **owls** hunt at night, swooping down silently on rabbits, mice and other prey. Their fringed wing feathers can beat the air without making a sound.

and hollow **trees** in which to lay their **eggs**. They do not build **nests**. They feed mainly on small **rodents**.

The long-eared owl's tufted 'ears' are not ears at all, just feathers. But they help in the recognition of this bird, which is found in most of **Europe**, northern **Asia** and North America.

Oxygen

Oxygen is a **gas**. It is colourless and odourless, and one of the most abundant **elements** on **earth**. It makes up one part in every five of **air**. Oxygen is found in **water** and many different **rocks**. Most of the **weight** of water, and half that of rocks, comes from the oxygen in them.

Fire needs oxygen to burn. Almost all living things need oxygen for **breathing** and to give them the **energy** just to stay alive. **Animals** need extra oxygen to move about. **Plants** give out oxygen into the air.

Oyster

Oysters are **molluscs** with a soft body protected by a broad, hinged shell. This is rough on the outside. The inside of a pearl oyster's shell is smooth, shiny mother-of-pearl. Pearl oysters make pearls.

Several kinds of oyster are eaten as a **food**. They are farmed in shallow coastal **water**. Oysters cling to empty shells, **rocks** or wooden posts on the seabed. When they have grown large enough, they are harvested.

An oyster makes a pearl when there is a foreign object, such as a grain of **sand**, inside its shell. To stop the irritation caused by the sand, the oyster deposits a substance called nacre around it, which gradually builds up to form a pearl.

Ozone layer
see **Global warming**

▷ When this girl touches the spines on a cactus, it causes her **pain**. Special nerves in her finger send a warning signal to her central nervous system. A message is sent back to the nerves that control the muscles of her arm, making her jerk her hand away.

Pacific Ocean

This is the largest and deepest of all the **oceans**. Its waters cover more than one-third of the world's surface. All the **continents** on **earth** would fit inside the Pacific Ocean with room to spare. Its deepest part is deep enough to drown the world's highest **mountain**, Mount **Everest**.

The Pacific Ocean lies west of the Americas, and east of **Australia** and **Asia**. It stretches from the frozen **Arctic** to the frozen **Antarctic**. There are thousands of tiny **islands** in the Pacific. Most were formed when **volcanoes** erupted from the seabed. Sometimes **earthquakes** shake the seabed and send out huge tidal waves.

△ The **Pacific Ocean** is the largest ocean on earth. Its average depth is 4,300 m, but the deepest part is the Challenger Deep in the Mariana Trench, which is 10,915 m.

Pain

Pain is an unpleasant feeling. It is a warning that something is wrong somewhere in your body. You feel pain if something burns or presses hard on the ends of certain **nerves**. Those parts of the body with the most nerve endings, such as your hands, feel pain most easily. The nerves carry the pain signals to the central nervous system.

Sometimes pain is useful because it teaches you to avoid what caused it.

For example, if you prick yourself with a pin, you learn not to do it again, and toothaches tell you it is time to go to the dentist. Chemists have invented painkillers to deaden pain caused by **disease** and injury.

Paint

Paint is used to decorate a surface and protect it from rotting. When paint is spread over a solid surface such as plaster, **wood** or **paper**, it forms a thin coat. The paint then dries by evaporation. Oil-based paints are coloured powder in oil or resin. Emulsion paints are powder and drops of **oil** or resin in **water**. Traditionally, paints and **dyes** were produced from natural substances such as earth, fruits or flowers. Today, most are mass-produced.

In the factory, **paint** is made by grinding powdered colours called pigments and a liquid medium such as oil between huge rollers.

PAKISTAN

Government: Military dictatorship
Capital: Islamabad
Area: 796,095 sq km
Population: 134.8 million
Languages: Urdu and English
Currency: Rupee

▽ Pakistan's Punjab area is where archaeologists excavated the prehistoric city of Harappa (recreated here) in 1826. This early river settlement grew into one of the largest cities of its time – well over 1 sq km in area. It was occupied c.2300–1750 BCE.

Painting can be a long, hard task, but rewarding for both the painter and the generations who follow. In 1508, the Italian Renaissance artist Michelangelo was asked by Pope Julius II to paint the ceiling and altar wall of the Sistine Chapel in the Vatican in Rome. It took him many years to complete his work.

Painting

Painting is a form of **art** in which people use coloured **paint** to make pictures on canvas, plaster, **wood** or **paper**. Today, many people paint for their own pleasure, but in the past this was not always the case.

Stone Age hunters probably used painting as **magic**. They drew wounded wild beasts on their **cave** walls, maybe thinking that such pictures would help them kill real animals on the next hunt.

In the **Middle Ages**, most artists worked for the Church, and their paintings usually showed scenes from the **Bible**. Such paintings helped people who could not read to understand the stories in the Bible.

By the 1400s, Europe's rich princes and merchants were paying artists to paint pictures to decorate their homes. The pictures might be family portraits, still-life scenes of flowers and fruit, or landscapes showing their cities and country estates.

In the 1800s, many artists began trying out new ideas. For example, some tried to give a feeling of **light** and shade in a landscape. Others used bright, flat **colours** to bring out the patterns in still-lifes and landscapes. In the 1900s, Pablo **Picasso** and other artists began to experiment with abstract paintings. These concentrate on the basic shapes, colours and patterns of the things painted.

Pakistan

Pakistan lies between **India** and **Iran**. There are more than 130 million people living in Pakistan. Most of them follow the religion of **Islam**.

Much of Pakistan is hot and dry, but crops such as **wheat** and **cotton** grow with the help of **water** from the Indus River. The Indus flows from the **Himalayas** to the Arabian Sea. Until 1947, Pakistan was part of India, ruled at that time by the British. It then broke away to become an independent Muslim **republic**. In 1971, East Pakistan became **Bangladesh**. The military seized control in 1999 under General Pervez Musharraf, who intends to restore civilian rule.

The giant **panda** feeds mainly on bamboo shoots (as here), grasses and flowers such as irises and crocuses.

The red **panda** is a tree-dwelling mammal that is closely related to the giant panda.

Palestine

Palestine is a land on the eastern shore of the **Mediterranean Sea**. Historic Palestine covers an area of only 27,000 sq km, little more than a third the size of **Scotland**. People lived in Palestine at least 200,000 years ago, during the Old **Stone Age**. Most of the stories in the **Bible** took place there and Palestine gets its name from the Philistines who once lived in one particular area. By 1800 BCE, the Hebrews had made Palestine their home.

Later, the Hebrews ruled Palestine as two nations called **Israel** and Judah. Today, most of what used to be called Palestine lies in the nation of Israel. The rest is part of **Jordan, Lebanon** and **Syria**. In the 1990s, attempts were made to create a Palestinian state in territories occupied by Israel. But conflict between Palestinians and Israelis has continued into the 21st century.

Palm

The most familiar palm **tree** has leaves that sprout straight out of the top of its trunk. But there are more than 1,000 kinds of palm and not all are trees. Some are shrubs and some are vines. Most grow in warm **climates**.

Palms are useful **plants**. People make mats and baskets from their leaves, and eat the **fruits** such as coconuts.

Panama

Panama is a country about the size of **Scotland**. It occupies the narrow neck of land that joins **Central America** and **South America**. Panama has a damp, tropical **climate**, in which **rice**, **sugar**, bananas and pineapples are grown.

The Panama Canal cuts the country in half, and **ships** use the **canal** as a shortcut between the **Atlantic Ocean** and **Pacific Ocean**. Much of Panama's wealth comes from this **trade** and Panama City is an international finance centre because of it. Many ships are registered in Panama.

Sets of locks on the canal raise and lower ships as they cross the hilly countryside. In 1903, Panama granted the occupation and control of the canal to the **United States**. A new treaty in 1978 provided for the gradual takeover by Panama of the canal. The takeover was completed on 31 December 1999.

Panda

There are two kinds of panda. Both live in the forests of eastern **Asia**. The giant panda looks like a black and white bear. It lives in bamboo **forests** in **China**. The red panda is not much larger than a cat. It has a bushy tail and reddish fur. It is nocturnal – in other words it sleeps during the day and looks for food at night. Both kinds of panda eat mainly **plants**. Their nearest relatives are the **raccoons** of **North America** and **South America**.

PANAMA
Government: Republic
Capital: Panama City
Area: 77,529 sq km
Population: 2.8 million
Languages: Spanish and English
Currency: Balboa

Coconut palm

Coconut

△ The coconut **palm** can grow as high as 30m. Its fruit, which is covered with hairs, contains a hollow space filled with coconut 'milk'. The white meat, or kernel within the coconut is not only good to eat, but can be used in making soap, wax and oil.

243

PAPUA NEW GUINEA
Government:
Parliamentary democracy
Capital: Port Moresby
Area: 461,691 sq km
Population: 4.7 million
Language: English
Currency: Kina

PARAGUAY
Government:
Constitutional republic
Capital: Asunción
Area: 406,752 sq km
Population: 5.4 million
Language: Spanish
Currency: Guarani

△ **Parasites** like the greenfly suck the sap of plants such as roses, and can spread disease.

Paper

Paper gets its name from papyrus. The papyrus plant grows in swamps in **Egypt**, and the ancient Egyptians made a kind of paper from it. But the Chinese invented paper as we know it today. About 1,900 years ago, they learned to separate the fibres from mulberry bark. They soaked these, then dried them, making a flat, dry sheet on which they could write. Paper is still made of plant fibres. Some of the best paper is made from **cotton**. Newspaper is made from **wood**.

Papua New Guinea

Papua New Guinea is a country that occupies the eastern half of the **island** of **New Guinea**, north of **Australia**. The western half of the island, West Papua (formerly Irian Jaya), is Indonesian. Papua New Guinea gained its independence from Australia in 1975, and is a member of the **Commonwealth**. It is a hot, wet country, and the chief crops are coffee and cocoa.

Paraguay

Paraguay is a landlocked country in **South America**. It is divided into two by the Paraguay River, and much of the **population** is in the east. Most Paraguayans are mestizos, people of mixed Indian and Spanish descent. They farm soybeans, **cotton**, **sugar** cane, **tobacco**, **rice** and **fruit**. Many of the people living in Paraguay are farmers, and they produce barely enough to feed themselves.

General Alfredo Stroessner became president in 1954 and ruled as a

1 Bark is stripped from tree trunks
2 Wood is made into chips
5 Pulp from recycled paper added
3 Chemicals added and mixture cooked
4 Pulp beaten to break down fibres
6 Pulp cleaned and bleached to make it white

◁ **Paper** is made by boiling wood chips with caustic soda or another chemical to soften them and strip them of everything but their long, stringy fibres. This pulp is spread over a conveyor belt, blasted with air, then squeezed between rollers to turn it into dry paper.

dictator until he was deposed in 1989. Democratic government was restored and three **elections** held in the 1990s.

Parasite

Parasites are living things that live and feed on and in creatures larger than themselves. Animal parasites include **fleas**, lice, ticks and mites. Different kinds live on different **birds** and **mammals**. Most suck **blood**, and some spread **germs** that cause **disease**. Certain kinds of **worm**, including the tapeworm, get inside the body of the animal off which they are feeding, and live in their intestines or burrow deep into their **muscles**.

Greenfly and some other creatures live as parasites on **plants**. Plant parasites include many kinds of **fungus** that cause disease in plants or animals. Mistletoe is a parasite. It feeds off the trees on which it grows.

Paris

Paris is the capital of **France**, and the country's largest city. More than nine million people live in Paris and its suburbs. The Seine River divides the city into the Left and Right Banks.

From the top of the Eiffel Tower, you can see parks and **gardens**, fine squares and tree-lined avenues. Other famous landmarks are the cathedral of Notre Dame, the basilica of the Sacré Coeur, the Arc de Triomphe (built by **Napoleon**) and the Louvre Palace, now a museum and art gallery.

Paris is known for its **fashion**, perfume and **jewellery**. Another important industry is the manufacture of cars.

△ **Paris** is dominated by the Eiffel Tower, designed by Gustave Eiffel (1832–1923) and erected for the Paris Exhibition of 1889. It was the tallest building in the world until 1930.

Parliament

A parliament is the highest meeting of people held to make a nation's **laws**. The word 'parliament' comes from the French word *parler* meaning 'to talk'. One of the first parliaments was the Althing in **Iceland**, founded more than 1,000 years ago.

Parliaments exist in many countries around the world. In **Great Britain**, the Houses of Parliament in **London** are the seat of the British Parliament, started in 1265. It grew gradually out of a meeting of nobles who advised the king. By the 1700s, Parliament had become more powerful than the king. Congress, which meets in the Capitol Building in **Washington D.C.**, is the equivalent in the **United States**.

◁ The **Parthenon** in Athens was built with the best white marble to please the gods for whom it was erected. The huge stone blocks were carried to the site on ox-drawn carts and hauled up to the builders on ropes and pulleys.

The scarlet macaw is the world's largest **parrot**. It lives in the treetops of the jungles of Central and South America and feeds on fruit.

Parrot

These tropical **birds** have brightly coloured **feathers**. They use their strong, curved beaks as 'hands' to help them climb from branch to branch. Their beaks can also crack open nuts and bite off chunks of **fruit**.

There are hundreds of different kinds of parrot. Cockatoos, macaws and lovebirds all belong to the parrot family. Budgerigars and other parrots can learn to 'talk' by imitating **speech**, and one African grey parrot was taught to speak over 900 words.

Parthenon

The Parthenon is one of the world's most famous buildings. The ruins of this great white **marble** temple stand on the **Acropolis**, a hill that overlooks the Greek capital, Athens.

The Athenians built the Parthenon between 447 and 433 BCE in honour of Athena Parthenos, the **goddess** of war and their patron. They used the finest materials and the best craftsmen to please her. Rows of columns like huge tree trunks held up the sloping roof. Elegant statues, tall columns and painted friezes decorated the outside. Inside, the rooms were filled with treasures, dominated by a huge **gold** and **ivory** statue of Athena made by the sculptor Phidias.

In 1687, the Parthenon was damaged by a shell during the Turkish-Venetian war, and more recently, it has suffered from air **pollution**, but its ruins still dominate the city of Athens.

Passover

This Jewish **festival** celebrates the Israelites' escape from **slavery** in **Egypt**. The **Bible** tells how God punished the Egyptians ten times before they freed the Israelites. The tenth time, an angel killed the eldest child in each Egyptian family, but passed over the Israelites' homes without harming them. The Passover feast, or Seder, is led by the head of the family on the first two nights of the eight days of Passover.

Pasteur, Louis

The French scientist Louis Pasteur (1822–1895) proved that **bacteria** and other **germs** cause **diseases**. Pasteur injected weakened germs into animals and people to stop them catching the diseases those germs usually caused. He also invented pasteurization, a way of heating **milk** and cooling it quickly to stop it going bad. He discovered how **yeast** cells turn **sugar** into **alcohol**.

Peacock

Peacocks are male peafowl. Peafowl are large **birds** that live in **Asia**. Peacocks attract their mates by spreading out

Weight

Pendulum swinging

◁ The swing of the **pendulum** makes the weight in a grandfather clock fall evenly. As the weight falls, tiny toothed gearwheels turn and move the hands around the clock face.

△ Louis **Pasteur** developed vaccines against cholera, rabies, anthrax and other deadly diseases.

their long, blue-green **feathers** that grow just above the tail. Big spots on the feathers look like rows of eyes. As the peacock struts before the female it looks extremely proud, hence the term 'proud as a peacock'.

Pendulum

This is a hanging weight that is free to swing backwards and forwards. When the weight is pulled to one side and then released, **gravity** sets it swinging to and fro in a curved path called an arc. Each swing takes the same amount of **time**, no matter whether the swing is big or small. This makes pendulums useful for keeping time in **clocks**. After a while, a pendulum will stop moving. But a pendulum clock keeps its pendulum swinging with a mechanical device called an escape wheel. This is what makes the 'tick-tock' sound.

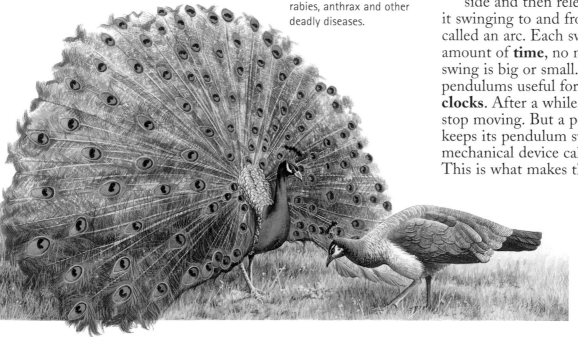

◁ Only the **peacock** has the spectacular tail with its 'eyes'. The peahen is much less colourful and has a short tail.

Emperor　　*King*　　*Chinstrap*　　*Rockhopper*　　*Gentoo*

◁ There are 17 types of **penguin**, and many of them live in huge groups called colonies. All five types shown here live in Antarctica. Tough feathers and a thick layer of fat keep penguins warm in the icy conditions of the frozen continent.

Penguin

Penguins are **birds** that swim. They cannot fly because their wings are shaped as flippers. Penguins use their wings to 'row' themselves through the sea. They swim and dive very well.

All penguins come from the southern part of the world. Emperor penguins live in **Antarctica**. In winter, the female lays one **egg** on the ice. Her mate rolls the egg onto his feet and keeps it warm for two months until it hatches.

Pepys, Samuel

Samuel Pepys (1633–1703) was an English **government** official who became Secretary of the Admiralty. He doubled the size of **England**'s navy and helped make it very strong. He also wrote a famous diary describing life in **London** under Charles II (1630–1685). Pepys wrote about the fire that burned down much of London in 1666. He recorded gossip about the king, described family quarrels and told of visits to the theatre.

Perfume

Perfumes produce a pleasant **smell** and people use them on their bodies. Factories add perfumes to products such as **soap** and **detergent**. Natural perfumes are **oils** squeezed from **flowers**, leaves or stems and mixed with substances like musk. Factories make synthetic perfumes from substances including coal tar.

Eva **Perón** was dearly loved by the people of Argentina – so much so that she became the subject of the musical *Evita*, which has been turned into a film.

PERU
Government: Multi-party republic
Capital: Lima
Area: 1,285,216 sq km
Population: 25.2 million
Language: Spanish
Currency: New sol

Perón, Eva

Eva Perón (1919–1952), also known as Evita, was born in **Argentina** and was an actress before her marriage in 1945. Her husband, Juan Perón (1895–1974), was a soldier and later president of Argentina. Evita became a powerful political figure.

Peru

Peru is the third largest nation in **South America.** You could fit **France**, the **United Kingdom** and **Germany** inside it with room to spare.

Peru shares borders with five other countries and its western coast is washed by the **Pacific Ocean**. The sharp, snowy peaks of the high **Andes** mountains cross Peru from north to south like a giant backbone. Between the **mountains** and the **ocean** lies a thin strip of **desert**. East of the mountains, hot, steamy **forests** stretch for vast distances around the **Amazon River**.

People have been building towns in Peru for several thousand years. The most famous people were the **Incas**, who established an empire in the mountains. In the 1530s, the Spaniards seized Peru. Since the 1820s, Peru has been an independent nation.

Today, Peruvians grow **sugar** cane and **coffee**. **Sheep** and **llamas** are kept to produce wool and meat. Peruvian mines are worked for **copper**, **iron** and **silver** for export, and the fishing-grounds usually hold plenty of **fish**.

When the **pharaoh** sat on the throne holding the symbols of authority – the crook and the flail – the Egyptians believed that the spirit of the god Horus entered him and he spoke to them as a god on earth.

PHILIPPINES
Government: Republic
Capital: Manila
Area: 300,000 sq km
Population: 74.3 million
Language: Filipino and English
Currency: Peso

Pharaoh

The word 'pharaoh' is used to mean 'king' when describing the kings of Ancient **Egypt**. (The ancient Egyptians gave their kings other titles as well.) 'Pharaoh' comes from the Egyptian word *peraa*, which means 'great house' and was the royal palace where the pharaoh lived. When he died, he was preserved in a **pyramid**.

Egyptians believed that pharaohs were descended from Ra, the sun **god**. The pharaoh was said to look after all the needs of his people and he was king of a united Upper and Lower Egypt. The pharaoh owned all the land and Egypt's nobles, priests and soldiers were supposed to obey him. In reality, the priests and nobles ran the country.

Philippines

The Philippines is a large group of **islands** in **Southeast Asia**. The largest islands are Luzon and Mindanao. Manila, the chief port and largest city, is the capital. Most of the people live in small villages and make their living from **farming**. They grow **sugar** cane, **fruits**, **rice**, coconuts and **vegetables**.

Spanish **explorers** named the islands after King Philip II of **Spain** (1527– 1598). In 1898, after the Spanish–

American War, the islands were turned over to the **United States**. They became independent in 1946, but the Philippines still has close links with the USA.

Ferdinand Marcos (1917–1989) was elected president in 1965 and restricted the activities of his opponents. In 1986, he was forced to flee the country. The following governments faced economic problems and widespread poverty.

Philosophy

The word philosophy comes from the Greek *philosophia* meaning 'love of wisdom'. Philosophers are thinkers who search for truth and knowledge about the **universe**. They do this by reflecting, reasoning and argument, and ask questions such as: How much can we really know about anything? If we argue that something is what we say it is, how can we be sure that our ideas are really right? When we say that God exists, what do we mean by 'God' and what do we mean by 'exists'? The first great philosophers were Greeks and included Socrates, **Plato** and **Aristotle**.

Photocopier

A photocopier is a **machine** that can copy a page of a **book** or a letter in only a few seconds. When you press the button on a photocopier, a bright **light** lights up the page. A **lens** inside the machine shines an image of the page onto a smooth metal drum which is electrified all over (*see* **electricity**). When the image shines on it, the light in the bright parts destroys the electric charge, while the dark parts of the drum are still electrified.

A black powder is then dusted over the drum. This clings only to the parts of the surface of the drum that are electrified. When a sheet of **paper** is pressed against the drum, the powder comes off onto the paper and this produces a copy of the page. This process is called xerography.

Photography

The word photography comes from the Greek words *photos* for 'drawing' and *graphien* for 'light', and means 'drawing with light'. When you take a photograph, rays of **light** produce a picture on the **film** in the **camera**.

First you look through a viewfinder at the subject you want to photograph. Then you press a button or lever that opens a shutter to let light from the subject enter the camera. The light passes through a **lens** that produces an image of your subject on a film in the camera. But the image shows up only when the film is developed (treated with chemicals). A developed film is called a negative. This shows black objects as white, and white objects as black. From negatives, you can print positives, the final photos, either as paper prints or slides.

Photosynthesis *see* Plant

Physics

Physics is a **science** and physicists are interested in **matter** – in solids, **liquids** and **gases** – and in the tiny **atoms** that make up all matter. They are also interested in the different forms of **energy** – electrical, light, sound, mechanical, chemical and nuclear. Some of the major fields of study in physics include mechanics (forces and motion; solids, liquids and gases); optics (**light**); acoustics (sound); **electricity** and **magnetism**; atomic, molecular and nuclear physics; and cryogenics (the study of extremely low **temperatures** and their effects, including superconductivity).

Physicists try to find things out by doing experiments. They carefully record the results of their experiments so that other people can test them for themselves. Physics covers a very large field and no single physicist today understands all the different parts of the subject. For example, nuclear physicists who study the tiny atom in detail may know little about outer space and the movements of **planets**, **stars** and **galaxies** because these are studied by astrophysicists. But one subject all physicists must understand is **mathematics**.

Two of the greatest physicists who ever lived were Isaac **Newton** and Albert **Einstein**.

Piano

Piano is short for the Italian word *pianoforte*, meaning 'soft' and 'loud'. The piano was invented by Bartolomeo Cristofori in 1709. The name refers to the piano's great range when compared with the harpsichord, in use before the piano was invented. The earliest instruments had strings that extended horizontally away from the keyboard, like the modern grand piano (below). The upright piano, with vertical strings, was not developed until the 1800s.

A modern standard piano has 88 keys. It also has two pedals that can be used to soften or sustain (prolong) the notes.

△ The first **photographs** were very different from today's snapshots. They were made by exposing large metal plates covered in tarlike chemicals to light. Photos such as the one above could take several minutes, during which the subjects had to stay very still.

▽ **Pianos**, like this grand, are played by hitting the keys. The lever movement of the key is transmitted to a felt-covered hammer that strikes the piano string. A damper stops the note from sounding after the key is released.

△ Pablo **Picasso** was a very influential artist whose work dominated early 20th-century art.

1

2

3

4

△ There are many different breeds of **pigs**. The ones shown are 1) Gloucester Old Spot, 2) Poland, 3) China and 4) Tamworth.

▽ **Pigeons** have a plump body, rounded tail, and soft brown, pink or grey-blue feathers.

Picasso, Pablo

Pablo Picasso (1881–1973) was the most famous artist of the 20th century. He was born in **Spain** but lived mostly in **France**. It is said Picasso could draw before he even learned to talk. At the age of 14, he spent one day on an **art** school test that most people needed a month to take, and by 16, had passed all the tests that Spain's art schools could offer. He disliked **paintings** that looked like **photographs**, and admired the curving shapes of African **sculpture**. His style developed over the years, until he began painting people as simple shapes – as cubes – and he became the most influential painter of the Cubist art movement. He also produced sculpture and **pottery**.

Pig

These farmyard **animals** have a long, heavy body, short legs ending in hoofed toes, a long snout and a short, curly tail. Males are called boars. Females are called sows. The heaviest boars can weigh over a tonne.

Domestic pigs are descended from the wild boar of Asian and European **forests**. They provide us with bacon, ham, pork and lard. Different parts of a pig's body are used to make brushes, **glue**, **leather** and **soap**. The wild boar is a tough, fierce animal, unlike most of its domestic relatives.

Pigeon and Dove

Pigeons and doves are **birds** that eat **seeds** or **fruit**. Many make soft cooing sounds. Pigeons are larger than doves. The crowned pigeon is bigger than a chicken, but the diamond

△ The **Pilgrim** Fathers sailed on the *Mayflower*, a galleon of around 180 tonnes that was probably only about 35 m long. The journey took 66 days. One passenger died during the voyage, but two were born.

dove is almost as small as a lark.

Tame pigeons are all descended from rock doves, which nest on cliffs. Pigeons and doves have become domesticated. Some are pets, others are used for racing. Homing pigeons will fly great distances to return home – one once flew 1,300 km in one day.

Pilgrim

A pilgrim is a person who makes a journey to a place, often holy, as an act of religious faith. The journey is known as a pilgrimage. Among Christians, pilgrimages were highly organized in the **Middle Ages**, and included trips to the Holy Land, **Rome**, and shrines to saints such as the one to Bernadette at Lourdes in southern **France**.

Some groups of people who settle in foreign lands are also described as pilgrims. In 1620, a group of English Puritans seeking religious freedom sailed from **England** across the **Atlantic**. They landed on the coast of what is now Massachusetts in the **USA** and founded a colony there.

The 102 men, women and children are known as the Pilgrim Fathers.

There are still many pilgrimages today. The birthplace of the Prophet **Muhammad** is **Mecca** in **Saudi Arabia**. It is a holy city and a place of pilgrimage for more than two million **Muslims** every year. Muslim men and women are expected to make at least one pilgrimage there in a lifetime.

Pine *see* Conifer

Plague

The word plague comes from the Latin *plaga* meaning 'disaster' or 'pestilence'. Since ancient times, terrible diseases have swept through **Europe**, **Asia** and **Africa** from time to time. Bubonic plagues, such as the **Black Death**, have wiped out hundreds of thousands of people over the centuries.

The word plague is also used to describe an overwhelming invasion by something that is not welcome, for example 'a plague of tourists' or 'a plague of locusts'.

Planet

The word 'planet' comes from the Greek word *planetes* meaning 'wanderer'. Long ago, skywatchers gave this name to 'stars' that appeared to move. We now know that planets are not **stars**, but are bodies that travel around stars.

The earth and other planets of our **solar system** travel around the star we call the **sun**. Each planet travels in its own orbit, but they all move in the same direction, and, except for Pluto and Mercury, lie in the same plane.

Astronomers think the planets came from a band of **gas** and dust that once whirled around the sun. They think that **gravity** pulled parts of this band together as masses that became planets. The nine planets in our solar system are **Mercury**, **Venus**, **earth**, **Mars**,

△ A **plague** of locusts so big that it blocked out the sun devastated Africa in the summer of 1988. As many as 50 billion hungry insects ate thousands of tonnes of crops and the people faced famine.

△ **Plankton** often have beautiful and complex structures despite their tiny size. These diatoms have shells that are made up of silica, a protective hard, colourless solid.

Jupiter, **Saturn**, **Uranus**, **Neptune** and **Pluto**. Mercury is closest to the sun and Pluto usually farthest away. Viewed from earth, the other planets shine because of reflected sunlight.

Plankton

Plankton is the mass of tiny **plants** and **animals** that drifts about in the sea and inland **waters**. Most plankton are so small they can be seen only with a **microscope**.

Planktonic plants are called phytoplankton. They live near the surface of the water, where they find the **light** they need. Some tiny plants swim by lashing the water with little whiplike organs. Others have spiky **shells** that look like glass.

Planktonic animals are called zooplankton. Some live deep down and rise at night to feed. Zooplankton includes tiny one-celled creatures, and baby **crabs** and **fish**.

Plankton forms the base for the ocean **food chain**. All sea creatures depend directly either on plankton for food or on animals that feed on plankton.

PLANTS

Plants are living organisms that harness the energy of the sun to feed themselves and build up living matter. They take in carbon dioxide gas from the air and give out oxygen. Without plants, our planet would be a lifeless world. Plants release all the oxygen that animals need to breathe. They also provide food for animals and form the basis for the habitats in which they live.

△ *The violet is an example of a very versatile plant. It is used in the production of perfumes. It can be eaten in salads, fried in oil and candied. It is also used to treat skin complaints and in poultices for ulcers.*

There are more than 375,000 different kinds of plants, ranging in size from tiny mosses only a few millimetres long to giant redwood trees, which grow to over 100 m tall. Plants live in nearly all the regions of the world, although half the known plant species grow in tropical forests – this large mass of plants produces so much oxygen that the forests are often described as the lungs of the planet. Each plant has adapted to its own habitat, sometimes in extreme conditions. Desert plants such as cacti and succulents have long, widely spreading roots to collect water, which they store in their fleshy stems and leaves. Plants in cold places grow in low, thick clumps which protect them from the cold and wind.

PLANT GROUPS

There are several different plant groups. Liverworts and mosses grow in moist places with no roots, flowers or seeds, just simple leaves. Horsetails are an ancient group of plants that are found in damp, shady areas, and have small leaves and hollow stems. Ferns have curled stems and feathery leaves known as fronds. They reproduce by spreading spores from packets on their leaves.

Conifers (gymnosperms) such as pines and firs are cone-bearing plants. They produce bare seeds that are contained in cones, and they were the earliest seed-bearing plants to evolve. Many conifers grow in relatively dry, cold places. Flowering plants (angiosperms) produce covered seeds. They are divided into two classes: monocotyledons and dicotyledons. Monocotyledons grow from seeds which contain only one seed leaf, or cotyledon. They have long, narrow leaves, and include grasses, bamboos, palms, lilies and bluebells. Dicotyledons grow from seeds which contain two seed leaves. They are the largest group of plants with over 200,000 species, including oak, apple, beech, cacti, daisies and potatoes.

Sunlight

△ *Leaves are the plant's food-making factories. In the leaves, cells are arranged so they absorb as much sunlight as possible.*

FOOD FACTORIES

Plant cells contain a green pigment called chlorophyll. This pigment absorbs energy from sunlight to make glucose – a type of sugar – from carbon dioxide gas in the air and water in the soil. This process, unique to plants, is called photosynthesis. The glucose molecules made in photosynthesis are joined together to form other substances. One of these is cellulose, which is used for growth and to build new cells, and the other is starch, which is used as a reserve food store.

Stem

Pollen sac

▷ *Flowers have reproductive parts called carpels and stamens. The stamens are male and the carpels are female. Each stamen has an anther, which produces tiny grains of pollen. Here, honey bees are collecting pollen from this lily in pollen sacs and carrying it from plant to plant to pollinate.*

PARTS OF A PLANT

Flowers contain the reproductive parts of a plant. They are often brightly coloured or scented. The stem carries water and minerals to the leaves. In trees and other woody plants the stems are stiffened by wood – the branches and trunk. Roots take in water and minerals from the soil, and anchor the plant into the ground.

Anther

Carpel

Stamen

Petal

HOW PLANTS REPRODUCE

Most flowers have male and female organs. The male parts, the stamens, make pollen, which is transferred to the female part, the stigma, usually of another flower. This is called pollination. Some plants spread their pollen using the wind. Others use animals such as insects to carry it for them.

Plants spread their seeds in a huge variety of ways. Some seeds are small and light and carried by the wind. Others have hooks or sticky coatings which allow them to be carried by animals, and many are eaten by animals attracted to the fleshy fruit. Some, such as the squirting cucumber, actually fire their ripe seeds into the air. Many plants can also reproduce without seeds, just by growing mini versions of themselves.

Runner bean seed germinating

GERMINATION

Germination is the development of a seed into a young plant, and it happens when the conditions of temperature, light and moisture are just right. First the seed absorbs water, swells and splits. It sends out an embryo root, which pushes downwards into the soil. A shoot then pushes upwards, growing towards the sunlight.

TREES

Trees can be coniferous or deciduous. They are a vital part of many habitats and a single tree can support thousands of creatures which rely on it for food and shelter. They also protect the land from erosion, as their leaves and branches absorb heavy rains and their roots bind the soil and stop it from being washed or blown away.

Trees have woody stems and bark. When a tree is sliced across, you can see the annual growth rings in the trunk. The inner rings are alive and growing. The bark is a layer of dead tissue which protects the living parts inside.

▷ *Deciduous trees are broad-leaved and have spreading crowns and roots. Their spring flowers develop into fruit.*

PEOPLE AND PLANTS

People use plants in all kinds of ways. Food crops, such as cereals, vegetables and fruit, feed people and their livestock. Many useful substances, such as timber, rubber and cotton, come from plants, as well as life-saving medicines. People also cultivate plants to create a pleasant environment in their gardens, towns and parks. Today, many thousands of wild plants are endangered as their habitats are under threat, so it is important to protect them.

> **SEE ALSO**
> Air, Cell, Conifer, Flower, Fruit, Gas, Leaf, Light, Medicine, Oxygen, Reproduction, Seed, Temperature, Tree, Vegetable, Water

Plastic pellets

Mould

Heating element

Finished bowl

Plunger

INJECTION MOULDING

◁ **Plastic** objects can be made by a process called 'injection moulding'. Plastic pellets are heated and then injected into a mould. There is another common method for moulding plastic. This is used to make rods or sheets of plastic. It is called hot extrusion, and the plastic is forced through openings.

Plastic

Plastics are manufactured substances and can be moulded into different shapes. They are used to make anything from furniture and car seats to shoes and bags, cups and plates.

Most plastics are largely made from chemicals obtained from petroleum **oil**. **Coal**, limestone, **salt** and **water** are also used. Plastics can be hard, soft or **liquid**. They can be made to look like **glass**, **metal**, **wood** or other substances.

Hard plastics are used in **radio** and **camera** cases. But fine threads of the hard plastic nylon make soft stockings. Some bags and bottles are made of soft plastics like polyethylene. The first plastic was celluloid, which was discovered in the 1800s.

Plato

Plato (c.427–347 BCE) was a great Greek thinker, whose ideas were very important in the establishment of the field of **philosophy**. Plato believed that the things we see around us are only poor copies of the perfect things in an ideal world. He developed ideas such as the notion of justice, and in his book *The Republic*, described his idea of a perfect nation, or Utopia, ruled by philosopher-kings. Plato travelled widely before settling in Athens, where he founded his own academy, with **Aristotle** as one of his pupils.

△ As a **plough** travels up and down the field, it turns up the soil, leaving ridges and furrows.

▽ The duck-billed **platypus** is just one of a number of very unusual animals found only in Australia and New Zealand. These land masses were cut off millions of years ago, when the continents drifted apart. The animals there evolved in isolation from those elsewhere.

Platypus

The platypus is an Australian **mammal** that lays eggs. Its name means 'flat-footed'. The platypus uses its webbed feet to swim in **rivers**, and its ducklike beak to grub for **worms** and **insects** underwater. It lives in a burrow in river banks. The female lays her soft-shelled eggs in a nest. They are as small as marbles.

Plough

This farm **machine** has blades which turn over the surface of the soil. It is used to bury weeds, stubble and other **plants** on the surface in preparation for the cultivation of a new crop.

Pluto

The **planet** Pluto is named after the Greek **god** who ruled the dreary world of the dead. Pluto must be bitterly cold, because it is farther away from the **sun** than any of the other planets. It is almost 40 times farther from the sun than the **earth** is.

Pluto spins and moves around the sun much more slowly than the earth. A day on Pluto may equal nearly a week on earth. One year on Pluto lasts almost 248 earth years. Pluto is only half as big as the earth, and weighs one-sixth as much.

Pocahontas

Native American Pocahontas (c.1595–1617) was the daughter of Chief Powhatan. According to John Smith, one of the English founders of the Jamestown settlement of Virginia, Pocahontas saved his life twice when he was at the mercy of her tribe. In 1613, Pocahontas was taken captive by the Jamestown colonists and while a prisoner, became a Christian and took the name Rebecca. The following year, she married James Rolfe, a tobacco planter. She travelled to **England** with her husband in 1616, where she was received by royalty. She became ill and died of smallpox just as she set out on a ship to return to America.

Poetry

Poetry is the oldest form of literature. Before people developed a system of writing, they found that the best way to remember a story was to sing it or put it in a rhyming pattern. Poets choose words carefully, for their **sound** as well as their meaning. Poetry can be compared to music because it creates beautiful sounds with words.

Much poetry is written in rhyme. This means that the words at the ends of lines have the same final sound. Rhyme is not necessary in poetry,

△ Many **poisons** are so dangerous that they have to have a clear warning sign when they are being transported from one place to another or stored. The international symbol for poisonous substances is a skull and crossbones. The other symbol shows that the contents of the barrel are radioactive.

however. Poets use rhyme in some poems and not in others. Poems are usually divided into parts, or verses. The lines of a verse have a rhythm that is built up by strong and weak sounds.

There are three main types of poetry. They are narrative, lyric and dramatic. Narrative poetry tells a story. Lyric poetry tells of the poet's own feelings. Dramatic poetry has characters who tell a story, just as a play does. Shakespeare wrote many of his plays in verse.

Poisons

Poisons are chemical substances that kill or damage living things. Some poisons get into the body through the **skin**. Some are swallowed. Poisonous **gases** are harmful if someone breathes them in with **air**. Different poisons work in different ways. Strong **acids** or alkalis 'burn'. **Nerve** poisons can stop the **heart**. Some other poisons can make the body bleed inside. If they are administered in time, **drugs** called antidotes can cure people who have ingested certain poisons.

▽ **Pluto** has one moon, Charon (left), which is about half as large as the planet it orbits. Many astronomers think that they are twin planets rather than a planet with a moon.

PLUTO FACTS	
Average distance from sun:	5,900 million km
Nearest distance from earth:	5,800 million km
Average temperature:	−230°C
Diameter across the equator:	3,000 km
Atmosphere:	None?
Number of moons:	1 known
Length of day:	6 days 9 hours
Length of year:	247.7 earth years

Poland

Poland lies in eastern **Europe**, south of the Baltic Sea, and is the seventh largest country in Europe. Most of Poland is low farmland, although **forests** sprawl across the Carpathian **Mountains** in the south. Poland's largest **river** is the Vistula. It rises in the mountains and flows into the Baltic Sea. Rivers often freeze in Poland's cold, snowy winters.

There are more than 38 million Poles. Most of them speak Polish, and most are Roman Catholics.

In 1989, Poland had the first free **elections** in 40 years. The independent trade union Solidarity swept into power and Poland became the first non-communist country in the former eastern bloc. In 1999, Poland joined **NATO** and it seems likely that it will move closer to countries in the West.

POLAND
Government: Democratic state
Capital: Warsaw
Area: 312,677 sq km
Population: 38.7 million
Language: Polish
Currency: Zloty

Police

Police are employed by a **government** to enforce the **laws** of a country and maintain order. Part of this job is protecting people's lives and property. They patrol streets, direct traffic, control crowds, find missing persons

△ The modern **police** rely heavily on contacts with members of the public. When officers patrol, it can be on horseback (like this officer in New York), on foot, or in a car.

◁ **Pollution** such as this oil spill at sea can harm wildlife and permanently damage the ecology of an area. These seabirds stand little chance of survival.

and help people hurt in accidents. Police officers try to prevent crime, and track down and capture criminals. This can be dangerous and sometimes officers are killed. Most police forces today are armed with weapons of some kind, and many carry **guns**.

Other branches of police work include forensics (the scientific investigation of a crime that includes fingerprinting and the analysis of clues) and criminology (the study of criminals, their crimes and the way that their minds work).

Pollution

Pollution happens when harmful substances are released into the environment in such large quantities that they cause damage to people, wildlife or **habitats**. Before the **Industrial Revolution** in **Europe**, most of the wastes produced by living things had been used by other living things. Today, people produce more waste matter than can be coped with naturally and more and more pressure is being put on **governments** to control industry and combat pollution.

Cars and factories pour smoke and fumes into the air. Chemical **fertilizers** and pesticides can kill off wild **plants** and **animals**. Poor sewage disposal and spilt **oil** devastate seas and **rivers**. International agreements have been drawn up to reduce such pollution and stop countries dumping waste at sea.

Polo, Marco

Marco Polo (1254–1324) was an Italian who travelled to **China** at a time when the people of **Europe** knew little about the East. His father and his uncle were merchants in **Venice** and they decided to take the young Marco with them on their second journey to the East in 1271. They crossed Persia (today's **Iran**) and the vast Gobi

Desert. In 1275, the Polos reached Peking (today's **Beijing**) and were welcomed at the court of **Kublai Khan**, a great **Mongol** conqueror. The Polos stayed for many years during which Marco travelled all over China as an envoy in the service of the Khan. They left China in 1292 and arrived home in Venice in 1295. Later, Marco Polo wrote down his adventures in a book, *Travels of Marco Polo*.

Pompeii

Two thousand years ago, Pompeii was a small Roman city in southern **Italy**. A sudden disaster killed many of its citizens and drove out the rest. But the same disaster preserved the streets and buildings. Today, visitors to Pompeii can learn a great deal about what life was like inside a Roman city.

In 79 CE, the nearby **volcano** of **Vesuvius** erupted and showered the town of Pompeii with volcanic ash and cinders. Poisonous **gases** swirled through the streets. About one citizen in every ten was poisoned by fumes contained in clouds of hot ash that swept down the volcano's slopes. Their remains were buried by ash and pumice-stone, which also covered their homes. In time, people forgot that Pompeii had ever existed.

For centuries, Pompeii's thick coat of ash, which was 6–7 m deep, hardened and protected it from the **weather**. Finally, in the 1700s, people began to dig out the city. The excavation continues today. Archaeologists have discovered whole buildings, streets, tools and statues. They have even found hollows in the ash left by the decayed bodies of people and dogs that were killed by the eruption. The archaeologists poured plaster into these hollows, allowing it to harden. Then they cleared away the ash to reveal life-size plaster models of the dead bodies. Part of the city still remains buried, and the modern town lies to the east.

Pope

'Pope' is a title of the head of the Roman Catholic church. (The word 'pope' comes from the Italian word *papa*, which means 'father'.) The Pope is also the Bishop of **Rome**. He lives in the **Vatican City** inside Rome.

Roman Catholics believe that Jesus made St Peter the first Pope. Since then, there have been many Popes. Each time one dies, church leaders choose another. The Pope makes Church laws, chooses bishops and can declare people saints.

△ Archaeologists have uncovered almost half the city of **Pompeii**. Bodies of the people trapped in the ash while fleeing have been recreated by making plaster casts of their imprints in the ash.

Pop music

Pop **music** is short for 'popular music'. Modern pop music has strong, lively rhythms, and simple, often catchy, tunes. Most pop tunes are songs. A pop group usually has one or more singers with musicians who play such instruments as electric **guitars**, synthesizers and electronic organs. Many people start pop groups when they are still at school, and a few have achieved success by being 'discovered' and given recording contracts. Pop groups often need vans to carry their heavy equipment, as well as people to set it up, take it down and do repairs.

Elvis Presley was one of the first rock and roll stars to become a cult hero. Famous pop groups and stars like the Beatles, Madonna, Michael Jackson and Britney Spears have attracted huge audiences to concerts all over the world. Millions of people watched the Live Aid concert on television in 1985.

△ As the current **Pope**, John Paul II is recognized by Roman Catholics as the representative of Jesus Christ on earth. He is also head of the Vatican City state, the smallest state in the world.

257

△ The **potato** is a root crop. The tubers – the part that we eat – vary greatly in size, shape, colour and flavour, depending on the variety of potato. Potatoes can be cooked and eaten as a vegetable, or processed to make crisps or chips.

PORTUGAL
Government: Parliamentary democracy
Capital: Lisbon
Area: 92,082 sq km
Population: 10 million
Language: Portuguese
Currency: Euro

Population

All the people living in a place make up its population. That place may be a village, a city, a country or the world. In the **Stone Age**, the whole world held only a few million people. Their numbers were kept down by lack of **food**, injury and **disease**. As people have solved these problems, the **population** of the world has increased.

Between 1 CE and 1650, the world's population doubled. It doubled again in only 150 years after 1650. Since then it has risen even faster. In 1930, the world had two thousand million people. It passed the six thousand million mark on the eve of the 21st century and it is still increasing fast.

Porcupine

Porcupines are named from the Latin words for 'spiny pig'. A porcupine is really a **rodent** with many **hairs** shaped as long, sharp spines or quills. If a porcupine is attacked, it backs towards its enemy and lashes its tail. Some of the spines stick into the attacker and cause painful wounds or even death.

Ground-living or terrestrial porcupines are found in southern **Asia**, **Africa**, southern **Europe** and the East Indies. A tree-living or arboreal species is found in both **North America** and **South America**.

Porpoise *see* Dolphin

Portugal

This is a long, narrow, country in southwest **Europe**. It is sandwiched between the **Atlantic Ocean** and **Spain**, a country four times the size of Portugal. Much of Portugal is mountainous. **Rivers** flow from the **mountains** through valleys and across plains to the sea.

Portugal's mild winters and warm summers help its people to grow olives, oranges and **rice**. Its grapes produce port, a **wine** named after the Portuguese city of Oporto. Portugal's **woods** yield more cork than those of any other nation. Its fishermen catch sardines and other sea **fish**. Portugal also has mines that produce **minerals** such as **copper** and **tin**, and factories for products such as textiles, leather and electrical machinery.

There are nearly 10 million people in Portugal. They speak Portuguese, which is also the official language of **Brazil**. The capital of Portugal is Lisbon.

Potato

Potatoes are valuable **foods**. They are rich in **starches** and contain **proteins** and different **vitamins**. Potatoes must be cooked to give the nourishment that our bodies can use. Potato **plants** are related to tomatoes. Each plant is low and bushy with a soft stem. Each potato grows on a root as a kind of swelling called a tuber. When its tubers have grown, the plant dies, but new plants spring up from the tubers.

Potatoes were first grown by South

▽ The North American **porcupine** is not hurt by losing some of its quills. They are part of its defence system, and soon grow back.

American Indians. Spanish **explorers** brought potatoes back to **Europe**. After **wheat**, **rice** and maize they are the world's most important crop.

In 1845 and 1846, the Irish potato crops failed because of a plant **disease**. As a result, thousands of Irish people died of starvation and many more emigrated to the **United States**.

△ On farms, **poultry** like these chickens can be kept roaming free – free range – or raised intensively in battery units.

Pottery

All kinds of objects made of baked **clay** are called pottery. Many cups, saucers, plates, bowls, pots, vases and other objects and ornaments are made of this very useful substance.

People have been making pottery for thousands of years. Early pots were thick and gritty. They leaked, and they cracked if heated. In time, people learned to make pottery that was more useful and more beautiful. Today, the two main kinds of pottery are porcelain and stoneware. Porcelain is fine pottery made of white China clay. It is so thin that it lets the light show through. Stoneware is usually much thicker.

To make a pot, a potter puts a lump of moist clay on a spinning disc called a **wheel**. He uses thumbs and fingers to shape the clay into a pot, then leaves it to dry. Next, he may coat it with a wet mixture called a glaze. Then he fires (heats) the pot with others in an oven called a kiln. Firing makes the pots rock-hard and turns their glaze into a smooth, hard, shiny coat. Different glazes produce different **colours**. Some glazes even produce a metallic sheen on a pot.

Most pottery today is mass-produced in factories, because it can be shaped, fired and decorated quickly and cheaply on an assembly line.

△ **Pottery** objects like these jugs can be made by pouring 'slip', or liquid clay, into a mould. They can also be shaped on a potter's wheel. The jug on the right has been fired and glazed.

Poultry

All birds kept for meat or eggs are known as poultry. To most people, poultry means chickens, **ducks**, geese and turkeys, but **ostriches**, partridges, guinea fowl, **peacocks**, pheasants and **pigeons** are kept as poultry too.

Chickens outnumber other kinds of poultry. There are probably more chickens than people in the world, and they lay enough **eggs** to give everyone on earth several hundred eggs each year. And the meat from chickens is produced more cheaply than **sheep** or **cattle**.

Power station

Power stations are places where the **energy** in **heat** or in flowing **water** is changed into electrical energy for use in homes and factories. Most power stations obtain their energy from a **fuel** which makes steam that works a **generator** or a group of generators.

The generators produce **electric current** that often travels overland through **wires** slung between tall **metal** towers called pylons. First, the current passes through a transformer. This raises the voltage (pressure) of the current and so reduces the amount that leaks away as the current flows. The voltage is reduced again before it reaches the homes and factories.

▽ A coal-fired **power station** transforms the energy locked in coal into electricity. Coal, oil and natural gas are fossil fuels and these fuels are used in the vast majority of power stations around the world. Most power stations burn vast quantities of fossil fuels to produce steam from water.

Cooling tower

Supply of coal

Generator

Water is turned to steam in boiler

Turbine

◁ Ornithocheirus *was
a coastal pterosaur with
a 12 m wingspan – almost
five times bigger than the
largest living bird. Behind it,
the pterosaur* Tapejara *and some
early birds throng the cliffs.*

PREHISTORIC ANIMALS

Prehistoric animals are those that lived more than 5,000 years ago. The fossils (preserved remains) of many animals have been found all over the world. Some are hundreds of millions of years old.

▽ Meganeura, *one of the first flying
insects, had a wingspan of up to
70 cm. It lived in warm forests at the
same time as the early reptiles,
around 300 million years ago.*

△ *Trilobites were among the first animals
to develop a tough protective shell.*

SIGNS OF LIFE
The earliest animals appeared in seas and oceans about 3,500 million years ago. Most of them were single-celled organisms that drifted in the water. Around 550 million years ago, the first complex animals evolved – soft-bodied invertebrates (animals without a backbone) such as jellyfish and worms.

ARMOURED ANIMALS
Some of the early soft-bodied sea creatures developed shells or hard, jointed limbs. These included shellfish, corals and ammonites. Shelled trilobites were once the most common sea animals on earth, between 570 and 245 million years ago. The hard parts of their bodies were often preserved as fossils.

△ Dimetrodon *was a fierce, meat-eating reptile that
lived around 275 million years ago. The large fin on
its back helped this animal control its body temperature.*

THE FIRST FISH
The earliest fish evolved around 500 million years ago. They were the first vertebrates, or animals with a backbone. At first they had no jaws and could only draw in specks of food through their sucker-like mouths. Then some fish developed bony armour and strong, movable jaws equipped with sharp teeth. These adaptations allowed fish to take over from giant, 2 m-long water scorpions as masters of the oceans.

FROM WATER TO LAND
Around 380 million years ago, some fish began to crawl on to dry land to find new sources of food. They had primitive lungs and muscular fins that were strong enough to pull their bodies out of the water. At first these adventurous fish may have been able to stay on land for only a few hours before struggling back to the water, but gradually they evolved into the first amphibians – animals that can live in both water and on land. Some of them may have looked like large newts or salamanders.

EARLY REPTILES

Reptiles evolved from amphibians. They had thicker skins and laid eggs with thick shells, which allowed them to live far from water. Some reptiles, called pterosaurs, developed leathery wings and learned to fly. Others, such as the ichthyosaurs, returned to the sea. During the Triassic, Jurassic and Cretaceous periods – between 230 and 65 million years ago – the dominant land reptiles were the dinosaurs.

INSECTS AND BIRDS

Insects were the first animals to take to the air, about 300 million years ago – long before the pterosaurs. The largest flying insect was *Meganeura*, which looked like a giant dragonfly. The first bird, *Archaeopteryx*, is believed to have evolved from a dinosaur about 150 million years ago.

SMALL MAMMALS

The first mammals evolved from reptiles around 230 million years ago. During the reign of the dinosaurs they remained small and rat-like, living on worms, insects and dinosaur eggs. Once the dinosaurs had become extinct, some mammals began to grow larger and take on different shapes. Before long, they had taken over as rulers of the earth.

▽ *This scene from South America one million years ago shows just how varied mammals became after the demise of the dinosaurs. Toxodon, for example, was a thick-skinned plant-eater about the size of a rhinoceros.*

△ *Archaeopteryx was the size of a magpie. It had bird-like feathers, but also the teeth and long, bony tail found in many reptiles.*

THE WORLD OF MAMMALS

Prehistoric mammals were all shapes and sizes. An early horse, *Hyracotherium*, stood just 20 cm tall at the shoulders. One group of large mammals, the brontotheres, had a massive forked horn on their snouts. *Baluchitherium* was probably the largest mammal ever to live on land. This giant, giraffe-shaped rhinoceros carried its head about 8 m above the ground.

SABRE-TOOTHED CATS

Sabre-toothed cats lived in many parts of the world during the last 25 million years. Their huge canine teeth measured up to 15 cm long – ideal for piercing the thick hides of large plant-eating mammals. The last sabre-tooths died out a few tens of thousands of years ago.

SEE ALSO
Amphibians and Reptiles, Birds, Cat, Dinosaur, Elephant, Evolution, Fish, Forest, Horse, Insects, Mammals, Teeth

PREHISTORIC ELEPHANTS

Elephants were among the most common and varied of prehistoric mammals. Pig-sized elephants lived in the Mediterranean region, while the woolly mammoths of Europe and Asia and the mastodonts of America stood up to 3 m tall. The mammoths and mastodonts adapted to the severe cold of the ice ages by developing a coat of long, thick fur. These animals were among the last prehistoric species to die out, around 10,000 years ago. They were probably wiped out by early human hunters.

▷ *Megatherium, a 5 m-tall sloth, died out 11,000 years ago.*

▽ *Glyptodon was a slow-moving, armoured mammal that was probably hunted by sabre-toothed cats.*

△ About 20,000 years ago, **prehistoric people** lived in caves or crude huts built of wood or hides. They used tools of stone and bone for hunting and preparing food, as well as for making clothing and shelters. During the Stone Age, it has been estimated that only a few thousand people lived in the whole of Africa and another few thousand in Asia.

△ Of all the **prehistoric peoples**, *Homo habilis* was probably the first human being to make and use tools, such as flint knives.

Prehistoric people

Prehistoric people lived long ago before there were any written records of **history**. We know about them from their remains. Prehistory is divided into the **Stone Age**, the **Bronze Age** and the Iron Age. The ages are named after the materials that people used to make their tools and weapons.

The Stone Age lasted for a long time. It began around 2.5 to 3 million years ago when human-like creatures began to appear on the earth. They were different from the ape-like animals that lived at the same time. They had larger **brains**, used stone tools and could walk upright.

Around 1.5 million years ago, a more human-like creature appeared. Scientists call this early human *Homo erectus*, meaning 'upright man'. *Homo erectus* is probably the ancestor of more advanced types of human called *Homo sapiens*, meaning 'intelligent man'. One kind of *Homo sapiens* was Neanderthal man, who appeared about 100,000 years ago. Modern man, *Homo sapiens sapiens*, first appeared in Europe and Asia around 35,000 years ago.

Towards the end of the Stone Age, prehistoric people began to use **metals**, the first of which was **copper**. They made copper tools about 10,000 years ago. About 5,000 years ago, people invented **bronze**, a hard **alloy** of **copper** and **tin**. This development signalled the start of the Bronze Age, when the earliest civilizations began. The Bronze Age ended about 3,300 years ago in southeastern Europe, when people learned how to make tools from iron. Iron is much harder than bronze, and with it, people were able to develop farming and building methods.

President

A president is the elected head of a state or republic, and in some countries, he or she is also the head of the government. In the **United States**, the president – the most powerful elected person in the world – is head of the government. In **France**, on the other hand, the president is the head of state, and appoints a prime minister to head the government. The title of president is also given to heads of clubs, business organizations and societies.

Printing

Printing is a way of copying words and pictures by mechanical means. It is used to produce **books**, **newspapers**, magazines, and other items such as **food** labels and printed carrier bags. It can also be used to print on fabrics.

The earliest printing, using carved wooden blocks, was in China, probably as early as the eighth century. Around 1455, Johannes **Gutenberg** of **Germany** invented the first printing press, using moveable type, which has raised **metal** letters that can be used again and again. The process is known as relief printing, and ink is put onto the raised letters, which are then pressed against **paper**.

The most common relief method today is letterpress printing, but there are many other kinds of printing.

In intaglio or gravure printing, often used by artists, the image is not raised. Instead it is etched, or cut away.

In other kinds of printing, the ink is put onto a flat surface. Offset lithography uses printing plates that are made photographically. The plates are treated with chemicals so that the greasy ink sticks only to the images to be printed. This method, invented in the early 1900s, made mass-production **colour** printing possible.

Today, most publications are printed from **computer**-generated pages. **Laser** printers work by spraying ink onto a page, while dot matrix printers form images from tiny dots.

Protein

Proteins are substances in **food** which are vital to life. They contain **carbon**, **hydrogen**, **oxygen** and nitrogen. They build up body tissue, especially **muscle**, and repair broken-down **cells**. They also give **heat** and **energy**, help us to grow, and they protect us from **disease**. Our bodies do not store extra protein, so we must eat a regular supply.

Proverb

A proverb is a short sentence containing a piece of wisdom. The **Bible** contains a **book** called Proverbs. All the peoples of the world have proverbs and many are international. 'A bird in the hand is worth two in the bush' is first found in English in a manuscript of about 1470. The Spanish version is 'A sparrow in the hand is worth a vulture flying', and the German, 'A sparrow in the hand is better than a stork on the roof.'

Psychology

Psychology is the scientific study of the mind and behaviour of **animals** and **humans**. Psychologists are interested in how the mind and **senses** work and can measure some things, such as **intelligence**, by using special tests.

There are several branches of psychology. Child psychology is the study of how children behave and what they do at different ages. Psychiatry is a similar science, but psychiatrists are doctors who cure mental illness and abnormal kinds of behaviour such as drug addiction and depression.

△ Most of the **protein** we need is found in foods that come from animals – meat, fish, eggs and cheese are all good sources. But some plant foods such as groundnuts, peas and beans are also rich in protein.

▽ In **printing** that uses offset lithography, rubber rollers are offset (stamped) with a printing image, for example a butterfly. There is one roller for each of four basic colours – yellow, magenta, cyan (blue) and black. Paper is then printed with the coloured inks in turn until the complete four-colour picture is built up.

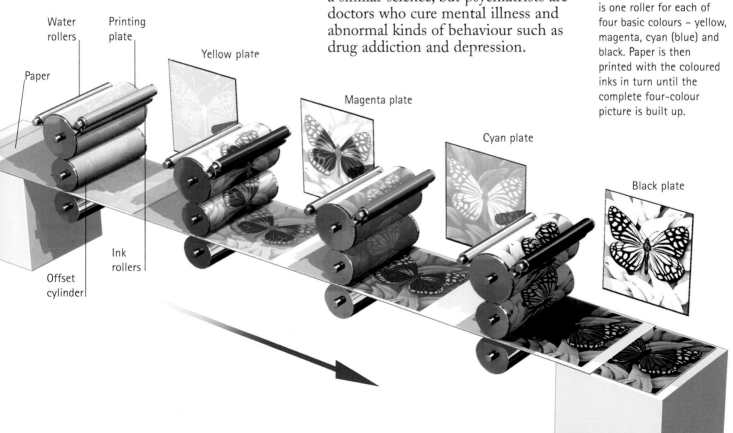

Water rollers

Printing plate

Paper

Yellow plate

Magenta plate

Cyan plate

Black plate

Ink rollers

Offset cylinder

PUERTO RICO
Government: Self-governing commonwealth of the USA
Capital: San Juan
Area: 8,897 sq km
Population: 3.8 million
Languages: English and Spanish
Currency: US dollar

Puerto Rico

Puerto Rico is a tropical **island** in the **Caribbean**. It is a **commonwealth** that governs itself, but it benefits from the military protection of the **United States**. Puerto Ricans are US citizens, but they cannot vote in American **elections**. Puerto Rico is densely populated and many people have emigrated to the United States. One of the main industries is tourism.

Pulley

A pulley is a simple **machine** consisting of a **wheel** on a fixed axle. A rope or belt passed over the wheel is tied to a load. When the rope is pulled, the load is raised into the air.

A moveable pulley runs along a rope which has one end fixed to a support. The load hangs from the pulley itself. When the other end of the rope is pulled, the pulley moves the load along the rope. Pulleys are used in machines such as cranes.

Piston
Valve
Cylinder
Air in   Air out
Valve

Pulsar

Sometimes a huge star, several times larger than earth's **sun**, becomes so hot that it explodes. For a few days, it sends out as much **energy** as a whole **galaxy** of stars. It has become a supernova. After such an explosion, all that is left is a very hot ball of **matter** a few kilometres across. This spins at a tremendous rate and sends out a beam of **light** and **radio** waves like a revolving searchlight. The beam seems to 'pulse' on and off, so it is called a pulsar. Most pulsars are too faint to be seen except with a very large **telescope**, but they give out powerful radio waves.

△ **Pumps** like this one, which is used to inflate a bicycle tyre, are simple mechanisms. Air is pushed into the tyre by a piston which is pumped up and down in a cylinder. A valve inside the cylinder allows the air to flow only one way. There is a second valve on the tyre, so it will remain inflated when the pump is taken away.

Pulse

The pulse is a rhythmic beat or throb in the body's **arteries**. These blood vessels carry blood away from the heart. A pulse beat occurs as the heart contracts (becomes smaller) and **pumps** blood into the arteries.

Doctors measure pulse rates to find out if the heart is beating normally. They usually feel the radial artery in the wrist. But the pulse can be felt wherever an artery passes over a **bone**. The normal pulse rate for men is 72 beats per minute. For women, it is 76 to 80 beats. But pulse rates between 50 and 85 are considered normal. Children have faster pulses.

Pump

Most pumps are used to move **liquids**, but some move **gases**. There are several kinds of pumps. For example, a **bicycle** pump is a simple reciprocating pump – it has a piston which moves up and down inside a cylinder. A similar pump is the lift pump which can raise water about nine metres from the bottom of a well. It has an upright barrel with a close-fitting piston worked by a handle. Force pumps are used to raise water from greater depths.

Pyramid

Pyramids are huge, four-sided buildings with a square base. The sides are triangles that meet in a point at the top.

The Egyptians built pyramids as

◁ As a **pulsar**, or neutron star, spins, its signal sweeps through space like the beam of light from a lighthouse. The signal reaches the earth once in every rotation, and can be photographed or picked up by radio. Over millions of years, pulsars slow down.

royal tombs. The first, which was built in about 2650 BCE at Sakkara, is 62 m high. The three most famous pyramids are near Giza. The Great Pyramid, built in the 2600s BCE by the **pharaoh** Khufu, is 137 m high. Khafre, who ruled soon after Khufu, built the second, at 136 m high. The third, built by Khafre's successor Menakaure, is 73 m high. About 80 pyramids still stand in Egypt.

Central and South American Indians also built pyramids as temples during the first six centuries CE. One huge example is at Cholula, near Mexico City, which is about 54 m high.

△ The huge **pyramids** built thousands of years ago in Egypt are great feats of engineering but it took countless numbers of slaves to move the great blocks of stone.

over 3,000 m, though most average about 1,100 m. The highest is Pico de Aneto at 3,404 m. On the southern slope of the eastern Pyrenees lies the tiny republic of **Andorra**.

Python

Pythons are large **snakes** that are egg-laying members of the boa family. They live in **Africa**, southeastern **Asia** and a few species are found in **Australia**. Some grow as long as 9 m. They are constrictors. This means that they squeeze prey such as **hares**, **rats** and **antelopes** to death, before swallowing it whole.

Pyrenees

The Pyrenees are a chain of **mountains** that lie between **France** and **Spain**. They stretch about 435 km from the Bay of Biscay to the **Mediterranean Sea**. They have always formed a natural barrier between France and Spain, so that most of the trade between the two countries has been by sea. **Iron**, **lead**, **silver** and cobalt are mined in the mountains, and the beautiful scenery attracts many tourists.

The peaks of the Pyrenees rise to

▷ The African rock python lives on grasslands and in forests, where it preys on everything from birds to mammals the size of this zebra. Its pattern and colouring are well-matched to its surroundings, so it is difficult for prey to avoid it. It is one of the longest snakes in the world.

Quakers

The Quakers are a religious movement also known as the Society of Friends. They are a Protestant group that was begun by George Fox (1624–1691) in **England** during the 1650s.

They were called Quakers because some of them shook with emotion at their meetings. Early Quakers were often badly treated because of their belief that **religion** and **government** should not be mixed. Quakers have simple religious meetings and they appoint elders, not priests.

Quantum

We think of **light** and other forms of **energy** such as **radio** waves and **X-rays** as travelling in waves. Light can also be thought of as a stream of tiny quanta (the plural of quantum) or photons. The energy of each photon depends on the wavelength and therefore the **colour** of the light. A photon of white light has more energy than a photon of red light. Scientists combine the two ways of thinking about light. They think of light streaming out in packets

△ The **Quaker** Society was founded in England in the mid-17th century. They were puritans and disliked priestly control of the church. Quakers, including women, were encouraged to preach and speak out.

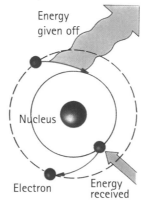

△In **quantum** theory, the electrons orbiting the nucleus of an atom can absorb energy and move from a normal orbit to a high one. If they move back again they give off energy. The amount of energy given off is measured in quanta.

of waves, each packet being a quantum or photon. They also think that tiny particles of **matter** such as electrons behave like waves as well as behaving like solid particles.

When you look at the light from a light bulb, it seems to be quite steady. Actually, light is not as steady as it seems. It is given off in a vast number of tiny packages of energy, like the bullets from a machine-gun. Each package is a quantum.

Quarrying

Quarries are huge pits where **rocks** are cut or blasted out of the ground. As long ago as prehistoric times, people had quarries where they dug up **flint** to make into tools and weapons.

Today, rock is quarried in enormous quantities. **Explosives** blast loose thousands of tonnes at a time. This is scooped up by bulldozers and diggers and carried to crushers. The rock is ground into stones for use in **roads**, **railways**, **concrete** and cement.

Not all rock is removed in this way. Stone that is used in building and paving is cut out of the ground rather than blasted. Electric cutters, wire saws and drills are used to cut the rock.

Quartz

Quartz is one of the most common **minerals** in the world and is found everywhere. **Sand** is mostly made of quartz, and many **rocks** contain quartz.

Quartz forms six-sided crystals. It is a very hard substance, harder even than **steel**. In its pure form, it is called rock crystal and has no colour and is as clear as glass. Most quartz is smoky white or tinted with various **colours**. Many semiprecious **gems**, such as agate, amethyst, opal and onyx, are quartz.

Quartz is an important mineral. It is used in many things, including abrasives such as sandpaper, cement, **lenses**, **clocks** and **electronics**.

Quasar

Quasars are very distant, very powerful objects farther out in space than the most remote **galaxies**. Quasars were not discovered by astronomers until the 1960s. They may be galaxies with some extra-powerful **energy** source at their centre. Quasars send out strong **radio** waves, **X-rays**, **infrared rays** and light. All quasars are millions of light years away, and we see them now as they were that long ago. From **earth** they look like very faint **stars**.

Quebec

Quebec is the largest province in **Canada**. It stretches from the St Lawrence River in the south to the Hudson Strait in the north. Much of northern Quebec is a forested wilderness, so most people live in the south, in cities such as Montreal and Quebec City. The province is the centre for French culture in Canada. Jacques Cartier claimed the Quebec region for France in 1534 and Quebec joined the Canadian confederation in 1867. In 1980, the people of Quebec voted against a plan to make their province politically independent. Quebec's industries include the manufacture of **cars**, machinery, **aircraft**, and chemical and petroleum products. The lumber business and tourism are other important industries.

△ **Quasars** are among the most powerful objects in the universe. It is believed that a huge black hole lies at the centre. As the gas, and possibly complete stars, are sucked into the black hole, huge amounts of energy in the form of radio waves, infrared, light and X-rays are sent into space.

△ Pure **quartz** crystals are colourless, but when they are mixed with other substances they take on many different shades.

◁ **Quarrying** is usually carried out by using dynamite or other explosives to break up the rock. Diggers load it into lorries for transporting to the crushing plant. There the rock is broken down still further for use on railway lines, road beds and as cement for concrete buildings. The world's largest quarry is Bingham Canyon copper mine in Utah, USA. It is about 770 metres deep.

All types of **rabbit** have been bred from the Mediterranean wild rabbit (left). Today, they are all kinds of colours, shapes and sizes. The tiny dwarf lop-eared rabbit has ears that droop. The Himalayan rabbit is not really from the Himalayas. It just means a certain type of coat marking with darker face, ears, legs and tail.

Rabbit

Rabbits were originally found only in southern **Europe**. Humans have now introduced them throughout the world. They are small **mammals** with a short tail and long, pointed ears. Rabbits live in burrows in the ground. Each burrow is the home of a single rabbit family. A group of burrows is known as a warren.

Raccoon

Raccoons live in **North America.** They have long fur, a short, pointed nose, a black mask across the **eyes** and a bushy tail with black rings.

▽ **Raccoons** are often thought of as pests in the United States, and are sometimes hunted. Davy Crockett's famous hat was made of raccoon fur, with the striped tail left hanging down at the back.

Raccoons may grow to as much as 90 cm from nose to tail.

Raccoons live in **forests.** They make their homes in holes in **trees** and are good climbers. At night, they leave their hollows to hunt for **food.** They will eat almost anything – **fruit** and **plants**, **eggs**, **insects**, **fish**, **birds** and small **mammals** – but their main food comes from **rivers**, so their tree-holes are usually found close by. These mammals also scavenge for food in towns, and can often be heard scampering across rooftops at night.

Race

All the people on earth belong to the **human** race. But 'race' also means any group of people who look alike in particular ways. It is not known when and how the different races came into being, but there are three main ones – Mongoloid, Caucasian and Negroid.

The Mongoloid race is known for its straight dark **hair**, yellow-brown **skin** and almond-shaped **eyes.** Caucasians have hair **colour** that ranges from blond and red to black, are fair-skinned or dark-skinned, and are round-eyed. The Negroid race has dark, tightly

Bad weather detected from radar in nose of aircraft warns pilot

Pulses sent and received from secondary scanner

Pulses sent and received from primary radar scanner

Radar altimeter measures height of aircraft above ground

Receiver

Oscillator

Transmitter

Antenna

Antenna

Radar is used by air traffic controllers at airports. They need to know the height and position of aircraft to prevent collisions. They have small screens to relay the information they have found. Large aircraft have on-board radar to detect other planes and bad weather.

curling hair and dark skin colour.

In addition to the three main races, there are also a number of smaller groups. Because thousands of years of migration, conquest and marriage have mixed all the races, the pure racial types probably do not exist any more.

Racism

Racism is a form of discrimination against people because of their **race**. It is practised by people who believe that their race is superior to that of another group. For centuries in many parts of the **United States**, white people discriminated against black people. In **World War II**, **Hitler** practised racism against minority groups in **Germany**. South African **apartheid** was also a form of racism.

Radar

The name radar comes from the phrase 'radio detecting and ranging'. Radar is a system for tracking objects using **radio** beams. It is a very useful **invention**, because it works in the dark and in fog, and it can detect objects thousands of kilometres away.

Radar works by sending out a narrow, high-powered beam about 500 times a second. It travels at a steady 300 metres every millionth of a second. When the beam strikes an object a faint **echo** bounces back. The echo is picked up and turned into a 'blip' of **light** on a screen. A radar operator can tell by studying the blip

how far away the object is, in what direction it is moving and at what speed. Radar is used by the military to track **missiles** and planes, and by **weather** stations to find and follow the path of storms. **Satellites** fitted with radar can map the **earth** from space.

Radio

The common household object we call a radio is only the receiving end of a large system of radio **communications**. A radio programme begins in a studio. There, voices and music are turned into **electronic** signals. These are amplified (made stronger), and then sent out from tall masts as radio waves. The waves are picked up by a radio in the home and changed back into **sounds**. Radio waves travel at the speed of **light** – so fast that a signal can circle the world 7.5 times in one second.

The first person to generate radio waves, in 1887, was Heinrich Hertz (1857–1894). Guglielmo **Marconi** sent the first messages in 1894.

Radioactivity

The atoms of some substances shoot off tiny particles and rays that we cannot see or feel. This radioactivity was discovered in 1896 by Marie and Pierre **Curie**, who found that, in time, these radioactive substances changed into other substances, and that they did this at a steady rate.

△ A **radio** broadcast is turned into a vibrating electric current which is sent through the air to a transmitter (above). The transmitter mixes the vibrating current with another faster current, turning them into a radio wave that is then beamed out through the air.

▽ The three forms of **radioactivity** are alpha, beta and gamma radiation. Their different abilities to penetrate substances are illustrated here.

Alpha particle
Beta particle
Gamma ray

Steel

Aluminium

Paper

continued on page 272

RAILWAYS

Railways are networks of smooth metal tracks on which trains run. This system of transport expanded rapidly during the 19th century – it enabled goods and people to travel long distances at speed. Today, railways are used to transport people and goods in nearly every country in the world.

△ *The Native Americans called the train the 'iron horse', and it crossed the continent of North America for the first time in the 1860s. A typical engine was powerful enough to haul 40 tonnes of train. Behind the engine, the tender carried wood for the fire, and a large metal 'cowcatcher' was fitted at the front of the train. This nudged stray cattle off the tracks and cleared snowdrifts or loose rocks.*

THE FIRST RAILWAYS

The first passenger railway, the Stockton and Darlington in northeast England, was designed in 1825 by British engineer George Stephenson (1781–1848). The Liverpool to Manchester railway opened soon afterwards, in 1829. By 1900, most of the developed countries of the world had extensive railway networks and millions of people were travelling by train.

△ *In 1829, Stephenson and his son Robert designed and built the* Rocket *for trials on the Liverpool and Manchester Railway. It reached a speed of 40 km/h.*

POWERING UP

The first trains were powered by steam engines. In 1804, mine-owner Richard Trevithick (1771–1833) developed a steam engine to carry heavy loads. George Stephenson urged the owners of the first railways to use steam engines, and they were a great success. Today's trains can travel at high speeds and most are powered by electricity from wires overhead, or by diesel engines. Maglev trains are powered with magnets that lift the train above the tracks – these 'floating' trains are able to travel very fast and create little noise.

△ *Railways operated by electricity run underground in many cities today. There is usually an interchange system so that people can continue their journey by road, rail, bus or taxi.*

SIGNALS AND TRACKS

Trains run on steel railtracks, switching from one track to another at points – moving rails where tracks divide or join together to make a train change direction. Railway lines are divided into sections with a signal at the beginning of each section. The signals and points are controlled from signal boxes with the aid of computers, and the computers ensure that only one train is travelling on a section of track at a time. Signals work like traffic lights.

UNDERGROUND RAILWAYS

Many cities around the world have railways that run in tunnels under the streets. These railways are extremely useful for avoiding congestion on the roads above. The first underground railway was the Metropolitan, which opened in London in 1863. Soon after, other cities began to build underground railways – Boston in 1895, Budapest in 1896, Paris in 1898 and New York in 1904. Today, there are more than 60 underground railways throughout the world.

▷ *At a busy junction, the signal controllers keep the line free for high-speed passenger trains, or express trains, by moving local and freight trains on to sidings (tracks on the side).*

Sidings

High-speed passenger train

Signals

Signal control box

Local passenger train

Diesel freight train

Points

SEE ALSO
Computer, Diesel engine, Electricity, Engine, Industrial Revolution, Magnetism, Steam engine, Underground railway

RAILWAY HISTORY
1765 Standard gauge (width of track) established at 4ft 8½ in (1.44 m)
1804 Trevithick's first working steam train
1814 Stephenson's Blucher train begins working at a colliery
1825 Opening of the Stockton and Darlington Railway
1829 Stephenson's *Rocket* wins best steam engine at the Rainhill Trials 1830; first US railway, South Carolina
1859 First Pullman sleeping cars (USA)
1863 World's first underground railway opens in London
1869 Railway across the USA completed
1879 First electric railway (Germany)
1925 First diesel-electric train (Canada)
1938 *Mallard* set the steam speed record of 201 km/h
1964 First high-speed train Bullet trains (Japan)
1981 French TGVs start running, travelling up to 270 km/h
1984 First regular passenger maglev train service opens in UK
1994 Channel Tunnel opens; Eurostar trains take passengers between London, Paris and Brussels

continued from page 269

For example, if a piece of radioactive **uranium** was left for millions of years, it would 'decay' and turn into a piece of **lead**. Scientists measure the rate of decay in radioactive **carbon** in **animal** and **plant** remains to find out how many thousands of years ago the animals and plants lived.

Radioactive materials can be highly dangerous – a nuclear explosion causes life-threatening levels of radioactivity.

Radium

Radium is an **element**. It is found only in **uranium** ore and was first discovered by Marie **Curie** in 1898. She was examining uranium and realized that it had much more **radioactivity** than it should have had. Radium is very radioactive and dangerous to handle.

In its pure form, radium is a whitish **metal**. About five tonnes of uranium ore have to be mined (see **mining**) to produce just 1 gramme of radium. Each year, less than 75 gramme of uranium are produced in the entire world, mostly from **Zaire** and **Canada**. Radium is used in **medicine** to treat **cancer**. **Compounds** of it are used to make luminous dials glow in the dark.

Railway *see* pages 270–271

Rainbow

The wonderful **colours** of a rainbow are formed by sunlight shining on drops of rain. The best time to see a rainbow is immediately after a shower, when the clouds break up and the sunlight streams through.

Rainbows can be seen only when the **sun** is behind you and low over the horizon. When the sun's rays strike the raindrops, each drop acts as a prism and splits the **light** into a **spectrum** of **colours** ranging from red to violet. The lower the sun, the higher the rainbow and the fuller its curved arch.

Towards the end of **Ramadan**, the ninth and most holy month in the Muslim year, people search the night skies with small telescopes or binoculars. They are trying to see the crescent of the new moon because this will signal the end of the festival.

△ It is said that there is a crock of gold at the end of a **rainbow**. Nobody has ever found the treasure because a rainbow really has no end. It is a full circle. The bottom half of the circle lies below the horizon and out of sight.

Rainforest *see* pages 274–275

Ramadan

In **Islam**, Ramadan is the ninth month of the Muslim year, during which Muslims fast (go without **food**) between sunrise and sunset. The fast is one of the five 'pillars', or basic duties, of Islam and ends with **Eid**-ul-Fitr, the Festival of the Breaking of the Fast.

Rat

Rats are **rodents**. They are found all over the world in enormous numbers, and can live equally successfully in towns and the countryside. Both the black and more common brown rat will eat almost anything. They are harmful to people because they spoil **food** and they spread **disease**. Some rats carry a type of **flea** which can cause bubonic **plague** in **human beings**.

Like all rodents, rats have a set of four sharp front **teeth** called incisors. These work like chisels and they are used to graw food, chop up nesting material and get through anything that obstructs their way. Female brown rats can breed when they are only two months old and will produce as many as 12 babies a time and up to five litters a year.

In the country, most **rats** live outside and do not represent much of a health risk. But rats in cities steal food intended for humans, and are a major health hazard.

Recording

Sound can be recorded in a number of ways – on magnetic tape, tape cassettes, CDs and DVDs.

A CD is a disc on which sound information is recorded using a **laser** beam. The digital signals are represented by a series of depressions on the surface of the disc, which can then be played back using another laser. This technology is also used to create **video** discs and DVDs.

A tape recorder works by changing sound waves into **magnetism**. The sound is recorded as a magnetic pattern along the recording tape. When the tape is played, the magnetic pattern is turned back into sound.

You use a video cassette to record a **television** programme on a video recorder. The video cassette contains tape just like a sound cassette. It records the electric signal coming from the television aerial. Sound recording was pioneered by Thomas **Edison**.

To make a CD, a **recording** is fed onto a disc. Each track on the CD contains a sequence of pits which store sounds in digital form. As the disc spins in a laser beam inside the CD player, the pits reflect pulses of light onto a light-sensitive detector. This detector converts the code signals into electrical pulses. These are then changed back into reproductions of the original sounds.

Red Sea

The Red Sea is a narrow strip of **water** that is part of the **Indian Ocean**. It stretches for 1,900 km, dividing Arabia from northeast **Africa**. It has an area of about 440,300 sq km. At its northern end, it is linked to the **Mediterranean Sea** by the **Suez Canal**. Its southern end is guarded by the narrow straits of Bab el Mandeb. The Red Sea is quite a shallow body of water. As there are no major currents that flow through it, it is also very warm and salty.

Reformation

The Reformation is the name given to the period of great religious upheaval that began in **Europe** in the 1500s.

Most people think that the **refrigerator** is a recent invention. However, the one above was invented by Ferdinand Carré in France in 1858. And ice-making machines were slipped through the Union blockade of the South during the American Civil War in the 1860s.

At that time, a revolt occurred in the Roman Catholic Church. In protest at what they saw as bad practice and errors in the Church, some groups of the protesting people broke away to set up their own churches. They became known as Protestants.

What many Protestants wanted was a simpler, more basic form of **Christianity**, allowing them greater freedom to worship as they chose. As the number of Protestants grew, many rulers saw the new movement as a chance to broaden their power at the expense of the Church. They were happy to support the Protestant cause because the religious protest helped them to gain more influence. The Reformation led to wars between Protestant and Roman Catholic rulers.

Refrigerator

Refrigerators are used to keep **food** cold. The simplest ones are really just boxes, with an electric **motor** running a cooling system. Refrigerators are made from insulating material that keeps the inside of the box cold for some time, even when the motor is not running. The average **temperature** inside a fridge is between 2°C and 7°C.

The cooling system has a special **gas** in it. This gas is first compressed (squeezed) to turn it into a **liquid**. The liquid flows through hollow tubes inside the fridge into an evaporator, which turns it back into gas. The gas is then pumped on around the system. As it goes round, it draws out any **heat** from within the refrigerator.

When it is pumped outside the fridge the gas is compressed again. This turns it back into a liquid and it gives out the heat it picked up on the inside. The liquid is pumped round and round, turning from liquid to gas and back again. The **air** inside the fridge becomes colder and the heat is carried to the outside. The process works like a sort of heat sponge.

RAINFOREST

Tropical rainforests are found in an area called the tropics, around the equator, where the weather is hot and rainy. These forests are home to over half of the world's ten million species of animals and plants, and they are some of the oldest places on earth. There are tropical rainforests in South and Central America, Africa and parts of Southeast Asia and Australia. Each rainforest is different. Some animals and plants can only be found in rainforests in one area. Lemurs, for example, which are related to monkeys, are only found in the rainforests on the island of Madagascar.

▷ *All kinds of animal live in the canopy of a rainforest – birds, monkeys, snakes, butterflies and tree frogs find plenty to eat and places to shelter. Giant woody plants called lianas loop from one tree to another and hummingbirds feed on the nectar and pollen in orchid flowers.*

Emerald tree boa

Bromeliad

Tamandua

LAYERS OF A RAINFOREST

Rainforests are made up of millions of trees. It rains nearly every day and many plants and trees grow quickly, becoming very tall. The tallest trees in a forest are known as the emergents. Below them, the canopy is made up of the tops of the smaller trees. The canopy is home to insects, birds, reptiles, amphibians and more than half the mammals of the rainforest.

The area between the canopy and the forest floor is called the understorey. This is a darker, cooler environment below the branches and leaves of the trees. Because of all the foliage, it can take up to 10 minutes for rain to reach the forest floor. All kinds of animals live here, including anteaters, lemurs and tree kangaroos. The forest floor is full of small forms of life, especially insects, as well as large animals, such as forest elephants. Many of the animals are nocturnal – they only come out to hunt for food at night.

RAINFOREST FOOD AND MEDICINE

The rainforest is a treasure trove of millions of plants. At least 80 percent of the developed world's diet originated in a rainforest environment. These foods include coffee, cacao beans for chocolate, bananas, pineapples, vanilla, peanuts, potatoes, pepper and sugar. There are at least 3,000 types of fruit in the Amazon rainforest. In the West, we grow and eat only 200 of them, while the local people use 2,000.

Many of the plants have medicinal properties that have not yet been fully researched. An extraordinary quarter of the world's medicines are derived from rainforest ingredients, and yet only one percent of the tree and plant species have been tested by scientists. Many rainforest plants are disappearing. For example, the rosy periwinkle, originally from the island of Madagascar off the coast of Africa, is used to make a medicine to treat a type of cancer called leukaemia. Unfortunately, it is now extinct in the wild.

▷ *The high branches of the trees are covered with plants and flowers called epiphytes. Some have spongy roots that hang from the branches and absorb moisture from the air. Bromeliads collect water in overlapped leaves at their base. More than 28,000 different kinds of epiphyte grow on rainforest trees.*

Harpy
eagle

Toco toucan

Spider
monkeys

Liana

Sloth

Hummingbird

Tree frog

IN DANGER

Rainforests are very important. Without them, weather patterns change – there is less rain, fewer plants, and when it does rain, there can be more flooding because there are fewer trees to soak up the water. Rainforests also remove carbon dioxide from the atmosphere and help prevent global warming – the greenhouse effect.

But rainforests are under threat. In 1950, they covered 14 percent of the world's land surface, but now they cover just 6 percent. They are being cut down for wood and to clear land for farming and grazing animals, especially in poor countries. Scientists estimate that we lose over 137 species of rainforest plants, animals and insects every day. This amounts to 50,000 species a year. Rainforests are disappearing at such a rate that they may vanish completely by 2040.

There are many groups of people living in tropical rainforests around the world. Some of them, such as the Yanomamo tribe of the Amazon forests of Brazil and southern Venezuela, have lived in villages there for hundreds, sometimes even thousands, of years.
The populations are declining either because of diseases caught from non-rainforest people or because of government land seizure. If indigenous people die out, a whole way of life and a massive amount of plant and animal knowledge dies with them.

SEE ALSO
Amazon River, Amphibians and Reptiles, Birds, Global warming, Insects, Madagascar, Mammals, Medicine, Plants, Trees, Weather

One result of hostility between the Arabs and the Jews in 1948 was the migration of nearly one million Arabs from Palestine. They left their homes and became **refugees** because they were afraid of the action Israel might take after the war with the Arab League.

Rembrandt excelled as a portrait painter, and many of his portraits were of himself. This one was painted late in his life, in 1661–1662.

Refugee

A refugee is a person who seeks shelter or protection from danger or trouble in another country. They may be trying to escape religious or political persecution, **famine** or **flood**. There are many refugee organizations today that provide international assistance to people who have had to leave their own country. The main one is the **United Nations** High Commissioner for Refugees (UNHCR), which gives protection and assistance to more than 22 million refugees and displaced people around the world, the majority of whom are women and children.

Relativity

If you are travelling in a **car** at 60 km/h and you are overtaken by another car travelling at 80 km/h, the second car pulls away from you at 20 km/h. Its true speed relative to the ground is 80 km/h, but its speed relative to you is 20 km/h. This is the basic idea of relativity. Assuming you are not moving, it works out the speed of something that is moving relative to you.

At the end of the last century, scientists discovered that the speed of **light** is always the same, no matter how fast the source of the light is moving. In 1905, Albert **Einstein** put forward his special theory of relativity to explain this strange fact. His theory concerns, among other things, the effect of motion on **time**, length and mass. For instance, the theory predicts that, in a spaceship hurtling across the **universe** at nearly the speed of light, time would pass more slowly, the spaceship's length would become smaller and its mass would become greater than on a similar spaceship stationary on **earth**. Later, in 1915, Einstein produced his general theory of relativity. This theory has helped scientists understand more about space, **gravity** and the nature of the universe.

Religion

The five great religions today are **Buddhism** (based on the teachings of **Buddha**), **Christianity** (based on the teachings of **Jesus**), **Hinduism** (followed by Hindus), **Islam** (followed by Muslims) and **Judaism** (followed by Jews). All are very ancient. The most recent is Islam, which was founded about 1,300 years ago by **Muhammad**. The largest religion, Christianity, has about two billion followers.

There are also some people who follow ancient religions based on the worship of **gods** and spirits. Often these gods are seen as part of the natural world – rocks, trees and lakes.

Buildings that are devoted to religious worship include magnificent shrines, temples and **churches**. Statues and works of art are used to give religious messages or tell stories. Specially trained priests and holy people say prayers and lead religious ceremonies. They also study the **laws** and teachings of the religion. These are often written down in holy **books**, for example, the **Bible** and the **Koran**.

Rembrandt

Rembrandt van Rijn (1606–1669) is one of the most famous of all Dutch painters. Helped by assistants in his large studio, he produced an amazing 650 oil **paintings**, 2,000 drawings and studies, and 300 etchings.

Rembrandt is best known for his portraits of the wealthy townspeople of **Holland**, particularly in Amsterdam, where he lived most of his life. Unlike many other painters, he became very successful while he was still alive. However, later in his career, many of the wealthy people no longer bought his pictures because they did not like the way his style of painting had changed. In the end, he was living in poverty, but it was at this time that he painted some of his best works.

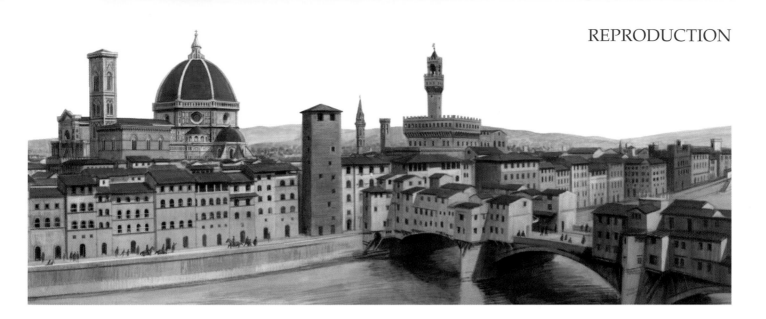

Renaissance

The Renaissance is the name given to a period of about 200 years in the **history** of **Europe**. The word means 'rebirth' in French, and the Renaissance was the time when people again became interested in every aspect of **art**, **science**, **architecture** and literature.

Since the times of the ancient Greeks and Romans there had been little interest in new ideas. Then, during the 1300s, Italian scholars began to take a fresh interest in the past. They also looked for new scientific explanations of the mysteries of the world and the **universe**. During the Renaissance, a great number of painters, sculptors and architects were at work in **Italy**. The works of art of Leonardo **da Vinci** and **Michelangelo** are among the most famous achievements of this time. From Italy, the ideas of the Renaissance quickly spread to the rest of Europe.

There was a great growth in **trade** at the same time as all these artistic and scientific ideas. Later, there were voyages to explore **Africa** and **India**, and in 1492, **North America** was discovered by Christopher **Columbus**.

Reproduction

Reproduction is the process by which **plants** and **animals** make new plants and animals like themselves. Some plants and animals can reproduce on their own by simply splitting in two. Many plants reproduce asexually by producing buds that drop off and plant themselves. Others produce spores that may be carried away by **wind** or **water**, or on an animal's fur.

In sexual reproduction, a male **cell** called a sperm joins with, or fertilizes, a female cell called an ovum or **egg**, to form a new fertilized cell. This cell divides over and over again until a whole new organism has been formed.

Most female **fish** lay their eggs in the water. The male swims over the eggs and releases his sperm on them. The developing fish, or embryo, grows while using the store of food inside the egg.

In many animals, fertilization takes place inside the female's body. After fertilization, the female **bird** or **reptile** lays her eggs. The embryo develops inside the egg until it is ready to hatch out. In **mammals**, fertilization also takes place inside the female, but the embryo develops inside its mother, receiving food from her bloodstream until it is ready to be born. After birth, the mother feeds it with her **milk**.

The number of offspring a mother gives birth to at one time depends on the number of eggs fertilized. In human mothers, usually only one egg is fertilized. If more than one is fertilized, there may be twins or triplets.

△ During the **Renaissance**, Florence was the cultural and intellectual centre of Italy. Revived interest in classic art and architecture began in Florence, and the first academy of art was founded there in 1563.

▽ For **reproduction**, the parts of the body are very different in women and men. The woman produces eggs in her ovaries. These travel down the oviducts and, if fertilized by sperm provided by a man during sexual intercourse, may develop into a baby in the woman's uterus, or womb (below). Men produce millions of sperm in their testicles. The sperm and the egg each contain half of what is needed to make another human being.

Reptile
see **Amphibians and Reptiles**

Republic

A republic is a form of **government** in which the people are supposed to rule themselves. Usually they hold **elections** to choose their leaders. Many republics have been formed to take over powers from rulers who are considered to be reigning unfairly. The first republics were in Ancient **Greece** and Rome (see **Roman Empire**), but many of the people in these countries were slaves (see **slavery**). Today, some republics are run by people who have not been elected by the people. There are both communist (see **communism**) and democratic (see **democracy**) republics.

Revolution

A revolution is the usually violent overthrowing of a **government** or political system by those who are governed, for example the American **Revolutionary War**. Sometimes revolutions are peaceful but effective rejections of a system. For instance, there can be a revolution in ideas – a complete change in a way of thinking about a particular subject.

Revolutionary War, American

The Revolutionary War was fought between Great Britain and her 13 American colonies from 1775 to 1783. The colonies won their independence from Britain and became a new nation, the **United States of America**.

For many years before the war, Britain and the American colonies had disagreed about a number of things, in particular **taxes**. The British tried to force the colonies to pay, but would not allow them any representation in

British grenadier c.1775

American revolutionary soldier c.1775

▽ **Rhinoceroses** have poor eyesight, and this would make them an easy target for hunters, except that they have heightened senses of hearing and smell.

the British **parliament**. The colonies responded by insisting on 'no taxation without representation'.

The first shot in the war was fired at Lexington, Massachusetts, on 19 April 1775. In July, George **Washington** was made commander of the American forces. On 4 July 1776, the colonies declared their independence.

At first the war went badly for the Americans, but in October 1777, the British were defeated at the Battle of Saratoga, in New York. This was the turning-point. On 19 October 1781, a British army under Charles Cornwallis (1738–1805) surrendered to Washington. The final peace treaty, the Treaty of Paris, was signed in 1783.

Rhinoceros

Sometimes described as a 'tank on legs', the rhinoceros is one of the largest and strongest of all land **animals**. A fully grown male can weigh as much as 3.5 tonnes. This massive beast has a tough leathery skin and sprouts one or two **horns** (actually made of hair) on its snout. These may grow as long as 127 cm.

The rhinoceros lives in **Africa** and **Southeast Asia** where it feeds on leafy twigs, shrubs and **grasses**. Although an adult rhino has no natural enemies, it is so widely hunted for its horns that it has become an endangered species. When ground into a powder, rhino horn is believed, wrongly, to be a powerful **medicine**.

Rice

Rice is a member of the **grass** family. It is one of the most important **cereal** crops in the world, and it is the main **food** of most people in southern **Asia**. Young shoots of rice are planted in flooded areas called paddy fields, where they grow in 5 to 10 cm of **water** until they are ready to be harvested. Young rice has long, narrow leaves and clusters of **flowers** that turn into the grains we eat.

Over hundreds of years, **rivers** carve valleys out of the land as they flow towards the sea. From tiny mountain streams of melted snow, they grow and swell, picking up mineral and other deposits as they flow through the landscape. These deposits sink to the bottom when the rivers slow down as they near the sea, forming great deltas.

River

Rivers are one of the most important geographical features in the world. They range in size from small streams to waterways that flow for thousands of kilometres. The greatest rivers in the world are the **Amazon**, the **Mississippi** and the **Nile**. They all drain huge areas of land. The basin of the Amazon stretches over an area larger than all of western **Europe**. Some rivers serve as transport links that allow ocean-going **ships** to sail far inland. In tropical **rainforests** they are often the only way to travel. Rivers with **dams** supply power to produce **electricity**. **Water** from rivers is also used to irrigate farmland in **desert** lands and other dry parts of the world (see **irrigation**).

Road

The Romans were the first great road-builders, and some of their long, straight roads survive. They made their roads with gravel and stones. The surface paving stones were arched so the rain would run off into ditches.

Modern road building began during the **Industrial Revolution**. In the early

▽ Modern **roads** are made up of a smooth layer of concrete, or of asphalt and small stones, over a base course of 4 cm stones and a sub-base of stone to even the ground.

This Japanese industrial **robot** can do a variety of jobs depending on how it is controlled. The automated arm can weld metal, use a paint spray or move objects from place to place.

1800s, a Scottish engineer, John McAdam (1756–1836), became the pioneer of modern road-making, but the stony surfaces of his roads were not good for vehicles with rubber tyres. Later, 'macadamized' roads were built. They are covered with tar or asphalt to make them smooth. Many roads, especially motorways, are now made of concrete.

Robot

In films and books set in the future, robots often look like **metal** people and they can walk, talk and even think. Real robots are very different. They are **machines** with limbs that can move in several directions. They are made in various different shapes – some like people, and others like **insects**. They are programmable. This means they can be instructed to carry out different tasks. The instructions, or programs, are stored in the robot's **computer** brain. Most robots work in industry and do jobs such as paint spraying, welding, and heavy lifting and loading. Some robots work in places that are dangerous for humans, such as nuclear **power stations** and space.

Rock

Rocks consist of grains of **minerals**. Igneous rocks form when magma (molten rock) hardens. Some harden on the surface to form rocks like basalt and obsidian, while others harden underground to form rocks like **granite**. Sedimentary rocks are composed of sediments, like **sand**. For example, conglomerates are rocks made up of pebbles and sand and many limestones are made of sediments formed mainly from the remains of dead **plants** and **animals**. Metamorphic rocks are igneous or sedimentary rocks that have been changed by great **heat** and pressure – limestones may be metamorphosed (changed) into **marble**.

Rocket

A **firework** rocket and the rockets that took astronauts to the **moon** (see **space exploration**) work in much the same way. Both burn **fuel** to produce hot **gases**. The gases shoot out backwards and this creates a force that thrusts the rocket forwards. Rockets do not need **air** for their **engines**, unlike **jets**, so they are ideal for moving in space where there is no air.

The Chinese used rockets as weapons as early as the 1200s. Rockets used to launch **satellites** and spacecraft were developed after **World War II**. They

Soil
Hardened rock
Molten granite

are multi-stage rockets, which means several rockets joined together. Each stage fires in turn.

Fuel for early rockets, such as **Germany**'s V2 in **World War II**, was a mixture of kerosene and **oxygen**. Today's space rockets use **liquid** fuels – usually a liquid called hydrazine or liquid **hydrogen**. In a liquid-fuel rocket, the fuel needs oxygen before it will burn. The fuel and the oxidizer are stored in separate tanks. When they are both pumped into a combustion chamber, they burn explosively and produce the gases that rush out of a nozzle and give lift to the spacecraft.

Rocky Mountains

The Rocky Mountains are a huge range of **mountains** 4,800 km long in **North America**. They stretch from **Alaska** through western **Canada** and the **USA**, as far south as New Mexico. The highest peak, Mount Elbert, is in the USA, 4,399 m above sea level. In Canada, the highest point is Mount Robson at 3,954 m. The 'Rockies' have several national parks, including Yellowstone, Banff and Glacier, and many wild **animals** live in them.

Rodent

Rodents are a group of gnawing **animals**. They have large, sharp front **teeth** that grow all the time. They wear down these teeth by gnawing their **food**. They also use their teeth to dig burrows in the ground for their homes and **nests**. **Beavers** are able to cut down large trees for their **dams** with their gnawing teeth.

The 2,000 or so rodents include mice, **rats**, **porcupines** and **squirrels**. The South American capybara is the largest rodent. It looks like a giant **guinea pig**, grows to a length of 1.25 m and weighs over 45 kg. The smallest rodent is the European harvest **mouse**. It grows only about 7 cm long.

Command module

THIRD STAGE

Liquid oxygen

Liquid hydrogen

SECOND STAGE

Liquid oxygen

Liquid oxygen

FIRST STAGE

Liquid oxygen

Kerosene fuel

△ The **rocket** *Saturn V* took the US *Apollo 11* crew to the moon in 1969. It had three separate sections, or stages. After the powerful first stage ran out of fuel, it fell away and the second stage engines ignited. When the fuel in this stage was used up, the third stage engines helped it complete its journey to the moon.

◁ This section shows an igneous **rock** – granite – in its molten form rising towards the surface. As it goes, it pushes the layers of already hardened rock and soil above it into a dome shape.

Rodeo

Rodeos are exciting shows where American **cowboys** show off their skills. In bareback riding, a cowboy rides a bronco (a half-wild or bad-tempered **horse**). In saddle-bronco riding, the cowboy rides one-handed, using one rein, a saddle and a halter. Bull-riding and calf-roping are other events. In steer wrestling, the cowboy chases a young bull, or steer, on horseback, grabs its head and pulls the steer down. The first recorded rodeo was held in 1869.

Roman Empire
see **pages 282–283**

Romania

Romania is a small country in southeast **Europe**. It has beautiful **mountains** and many **forests**. Most of its people farm, but there is also **mining** and **oil** production. In 1989, the Romanians overthrew the corrupt communist **government** (see **communism**). A new democratic constitution (see **democracy**) was introduced in 1991 and free **elections** were held in the 1990s.

Rome

Rome is the capital of **Italy**. With a population of 2,645,000, it is also Italy's largest city. Rome stands on the Tiber **River**, about 27 km from the **Mediterranean Sea**. Many tourists visit Rome to see the great ruins of ancient Rome (see **Roman Empire**), and the beautiful **churches**, fountains, palaces and art galleries.

Roosevelt, Franklin D.

Franklin Delano Roosevelt (1882–1945) was the 32nd **president** of the **USA**. Born in **New York** into a

wealthy family, he trained as a lawyer. By 1923, he had become paralysed, but this did not stop him becoming governor of New York in 1928. He was elected president in 1932, and was immediately faced with the economic crisis known as the Great Depression. Roosevelt responded with a 'New Deal' programme which was so successful that he was re-elected by a landslide victory in 1936 and secured a third term in 1940 and a fourth in 1944. He took his country into **World War II** on the side of the Allies and met with **Churchill** and **Stalin** at Tehran in 1943 and Yalta in 1945.

Roses, Wars of the

The Wars of the Roses was the name given to a struggle between Lancaster and York for control of the English throne in the 1400s. The wars were named after emblems, a red rose for Lancaster and a white rose for York.

For many years, York was the winning side. Not until Lancastrian Henry Tudor defeated Richard III at Bosworth Field in 1485, and married Elizabeth of York, did the two houses unite. The crown passed to the Tudors.

A **rodeo** gives the cowboy a chance to show off riding and roping skills. However, many are thrown out of the saddle in the bucking bronco contests.

ROMANIA
Government: Republic
Capital: Bucharest
Area: 237,500 sq km
Population: 22.5 million
Languages: Romanian, Hungarian and German
Currency: Leu

◁ *This map shows the extent of the Roman Empire c.100 CE. The Romans – citizens of Rome – became so powerful that they began to conquer lands around them. By 100 CE, they ruled a huge empire, and were one of the mightiest peoples in the ancient world.*

▷ *Most Roman soldiers had to stay in the army for 25 years. Those who were Roman citizens were luckier – they could leave after just 20. They were far from home, and had to put up with danger, tough training and harsh punishments.*

Roman Empire

The Roman Empire (c.449 BCE–476 CE) was one of the most powerful ancient civilizations ever to have existed. At the height of its power, it controlled all the land from the Mediterranean in the south to Germany in the north, and from England in the west to central Asia in the east. At its centre was the capital, Rome, the largest city in the world with an estimated one million inhabitants.

RULED BY THE SENATE

Rome was ruled by a senate, an assembly that was governed mainly by the rich aristocracy in Rome. The highest office in the senate was that of consul. Two consuls ruled together for a year, ensuring that no one man could achieve total rule over the state. The rights of the poor were protected by two other offices in the Senate called the tribunes.

THE EMPIRE IS BORN

In 45 BCE, Julius Caesar (c.100–44 BCE) received the title 'Father of

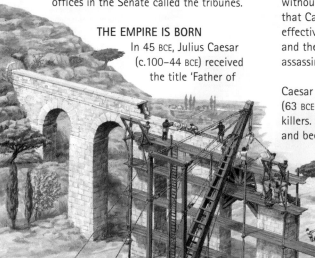

his Country'. He was also made consul for ten years and granted the office of Perpetual Dictator by the Senate. It was the greatest honour that could be bestowed on an individual, and it allowed him to act without approval from the senate. The fact that Caesar was made dictator in perpetuity effectively meant the end of the Roman Republic and the start of the Empire. In 44 BCE, Caesar was assassinated by his rivals.

Caesar was followed by his adopted son Octavian (63 BCE–14 CE) who successfully pursued his father's killers. Octavian then changed his name to Augustus and became the second Emperor of Rome.

◁ *The inventive ability of the Romans was shown time and time again. These aqueducts were built in around 128 CE to provide Romans with water every day.*

TIME OF CHANGE

It was in Augustus' reign that a huge project to improve the city was started in Rome. Augustus believed that Rome should be an example to the Empire of the power and might of the Romans. He famously claimed that he had found Rome a city of wood and left it a city of marble.

The Caesars continued to rule Rome in a dynasty that lasted many generations. During this time the living conditions in the Empire changed dramatically. Many of the nations that were conquered by the Romans were, to use the Roman word, extremely 'barbaric'. The Romans introduced many things that changed life in the provinces forever. Central-heating, baths, wine and paved roads are all Roman inventions.

GLADIATORS AND AMPHITHEATRES

Another famous Roman creation was the Games. The Romans celebrated the lives of famous citizens by holding gladiatorial contests in amphitheatres – notably the Colosseum in Rome. In these contests, slave gladiators would fight to the death for the pleasure of the Roman people. There would also be the public execution of prisoners and the matching of men against terrifying foreign beasts such as the tiger and hippopotamus. Another popular form of public entertainment was the staging of historical battles on a lifelike scale, with real combatants. Famously, this included the staging of sea battles on a huge flooded plain.

A NATION OF SLAVES

In many ways, the Roman Empire only survived because of its huge slave population. The Romans forced most of their conquered opponents into slavery, and the slaves did most of the manual labour in the Empire, working on the farms and in the highly dangerous mines, as well as in the houses of the rich Romans.

THE FALL OF THE ROMAN EMPIRE

Over time, the Roman Empire changed a great deal. The Emperor Constantine (ruled 324–337 CE), was the first emperor to tolerate Christianity. Gradually the whole Empire also became Christian. The seat of the Empire also moved from Rome to Byzantium, later Constantinople (modern Istanbul). This became the eastern Roman Empire.

It became harder and harder to defend the borders of the Empire, until in 455 CE, the Vandals from Germany finally managed to sack the city of Rome. The last Roman emperor Romulus Augustus was deposed in 476 CE and his throne taken by a German chief, Odoacer (d.493). This event marked the end of the Roman Empire and the beginning of the 'Dark Ages'. Some of the Roman colonies, such as Great Britain, returned to pre-Roman ways, losing the technological advantages that they had gained under Roman rule.

△ On special days of the Roman calendar, people flocked to see spectacular shows at the amphitheatre. Christians, criminals and slaves were thrown into a ring with lions and other animals, and were chased, wounded and killed.

▽ Rome's spiritual heart was the forum or market-place where Romans met to conduct business.

SEE ALSO
Caesar (Julius), Calendar, Christianity, Colosseum, Dark Ages, Dictator, Gladiator, Italy, Republic, Road, Rome, Wine

RUSSIA
Government: Republic
Capital: Moscow
Area: 17,075,000 sq km
Population: 146.2 million
Language: Russian
Currency: Rouble

RWANDA
Government: Republic
Capital: Kigali
Area: 26,338 sq km
Population: 8.3 million
Languages: French and
Kinyarwandu
Currency: Rwanda franc

▷ During the **Russian Revolution**, armed workers were supported by soldiers and sailors. On 6 November 1917, they attacked the Winter Palace in Petrograd (today's St Petersburg). Although it was the headquarters of the tsar's government, it was weakly defended and soon in their hands.

Rubber

Rubber is an important material with many uses in industry and the home. Most natural rubber comes from the rubber **tree**. When the bark of the tree is cut, a white juice called latex oozes out. The juice is collected and made into rubber. Today, most natural rubber comes from **Malaysia** and **Indonesia**.

Scientists found ways of making synthetic rubber during **World War I**. Synthetic rubber is made from **oil** and **coal**. About two-thirds of the rubber used today is synthetic rubber.

Rugby *see* Sport

Russia

Russia is by far the largest of the countries that formed from the former **Soviet Union**. It contains more people than the other states put together and has most of the great cities, including **Moscow** and St Petersburg. It is rich in **mineral** resources and is industrially powerful. **Farming**, including **cereal** crops and **cattle**, is also important.

Russian Revolution

The Russian Revolution was, in fact, two revolutions in one year. In 1917, Russia was ruled by Tsar Nicholas II

(1868–1918), the peasants were repressed and the urban poor had no civil rights. After mass demonstrations by workers and soldiers in Petrograd, the tsar was forced to abdicate in February, and a short period of democratic rule by the middle classes followed (see **democracy**). However, there were still many social problems and **Lenin**, leader of the Communist Party (see **communism**), took advantage of this to start an uprising in many major cities. In November 1917, Lenin seized power and established the first Soviet **government**. The tsar and his entire family were shot in 1918.

Rust

Rust is a brownish-red crust that forms on ordinary **iron and steel** when they are left in damp air. As rust forms, the surface of the **metal** is eaten away. Grease, **oil** and paint protect the **metal**.

Rwanda

Rwanda is a small country in central **Africa**. Much of the country is mountainous and the **climate** is cool and pleasant. The Rwandan people farm, producing **coffee**, **tea**, maize and beans. They also raise **cattle**. The country is one of the most densely populated in Africa. Rwanda became independent in 1962. In 1994, it was torn apart by **civil war**.

S

Sailing a boat takes great skill. The boat is steered with a lever called a tiller. This moves the rudder – a board at the back of the boat.

Sailing

At one time, nearly all types of **ship** used sails. But by the mid-1800s, sailing ships had been largely replaced by steamships. Today, people sail mostly for pleasure or **sport**.

Sailing boats vary in size from small dinghies to large yachts. The hull, or body, of the boat is made of fibreglass or moulded plywood. The sails are usually made of a synthetic material such as nylon. They can be moved to catch the **wind** by pulling on ropes, called rigging. Sailing boats can sail in any direction, except straight into the wind.

One of the most famous sailing races is for the America's Cup, which began in 1870. Sailing has been an **Olympic** sport since 1908.

Strangely eroded rocks, sand and salts shimmer in the heat of the Libyan Desert. This harsh, dry landscape is part of the enormous **Sahara Desert**, in northern Africa.

Sahara Desert

The Sahara is the world's largest hot **desert**, covering about 9.1 million sq km of northern **Africa**. It extends from the **Atlantic Ocean** in the west to the **Red Sea** in the east. In the north, it stretches to the **Mediterranean** coast of **Libya** and **Egypt**. In recent years, very little **rain** has fallen on the lands south of the Sahara. Because of this, the desert is spreading southwards.

About a third of the Sahara is covered by **sand**. Other parts are covered by gravel and stones, or by bare **rock**. The Sahara is the hottest place on **earth** – the world's highest air **temperature** in the shade, 57.7°C, was recorded there.

Salamander and Newt

Salamanders are **amphibians** with short legs and long tails. As adults, some salamanders live in damp woods, while others spend their lives in ponds and streams. Most salamanders feed on **worms** and **insects** and have smooth, shiny **skin**.

Salamanders in **Europe** and **North America** that spend long periods in **water** are called newts. Many adult newts have webbed tails, and some males grow a crest down their backs at breeding time. Most male newts perform a complicated dance to attract a female.

△ Most **salamanders** produce poison from glands in their skin. This fire salamander's bright colours are a warning to predators to stay away.

▽ Two **salmon** leap up a waterfall on their way to their breeding grounds. Salmon use so much energy during the journey that they can lose half their body weight.

Salmon

Salmon are **fish** that breed in shallow **rivers**. After the **eggs** hatch, the young fish swim down the river to the sea. The salmon spend their adult lives in the sea, before returning to their birthplace to breed.

Pure **salt** crystals are cube shaped. We need to eat some salt every day, because the body loses it all the time – in sweat for example.

△ In 1906, the San Andreas fault moved 6.5 m, causing an earthquake that devastated San Francisco. Much of the city burned down as the gas mains broke and caught fire.

This may mean a journey of hundreds or even thousands of kilometres. Most salmon die after laying their eggs.

Salt

The chemical name for the salt we eat is sodium chloride. We need some salt to stay healthy, but not too much. Salt is also used to preserve **foods** and to make **dyes**, **paper**, **pottery**, **leather** and many **medicines**. Much of our salt comes from sea **water**, but some is mined from deposits in the ground.

Sand

Sand is a loose material made up of small grains of **rock**. Sand grains are smaller than those in gravel, but larger than those in silt or mud. On **seashores**, sand piles up to form sandy beaches. Inland, in dry places, it forms hills called dunes. Sand is also an important ingredient in **soil**. Layers of sand in the ground may be pressed together to form a hard rock called sandstone – the second most common rock in the world. The main **mineral** in sand is **quartz**.

▽ Weather **satellites** take photographs of weather conditions from space. The information they send back to earth allows accurate weather forecasts to be made several days in advance.

San Francisco

San Francisco, in California, is a hilly city that lies on the **Pacific** coast of the **United States**. It is a major port and financial centre, and has a **population** of 732,000. The most famous of the five **bridges** that cross San Francisco Bay is the Golden Gate Bridge, a suspension bridge built in 1937.

San Francisco has suffered several strong **earthquakes** because it is built across the San Andreas fault. In 1906, most of the city was destroyed by severe tremors and raging fires. The most recent strong quake was in 1989.

Satellite

A body that moves in **orbit** around another body is called a satellite. The **earth** and the other **planets** in the **solar system** are satellites of the **sun**. The **moon** is just one of earth's many satellites. The others are artificial satellites launched by **rockets** into fixed orbits. **Weather** satellites have **cameras** that send back pictures of cloud and storm formations. **Communications** satellites relay **television** and **telephone** signals around the world. They have **radio** and other equipment powered by **batteries** charged by the sun's rays. The satellites receive a signal from a transmitting station on earth, amplify it, and beam it down to another earth station, which may be many thousands of kilometres away.

The first artificial satellite was *Sputnik 1*, launched by the former **Soviet Union** in 1957.

Saturn

Saturn is the second largest **planet** in the **solar system** after **Jupiter**. It measures about 120,200 km across. Saturn is famous for the rings that circle it. These are very thin, and are made of billions of icy particles.

The particles in the rings may be the remains of a **moon** that drifted too close to Saturn and broke up.

To the naked eye, Saturn looks like a bright **star**. The planet is actually mostly made up of light **gases**, and it is less dense than **water**, but scientists think that it may have a solid core. Saturn has at least 23 **satellites**. The largest, Titan, measures about 5,200 km across – larger than **Mercury**. Titan is the only known moon to have an atmosphere – a layer of gases surrounding it.

Saudi Arabia

Saudi Arabia is a large country that occupies most of the Arabian peninsula in southwest **Asia**. It is named after the Saudi family which has ruled the country since it was founded in 1932. In 1933, **oil** was discovered along the Persian Gulf coast. Today, it is estimated that Saudi Arabia has about one-quarter of the world's oil reserves. The money from oil has been used to modernize the country. During the **Gulf War** (1991), Saudi Arabia was the base for the Allied forces' liberation of Kuwait.

Savanna

Savanna is a large area of tropical grassland. The land is flat or gently rolling and covered by **grasses**.

Trees and bushes are scattered among the grasses or clustered along streams and **rivers**.

Savanna is found in southern **Brazil** and **Australia**, but mainly in **Africa**. These regions have wet and dry **seasons**. The grasses grow quickly, flower and produce **seeds** in the short wet season. They die back or do not grow in the longer dry season.

On the African savanna, the **temperature** is hot all year round. Herds of grazing **animals**, such as **zebra**, wildebeest and **elephants** wander across the savanna in search of **food** and **water**. These animals are hunted by predators such as **lions**, cheetahs and **hyenas**.

School

Nearly all countries try to provide enough schools to give their children some education. In many countries, it is the **law** that children have to go to school between certain ages, such as between 5 and 16. But some poorer countries do not have enough schools or teachers. They try to make sure that children go to school for long enough to learn to read, write and use **numbers**. However, nearly a third of the world's people over 15 cannot read or write.

Saturn's rings are less than 30 m thick, and are made up of pieces of ice, rock and dust. They form a band that, measured across, is more than 20 times the diameter of the earth.

SAUDI ARABIA
Government: Monarchy
Capital: Riyadh
Area: 2,149,690 sq km
Population: 20,198,000
Language: Arabic
Currency: Riyal

Science

The main divisions of science are **astronomy**, **biology**, **chemistry**, **geology**, **mathematics**, **medicine** and **physics**, which deals with the different types of **energy**.

Modern scientists use the scientific method. First they observe, or look at, something carefully to find out everything they can about it. Then they make a theory which explains what the thing is made of, or how it works. Then they test the theory with experiments. If the experiments agree with the theory, it becomes a **law** of science. Sometimes a law is changed when scientists discover new facts about something. Science is always changing.

Scientific studies began in early times. Great advances were made during the first civilizations, especially in Ancient **Greece** and **China**. Science nearly died out in **Europe** in the **Middle Ages**, but during the **Renaissance**, scientists began making discoveries that changed the way people thought and lived. This process accelerated during the **Industrial Revolution**, and scientific research has been speeding up ever since.

The French author Jules Verne wrote some of the first **science fiction** stories. This illustration is from *20,000 Leagues Under the Sea*, published in 1870.

Science fiction

Stories which are set in the future or on other **planets** are called science fiction. The writers often use new scientific discoveries in their stories. They imagine how these discoveries might change the world in the future.

Many science fiction stories are about space travel and **time** travel, and meetings with or between creatures from other planets.

Jules Verne (1828–1905) and H. G. Wells (1866–1946) were two of the first great science fiction writers. Recent writers include Isaac Asimov, Ray Bradbury and Arthur C. Clarke.

Scorpion

Scorpions are related to **spiders**, and mostly live in warm, dry places. They have four pairs of legs, a pair of large claws and a poisonous sting in their tail. Scorpions use the sting to stun or kill their prey. The **poison** can make people ill, but it very rarely kills them.

Scotland

Scotland is part of the **United Kingdom**. Most Scots live in the south of the country, in Glasgow, Scotland's largest city, and Edinburgh, the capital. Most of Scotland's industry is also found in the south. The Highlands have very few people and many beautiful **mountains** and lochs. Ben Nevis, at 1,343 m, is the highest mountain in the UK. There are many **islands** off the Scottish coast, such as the Hebrides, Orkneys and Shetlands.

Scotland joined with **England** and **Wales** in 1707, but, in 1997, the Scots voted in favour of having their own **parliament**. In 1999, the people elected the parliament, which has powers to vary its **taxes** and run its own **health** and education services. Scotland has its own executive (cabinet), which is headed by the First Minister.

▽ Baby **scorpions** hatch inside the mother's body, and then cling to her back for the first week or two of their lives. Once they climb down, they live on their own.

Scott, Robert Falcon

Captain Robert Falcon Scott (1868–1912) was an English naval officer and an **explorer** of the **Antarctic**. His first expedition was in 1901–1904. In 1911, he began a march to the **South Pole** with four companions. After a great struggle, he reached the Pole on 17 January 1912, but he was disappointed to find that Roald **Amundsen**, of **Norway**, had been there just a month earlier. Scott and his companions died in a snowstorm on the journey back.

Scott, Walter

Sir Walter Scott (1771–1832) was one of the most popular writers in the English **language**. Born in Edinburgh, **Scotland**, he became a lawyer, but was more interested in Scottish **history** and folklore. He wrote **poetry** and many novels of historical adventures, including *Rob Roy* and *Ivanhoe*.

Scouting

Scouting is an international movement for boys and girls. It was founded in **England** in 1907 by Robert Baden-Powell (1857–1941) for boys only. In 1910, a similar organization, the Girl Guides, was founded. The movement spread rapidly to other countries.

Children from the age of 6 or 7 to 11 belong to the Cub or Brownie units. Teenagers from 14 upwards become Venture Scouts or Ranger Guides.

One aim of scouting is to build character and self-reliance in young people throughout the world. Another is to teach helpfulness to others.

Screw

A screw is a simple **machine**. There are many kinds of screws, but the best known are the **metal** ones used to join things together. The spiral part of a screw is called the thread. When a

△ **Screws** can be twisted by a tool called a screwdriver – a kind of lever that moves in a circle. When you turn the handle, the force of the turn travels down the shaft to the blade of the screwdriver, and then into the screw.

screw is turned round in a piece of **wood** by a screwdriver, the thread pulls the screw into the wood.

Sculpture

Sculpture is a way of making attractive models, statues and objects as works of **art**. They may be carved from stone or **wood**, or they may be made by casting. To make a cast, the sculptor first makes a model in **clay** or wax. This model is used to make a mould. Hot molten **metal**, such as **bronze**, is then poured into the mould. When the metal has cooled and hardened, it is taken out of the mould. The metal 'cast' is a perfect copy of the original model.

Early Greek statues were models for **Renaissance** sculptors such as **Michelangelo**, who was possibly the finest sculptor ever. Many modern sculptors have moved away from lifelike figures. Great artists, such as Henry Moore (1898–1986), have made **abstract** figures and groups.

△ *The Thinker* (1880) is one of the best-known **sculptures** by the French artist, Auguste Rodin (1840–1917).

Sea anemone

Sea anemones are soft-bodied, tube-like **animals**. They are closely related to **corals**, but they do not build a hard cup around themselves as corals do. Sea anemones cling to **rocks**. Many live on or near the **seashore**. They have one or more rings of petal-like tentacles around their mouths.

A **sea anemone** attaches itself to rocks with a suckerlike disc. When the anemone is covered by the tide, its tentacles float in the water. When the tide goes out, the anemone pulls in its tentacles to stop them drying out.

△ **Sea horses** swim upright. To feed, they hold on to seaweed with their tails and pick food out of the water as it floats past.

△ **Seals** are wonderful swimmers, but on land they move slowly. They spend most of their time at sea, but come ashore to breed.

The tentacles have stinging **cells**, and trap small **fish** and other tiny animals that float by. The sea anemone then pulls the **food** into its **stomach** through its mouth, and digests it.

Sea horse

Sea horses are unusual, delicate **fish** with bony bodies. They are called sea horses because of their horse-shaped heads. Most species grow to between 15 and 25 cm long.

Sea horses swim by waving the fin on their backs. They often cling to **seaweed** with their tail. The males look after the **eggs**, keeping them in a pouch on their belly until they hatch. Sea horses are found all around the world in tropical and warm seas.

Seal and Sea lion

Seals and sea lions are large sea **mammals**. Many of them live in icy waters. They spend most of their time in the sea, but sometimes come ashore to lie in the sun. They also give birth to their young, called pups, on land. Seals can swim fast because they have streamlined bodies and strong flippers. They also have a thick layer of **fat**, or

blubber, under their **skin** to protect them from the cold. Seals and sea lions eat **fish** and other sea creatures. Sea lions have small **ears** outside their heads and fur all over their bodies. The males often have a shaggy mane. The California sea lion is the smallest and can often be seen in **zoos**.

Seashore

The shores surrounding **earth**'s seas and **oceans** are shaped by **water**. Along some shores, fierce **waves** hammer at **rocks** and carry away stones and soil. Along others, the waves and **tides** bring in pebbles and **sand** and dump them.

There are several kinds of seashore. They can be made of rock, sand, mud, pebble or a mixture. All shores are home to many living things.

Limpets, winkles, whelks, barnacles, **sea anemones** and **sponges** are some of the creatures found on rocky shores. All these animals cling to rocks and eat tiny pieces of **food** that float by in the water. Others, such as cockles, razor shells, mussels and **crabs**, live on sandy and muddy beaches.

Seashores have their own **plants**, many of which are **seaweeds**, but other plants also grow in these wet, salty places. Most shore plants and animals are able to live both in and out of water. When the tide is in, they are

▽ Some of the many animals found along the **seashore** include: (1) Oystercatcher (2) Common shore crab (3) Limpet (4) Edible lobster (5) Shrimp (6) Hermit crab (7) Goby (8) Mussel (9) Masked crab (10) Tellin (11) Razor shell (12) Lugworm (13) Starfish (14) Black-headed gull (15) Curlew (16) Jellyfish.

21 December
The South Pole tips towards the sun.

23 September

21 March

21 June
The North Pole tips towards the sun.

summer and winter, happen when the earth is between its summer and winter positions.

At the poles, there are only two seasons – summer and winter. During winter, the sun never rises and days are dark. In summer, the sun shines all the time and there are no real nights.

Farthest from the poles, at the **equator**, the earth's tilt has no effect. There are no clear differences between the seasons in this part of the world.

often underwater, but when the tide is out, they are left on land.

Many **birds** live along the seashore. Some shore birds use their long beaks to dig for **worms** and **insects** in the mud. Others catch **fish** in the sea.

Season

The **year** is divided into four seasons. They are spring, summer, autumn and winter. Each season has its own kind of **weather**.

In spring, for example, the **days** become warmer, **plants** begin to grow again after the winter cold and most **animals** have their young. In autumn, the days are cooler, **leaves** fall from the **trees** and many **birds** fly to warmer places for the winter.

Seasons happen because the **earth** is tilted on its axis (an imaginary line through the centre of the planet between the North and South poles). As the earth travels around the **sun,** first one pole, then the other, leans towards the sun. When the **North Pole** tips towards the sun, it is summer in the northern half of the world and winter in the southern half. Six months later, it is the **South Pole**'s turn to lean towards the sun, making it summer in southern lands and winter in northern ones. Spring and autumn, the halfway seasons between

In the northern half, or hemisphere, of the earth, summer officially begins on 21 June. The other **seasons** begin on 23 September (autumn), 21 December (winter) and 21 March (spring). In the southern hemisphere, the seasons are reversed.

Seaweed

Seaweeds are a group of **plants** that live in the sea. They grow on **rocks** or on the seabed. Seaweeds do not have **leaves** or **flowers**. Instead, they have tough, leathery fronds. Like most plants, seaweeds need sunlight to make **food**. Because the **sun**'s rays do not reach very far down into the sea, there are no seaweeds in deep **water**.

In some countries, such as **China** and **Japan**, people eat different types of seaweeds as **vegetables**.

▽ **Seaweeds** all belong to the class of simple plants called algae. They live in shallow water where they give out oxygen. Seaweeds provide food and shelter for many animals such as crabs, sea snails and shrimps.

Oarweed

Serrated wrack

Sugar kelp

Thongweed

Dulse

Carragheen

Seed

Seeds are the most important part of a **plant**; each one is able to grow into a new plant under the right conditions. A seed forms when pollen reaches the female part of a **flower**. The new seed grows inside a **fruit**, which protects it. In a grape, for example, the fleshy part is the fruit and the pips are the seeds.

Seeds have to be scattered to find new ground to grow on. Some fruits have wings and are carried by the **wind**. Others are prickly and stick to the fur of passing **animals**. Many seeds contain the baby plant and a small supply of **food**. When the seed begins to grow, the baby plant takes in this food until it has roots and **leaves** and can make its own food.

Semiconductor

Some materials, called conductors, allow **electricity** to pass through them easily. Most of these materials are **metals**. Other materials do not allow electricity to pass – they are insulators. Semiconductors are materials such as silicon and germanium, which are neither conductors nor insulators. When small amounts of other **elements** are added to semiconductors, important **electronic** devices can be made. These devices – such as the **silicon chip** – can be made to pass different amounts of electric current, to block it completely, or to allow it to pass only in one direction. **Transistors** are made from semiconductors.

Senegal

The country of Senegal lies on the west coast of **Africa**. Neighbouring **Gambia** is surrounded on three sides by Senegal. Peanuts, **rice** and millet are Senegal's main crops, and **fishing** is an important industry.

Senegal was the first French colony in Africa. Independence came in 1960.

SENEGAL
Government: Republic
Capital: Dakar
Area: 196,192 sq km
Population: 9.3 million
Language: French
Currency: CFA franc

**UNION OF SERBIA
AND MONTENEGRO**
Government:
Federal republic
Capital: Belgrade
Area: 102,168 sq km
Population: 10.6 million
Languages: Serbian
and Albanian
Currency: Dinar

Senses *see* Hearing, Sight, Smell, Taste, Touch

Serbia and Montenegro, Union of

Serbia and Montenegro were formerly the last two **republics** of Yugoslavia. In 2002, the Yugoslav **parliament** voted to form a new country, the Union of Serbia and Montenegro.

In the early 1990s, Serbia fought **wars** against **Slovenia**, **Croatia** and **Bosnia-Herzegovina**. A peace agreement was signed in 1995, but in Kosovo, a region in the south of Serbia, the Albanian-speaking people called for independence. Serbian troops attacked the Albanians. As a result, a **NATO** force bombed the Serbs, who withdrew from Kosovo in 1999.

Seven Wonders of the World

The Seven Wonders of the World were seven outstanding objects that were built in ancient times. They were so-called because people marvelled at their size or beauty. Only one of these wonders, the **pyramids**, exists today. The others have all been destroyed.

The Hanging Gardens of **Babylon** were built high up on the walls of temples. They were probably a gift from Nebuchadnezzar II (c.630– 562 BCE) to one of his wives.

▽ The Hanging Gardens of Babylon were one of the **Seven Wonders of the World**. Babylon stood on the banks of the Euphrates River (now in Iraq).

The Temple of Artemis at Ephesus (now in **Turkey**) was one of the largest temples in the ancient world. Some of its **marble** columns are in the British Museum in **London**.

The Statue of Zeus at Olympia, a valley in **Greece**, showed the king of the **gods** on his throne. It was made of **gold** and **ivory**.

The tomb at Halicarnassus (now in Turkey) was built for Mausolus (d. 353 BCE), a ruler in Persia. It was so massive and became so famous that all large tombs are now called mausoleums.

The Colossus of Rhodes, in Greece, was a huge, bronze statue of the **sun** god, Helios. It stood towering high over the harbour entrance.

The Pharos of Alexandria, in **Egypt**, was the first modern lighthouse. It was built in 270 BCE on the **island** of Pharos, outside Alexandria harbour. It had a wood **fire** burning on top.

Seychelles

The **islands** of the Seychelles make up a small country about 1,600 km off the east coast of **Africa**, in the **Indian Ocean**. The country has volcanic **mountains**, sandy beaches and coconut **palm** plantations.

The islands were ruled by Britain until they gained independence in 1976. The inhabitants are of mixed African and European ancestry. Tourism is an important business.

Shakespeare, William

William Shakespeare (1564–1616) is thought by most people to be **England**'s greatest writer. He is most famous for his plays – about 40 altogether – which include *A Midsummer Night's Dream*, *Hamlet*, *Macbeth* and *Romeo and Juliet*.

Very little is known about Shakespeare's life. He was born in Stratford-upon-Avon and was the son of a glovemaker. When he was 18,

he married Anne Hathaway, a farmer's daughter. They had three children. At the age of 20, he left Stratford and went to **London**, where he became an actor and playwright. Towards the end of his life he returned to Stratford.

Shakespeare's plays are acted and studied all over the world. Many of the words and phrases we use today were first used by Shakespeare.

Shark

The shark family includes the world's largest and fiercest **fish**. Many sharks have a wedge-shaped head, a long body and a triangular back fin that sometimes sticks out of the **water**. Their **skeletons** are made of rubbery gristle, not **bone**. Most sharks live in warm seas. They vary greatly in size. The dogfish, one of the smallest sharks, is only 60 cm long. The largest fish in the **oceans**, the whale shark, measures over 15 m – longer than a bus.

The whale shark and the basking shark are harmless to people and other **animals** because they live on **plankton**. But many sharks are killers with rows of razor-sharp **teeth**, and several will attack humans. The great white shark even swallows its prey whole. The remains of large animals, such as **dolphins**, **seals** and other sharks, have been found in its **stomach**.

Other dangerous sharks are the blue shark, the tiger shark and the leopard shark, which has leopardlike spots. The smell of **blood** in water can cause these sharks to attack anything nearby, even other sharks.

SEYCHELLES
Government: Single party republic
Capital: Victoria
Area: 280 sq km
Population: 80,000
Languages: English and French
Currency: Rupee

▽ The great white **shark** grows up to 8 m long. Like most sharks, it can pick up the electrical signals given off by the twitching muscles of other animals in the sea.

Sheep

Sheep have been kept as domestic **animals** for thousands of years. At first, they were kept for their **milk** and **skins**. The milk could be made into **cheese** and the skins were used for **clothing**. Then people discovered that the animals' thick coats could be sheared (shaved off) and the **wool** woven into cloth. Today, sheep are kept mostly for wool and for meat (mutton or lamb).

Modern **sheep** have been specially bred to give the best combination of wool and meat.

Shells and Shellfish

Many **animals** live inside shells. This is because they have soft bodies that need protection. Shells are usually hard and are all sizes and **colours**. The shells of some sea **snails** are no larger than a grain of **sand**, but the giant clam of the **Pacific Ocean** has a shell 120 cm across.

Some land animals such as snails have shells, but most creatures with shells live in the sea. These include **molluscs** and **crustaceans**. Some of these, such as **oysters**, scallops and **lobsters**, can be eaten. They are often called shellfish, although they are not really **fish** at all. Shellfish have been an important **food** for thousands of years. In some places, the kitchen rubbish of **prehistoric people** has been found that consists entirely of enormous mounds of shells, as high as a two-storey **house**.

△ **Shrews**, such as this pygmy shrew, are very fierce mammals. They often use their sharp teeth to attack mice and other shrews.

Shinto

Shinto is a Japanese **religion**. The word 'Shinto' means 'the way of the **gods**'. Unlike other religions, Shinto does not teach that there is one supreme being. It says that there is an eternal truth called *kami*. *Kami* is to be found in every form of nature and in **rivers, mountains** and **lakes**. All over **Japan** there are shrines, large and small, dedicated to different *kami*.

Ship and Boat

Today, most ships are cargo vessels. They are usually built to carry a certain type of cargo. Tankers carry **liquids** such as **oil** or **wine**. Some oil tankers are so long that the crew can ride **bicycles** around the deck. Bulk carriers take dry cargoes, like **coal** and **wheat**, that can be loaded loose. Container ships carry all kinds of goods packed into large boxes called containers. **Refrigerator** ships are for carrying fresh **food** such as **fruit** and meat.

Planes have replaced most passenger ships for long journeys, but ferries still carry people, **cars** and lorries across smaller stretches of **water**. There are also luxury cruise liners. Various kinds of warship are used by the navy.

Shrew

Shrews are furry **animals** about the size of a mouse. They have pointed snouts and are seldom seen because they only come out at night. Shrews are very active animals and have to eat **insects** and **worms** almost continually to stay alive. They often fall prey to larger night hunters, such as **owls, cats** and even **badgers**.

▷ The largest passenger **ship** in the world, a cruise liner called the *Grand Princess*, carries 2,600 people on 12 decks. The facilities on board include a library offering CD-ROM and internet access, a virtual reality games area, a swimming pool that can be protected by a moving roof, and a casino decorated with holograms.

Siberia

Siberia is a vast region that covers most of Russian **Asia** east of the Ural **Mountains**. It is a very cold land. Along Siberia's northern coast lies the **tundra**, a cold semi-**desert**. **Forests** cover about a third of the 15 million sq km that make up the area. Towards the Mongolian border lies Lake Baikal, the largest freshwater **lake** in Asia or **Europe**.

During the period when **Russia** was part of the **Soviet Union**, the communist **government** encouraged people to settle in and develop Siberia.

Sierra Leone

Sierra Leone is a country on the west coast of **Africa**. It is about the size of **Scotland**, with a **climate** that is hot and damp. Around Freetown, the capital, about 380 cm of **rain** falls each year. Most people are farmers, producing **rice**, **palm** kernels, ginger, **coffee** and cocoa. **Iron** ore, bauxite and **diamonds** are mined.

Sierra Leone was a British colony. It became an independent state in 1961 and a **republic** in 1971, but **civil war** broke out in the 1990s. A peace agreement was reached in 1999.

Sight

Sight is the sense that allows people and **animals** to see things. The sense organ that makes this possible is the **eye**. Sight is the most important sense for most animals, because it allows them to look for **food** and a mate, and to watch for danger.

Most **invertebrates** (animals without backbones) have simple eyes that give only a rough picture of what is around them. Animals with backbones (**vertebrates**) are able to see clearly. Only humans and a few types of animal can see in full **colour**.

Sikhism

Sikhism is a **religion** that began in the Punjab region of northern **India**. Followers of Sikhism are called Sikhs. The first Sikh guru (teacher) was **Nanak** (1469–1539). The teachings of the gurus were written in the Sikh sacred book, the *Granth*.

Sikhs are taught three main things. Firstly, they should remember God by saying his name often. Secondly, they should work hard to earn an honest living. Thirdly, they should share their earnings and help others.

The Golden Temple, in Amritsar, India, is sacred to the followers of Sikhism. It was built to house the Sikh sacred book, the *Granth*.

SIERRA LEONE
Government: Republic
Capital: Freetown
Area: 71,740 sq km
Population: 4.9 million
Language: English
Currency: Leone

GRAND PRINCESS

Silicon chip

Silicon chips are tiny pieces of the **element** silicon. (Silicon is a **semiconductor**.) The chips can be made to carry very small electrical circuits called microcircuits. These are used in **radios**, digital watches, **calculators** and **computers**. Because the chips are so small, the **electronic** devices in which they are used can be small too.

Silk

Silk is a natural fibre made from the cocoon of one kind of **moth**. Silkworms, which are really **caterpillars**, are kept in special containers and fed on mulberry **leaves** for about four weeks. At the end of this time, they spin their cocoons and start to turn into moths. Then they are killed and each cocoon is unwound as a long thread between 600 and 900 m long.

Silk was first used in **Asia** centuries ago, especially in **China** and **Japan**. Silk **weaving** in **Europe** began in the 1400s. Silk makes a very fine, soft material. It was used for stockings before nylon was invented. Silk can be made into other fabrics such as satin and chiffon, and can be dyed many beautiful **colours**.

Silver

Silver is a precious **metal**. It has been used by people all over the world for thousands of years. Although many countries have silver deposits, the **mining** process is very expensive.

Silver bends very easily, and can be beaten into many shapes and patterns. Like **gold**, it can be hammered out into thin sheets. It is used to make useful and decorative things such as spoons and forks, bowls and **jewellery**. Sometimes it is used as a coating on cheaper metals such as **copper** or nickel, to make them look like silver.

SINGAPORE
Government: Republic
Capital: Singapore
Area: 581 sq km
Population: 3.9 million
Languages: Chinese, Malay, Tamil and English
Currency: Singapore dollar

The **skeleton** of an adult human has about 206 bones. Babies are born with about 350 bones, but as a child grows, some of these bones join together.

Silver is used in industry because it carries **electricity** well. Some chemicals made from silver react to **light** and are used in **photography**.

Singapore

Singapore is a small country in **Southeast Asia**, off the southern end of the Malay peninsula. Three-quarters of the **population** are Chinese, but people from all over the world live there.

The capital city is also called Singapore. It has one of the busiest ports in the world and trades with many countries. For a short time Singapore was part of **Malaysia**, but now it has its own **government**. It is a member of the **Commonwealth**.

Skating

Roller-skating and ice-skating are both popular **sports**. Roller skates have four **wheels** made of **steel** and **rubber**. Ice skates have a thin steel blade.

There are two main kinds of ice-skating. Figure-skating and ice-dancing to **music** are **Olympic** sports. Speed skaters race against each other.

The first ice skates had runners, or blades, of **bone**. Today, figure skates have jagged teeth at the front to help grip the ice when starting and stopping. Speed skates have longer blades. Skates are also worn by ice hockey players.

Skeleton

Our skeleton is made up of **bones**. Without a skeleton, our bodies would be shapeless blobs. The skeleton protects our vital organs, such as the **heart**, **liver** and **lungs**. It is also an anchor for the **muscles**.

In humans and other **vertebrates** (animals with backbones), the skeleton is inside the body, covered by flesh and **skin**. In other animals, such as **insects** and **spiders**, the skeleton is like a hard crust on the outside of the body. It is called an exoskeleton. Some animals, such as the **jellyfish** and **octopus**, lack a skeleton. Their bodies are supported by the **water** in which they live.

There are more than 200 bones in the human skeleton. These include the bones of the spine, skull (which protects the **brain**), breastbone, ribs, pelvis and limbs. Joints are places where bones meet. Some joints, such as those in the skull, do not move. Others, like those in the shoulders and hips, help us to move about. Muscles across the joints tighten, or contract, to move the bones.

Skiing

Skiing is a way of moving across **snow** on long runners, or skis. It probably started around 3000 BCE. The oldest skis ever found date back to 2500 BCE, and we know that the **Vikings** used skis. Today, skiing is a popular **sport** and is part of the Winter **Olympic Games**.

There are four main kinds of skiing: downhill, cross-country, slalom (a type of obstacle course) and ski-jumping. Downhill skiing, in which the skier glides down a steep **mountain** run at high speed, is especially popular. There are special ski resorts in the mountains of **Australia**, **Europe** and **North America**, where people can enjoy skiing holidays.

Skin

Skin is a waterproof, stretchy covering on the outside of the body. It protects the body from dirt and **germs** and can even repair itself. Skin is sensitive to **heat**, cold and **pain**. Human skin can be quite thick and hard on places that get a lot of wear, such as the soles of the feet. In other places, such as the eyelids, it can be very thin.

Human skin is made up of two layers. The outer layer, the epidermis, is made up of dead skin **cells** and has a chemical called melanin which gives skin its **colour**. The inner layer, the dermis, contains **nerves**, **blood** vessels, sweat **glands** and the roots of **hairs**. The skin of an adult human covers an area of about 1.7 sq km.

Skunk

Skunks are **mammals**, members of the same family as weasels and **badgers**. There are three kinds: the hog-nosed, the spotted and the striped skunk. They all live in **North America**. The best known is the striped skunk, which is black with white markings on its back. All skunks are able to drive away enemies by squirting a stinking **liquid** from a **gland** under their tails. If another **animal** is hit by this liquid, the smell will cling to its fur for days.

Skunks eat most kinds of **food**, including **insects**, **rats**, **mice**, **birds**, **eggs** and **plants**. They feed at night and sleep in burrows during the **day**.

△ **Skunks** are quite harmless if left alone, but if they feel threatened, the foul-smelling liquid they squirt drives off any attacker. Before a skunk sprays, it gives a warning by stamping its front feet and hissing.

▷ Downhill **skiing** is a popular sport. The skiers wear protective helmets and smooth, tight-fitting costumes to reduce resistance from the wind.

Skyscraper

'Skyscraper' is a name for a very tall building. The first one was built in 1884 in Chicago in the **United States**. It was designed by William Le Baron Jenney, and had an **iron** frame. All the early skyscrapers were built in **New York** and Chicago. Now they are built all over the world.

For many years the tallest skyscraper was the Empire State Building in New York, at 102 storeys high. Today, the world's tallest skyscrapers are the Petronas Twin Towers in Kuala Lumpur, **Malaysia**. Completed in 1996, the buildings stand 451.9 m high.

△ The Empire State Building (left), in New York, was the world's tallest **skyscraper** when it was completed in 1930. It stands 381 m high. The Sears Tower (right), in Chicago, was built in 1970–1973 and is 443 m high.

▽ African people captured for **slavery** suffered terrible treatment. They were rounded up in gangs and marched to the coast. As they boarded ships, the slaves were held in leg-irons, with their hands tied behind their backs.

Slavery

Slavery is when one person becomes the property, or slave, of another. Slaves can be bought and sold. In ancient civilizations, prisoners captured in **war** were often made into slaves, and poor people sometimes sold their children as slaves.

From the 1500s, the Spanish took people from **Africa** as slaves for their colonies in the Americas. By the 1770s, the British were also carrying slaves to the Americas. They were packed tightly into **ships**, in terrible conditions and many of them died on the way.

Britain abolished the slave trade in 1833. In the **United States**, slavery was ended in 1865, after the **Civil War**. But racial discrimination continued even after **civil rights** laws were passed to guarantee equal rights for black people.

Sleep

Sleep is a time when we are unconscious and resting. People and some **animals** need sleep to stay healthy. Without it, people become bad-tempered, and after a long time, they may start having hallucinations – seeing things that are not there.

There are four different stages of sleep. At each stage the electrical **waves** given off by the **brain** change. When we are deeply asleep, these waves are slow and large. When we are only lightly asleep the waves are faster. This is the time when we – and all **mammals** – have **dreams**.

Sloth

Sloths are a group of **mammals** that live in **South America**. They move very slowly, usually at night. Sloths spend most of their lives hanging upside down in **trees**. They eat **leaves**, buds and twigs. Their fur is often covered with a mass of tiny green **plants** called algae. There are two main kinds of sloth – those with two toes on their front feet and those with three.

Slovakia

This country in eastern **Europe** was once part of the country known as Czechoslovakia. The territory was ruled for many centuries by the Hungarians, but in 1918 the Slovak and Czech regions were joined into Czechoslovakia. The country came under communist rule in 1948.

A democratic **government** took over after the communists fell in 1989. However, the Slovak people soon felt that they were being treated unfairly, and called for independence. The country split into Slovakia and the **Czech Republic** in 1993.

Slovenia

Slovenia was the most westerly **republic** of the former country of Yugoslavia. It declared its independence in 1991. Until 1918, Slovenia was ruled by **Austria**. It is the most westernized of the former Yugoslav republics and its people are mainly Roman Catholic. Ljubljana, the capital of Slovenia, is also an important industrial centre.

Smell

Smell is an important sense, like **sight** and **hearing**. **Humans beings**, like other **mammals**, smell through the nose. We sniff the **air**, and the scents given off by things around us are picked up by special **cells** in the nose. These cells send messages to the **brain**.

Our sense of smell is useful when we are eating. It helps us to **taste** things. It can also let us know when **food** is bad. Most other **animals** have a much better sense of smell than humans. **Dogs** can use their sense of smell to track down and follow prey. **Moths** do not have noses, but they can still smell things. Some male moths can smell a female moth many kilometres away.

Snail and Slug

Snails are **molluscs** with a coiled **shell** on their backs. There are more than 80,000 kinds in the world. Some live on land, some in fresh **water** and some

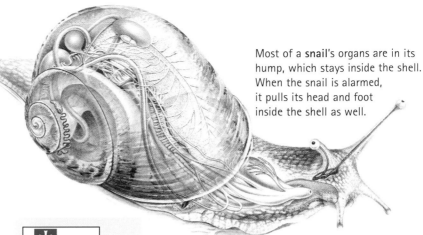

Most of a **snail**'s organs are in its hump, which stays inside the shell. When the snail is alarmed, it pulls its head and foot inside the shell as well.

SLOVAKIA
Government: Republic
Capital: Bratislava
Area: 49,035 sq km
Population: 5.4 million
Languages: Slovak and Hungarian
Currency: Koruna

SLOVENIA
Government: Republic
Capital: Ljubljana
Area: 19,991 sq km
Population: 1.9 million
Language: Slovenian
Currency: Tolar

in the sea. Most snails are less than 3 cm long, but one of the largest, the giant land snail, is about 20 cm long.

Unlike a snail, a slug does not have a large shell on its back. Some slugs have a small, flat shell under their **skin**. Both slugs and snails glide along on a muscular part of their body called the foot, and they both have one or two pairs of tentacles.

Snake

Snakes are **reptiles**. They are long and thin and have no legs. They move along by wriggling their bodies.

Snakes have a dry, smooth **skin**. Most live in warm places. Those that live in colder **climates** spend the winter in **hibernation**.

A few snakes give birth to live young, but most hatch from **eggs**. A female snake lays up to ten eggs at a time.

Some snakes can inject **poison** into their prey through large **teeth** called fangs. The rattlesnake and the cobra are both poisonous snakes.

The largest snakes are pythons and anacondas, which can grow up to 10 m long. Both these snakes suffocate their prey. They coil their massive bodies around their victims and squeeze.

Soap

Soap is used for cleaning things. It is made by mixing **fat** or vegetable **oil** with a chemical such as caustic soda. It loosens dirt in clothes and then carries it away. Today, chemical cleaners called **detergents** are often used instead. Detergents clean better than soap in hard water.

Soil

Soil is a layer of small **mineral** particles on the surface of the **earth**. It covers the **rocks** the earth is made of and is sometimes quite thick. Soil is made up of small pieces of rock, the rotted remains of **plants** (called humus), **fungi**, **bacteria** and many tiny **animals**.

Good soil is a mixture of **clay**, silt and **sand**, with plenty of humus. People often add animal manure or chemical **fertilizers** to poor soil to makes it richer in certain minerals.

Solar energy

Solar energy is **energy** from the **sun**. It reaches the **earth** as **light** and **heat**. Without these things there could be no life on earth.

Only about 15 per cent of the sun's energy that reaches earth is absorbed by the earth's surface. Much of it bounces back into space. Solar energy can be collected by special panels and **mirrors** and used to make **electricity**.

Solar system

see **pages 302–303**

Somalia

Somalia is a country in the east of **Africa**, on the coast of the **Indian Ocean**. It is a poor country, and most

△ Solar panels use **solar energy** to heat water for houses and other buildings.

SOMALIA
Government: Republic
Capital: Mogadishu
Area: 637,657 sq km
Population: 9.4 million
Languages: Somali and Arabic
Currency: Somali shilling

of the people are **nomads**. Low rainfall means that farming is possible only around the Shebelle and Juba **Rivers**. The chief crops are **sugar**, bananas, sorghum and incense. Since the early 1990s, the country has suffered from drought and **civil war**.

Sonar

Sonar stands for '*so*und *na*vigation and *r*anging'. It is used in **ships** to find the depth of anything beneath them. It can measure the depth of the seabed as well as locate **submarines** and shoals of **fish**. It works like **radar**, except that sonar uses **sound** signals instead of **radio** signals.

The sonar device on a ship turns electric signals into pulses of sound. These travel down through the **water**. Any object in the water struck by the sound pulses sends back an **echo**. The sonar equipment turns the echoes back into electric signals (see **electricity**) and measures the time delay. This indicates how deep the object is in the water. The depth is shown on a screen.

▽ **Sonar** can be used on ships to map the bottom of the sea and to find shoals of fish. Whales and dolphins use a type of sonar to locate their prey.

Vertical sonar detects seabed

Shoal of fish

Shoal of fish

Sound

Sound is made by vibrating objects that send sound **waves** through the **air**. When these vibrations reach our **ears**, we hear them as sounds.

Sound travels through air at about 334 m per second. This is slow enough for us to see a far-off explosion, for example, before we hear it. The sound takes time to reach us.

The speed of the vibrations makes a difference to the kind of sound we hear. If the vibrations are very fast, they are said to be 'high frequency' and the sound we hear is high-pitched. If they are slow, the sound is said to be 'low frequency' and the sound we hear is low-pitched.

South Africa

South Africa is a country in southern **Africa**. Most of the country is tableland, a high region of flat-topped hills. Around the coast is a narrow plain. The **climate** is warm and dry.

South Africa is a rich country, with factories making a wide range of goods. Mines produce **gold, diamonds, uranium, copper, iron** and other **minerals**. Farms grow large crops of maize, **wheat** and **fruit**.

Over 42 million people live in South Africa. Almost three-quarters of them are black Africans. There are fewer than five million whites. The whites, who are descended mainly from Dutch and British settlers, used to control the country's **government** and **money**. From the 1940s, South Africa had a policy of **apartheid** or 'apartness'. This meant that whites and non-whites lived separately. In 1991, the government ended apartheid, and in 1994, the majority black African National Congress (ANC) won the South Africa's first non-racial **elections**. Its leader, **Nelson Mandela**, became **president**. Mandela retired in 1999 and was succeeded by Thabo Mbeki.

South America

see pages 306–307

Southeast Asia

Southeast Asia is a large area that lies to the south of **China** and to the east of **India**. It is made up of many countries. Joined to the Asian mainland are **Myanmar, Thailand, Malaysia, Singapore, Cambodia, Vietnam** and **Laos**. Farther east and south lie chains of **islands** that are divided into the countries of the **Philippines, Indonesia** and Brunei.

Southeast Asia is mainly mountainous. It has a tropical **climate**, with heavy rainfall in the wet **season**. Most of the people are farmers. They grow **rice, tea,** maize, **rubber** and **sugar**cane. **Mineral** resources include **oil, tin** and bauxite (**aluminium** ore). Although many Southeast Asian people live in small villages, there are also large cities such as Bangkok in Thailand, Kuala Lumpur in Malaysia, Ho Chi Minh City in Vietnam, and Singapore, one of the world's greatest ports.

Southeast Asia is densely populated. Its people belong to a variety of ethnic groups and speak many **languages**. Their lifestyles also vary greatly.

SOUTH AFRICA
Government: Republic
Capitals: Cape Town (legislative), Pretoria (administrative) and Bloemfontein (judicial)
Area: 1,223,412 sq km
Population: 42.1 million
Languages: Afrikaans, English and 9 Bantu languages (all official)
Currency: Rand

This dancer is from the small Indonesian island of Bali, in **Southeast Asia**. Dancers perform in villages across the island. Some dances are religious, while others are for the entertainment of friends, family and tourists.

SOLAR SYSTEM

The solar system is the sun and the family of objects that orbit it. They stay together because of the sun's strong gravity.

THE POWERFUL SUN

The sun, our local star, is the largest object in the solar system. It is made up of over 95 percent of all the material in the system. The rest is used up in the objects that orbit the sun. These are nine planets, more than 80 moons, billions of asteroids and billions of comets. Because of the sun's great size, it has a powerful gravitational pull. This pull keeps the solar system together and controls the movements of the planets.

BIRTH OF THE SOLAR SYSTEM

About five billion years ago, the solar system was born from a great cloud of gas and dust called the solar nebula. This material was left over from the formation of the Milky Way galaxy. The nebula began to condense into a nursery of proto-stars. One of these proto-stars started to develop into the young sun. Gas and dust collected around the sun in a disc. The disc cooled and grains of solid matter began to freeze and stick together. Over thousands of years, these lumps of matter merged to form the planets.

A STABLE SYSTEM

Little has changed in the solar system over the past four billion years. The sun has brightened slightly, a few comets and asteroids have crashed, but the nine planets have remained in stable orbits. Only the earth has changed significantly as life developed on its surface.

Moon

Mercury

Venus

Earth

Sun

Mars

ROCKY WORLDS AND GAS GIANTS

Most of the matter from which the planets formed consisted of hydrogen and helium. The planets nearest the sun – Mercury, Venus, earth and Mars – were too warm to hold on to these plentiful light gases. Instead, they became small worlds of rock and metal. Farther from the sun, where temperatures were very low, the planets attracted huge amounts of hydrogen and helium. They became the gas giants Jupiter, Saturn, Uranus and Neptune. Pluto is the smallest planet, and farthest from the sun. It is more like a moon than a major planet. Some astronomers believe there is a tenth planet, known as Planet X, yet to be discovered.

Asteroids

THE PLANETS OF THE SOLAR SYSTEM

Name	Av. distance from sun (million km)	Diameter (km)	Length of day	Length of year	Moons
Mercury	58	4,878	59 days	88 days	0
Venus	108.2	12,103	243 days	225 days	0
Earth	149.6	12,714	23 hrs 56 mins	365.26 days	1
Mars	228	6,794	24 hrs 37 mins	687 days	2
Jupiter	778	142,800	9 hrs 50 mins	11.9 years	28
Saturn	1,427	120,200	10 hrs 14 mins	29.5 years	23
Uranus	2,871	51,118	17 hrs 14 mins	84 years	21
Neptune	4,497	48,400	18 hrs	164.8 years	8
Pluto	5,900	3,000	6 days 9 hrs	247.7 years	1

Comet

Pluto

DISTANT SOLAR SYSTEMS

There are many more
stars like the sun in the
universe. Astronomers
have always thought it
was possible that one of these had a system of
planets orbiting around it. But the stars are so
distant and so bright that detecting a dull planet
close to a star was impossible for a long time.

During the 1980s, astronomers discovered the first
stars surrounded by discs of gas and dust. A decade
later, the first solar systems other than our own
were discovered. The first was in 1995, around
a star called 51 Pegasi. The planet is at least
150 times more massive than earth, and
20 times closer to its star than earth
is to the sun. It orbits every 4.2 days.

About 15 other stars with a planet
have now been found. Astronomers
cannot see the planets directly, but
they can detect a small wobble in
the star. This is produced by the
pull of the planet's gravity as it
orbits round the star.

ASTEROIDS AND COMETS

Between the orbits of Mars and Jupiter is a gigantic
belt made up of more than 4,000 lumps of rock.
These are asteroids. They range in size from a
few metres across to the biggest, called Ceres,
which is about 1,000 km across. The outer
edge of our solar system is marked by a
huge cloud of billions of frozen comets called
the Oort Cloud. Scientists think the cloud may be
debris left over from when the solar system formed.

Neptune

Saturn

Uranus

Jupiter

SEE ALSO
Asteroid, Astronomy, Comet,
Earth, Eclipse, Galaxy, Gravity,
Jupiter, Mars, Mercury, Meteor,
Milky Way, Moon, Neptune,
Planet, Pluto, Saturn, Solar
energy, Universe, Uranus, Venus

Supply planes land at the **South Pole** almost every day. No people live permanently in Antarctica, but research bases are visited by teams of scientists.

South Pole

The South Pole is the point on a **map** that marks the southern end of the **earth**'s axis. The **North Pole** marks the northern end. The South Pole lies among high, frozen **mountains** in the middle of the **Antarctic**. The first person to journey to the pole was the Norwegian **explorer**, Roald **Amundsen** (1872–1928), in December 1911.

In 1956, the **United States** set up a scientific base at the South Pole. They called it the Amundsen–Scott Station.

Soviet Union (former)

The vast area that was the Soviet Union in 1990 is now a complex of independent states. The three **Baltic States** – Latvia, Lithuania and Estonia – declared their independence from the Soviet Union at the end of 1991.

By 1992, eleven of the remaining **republics** that had formerly made up the Soviet Union had become members of the Commonwealth of Independent States (CIS). They were: Armenia, Azerbaijan, Belarus, Kazakhstan, Kyrgyzstan, Moldova, **Russia**, Tajikistan, Turkmenistan, **Ukraine** and Uzbekistan. Georgia, the final former Soviet republic, joined later. However, each country is now fully independent,

with its own **government**, military and **economic** system. The CIS has been dominated economically and militarily by Russia under the leadership of Boris Yeltsin (b. 1931) and, from 2000, Vladimir Putin (b. 1952).

Before 1922, the Soviet Union was called Russia. It was ruled by tsars, or emperors. After a **revolution** in 1917, a communist government took over (see **communism**), led by Vladimir **Lenin**. Russia was nearly destroyed by a **civil war** between the communists and their enemies. The communists won, and began to turn the Soviet Union into a great industrial nation.

During **World War II**, the Soviets occupied **Hungary**, **Bulgaria**, **Romania**, **Czechoslovakia**, **Poland** and part of **Germany**. Communist governments closely tied to the Soviet Union were set up in these countries after the war.

From the 1950s, the **United States** and the Soviet Union grew to distrust each other and the so-called Cold War developed. Under its last leader, Mikhail **Gorbachev** (b. 1931), the Soviet Union entered a period of change and unrest. When the country began to break apart in 1991, the Communist Party was disbanded. **Food** shortages became widespread as the economy worsened.

The former Soviet states are rich in **minerals**. They have great deposits of **coal**, **oil** and natural **gas**, **iron**, **lead**, chromium and manganese. Farmers grow a variety of crops, including **wheat**, rye and barley. They also grow **vegetables**, **fruit**, **tea** and **cotton**. **Fishing** and forestry are also important.

Space exploration
see **pages 310–311**

Spain

Spain lies in southwest **Europe**, beyond the **Pyrenees**. Most of the country is covered by high plains and

SPAIN
Government: Constitutional monarchy
Capital: Madrid
Area: 504,782 sq km
Population: 39.4 million
Language: Spanish
Currency: Euro

mountains, with a low plain around the coast. The highlands have hot summers, cold winters and little **rain**. The coast is milder and wetter, especially in the north.

Many people work on farms, growing potatoes, **wheat**, grapes, olives and **fruits**. **Wine**, olive **oil** and oranges are exported. Many Spaniards who live on the coast are fishermen. Others work in the tourist trade. Each year, millions of tourists visit Spain to enjoy its sunny beaches. The two main industrial areas are around Bilbao in the north and Barcelona in the northeast.

Spectrum

Where do the **colours** in a **rainbow** come from? The answer was found in 1666, when Sir Isaac **Newton** put a triangle-shaped block of glass called a prism in front of a beam of sunlight. The prism bent the **light** and separated it into the different colours of the rainbow. Newton showed that sunlight is made up of different colours – a spectrum of colours. Sunlight is white because it contains all the colours of the rainbow, mixed together.

The spectrum of light is only one small part of the whole electromagnetic spectrum. This is arranged according to the wavelength (distance between **waves**) and frequency (number of waves per second) of the waves. **Radio** waves have the lowest frequency and the longest wavelength. Gamma rays have the highest frequency and shortest wavelength. In between these come **ultraviolet** rays, **X rays** and other rays.

Speech

Once, the only sounds people could make were grunts and yells. Then, over tens of thousands of years, people learned to form words. **Languages** slowly developed.

△ In **speech**, the vocal cords are tightened and loosened. When the vocal cords are relaxed (top), they produce low notes. When they are taut (bottom), the vocal cords produce high notes.

▽ The electromagnetic **spectrum** covers a huge range of energy waves. The only waves that humans can see are light waves, but unseen waves are around us all the time. Different wavelengths of the electromagnetic spectrum are used for different things, and have many different effects.

Speech sounds are made by **air** from the **lungs** passing around two membranes called vocal cords. We change the pitch of the sound by altering the tension of the vocal cords, just as the pitch of a **guitar** can be altered by tightening or loosening the strings. By changing the shape of the passages in our throat, mouth and nose, and by using our **tongue**, we can alter the sounds produced. This allows us to make the words of speech.

Spice

Pepper, ginger, cloves, cinnamon and nutmeg are common spices. Spices have a strong **taste** and **smell** and are used to flavour **foods** and drinks. They are the dried parts of **plants**, usually ground into a powder. Most spice plants grow in hot places such as **Africa**, **India** and **Southeast Asia**.

Gamma rays, used to detect cracks in metal

X rays, used to look inside the body

Ultraviolet rays, used in sunbeds

Visible light, from red to violet

Infrared rays, used in heat sensitive cameras

Shorter microwaves, used in a microwave oven

Longer microwaves, used in radar

Ultra high frequencey (UHF) radio waves for TV transmissions

Radio waves used in radio broadcasts

SOUTH AMERICA

South America is the world's fourth largest continent. It stretches from Colombia in the north to the southernmost tip of Chile. It contains the world's longest mountain range and its largest area of rainforest.

▷ Skilled cowboys called gauchos *herd their cattle on the vast grasslands of Argentina.*

MOUNTAINS AND RAIN FOREST

South America has an amazing variety of landscapes. The Andes mountain range runs along the Pacific coast for over 8,000 km. It includes the continent's highest peak, Mount Aconcagua in Argentina, which is 6,960 m above sea level. High in the Andes is the starting-point of the Amazon River, one of the world's greatest waterways, which travels for 6,540 km across the continent before emptying into the Atlantic Ocean in Brazil. The Amazon basin is a huge area which includes a massive region of tropical rainforest, home to an enormous variety of plant and animal life. This important natural habitat is being reduced in size every day as a result of deforestation.

GRASSLAND AND COLD DESERT

Although much of the east of the continent is made up of lush jungle, there are immense regions of grassland further south. On the grasslands of Argentina and Venezuela there are vast cattle ranches and fertile arable land. South America also has cold desert areas – the Atacama Desert in northern Chile is one of the world's driest places. In the far south of the continent lies the Patagonian Desert in Argentina and Chile, a desolate and inhospitable region.

△ *Fishermen on coasts of the Pacific Ocean fish for anchovies. Sardines and tuna are also canned for export worldwide.*

PEOPLE THROUGH THE AGES

The earliest settlers in South America were the Native Americans. There is evidence that they came across the Bering Straits from Asia, and had migrated down through North America into South America by c.9000 BCE. These people formed some of the most extraordinary ancient civilizations in the world, including those of the Aztecs and Incas. These two civilizations were destroyed by invading Europeans in the 1500s.

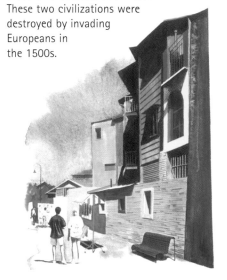

△ *La Boca, with its colourful houses, is the artists' quarter of Buenos Aires, in Argentina. The area was settled by Italians from Genoa in the 1800s.*

CONQUEST AND PLUNDER

In the late 1500s, Europeans conquered much of South America. They were attracted by the gold and other precious minerals they found there. European adventurers plundered much of the continent's riches. They also transmitted many European diseases to the native people, many of whom died after contact with the invaders.

TODAY'S PEOPLES

There are twelve independent countries in South America. The largest of these, Brazil, takes up half the continent, including most of the Amazon basin. Most of the peoples of South America speak Spanish, reflecting their Spanish colonial past. However in Brazil, Portuguese (the language of its conquerors) is the national language, and in Guyana, English is spoken. In Andean countries such as Bolivia and Peru, native peoples still make up a large part of the population. Argentina's population is largely white, while Brazil's population includes many descendants of African slaves.

NATURAL RESOURCES

The continent is rich in a variety of natural resources. The Andes mountains are full of minerals, such as silver in Peru, tin in Bolivia and copper in Chile. Venezuela is a source of vast amounts of oil. Brazil produces a third of all the world's coffee, and the grasslands of Argentina, Uruguay and Paraguay support the sheep and cattle that feed much of the continent. Many life-saving medicines have been developed from rainforest plants.

CULTURE AND SPORT

South America is home to some of the world's most vibrant and exciting people and cultures. The continent is obsessed with football and two of the world's greatest national teams, the Brazilians and the Argentinians, are South American. Pelé, one of the greatest players of all time, played for Brazil.

Brazil is also the venue for the world's biggest carnival, in Rio de Janeiro. During the carnival celebrations in February or March, millions of people take to the streets to celebrate and to watch the amazing processions as they move through the city. It is by far the largest single party in the world.

◁ *Many native peoples in remote areas follow an ancient way of life. This Amazonian boy is hunting by shooting a poison arrow.*

Caribbean
Sea

CARACAS

VENEZUELA

GEORGETOWN
GUYANA
PARAMARIBO
CAYENNE
SURINAME
FRENCH
GUIANA

BOGOTÁ

COLOMBIA

ATLANTIC
OCEAN

QUITO

ECUADOR

Amazon

B R A Z I L

A N D E S

P E R U

LIMA

BOLIVIA

BRASÍLIA

LA PAZ

SUCRE

P A R A G U A Y

PACIFIC
OCEAN

Atacama

RIO DE JANEIRO

ASUNCIÓN

C H I L E

SÃO PAULO

SOUTH AMERICA FACT FILE
Area: 17,800,000 sq km
Highest mountain: Aconcagua, 6,960 m
Lowest point: Peninsula Valdes, Argentina,
40 m below sea level
Largest lake: Maracaibo, 13,512 sq km
Longest river: Amazon, 6,437 km
Largest desert: Atacama
Number of countries: 12
Largest country: Brazil
Smallest country: Uruguay
Largest city: Sáo Paulo, Brazil, 17 million
Total population: 350 million

URUGUAY

SANTIAGO

MONTEVIDEO

BUENOS AIRES

A R G E N T I N A

ATLANTIC
OCEAN

Falkland Islands
(Islas Malvinas)
(UK)
STANLEY

Terra
Del Fuego

SEE ALSO
Amazon River, Andes, Argentina, Aztecs,
Bolivia, Brazil, Chile, Cowboy, Ecuador,
Equator, Fishing, Inca, Paraguay, Peru,
Rainforest, Sport, Uruguay, Venezuela

△ *An imposing statue of*
Christ stands high above
Rio de Janeiro, in Brazil.

307

Bird-eating **spiders** are among the largest spiders in the world, with a leg span of up to 25 cm. All spiders have two body parts – an abdomen (back end) and a cephalothorax (head and chest). The brain and stomach are in the cephalothorax. The heart and silk spinners are in the abdomen.

Prairie dogs are ground **squirrels** that live in large groups in huge burrow systems. Members of the group take it in turn to do jobs that benefit the whole group. This prairie dog is standing guard at the entrance to its burrow.

Spider

Spiders are small **animals**. They are not **insects**, although many people think they are. An insect has six legs and a body made up of three parts. A spider has eight legs and a body with two parts.

All spiders spin **silk** threads. Many of them use the threads to make a sticky web for catching insects. Others are hunters and chase their prey; some lie in wait, then pounce. When a spider catches something, it stuns or kills it with a poisonous bite. All spiders can inject **poison**, but in most cases it does not hurt **human beings**.

There are about 30,000 kinds of spider. The comb-footed spider is no larger than a pinhead, but some **bird**-eating spiders can grow to 25 cm across. Some spiders live for only a year, others for 20 years. Some mate in winter, others in spring. Tiny spiders lay a few **eggs**, sometimes only one, but the largest lay up to 2,000.

Sponge

A sponge is a simple water **animal**. Most sponges live in warm seas and **oceans**, but some are found in cold seas. A few are freshwater creatures.

A sponge's body is a mass of jelly-like flesh full of tiny tubes, which lead to small surface holes. **Water**, carrying **oxygen** and pieces of **food**, flows in through the holes and travels along

the tubes. This is how the animal breathes and feeds. Waste products are taken away through other tubes.

When a sponge dies, the flesh rots and leaves behind the **skeleton**. Some skeletons are soft, and are used in homes as bath sponges. Today, most bath 'sponges' are not real – they are made from **rubber** or **plastic**.

Sport *see* pages 314–315

Squid

Squid are **molluscs** related to the **octopus**. Many live deep in the sea by day but rise to feed at night. A squid uses its ten tentacles to catch **fish** and feed them into its beaklike mouth. Some squid are no bigger than a thumb, but the giant squid grows up to 12 m in length.

Squirrel

Squirrels are **rodents** that are active during the day, unlike most small **mammals**. The most common squirrel in Britain is the grey squirrel.

Tree squirrels have sharp claws for climbing and a long, bushy tail for balance. They can leap 3 m from tree to tree. Flying squirrels jump up to 30 m. They have flaps of **skin** between their front and back legs. When a flying squirrel jumps and spreads its limbs, the flaps form a parachute. Both tree squirrels and flying squirrels feed on **leaves**, twigs and **seeds**.

Ground squirrels live in underground burrows. They include prairie dogs, chipmunks and woodchucks, which all live in **North America**.

Sri Lanka

Sri Lanka is an **island** country off the southern tip of **India**. Until 1972, Sri Lanka was called Ceylon. The island is near the **equator**, so the **climate** is

(1) A nebula (cloud of dust and gas) is the birthplace of a star.

(2) The gas and dust condense. The star begins to form.

(3) Nuclear reaction takes place – hydrogen changes to helium.

(4) The new star gives off light and heat.

(5) The yellow star remains stable for billions of years.

tropical. Most of the **trees** and shrubs have been cleared away to make room for crops, but there are still bamboo and **palm** trees. **Elephants, leopards, monkeys, snakes** and colourful **birds** live in the wilder areas. Sri Lanka's crops include **tea, rubber** and coconuts.

There is continuing unrest between the ruling Sinhalese, who are mainly Buddhist (see **Buddhism**), and the Tamil people, most of whom follow the **religion** of **Hinduism**.

Stalin, Josef

Josef Stalin (1879–1953) ruled the **Soviet Union** from 1929 to 1953. After **Lenin** died, Stalin made the Soviet Union one of the two most powerful nations in the world. He was a **dictator** who killed or imprisoned millions who disliked him or disagreed with his kind of **communism**.

Stamp

A stamp can be a special mark, or a piece of printed **paper** with a sticky back. A passport must bear the correct **government** stamp. Postage stamps are stuck on letters and parcels to be carried by the post office. Each nation has its own postage stamps.

Star

The stars we can see from **earth** are just a few of the many billions scattered through space. Stars look small because they are so far away, but most are huge, fiery balls of **gas** like the **sun**.

Stars begin as clouds of gas. **Gravity** pulls the gas particles in towards the middle of each cloud. There, the particles collide and grow hot. More and more particles press in until a star forms. **Hydrogen** atoms inside the star change into helium **atoms** by a process called nuclear fusion. This gives off **nuclear energy**, which makes the star glow brightly.

When all the hydrogen at the centre of a star is used up, the outer layers swell until the star is much larger than before. Astronomers (see **astronomy**) call such stars red giants. Red giants later shrink into tiny, white-hot stars called white dwarfs. In time, these cool and fade into the darkness of space.

Starch

Starch is a substance found in **plants**. **Cereals** such as **wheat, rice** and maize are particularly rich in starch. Other plants that contain it are peas, beans and potatoes. Starch is a carbohydrate, which means that it is made up of **carbon, oxygen** and **hydrogen**, the same ingredients found in **sugar**. It is important to have starch in the diet because it gives **energy**.

Pure starch is a white powder used in the making of many **food** products. It is also used to give some types of **paper** a shiny coating and to stiffen **cottons**, linens and other materials.

△ A **star** forms from a cloud of gas and dust, and then shines steadily for billions of years.

SRI LANKA
Government: Republic
Capital: Colombo
Area: 65,610 sq km
Population: 19 million
Languages: Sinhala and Tamil
Currency: Rupee

Josef **Stalin** ruled the Soviet Union as a dictator. The name Stalin means 'man of steel'.

SPACE EXPLORATION

Space exploration began in 1957 with the launch of the first artificial satellite. The Americans put the first man on the moon in 1969. Today, probes search ever further throughout the universe and the first tourist space flights have taken place.

△ *After intense competition between the Americans and Soviets, US astronaut Neil Armstrong walked on the moon in 1969.*

WARLIKE BEGINNINGS

The technology that fuelled early space exploration originated in World War II, with the development of an unpiloted rocket engine, the German V2 rocket. After the war, many of Germany's best scientists emigrated to the United States. As the Cold War between the United States and the Soviet Union escalated, both superpowers wanted to develop the capability to launch a decisive strike from space.

The United States and the Soviet Union raced to become the first to launch a satellite into space. They built on the technology of the V2 rocket, albeit on a greater scale.

On 4 October 1957, the Soviets successfully sent a satellite, *Sputnik*, into orbit. The radio messages it relayed back to earth were proof of the Soviet Union's achievement.

FIRST MAN IN SPACE

In the USA, NASA (the National Aeronautics and Space Administration) started to recruit pilots to train as astronauts. Seven men were chosen, keen to be the first humans in space. But on 12 April 1961, the Soviet Union strengthened their lead when they launched the cosmonaut (Soviet astronaut) Yuri Gagarin into orbit around the earth. The first words uttered by a human in space were, 'I see earth. It's so beautiful.'

The United States were not far behind, and on 5 May 1961, launched astronaut Alan Shepard into orbit in the *Mercury* space capsule. On 25 May 1961, US president John F. Kennedy, worried at the lack of progress made by the Americans, promised that the USA would put a man on the moon by the end of the decade.

▷ *Space rockets are made of three parts, or stages, each with its own fuel tank. The first stage falls away as the rocket leaves the earth's atmosphere and the second is dropped at 190 km.*

TARGETING THE MOON

The fact that the Americans had lost the race to put the first human in space made them all the more determined to be the first to the moon. By the late 1960s, the US was ready to attempt a moon landing.

ONE GIANT LEAP

Following numerous setbacks, the US scientists and engineers finally got everything right with *Apollo 11*. On 20 July 1969, astronaut Neil Armstrong became the first human ever to step on the surface of the moon. His words have become legendary: 'One small step for man, one giant leap for mankind.' His steps were watched on TV by millions around the world.

VOYAGES OF DISCOVERY

The Americans launched several more manned flights to the moon, but from the 1970s the space programme began to concentrate instead on sending unmanned satellites into space, both for scientific research and also for defence purposes. The *Voyager* satellites began their vast journeys through the solar system in 1977. They passed the planet Neptune in 1989 and are still travelling through the universe today, heading towards the outer boundary of the solar system. Images sent back from these satellites are beautiful, and invaluable in helping scientists to find out more about objects in space.

▷ *The Hubble Space Telescope, launched in 1990, has two large, flat solar panels to power it.*

SPACE SHUTTLE

Space travel is enormously expensive. To save on costs, American scientists in the 1970s and early 80s worked on designing a craft that was launched in the conventional way but landed like an aeroplane. The space shuttle *Columbia* made its maiden flight in 1981. Shuttle missions gave astronauts an unprecedented opportunity to conduct experiments in space. The space shuttle programme suffered a tragic disaster on 28 January 1986, when the shuttle *Challenger* exploded seconds after launch. All seven of the crew died in the explosion.

INTERNATIONAL SPACE STATION

Since the end of the Cold War in the 1990s, American and Russian scientists have worked together to construct an international space station. It is hoped that this will provide a permanent platform for experiments in space, and a base for the next stage of space exploration. There have even been tourist space trips – Dennis Tito was the first, paying $20 million to join a Russian space flight in 2001.

SPACE EXPLORATION FACT FILE
First satellite: *Sputnik 1*, 1957
First animal in space: Laika the dog, 1957
First space probe: *Luna 2*, 1959
First man to orbit earth: Yuri Gagarin, 1961
First woman to orbit earth: Valentina Tereshkova, 1963
First space walk: Alexei Leonov, 1965
First men on moon: Neil Armstrong and Buzz Aldrin, 1969
First space station: *Salyut 1*, 1971
First space shuttle flight: *Columbia*, 1981
First space tourist: Dennis Tito, 2001

▽ *The third stage of the rocket is designed to fire twice before releasing the Apollo spacecraft and lunar modules towards the moon.*

▽ *The International Space Station is being built by scientists from 16 nations including the USA, Russia, Japan and the UK. The picture shows what the finished station may look like.*

SEE ALSO
Astronomy, Atmosphere, Gagarin (Yuri), Kennedy (J. F.), Mars, Moon, Planet, Rocket, Solar system, Soviet Union, Telescope

Starfish

Starfish are **animals** that live on the seabed. Most have five arms that stick out like the spokes of a wheel. Starfish do not have a backbone, but they do have a **skeleton** made up of bony plates. They move slowly on tiny tube feet arranged along the underside of their arms.

A starfish can open and eat a cockle. It grips both halves of the cockle's **shell** with its tube feet, and then pulls the shell open. The starfish pushes part of its **stomach** out of its mouth, which is under the middle of its body. The stomach slips inside the cockle shell and digests the cockle's soft body.

Common **starfish** have five arms, which can regrow if they are cut off. A starfish has no head or brain, although it has a network of nerves in its body. The mouth is on the underside.

Steam engine

Boiling **water** turns into steam. Steam will fill 1,700 times more space than the water that it came from. So, if steam is squashed into a small container, it presses hard against the sides. If one side is free to move, the steam pressure will push it outwards.

In the 1700s, British inventors such as Thomas Newcomen (1663–1729) used this fact to build **engines** powered by steam. In Newcomen's engine, a furnace heated water in a boiler. The water gave off steam that pushed a piston up inside a cylinder. When the steam cooled and turned back to water, **air** pressed the piston down again. The engine was used to pump water from flooded mines.

James **Watt** built a more powerful engine where steam pushed the piston first one way and then the other. Rods from the piston spun a **wheel**. By the early 1800s, such engines were moving heavy loads faster than **horses** could.

Steam engines powered factory machines that made the **Industrial Revolution** possible. They also powered locomotives and steamships.

The internal combustion engine has largely taken the place of steam engines. But many **ships**' propellers and power station **generators** are worked by steam which spins wheels called **turbines**.

▽ Until the 1950s, most trains were hauled by locomotives powered by **steam engines**. This picture shows the world's fastest steam engine, the *Mallard*. In 1938, this streamlined locomotive reached a record speed of 201 km/h.

Steel *see* Iron and Steel

Stevenson, Robert Louis

Robert Louis Stevenson (1850–1894) was a Scottish author of adventure stories such as *Treasure Island*, an exciting tale about a hunt for pirate treasure, and *Kidnapped*, an adventure story set in the wilds of **Scotland** in the 1700s. Stevenson also wrote *A Child's Garden of Verses*, a collection of poems especially for children.

Stock exchange

A stock exchange is a place where people called stockbrokers buy and sell stocks and shares – pieces of paper that show that someone owns a share in a **company**. A company's stock tends to cost more if the company does well, and gets cheaper if it does badly. People buy stock hoping to sell it at a higher price later. Millions of stocks change hands each day in the exchanges of **London**, **New York** and **Tokyo**.

Stomach

The human stomach is a muscular bag, open at both ends and shaped like a fat letter J. It plays an important part in the **digestion** of **food**.

When you eat a meal, food travels down the throat to the stomach. Juices produced in the stomach kill **germs** in the food. They also moisten and start to break down the food. Stomach **muscles** churn the mixture, then force it into tubes called the small intestine.

Stone Age

The Stone Age was the long period of time before people learned how to make **metal** tools. Stone Age people used stone, **wood** and **bone** instead of metal. The Stone Age probably began more than three million years ago. It ended when the **Bronze Age** began in **Iraq** and **Egypt** about 5,000 years ago.

The Stone Age had three parts: Old, Middle and New. In the **Middle East**, the Old Stone Age lasted until 10,000 years ago. When it began, hunters could barely chip stone well enough to sharpen it. When the Old Stone Age ended, people had learned to chip **flint** into knives, spearheads and scrapers.

In the Middle Stone Age, hunters used tiny flakes of flint in their arrows and harpoons.

The New Stone Age began in the Middle East about 9,000 years ago. New Stone Age people made smooth axe heads of ground stone. During this period, **farming** took over from hunting as the main way of collecting **food**.

▷ Archaeologists can tell that some of the huge stones that form **Stonehenge** were dragged from a site over 400 km away. This task must have taken our prehistoric ancestors years to complete.

Stonehenge

Stonehenge is a huge prehistoric temple on Salisbury Plain, in southern **England**. The main part is a great circle of standing stones. Each is more than twice as tall as a person and weighs nearly 30 tonnes. Flat stones were laid across the tops of the standing stones to form a ring. Inside the ring stood smaller stones, and a great block that may have been an altar. The large stones were raised 3,500 years ago, but some parts are older.

Stork

These large **birds** have long beaks and legs. They wade into swamps to catch **fish** and **frogs**. Some storks prefer to feed on dead **animals**. More than a dozen kinds of stork live in the warm parts of the world

The white stork is the best-known species. In summer, white storks nest in **Europe** and central **Asia**. In autumn, they fly south. Storks soon become tired flapping their wings, so they prefer to soar and glide.

△ In northern and eastern Europe, pairs of white **storks** often build their nest on a rooftop. The female usually lays four eggs, which take about five weeks to hatch.

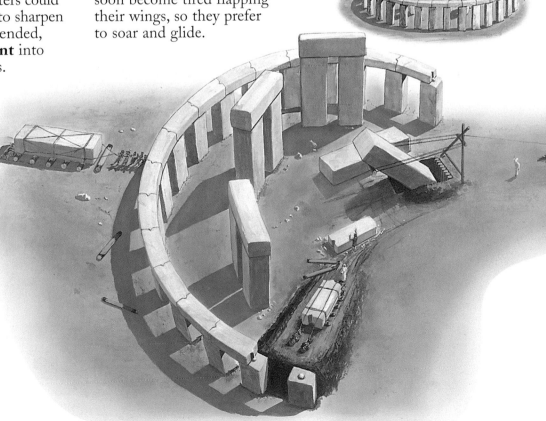

SPORT

A sport is a game or activity involving physical skill, usually in competition. Sports are enjoyed by millions of people around the world and provide big-business entertainment.

High jump

Landing area

Pole vault

△ *A discus thrower spins around before releasing the discus from his hand.*

COMPETITION

Hundreds of different sports are played throughout the world, pitting individuals or teams against each other and challenging participants to perform at their physical best. Sports offer fun and exercise for the casual athlete or at an amateur level, while professional sport is a multi-million-dollar business. The stars of many sports, such as basketball's Michael Jordan, golf's Tiger Woods or football's David Beckham, are worldwide celebrities.

In ancient times, sporting contests were tests of strength, bravery or proficiency at the skills needed to hunt, fight and flee. The ancient Egyptians played forms of handball, hockey, fencing, tug-of-war and long-distance running. The greatest sporting event of ancient times was the Olympiad, held every four years at Olympia in Greece. Today's Olympic Games, featuring dozens of sports and thousands of athletes, is a modern version of this ancient event.

△ *Ice hockey players speed across the ice and drive a hard, disk-shaped puck to score a goal.*

TRACK AND FIELD

Athletics events are held on and around a 400m-long oval track. Many of the events date from ancient times and are about being the fastest, the strongest, the highest and the furthest – the winner of the 100m sprint is known as the fastest person on earth. Track events include sprints over 100m, 200m or 400m, races over hurdles, and middle- and long-distance running events. Field events include four throwing events – the discus, the javelin, the shot put and the hammer throw – and three jumping events – the high jump, the long jump and the pole vault.

◁ *Baseball, played in the United States since the 1800s, is one of the world's most popular games. Thousands of people watch World Series matches, supporting teams such as the New York Yankees and the Toronto Blue Jays.*

FOOTBALL

Football is simple to understand and start playing, and is the most played sport in the world. The full game is played by two eleven-a-side teams for two halves of 45 minutes each. Players can use any part of their body except their hands and arms to get the ball into the opponent's goal. The one exception is the goalkeeper, who can handle the ball to prevent it going in the goal. Football has been an organized sport since the late 1800s, and by the 1930s over a hundred countries had their own football competitions. The very best footballers are picked to play for their country in international competitions such as the European Championships, the African Nations Cup and the biggest football event of all, the World Cup.

◁ *Influenced by wrestling in both China and Korea, sumo wrestling developed in Japan between 300 and 200* BCE. *Amidst much ceremonial and ritual, the two competitors must attempt to wrestle the other out of the circle.*

◁ *Heading the ball is a useful skill in football. Players use their foreheads to direct the ball – out of danger if they are defending, or into the goal if they are on the attack.*

▽ *Basketball is the most popular indoor team sport in the world. The best players, such as Michael Jordan and Magic Johnson, earn huge salaries and are national heroes in the USA.*

AMERICAN FOOTBALL

American football is a tough contact sport that developed from rugby and football. Two teams compete to get the oval-shaped ball over the opponent's goal line and score a touchdown. Each team consists of up to 45 players divided into three units – one for offence when their team have possession of the ball, one for defence, and a special team for taking kicks. Players advance the ball up the pitch by running with it or throwing it to a team-mate. In the United States, professional teams compete over each season to reach the two-team final, the Superbowl.

SEE ALSO
Baseball, Basketball, Boxing, Danger sports, Golf, Gymnastics, Horse-riding, Ice hockey, Marathon, Martial arts, Olympic Games, Rowing, Sailing, Skating, Skiing, Swimming, Table tennis, Tennis, Weightlifting

A **submarine**'s smooth shape helps it slip through the water with the least resistance. The submarine is steered by rudders, while its depth is controlled by winglike hydroplanes at the front and back.

Stowe, Harriet Beecher

Harriet Beecher Stowe (1811–1896) was an American author whose most famous **book**, *Uncle Tom's Cabin*, described the suffering of slaves in the south of the **United States**. The novel became a best-seller and played an important part in the struggle to bring an end to **slavery** in the USA.

Submarine

Submarines are **boats** that can travel underwater. A submarine floats on the surface when its large ballast tanks are full of **air**. If **water** is pumped into the tanks, the submarine begins to sink. To come back to the surface, compressed air is pumped back into the ballast tanks, forcing the water out.

Early submarines were hand-powered and slow. A steam-powered submarine was invented in the 1870s, but each time it dived, the crew had to pull down its chimney and put out the **fire** that heated water to produce steam.

By 1900, the American inventor John P. Holland had built the first truly successful submarine. Petrol **engines** drove it on the surface. Because petrol needs **air** to burn, underwater the boat ran on **battery**-driven **motors**.

In 1955, the first nuclear-powered submarine was invented (see **nuclear energy**). These can travel around the world without having to surface. In 1958, the nuclear submarine *Nautilus* of the **United States** navy made the

This one-person **submarine** can withstand the crushing effect of water pressure. It allows divers to work at a depth of up to 300 m.

SUDAN
Government: Military regime
Capital: Khartoum
Area: 2,505,813 sq km
Population: 28.9 million
Language: Arabic
Currency: Sudanese dinar

first submerged crossing under the **North Pole**. The largest modern nuclear submarines weigh more than 20,000 tonnes, and have room for about 150 crew members and 16 nuclear **missiles**.

Sudan

Sudan, the largest African nation, is nearly four times the size of **France**. It is a hot country in northeast **Africa**. **Desert** sprawls across the north and there are flat grasslands in the centre. The south has **forests** and huge swamps.

Most Sudanese people live near the **Nile River**, which flows north across the country. Khartoum is the capital city. A **civil war** has been fought between the north and south of the country since 1988. The war, together with severe droughts, is threatening the traditional way of life of many tribes.

Suez Canal

The Suez **Canal** crosses **Egypt** between Port Said on the **Mediterranean Sea** and Suez on the **Red Sea**. It is the world's longest canal that can be used by large **ships**. It measures 160 km from end to end and 60 m across its bed. Ships use it as a shortcut on voyages between **Europe** and **Asia**. This saves them from sailing 9,000 km around southern **Africa**.

The canal was begun in 1859 by a French engineer, Ferdinand de Lesseps (1805–1894). More than 8,000 men and hundreds of **camels** worked on it for ten years. **France** and the **United**

Kingdom operated the canal until Egypt took it over in 1956. Sunken ships blocked the canal for eight years after Egypt's **war** with **Israel** in 1967.

Sugar

Sugar is a sweet-tasting **food**. It is an ingredient in ice cream, sweets and soft drinks. We use sugar crystals to sweeten **cereals, coffee** and **tea**. Sugar gives the body **energy** more quickly than any other food, but eating too many sugary things can cause tooth decay.

Sugar contains **carbon, hydrogen** and **oxygen**. Different groupings of these **atoms** produce different kinds of sugars. The kind we eat most of is known as sucrose.

Every green **plant** produces sugar. Most of the sugar that we use comes from two plants: sugarcane, a type of giant **grass**, and sugar beet, a plant with a thick root rich in sugar.

Sulphur

Sulphur is an **element** often found as yellow crystals lying at the mouth of **volcanoes** and hot springs. Cabbages, **eggs** and other **foods** contain some sulphur. **Plants** and **animals** need a little sulphur in order to grow well.

Sulphur is used to make **fertilizer**, **drugs**, gunpowder and many other useful chemicals.

Sun

The sun is just one of many millions of **stars** in the **Milky Way**. It is also the centre of the **solar system** – the **planets** and their **moons** all whirl around it. The **heat** and **light** given out by the sun make it possible for **plants** and **animals** to live on **earth**.

The sun seems small because it is so far away. A spacecraft that took an hour to fly around the earth would need five months to reach the sun. In fact, the sun is so big that you could

fit a million earths inside it with room to spare. A bucketful of the material that makes up the sun would weigh far less than a bucketful of **rock** from the earth. But the whole sun would weigh over 750 times more than all the planets put together.

The sun is a great glowing ball of **gases**. In the middle of the sun, a process called nuclear fusion turns **hydrogen** gas into helium gas. The change releases huge amounts of **nuclear energy**. The sun beams out this energy in all directions as electromagnetic **waves**. Some of these waves give us heat and light. But there are also **radio** waves, **ultraviolet** rays, **X-rays** and others.

The sun was formed from an immense mass of gas and dust five billion years ago. It contains enough **fuel** to keep it glowing for about another five billion years.

Sulphur is a bright yellow element. A molecule of sulphur contains eight atoms in a ring.

The shining surface of the **sun** is called the photosphere. The dark patch is a cooler area called a sunspot.

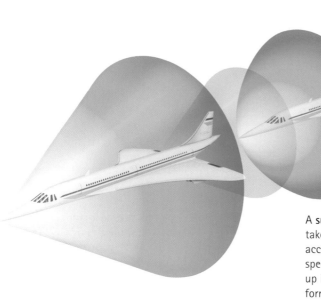

A **supersonic flight** takes place when a jet accelerates through the speed of sound. Air piles up in front of the jet, forming a shock wave. A second shock wave forms at the tail. The shock waves reach the ground, making a double bang, or sonic boom, as they pass over.

Superconductivity

Some materials allow **electricity** to flow through them more easily than other materials. These good conductors, such as **copper** and **silver**, have little resistance to an electric current, but they do have some – electricity struggling to pass through them makes them warm. In 1911, it was discovered that a **metal** called **mercury** loses all its electrical resistance when it is cooled to minus 273°C – the coldest possible **temperature**. The mercury became a superconductor, but it was very expensive and difficult to produce such a low temperature.

Today, scientists have created ceramic (**clay**-based) materials that superconduct at higher temperatures. They use dry ice (solid **carbon** dioxide) to cool the ceramics to minus 78.5°C. Now the race is on to find materials that are superconductors at room temperature. If this is achieved, the whole **electronics** industry will be changed. **Computers** will become smaller and faster, and **machines** such as medical scanners will be much cheaper to produce and run.

Supersonic flight

'Supersonic' flight means flying faster than the speed at which **sound** travels through the **air** – about 1,225 km/h at sea level. Higher up, sound travels at a slower speed.

When a plane flies slower than the speed of sound, the air ahead has time to divide smoothly and flow around the plane. But with supersonic flight, the air ahead has no time to prepare for the arrival of the plane. Instead, the air is disturbed so much it forms a shock **wave** that makes a loud bang and may badly buffet the plane.

Aircraft builders prevented buffeting by building planes such as *Concorde* with long, sharp noses and thin, swept-back wings. One supersonic plane has flown six times faster than sound.

Surgery

Surgery involves cutting into a person's body to remove or mend a damaged part. Surgery is performed in a **hospital** by a specially trained doctor called a surgeon. **X-ray** and other tests help to show the surgeon how best to operate. Before an operation, a patient is given an anaesthetic so that he or she feels no **pain**.

The surgeon cuts the patient open with a sharp knife called a scalpel, or with a delicate **laser**. Other tools help prevent bleeding and hold back flaps

During **surgery**, the surgeon and his team all wear sterile gowns, gloves and masks. This makes sure that they neither receive nor transmit germs.

of **skin**. After operating, the surgeon closes the wound with a special tape or by sewing its edges together.

Surinam

Surinam is a small country on the northeast coast of **South America**. People of many races live there. They grow **rice**, bananas, cocoa, **sugar** and **fruits** on the coastal plains. Surinam's most important product is bauxite, from which **aluminium** is made.

Surinam became a Dutch possession in 1667, when Britain handed it over in exchange for the Dutch colony of New Amsterdam (now **New York**). Surinam became independent in 1975.

Surveying

Surveying means using measuring instruments and working out certain sums to find out the exact positions of places on the **earth**'s surface. This kind of information makes it possible for people to make **maps** and charts and to build **bridges**, **roads** and buildings.

Swan

These large, graceful water birds are among the heaviest **birds** ablc to fly. To take off, they need a long, clear stretch of **water**. Some species of swan fly south in V-shaped flocks in spring and autumn.

Swans swim with webbed feet, and lower their necks to feed on underwater **plants**. They build bulky **nests** by pools or **rivers**. Young swans are known as cygnets.

Sweden

Sweden is the fifth largest nation in **Europe**, lying between **Norway** and the Baltic Sea. **Mountains** rise in most of the west, and **forests** cover more than half of the land. Their **conifer** trees yield much of the world's

Mute **swans** are heavy birds, but their long, wide wings and powerful breast muscles allow them to fly well. They need a long running start, on land or water, to take off.

SURINAM
Government: Republic
Capital: Paramaribo
Area: 163,265 sq km
Population: 413,000
Languages: Dutch, Sranan and English
Currency: Guilder

SWEDEN
Government: Constitutional monarchy
Capital: Stockholm
Area: 449,964 sq km
Population: 8.8 million
Language: Swedish
Currency: Swedish krona

softwood. Most of Sweden's **electricity** comes from fast-flowing mountain **rivers**. Farmers produce **milk**, meat, **cereals** and **sugar** beets on farmland near the coast. The north is too cold for farming, but it has rich **iron** mines. **Fishing** is also an important part of the Swedish economy.

Most of the 8.8 million Swedes live in the south of the country. The capital city is Stockholm.

Swift, Jonathan

Jonathan Swift (1667–1745) was an English writer, famous for **books** that poked fun at the silly, cruel behaviour of people and **governments**. Swift's most famous book is *Gulliver's Travels*, which tells of voyages to very strange lands. On his first voyage, Gulliver reaches the land of Lilliput, where the people are only 2 cm tall. Then he travels to a land of giants.

Swimming

Swimming is the skill or **sport** of moving through **water**. Many **animals** know how to swim from birth, but people have to learn, usually with the help of a trained instructor.

Swimmers usually use one or more of four main strokes. These are called the breaststroke, butterfly stroke, backstroke and crawl. Swimming is one of the best forms of **exercise**, because the water supports the body.

SWITZERLAND
Government: Federal
state
Capital: Bern
Area: 41,288 sq km
Population: 7.1 million
Languages: German,
French and Italian
Currency: Swiss franc

SYRIA
Government: Republic
Capital: Damascus
Area: 185,180 sq km
Population: 15.7 million
Language: Arabic
Currency: Syrian pound

▷ The battle of Yarmuk was
fought in **Syria**, in 636.
Muslim forces defeated a
Byzantine army twice their
size. The Muslims captured
Syria and Palestine, the
most prosperous part of
the Byzantine Empire.
They took Jerusalem, and
established the beginnings
of a large empire.

Switzerland

This small, mountainous country lies
in central **Europe**. The snowy peaks of
the **Alps** and their steep-sided valleys
fill most of southern Switzerland.
Tourism is an important industry –
many people visit the **mountains** for
skiing and walking holidays.

Most of the country's crops are
grown where the mountains meet the
lower land of the Swiss plateau. Here,
too, are most of Switzerland's cities,
including Bern, the capital. Swiss
factories make chemicals, machinery
and watches. **Chocolate** and **cheese**
are made from the **milk** of **cattle** that
graze in the Alpine meadows.

The seven million Swiss speak
mainly German, French or Italian.
The Swiss people are among the
wealthiest in the world.

Sydney

Sydney is the largest city in **Australia**,
and the capital of New South Wales.
More than three million people live in
Sydney. It stands on a natural harbour
(Port Jackson) crossed by a famous
steel-arch **bridge**. Sydney makes
chemicals, machinery and **ships** and
is an important port. It was founded
in 1788 as a settlement for convicts
sent there from **England**.

Synagogue

The building where Jews (the followers
of **Judaism**) gather to study and pray is
called a synagogue. The main prayer
services take place on the Jewish
Sabbath – from sunset on Friday to
sunset on Saturday. They are often led
by a rabbi (teacher). Children come to
the synagogue to learn the Hebrew
language and study the *Torah*, the
holy **book** of Jewish teachings.

Syria

This Arab country lies just east of the
Mediterranean Sea. Much of Syria is
covered by dry plains that are hot in
summer and cold in winter. **Nomads**
drive flocks of **sheep** and **goats** over
the dry lands. Farmers grow **cereals**,
grapes and apricots in areas where
rivers or **rain** provide **water**.

Most Syrian towns grew up on the
roads used long ago to bring goods
from the east. From 1516, Syria was
was ruled by **Turkey** for 400 years.
After **World War I**, the French ruled
the country on behalf of the League
of Nations. Syria became fully
independent in 1946. In 1967, Syria
lost an area called the Golan Heights
to **Israel**. Unsuccessful negotiations for
the return of this disputed area took
place in the late 1990s.

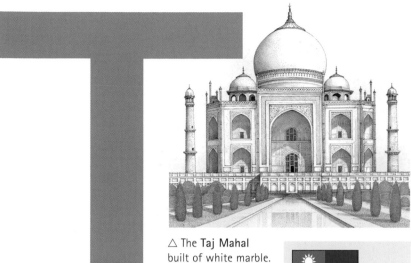

△ The **Taj Mahal** built of white marble. Its four sides are identical, with a minaret, or tower at each corner

Table tennis

Table **tennis** is a fast-moving indoor game played by hitting a small, light **plastic** ball backwards and forwards across a table. Each player has a **rubber-**covered bat. The ball has to be hit so that it will clear the net across the middle of the table, bouncing once on the other side of the net. If a player fails to return the ball, the other player scores a point.

The game was invented in **England** in the early 1900s as an after-dinner game. It is now a popular **sport** around the world and has even become an **Olympic** event.

Taiwan

Taiwan, once called Formosa, is an **island** country 140 km off the coast of **China**. **Rice** is the main crop. Most Taiwanese are Chinese whose ancestors emigrated to the island in the 1700s. Others are Chinese who fled from the mainland after the communist (see **communism**) takeover of China in 1949. Taiwan held the Chinese seat in the **United Nations** until 1971, when China was admitted and Taiwan expelled. China regards Taiwan as part of China, but many Taiwanese prefer to keep their island separate from the mainland.

TAIWAN
Government: Democracy
Capital: Taipei
Area: 36,000 sq km
Population: 22 million
Languages: Chinese, Taiwanese and Hakka
Currency: Taiwan dollar

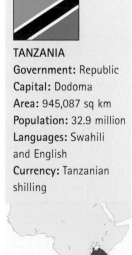

TANZANIA
Government: Republic
Capital: Dodoma
Area: 945,087 sq km
Population: 32.9 million
Languages: Swahili and English
Currency: Tanzanian shilling

Taj Mahal

This is the world's most beautiful tomb. It stands on the Jumna **River** at Agra, in northern **India**. The emperor Shah Jahan (1592–1666) built it for his favourite wife, Mumtaz Mahal (1598–1631). The graves of both the emperor and Mumtaz Mahal are inside the tomb.

The building of the Taj Mahal began in 1632. More than 20,000 people worked daily on the tomb, and the building was completed in 1648.

Tanzania

Tanzania consists of two parts – Tanganyika on the east African mainland, and the **islands** of Zanzibar and Pemba off the coast. They joined to form one country in 1964. Tanzania contains part of **Africa**'s largest **lake**, Lake Victoria, and Africa's highest **mountain**, Mount Kilimanjaro (5,895 m). The country has much wildlife and beautiful scenery. **Diamonds** are the country's most valuable **mineral**. **Gold** is also mined (see **mining**). Tanzania's former capital and largest city is Dar es Salaam.

Tape recorder

A tape recorder (see **recording**) turns **sound** waves into a magnetic (see **magnetism**) pattern on tape. When played, the pattern changes back into sound.

A **microphone** inside or connected to the recorder changes sound into an electrical signal (see **electricity**). This is amplified (made stronger) and fed to the recording head. The recording head produces a magnetic field which magnetizes the tape as it passes the head.

When playing back the tape, the magnetic field produces an electrical signal which goes to an amplifier and **loudspeaker**.

Tapestry

Tapestries are designs or pictures woven in cloth. Making tapestries is a very old craft. The Egyptians made tapestries about 1,700 years ago.

Tapestries are made by **weaving** coloured **silk** thread across rows of strong linen or **wool** threads held in a frame.

The tapestry design is drawn onto the linen threads with ink. The weaver works from the back of the tapestry.

In the Middle Ages, colourful **tapestries** decorated the walls of wealthy people's homes.

Taste

We can taste **food** because we have taste buds on our **tongues**. The tongue is covered in tiny bumps called papillae, and the taste buds are buried in the sides of these bumps. There are 10,000 microscopic taste buds, which are scattered in clusters on the back, tip and sides of the tongue. Each taste bud is a tiny pit containing a ball-shaped cluster of 20 to 30 gustatory (taste) **cells**. As the flavour of the food being eaten dissolves in the mouth, the cells in the taste buds trigger signals along **nerves** running from the buds to the **brain**. This tells you whether the food you are eating is sweet, sour, bitter or salty.

Flavour is a mixture of the taste and the **smell** of food. If you have a bad cold and your nose is blocked, food hardly tastes of anything because you cannot smell it. The most comfortable way to take bad-tasting **medicine** is to hold your nose while you swallow.

Bitter

Sour

Salty

Sweet

Taste has only four main kinds of flavours – sweet, salty, sour and bitter. Each patch of taste buds on the tongue picks up one kind of flavour, with the tip of the tongue most sensitive to sweetness. The middle of the tongue has hardly any taste buds.

Tax

The **government** of a country must have money to carry on its work. It gets most of this money by taxing people. Direct taxes, called income tax, on an income are those that people pay directly to the government. How much income tax a person pays depends on several things. The higher a person's income, the more he or she pays in tax, and a married person may pay less than a single person with the same income. Indirect taxes are those charged on some goods bought in shops or elsewhere. This tax is called Value Added Tax (VAT) in **Europe** and sales tax in the **United States**. Some countries impose these taxes on luxury goods such as **alcohol** and cigarettes, which makes them expensive to buy.

The taxes that people pay are used to keep essential services running so that they are available to everyone. These services may include the emergency services (ambulance, police and fire services), **schools**, **hospitals**, **road** building and defence (**army**, navy and air force). The spending of money raised by taxes differs from country to country.

Tchaikovsky, Peter Ilyich

Peter Tchaikovsky (1840–1893) was one of the most famous and popular musical composers. He was born at Votkinsk in **Russia** and studied **music** at the conservatory in St Petersburg. Tchaikovsky lived in great poverty until a wealthy lady, Nadezhda von Meck, offered to support him with a yearly allowance of **money**. Tchaikovsky never met Madame von Meck, but they wrote many letters to each other.

Tchaikovsky was a lonely man and very unhappy, but his music was full of warmth. He made several tours abroad, but he preferred to be at home in the countryside. Among his best-known works are the **ballets** *Swan Lake*, *Nutcracker* and *Sleeping Beauty*, his First Piano Concerto, the Violin Concerto in D Major and his Symphony No. 6, the '*Pathétique*'.

Tea

Tea is a refreshing drink that is made by pouring boiling **water** over the dried, chopped leaves of the tea **plant**.

Tea was first grown in **China**. It was brought to **Europe** by Dutch traders in the 1660s. Today, most tea is grown in northern **India**, China and parts of **Sri Lanka**.

A tea plant at full height can reach 10 m. As a crop, the plant is kept small and bushy by regular pruning, so that all of its **energy** goes into growing new leaves for use in tea production.

Teeth

Teeth cut, tear or crush **food** so that it can be swallowed (see **digestion**). Cutting teeth are called incisors, tearing teeth are called canines and crushing teeth are called molars. Meat-eating **animals**, such as **carnivores**, have large canines for tearing flesh. Plant-eating animals, or **herbivores**, have sharp incisors and large molars for snapping off and grinding stringy stalks. **Human beings** have all three kinds of teeth because we are omnivores – in other words, we eat all kinds of food.

In Japan, there is an ancient **tea** ceremony called *chanoyu*. The tea is made slowly, and sipped so carefully that it can take all afternoon to drink a cup.

People have three kinds of **teeth** – molars, canines and incisors. Each tooth has three layers. At the centre is a space full of nerves and blood vessels, and around that is a bony wall of dentine. On top is a layer of hard, shiny enamel.

Dentine   Enamel

Molar teeth grind up food into smaller pieces for swallowing

Incisor teeth slice food into mouth-sized pieces

Canine teeth tear food into chunks

Blood vessels

Nerve

There are two parts to a tooth. The root, which has either one, two or three prongs, is fixed in the jawbone. The crown is the part you can see. Tooth decay happens when **bacteria** mix with **sugar**. This mixture dissolves the tooth enamel, making holes that let infection get inside the tooth.

A human being's first set of teeth are called milk teeth. There are ten on top and ten on the bottom. As you grow, these teeth become loose and fall out. They are replaced by a permanent set of teeth – 32 in all.

Telecommunication

The Greek word *tele* means 'far off'. Telecommunication refers to long-distance **communication** by **radio**, telegraph, **telephone** and **television**. Most of today's long-distance communication is **electronic**.

Telecommunication is very fast because the **sound** and picture signals travel as electric currents along **wires**,

323

radio waves through the **air** and space, or **light** waves along **glass** fibres. Radio waves and light waves travel at 300,000 km a second. Electric signals travel almost as fast. Cable, telephone and radio networks use communications **satellites** orbiting in space high above the **earth**.

The rapid growth of the **internet** has revolutionized the telecommunication industry. An electronic mail (email) sent from one country to another can travel by several routes. For example, an email sent by **computer** travels by **fibre-optic** cable, then is transmitted via microwaves to a satellite, before arriving at the receiver by cable.

Telex and fax **machines** also play a part in today's communications. A fax machine is equipped with a telephone. When sending a message, the scanner inside the fax machine reads the page and converts it into electronic signals that can be sent down the phone line. The machine at the receiving end then translates the signals and prints out a copy.

Earpiece

Diaphragm

Mouthpiece

Number pad sensors

△ A **telephone** handset has a mouthpiece into which you speak, and an earpiece that you hold to your ear to listen.

▽ People use many **telecommunication** systems in their homes. Computers use telephone networks to send and receive electronic mail (email), and to connect to the internet. Most homes have a radio, television and telephone.

Telephone

Telephones let you speak to someone who is far away. When you pick up a telephone receiver, a weak electric current is switched on. When you speak into the mouthpiece, you speak into a **microphone**.

Sound waves from your voice hit a **metal** disc, the diaphragm, inside the microphone and make it vibrate. These vibrations travel along the telephone **wires** as electrical waves. When they reach the other end, they hit another diaphragm in the earpiece. This changes the vibrations back into sound waves, which the person you are calling hears as your voice.

The first electric telephone, made by Alexander **Bell** (1847–1922) in 1876, produced only a very weak sound over a long distance. Today, telephone networks use a worldwide system of cables and **communication satellites**. One of the most popular ways to contact people is by mobile phone. These handy pocket-sized phones use **radio** waves to put people in touch with one another from almost anywhere around the world. Mobiles also use radio waves to send text messages from one mobile to another. Some mobiles can even connect to the **internet**.

Telescope

Telescopes make things that are far away look nearer. They work by gathering the **light** from an object and bending it to make a tiny image. The image is then made larger so we can see it.

There are two kinds of telescope. The **lens** or refractor telescope uses two lenses fixed in a tube to keep out unwanted light. A large lens – the object lens – at one end of the tube collects the light. A smaller lens – the eyepiece – makes the image larger. The image seen through this kind of telescope is upside-down. To turn the image the right way around, a third lens is needed.

The other kind of telescope is called a reflecting telescope. Instead of a lens, it has a curved **mirror** to collect light. The mirror is shaped so that the light rays bouncing off it are directed at a second mirror that reflects the ray towards the eyepiece.

Television

Television is a way of sending **sounds** and pictures through the **air**. Scientist John Logie Baird (1888–1946) demonstrated the first television in 1926.

Cathode ray tube

Electron guns

Phospor strips

Television screen

▷ The main part of a **television** set is the cathode ray tube. The large end is the television screen. The narrow end contains three electron guns that fire electrons onto the phosphor strips on the screen. As each electron hits the screen, it lights up a dot. These tiny flashes of colour build up the picture on the screen. All the colours on a colour television screen are made up from three colours - red, blue and green. Each of the colours is supplied by one of the guns.

▽ The Keck **telescopes** on top of Mount Kea, Hawaii, each have 36 six-sided mirrors joined together to make one large mirror, 10 m wide.

The first television service began in 1936 in the **United Kingdom**. To begin with, all television was black and white. **Colour** television was introduced in the **United States** in 1956.

Television works by changing **light** waves into electric signals (see **electricity**). This happens inside a television **camera**. A picture of what is happening in front of the camera forms on a screen behind the **lens**. Behind the screen is an electron gun. This scans the screen. It moves from left to right to cover each part of the picture. Each part is turned into an electric signal

The temperature of the dome is kept near freezing to stop the glass warping.

The first mirror is made up of 36 small mirrors.

The second mirror reflects light towards the eyepiece.

Keck telescopes

that is made stronger, then sent to a transmitter. All the signals are broadcast by the transmitter as **radio** waves. They are beamed via **satellite** or sent along cable networks, and changed back into electric signals, which are sent directly into television sets in homes.

Live television programmes show you what is happening as it happens. Most programmes are recorded on **film** or videotape and sent out later.

Recently, the quality of television sound and vision has improved greatly with the introduction of digital technology, which produces a clearer sound and image.

Temperature

Temperature is the measurement of **heat**. It is measured on a scale marked on a **thermometer**. Most people in the world use the Celsius scale. The Fahrenheit scale is most often used in the **United States**.

Some **animals**, including **mammals** such as **human beings**, are warm-blooded – their temperature stays much the same. A healthy person's normal body temperature is 37°C. When he or she is ill, their temperature might go up to 41°C or more.

Other animals, such as **snakes** and **frogs**, are cold-blooded – their body temperature goes up and down with the temperature of their surroundings.

Tennis

Tennis is a **sport** for two or four people played on a specially marked court, which is divided in half by a net 91 cm high. If two people play, it is called a singles match. If four people play, it is called a doubles match.

Tennis balls must be about 63 mm in diameter and weigh about 56.7 g. Most tennis racquets are 68 cm long.

A tennis match is divided into sets. Usually, women play the best of three sets and men the best of five. Each set has at least six games. To win a game a

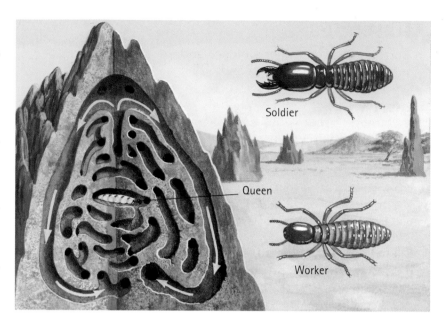

Soldier

Queen

Worker

△ Many **termites** build their nests inside huge mounds of earth. Inside the nest is a maze of tunnels and chambers where the workers look after the young. The queen is at the centre of the nest. Soldier termites defend the nest against attack.

△ Many cold-blooded animals, such as lizards, can survive when their body **temperature** drops almost to freezing-point. The body temperature of a lizard in the desert is hot during the baking heat of the day and cold during the chilly night.

player, or pair of players, must score at least four points. The object of tennis is to hit the ball into the opponent's court so that it cannot be returned. Modern tennis is a version of an old French game called 'real' tennis or royal tennis.

Termite

Termites are **insects** that eat **wood**. They have soft, pale bodies and thick waists, and live in the warmer parts of the world. Some termites burrow underground or tunnel into house timbers, causing a lot of damage. Others live in huge mounds of earth.

All termites live in large groups called colonies. Each colony has a queen, her king, soldiers and workers. Most termites are workers, and are small, blind and wingless. They dig the tunnels or build the mound and find food for the rest of the colony.

Soldier termites have large, strong heads, and are also blind and wingless. They defend the colony from attack. The queen is many times larger than the other termites, and her role is to lay **eggs**. She is kept in a chamber in the middle of the colony, with her king. The workers feed her and look after the eggs until they hatch.

Terrorism

Terrorism is the use of violence and terror to achieve political ends. There has been a marked increase in terrorism throughout the world since the end of **World War II**. Terrorists murder by bombing and shooting, they hijack **aircraft**, they kidnap people and hold them as hostages, they rob **banks** and often take part in **drug** trafficking.

Terrorism is a worldwide problem. On 11 September 2001, four US planes hijacked by terrorists crashed in **New York**, **Washington D.C.** and Pennsylvania, killing more than 3,000 people in a matter of hours. Since then, the US declared a **war** on terrorism, and countries around the world are working together against terrorist groups.

Textile

A textile is any cloth made by **weaving.** Before the **Industrial Revolution**, all cloth was made by hand from natural fibres of **wool**, **silk**, **cotton** or linen. Since this time, scientists have developed many kinds of manufactured fibre. Rayon is made from **wood**. Nylon comes from **oil**. There are even some fibres made from **glass**. Manufactured fibres are cheaper to produce, and often easier to wash and take care of. Sometimes, they are mixed with natural fibres to get the best of both materials. Some fabrics are treated to keep them from creasing or fading.

THAILAND
Government: Constitutional monarchy
Capital: Bangkok
Area: 514,000 sq km
Population: 60.2 million
Language: Thai
Currency: Baht

Thailand

Thailand is a country in **Southeast Asia**. It is surrounded by **Myanmar** (once Burma), **Laos** and **Cambodia**. The south coast opens onto the Gulf of Thailand, which is the westernmost part of the South China Sea.

Thailand is a tropical landscape of **mountains** and **rainforests**, with plains in the centre of the country, where most of the **population** live. Many **rivers** flow through this area, making it very fertile. Most people are farmers, and **rice** is their main crop. They also grow **cotton**, **tobacco**, corn, coconuts and bananas. In the north, there are large **forests** of teak (see **wood**), which is a major export. The peninsula in the southwest of Thailand is very rich in **minerals**, especially **tin**.

Most Thais are Buddhists (see **Buddhism**). Many Thai men live for a time as monks in one of the many Buddhist temples. They wear distinctive bright orange robes.

Thailand was called Siam before 1939. Thai means 'free', so Thailand means the 'land of the free'. There is a king, but the country is ruled by an elected **government**.

◁ Airports and planes are targets for **terrorism**. In the past, planes have been hijacked or bombed. Airports now have increased security, and detect bombs and weapons with metal detection equipment and X-ray machines.

327

Thanksgiving

Thanksgiving is a national holiday in the **United States** celebrated on the fourth Thursday of November. The **festival** originated in autumn 1621 and President Abraham **Lincoln** declared it a national holiday in 1863. People gather to give thanks for the harvest and share a traditional meal, which is usually a feast of turkey and pumpkin pie. **Canada** adopted Thanksgiving as a national holiday in November 1879, and it is now celebrated on the second Monday in October.

Theatre

A theatre is a place where plays are performed by actors and watched by an audience. The theatre may be just a patch of ground or a large building.

The earliest theatres were in Greece (see Ancient **Greece**). The Greeks cut a half-moon shape in the hillside and lined it with rows of stone seats that looked down on a round, flat stage.

The Romans (see **Roman Empire**) copied the Greek pattern, but they built most of their theatres on flat ground. The rows of seats were held up by a wall.

△ The first **Thanksgiving** was celebrated in 1621 by the Pilgrims at Plymouth Colony in Massachusetts, USA. A number of Native Americans joined the feast.

▽ The Metropolitan Opera House, known as the 'Met', is a **theatre** in New York, USA, that stages both opera and ballet. Each time a performance is put on, the theatre employs a team of about 1,000 people.

In **Europe**, before the 1500s, troupes of travelling actors used their carts as stages. Later, they performed in wealthy people's houses and in courtyards. The first theatres were made of **wood**. The stage jutted out into a large yard and galleries of seats ran all round the sides. There were seats on the stage, but only for rich people. These theatres had no roofs. When it rained, the groundlings – people who stood around the edge of the stage – got wet. **Shakespeare**'s plays were performed in theatres like this.

In the 1800s, music halls became popular. They staged shows featuring actors, singers and comedians. Lavish **opera** and **ballet** productions also became increasingly popular at this time. Towards the end of the 1800s, electric lighting (see **electricity**), revolving stages and special effects with **water** and smoke were used to add excitement to some shows.

Today, theatres range from a huge professional theatre offering the latest **electronic** effects, lighting and **sound** systems to simple productions by amateurs in small halls and **schools**. Modern theatre productions cover a huge range of entertainments, including opera, ballet, historical and modern drama, and comedy.

Entrance hall | 3,800 seats in auditorium | Stage | Slip stage with scenery for next act

Thermometer

A thermometer is an instrument that measures **temperature**. It is usually a **glass** tube marked with a scale. Inside is another, thinner glass tube, which ends in a bulb containing **mercury** or **alcohol**. When the temperature goes up, the mercury or the alcohol gets warm and expands (grows bigger). It rises up the tube. When it stops, the temperature can be read on the marked scale. When it gets cold, the mercury contracts (grows smaller) and sinks down the tube. If alcohol is used in a thermometer it is usually coloured red. Most thermometers measure temperatures between the boiling and freezing points of **water**. This is between 0° and 100° on the Celsius scale. Most countries use the Celsius scale, but some, such as the **United States of America**, also use Fahrenheit, in which the freezing point of water is 32° and the boiling point is 212°.

Medical thermometers are small enough to go in your mouth, and measure the **heat** of your **blood**.

Thermostat

A thermostat is an instrument which keeps a **temperature** steady. It is usually part of a central heating system (see **heat**). It switches the boiler on or off when the temperature gets too low or high. Thermostats are also fitted in kettles, **cars**, spacecraft, ovens, hot **water** heaters and many other **machines**.

Until recently, thermostats were made with **metal** strips inside. When the strips got hot, they expanded. They had to bend to fit into their space. When they bent, they broke electrical contacts. This switched off the boiler or heater. Modern thermostats are **electronic** and can work in temperatures that would melt most metals.

△ **Thunderstorms** are most frequent in the tropics. In some areas, they may occur on as many as 200 days a year.

Alcohol

△ Household **thermometers** measure how warm or cold the air is inside or outside buildings. Most of these thermometers contain alcohol because it is cheaper to use than mercury.

Thunderstorm

Thunderstorms are caused by **electricity** in the **air**. Different electrical charges build up inside large **rain** clouds. When the charges are strong enough, a spark leaps from one charged part of the cloud to another. Sometimes the spark jumps from the cloud to the ground, and we see the spark as **lightning**. Lightning heats up the air. The air expands so quickly that it explodes, making the crashing noise we call thunder.

Since **sound** travels much slower than **light**, you always hear thunder after you see lightning. It takes the noise of thunder about three seconds to travel 1 km. To find out how many kilometres away the storm is, count the seconds between seeing the lightning and hearing the thunder, and divide the number by three.

△ Lhasa in **Tibet** is the world's highest city, at 3,600 m above sea level. It was the home of the Dalai Lama, the head of the Tibetan Buddhists, until he sought exile in India in 1959.

Spring tide

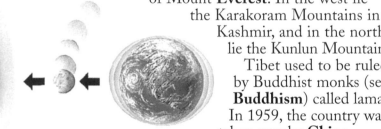

Neap tide

△ Spring **tides** are caused by the combined pull of the sun and moon. Neap tides occur when the sun and moon are at right angles to each other. The red arrows show the pull of gravity.

Tibet

Tibet is a region in Central **Asia**. It is the highest country in the world at 4,900 m above sea level – as high as the peaks of the **Alps**. Enormous **mountain** ranges surround the flat plain in the country's centre. In the south lie the **Himalayas** – the home of Mount **Everest**. In the west lie the Karakoram Mountains in Kashmir, and in the north lie the Kunlun Mountains. Tibet used to be ruled by Buddhist monks (see **Buddhism**) called lamas. In 1959, the country was taken over by **China**.

Tide

Tides are regular movements of the **oceans**. They are mainly caused by the **moon**. The moon's **gravity** is like a giant magnet (see **magnetism**). It tugs the oceans towards it as it loops around the **earth**. The earth is spinning at the same time, so most places get two high tides and two low tides about every 24 hours.

High tide happens when the **water** flows as far inland as it can. Low tide happens when it flows out as far as it can.

When the sun's gravity and the moon's gravity pull in the same direction, their combined force causes a very high, or spring, tide. These tides occur when there is a full or new moon. Twice a month, when the sun and moon pull against each other at right angles, a very low, or neap, tide occurs.

Tiger

Tigers are the largest members of the **cat** family. Siberian tigers of a remote region in southeastern **Russia** can be up to 4 m long, and weigh over 300 kg.

Tigers live in the thick **forests**, rocky **mountains** and swampy plains of **Asia** and **Indonesia**, in both tropical and very cold regions. They hunt **deer, fish, turtles** and **cattle**. They usually lie still during the day, and hunt alone during the evening and night. These powerful hunters stalk their prey near trails and waterholes, then drag their kill to a quiet spot to eat. One tiger can pull a dead buffalo that is too heavy for a group of people to move.

Until the 1800s, thousands of tigers roamed through the forests of Asia. Then hunters began to shoot them both for sport and for their skins. Today, tigers are hunted for their body parts, which are highly prized ingredients in some traditional Chinese **medicines**. Also, the forest **habitats** in which they live are slowly being destroyed. As a result, all kinds of tiger are now endangered.

Time

Nobody has ever really explained what time is, but people have invented many ways of measuring it. First, they divided up the **years** and months by natural things that happened regularly, such as the **season**, and the size and shape of the **moon**. The position of the **sun** in the sky told them the time of day.

The very first **clock** – a sundial – was probably invented by the Egyptians (see **Egypt, Ancient**). As the sun moved across the sky, an upright rod in the middle of the dial cast a shadow onto a scale of hours drawn around it. However, this was no use at night.

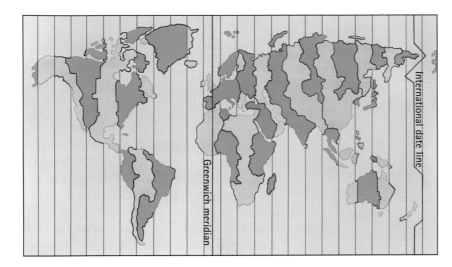

Greenwich meridian

International date line

make clocks more accurate. Modern clocks are very accurate. They work by **electronics**. Scientists need ever more accurate timekeeping. They use atomic (see **atom**) clocks that are accurate to 10 millionths of a second.

We think of time as being something that is the same in all situations, but this is not necessarily so. Albert **Einstein** showed that the rate at which time passes varies according to the speed at which we are travelling. On a **supersonic** jet, clocks and watches move very slightly slower than they do on the ground. The difference would only be noticeable, however, in a spacecraft travelling at close to the speed of **light**.

Because of the rotation of the **earth**, sunrise in, for example, the eastern **United States** occurs three hours earlier than in the western part. For this reason, the world has been divided into 24 time zones. At the International Date Line, the date changes.

Other ways of telling the time, without the sun's help, were invented, for example, the hour glass. This was two **glass** bulbs joined together. **Sand** in one bulb took exactly one hour to trickle through a hole into the other bulb. Mechanical clocks, driven by **weights**, were not made until the 1200s. Clocks worked by springs were made in the 1500s, and in the early 1600s, the **pendulum** was used to

△ The world is divided into 24 **time** zones, starting at the prime meridian at Greenwich, in the UK. Each zone west of the meridian is an hour earlier than the last. Each zone to the east is one hour ahead.

▽ The Siberian **tiger** is the largest and rarest type of tiger, with less than 400 left in the wild.

△ **Tokyo** is Japan's centre of culture as well as being the largest built-up area in the country. More than ten percent of Japan's population live in this bustling city.

Tin

Tin is a soft, white **metal**, and can be mixed with **copper** to make **bronze**. It is one of the oldest metals known to us – people were mining tin before **iron** was discovered. Tin was mined in Mesopotamia (present-day **Iraq**) and **Europe** over 4,000 years ago. An ancient people called the Phoenicians sailed from the **Mediterranean Sea** to **England** to **trade** goods such as cloth and precious stones for it. Today, the main tin mines are in **Bolivia**, **Southeast Asia** and West **Africa**.

Tin is not a common metal, but is very useful. It is used for packaging because it does not **rust**, and for plating other metals to give a bright, shiny surface. Tin cans are made from sheets of steel that have been coated with tin. Mixed with antimony and copper, tin makes pewter – a soft **alloy** once used for most tableware.

△ In the 1600s, European settlers in America grew **tobacco**, as well as other crops such as wheat and cotton.

Toad *see* Frog and Toad

Toadstool
see **Mushroom and Toadstool**

Tobacco

Tobacco is made from the dried leaves of the **plant** *Nicotiana*, which belongs to the same family as potatoes. It is a native plant of **Central America** and **South America**, but is now grown all over the world. The Spanish **explorer** Francisco Hernandez (d. 1517) carried it to **Europe** in 1599.

Tobacco leaves are picked, dried and can be rolled together to make cigars, or shredded up to be smoked in pipes or cigarettes. Tobacco is also chewed and is made into snuff – a powder that can be sniffed. All these forms of tobacco are harmful to people's **health**. It is particularly harmful to the **lungs**, **heart** and **blood** vessels.

Tokyo

Tokyo is the capital of **Japan**, and is situated on the southeastern coast of Honshu – Japan's main **island**. It is one of the largest cities in the world. The **population** of Tokyo and the surrounding area is 26 million. Tokyo's **houses**, buildings and factories sprawl along the western side of Tokyo Bay.

Tokyo is Japan's leading centre for business, finance and manufacturing, producing a large variety of products, including electrical and **electronic** goods, **cameras** and **cars**. Its location near the sea makes it a busy shipping port. There are also huge shipyards and **oil** refineries on the coast.

Tolstoy, Leo

Leo Tolstoy (1828–1910) was a Russian author who is known particularly for his novels *War and Peace* and *Anna Karenina*. He was born into a noble family and fought in the Crimean War (1854–1856). Tolstoy hated the greed and selfishness he found on his travels. He turned away from the Russian Orthodox Church and followed a way of life that was based on **Christianity** and the teachings of **Jesus** Christ. He felt that all violence, and having wealth, was wrong – only love and pity would bring happiness.

Leo Tolstoy had very advanced ideas for his time. He made sure the people who worked for him had proper homes and education.

Tolstoy died at the age of 82. He was refused burial by the Church, but people thronged to his funeral, seeing him as a man who had done his best to improve their lot.

Tomato

Tomatoes are round, red, fleshy **fruits**. They contain a very good supply of some of the **vitamins** people need, especially the vitamins A and C.

Tomatoes were first grown thousands of years ago in **South America**. In 1596, the Spanish carried them to **Europe**. At first, no one would eat tomatoes because people thought they were poisonous, so they were kept as ornamental **plants**. For a long time, tomatoes were called 'love apples' or 'golden apples'.

Although tomatoes are fruit, they are almost always eaten as **vegetables**. In the 1900s, they became a popular **food**. Now they are grown all over the world.

△ **Tomatoes** develop from clusters of small yellow flowers. After the flowers are pollinated, the seeds of the fruit start to develop. The whole process, from flower to ripe tomato, takes 40 to 75 days.

Tongue

The tongue is a muscular, flexible flap fixed inside the mouth. Only **vertebrates** have tongues. Our own tongues help us to **taste** and eat **food**, and to talk. The letters T and D, for instance, cannot be said without using the tongue in a certain way.

In toads, the tongue is fixed to the front of the mouth. **Cats'** rough

tongues are covered in tiny hooks of flesh called papillae. They help the cat lap up **liquids** and keep its fur clean.

Many **reptiles**, such as **snakes**, have split or forked tongues, which flick in and out of their mouths to 'smell' the **air**. Some **amphibians** and **lizards** have long sticky tongues that shoot out of their mouths to catch **insects**.

Tonsils

Tonsils are two small lumps at the back of the throat, one on each side. They help to protect the body from **germs** coming in through the mouth.

Children have very large tonsils. These gradually shrink as they grow older. Sometimes, tonsils can become infected. They swell up and are very painful. This illness is called tonsillitis. The tonsils may have to be taken out by doctors in a **hospital**. Having tonsils taken out does not seem to harm our bodies in any way.

Tornado

Tornadoes are violent, whirling windstorms (see **wind**). Most of them happen in **North America**, but they can occur anywhere in the world.

Hurricanes are strong winds that build up over the sea, whereas tornadoes build up over land. Tornadoes happen when large masses of cloud meet. The clouds begin to whirl around each other, and gradually join together to make a gigantic, twisting funnel. When this touches the ground, it sucks up anything in its path – **trees**, houses or people.

At the tornado's centre, wind speeds can reach almost 650 km per hour.

▽ This grass snake has a forked or split **tongue** that can 'smell' the air.

Tortoise

Tortoises are slow-moving **reptiles**. They can walk only about 5 m in a minute. When frightened, they pull their heads and legs inside their domed shells. There are 40 or so species of tortoise and they live on land, mostly in warm parts of the world. They are similar to **turtles** and terrapins, but those reptiles live in **water**.

Giant tortoises live in the Galapagos Islands and **islands** in the **Indian Ocean**. They can weigh up to 225 kg and be 1.8 m long. Some large tortoises live for over 150 years.

Touch

There are different **nerve cells** in **skin** called receptors that respond to five main kinds of sensation – light touch, heavy touch (pressure), pain, **heat** and cold. Receptors pass sensations along nerves to the **brain**.

Pain receptors are the most numerous, and cold receptors the least numerous. Some parts of the body, such as the **tongue** and fingertips, have more receptors than others.

There are also receptors inside the **human body**. Usually, we do not realize that these are working, except when they produce sensations such as hunger or tiredness.

△ This odd body shows which areas of our body are most sensitive to **touch**. The enlarged body parts – mouth, feet and hands – are the most sensitive.

△ The most visible **trade** is carried out by ships on waterways. They transport goods cheaply, packed in large containers.

▽ Desert **tortoises** are up to 35 cm long and live in the American deserts. As long as they have juicy cacti to eat, they do not need to drink.

Trade

The buying and selling of goods and services is called trade. Trade also includes barter, which is the exchange of one type of goods for goods of a different kind. Domestic trade is trade that takes place within one country. **Companies** that buy goods in large quantities and then sell them to shopkeepers are called wholesalers. Companies that sell the goods to shops are called retailers.

International trade is trade between countries. Imports are things that a country buys. Exports are things that a country sells. Some imports and exports are said to be 'visible'. These include raw materials, such as **iron** ore, and farm products, such as **wheat**. They also include factory-made goods, ranging from pencils to jet **aircraft**. Other imports and exports are invisible. These include banking (see **bank**) and **insurance**, transport services and **money** spent by tourists.

The chief trading nations are those with the most industries. But nearly every country now depends on trade.

Transistor

Transistors are small **electronic** devices. They are usually made to amplify (strengthen) electric currents in electronic equipment such as **radios, televisions, computers** and **satellites**. They can also switch electric currents on and off. Transistors have largely replaced valves, which were once used for the same purpose.

Today, complicated circuits containing thousands of transistors can be put into **silicon chips** that are only a centimetre square. The first practical transistors were developed in the 1940s by the US scientists Walter Brattain (1902–1987), John Bardeen (1908–1991) and William Shockley (1910–1989). The invention of transistors completely revolutionized electronics, and millions of these devices are now made every year.

Electric circuit

△ **Transistors** can act as switches or amplifiers in an electric circuit. These circuits contain many electronic components through which an electric current flows to make an electrical device, such as a toaster or computer, work.

transistors

Tree

Trees are beautiful to look at and are also very useful **plants**. Some trees give us **fruits** and nuts. Many trees, especially the **conifers**, are grown for timber. **Wood** is not only a valuable building material. It is also used to make **paper** and in some countries it is burned for **fuel**. Trees are vital to the environment, as they enrich the **atmosphere** with **oxygen**, and help protect the **soil** from erosion by **wind** and **rain**.

Trees are the largest and oldest living things on **earth**. The largest tree is a type of sequoia, which can grow to over 100 m in height. One bristlecone pine in Nevada, USA, is thought to be at least 4,900 years old.

▽ Different **tree** species can be identified through their characteristics. Each type of tree has a certain combination of bark colour and pattern, seed and leaf shape and colour. At a distance, some trees can also be identified by their distinctive shape.

There are two main kinds of tree – conifers, or softwood trees, and deciduous trees, or hardwoods. Conifers, such as pines, firs, larches, hemlocks and spruces, have needle-like leaves. They are also called evergreens because they keep their leaves throughout the year. Conifers produce **seeds** on the woody scales that make up their cones.

Deciduous trees, such as oak, ash, maple, elm, beech and horse chestnut, are broad-leaved, flowering trees that shed their leaves in the autumn. Deciduous trees have **flowers** that develop into fruits. The seeds of the trees are within the fruits.

The outer layer of wood on the trunk and branches of a tree is the bark. Bark is dead wood. It is tough and waterproof, and protects the living wood underneath. In this way, it has the same purpose as the outer layers of **skin** on our bodies.

As trees grow, they form layers, or rings, of new wood and become thicker. When this new wood is formed inside a tree, it pushes against the dead bark and makes it crack and peel off.

Red oak

Deciduous tree that is a bushy, round shape

Leaves turn red in autumn

Silvery grey bark

The fruits of an oak are nuts called acorns

Brewer's weeping-spruce

Needle-like leaves

Evergreen tree that is shaped like a cone

Seeds are held within a long brown cone

335

Trinidad and Tobago

Trinidad and Tobago is a country made up of two **islands** in the **Caribbean**. The islands lie near the coast of **Venezuela**. The **climate** is warm and damp, and the main occupation is **farming**. Trinidad is a large producer of **oil**, and this brings in most of the island's wealth. An annual carnival attracts many tourists, who come to hear the steel bands and calypsos for which Trinidad is famous.

TRINIDAD AND TOBAGO
Government: Parliamentary democracy
Capital: Port of Spain
Area: 5,130 sq km
Population: 1.3 million
Language: English
Currency: Trinidad dollar

Trojan War

The Trojan War was fought in about 1200 BCE between the Trojans of Troy, a city in what is now **Turkey**, and the Greeks. It lasted for ten years. The poet **Homer**, in his poem the *Iliad*, tells the story of only a few days of the war. We know about the rest from other writings.

Paris was a prince of Troy. He fell in love with **Helen**, the wife of King Menelaus of Sparta in **Greece**. Paris took Helen to Troy, and Menelaus with other Greek kings and soldiers went to get her back. They besieged Troy for years. In the end, they won by tricking the Trojans with a huge wooden **horse** filled with Greek soldiers, which they left standing outside the city. The Trojans, thinking that the horse was a gift, took it inside the city walls. The Greek soldiers then opened the gates and Troy was destroyed.

No one knows if the story is true. But in the late 1900s, archaeologists in Turkey discovered the remains of a walled town that had suffered a siege, violence and fire about the time the Greeks destroyed Troy.

△ According to Homer's poem, during the **Trojan War**, the hero Odysseus and other men from the Greek army hid inside a wooden horse.

Tropical fish

Tropical **fish** are among the most colourful fish in the world. They live in the warm seas of tropical regions, often along the edges of **coral** reefs. The bright **colours** are to warn predators to stop them attacking the fish.

Many small, brightly coloured freshwater tropical fish are popular aquarium pets. Marine fish can also be kept, but they are more expensive and difficult to look after. They have to have **salt** water containing just the right amount of salt in which to live.

Most tropical fish tanks have a heater to keep the **water** at around 24°C. A cover on the tank holds in the **heat** and stops the water from evaporating. Electric **light** bulbs in the cover light the tank and also heat the water. Most aquariums have air **pumps** that add **oxygen** to the water and filter it to keep it clear. Water **plants** also provide oxygen. Special **food** for tropical fish can be bought at pet shops.

The most common species of tropical freshwater fish is the guppy. Others include angelfish, barbs, neon tetras and cichlids.

Parrotfish

Imperial angelfish

Angelfish

◁ Thousands of species of **tropical fish** live on coral reefs. Many have dazzling colours and bold patterns.

Butterflyfish

Triggerfish

Clownfish

Tuna

The tuna, also called tunny, is a large **fish** whose firm flesh is rich in **proteins** and **vitamins**. Most tuna live in warm seas, but they may swim into northern waters in summer. Different kinds of tuna include the bluefin, which may be 3 m long, and the albacore. Tuna are the only fish whose body **temperature** is higher than that of the **water** around them.

Tundra

Tundra is the word used in **geography** to describe the vast treeless plains of northern **North America**, **Europe** and **Russia**, where it is too cold for **trees** to grow. Tundra regions lie just south of the ice-capped polar regions.

△ Temperatures on the **tundra** rise above freezing point for only two to four months each year. Despite this, the land supports a variety of plants.

△ **Tuna** is one of the most important food fish. It has been an important source of food to the people of the Mediterranean since the time of the Ancient Greeks.

Winters are long on the tundra, where the **sun** may not rise for several weeks or months. Snow covers the land at this time and the ground is frozen solid. The average **temperature** in summer is around 10°C.

Despite the harsh **climate**, hardy **plants** including **mosses**, dwarf shrubs and **lichens** manage to grow. The land is also home to a large variety of **insects**, which provide a rich source of food for **birds**, such as **swans**, geese and **ducks**. In summer, the tundra attracts migrating **animals**, such as musk oxen and caribou or reindeer, escaping from winter. Other animals that live on the tundra include Arctic **foxes**, **bears**, **hares**, wolves and lemmings.

Only a few people, including **Inuit**, live on the tundra. The tundra is a source of **minerals**, such as **oil** and natural **gas**.

TUNISIA
Government: Republic
Capital: Tunis
Area: 163,610 sq km
Population: 9.5 million
Languages: Arabic and
French
Currency: Tunisian dinar

Tunisia

Tunisia is a warm country in North **Africa**. Its beaches attract many tourists from **Europe**. The north is rugged and has the most rain. The south is part of the dry **Sahara**. **Farming** and tourism are the main industries in Tunisia, but **oil** and phosphates are important exports.

Over 9 million people live in Tunisia, most of whom are Muslims (see **Islam**). Near the capital, called Tunis, are the ruins of Carthage. Carthage was a great **Mediterranean Sea** power until it was destroyed by the **Roman Empire** in 146 BCE.

Tunnel

Tunnelling is important in **mining**, transport and **water** supply. The Romans built long tunnels to carry water (see **Roman Empire**). And today, a tunnel that brings water to **New York**, in the **USA**, is the world's longest at 169 km.

Different methods are used to build tunnels. In hard **rock**, the tunnel is blasted out with **explosives**. Cutting **machines**, such as those used to drill **oil** wells, are used in softer rock. In the softest rocks, tunnel shields are used. These are giant **steel** tubes, the same size as the intended tunnel. The front edge of the shield is sharp and is pushed into the earth. The earth is dug out, and the tunnel behind the shield is lined to stop it from caving in.

Some tunnels under **rivers** are built by lowering sections of tunnel into the river. Divers join them together. When the tunnel is complete, the water is pumped out. Underground **railway** tunnels can be built in deep trenches. When they are finished, the tunnel is covered over. The largest tunnelling operation of recent years is the digging of the world's longest rail tunnel under the Gotthard **mountain** range – part of the **Alps**, in **Switzerland**. It is due to be finished in 2006, and will be 58 km long. The tunnel will allow express trains to travel at high speed from Milan in northern **Italy**, to Zurich, Switzerland.

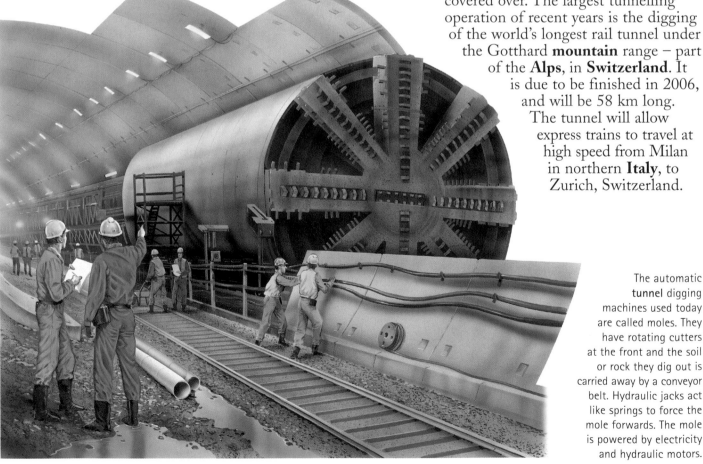

The automatic **tunnel** digging machines used today are called moles. They have rotating cutters at the front and the soil or rock they dig out is carried away by a conveyor belt. Hydraulic jacks act like springs to force the mole forwards. The mole is powered by electricity and hydraulic motors.

Turbine

A turbine is a **machine** in which a **wheel**, drum or **screw** is turned around by fast-flowing **water**, or by steam, **wind** or **gas**, to produce **energy**. Water wheels and **windmills** are simple turbines.

Water turbines are used at hydroelectric **power stations**. These stations are next to **dams** or **waterfalls**. The force of falling water carried through a pipe from a dam turns the turbine. The turbine does not produce **electricity** itself, but as it spins, it drives a **generator**, which produces the electricity. Some turbines are wheels or drums, with blades or cup-shaped buckets around their edges. Others are shaped like screws or propellers.

Steam turbines are operated by jets of steam. They have many uses. They are used to produce electricity in power stations, to propel **ships** and to operate **pumps**.

Gas turbines are turned by fast-moving jets of gas. The gases are produced by burning **fuels** such as **oil**. The force of the expanding hot **air** escaping from the combustion chamber within the gas-turbine system is used to make the turbine rotate. Gas turbines are used to turn the propellers of **aircraft**.

Tiny air turbines driven by compressed air are used for dentists' drills. These turbines drive the drill at more than 250,000 revolutions per minute, so the drilling of a tooth is done quickly.

Wind turbines are a great source of renewable **energy** because they generate electricity through wind power, so they do not need **fuel** to generate power.

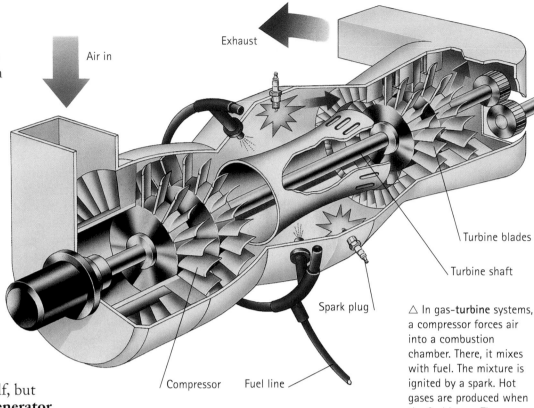

Air in

Exhaust

Turbine blades

Turbine shaft

Spark plug

Compressor

Fuel line

△ In gas-**turbine** systems, a compressor forces air into a combustion chamber. There, it mixes with fuel. The mixture is ignited by a spark. Hot gases are produced when the fuel burns. They expand and drive a series of fan blades – the turbine. The rotation of the turbine can be used to drive a generator.

Turkey

Turkey is a country that is partly in **Europe** and partly in **Asia**. The small European part covers three percent of the land. It lies west of the waterway which links the Black Sea to the **Mediterranean Sea**. This part includes the largest city, Istanbul, which was once called **Constantinople**. The Asian part, which is sometimes called Anatolia or Asia Minor, includes the capital, Ankara.

Most of Turkey's people follow the religion of **Islam**. Much of the land is mountainous and large areas are covered by dry plateaux (tablelands), but the coastal plains are fertile and **farming** is the main industry. Turkey also produces chromium – a **metal** used to strengthen **iron** and **steel**.

Turkey was once part of the **Byzantine Empire**, which was the eastern part of the **Roman Empire**. After Constantinople fell in 1453, the **Muslim** Ottoman conquerors built

TURKEY
Government: Republic
Capital: Ankara
Area: 780,576 sq km
Population: 64.4 million
Language: Turkish
Currency: Turkish lira

A niche in the wall marks the direction of Mecca

◁ The Blue mosque in Istanbul, **Turkey**, is one of the most beautiful religious buildings in the world. It was built between 1609 and 1616 on the orders of Sultan Ahmet I.

People are called to prayer from balconies on the minarets

European pond terrapin

up a huge empire. At its height, it stretched from southern **Russia** to **Morocco**, and from the Danube **River** to the Persian Gulf. But it slowly declined after 1600 and collapsed in **World War I**. After that war, Turkey's **president**, Kemal Atatürk (1881–1938), modernized the nation. Atatürk means 'Father of the Nation'.

▽ Green **turtles** spend almost all their lives at sea. They feed on seagrass and seaweed.

△ **Terrapins** live in ponds, lakes, rivers, marshes and coastal waters. They eat various freshwater animals, such as frogs and fish.

Turtle and Terrapin

Turtles and terrapins are **reptiles** of a type that have existed on **earth** for over 200 million years. Some people give the name 'turtle' to all shelled reptiles, including **tortoises**, but generally, the name is just used for those that live in **water**. Small freshwater turtles are called terrapins. The largest number of turtles are found in the southeastern **United States** and **Southeast Asia**.

All turtles have a scaly **skin** and a protective shell that covers most of the body. The shells of turtles are similar to those of tortoises – they are both made of bony 'plates' which are covered by large horny scales. They have a horny beak instead of **teeth**.

Marine, or sea, turtles spend most of their lives in warm seas, and feed on many marine **plants** and **animals**, including **jellyfish**. They swim great distances to find food, and many of them have webbed toes or flat, flipper-like legs to help them swim. The green turtle can hold its breath underwater for over an hour.

Turtles go ashore once a year to lay their **eggs**. They usually bury them in **sand**, or hide them among **weeds**. When the baby turtles have hatched, they dig themselves out of their nest and head for the sea. At this time, they are in great danger from predators such as **birds** and **crabs**.

There are several kinds of marine turtle. The largest is the leatherback turtle, which can weigh over 725 kg and be up to 1.8 m long. The green turtle is hunted for use in turtle soup, and its eggs are eaten in Asian countries.

Snapping turtles are the largest freshwater turtles at over 60 cm long and 90 kg in weight. However, they are not very good swimmers, and usually walk on the beds of the **rivers** and **lakes** where they live. They are found in central and eastern parts of the United States and in some parts of **Central America**.

△ In 1922, archaeologist Howard Carter found the entrance to **Tutankhamen**'s tomb. On the left is the chamber full of the pharaoh's belongings The burial chamber is in the centre and the treasure room with a shrine is on the right.

Tutankhamen

Tutankhamen was a **pharaoh** of Ancient **Egypt**. His tomb was discovered in 1922 by a British archaeologist, Howard Carter (1873–1939). Carter and the Earl of Carnarvon (1866–1923) were digging in the Valley of the Kings, in Egypt. The discovery was an exciting one, because they had found the only tomb of a pharaoh that had not already been robbed of its treasures. In the tomb were a golden throne, caskets, statues, precious stones and furniture. There were four **gold** shrines, one inside another, in the burial chamber.

Tutankhamen became pharaoh when he was about 11 years old. He probably became ruler because, as a child, he had married the daughter of the pharaoh Akhenaton. Akhenaton was a worshipper of the **sun** god Aton and had set up a new capital at Amarna. Tutankhamen brought back the old **religion** and moved the capital back to Thebes. He died in 1352 BCE, having ruled for about eight years.

Twain, Mark

Mark Twain was the pen-name of Samuel Langhorne Clemens (1835–1910), whose most famous books are *The Adventures of Tom Sawyer* and *The Adventures of Huckleberry Finn*. Twain grew up in Hannibal, Missouri, on the **Mississippi River, USA**. He had various jobs, including steamboat worker. It was from this experience that he took his pen-name. The steamboat expression 'mark twain' means 'two fathoms' (a fathom is a nautical measure equal to 1.8 m). Twain lectured all over the world, and wrote about his travels and life on the Mississippi.

◁ The body of **Tutankhamen** was protected by a nest of human-shaped mummy cases. The cases were put inside a big stone coffin called a sarcophagus. Each mummy case was decorated with gold and jewels. The mummy itself was wearing a beautiful mask made of solid gold. The coffins provided a home for Tutankhamen's spirit, or *ka*.

341

Uganda

Uganda is a small **republic** in East **Africa**. It was ruled by the **United Kingdom** until 1962, when it became independent. General Idi Amin (born c. 1925) seized power in 1971, but in 1979, Ugandan and Tanzanian troops (see **Tanzania**) took over Uganda, and Amin fled to **Saudi Arabia**. Most Ugandans are farmers. They grow **coffee**, **tea** and **cotton**. Coffee is one of the country's main exports.

UGANDA
Government: Republic
Capital: Kampala
Area: 236,036 sq km
Population: 21.5 million
Languages: Luganda, Swahili and English
Currency: Ugandan shilling

Ukraine

Ukraine became independent in 1991, following the break-up of the **Soviet Union**. The land varies from fertile plains to forested **mountains**. Ukraine has great **mineral** wealth. Its factories produce **steel**, chemicals and cement.

UKRAINE
Government: Republic
Capital: Kiev
Area: 604,000 sq km
Population: 50 million
Language: Ukrainian
Currency: Kryvna

Ultrasound

Ultrasound is the use of high-frequency **sound** (ultrasonic) waves, which can produce pictures of parts within the **human body**. Ultrasonic waves are too high-pitched to be heard by **human beings**. They are produced by sending a high-frequency electric current (see **electricity**) through a crystal of **quartz**, causing the quartz to vibrate.

Ultrasound pictures can help doctors detect tumours and **blood** clots. They can also help make sure that a baby is developing well within a mother's womb.

Ultrasound is also used in **sonar** to detect underwater objects such as **submarines**, and to map the seabed.

Ultraviolet light

If **light** from the **sun** shines through a prism, it splits up into a rainbow of colours called a **spectrum**. Red is at one end of the spectrum and violet at the other. Ultraviolet (UV) light lies just beyond the violet end of the spectrum. **Human beings** cannot see it, but it blackens photographic film (see **photography**) and makes some chemicals glow. Most ultraviolet light from the sun is lost in the **atmosphere**, but enough rays reach **earth** to give people suntans. If more ultraviolet rays reached us, they would be very harmful.

Ultraviolet light has many uses. It is a powerful **germ**-killer and can be used to sterilize **food** and medical equipment. Forged documents can be detected by shining ultraviolet light on them – the different kinds of ink on a document can give off a certain glow.

Uluru

Uluru is the **aboriginal people**'s name for the world's largest isolated **rock** formation. Sometimes known as Ayers Rock, it is 440 km southwest of Alice Springs in **Australia**. The rock is 335 m high and 10 km around its base.

◁ **Ultrasound** is most commonly used to monitor a baby's development within the mother's womb.

▽ **Underground railway** stations have a network of tunnels, stairs and escalators so that passengers can get up to the surface, and can move from one train line to another.

UNITED ARAB EMIRATES
Government: Federation
Capital: Abu Dhabi
Area: 83,600 sq km
Population: 2.8 million
Language: Arabic
Currency: Dirham

Underground railway

Every day, millions of people use underground **railways**. Underground electric trains (see **electricity**) carry passengers across cities much faster than **cars** and buses driving through the busy streets above. Most underground railways run through **tunnels** excavated out of the **rock** beneath a city.

The best-known underground railways are in **London**, **New York**, **Moscow** and **Paris**, because they were the first cities to have this railway system. The world's first underground railway opened in London in 1863. Today, there are over 60 underground systems in the world. The London and New York undergrounds are the longest networks, each having around 400 km of track. New York is the busiest underground – one billion people travel on it every year. The largest and most beautifully decorated underground stations are in Moscow.

The underground railway is known as the 'tube' in London, the 'metro' in Paris and the 'subway' in New York.

United Arab Emirates

The United Arab Emirates is made up of seven small states – Abu Dhabi, Ajman, Dubai, Fujairah, Sharjah, Umm al-Qaiwain and Ras al-Khaimah. Most of the country is hot, dry **desert**, but **oil** in Abu Dhabi and Dubai make the area one of the richest in the world. Each state is led by a sheikh (ruler), and each sheikh sits on a governing council for the whole country, with one sheikh as **president**.

United Kingdom

The United Kingdom of Great Britain and Northern **Ireland** is the eleventh largest nation in **Europe**. **England**, **Wales** and **Scotland** make up Great Britain. Northern Ireland, Scotland and Wales are mountainous – the highest **mountain** is Ben Nevis in Scotland. Plains and valleys cover much of England. The longest **river** is the Severn, which flows through parts of England and Wales, and the **climate** is mild.

UNITED KINGDOM
Government:
Constitutional monarchy
Capital: London
Area: 244,100 sq km
Population: 59.5 million
Languages: English and Welsh
Currency: Sterling pound

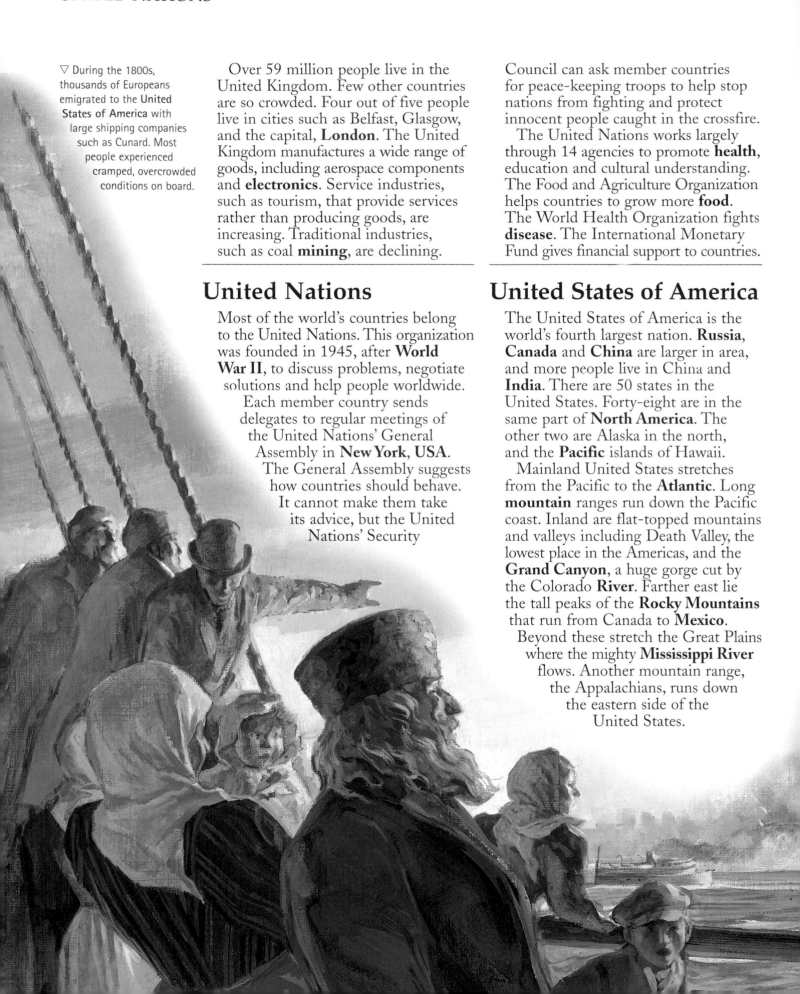

▽ During the 1800s, thousands of Europeans emigrated to the **United States of America** with large shipping companies such as Cunard. Most people experienced cramped, overcrowded conditions on board.

Over 59 million people live in the United Kingdom. Few other countries are so crowded. Four out of five people live in cities such as Belfast, Glasgow, and the capital, **London**. The United Kingdom manufactures a wide range of goods, including aerospace components and **electronics**. Service industries, such as tourism, that provide services rather than producing goods, are increasing. Traditional industries, such as coal **mining**, are declining.

United Nations

Most of the world's countries belong to the United Nations. This organization was founded in 1945, after **World War II**, to discuss problems, negotiate solutions and help people worldwide. Each member country sends delegates to regular meetings of the United Nations' General Assembly in **New York**, **USA**. The General Assembly suggests how countries should behave. It cannot make them take its advice, but the United Nations' Security

Council can ask member countries for peace-keeping troops to help stop nations from fighting and protect innocent people caught in the crossfire.

The United Nations works largely through 14 agencies to promote **health**, education and cultural understanding. The Food and Agriculture Organization helps countries to grow more **food**. The World Health Organization fights **disease**. The International Monetary Fund gives financial support to countries.

United States of America

The United States of America is the world's fourth largest nation. **Russia**, **Canada** and **China** are larger in area, and more people live in China and **India**. There are 50 states in the United States. Forty-eight are in the same part of **North America**. The other two are Alaska in the north, and the **Pacific** islands of Hawaii.

Mainland United States stretches from the Pacific to the **Atlantic**. Long **mountain** ranges run down the Pacific coast. Inland are flat-topped mountains and valleys including Death Valley, the lowest place in the Americas, and the **Grand Canyon**, a huge gorge cut by the Colorado **River**. Farther east lie the tall peaks of the **Rocky Mountains** that run from Canada to **Mexico**. Beyond these stretch the Great Plains where the mighty **Mississippi River** flows. Another mountain range, the Appalachians, runs down the eastern side of the United States.

The United States is a young country – in 2001, it was just 225 years old. The original 13 colonies declared their independence from Britain in 1776, and George **Washington** was elected first **president** in 1789. By the mid-1800s, the United States had grown to much the same size as it is today. **Explorers** had added new land to the original colonies, and the country stretched as far west as the Pacific. From 1861 to 1865, a **civil war** was fought between the South, which believed in **slavery**, and the North, which wanted every man to be free. The northern states won and slavery was abolished.

Between 1870 and 1900, thousands of Europeans (see **Europe**) came to seek land and a new life in the United States. By 1900, the country's **population** had doubled. The 268 million citizens of the United States include **Native Americans**, **Inuit**, Polynesians and people whose ancestors came from Europe, **Africa** or **Asia**. Out of every 100 Americans, 76 live in cities and large towns. **Washington D.C.** is the capital, but **New York** is the largest city. Other large cities include **Los Angeles**, Chicago and **San Francisco**.

◁ Immigrants who sailed into the **United States of America** by New York Harbour were greeted with the sight of the Statue of Liberty. The statue was a gift from France in 1884 to commemorate 100 years of US independence.

The United States is one of the world's richest countries. Its huge farms produce large **wheat** crops, and more oranges, meat, **eggs** and **cheese** than any other country. American miners extract **coal**, **copper**, **lead** and **uranium** (see **mining**), and the United States is the world's largest manufacturer of **cars** and chemicals. California, on the country's west coast, is a major centre of high-technology industries such as **computer** and software design.

Universe

The universe is made up of the **stars**, **planets**, **moons** and other **matter** scattered through space. The **earth** is just a tiny part of the **solar system**, in a great group of stars – a **galaxy** – known as the **Milky Way**. Beyond our galaxy lie possibly 10,000 million other galaxies. Some are so far away that the light from them takes thousands of millions of years to reach us.

Scientists think that all matter in the universe was once squashed together as a fireball that exploded, shooting the matter out in all directions. As the matter spread, it cooled, and clouds of **gas** and dust came together to form the stars, planets, moons and so on. This idea is called the Big Bang theory.

Scientists are trying to work out the future of the universe. In the 'never-ending universe' theory, galaxies will continue to fly apart until space is almost all black emptiness. In the 'big crunch' theory, the galaxies stop moving apart. Their **gravity** will then pull them inwards again until they collide and explode.

UNITED STATES OF AMERICA
Government: Federal republic
Capital: Washington D.C.
Area: 9,373,614 sq km
Population: 278.2 million
Languages: English, Spanish and many others
Currency: US dollar

▽ Scientists think the **universe** was created by a huge explosion, called the Big Bang, 15 billion years ago. It generated a huge amount of heat and sent gases and other matter out into space.

345

▽ On 26 April 1986, a nuclear reactor exploded in Chernobyl power station, in the Ukraine, sending radioactive elements, including uranium, into the surrounding area. About three million people were affected by the disaster.

University and College

Universities and colleges began in the **Middle Ages** when societies of scholars banded together. As the institutions grew, buildings were bought to house the scholars. **Europe**'s first university was founded in the 1000s at Bologna in **Italy**. Soon after, universities were founded at **Paris** in **France**, Salamanca in **Spain** and Oxford in **England**. Today, most countries have colleges and universities.

Once people leave secondary school, they may choose to study further at a college or university. At these places of learning, a student usually studies only one subject. He or she goes to talks called lectures, and smaller study groups known as tutorials or seminars.

The student may have to write essays, produce projects and maybe carry out experiments in a laboratory. Colleges and universities have **libraries** that students use for study and research.

After three years or so, students take their final examinations. If they pass, they are given a degree, such as a Bachelor of Arts or a Bachelor of Science. If they continue their studies they can earn higher degrees.

Uranium

This rare, whitish **metal** is one of the heaviest of all known **elements**. It was named after the planet **Uranus**, which was discovered at the same time as uranium in the 1780s. Uranium gives off **radioactivity**. As it loses atomic particles (see **atom**), it decays, ending up, after millions of years, as **lead**. People working with uranium need protective **clothing** to shield their bodies from radiation damage.

Uranium had very few uses until 1940, when scientists found a way of obtaining **energy** from it. Uranium is the **fuel** used to make **nuclear energy** in atomic bombs and nuclear **power stations**. One tonne of uranium can produce as much energy as 30,000 tonnes of **coal**, and is therefore a very valuable metal. It is mined in many countries (see **mining**). Most of the western world's uranium comes from the **United States** and **Canada**.

Uranus

The **planet** Uranus is 19 times further away from the **sun** than the **earth**. It was the first planet discovered with the help of a **telescope**. Although it is four times the size of earth, Uranus looks like a tiny greenish-blue disc when seen through a telescope.

Unlike our planet, Uranus is mainly made up of **gases**. It has a rocky core surrounded by **water**, and its dense atmosphere is made up of the gases helium, **hydrogen** and methane. The methane gas gives the planet its distinctive blue-green **colour**.

Uranus spins at a speed that makes one of its days about the length of 17 earth hours, and one of its years lasts 84 earth years. It is the only planet in our **solar system** to rotate at right angles to its **orbit** around the sun. This gives Uranus strange **seasons** – the poles are the warmest places on the planet, with a summer lasting 42 years on the south pole where the sun never sets. At the same time, the north pole is plunged into 42 years of darkness.

No one knew what the surface of Uranus looked like until 1986, when *Voyager II* flew close to Uranus and took pictures. The pictures it sent back showed there are clouds on the surface, with **winds** blowing at up to 300 km per hour. The planet is circled by eleven rings of very dark, boulder-sized fragments. The planet also has at least 21 **moons**, one of which – Miranda – has **mountains** 26 km high.

Uruguay

Uruguay is one of the smallest countries in **South America** and is only 500 km from north to south. It lies in the southeast, between the **Atlantic Ocean** and its two large neighbours, **Argentina** and **Brazil**. Uruguay was a province of Brazil, but it became independent in 1825.

Low, grassy hills and lowlands cover

△ **Uranus** viewed from Miranda, its smallest moon. Miranda's surface is covered with craters, mountains and ice cliffs.

URANUS FACTS
Average distance from sun: 2,871 million km
Nearest distance from earth: 2,650 million km
Average temperature (clouds): -200°C
Diameter across the equator: 51,118 km
Atmosphere: Hydrogen, helium, methane
Number of moons: 21 known
Length of day: 17 hours 14 minutes
Length of year: 84 earth years

URUGUAY
Government: Republic
Capital: Montevideo
Area: 176,215 sq km
Population: 3.3 million
Language: Spanish
Currency: Peso

most of Uruguay. Many streams and **rivers** flow into the large Uruguay River or into the river mouth called the Plate River. Uruguay has mild winters and warm summers.

Most of Uruguay's inhabitants are descended from Spanish or Italian settlers. More than one in three of them live in the capital, Montevideo. Its factories make **clothing**, furniture and other goods. But most Uruguayans work in meat-packing plants, **wool** warehouses or on country ranches. Cowboys called *gauchos* herd the millions of **sheep** and **cattle** that graze on these ranches. Sheep- and cattle-rearing is one of the most important industries, and wool is Uruguay's most valuable export.

V

Vaccination *see* Immunity

Vacuum

A vacuum is a space with nothing in it. It gets its name from *vacuus*, the Latin word for 'empty'. In fact, there are no complete vacuums. When you try to empty a container by pumping out the **air**, a small amount of air always stays behind. This partly empty space is called a partial vacuum and new air always rushes in to fill the space. This is how your **lungs** work. When you breathe out, you make a partial vacuum in your lungs. Air rushes to fill the space, making you breathe in. However, the space does not always fill up with air. When you suck in air from a straw dipped in lemonade, it is the lemonade that rushes to fill the vacuum and so reaches your mouth. It is a partial vacuum that helps to keep **aircraft** in the air. As an aeroplane flies along, its wings are so shaped that they make a partial vacuum just above them. Air underneath the wings pushes them up to fill the space.

▽ Suction pulls dirty air into a **vacuum** cleaner. A swirling vortex of air spins the dirt out. The dirt is trapped in the machine, while the air is pushed out. The red arrows show the direction taken by the dirty air.

Dirty air is sucked in

Clean air is pushed out of the machine

van Gogh, Vincent

Vincent van Gogh (1853–1890) was a Dutch painter who worked mostly in the south of **France**. Van Gogh lived a troubled life. Only his brother Theo (1857–1891) believed in his genius while he was alive. Now van Gogh's **paintings** are famous all over the world.

Van Gogh failed in every career he attempted. He turned to **art** to express his strong religious feelings, but it was not until 1880 that he decided to become a painter. In 1886, he went to **Paris** to visit his brother, a director of an art gallery, and was immediately attracted to the work of the Impressionists (see **Impressionism**) he saw there. Influenced by this work, he began painting with vibrant **colour** and distinctive brushwork. In 1888, van Gogh moved to Arles in the south of France, where he did most of his most best-known paintings. During his last years, he suffered from terrible fits of depression. He sold his first painting in 1890, but committed suicide in July of that year.

During his short life as an artist, van Gogh produced some 750 paintings and 1,600 **drawings**. A great deal is known about his life because of 700 letters he wrote to his brother Theo and others.

St Peter's Basilica

Sistine Chapel

Papal Palace

Vatican City

Vatican City is the world's smallest country – only the size of a small farm – and about 1,000 people, mainly priests and nuns, live there. Located on Vatican Hill in northwest **Rome**, **Italy**, it is the **pope**'s home, and headquarters of the Roman Catholic Church (see **Christianity**). Despite its small size, the city has its own **flag**, **radio** station, banking system and **railway**. It also issues its own **stamps**.

Vatican City is surrounded by walls and contains many famous buildings. These include the Vatican Palace, which has more than 1,000 rooms; the Sistine Chapel, decorated by **Michelangelo**; and St Peter's Basilica – the world's largest Christian **church**.

Vegetables

Vegetables are **plants** with parts that we can eat. They taste less sweet than the plant **foods** we call **fruit**. Vegetables such as lettuce and spinach are eaten for their leaves. Other vegetables are eaten for their roots or stems. Carrots and parsnips are roots. Celery and asparagus are stems. Peas, beans and sweetcorn are **seeds**. **Tomatoes** and squash are really fruits, but are sometimes described as vegetables.

Seeds supply body-building **proteins**. Leafy and root vegetables provide **vitamins**, **minerals** and fibre to help keep our **digestion** working properly. Potatoes contain **starches**, which the body can burn up to make **energy**.

Canned vegetables often lose their vitamins and minerals, but frozen and dried vegetables can keep them. Vegetables can lose their valuable vitamins and minerals, and also their flavour, if they are overcooked. The best way of eating many vegetables is raw in salads, by baking or steaming, or if they are cooked quickly in a stir-fry. Some vegetables, including potatoes, cannot be eaten raw and have to be cooked before they are eaten.

Many people are vegetarians – they do not eat the flesh of **animals**, including red meat, **poultry** and **fish**. Vegetarians eat a diet of vegetables, **cereals**, nuts, seeds and fruits. Soya beans are a good source of protein. People who eat a well-balanced vegetarian diet generally have lower **blood** pressure and less excess **fat** than those who eat meat. Vegetarians must take care, however, to consume enough proteins and vitamins to keep themselves healthy.

△ Vatican City's buildings include St Peter's Basilica, which was built between 1506 and 1614. Next to it stands the Papal Palace and the Sistine Chapel, which is decorated with frescoes by the painter Michelangelo.

▽ There are many different **vegetables** that can be eaten as part of our daily diet. Most are grown from seeds, bulbs or tubers, then harvested within a year. A few grow on long-lived plants.

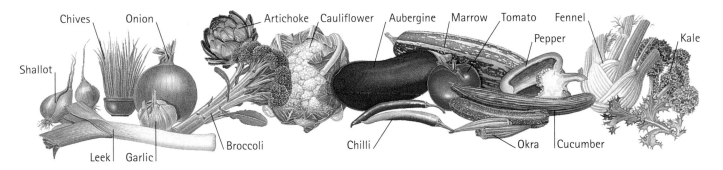

Chives Onion Artichoke Cauliflower Aubergine Marrow Tomato Fennel

Shallot Pepper Kale

Leek Garlic Broccoli Chilli Okra Cucumber

Inner layers
of vein wall

Muscle

Outer layers
of vein wall

Red blood cell

White blood cell

△ **Veins** carry blood
towards the heart so it
can be pumped to the
lungs and then out to
the rest of the body.

Vein

Veins are narrow tubes that carry used
blood from all parts of your body back
to the **heart**. Blood flowing through
the **arteries** is pushed along by the
pumping of the heart. Blood in the
veins has nothing to push it along.
So many veins have flaps, or valves,
inside them which close the tube if
the blood begins to flow backwards.

Venezuela

Venezuela is a large country on the
north coast of **South America**. Its
name means 'little Venice' in Spanish
because its many rivers reminded the
explorer who named the country of
the **canals** of Venice. In the northeast,
Venezuela is covered by high, flat-
topped **mountains** – part of the
Andes range. The Guiana Highlands
in the southeast are covered with dense
rainforest. Here, the Angel Falls –
the highest **waterfall** in the world –
plunges down 979 m. Grassy plains
called *llanos* stretch across the middle
of the country on either side of the
Orinoco **River**. Thousands of **cattle**
are raised on the plains.

Most Venezuelans live in towns and
cities along the coast. Venezuela grows
coffee, **cotton** and cocoa. Its **minerals**,
especially **oil**, make it the richest
country in the continent.

Beautiful masks, gowns
and cloaks are worn by
people during the annual
carnival in **Venice**. Many
of the costumes are based
on designs from the 1700s,
when the festival was at
its most grand.

VENEZUELA
Government: Federal
republic
Capital: Caracas
Area: 912,050 sq km
Population: 23.2 million
Language: Spanish
Currency: Bolívar

Venice

Venice is a beautiful city in **Italy**,
on the Adriatic Sea. It is built on
a cluster of about 120 low, mud
islands. The houses are built on
wooden posts driven into the mud.
A causeway of just over 4 km connects
the city with the mainland, and carries
a **road** and a **railway**. Within the city,
there is a network of over 180 **canals**
instead of roads. Ferry boats take
people into the centre of the city.
There are also elegant, black, flat-
bottomed gondola boats for hire, which
are propelled by an oarsman called a
gondolier. These boats are very popular
with the thousands of tourists who
travel to the city every year.

For hundreds of years, Venice was
the most important centre for sea **trade**
between **Europe** and the empires of
the East. The city became very rich,
and is full of palaces and fine houses
built by merchants.

Venus

The **planet** Venus is named after the
Roman **goddess** of beauty and love.
Venus is the brightest planet in the
solar system. We see it as the morning
star or the evening star, depending on
where it is on its journey around the
sun. If you look at Venus through
binoculars, you may see it looking like
a small **moon**, showing just the part
that is lit by the sun.

Venus takes only 225 days to go
around the sun, so more than three
years pass on Venus for every two on
earth. But Venus itself spins so slowly
that one day there lasts for 243 days on
earth. It is the only planet in our solar
system to spin in the opposite way to
the direction of its **orbit**.

Venus is about the same size as earth, and is made up of volcanic **rock**, but this planet has one of the most hostile environments in the solar system. The surface of Venus is hidden under a dazzling white cloak of cloud, which may be made up of tiny drops of sulphuric **acid**. Since it is the second planet from the sun, its surface is much hotter than earth. The atmosphere on Venus consists mainly of the **gas** carbon dioxide, which acts like a greenhouse, trapping in the sun's **heat** (see **global warming**). The average **temperature** on Venus is 480°C – hotter than boiling **water**. Fierce **winds** above the surface blow at over 320 km/h, and chemical reactions in the atmosphere create electrical storms.

◁ In 1982, the Russian space probe *Venera 13* landed on **Venus** and sent back pictures and information to earth. Soon after landing, the probes were destroyed by the terrible climate on the planet.

VENUS FACTS
Average distance from sun: 108.2 million km
Nearest distance from earth: 42 million km
Average temperature: 480°C
Diameter across the equator: 12,103 km
Atmosphere: Carbon dioxide, nitrogen
Number of moons: 0
Length of day: 243 earth days
Length of year: 225 earth days

Verb

Verbs are 'doing' or 'being' words, such as go, hit, choose, have and be. Verbs describe what people or things are doing, or what is happening to them.

Here are three examples of verbs in sentences: 'It is a cold night. Tom ate the hamburger. Jill was drinking a milkshake.' In the first two examples, the verb is one word – 'is' and 'ate'. In the third example, it is two words – 'was drinking'.

In the first sentence, the verb is describing something happening in the present. We call this the use of the present tense. If the action happened in the past, the verb

changes: 'It was a cold night.' Similarly, if the action is to happen in the future: 'It will be a cold night.'

Verbs can also be active or passive. In the sentence 'Tom ate the hamburger', the verb 'ate' is active. If we said 'The hamburger was eaten by Tom', the verb 'was eaten' is passive.

Versailles

Versailles is a famous palace in **France**. It stands in a town, also called Versailles, just outside **Paris**.

The palace at Versailles was begun by **Louis XIV** (1638–1715) in 1661, as a kind of 'holiday home' for the king and his court. The most famous architects, sculptors and gardeners of the time worked on the palace and its park to enable the king to live in greater luxury than any other **monarch** at the time.

The palace is built of pink and cream stone, and is more than 800 m long. Inside are hundreds of beautiful rooms. The most famous is the Hall of Mirrors, which is lined with 483 enormous mirrors, and is full of **paintings**. Louis XIV spent enormous sums of **money** on the palace. The great expense and luxury of the palace at Versailles was one of the causes of the **French Revolution** a century later.

Today, the palace is a museum and attracts tourists from all over the world.

▽ Louis XIV wanted **Versailles** to be the most splendid palace in France. He spent £58 million on the building – an enormous sum at that time.

VIKINGS

From about 800 CE, people called Vikings began to leave their homes in Norway, Denmark and Sweden in search of new farmland. Their strength and seamanship became legendary in Europe.

Viking chieftains, or jarls, had weapons of high quality with carved gold or silver hilts.

△ *The Viking Althing in Iceland. This assembly made laws and agreed important issues.*

SHIPS

The Vikings were amazing seamen. For long sea journeys, they sailed longships, which were extremely fast and had prows that were carved into fierce figureheads. They were known as 'dragon ships' by the people who saw them. Longships were sleek and built of thin, overlapping planks that flexed in rough seas. The boats were light and had low sides, so the Vikings could sail up rivers as well as over seas. The Vikings were the first Europeans to build ships with sails, which meant their ships sailed very fast. Longships could also be rowed when there was no wind or when the ship sailed close to the coast in preparation for landing. They also built wider, deeper ships for trade and small rowing boats for coastal sailing.

EXPLORERS AND SETTLERS

The Vikings were a farming community, and the need to find more suitable farmland drove them to travel and explore. They used their skills as sailors to voyage over much of the north Atlantic – an ocean known for its rough and treacherous waters. The Vikings discovered and then settled in Iceland and Greenland. According to legend, the Viking Eric the Red (c.950–1003) named the lush green island Iceland in order to put off any potential raiders. Within 60 years of settling in Iceland (c. 874), the Vikings had already set up a national assembly, which is now the oldest parliament in the world. Many of England's great northern cities, such as York, were founded by the Vikings. It is now also believed that the Viking explorer Leif Eriksson landed in North America in 1003 CE, about 500 years before it was settled by Christopher Columbus (1451–1506) in 1492.

TRADE

Vikings were very successful traders. They founded many great trading posts, such as Dublin in Ireland and York in England, from which goods flowed back into the Viking homelands. These trading routes also expanded east into Kiev and Novgorod in Russia, and as far south as Iraq and Syria. This allowed the Vikings access to goods that could never be produced in their own lands, such as silk, honey and oriental spices.

▷ *Runestones were set up by Vikings. These were tall standing stones carved with runes (letters) and beautiful patterns.*

◁ *Most Viking settlements were located near to water, and traders could often be seen unloading goods on the shore.*

VIKING SOCIETY

Viking homelands were divided into several kingdoms with a king at the head. However, people were more loyal to their local chieftains, or jarls, than to their king. The jarls, therefore, were the most wealthy and powerful people in society. They ruled over an area of land and had their own band of warriors which they could call upon to go raiding with. The largest group of people in Viking society were the karls – free men and women who were farmers or craftsmen. The poorest people were the thralls – slaves who were captured in raids or karls who had committed a crime. They worked as servants of farmworkers.

LONGHOUSES

Most Viking families lived in large, low rectangular buildings called longhouses. Each house had one main room where the family lived and slept. In the middle of the room was a huge fireplace, which provided heat and light, and was used for cooking food. Smoke from the fire escaped through a small hole in the roof. Family life centred around the fire. Women and girls did most of the household chores, such as cooking. They also spun wool and flax, which was then woven on a loom to make cloth.

WARRIORS

The Vikings earned a reputation for being bloodthirsty warriors, and were feared throughout Europe. Every able-bodied Viking man was trained to fight. Warriors were led by their chieftain, and went raiding or trading in summer. The warriors did not fear dying because death in battle meant that they would be taken to Valhalla (the god Odin's great hall), and feast and drink forever. So they fought ferociously and bravely with their weapons, which included swords, axes, spears and wooden shields. Rich warriors wore protective chainmail shirts and metal helmets.

▷ *Viking raids involved up to 60 longships filled with warriors. They targeted treasure-filled churches, and plundered coastal towns.*

RELIGION

Vikings worshipped many gods and goddesses in the open air beside natural landmarks such as waterfalls or large rocks. Different gods controlled different aspects of their lives, and Odin, the king of the gods, ruled over all things. Vikings believed the gods also controlled what happened to them after they died. By the 1100s, many Vikings had converted to Christianity.

▷ *When a jarl died, he had a spectacular burial. His body was placed in a boat, which was then set alight.*

Inside a longhouse

ENTERTAINMENT

In the evenings, Viking households settled down to entertainment. Vikings were excellent storytellers and loved to recite poems and stories called *sagas*. These were learned by heart because Vikings had no pens or paper with which to write them down. The tales told of the great deeds of gods and famous warriors. Vikings also enjoyed playing board games similar to chess or draughts, and enjoyed competitive sports such as wrestling and skiing.

END OF THE VIKING AGE

The power of the Vikings started to come to an end around 1066 when the king of Norway, Harald Hardrada (1015–1066), was killed at the battle of Stamford Bridge in England by the Anglo-Saxon King Harold of England (1020–1066). When Harold himself was killed later in the same year during the Battle of Hastings with William the Conqueror of Normandy (1028–1087), it signalled the end of the Viking age and the beginning of Norman power in Europe.

SEE ALSO
Anglo-Saxons, Christianity,Dark Ages, God and Goddess, Myths and Legends, Ship and Boat, Weaving, William the Conqueror

Vertebrate

Around 520 million years ago, Pikaia (centre) was the first fish and the first **vertebrate**, or animal with a backbone.

Vertebrates are **animals** with a backbone or spine. The backbone is made up of short **bones** called vertebrae. This name comes from a Latin word that means 'to turn'. Most vertebrates can bend and straighten their backbones by turning their vertebrae slightly.

Many things make vertebrates different from other animals. Most have a bony case to protect their **brain**, ribs to protect their **heart**, **lungs** and other delicate parts, and one or two pairs of limbs. And most vertebrates have a **skeleton** made of bone.

There are seven main groups of vertebrate. The simplest group includes the lampreys. Lampreys are eel-like **fish** with no jaw. They have a spine but no skeleton. Next come **sharks** and skates, which have a skeleton of a light, bendy material called cartilage. All other vertebrates have bones. They are the bony **fish**, **amphibians**, **reptiles**, **birds** and **mammals**.

Queen **Victoria**'s character and long reign, from 1837 to 1901, restored strength and popularity to the British monarchy.

Vesuvius

Vesuvius is one of the world's most famous **volcanoes** and the only active volcano on the mainland of **Europe**. The **mountain** rises over the Bay of Naples in southern **Italy**. It is about 1,200 m high, but gets shorter every time it erupts.

The first eruption happened in 79 CE. Nobody realized that it was an active volcano and so people had built towns close by and farmed the slopes of the **mountain**. For three days, Vesuvius threw out ash and lava that buried the Roman cities of **Pompeii** and Herculaneum. There have been nine large eruptions in the last 200 years. The worst in recent years happened in 1944 during **World War II**. One village was destroyed and Allied troops helped people to escape from the flowing lava.

This picture shows the first eruption of **Vesuvius** in 79 CE.

Victoria, Queen

Queen Victoria (1819–1901) ruled the **United Kingdom** and British empire for 64 years – longer than any other British **monarch**. During her reign, the nation grew richer and its empire larger than ever before. She was the queen of many countries, including **Australia**, **New Zealand**, **Canada** and **South Africa**, and she was the empress of **India**.

Victoria was the daughter of Edward, Duke of Kent (1767–1820). George III (1738–1820) was her grandfather. She was just 18 when she inherited the throne from her uncle, William IV (1789–1837), in 1837. Two years later, she married her German cousin, Prince Albert (1819–1861). They had four sons and five daughters. Prince Albert died of typhoid fever in 1861. His death left the queen deeply unhappy. For many years, she wore only black clothes to show her grief. She also stopped going to public ceremonies.

Victoria was very popular with her people. In 1887, she had been queen for 50 years. All over the British empire there were huge parades and parties to celebrate this Golden Jubilee. In 1897, there were more celebrations for her Diamond Jubilee. Her reign is known as the Victorian Age.

Video

A video is a **recording** of moving pictures and **sound**. Most of the programmes you see on **television** are video recordings.

Videotape was invented in 1956. A videotape is played in a video recorder that is connected to a television, and the video appears on the television screen. A video recorder can record television programmes on tape in much the same way as a tape recorder records sound (see **recording**). Old recorded programmes can be erased and new ones recorded on the same tape.

Many people record their own home videos using camcorders, or video **cameras**, which are hand-held devices. Electric signals (see **electricity**) from the camera or from a television programme are recorded on magnetic tape (see **magnetism**). The main difference from a tape recorder is that the record and replay heads in a video recorder spin round as the tape passes. This allows the head to move over the surface of the tape at high speed, giving the high recording speed needed to record picture signals. Recorded camcorder images can be played back through a television.

Video images and sounds can also be stored on Digital Versatile Discs (DVDs), which are similar to compact discs (CDs). However, DVDs can hold seven times more data and so a whole film can be recorded onto one DVD. The signals are stored in small pits and bumps on the surface of the DVD and can be played back by a **laser** in a DVD player. DVDs have a much clearer sound and picture quality than video tapes. There are also DVD recorders that can record video onto DVDs. However, each disc can be recorded on only once.

Lens
Decoder
Microphone
Lens
Light
Lens
Videotape

△ **Videos** can be recorded onto video tape using a hand-held device called a camcorder. Many people use them on holiday, or to record events such as weddings or birthdays.

Vienna

Vienna is the capital city of **Austria** and stands in the east of the country on the Danube **River**. It is a very ancient site. **Celts** settled there more than 2,000 years ago.

Then the Romans (see **Roman Empire**) built a city called Vindobona. Many buildings from the **Middle Ages** still stand in Vienna. The most famous is St Stephen's Cathedral. Until the end of **World War I**, it was the home of the powerful **Hapsburg** family.

Vienna has always been popular with artists and musicians – **Beethoven** (1770–1827) and **Mozart** (1756–91), among many other famous musicians, lived there. Great men of **science** and **medicine**, such as Sigmund **Freud**, also lived there. Today, more than 1.5 million people live in the city.

Vienna is an important centre for industry, **trade** and **communications**. Its main products are electrical goods, **paper** and **clothing**. Tourism is one of the most important industries.

▽ The Austrian city of **Vienna** is known for its beautiful architecture as well as its music. In the 1800s, when Beethoven lived in Vienna, opera houses and other magnificent buildings were built.

Vietnam

Vietnam is a small country in **Southeast Asia**. It has a hot and damp **climate**.

Vietnam was once ruled by **France** as part of Indochina. After **World War II**, it was divided into two countries – North Vietnam and South Vietnam. Hanoi was the main city in the North, and Saigon (now called Ho Chi Minh City) the capital of the South. From the 1950s, the communist North (see **communism**) was at **war** with the South, which was helped by the **USA**. The war ended in 1975, with more than one million Vietnamese casualties and the deaths of 58,000 US soldiers. North and South Korea were then united under a communist **government**.

VIETNAM
Government: Communist
Capital: Hanoi
Area: 329,556 sq km
Population: 76.5 million
Language: Vietnamese
Currency: Dong

Vikings *see* **pages 352–353**

Violin

The violin is a **musical instrument**. It belongs to the string family and is usually the smallest string instrument in an **orchestra**.

A violin is a curved wooden box, shaped like a figure eight. A long neck is fixed to one end of the box. Four strings, made of gut or nylon, are stretched from the top of the neck to the bottom end of the box.

Chin rest · Bow · Bridge · Neck · Tuning peg · Strings of gut or nylon · Ribbon of horsehair · F-hole · Back

◁ The wooden body of a **violin** amplifies (makes louder) the sound, which comes through two curved soundholes called f-holes.

Virus · Cell

△ A **virus** spreads in the body by using the body's cells to make copies of itself. As the replicas break out, they destroy the cell and each virus starts again.

The violin is played with a bow that has a flat ribbon, made up of about 150 horsehairs. When this is drawn across the strings, they vibrate to make musical **sounds**. The strings can also be plucked.

Virus

Viruses are very small living things that cause **diseases** in **plants** and **animals**. They are smaller than **bacteria** and can be seen only with a very powerful electron **microscope**.

You can be infected with viruses by swallowing them or breathing them in. Some **insects** carry viruses, which they pass on when they bite you. Once inside the body, a virus travels around in the bloodstream (see **blood**). It gets inside a living **cell**, where it produces more viruses. Sometimes the cell is entirely destroyed by the viruses.

Diseases caused by viruses include measles, chicken pox, mumps, **AIDS**, influenza and colds. Viruses are very hard to kill. **Inoculation** helps to prevent some of these diseases.

When a virus enters the body, the blood produces substances called antibodies. After a while, there are usually enough antibodies to kill all the viruses, and the patient recovers.

Vitamins and Minerals

Vitamins are chemicals that **human beings** need to stay healthy. They are found in different kinds of **food**. The six kinds of vitamins are A, B, C, D, E and K. Vitamin B is a group of vitamins.

The first people to realize that certain kinds of food were important to **health** were sailors. On long voyages, they got a **disease** called scurvy, caused by a lack of vitamin C, if they could not eat fresh **fruit** and **vegetables**. From the 1700s, English sailors were given limes to eat to prevent scurvy, and were nicknamed 'limeys' by the Americans.

No single food has all the vitamins a person needs. That is why it is important to eat a mixture. Some people take their vitamins in pills, but no one really needs pills if they eat a varied, healthy diet. Very old people, babies and pregnant women all need to take more vitamins than usual. However, too much of some vitamins, such as vitamin A, can be harmful.

Human beings also need minerals in small amounts. Calcium, found in **milk** and **cheese,** builds healthy **bones** and **teeth**. Iron is needed for haemoglobin – the part of red **blood cells** that carries **oxygen** from your **lungs** to tissues. Other minerals needed are iodine, phosphorus, sodium and potassium.

△ Limes are a valuable source of **vitamin** C.

▽ Far below the surface of a cone **volcano** is a chamber containing magma (molten rock), and hot, bubbling gases. During an eruption, the magma shoots up through a chimney-like vent, and lava and ash explode out of the volcanic cone.

Volcano

A volcano is an opening in the surface of the **earth**. Burning **gas**, molten **rocks** and ash escape from this opening. Sometimes they trickle out, sometimes they explode. An explosion is called an eruption.

Some volcanoes are gently sloping **mountains** with cracks, or fissures, in them. Hot, **liquid** rock called lava flows out through the fissures. Other volcanoes are steep-sided mountains with a large hole at the top. These are called cone volcanoes. They are the kind that explode when they erupt.

Erupting volcanoes can do a lot of damage. The Roman city of **Pompeii** was destroyed by **Vesuvius** in 79 CE. In 1883, Krakatoa, a volcano in **Indonesia**, erupted, causing a tsunami (tidal wave) that killed 36,000 people. Volcanoes can also make new land. An **island** called Surtsey, south of **Iceland**, was made by a volcano erupting under the sea in 1963.

Volcanoes appear in long mountainous chains. These chains mark the edges of the huge 'plates' that form the earth's surface. They are the most unstable parts of the earth's

crust. One chain, called 'the ring of fire', goes right around the **Pacific Ocean**. **Earthquakes**, **geysers** and hot springs are all found in the same areas as volcanoes.

Volume

The volume of an object is the amount of space it takes up. You can find out the volume of a solid by measuring its height, width and depth, and multiplying the figures together. So a block with equal sides, each 10 cm long, has a volume of 1,000 cubic cm (1,000 cc) – that is, 10 cm x 10 cm x 10 cm.

It is easy to find out the volume of boxes or bricks or anything with straight edges. Measuring the volume

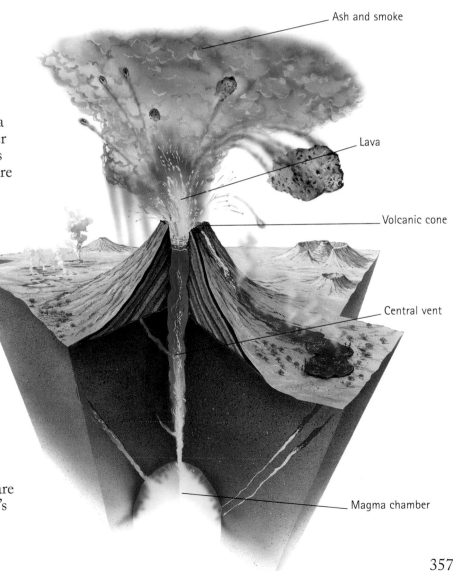

Ash and smoke

Lava

Volcanic cone

Central vent

Magma chamber

357

of something with an irregular shape is more difficult. A very simple method was discovered by Archimedes (c.290–211), the Greek scientist. A story told about him says that he was getting into his bath, which was full to the brim, and **water** spilled over the side. He suddenly realized that the volume of water that had spilled over must be exactly the same as the volume of his body. This means that any irregular object can be measured by plunging it into **water** and measuring the rise in the water level.

Vowel

Vowels are the letters A, E, I, O and U. Sometimes, the letters Y and W are used as vowels. Vowels are pronounced with the mouth open. What they sound like depends on the position of your **tongue** in your mouth. The shape your lips make is also important. If they are pushed forward, as if you are whistling, you make an 'oo' **sound**. If they are pulled right back, you make an 'ee' sound.

The tongue and the lips can shape themselves in hundreds of different ways, so there are hundreds of different vowel sounds.

Sometimes, two or three vowel sounds are run together to make a new sound. The vowel sounds in one **language** are often very difficult for speakers of another language to say.

The pronunciation of vowel sounds changes over the years. The author Geoffrey Chaucer (c.1342–1400), pronounced 'do' with the vowel sound we use for 'go'. He pronounced 'bee' with the vowel sound we use for 'bay', 'by' the way we say 'bee', and 'cow' as we pronounce 'coo'.

Vulture

Vultures are large **birds** of prey. They live in the warm parts and **mountains** of **Asia**, **Africa**, **North America**, **South America** and southern **Europe**. The largest land bird in **North America** is a type of vulture – the California condor. When its wings are spread out, they measure up to 3 m from tip to tip.

Vultures do not hunt for their **food**. They live on carrion – the rotting bodies of dead **animals**. Sometimes, vultures have to wait for their meal until a large hunter such as a **lion** has made a kill and eaten its fill. Vultures may spend hours soaring high on their long wings, waiting for an opportunity to eat. When one vulture swoops down, others follow it and join in the feast.

Most vultures have bald heads and necks. This stops their **feathers** getting messy when they plunge their heads into large carcasses. Most vultures have strong beaks to tear into meat. They have very good **sight** and can spot dead or dying animals from far away. They also have a keen sense of **smell**.

Vultures nest in groups on cliffs, in trees or on the ground. They lay only one or two **eggs** at a time.

▽ **Vultures**, such as these African white-backed vultures, do a vital job because they clean up the carcasses left behind by predators. Once they spot a carcass, they glide down to feed. Some vultures have adapted to living in towns and scavenge on rubbish dumps.

W

Wagner, Richard

Richard Wagner (1813–1883) was a German composer whose **music** brought about great changes in **opera**. He believed that the music and the plot of an opera should be closely bound together, in the same way that the words and the plot of a play are. Unlike many other composers, Wagner wrote his own librettos (scripts) for his operas.

In 1848, Wagner took part in a political **revolution** in **Germany** and he had to escape to **Switzerland**. There he began his greatest work, *The Ring of the Nibelung*. This long piece consists of four music dramas based on old German legends. When Wagner returned to Germany he designed a **festival theatre** at Bayreuth especially for his operas. Today, people from all countries still go to Bayreuth to hear them.

Richard Wagner spent the last part of his life in debt. He died a year after his final opera *Parsifal* was performed.

Wales

Wales is part of the **United Kingdom** of Great Britain and **Northern Ireland**. It lies to the west of **England** and is a country of low **mountains** and green valleys. The highest mountain is

△ The **walrus** lives in the shallow Arctic seas. It has flippers but no tail. Although clumsy on land, the walrus can swim at speeds of about 24 km/h.

The Atlantic and the Pacific walruses both live in the cold Arctic. They are big animals. The male Atlantic walrus can be up to 4 m long and can weigh as much as 1,800 kg.

△ German composer Richard **Wagner**'s operas include *The Flying Dutchman, Tannhauser, Tristan and Isolde, Lohengrin, The Master-singers of Nuremberg* and *Parsifal*.

Snowdon (1,085 m above sea level) and Cardiff is the capital city.

English is the main **language** today, but more than a fifth of the people still speak Welsh as well.

Wallaby

Wallabies are small members of the **kangaroo** family. They live in **Australia**, **New Zealand** and parts of **New Guinea**. There are many different kinds of wallaby. Most are about the size of **hares**, though the biggest is about 1 m long with a 60-cm tail.

Wallabies feed mostly on **grass**. They also make good **food** for other animals. Two of their natural enemies are the dingo – the Australian wild **dog** – and the **eagle**. Some breeds of wallaby are hunted for their valuable fur.

Walrus

The walrus belongs to the **seal** family, and lives in the cold waters of the **Arctic** and northern **Atlantic Ocean**. Its enormous canine **teeth** look like two tusks, and can be up to 1 m long. The walrus uses them to scrape up the clams and **shellfish** that it eats. It also uses its tusks to fight, and even polar **bears** keep away from fully grown walruses.

WARFARE

Warfare is armed conflict between two countries or states, or between groups within a country or state. This type of conflict is common throughout the history of humankind, as nations and sometimes religions struggle for power.

△ *The Parthians (nomadic people from between 250 BCE and 350 CE) tricked their enemies by pretending to retreat, but then turned in their saddles and fired arrows at their pursuers.*

WHY GO TO WAR?

A war can start for many reasons. Often, a group may wish to gain something by conflict, such as food, land or natural resources. Ancient civilizations, such as the Romans, declared war on other nations to build up their empires. Some wars, such as the Crusades and the Thirty Years' War, were fought for religious reasons.

▽ *Galleons were important weapons of war in the 1600s. Here, an English galleon brings down the masts of a Dutch ship during a broadside attack in the Anglo-Dutch War.*

△ *The Battle of Agincourt in 1415 was a notable English victory. The French had at least three times as many heavily armed troops, but they were badly led and organized.*

WEAPONS THROUGH THE AGES

A war is usually won by the nation with the most powerful weapons. Early battles were fought with simple hand-held weapons such as spears and stone axes. Around 1000 BCE, iron swords were developed. Huge siege weapons, such as battering-rams and catapults, were used by the Romans from 200 BCE to 400 CE to batter down enemy defences. During medieval times, crossbows and hand-held weapons, such as maces, were popular. Then came the invention of gunpowder, which brought with it a new range of destructive weapons. Cannons were first used in European warfare in the 1300s,

and a hand-held firearm that could be used by one person was first developed in 1500. However, it was not until the development of steel and of machine tools in the late 1800s that firearms became really powerful and accurate. From then on, warfare has been dominated by machines.

MECHANIZED WARFARE

During the American Civil War (1861–1865), machine-guns that reloaded automatically were used. Vastly improved machine-guns in World War I (1914–1918) were able to fire explosive shells over 3,200 m. World War I also saw the first use of aircraft and tanks in warfare. During World War II, the first long-range rocket weapons – the German VI flying bomb and V2 rocket – were fired from aircraft. Weapons became far more destructive with the invention of the atomic bomb. World War II was brought to an end when the US dropped an atomic bomb on Hiroshima and Nagasaki in Japan, devastating both cities. In the 1960s, nuclear weapons were developed by the USA, USSR, UK, China and France.

CHEMICAL WARFARE

One of the most feared and deadliest forms of attack are by chemical weapons, which release gases or viruses. Poisonous gases were first used during World War I by the Germans. These either choke victims by attacking the lungs when breathed in, or blister the skin, causing horrific burns. Other forms of chemical weapons include nerve gases, which attack the muscles of the body and eventually make breathing impossible, and biological weapons, which can spread deadly contagious diseases such as anthrax or plague. Many countries want such weapons destroyed.

PEACE

Peace is when all fighting has stopped. Peace is often agreed between nations in a treaty – a written document that sets out the conditions in which peace has been agreed – which each nation signs. The United Nations was set up in 1945 to solve international disputes peacefully.

△ *Guerrillas like these are fighters who make hit-and-run raids on enemy forces during a war. They tend to fight in small groups.*

105-mm cannon

Machine-gun

Entrance hatch

Turret has sloped armour

Driver's seat

PRISONERS OF WAR

In all wars, rival armies have taken enemy soldiers prisoner, though the fate of these prisoners has varied from war to war. In 1864, the Geneva Convention was signed by most nations – this pact lays down strict rules regarding the treatment of prisoners of war to ensure that they are treated well and released at the end of the conflict. In World War II, many countries had prisoner-of-war camps where they sent captured enemy soldiers.

Caterpillar tracks instead of wheels

△ *The* Abrams M1 *is the main battle tank (MBT) of the United States. MBTs have heavy guns that can destroy strongholds, and thick armour to protect the crew. Their mobility allows them to drive across muddy or uneven terrain.*

SEE ALSO
Aircraft, Armour, Army, Castle, Civil war (American), Crusades, Guerrilla warfare, Gulf War, Gun, Hundred Years' War, Knight, Missile, Nuclear energy, Submarine, United Nations, World War I, World War II

Washington D.C.

Washington D.C. is the capital of the **United States**. It is named after the first **president**, George **Washington**, who chose its site on the Potomac River between Maryland and Virginia – a piece of land called the District of Columbia, which is why it is always called Washington D.C. It is not the largest city in America but it is the most important because it houses all the **government** buildings, the **White House**, and the headquarters of the United States armed forces. A third of Washington's workers are employed by the government. The city also has the embassies and legations of some 140 nations from all over the world.

△ In 1781, after a six-year war, the British finally surrendered to the American army at Yorktown, Virginia. George **Washington**, who had been commander-in-chief, went home to Mt Vernon. But he soon returned to public life and became first president of the new nation in 1789.

Washington, George

George Washington (1732–1799) was the first **president** of the **United States of America**. He commanded the victorious colonial troops in the **Revolutionary War** against the British. One of his officers said this about him in a speech to Congress: 'He was first in war, first in peace, and first in the hearts of his countrymen.'

George Washington was born on a farm in Westmoreland County, Virginia. In 1752, he inherited an estate called Mount Vernon and, for a while, he farmed his land. Then, in 1775, the Revolutionary War broke out and Washington was chosen to be commander-in-chief of the American troops. Despite many problems, the American colonies won their independence from Britain.

Washington tried to return to **farming**, but in 1787, he was asked to help in drawing up the Constitution. In the

first **election**, he became president. Altogether, he held office for ten years (1789–1797). When he finally retired from public life, he retired to his beloved Mount Vernon, where he died two years later.

Water

The world's surface is made up of 71 percent water – the majority is saltwater in the sea, with the remaining freshwater in **rivers**, **lakes** and **glaciers**. Without water, life would be impossible. Life first began in water, and the bodies of all living things are mostly water.

Water contains **minerals**, which are picked up from the surrounding **earth**

▽ The world's **water** is constantly being recycled in a process called the water cycle. Rain falls on land and into the oceans. The sun warms the earth and water evaporates back into the atmosphere. As this water cools, it condenses to form rain clouds.

Water falls as snow in the mountains

Water is transferred inland as clouds move with winds

Water evaporates from oceans

Water falls as rain on oceans

Water evaporates from lakes and rivers as it flows towards the ocean and **rocks**, and exists as ice, **liquid** or steam. At 0°C, it freezes into solid ice. At 100°C, it boils into steam.

Clouds (see also **weather**) are huge collections of water particles. At any time, clouds contain millions of tonnes of water, which falls back to earth as rain. Some of this water stays in the soil or underground for years, but most of it returns to the **oceans** eventually by rivers or streams.

The chemical formula for water is H_2O. This means that each molecule of water is made up of two **atoms** of **hydrogen** and one atom of **oxygen**. By using two electrodes to pass **electricity** through water, it can be separated into hydrogen and oxygen **gas**. This process is known as electrolysis.

△ The most famous **waterfalls** are Niagara Falls, between the USA and Canada, and the Victoria Falls in the Zambezi River, Africa.

Waterfall

Any sudden drop, or fall, in a **river** is catagorized geographically as a waterfall. These drops are made by the **water** slowly eroding (wearing away) the **rock** of the riverbed over which it flows. Some types of rock are more permeable (softer) than others, and so get worn away faster. When permeable rock is worn away, it leaves a cliff of non-permeable (hard) rock, over which the river's water pours.

There are waterfalls all over the world. The highest is Angel Falls in **Venezuela**. It is 979 m high. The Iguassu Falls lie on the boundary of **Argentina** and **Brazil**. The falls plunge over 82 m-high cliffs in separate cascades totalling over three km in width. The great Victoria Falls on the Zambezi River are more than 107 m high and about 1.6 km wide. Nearly 100 million litres of

▽ Pressure, produced by the steam, drove the various parts of James Watt's steam engine. His engines were first used to pump water from tin and copper mines in Cornwall, in England. Later, they were used in cotton mills.

water plunge over this drop every minute. If all this power was used, there would be enough energy to supply all the **electricity** for a city of five million people.

Watt, James

James Watt (1736–1819) was a Scottish engineer who spent most of his life developing **steam engines**. In early steam engines, steam was heated and cooled inside a cylinder but Watt designed a model in which steam cooled outside the cylinder. This made the engine much more powerful.

Watt made many other improvements to steam engines so that they could work all kinds of **machines**. But his steam engine was more efficient than other steam engines of his time. One of the improvements Watt made was to add a steam governor, using two heavy balls mounted on swinging arms. This steadied the speed of the engine by regulating the amount of steam admitted from the boiler.

Apart from the steam engine, James Watt invented other equipment such as the screw-propeller for use in **ships**.

Burning wood or coal generated heat which was used to boil water, which in turn created steam.

WEATHER

In most regions of earth, weather conditions – such as rain, wind and sunshine – are constantly changing. This is because the air in the lowest layer of the earth's atmosphere is always on the move.

△ Rainbows appear when the sun comes out from behind a cloud but it is still raining. The colours never change – red at the top, then orange, yellow, green, blue, indigo and violet.

THE TROPOSPHERE
The lowest 11 km of the atmosphere, called the troposphere, contains all the weather that we experience. The sun heats different areas of the troposphere to different degrees. For example, air over the oceans heats up and cools down more slowly than air over the land, while air at the equator is heated more strongly than air at the Poles. These differences in temperature drive the world's weather.

North Pole

Equator

South Pole

Winds blowing from the east are called trade winds.

AIR MASSES AND FRONTS
The boundary between two air masses of different temperature is called a front. Most changes in the weather occur at the front. A cold front forms when cold air catches up with a mass of warm air and rapidly pushes the warm air upwards. Then the weather is often showery. A warm front is created when warm air catches up with cold air and rises slowly above the cold air. This brings cloud and long periods of gentle rain. An occluded front is where cold and warm air masses mix. As this happens, the front weakens and disappears.

CLOUD COVER
Clouds are formed by rising and cooling air. When air cools, invisible water vapour begins to condense (turn to liquid). If it is cold enough, the water droplets freeze into ice crystals. Clouds are formed from these droplets and crystals.

△ The earth spins on its axis like a top, so the air that moves across the planet flows in a curve. This is called the Coriolis effect. Air moving from the poles to the equator curves to the west. Air moving from the equator to the poles curves to the east.

▽ Different types of cloud form when air rises and cools under different conditions.

Cirrus are the highest clouds in the sky and show unsettled weather

Altostratus are thin watery layers of cloud that sometimes form a mist

Cirrostratus have a colourful halo when sunlight hits ice crystals in the clouds

Cirrocumulus are tiny balls of icy cloud

Altocumulus are small, fluffy clouds that are linked together

Stratocumulus are long rolls of cloud made by cumulus clouds

Cumulonimbus can bring rain, thunder and lightning

Nimbostratus are thick, dark layers of rain clouds that can bring rain or snow

Cumulus are fuffy white clouds that can bring rain

PRECIPITATION

Water that falls from clouds – as rain, snow, sleet or hail – is called precipitation. In the tropics, raindrops form when air currents cause the water droplets, that make up a cloud, to bump into each other and join together. Eventually the droplets grow heavy enough to fall as rain. Outside the tropics, rain begins as ice crystals in very cold clouds. The crystals grow as water droplets freeze on to them, until they form snowflakes and start to fall. If the ground level temperature is below 0°C, the ice crystals reach the ground as snow. If the temperature is a few degrees above freezing, the crystals partially melt and fall as sleet. At higher temperatures, they melt completely and fall as rain. Hail forms when strong air currents carry ice crystals up and down between the two layers of a thundercloud. The crystals become larger until they fall to earth as hailstones.

▽ Hurricanes are large tropical storms that form over the ocean. Winds swirl around a calm centre (or eye of the storm) at speeds of up to 200 km/h. They bring very heavy rain and huge waves, and often cause severe flooding.

△ Weather forecasters use data from weather stations, high-altitude balloons, planes and satellites to track the movement of fronts and areas of high and low pressure across the globe. This allows them to make fairly accurate predictions of weather patterns for up to a week ahead.

△ Tornadoes (or twisters) are the most violent of all storms, and consist of winds that swirl in the shape of a funnel at speeds of up to 450 km/h. They form over land during a thunderstorm.

FUTURE WEATHER PATTERNS

Scientists predict that the average temperature of the earth's surface could rise by between 1°C and 5°C by 2100. This global warming is believed to be the result of the greenhouse effect – the build up of gases that trap more of the sun's energy in earth's atmosphere. This temperature change could cause sea levels to rise and more violent weather patterns to appear, amongst other things.

SEE ALSO
Acid rain, Air, Antarctic and Arctic, Atmosphere, Barometer, Climate, Earth, Gas, Global warming, Hurricane, Temperature, Thermometer, Wind

Wave

When the **wind** blows over the sea it raises waves. The size and speed of a wave depends upon the wind's strength and fetch (how far across the sea it blows). A light breeze causes gentle ripples, but a storm can whip up waves higher than a **house**.

Although ripples and waves move across the sea, the **water** itself does not travel with them. Instead, each passing wave just lifts the water particles that support floating objects (such as sea **birds** and bottles) up, forward, down and back again. This explains why these floating objects bob up and down but do not travel with the waves.

△ For thousands of years, **weaving** was slow work. First, the fibres were drawn out and twisted into a long thread (spinning). Then, rows of threads (the warp) were stretched lengthwise, side by side, on a frame called a loom. A crosswise thread (the weft) was then passed through from one side of the loom to the other, going over and under the warp. A large needle, the shuttle, was used to feed the weft through the warp.

◁ Surfers travel the world looking for the 'perfect **wave**'. The Polynesians (Hawaii, in the Pacific) invented surfing many centuries ago. They called it *he'e nalu* ('wave sliding').

The biggest waves are seismic sea waves or tsunamis. These are set off by underwater **earthquakes**, landslips or **volcanoes**. Tsunamis sometimes flood coasts and can cause a great number of human fatalities as a result.

Sea waves carry **energy** from the wind. This energy can be used to make **electricity**. One experimental machine for harnessing wave energy is called the nodding boom or 'duck'. The ducks have small generators inside them. As waves make the 'beak' of each duck move up and down, electricity is produced by the **generators**.

Weaving

Curtains and sheets, shirts and carpets, towels and suits are just some of the many useful articles made by a process known as weaving, where threads are joined together in a criss-cross pattern to make cloth.

People have been weaving cloth to make **clothing** since the **Stone Age**. The oldest fabric we know of was woven nearly 8,000 years ago in what is now **Turkey**. These weavers learned to make linen from flax (fibres from the linum **plant**). By 2000 BCE the Chinese were weaving cloth from **silk**. In **India**, people learned to use fibres from the **cotton** plant. Meanwhile **nomads** (travellers) from the **deserts** and **mountains** of **Asia** discovered how to weave **wool**.

Spinning **wheels** and looms were worked by hand until the 1700s. Then **machines** were invented for spinning and weaving. These machines worked far faster than hand looms, and cloth became cheap and plentiful.

Today, most woven fabrics are made by machine and fully automatic looms are now common in most countries, though hand looms are still used for very special woollen or silk fabrics. One man can easily operate 20 of today's fully automatic looms.

Website *see* Internet

Weed

A weed is any **plant** that grows where it is not wanted. On farms and in **gardens**, weeds damage crops and **flowers** by taking a large share of **water, minerals** and sunlight. In places where weeds grow thickly, cultivated plants do not develop properly – they may produce only a few flowers, small **seeds**, unhealthy leaves or weak roots.

There are several ways of controlling weeds. In gardens, people break up the **soil** with a hoe. This disturbs the weed roots and stops growth. They also pull the weeds out of the ground: this is called weeding. On farms, the soil is broken up by ploughing and harrowing. Farmers also spray their fields with weedkillers which are **chemicals** that destroy weeds. Most weedkillers are selective. This means the chemicals only affect certain plants, so they destroy weeds without harming crops.

Weeds grow in a variety of places. Black bindweed grows on cultivated land, the dandelion grows in fields and meadows, greater plantain grows on paths and purple loosestrife grows in damp places. Some weeds are edible and used in salads.

△ **Weeds** are only a nuisance when they interfere with cultivated plants. In woods and fields, away from gardens and farms, weeds are useful plants and food for many animals.

Weightlifting

Weightlifting is one of the **sports** included in the **Olympic Games**. In a weightlifting contest, the competitors lift very heavy **weights** from the floor to above their heads. Weightlifters, like **boxers**, are divided into classes according to their own body weight. Champion weightlifters can lift over 250 kg.

△ **Welders** have to protect their eyes from the heat by wearing masks.

Many other sportsmen, such as swimmers and footballers, do weightlifting as an exercise to strengthen their **muscles** and improve their **breathing**.

Weights and Measures

Weights and measures are used to work out how heavy something is, or the length, the width and the height. Length multiplied by width gives the area (amount of floor space in the case of a room) while length multiplied by width and height gives the **volume** (amount of space within something).

People first needed units of measurement when they began to build towns and to **trade** goods. In Ancient **Egypt**, people based their measurements on the proportions of the body. Four digits equalled one palm. Seven palms, or two spans (little finger to thumb tip) equalled one cubit (the distance from a person's fingertips to the elbow).

Most countries now use the metric system for measuring distances. The metric system is a decimal system based on the number 10 and was first used in **France** in the late 1700s. Another system – the imperial system – was originally used in Britain and the **United States**.

Welding

Welding is a way of joining metals by heating. The edges of two pieces of **metal** are heated (by **gas** or **electricity**) until they melt together. When they cool they form just one piece of metal. A join made by welding is extremely strong.

△ **Wheat** grows best in dry, mild climates. Farmers sow the seed in winter or spring. They harvest it when the grain is dry and hard.

▽ Modern **wheels** are different from the wheels invented 5,000 years ago. This illustration shows some of the wheels that have been used throughout history.

◁ The blubber under the skin of large **whales** can be up to 0.5 m thick. For hundreds of years, whales have been killed for this blubber. Oil was taken from it and used to make soap.

Whale

Whales are large sea **mammals** physically adapted for living in the water. A thick layer of fat (blubber) keeps out the cold. A whale's body is shaped for easy **swimming**. Its front limbs are flippers. It also has a broad tail flattened from top to bottom, not from side to side like a **fish**.

Unlike fish, whales must swim to the surface to breathe. Before **breathing** in, they blow out stale **air** through a blowhole (two slits on top of the head). Baby whales are born in water and must immediately swim up to the surface to take a breath of air.

The blue whale is the largest mammal in the world. It can grow as long as 30 m. The killer whale is a **carnivore**. It feeds on other whales, **seals**, **penguins** and **fish**. Bottle-nosed whales have beaks like some **dolphins**. They move around in schools of up to 50 animals. Humpback whales feed on fish, krill and **plankton**.

Wheat

Wheat is a valuable **food** crop. Grains of wheat are **seeds** produced by a certain kind of **grass**. Mills grind the seeds into flour for making **bread**, breakfast **cereals**, cakes, pies, noodles and spaghetti. Most wheat foods are good for us because each grain of wheat is largely made of **energy**-giving **starches**. It also contains plenty of body-building **protein**, as well as **fats**, **minerals** and bran.

Most wheat is produced from **China**, **India**, the **United States**, **France** and **Russia**. The world produces more wheat than any other kind of grain.

Wheel

The wheel is one of man's most useful **inventions**. This is because a wheel turning on an axle is a very good way to move loads. It is easier to move a heavy load with wheels than it is to lift the load or drag it on the ground.

Bronze Age people first invented the wheel about 5,000 years ago. The oldest known wheels looked like slices cut across a log. But each solid disc was made of three parts.

At first, the wheels were fixed on the axle, and it was the axle that turned in holes in the cart frame. Later, the axle was fixed and the wheels revolved on its ends.

Then people learned that a wheel with spokes was just as strong as a solid wheel, but much lighter in weight. Today, the wheels of **cars** and planes have hollow **rubber** tyres filled with air to make them springy.

Ball bearings keep wheel hubs turning easily on their axles. Wheels with notched edges turn one another within the gears that help to work all kinds of machinery.

Although the wheel was being used throughout a large part of the East by 1500 BCE, it is interesting that the wheel was unknown anywhere on the **American** continent until it was introduced by **Europeans** in the 1500s CE.

White House

The White House is the official residence of the **president** of the **United States** and is located in **Washington D.C**. This is where the president lives, works and entertains guests. Theodore **Roosevelt** was the first president to use the name – before it was simply called the President's House. In 1814, the British burned down the White House so today's building is the second White House.

Whitman, Walt

Walt Whitman (1819–1892) was the greatest American **poet** of the 18th century. He is best known for his *Leaves of Grass*, a collection of poems that he revised and added to over nearly 40 years.

William the Conqueror

William the Conqueror is another name for William I of **England** (1027–1087). He was England's first Norman king. William was born in **France**, where his father Robert was the

△ The **White House** is set in large formal gardens, where a variety of official occasions take place.

▽ People in many parts of England rebelled against **William's** rule. He built strong castles from which his knights rode out to defeat their Anglo-Saxon enemies. He also ordered a massive survey (the Domesday Book) of all the land and people in his new English kingdom.

Duke of Normandy. When William visited England in 1050, his relative Edward the Confessor allegedly promised him the throne of England. In 1064, William forced Edward's brother-in-law Harold to agree to help to make him king, but when Edward died in 1066, Harold had himself crowned king of England.

William set about invading England to seize it for himself. His Norman army defeated Harold's **Anglo-Saxon** army at the Battle of Hastings. He was crowned William I of England in Westminster Abbey on **Christmas** Day in 1066.

William and his nobles brought over their own language – Norman French – and the English ruling classes began to speak French as a result. Modern English contains many words that came from Norman French.

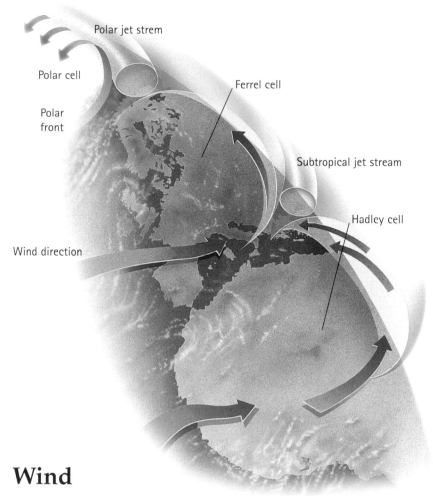

Polar jet strem

Polar cell

Polar front

Ferrel cell

Wind direction

Subtropical jet stream

Hadley cell

Wind

Wind is moving **air**. Slow winds are gentle breezes. Fast winds are gales. You can see the speed of the wind by its effect on **trees** and buildings.

Wind blows because some air masses become warmer than others. In warm air, the tiny particles of air spread out. A mass of warm air is lighter than a mass of cold air that fills the same amount of space, because warm air is so light it rises. As the warm air rises, cool air flows in to take its place. This causes the steady trade winds that blow over tropical **oceans**. **Climate** and **weather** are determined by the wind.

A scale of wind speeds was worked out in 1805 by Admiral Sir Francis Beaufort. It is called the Beaufort Scale. In it the force of the wind is shown by numbers from zero to 12. The number zero indicates calm weather (no wind). By the time it reaches four there is a breeze in which small branches are moving and **flags**

△ At each pole, cold air sinks and spills out, to be replaced by warmer air from above. This is a polar cell. Ferrel cells form between 30°C and 60°C. The cold air moving away from the poles meets warm **wind** from the subtropics and pushes the warm air back to the equator.

flap. At force seven, whole trees are moving and it is difficult to walk against the wind. Force 12 is something few of us will ever see. It is a full **hurricane**, with terrible damage to **ships** at sea and **houses** on land.

Wind vanes show the direction of wind. The arrow points in the direction of north, east, south or west.

Windmill

Windmills are **machines** that use the wind's **energy** to generate power. They were used in **Asia** as early as the 600s CE and came to **Europe** in the 1100s.

In early windmills, a **wheel** with long sails was fixed to a tower. The whole tower could often turn to face the **wind**. As the wind turned the **sails**, the turning wheel moved machinery inside the mill. This machinery was used to do useful work such as turning heavy stone wheels to grind corn or pumping **water** from wells.

Nowadays, people are using windmills as a way of generating **electricity**. These windmills, called wind **turbines**, are usually on a tower made of **steel** girders. Some have blades like aeroplane propellers (see **aircraft**) which turn at a high speed when the wind blows. The propellers work a **generator** which produces electricity.

Wine

Wine is a drink made from **plant** juice, containing **alcohol** produced by a process called **fermentation**.

Most wine is made from grapes. But you can make wine from other **fruit** as well. First the fruit is crushed. Then the juice is fermented in containers called vats. The wine is stored in casks until it is ready to drink. Sweet wines are rich in **sugar**. In dry wines most of the sugar has become alcohol.

◁ This **windmill** was used to grind corn. As the wind blew, the axle turned the millstones that ground the corn.

Grapes go through many processes before they reach your home as bottled wine. After fermentation, some wines are stored in cellars to 'mature' into fine wines. Cheaper wines are not allowed to mature. They are filtered, pasteurized (see **Pasteur, Louis**) and then bottled as soon as they are taken out of the casks.

Wire

Wire is **metal** that has been melted into a long thin rod that is easy to bend. Wire has many uses. Barbed-wire fences keep **sheep** and cows in fields. Wires twisted together form cables strong enough to hold up some of the world's largest **bridges**. Wires also carry electric currents. **Telephone** lines also use wires.

Metals used for making wire include **copper**, **iron**, **aluminium** and **silver**. Heavy blocks of metal are heated, and then passed through rollers that squeeze the part-melted metal into long narrow holes to make longer and thinner strips. Then the wire is wound around a turning drum. Finally, the wire is heated in a furnace to make it less brittle.

For centuries, wire was made by hand. The piece of metal to be drawn was beaten to a point and pushed through a small hole in a fixed metal block. The wiredrawer grasped it and pulled it through the hole to make wire. The fineness of the wire was therefore limited by the strength of the wiredrawer.

Witch

Many people once believed in witches (people with **magic** powers). It was claimed that witches worshiped the devil, and that they cast spells which 'bewitched' people, sometimes causing death or **disease**. Witches supposedly rode through the **air** at night on broomsticks and they met at secret meetings called sabbaths.

Long ago, many innocent women were burnt to death, accused of being witches. Today few of us believe in witches, but there are some people who still claim to practice magic – though they usually offer herbal cures and mix things such as 'love potions'.

Wolf

These **carnivores** include the grey wolf that lives in eastern **Europe** and parts of **North America**. Grey wolves used to be found in most of the northern hemisphere, but dwindling numbers, caused by humans hunting wolves almost to the point of extinction, are now only to be found in remote areas and dense **forests**. Grey wolves have thick fur, long legs, and powerful jaws. They can be up to 1.8 m in length. A pack of wolves can chase and kill a sick or injured **deer** much larger than themselves. They share their kill, but wolves have an order of seniority within each pack – young wolves must give way to larger, older animals. When grey wolves are hunting, they howl to signal to each other where they are.

A pack consists of a pair of adults with many generations of their young. Each spring, a she-wolf has four to six pups.

Throughout **history** (and in many countries) there have been stories of wolves raising human children from infancy.

△ The image of a **witch** as an ugly old women casting evil spells is still with us today – mainly through childrens' fairy tales.

▽ Like many other mammals, **wolves** live in family groups. They hunt together in packs led by a dominant male.

Women's rights

'Women's rights' is the term used when discussing the right of women to be full citizens, equal to men in every way. Until this century, women did not have these rights. In some countries today they still do not have equal citizenship with men.

At the beginning of the 20th century, women were not allowed to vote, so they were powerless to get changes through **parliament**. In 1903, Englishwomen Emmeline Pankhurst (1858–1928) and her daughter Christabel started the Women's Social and Political Union, which fought for

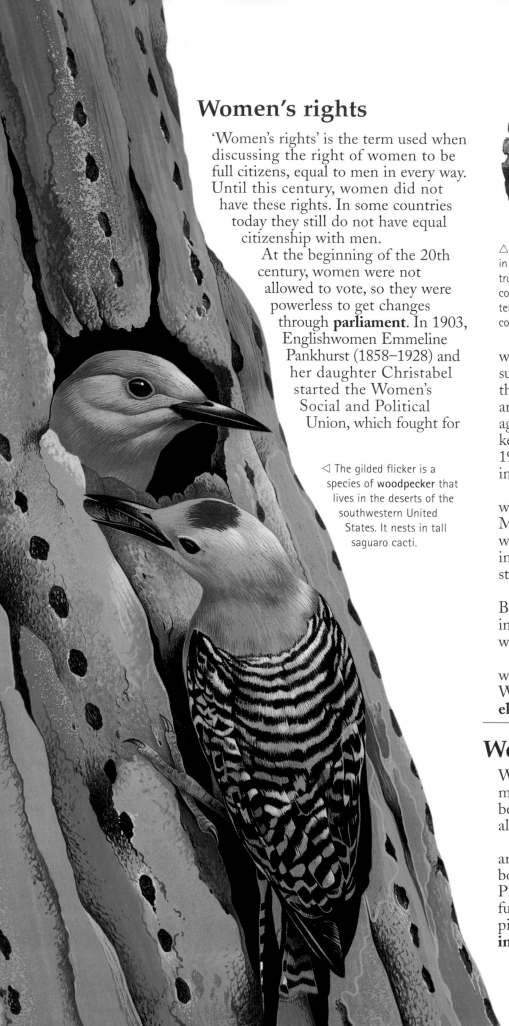

◁ The gilded flicker is a species of **woodpecker** that lives in the deserts of the southwestern United States. It nests in tall saguaro cacti.

△ Dendrochronology is the dating and study of rings in trees. If a tree is felled (chopped down) and the trunk cut in half, we can tell the age of the tree by counting the rings in the **wood**. Variation in the rings tells us about the variation in environmental conditions as the tree grew.

women's right to vote or suffrage. These suffragettes addressed crowds, chained themselves to railings, broke windows and set fire to pillar boxes. Again and again they were put in prison, but they kept on protesting. It was not until 1928 that women won the right to vote in the **United Kingdom**.

Today, most people accept that women should be judged as individuals. More women than ever go out to work. Many have professional careers in business, but in some fields women's struggle for equality is not yet complete.

Emmeline Pankhurst fought for the British woman's right to vote. She died in 1928, the year that women finally won equal voting rights in Britain.

However, the first country to allow women to vote was **New Zealand**. Women there voted in national **elections** from 1893.

Wood

Wood is one of the most valuable materials that people use. It can be sawn, carved and worked into almost any shape.

Thick timber is used for buildings and boats, while roughly cut logs and boughs are used as **fuel** for **fires**. Planks of wood are made into furniture, barrels and boxes. Seasoned pieces can be shaped into **musical instruments** and delicate ornaments.

The wood we use is the tough inner material of **trees** and shrubs and is protected by a thin layer of bark. It is very strong, supporting many times its own weight. The wood of a tree is made up of thick fibres that give it that strength.

Softwood, from **pines** and firs, is used mostly as pulp to make **paper**. Some is used for building. Hardwood, such as oak and mahogany, is used to make furniture.

Wood and wood products are made into sheets for building. Plywood is made up of thin sheets of timber glued together. Most modern furniture is made from plywood. Blockboard is used for making doors. Although it looks like plywood, it has blocks of softwood within it. Hardboard and chipboard, used in building and furniture-making, are made from wood chips. The chips are heated and rolled out into sheets.

Woodpecker

There are about 200 different kinds of woodpecker. They are found in many parts of the world, but most live in **North America, South America** and **Asia.**

Woodpeckers have sharp, powerful bills with which they drill holes through the bark of **trees**. They reach in with their long tongues to fish out **insects**. Some woodpeckers also nest in holes in trees.

Most woodpeckers have bright **colours** and markings, especially on their heads.

Wool

Wool comes from the fleece of **sheep** and some other **animals**. It is long, thick hair that can easily be turned into yarn. The yarn may be woven into blankets, carpets and **clothing**, or it can be knitted. Woollen cloth is heavy and warm.

Wool has been spun and woven since the **Stone Age**. Modern wool, however, comes from specially bred sheep that have good, fine wool. The best wool comes from Merino sheep. These are white sheep that originally came from **Spain**. Most wool is produced in **Australia**, **New Zealand**, **Argentina** and **Russia**.

△ The **wool** we wear comes from the fleece of sheep. Sheep were once clipped by hand, but the invention of electric shears makes it possible for farmers to clip over 200 sheep a day.

Worm

There are hundreds of different **animals** with soft flat bodies that are commonly called worms. Some, such as roundworms or flatworms, are very simple creatures. Others, such as earthworms, leeches and the larvae of some **insects**, are more complicated. Their bodies are divided into several segments.

Most of the simple worms are small. They usually live as **parasites** inside the bodies of animals or **plants**. Liver flukes and tapeworms are two such creatures.

△ The common earth**worm** has both male and female organs. Ragworms and lugworms live in muddy and sandy shores.

Wren, Christopher

Christopher Wren (1632–1723) was one of the most brilliant of all English architects (see **architecture**). He was responsible for many beautiful buildings, including the Royal Exchange, Kensington Palace and an addition to Hampton Court, **London**.

In 1666, the Great Fire of London destroyed St Paul's Cathedral. Christopher Wren designed its replacement, which still stands today.

Wren also designed the College of William and Mary, Virginia, **USA**. This is the oldest academic structure in America in continuous classroom use.

▷ As well as building the famous St Paul's Cathedral, Sir Christopher **Wren** built more than 50 other churches in his lifetime.

WORLD WAR I

World War I took place between 1914 and 1918 and involved 22 countries. More than 17 million people were killed.

△ The British Vickers FB 5 Gunbus was produced to stop the German Fokker E. III.

ALLIANCES

At the beginning of the 20th century, the relationships between the countries in Europe were strained. Germany was becoming increasingly powerful and France and Britain felt threatened. Austria-Hungary and Russia were rivals in the Balkans, which resented their outside interference. Based on these hostilities, alliances grew up with Austria-Hungary and Germany, known as the Central Powers, on one side, and France, Russia and Britain, known as the Allies, on the other.

△ A British recruiting poster at the start of World War I featured the war minister, Lord Kitchener.

WAR BREAKS OUT

War broke out in 1914 after Archduke Franz Ferdinand, the heir to the Austro-Hungarian emperor, was assassinated by a Serbian in Sarajevo in Bosnia (part of the Balkan States). Austria threatened Serbia with war, unless it submitted to Austrian rule. Serbia refused, and in July 1914, Austria declared war. Other countries became involved: Russia supported Serbia and in August Germany, Austria's ally, declared war on Russia and its ally France. Intent on invading France, Germany marched through Belgium, a neutral country since 1839. On 4 August, Britain declared war in defence of Belgium. Turkey joined the Central Powers in 1914, followed by Bulgaria in 1915. Italy joined the Allies in 1915, followed by Romania and Portugal in 1916 and the USA in 1917.

△ The German Fokker E.III carried a machine-gun rigged to fire forwards.

THE TREATY OF VERSAILLES

Russia withdrew from the war in 1917 and Germany then concentrated fully on the Western Front. The USA joined the Allies when Russia surrendered. In spring 1918, the Germans marched on Paris, but were halted by the Allies and gradually pushed back. By November 1918, the German army was defeated. In 1919, Germany signed the Treaty of Versailles, admitting guilt for the war and promising to pay compensation to the Allies for their losses.

◁ The war was fought from a system of ditches called trenches, protected by barbed wire and machine-guns, on the Western Front. However, until tanks were introduced in 1918 by the Allies, it was very difficult for either side to attack successfully without huge loss of life.

▷ Horses such as the Australian Waler were used as officers' mounts and for hauling artillery and ambulances.

WORLD WAR II

Twenty-one years after the Germans surrendered to the Allies in November 1918, a world war broke out in Europe once again. This time, technology was more advanced and everybody, civilians and military alike, in all countries, was directly affected by the mass destruction.

ADOLF HITLER

After World War I, Germany suffered humiliation and huge economic problems and many Germans were enthusiastic when military strength and national pride were championed by a party called the National Socialists, or Nazis, led by Adolf Hitler.

GERMANY MAKES A MOVE

In 1938, Hitler marched into part of the Czech Republic. At a meeting in Munich, Britain and France (the Allies) who wanted to avoid another major war, allowed Hitler to keep the area that he had annexed. Hitler then annexed the rest of the country and threatened Poland. Britain and France agreed to declare war if Poland was invaded. On 1 September 1939, Hitler matched into Poland, and the Allies declared war two days later. Germany allied with Italy and Japan in 1940 and 1941, and they were called the Axis Powers. The former USSR and the USA joined the Allies in 1941.

▷ *Japanese* kamikaze *pilots – kamikaze means 'divine wind' – died for their emperor by diving their aircraft, laden with bombs, straight into Allied ships.*

THE ARMISTICE

On 6 June 1944 – D-Day – the Allies landed in Normandy in northern France and forced the Germans to retreat. On 24 March 1945, they crossed the Rhine River and met the Russians coming from the east. Hitler committed suicide on 30 April 1945 and the war in Europe ended on 8 May 1945.

It continued in the Pacific until 14 August when the Japanese were devastated by US atom bombs dropped on the Japanese cities of Hiroshima and Nagasaki. The armistice, which ended the war, was signed on 2 September 1945.

THE HOLOCAUST

The word Holocaust means 'the wholesale slaughter or destruction of life'. It is also used as an historical term to refer to the mass murder of between 5.2 and 5.8 million Jews, and 5 million other people, such as the mentally ill, gypsies and political adversaries, killed by the Nazi Party.

△ *Between July and October 1940, the German air force (Luftwaffe) bombed British cities and attacked the British air force (RAF). Technology had moved on from World War I and fighters' top speeds rose from 580 to 870 km/h. Almost all of the new war-planes were monoplanes, such as the* Hawker Hurricane *(above).*

▽ *This photograph taken in 1938 shows Hitler triumphantly entering the town of Wildenan in the Sudetenland, a region in the west of the former Czechoslovakia. Hitler's armies went on to conquer the rest of the country.*

SEE ALSO
Aircraft, Army, Balloon and Airship, Bosnia-Herzegovina, D-Day, Europe, Fascism, Germany, Gun, Hitler (Adolf), Nuclear energy, Submarine, Warfare

△ It is said that Wilbur
Wright was twisting
a cardboard carton
containing a cycle inner-
tube when he noticed the
shape of the carton
changed but not the size.
This inspired the inventor
to make the wing-warping
mechanism that steered
the 1903 aircraft.

▽ The earliest **writings**
were on stone or clay and
only a few people could
read them.

Wright brothers

Wilbur and Orville Wright were two
American **bicycle** engineers who built
and flew the first powered **aircraft**.
Their successful **machine** was made
after years of testing models and gliders.
  The first actual flight took place at
Kitty Hawk, North Carolina, in
December 1903. Their simple
petrol-engined craft flew for
12 seconds. Five years later,
the brothers flew an
improved machine for
almost 75 minutes.
  The original Wright
Flyer I is in the
National Air and
Space Museum in
Washington D.C.

Writing

The earliest
forms of writing
were simple
picture messages.

Gradually, pictures that were used
again and again became simplified as
symbols such 'man' or 'house'. Egyptian
hieroglyphics were used in this way.
  In time, the symbols came to stand
for **sounds** and could be combined to
form words. Later still, **alphabets** of
these sounds came into being. **Vowels**
appeared in the **languages** spoken
by the ancient Greeks and Romans.
From their alphabets developed the
one used today in English.
  The Chinese invented **paper** in
105 CE. In 1824, Frenchman Louis
Braille (1809–1852) designed an
alphabet of raised dots (braille) on
paper enabling blind people to feel
words. Nowadays we can buy e-books
(electronic books). These are on disk
and are read on a **computer** screen
or a hand-held computer designed for
the e-book market.
  Words are powerful and many authors
use satire (a form of humour) to attack
people or ideas. *Gulliver's Travels* by
Jonathan Swift (1667–1745) pokes
fun at **human beings**.

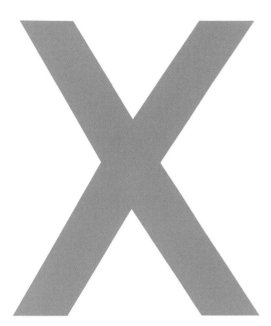

X-ray

X-rays are waves of **energy** like **radio** or **light** waves. They can pass through or into most living things. They can also leave an image on a photographic plate, making a picture of whatever they have passed through. Doctors use X-rays to take 'photographs' of the insides of people. This helps them find out what is wrong with patients.

Computerized tomography (CT) scanners also help diagnosis. A patient is moved slowly through the scanner as X-rays are beamed through their body from all angles. A powerful **computer** processes this information, displaying slices of the patient's body on its screens.

High doses of X-rays can damage body **cells**, but the harmful effects of X-rays are often used to help cure **cancers**. Radiographers target X-rays at cells in tumours, killing them off.

X-rays are produced inside a **glass** tube that has no **air** or other **gases** in it. At opposite ends of the tube are a cathode, which gives off electrons, and an anode or target. When the cathode is heated, electrons fly off it and strike the anode, producing X-rays.

A German scientist, Wilhelm Roentgen (1845–1923), discovered X-rays by accident in 1895 when he passed **electricity** through a gas.

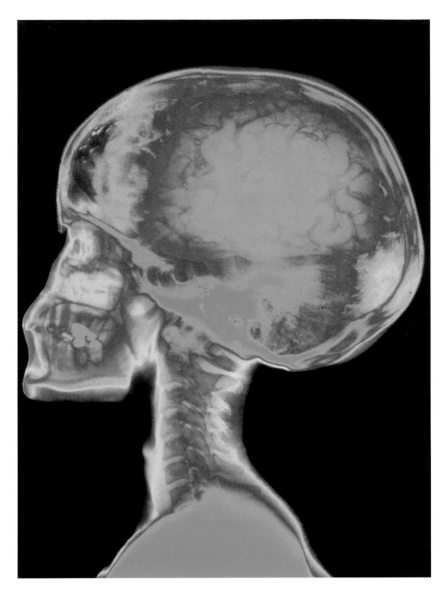

A radiographer has taken this **X-ray** of a human head. The resulting photograph has been coloured to show the skull and brain more clearly.

Xylophone

The xylophone is an odd-looking **musical instrument** that produces a crisp, bell-like **sound** when played. It consists of graded rows of solid wooden or **metal** bars that are fixed to a frame. Each bar is a different length and produces a different sound when struck with a hammer. The sound is produced by the **wood** or metal from which the xylophone is made. An electric version of the xylophone – the vibraphone – also exists.

The xylophone is used in **orchestras** and bands across the world. Resonators (metal tubes below each bar) help to amplify (increase) the sound.

The **xylophone** is a type of percussion instrument that has a clear, distinctive sound.

Yak

The yak is a large, shaggy kind of ox with a pair of long, thick **horns**. Yaks live in mountainous areas of **Tibet**, **China** and northern **Asia**. Wild yaks may be as tall as a man, but domestic yaks are about the size of a European cow (see **cattle**).

△ The **yak** was tamed over 2,000 years ago and gives Tibetan people milk, meat, leather, wool and transport. Yaks are sure-footed in rocky places and can survive harsh conditions.

Yangtze River (Chang Jiang)

The Yangtze River, or Chang Jiang, is the longest, most important **river** in **China** and the third longest river in the world. From its beginnings, high in the **mountains** of **Tibet**, it flows 6,380 km across the centre of China, emptying into the Yellow Sea near Shanghai.

The river takes its name from the ancient kingdom of Yang, which grew up along its banks 3,000 years ago. Today, the Yangtze is still one of the main **trade** routes in China, and the port of Shanghai, China's largest city, lies at its mouth. Large ships can

▽ Over thousands of years, the **Yangtze River** has created fertile farmland – leaving behind layers of rich silt when it floods. To protect their fields from flooding, farmers build giant dykes of earth.

sail up the Yangtze as far as Hankow, nearly 1,125 km inland. Smaller boats can reach I-Ch'ang, which is 1,600 km from the sea (see **ship and boat**).

Millions of people live and work on and near the Yangtze. Some people even live on the river itself in wooden sailing boats called junks.

Year

A year is the length of **time** it takes the **earth** to **orbit** (travel around) the **sun**. This journey takes 365 days and six hours (see **day and night**). A **calendar** year is only 365 days long, so every four years, the left-over quarter days are added together to make an extra day. These longer years of 366 days are called leap years.

The first people to measure the length of a year were the Ancient Egyptians (see **Ancient Egypt**). They noticed that the **Nile River** always overflowed its banks when Sirius – the brightest **star** in the sky – rose just before sunrise. They counted the days that went by until this happened again – 365 days had passed, a year.

Yeast

Yeast is a **plant** that is also a kind of **fungus**. The whole plant consists of just one **cell**, which is so tiny that you cannot see it without a **microscope**. Yeast is useful because it turns **sugar** into **alcohol** and carbon dioxide **gas**. This process is called **fermentation**. Yeast plants ferment because they do not produce their own **food** – they live on sugar instead. Today, yeast is grown in huge vats. It is then pressed into cakes or small pellets, ready to be sold.

In **wine**- and beer-making, yeast turns the sugar in grapes or malted barley into alcohol, while most of the gas it produces bubbles away. In **bread**-making, the carbon dioxide gas it creates forms bubbles, which make the bread dough rise.

Yemen, Republic of

The Republic of Yemen is a country on the coasts of the **Red Sea** and the Gulf of Aden. The **republic** was formed when North and South Yemen united in 1990, after years of political upheaval. Before then, North Yemen had been under Ottoman–Turkish rule for years until its independence in 1918. South Yemen was made up of the former British colony of Aden and the former British protectorate of South Arabia. It became independent in 1967.

Yemeni land is among the most fertile of the Arabian Peninsula, thanks to the **monsoon** rains that fall on its **mountains** each spring. Many Yemenis are farmers (see **farming**), growing **cotton**, **wheat**, **coffee**, millet and **fruit**. The port of Aden, on the south coast, has been a trading-post between the East and the West for 2,000 years. In 1994, **civil war** broke out between North Yemen and South Yemen, but ended when **government** forces took control of Aden. Despite this, kidnappings, bombings, and other acts of **terrorism** continued to disrupt the country into the late 1990s.

Yeti

The yeti, or abominable snowman, is a large, ape-like **animal** that is believed to live in the **Himalayas** – the highest **mountains** on **earth**. Several sightings have been reported since the late 1800s and photographs (see **photography**) of yeti footprints over 30 cm long have been published. Although the yeti is believed by many to exist, expeditions have so far failed to uncover evidence to back this belief.

Yom Kippur

Yom Kippur (the Day of Atonement) is the most important **festival** in the Jewish **calendar** (see **Judaism**). It comes at the end of a ten-day period of reflection. Yom Kippur is a festival of prayer and fasting (going without food or drink) that lasts for 25 hours. Jews spend the majority of the day in the **synagogue**, attending special services. Services begin early in the morning and continue until sunset. Jews pray to confess their sins from the past year and to ask for God's forgiveness. The end of the prayers is signalled by the blowing of a special **horn** called a *shofar* (ram's horn).

△ This is a photograph of what some people believe to be a footprint of a Yeti. It was taken by mountain climbers in 1951, and it is as long as the head of the ice-pick.

YEMEN
Government: Republic
Capital: Sanaa
Area: 527,928 sq km
Population: 17 million
Language: Arabic
Currency: Rial

Zambia

Zambia is a land-locked country in southern **Africa** that shares borders with the **Democratic Republic of Congo**, **Tanzania**, Malawi, **Mozambique**, **Botswana**, **Zimbabwe**, **Namibia** and **Angola**.

Zambia is named after the Zambezi **River** which runs across the western part of the country and along the border with Zimbabwe.

The majority of Zambians are farmers, but it is usually the women who cultivate the crops because most of the men work in the **mining** industry. The majority of the country's wealth comes from its **copper** mines.

Zambia was the British protectorate of Northern Rhodesia until it became an independent **republic** in 1964. It then became a one-party state in 1972, and democratic **elections** were first held in 1991.

Like many African countries, Zambia has a low life expectancy for its people: 37 years old for both men and women. This is because **AIDS** (Acquired Immune Deficiency Syndrome) ravages the continent of Africa – with 7,000 people dying every day.

△ Burchell's **zebra** is the most common type of zebra found in eastern Africa. This picture shows a newborn zebra foal, still covered with the afterbirth, suckling from its mother.

ZAMBIA
Government: Democracy
Capital: Lusaka
Area: 752,614 sq km
Population: 10.4 million
Languages: Bemba, Kaonda, Lozi, Tonga, English and others
Currency: Kwacha

Zebra

Zebra belong to the **horse** family. They live on the open grasslands of **Africa** to the south of the **Sahara Desert**. Zebra have creamy white coats covered with black or dark brown stripes. Each **animal** has a unique pattern of stripes.

Zebra live in herds. They feed on **grass**, and are often found roaming the grasslands with herds of **antelope**. Although zebra can run very fast, they are often hunted by **lions**, **leopards** and **hyenas**. Like other wild horses, the zebra depends on speed for survival. It can run at up to 40 km/h.

People also used to hunt zebra for their attractive **skins** and tasty meat, but this is now illegal in most countries.

Zimbabwe

Zimbabwe is a small country in southern **Africa**. It lies inland, about 240 km from the **Indian Ocean**. Almost 98 percent of the population are black Africans – the others are mostly white. In the north, Zimbabwe is bordered by the Zambezi **River**, famous for the Victoria Falls (see **waterfall**) and the Kariba **Dam**. The dam is part of a great **hydroelectric** operation that supplies power to both Zimbabwe and its neighbour, **Zambia**.

A wealthy empire first grew up in what is now called Zimbabwe from around the 900s CE through the **Middle Ages**. The great Zimbabwe stone ruins are an impressive reminder of this early civilization. It became known to the rest of the world in 1868 when it was discovered accidently by a hunting party.

Until 1965, Zimbabwe was the British colony of Southern Rhodesia. But white settlers seized power in Zimbabwe in that year and declared their independence from Britain. The settlers fought a bitter **civil war** with black African rebels. Rebel leader Robert Mugabe (b.1924) eventually took power, but violence flared again in the late 1990s when Mugabe began to confiscate land owned by white farmers, arguing that this land had been taken illegally from black Africans.

Zinc

Zinc is a hard, blue-white **metal** element. It has been used to make brass for over 2,000 years. Brass is an **alloy** of zinc and **copper**.

A large share of the world's zinc comes from **Canada**, **Australia** and the **United States**. Zinc mines usually contain other metals such as copper, **gold**, **lead** and **silver** as well. Most zinc is used to galvanize steel – putting a thin coat of zinc on steel to protect it. Zinc is also used to make cells in electric batteries (see **electricity**). As well as brass, zinc forms part of many other alloys including nickel and **bronze**. Zinc is always found combined with other substances.

We all need a small quantity of zinc in our diet. People who do not get enough zinc are anaemic (they do not have enough red **blood cells**) and their growth is retarded. A normal diet gives us all the zinc we need to grow and remain healthy.

Zoo

Zoos are places where wild **animals** are kept, often in a different country to the one from which they originated. The animals are cared for, bred, studied and sometimes saved from extinction (dying out) in zoos.

There are now more than 330 zoos in the world. The first were in Ancient **Egypt** – it is known that Queen Hatshepsut (c.1540–1481 BCE) kept a zoo that was running in 1500 BCE. More than 3,000 years ago, the emperors of **China** kept animals, **birds** and **fish** in natural **gardens** where they would feel at home. In the **Middle Ages** in **Europe**, kings gave each other presents of **apes**, **peacocks** and **lions**. Private collections of animals are called menageries. In the 1800s, travelling menageries were very popular, and toured through the towns of Europe.

Scientists have been interested in the study of animals since the 1700s. At that time, they began to sort animals into groups and give them Latin names, so that a particular animal would be recognized by the same name all over the world. Their work led directly to the building of the first public zoos. These were called 'zoological gardens' – shortened to 'zoo' later. One of the first was **London** Zoo, which was built in 1829.

ZIMBABWE
Government: Republic
Capital: Harare
Area: 390,759 sq km
Population: 13.1 million
Languages: Chishona, Sindebele and others
Currency: Zimbabwe dollar

▽ **Zoos** have done a great deal to save animals like this golden lion tamarin from extinction. These monkeys live in a heavily populated coastal region of Brazil, where less than 2 percent of the forest remains. There are only about 1,000 golden lion tamarins left in the wild. About 500 live in family groups in zoos worldwide.

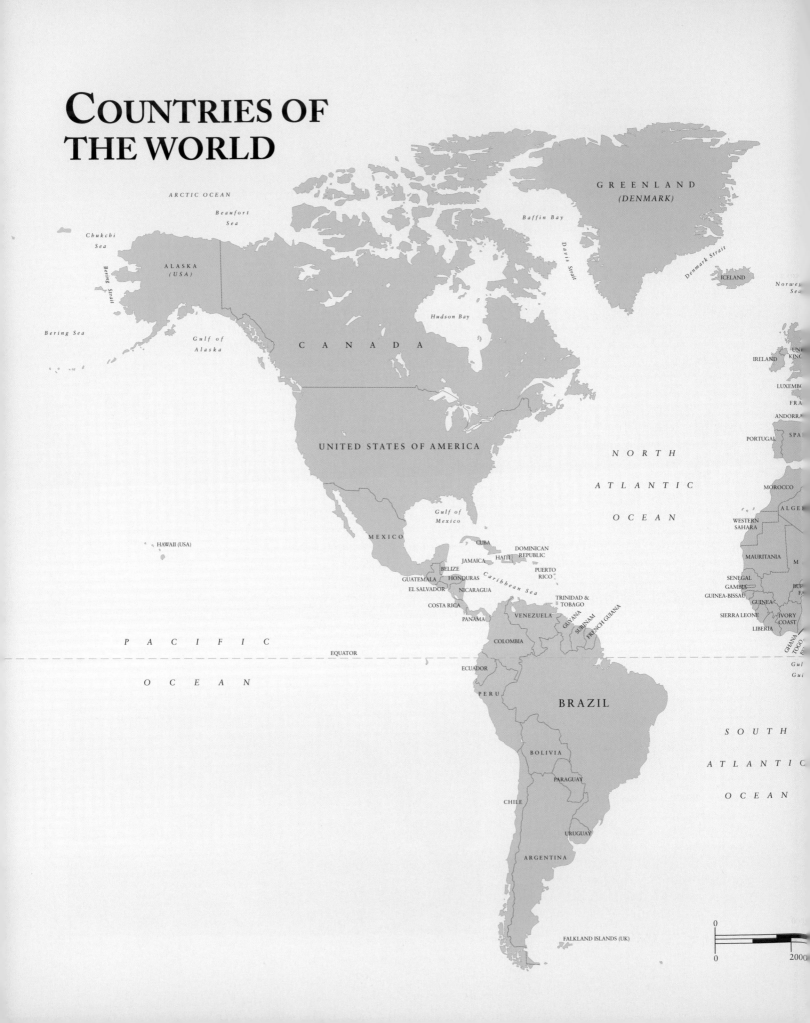

COUNTRIES OF THE WORLD

ARCTIC OCEAN

Beaufort Sea

Chukchi Sea

Bering Strait

Bering Sea

ALASKA (USA)

Gulf of Alaska

C A N A D A

Hudson Bay

GREENLAND (DENMARK)

Baffin Bay

Davis Strait

Denmark Strait

ICELAND

Norwe? Sea

UNITED STATES OF AMERICA

IRELAND

UNI KING

LUXEMBO

FRA

ANDORRA

PORTUGAL

SPA

N O R T H

A T L A N T I C

O C E A N

MOROCCO

ALGE

WESTERN SAHARA

Gulf of Mexico

HAWAII (USA)

M E X I C O

MAURITANIA

M

SENEGAL

GAMBIA

GUINEA-BISSAU

CUBA

JAMAICA

BELIZE

GUATEMALA   HONDURAS

EL SALVADOR   NICARAGUA

COSTA RICA

PANAMA

HAITI

DOMINICAN REPUBLIC

PUERTO RICO

Caribbean Sea

TRINIDAD & TOBAGO

VENEZUELA

GUYANA

SURINAM

FRENCH GUIANA

GUINEA

SIERRA LEONE

LIBERIA

IVORY COAST

GHANA

TOGO

COLOMBIA

Gul Gui

EQUATOR

P A C I F I C

O C E A N

ECUADOR

PERU

B R A Z I L

S O U T H

A T L A N T I C

O C E A N

BOLIVIA

PARAGUAY

CHILE

URUGUAY

ARGENTINA

FALKLAND ISLANDS (UK)

0

0   2000

ARCTIC OCEAN

ARCTIC OCEAN

Laptev Sea

East
Siberian
Sea

Barents Sea

Kara Sea

Chukchi
Sea

NORWAY

SWEDEN FINLAND

ESTONIA

Baltic Sea

LATVIA

LITHUANIA

DENMARK

RUSSIAN
FEDERATION

NETHERLANDS

BELARUS

GERMANY POLAND

CZECH
REP. SLOVAKIA

UKRAINE

LEICH.

AUSTRIA

SWITZERLAND HUNGARY MOLDOVA

SLOVENIA ROMANIA

CROATIA

UNION OF
SERBIA AND
MONTENEGRO

BOSNIA
HERZEGOVINA BULGARIA

ITALY

ALBANIA MACEDONIA

GREECE

TUNISIA

CYPRUS

LEBANON

ISRAEL

JORDAN

KUWAIT

LIBYA

EGYPT

SAUDI
ARABIA

BAHRAIN

QATAR

UNITED
ARAB
EMIRATES

OMAN

NIGER

CHAD

ERITREA

YEMEN

NIGERIA

SUDAN

DJIBOUTI

CENTRAL
AFRICAN
REPUBLIC

ETHIOPIA

SOMALIA

CAMEROON

EQUATORIAL
GUINEA

UGANDA

CONGO

GABON

DEMOCRATIC
REPUBLIC OF
CONGO

RWANDA

BURUNDI

KENYA

TANZANIA

ANGOLA

MALAWI

ZAMBIA

MOZAMBIQUE

Mozambique Channel

MADAGASCAR

NAMIBIA

ZIMBABWE

MAURITIUS

RÉUNION

BOTSWANA

SWAZILAND

LESOTHO

SOUTH
AFRICA

RUSSIA

KAZAKHSTAN

MONGOLIA

Aral
Sea

Caspian Sea

Black Sea

GEORGIA

ARMENIA

KYRGYZSTAN

TURKEY

UZBEKISTAN

AZERBAIJAN

TAJIKISTAN

CHINA

SYRIA

IRAQ

IRAN

AFGHANISTAN

Mediterranean Sea

Red Sea

PAKISTAN

NEPAL

BHUTAN

INDIA

BANGLADESH

MYANMAR

LAOS

Bay of
Bengal

THAILAND

VIETNAM

SRI
LANKA

CAMBODIA

Sea of
Okhotsk

Sea of
Japan

NORTH
KOREA

SOUTH
KOREA

JAPAN

Yellow
Sea

East
China Sea

TAIWAN

South
China
Sea

PHILIPPINES

Philippine Sea

Bering Strait

Bering Sea

PACIFIC

OCEAN

BRUNEI

MALAYSIA

Celebes
Sea

INDONESIA

PAPUA
NEW
GUINEA

SOLOMON
ISLANDS

INDIAN

OCEAN

Gulf of Aden

Coral Sea

VANUATU

FIJI

NEW CALEDONIA

AUSTRALIA

N

Tasman Sea

NEW
ZEALAND

2000   4000   6000   8000 miles (at equator)

4000   6000   8000   10 000   12 000 kilometres (at equator)

WEB ADDRESSES

There are hundreds of thousands of websites on the World Wide Web – so many, in fact, that finding the one you want can be quite a challenge. This is a guide to some of the most useful websites. All the websites listed here include links to other sites of interest.

The history of the internet and how it works is explained in a special feature on pages 168–169 of this encyclopedia.

SEARCH ENGINES
www.yahooligans.com
Yahoo's internet guide for children has links to thousands of websites, organized into categories to make searching easier.

directory.google.com/Top/Kids_and_Teens
This search engine from Google is specially designed for children, and is simple to use.

GENERAL REFERENCE
www.thinkquest.org/library/IC_index.html
The Thinkquest Library is a collection of over 5,000 websites designed by participants in the Thinkquest competitions.

www.EnchantedLearning.com/Home.html
Enchanted Learning is a valuable research tool that provides information on most subject areas.

www.bbc.co.uk/learning
Produced by the BBC, this site offers a wealth of educational material, and is ideal for school projects and homework.

about.com/homework
This homework guide produced by About.com has a list of links covering a wide range of subjects.

www.encyclopedia.com
The 14,000 articles contained in this easy-to-use website provide simple definitions and explanations.

www.infoplease.com/encyclopedia.html
The Infoplease online encyclopedia includes thousands of useful articles.

www.museumnetwork.com
This site is a directory to more than 30,000 museums across the world. There are also links to the museums' own websites.

GEOGRAPHY
www.altapedia.com
Altapedia is an online atlas that features world maps and detailed information on the countries of the world.

www.cyberschoolbus.un.org/infonation/index.asp
Infonation is the official children's site of the United Nations (UN), and has maps, facts and figures for all the UN's members.

PHYSICAL EARTH
kids.earth.nasa.gov/site.htm
This NASA site explores our own planet. It covers topics such as climate, volcanoes and movements of the earth's crust.

www.geography4kids.com
This educational website is packed with information about the physical geography of our planet.

NATURAL WORLD
www.kidsplanet.org/factsheets/map.html
Online fact sheets on many animals from all over the world.

www.EnchantedLearning.com/science/dictionary
This illustrated scientific dictionary has features on a wide variety of animals, plants and natural habitats.

www.worldwildlife.org/fun/kids.cfm
Produced by the World Wildlife Fund, this is an educational and fun website about wildlife and conservation issues.

www.bbc.co.uk/dinosaurs
This BBC site is full of useful information about dinosaurs.

HUMAN BODY
kidshealth.org/kid
This is a fun site that covers many aspects of the human body.

www.bbc.co.uk/health/kids/index.shtml
Visitors to this BBC website can do an online 'body tour'.

SCIENCE
www.physics4kids.com
www.biology4kids.com
www.chem4kids.com
These websites cover almost every aspect of science, and are full of interactive features that help explain difficult topics.

MATHEMATICS
mathforum.org/library/drmath/drmath.elem.html
'Dr Math' is a helpful site that explains topics such as arithmetic, geometry, measurement and special numbers.

INVENTIONS AND TECHNOLOGY

www.enchantedlearning.com/inventors
An A-Z of inventors and inventions from adhesive tape to zip.

howstuffworks.lycoszone.com
This Lycos site is packed with interesting articles that show how machines, gadgets and other useful objects work.

library.thinkquest.org/22522
Computer Chronicle describes the history of computing from the abacus to the invention of the silicon chip and powerful PCs.

www.aviation-history.com/right_index.htm
This site offers lots of information about the history of flight, plus data panels on different types of aircraft through the ages.

FOOD AND AGRICULTURE

museum.agropolis.fr/english/default.htm
The online Agropolis Museum describes the history of farming from prehistoric times to present-day intensive agriculture.

HISTORY

www.historyforkids.org
This website covers many periods of history from ancient civilizations to the 20th century.

www.bbc.co.uk/history/bytopic/index.shtml
This BBC site has information on almost every aspect of history.

www.thebritishmuseum.ac.uk/childrenscompass
Visitors to this site can see a varied selection of the British Museum's huge collection of artifacts, both ancient and modern.

library.thinkquest.org/C001692
'Voyage of Exploration' has details on explorers and expeditions throughout the world since ancient times.

RELIGION AND BELIEFS

www.bbc.co.uk/religion/religions/index.shtml
This BBC site offers an independent look at the world's major religions – Buddhism, Christianity, Hinduism, Islam, Judaism, Mormonism and Sikhism. It also explores other human beliefs.

www.windows.ucar.edu/tour/link=/mythology/mythology.html
This site is full of information about the myths, legends, folktales, gods and goddesses of many different cultures around the world.

LANGUAGE AND LITERATURE

library.thinkquest.org/26451
The history of communication is explored in this site, including the development of languages, writing, alphabets and computers.

uk.dir.yahoo.com/arts/humanities/literature/authors/children_s
Produced by Yahoo and regularly updated, this is a directory to websites about writers and books suitable for children.

ART AND ARCHITECTURE

www.tate.org.uk/home/default.htm
This site features a vast online database that allows you to learn about 50,000 works of art from the collections of the four Tate galleries in England.

www.louvre.fr/anglais/fr_g.htm
This is the English website of the Louvre, Paris, one of the world's greatest museums. Visitors can do an online tour to see a selection of paintings, drawings, sculpture and other objects.

www.greatbuildings.com
Key facts, photographs and 3-D models of 750 of the world's most important buildings are included in this site.

PERFORMING ARTS

www.empire.k12.ca.us/capistrano/Mike/capmusic/music_room/themusic.htm
The Music Room is an educational website produced by an American music school. It has features on musical instruments, famous composers and musical styles through the ages.

library.thinkquest.org/J002266F
'And They Kept On Dancing' provides all sorts of information about folk dance, ballet, tap, jazz and modern dance.

www.learner.org/exhibits/cinema
Discover how films are made at this fun interactive website.

SPORT

library.thinkquest.org/10480
Sports Central explains the rules of most major sports, and describes how different sports have changed over the years.

www.top-education.com/sports
SportsWorld has information about many sports and sporting events (including the Olympic Games and World Cup), plus biographies of famous sportspeople.

SPACE

kids.msfc.nasa.gov
This is a NASA site that introduces the wonders of space and space travel. Visitors can play games and take part in projects.

www.bbc.co.uk/science/space
This BBC site offers information on space and space exploration.

INDEX

Page numbers in **bold** refer to main entries

INDEX

ACKNOWLEDGEMENTS

The publishers wish to thank the following for supplying photographs for this book:

ABBREVIATIONS

(*t* = top; *b* = bottom; *c* = centre; *l* = left; *r* = right)

Illustrators

Susanna Addario, Anderson Geographics, Marion Appleton, Mike Atkinson, Julian Baker, Julie Banyard, Russell Barnett, Julian Baum, Richard Berridge, Mark Bergin, Simone Boni, Trevor Boyer, Peter Bull, John Butler, Robin Carter, Harry Clow, M. Coates, Dan Cole, Tom Connell, David Cook, Peter Dennis, Sandra Doyle, Richard Draper, Les Edwards, Bridget Ellison, Gill Elsbury, Dean Entwistle, Andy Farmer, James Field, Michael Fisher, Chris Forsey, Terry Gabbey, Luigi Galante, Lee Gibbons, Peter Goodfellow, Jeremy Gower, Craig Greenwood, Ray Grinaway, Alan Hancocks, David Hardy, Donald Harley, Keith Harmer, Gary Hinks, Adam Hook, Christian Hook, Richard Hook, Andre Hrydziusko, Ian Jackson, John James, Lovell Johns, Kevin Jones, Peter Kesterton, Martin Knowldon, Eddy Krahenbuhl, Mike Lacey, Ruth Lindsay, Bernard Long, Steiner Lund, Chris Lyon, Kevin Maddison, Shirley Mallinson, Janos Marffy, Shane Marsh, David Marshall, Joannah May, Jamie Medlin, Simon Mendez, Justin Moat, Chris Molan, Patrick Mulrey, Steve Noon, Nicki Palin, Alex Pang, Darren Patenden, Robert Payne, Andie Peck, John Porter, Sebastian Quigley, John Ridyard, Steve Roberts, Bernard Robinson, Susan Rowe, David Salariya, Claudia Saraceni, Mike Saunders, Chris Shields, Rob Shone, Nick Shewring, Guy Smith, Clive Spon, Roger Stewart, John Storey, Mike Taylor, Ian Thompson, Mike Trim, Bob Watton, Joanne Williams, David Wright

Picture libraries

Pages: 6: *(tr)* Powerstock/Zefa/Christie's Images; 27: *(tr)* The Bridgeman Art Library/Christie's Images, *(bl)* The Bridgeman Art Library/Galleria degli Uffizi, Florence, Italy; 30: *(tl)* Corbis; 66: *(tl)* ILN; 81: *(tc)* The Bridgeman Art Library/Christie's Images; 87: *(c)* ILN; 90: *(tc)* ILN; 104: *(tc)* ILN; 113: *(tl)* ILN; 152: *(bl)* ILN; 153: *(tc)* ILN; 155: *(tc)* Corbis; 225: *(tr)* Corbis/David Zimmerman; 250: *(tl)* ILN; 276: *(cl)* The Bridgeman Art Library/Kenwood House, London; 314–315: *(bc)* Corbis/Dmitri Lundt; 332: *(tl)* Corbis; 342: *(br)* Science Photo Library; 348: *(tc)* The Art Archive/Musée d'Orsay, Paris; 354: *(cl)* ILN; 375: *(cr)* ILN; 379: *(tr)* Science Photo Library, *(tr)* Corbis/Hulton–Deutsch; 383: *(br)* Corbis/Kevin Schaeffer

The publishers would also like to thank the following for their help in supplying information used as visual reference:

Pages: 14–15: Boeing Aircraft Corporation (Boeing 747 cutaway); 294–295: Princess Cruises (ship cutaway)

Every effort has been made to trace the copyright holders of the photographs. The publishers apologise for any unavoidable omissions.